THE BLACK EXPERIENCE

THE BLACK EXPERIENCE

An Anthology of American Literature for the 1970s

Edited with an introduction and notes by

FRANCIS E. KEARNS

Herbert H. Lehman College, City University of New York

Foreword by Arna Bontemps

THE VIKING PRESS / NEW YORK

CONTENTS

FOREWORD

In the early twenties the poet Countee Cullen recalled the genesis of a provocative quatrain he had written. It involved a personal story—perhaps a parable. An elegant white woman was visiting a black church in the ghetto. Young Cullen had been a confirmed Sunday-school boy, and the church happened to be one in which his foster parent was the minister.

The boy did not know, or possibly didn't remember, the circumstances that brought the visitor into their midst with such éclat that day, nor how it happened that she was invited, or volunteered, to teach a class of restless and inattentive youngsters, including himself. Nevertheless, for him the occasion was somehow embalmed.

When she realized that she was not getting complete attention, the visiting teacher resorted to a device she must have considered suitable. She began telling a dream she said she had recently experienced. She had been in heaven, as it seemed, and she went on to describe the beauties she had seen. These were right out of the scriptures, of course: streets paved with gold, rainbow walls, pearly gates, children petting lions and sheep at the same time, milk and honey flowing.

She had exhausted the narrative when a young Harlem imp raised his hand to ask a question. She paused, smiling, but the smile soon disappeared. The boy wanted to know whether or not she had seen any colored people up there. Not wanting to lie, and not wanting to discourage him either, she finally confessed that she had not seen any, but she quickly added for his comfort that this may have been because she had neglected to look into the kitchens.

Needless to say, a member of the class who had remained silent, Countee Cullen himself, went to his room in the parsonage and wrote what he thought might serve as a suitable epitaph for this visiting teacher's headstone:

> She even thinks that up in heaven
> Her class lies late and snores,
> While poor black cherubs rise at seven
> To do celestial chores.*

As a subject for a poem this was unusual enough in American letters, but it also suggests that young Cullen was already raising a question of prime relevance to the black experience in his time and ours: the difference in the ways things are apprehended through black eyes and white. Even so rarefied a concept as heaven could vary significantly.

Naturally it was a short step from that epitaph to Cullen's sonnet "Yet Do I Marvel." And from the latter to a reading of selected writings by black as well as white writers in the United States, a leap is now inevitable. Cullen had brought us to the brink of a problem, perhaps a crisis, which, though old, had not previously been seen as problem or crisis. Today it is, and the proliferation of black studies is a result. Not before, however, have examples been assembled in such quantity and with such thoughtful arrangement and knowledgeable selection as here. Perhaps the time had not come.

Read thus, confrontation may become to readers of today more than encounters of the meek of a rural region with men carrying cattle prods and supported by savage dogs. It may reveal a turmoil of the mind and heart. What disoriented the white Sunday-school teacher in the Harlem of half a century ago was not malice but something equally distorting. If an exploration of this wild terrain into which we have ventured does not give us pause, help us tame our passions, I suspect nothing will.

Arna Bontemps

New Haven, 1969

---

* "For a Lady I Know," from *On These I Stand* by Countee Cullen. Copyright 1925 by Harper & Brothers; renewed 1953 by Ida M. Cullen. Reprinted by permission of Harper & Row, Publishers.

INTRODUCTION

The literary significance of the black experience in America was indirectly suggested by Nathaniel Hawthorne when he wrote, not long before the Civil War, of the writer's difficulty in "a country where there is no shadow, no antiquity, no picturesque and gloomy wrong, nor anything but a commonplace prosperity." For since the 1830s, when critics first began to speak seriously of an American literature, each generation of writers has, with varying degrees of intensity and consciousness, been concerned with what Hawthorne indeed might have accurately termed "America's most ancient, picturesque, and gloomy wrong": slavery, that is, and its aftermath, or what George Washington Cable once called "the shadow of the Ethiopian." So significant has the theme of black experience been in American thought that it can be seen as a literary influence at least as pervasive as "the frontier experience" described by Frederick Jackson Turner.

The psychic impact of the black experience in a society which could cherish traditions of liberty and fraternity and at the same time regard part of its human population as mere property is, as Gunnar Myrdal suggests, too profound to be measured with the tools of statistical analysis. To come to grips with its implications one must turn to the nation's literature. One must consider, for example, the Calvinist habit of thinking in terms of broad allegorical blacks and whites, and the symbolic value given to black skin in Edgar Allan Poe's *Narrative of Arthur Gordon Pym* and Herman Melville's *Benito Cereno*. One must also consider Norman Mailer's view in "The White Negro" of the modern black American as a walking paradigm of all the psychopathological forces tearing at the fabric of contemporary American society. No serious study of the impact of Negro identity on American literature can ignore the recurrent quest for a "lost Edenic moment" in our writing. *Moby Dick, The Blithedale Romance, Huckleberry Finn, The Great Gatsby,* Faulkner's *The Bear,* and Ellison's *Invisible Man* have all reflected this effort to recover a moment in time when a special innocence between men was possible. One thinks immediately of Huck Finn's relation with Nigger Jim or Ike McCaslin's with Sam Fathers. Even in recognizing that the quest for innocence has not always been associated with the Negro, one can afford to bear in mind James Baldwin's caution: "If you don't know my name you don't know your own."

Part of the significance of the black experience for American literature can be seen in the highly emotional context in which this theme has appeared. Where the white author has not evaded the race issue by creating familiar black stereotypes, such as the "smiling Sambo" or the "noble savage," his approach to the Negro has often been affected by profound feelings of love, hate, terror, or shame. If Melville and Poe deal with blacks as vicious insurrectionists, Twain's Nigger Jim and Faulkner's Sam Fathers are among our most appealing father figures. Ambivalent feelings are often felt toward the same character. Although the Nat Turner created by G. P. R. James in *The Old Dominion* condones the murder of innocent children, he is also a romantic rebel chieftain straight out of Sir Walter Scott, with enough sensibility to spare the lives of the novel's white hero and heroine while actively promoting their love affair. James is unable to decide whether Turner should appear as hero or villain, and he ends the novel with the slave rebellion crushed but Turner still at large.

Caught in the same complex love-hate relationship, the black writer, in defining his own identity, has had to face the emotion-laden question of whether he can accept whites; and here the answers have been as diverse as Paul Laurence Dunbar's sometimes self-debasing efforts to court white favor, Claude McKay's readiness either to love or to die fighting, LeRoi Jones' revolutionary separatism, or Eldridge Cleaver's conclusion that "the price of hating other human beings is loving oneself less."

The theme of black identity has also been associated with the American writer's fundamental view of reality. In two of the most significant early works in our literature dealing with race, Poe's

Narrative of Arthur Gordon Pym and Melville's *Benito Cereno,* cruel and satanically clever black insurrectionists present themselves in the guise of benign primitives, suggesting not only the question of black identity but also the whole nineteenth-century literary problem of appearance versus reality: the anguish and terror which result when one can no longer trust the apparent meaning and order apprehended by the senses. One can also find correspondences between the slave rebellion as a cataclysmic alteration of reality and the natural disasters that come at the end of such nineteenth-century masterpieces as *Moby Dick,* in which Ahab tries to impose his transcendent will on reality, and "The Fall of the House of Usher," in which the acutely rational narrator finds reason unequal to the task of comprehending experience.

A more obvious way in which the literature on race has been associated with the problem of appearance and reality is in its dependence on stereotyped characterization. Inevitably, the simultaneous view of the Negro as both man and thing has resulted in the twisting of normal standards of verisimilitude. Sterling Brown, in "A Century of Negro Portraiture in American Literature," points out at least five principal stereotypes that were well established before the turn of the century: the "contented slave," the "comic minstrel," the "wretched freedman," the "brute Negro," and the "tragic mulatto."

One of the most revealing aspects of this literature is the picture it sometimes gives of a major white writer in literary undress— for what are we to make of the appearance of crude racial stereotypes in the work of an otherwise sensitive author? Fitzgerald, for instance, as a racial and religious outsider with social ambitions, was acutely aware of ethnic subtleties, yet in *The Great Gatsby* the narrator, Nick Carraway, points to a limousine driven by a white chauffeur and carrying "three modish negroes, two bucks and a girl," who roll their eyeballs "in haughty rivalry" as an illustration of his view that anything can happen in New York City. In *Tender Is the Night,* Fitzgerald offers a classic illustration of what Baldwin means by the phrase "Nobody knows my name." Without asking embarrassing questions, the hero, Dick Diver, disposes of the body of a virtually faceless Negro who had briefly wandered into the novel, and the episode is used to illustrate Diver's *savoir faire* and grace in the face of adversity. Inevitably the critic is tempted to read subtle ironies into what otherwise might be viewed as insensitivity on the author's part. Does the animal imagery used by Melville in describing the Negroes of *Benito Cereno* represent the author's real attitude, or is the novel a subtle antislavery argument demonstrating how slavery makes animals of both oppressed and oppressor? Are the knives and watermelons so prominently featured in Stephen Crane's "The Knife" intended to be another dimension of the racial stereotypes in the story, or was Crane consciously commenting on a role assumed by Negroes who, according to R. W. Stallman, are just as aware as Huck Finn of the necessity of disguised identity as a means of survival in America?

Perhaps an ultimate indication that the black experience has had a deep influence on American letters lies in the contention by some modern critics that the Negro, as "the prisoner," "the victim," "the outsider," and "the wearer of the mask," may in fact be seen as "America's metaphor," to use Richard Wright's words—as a figure of existential crisis, even as a twentieth-century Everyman. In his introduction to *Images of the Negro in American Literature* Seymour Gross writes:

> The image of the Negro in American literary criticism can, finally, be said to have undergone an exquisite reversal in the last one hundred years. For whereas our criticism began by locking the Negro into the fantasy construct of the stereotype, removing him from human consideration to a kind of psychological and moral no-man's land, one recent phase of criticism has interpreted him and his situation as archetypal, as "an image of man's fate."

Various social analysts, such as W. J. Cash and John Dollard, have pointed to the profound sexual emotions underlying the race question in America, emotions which have violently come to the surface in defenses of lynching, in cross-racial sexual aggression as an expression of supremacy or revenge, and in the fear of miscegenation that has served as a general rationale for segregation. Another aspect of the literature on race relations, as might be expected, is that it is one major area in American literature where the writer has felt free, even compelled, to explore the sexual implications of human character and condition.

For a society which has traditionally been known for its profound puritanism regarding sexual matters, white concern about Negro sexuality has met with surprisingly little censure. Whereas Hawthorne approaches the subject under a veil of allegory in *The Scarlet Letter*, William Gilmore Simms, in "Caloya; or, The Loves of the Driver," written some five years earlier, was quite open in describing a "black stud" and his campaign of seduction aimed at an Indian squaw. More recently, John Howard Griffin, a white writer who traveled in the South disguised as a Negro, reported in *Black Like Me* the abnormal curiosity of whites about his sexual practices, while Jack Kerouac and Norman Mailer both associate a sexual mystique with Negro life, which they regard as standing in stark contrast to the emptiness of white lives. This black sexual mystique envisioned by Mailer and the Beat writers has drawn sharply differing responses from black commentators, with Eldridge Cleaver in general accord, while Sterling Brown terms the mystique "a Greenwich Village refurbishing of old stereotypes."

The ways in which sexual matters have been approached are as varied as the talents of the writers engaged in the subject, but several major themes can be identified. The most familiar is what has been called the theme of "tainted blood." In works ranging from Boucicault's *The Octoroon* to Cable's *The Grandissimes* and Faulkner's *Light in August*, white writers have delivered implicit sermons against the dangers of racial mixing, either by dramatizing the tragic fate to be endured by the hero with mixed blood or by emphasizing the extraordinary viciousness of the mulatto villain. There have been exceptions among white writers, however. Sinclair Lewis's *Kingsblood Royal*, for instance, is an interesting attempt to debunk the whole theme.

Black authors have dealt with "tainted blood" too. In Langston Hughes's "Mulatto," a mulatto bastard revolts against his white father's refusal to recognize him, and in "Her Virginia Mammy," a story in Charles Chesnutt's *The Wife of His Youth*, the black mother of a girl who had been raised as a white conspires with her daughter's white suitor to keep the girl unaware of her "tainted blood." In "A Matter of Principle," another story in the same collection, light-skinned, bourgeois Negroes strive to dissociate themselves from darker members of their race.

A recent development, however, is the reversal of the "tainted blood" theme in the black revolutionary theater. *The Drama Review* for summer 1968, a special Black Theater Issue edited by Ed Bullins, presents several one-acters which expose the dangers of corrupting black blood. In Sonia Sanchez' *The Bronx Is Next*, for example, Black Bitch, a prostitute, is berated for consorting with a white policeman, and in Jimmie Garrett's *And We Own the Night*, a young black revolutionist shoots his mother, a black matriarch who had accepted white values to such an extent that she wished her husband were white.

Another sexual theme is what has been called the "forbidden fruit" motif, which centers around what is supposed to be the special but secret sexual attraction of each race for the other. The theme usually concentrates on the allure that white women supposedly represent for black men—probably the most enduring of all ideas in the complex of legend and myth surrounding race relations in America. Although it is usually associated with the type of Ku Klux Klan fiction of the Reconstruction era that influenced D. W. Griffith's film *The Birth of a Nation*, the fact that the white woman's special attractiveness for black men is still a potent literary topic can be seen in Eldridge Cleaver's elaborate analysis in "On Becoming," an essay in *Soul on Ice*, and in the charges leveled by the critics in *William Styron's Nat Turner; Ten Black Writers Respond*, that Styron had revived and mishandled the notion in his recent novel. Chester Himes's *Pinktoes*, on the other hand, exploits the obvious Rabelaisian possibilities of the theme by describing the farcical activities of a Harlem hostess who furthers race relations by bringing together pretentious liberal whites and bourgeois blacks for interracial seductions.

After considering even the few aspects of the literature of black experience and identity touched upon here, it seems evident that this body of writing represents a rich tradition deserving closer attention by the student of American literature as well as by the reading public in general. An even more urgent reason for closer familiarity with these writings is the personal insight they can provide into some of the complexities of the racial conflict that the country has experienced in recent years. For it would seem that only through confronting the myth and truth they offer, only in facing the love, hate, terror, and hope they associate with problems of racial identity, can we hope to survive with some measure of justice and compassion in an ethnically diverse society.

Although the anthology of black writing has been with us for almost half a century, and although journals such as *Phylon, The Crisis*, and *Freedomways* have long kept alive a scholarly interest in Negro literature, it is only recently that the general reader, either white or black, has come to realize the depth and diversity of the black literary tradition. Fortunately, with the recent publication of such anthologies as Herbert Hill's *Soon One Morning*, Arna Bontemps's *American Negro Poetry*, John Henrik Clarke's *American Negro Short Stories*, Langston Hughes' *The Best Short Stories by Negro Writers*, Abraham Chapman's *Black Voices*, and James A. Emanuel's and Theodore L. Gross's *Dark Symphony*, excellent collections of the work of black authors are now available.

Still largely unexplored is the large body of writing by white authors about the black experience in America. Although many of these writings are major works and have received much attention from students of such authors as William Faulkner and Flannery O'Connor, they have rarely been examined as part of a major literary tradition on race relations.

No new anthology has appeared that brings together both black and white writers. This is even more surprising when we consider that such black writers as Baldwin and Ellison have explicitly assessed their own works against a broad American tradition rather than an exclusively black one. Both writers have offered perceptive comments on Richard Wright. Baldwin, however, has also written tellingly on Faulkner and Harriet Beecher Stowe, while Ellison has produced first-rate criticism of Stephen Crane. One cannot ignore the influence of black and white writers on each other. Gwendolyn Brooks, for instance, has testified to the influence of Robert Frost, and Karl Shapiro and Allen Tate have expressed their profound admiration for the work of M. B. Tolson. Further, scholarship in the literature of black experience has traditionally dealt with the works of both black and white writers. *Images of the Negro in American Literature*, edited by Gross and Hardy, brings together both black and white critics on the works of both black and white writers, and Sterling Brown's recent essay, "A Century of Negro Portraiture in American Literature," is concerned with the outlook of both races. An anthology with this approach would seem to be especially needed at a time of rapidly growing black consciousness and increasingly open public discussion of racial tensions. One of the best ways of comprehending and exorcising prejudice and racist myth would appear to be directly confronting it as it is seen in a national literature created by both races.

In selecting works for this volume, my aim has been not only to chronicle the history of literary attitudes toward race in the United States, but also to suggest the importance of the black experience as a major influence on all American literary tradition. At the same time I have tried to offer a sampling of the works of black writers sufficiently wide to suggest the scope and achievement of the black literary tradition. In choosing individual works, my emphasis has been on artistic merit, although some pieces are clearly indispensable because of their historical and sociological significance (e.g., Boucicault's *The Octoroon* for its classic statement of the "tainted blood" theme, Stowe's *Uncle Tom's Cabin* for the historic influence of its abolitionist views, John Pendleton Kennedy's "The Quarter" for its pro-slavery bias, Irwin Russell's "Christmas-Night in the Quarters" for the representative quality of its important place in "the plantation tradition," and W. E. B. Dubois' *The Souls of Black Folk* for its major early statement of black consciousness). Since this is an anthology of imaginative literature, it consists almost exclusively of short stories, poems, plays, and extracts from novels, even though this has forced me to omit essays and speeches by important social commentators, politicians, and rights activists. The few essays included here are by major literary figures, such as Wright and Baldwin. I have also included Eldridge Cleaver because it seems to me that his social and political influence stems largely from his talent as a writer.

I have concentrated on works by major writers, and as a result there has been no room for such works as the once widely read fiction of Carl Van Vechten or the poems of Fenton Johnson, even though samples of these works might have added greater historical perspective to the anthology. The reader may note that a few of the selections seem to have little to do with race. I have included some of Claude McKay's nature poems not only because they are good poems, but also because they suggest what kind of poet he might have become had he not migrated to America and encountered our racial dilemma. Some of Countee Cullen's pieces on the function of poetry and the poet have been included because they represent his best work and again provide grounds for speculation on the question raised by his own "Yet Do I Marvel": what direction the writing of a major black literary figure might have taken had he not been so heavily influenced by the dimensions of "the race question."

In the end, no anthology can avoid the quirks of its editor. I have included two particular pieces because I feel they represent genuine "finds"—long-forgotten works now of considerable significance. The selection from G. P. R. James' *The Old Dominion* represents one of the earliest literary characterizations of Nat Turner published in America. It was written by one of the most prolific novelists of nineteenth-century England, a man who became Historiographer Royal and who served as British Consul in Norfolk on the eve of the Civil War. Yet so obscured has the book become that even its date of publication is misstated in historical summaries. Charles Chesnutt's "The Passing of Grandison," on the other hand, represents a work by a black author whose attainments are now coming to be appreciated by scholars and critics. Published in *The Wife of His Youth*, a long-neglected collection of Chesnutt stories, "Grandison" hardly deserves its obscurity, for it offers a delightfully ironic treatment of race roles played by both black and white, by both pro- and anti-slavery advocates, and its surprise ending is just as sophisticated as anything achieved with the same device by such better-known nineteenth-century writers as Bret Harte and O. Henry.

For their valuable advice on this book, I wish to thank David Aivaz, Robert Bush, Malcolm Cowley, Gerhard Joseph, and Charles Noyes.

Francis E. Kearns

NEGRO SONGS

The songs of the Southern Negro were not gathered for publication until the Civil War, when Northern antislavery advocates collected them partly in an attempt to enhance Negro cultural prestige. But an earlier interest in Negro songs had resulted from the adoption of such plantation melodies as "Oh, Susanna" by white minstrel-show singers and from the general interest in folk music promoted by Harvard Professor Francis J. Child's historic studies of English and Scottish ballads.

Colonel Thomas Wentworth Higginson, a student of Scottish ballads who commanded a colored regiment during the Civil War, published a landmark article, "Negro Spirituals," in the Atlantic in 1867. In the same year William Francis Allen, Charles Pickard Ware, and Lucy McKim Garrison brought out Slave Songs of the United States, the first book to gather words and music for the spirituals. Further interest in Negro spirituals was brought about by the tours through Northern states made by choral groups from Fisk University and Hampton Institute in the 1870s.

Several types of songs are associated with the American Negro, including plantation melodies, work songs, and the blues, but it is the spiritual, the religious folk lyric, that has the deepest roots in his emotional experience. Whether the spirituals originated with Negroes or were adopted from songs sung at camp meetings of white evangelical sects has long been debated, though the latter

view is generally held today. Two themes abide in these songs—
a Christian hope in an afterlife that will offer consolation for suffering in the world, and a yearning for freedom in this life that
looks for strength to the Old-Testament story of Israelite captivity
and endurance. Songs characteristic of the latter theme, such as
"Go Down, Moses" and "Didn' My Lord Deliver Daniel?" protest openly against slavery. This picture of social protest presented
in the socially sanctioned religious lyric offers an interesting contrast to the image of the unsophisticated and contented slave so
often found in Southern literature of the nineteenth century. It
also suggests the motifs of mask-wearing and role-playing which
have been central in Negro writing from Paul Laurence Dunbar to
James Baldwin.

"John Henry," which exists in many versions and dates from the
early 1870s, centers around one of the earliest confrontations of
man and machine. Roark Bradford brought together various tales
connected with the ballad in John Henry (1931), and Guy B. Johnson collected variants of the song in John Henry: Tracking Down
a Negro Legend (1931).

John Henry

John Henry was a li'l baby, uh-huh,
He sat on his daddy's knee;
Said: "De Big Bend Tunnel on de C. & O. road
Gonna cause de death of me,
Lawd, Lawd, gonna cause de death of me."

Cap'n says to John Henry,
"Gonna bring me a steam drill 'round,
Gonna take dat steam drill out on de job,
Gonna whop dat steel on down,
Lawd, Lawd, gonna whop dat steel on down."

John Henry tol' his cap'n
Dat a man wuz a natural man,
An' befo' he'd let dat steam drill run him down,

He'd fall dead wid a hammer in his han',
He'd fall dead wid a hammer in his han'.

John Henry sez to his cap'n:
"Send me a twelve-poun' hammer aroun',
A twelve-poun' hammer wid a fo'-foot handle,
An' I beat yo' steam drill down,
An' I beat yo' steam drill down."

John Henry started on de right han',
De steam drill started on de lef'—
"Before I'd let dis steam drill beat me down,
I'd hammer my fool self to death,
Lawd, Lawd, I'd hammer my fool self to death."

Sun shine hot an' burnin',
Wer'n't no breeze a-tall,
Sweat ran down like water down a hill,
Dat day John Henry let his hammer fall,
Lawd, Lawd, dat day John Henry let his hammer fall.

White man tol' John Henry,
"Nigger, damn yo' soul,
You might beat dis steam an' drill of mine,
When de rocks in dis mountain turn to gol',
Lawd, Lawd, when de rocks in dis mountain turn to gol'."

John Henry hammered in de mountains,
An' his hammer was strikin' fire,
He drove so hard till he broke his pore heart,
An' he lied down his hammer an' he died,
Lawd, Lawd, he lied down his hammer an' he died.

John Henry had a li'l baby,
Hel' him in de palm of his han'.
De las' words I heard de pore boy say:
"Son, yo're gonna be a steel-drivin' man,
Son, yo're gonna be a steel-drivin' man!"

John Henry had a pretty li'l 'ooman,
An' de dress she wo' was blue,
An' de las' words she said to him:
"John Henry, I've been true to you,
Lawd, Lawd, John Henry, I've been true to you."

John Henry had anothah 'ooman,
De dress she wo' wuz red.
De las' words I heard de pore gal say:
"I'm goin' w'eah mah man drapt daid,
I'm goin' w'eah mah man drapt daid!"

"Oh, who's gonna shoe yo' li'l feetses,
An' who's gonna glub yo' han's,
An' who's gonna kiss yo' rosy, rosy lips,
An' who's gonna be yo' man,
Lawd, Lawd, an' who's gonna be yo' man?"

Dey took John Henry to de graveyard,
An' dey buried him in de san',
An' every locomotive come roarin' by,
Says, "Dere lays a steel-drivin' man,
Lawd, Lawd, dere lays a steel-drivin' man."

Swing Low, Sweet Chariot

Swing low, sweet chariot,
Comin' for to carry me home;
Swing low, sweet chariot,
Comin' for to carry me home.

I looked over Jordan and what did I see,
Comin' for to carry me home?
A band of angels comin' aftah me,
Comin' for to carry me home.

If you git there before I do,
Comin' for to carry me home,

Tell all my frien's I'm a-comin', too,
Comin' for to carry me home.

The brightes' day that ever I saw,
Comin' for to carry me home,
When Jesus washed my sins away
Comin' for to carry me home.

I'm sometimes up an' sometimes down,
Comin' for to carry me home,
But still my soul feel heavenly-boun',
Comin' for to carry me home.

Nobody Knows De Trouble I See

Nobody knows de trouble I see,
Nobody knows but Jesus;
Nobody knows de trouble I see,
Glory, hallelujah!

Sometimes I'm up, sometimes I'm down,
Oh, yes, Lord;
Sometimes I'm almos' to de groun',
Oh, yes, Lord.

Altho' you see me goin' 'long so,
Oh, yes, Lord;
I have my trials here below,
Oh, yes, Lord.

All God's Chillun Got Shoes

You got shoes, I got shoes,
All God's chillun got shoes,
When I git to Heb'n goin' to put on my shoes

Goin' to walk all over God's Heb'n,
Heb'n, Heb'n, goin' to walk all over God's Heb'n.

I got a robe, you got a robe,
All God's chillun got a robe,
When I git to Heb'n goin' to put on my robe
Goin' to walk all over God's Heb'n,
Heb'n, Heb'n, goin' to walk all over God's Heb'n.

I got a crown, you got a crown,
All God's chillun got a crown,
When I git to Heb'n goin' to put on my crown
Goin' to walk all over God's Heb'n,
Heb'n, Heb'n, goin' to walk all over God's Heb'n.

I got a harp, you got a harp,
All God's chillun got a harp,
When I git to Heb'n goin' to play on my harp
Goin' to play all over God's Heb'n,
Heb'n, Heb'n, goin' to play all over God's Heb'n.

I got wings, you got wings,
All God's chillun got wings,
When I git to Heb'n goin' to put on my wings
Goin' to fly all over God's Heb'n,
Heb'n, Heb'n, goin' to fly all over God's Heb'n.

We Shall Overcome

We shall overcome,
We shall overcome,
We shall overcome, someday;
Oh, deep in my heart, I do believe
That we shall overcome someday.

We'll walk hand in hand,
We'll walk hand in hand,

We'll walk hand in hand, someday;
Oh, deep in my heart, I do believe
That we shall overcome someday.

We are not afraid,
We are not afraid,
We are not afraid, today;
Oh, deep in my heart, I do believe
That we shall overcome someday.

Go Down, Moses

When Israel was in Egypt's land,
Let my people go;
Oppressed so hard dey could not stand,
Let my people go.

Go down, Moses,
Way down in Egypt's land,
Tell ole Pha-roh,
Let my people go.

Thus saith de Lord, bold Moses said,
Let my people go;
If not I'll smite your first-born dead,
Let my people go.

No more shall dey in bondage toil,
Let my people go;
Let dem come out wid Egypt's spoil,
Let my people go.

Didn' My Lord Deliver Daniel?

God deliver'd Daniel from the lions' den,
Jonah from de belly of de whale,

And de Hebrew children from de fiery furnace,
An' why not every man?

Didn' my Lord deliver Daniel, deliver Daniel, deliver Daniel,
Didn' my Lord deliver Daniel, and why not every man?

Set my foot on de gospel ship,
An' de ship begin to sail,
It landed me over on Canaan's shore,
An' I'll never come back no more.

No More Auction Block

No more auction block for me,
    No more, no more;
No more auction block for me,
    Many thousand gone.

No more peck o' corn for me, [etc.]

No more pint o' salt for me, [etc.]

No more mistress' call for me, [etc.]

No more driver's lash for me,
    No more, no more;
No more driver's lash for me,
    Many thousand gone.

Free at Las'

Free at las', free at las',
I thank God I'm free at las';
Free at las', free at las',
I thank God I'm free at las', free at las'.

Way down yonder in de graveyard walk,
I thank God I'm free at las';
Me an' my Jesus gwineter meet an' talk,
I thank God I'm free at las', etc.

On a my knees when de light pass by,
I thank God I'm free at las';
Tho't my soul woulda rise an' fly,
I thank God I'm free at las', etc.

Some o' dese mornin's bright an' fair,
I thank God I'm free at las';
Gwineter meet my Jesus in de middle of de air,
I thank God I'm free at las', etc.

EDGAR ALLAN POE

(1809–1849)

The son of professional actors, Poe was born in Boston, but at the age of two he was taken as a foster child by John Allan, a wealthy resident of Richmond, Virginia, when he was orphaned in that Southern city by the death of his mother. He attended school in England, where the Allans lived for several years, and then entered the University of Virginia, but was forced to withdraw because of gambling debts and Allan's refusal to provide adequate financial support. After publishing his first volume of poems in 1827, Poe enlisted in the United States Army and later served briefly as a West Point cadet. Over Allan's strong opposition, Poe committed himself to a career as a professional literary man. Deprived of financial assistance from his foster father, he was in desperate economic circumstances for most of his remaining years, though he served with distinction as an editor of such journals as the Southern Literary Messenger, Burton's Gentleman's Magazine, Graham's Magazine, and the Broadway Journal.

Poe's social position was insecure throughout his early life. Although he had received an excellent education from the Allans and acquired their aristocratic outlook—the narrators of his tales are almost invariably men of independent means—he was never formally adopted by Allan, and he had no other socially advantageous family connections. His precarious position seems to have been sensed by Allan's Negro servants, for in one letter to his foster father he complains, "You suffer me to be subjected to the whim & caprice, not only of your white family, but to the complete authority of the blacks."

In reviews of works such as J. K. Paulding's Slavery in the United States Poe offered typical Southern commentary on the loyalty and devotion of Negro slaves, and in his story "The Gold Bug" his characterization of Jupiter, the narrator's servant, helped to advance the stereotype of the faithful but ignorant and craven "darky." Poe's latent hostility toward Negroes sometimes took a stronger tone than benign paternalism and is especially evident in reviews he wrote of works by Northerners such as James Russell Lowell who sympathized with the plight of the slaves.

In The Narrative of Arthur Gordon Pym (1838), Poe's only novel, the fictitious Pym relates his experiences aboard the whaler Grampus, on which he had sailed from Nantucket in 1827 with Dirk Peters, a half-breed Indian from the Black Hills. After a mutiny in which the whaler's black cook played a leading part, and a shipwreck, Pym and Peters are rescued by the merchant ship Jane Guy, aboard which Pym is able to persuade Captain Guy to continue a southward direction in hopes of discovering an Antarctic continent.

A major influence on the novel was An Address on the Subject of a Surveying and Exploring Expedition to the Pacific Ocean and the South Seas (1837) by Jeremiah N. Reynolds. Reynolds had here advanced a scheme to send an expedition to discover the South Pole and claim Antarctica for the United States and his proposal had led to considerable popular interest in the South Pole. Poe reviewed Reynolds's address in the same issue of the Southern Literary Messenger which began his serialization of Pym, and, strangely enough, it was Reynolds's name that he called, years later, on his deathbed.

Another significant influence on the novel was the fear of slave insurrection which ran through the South following several uprisings in the early nineteenth century, the most notable of which was Nat Turner's rebellion of 1831 in Poe's own Virginia. The novel may also have been influenced by the figure of the white albatross in Coleridge's "Rime of the Ancient Mariner." In its turn, Poe's use of whiteness may have influenced Melville's Moby

Dick (1851). *Leslie Fiedler writes that in* The Narrative of Arthur Gordon Pym *Poe "rather prophetically anticipates than initiates a long line of American books, in which certain gothic writers exploit the fear and guilt which the comic Negro of popular art attempts to laugh out of existence."*

From The Narrative of Arthur Gordon Pym

Chapter XVIII

January 18. This morning we continued to the southward, with the same pleasant weather as before. The sea was entirely smooth, the air tolerably warm and from the northeast, the temperature of the water fifty-three. . . .

January 19. To-day, being in latitude 83° 20′, longitude 43° 5′ W. (the sea being of an extraordinarily dark colour), we again saw land from the masthead, and, upon a closer scrutiny, found it to be one of a group of very large islands. The shore was precipitous, and the interior seemed to be well wooded, a circumstance which occasioned us great joy. In about four hours from our first discovering the land we came to anchor in ten fathoms, sandy bottom, a league from the coast, as a high surf, with strong ripples here and there, rendered a nearer approach of doubtful expediency. The two largest boats were now ordered out, and a party, well armed (among whom were Peters and myself), proceeded to look for an opening in the reef which appeared to encircle the island. After searching about for some time, we discovered an inlet, which we were entering, when we saw four large canoes put off from the shore, filled with men who seemed to be well armed. We waited for them to come up, and as they moved with great rapidity, they were soon within hail. Captain Guy now held up a white handkerchief on the blade of an oar, when the strangers made a full stop, and commenced a loud jabbering all at once, intermingled with occasional shouts, in which we could distinguish the words *Anamoo-moo!* and *Lama-Lama!* They continued this for at least half an hour, during which we had a good opportunity of observing their appearance.

In the four canoes, which might have been fifty feet long and five broad, there were a hundred and ten savages in all. They were about the ordinary stature of Europeans, but of a more muscular and brawny frame. Their complexion a jet black, with thick and long woolly hair. They were clothed in skins of an unknown black animal, shaggy and silky, and made to fit the body with some degree of skill, the hair being inside, except where turned out about the neck, wrists, and ankles. Their arms consisted principally of clubs, of a dark, and apparently very heavy wood. Some spears, however, were observed among them, headed with flint, and a few slings. The bottoms of the canoes were full of black stones about the size of a large egg.

When they had concluded their harangue (for it was clear they intended their jabbering for such), one of them who seemed to be the chief stood up in the prow of his canoe, and made signs for us to bring our boats alongside of him. This hint we pretended not to understand, thinking it the wiser plan to maintain, if possible, the interval between us, as their number more than quadrupled our own. Finding this to be the case, the chief ordered the three other canoes to hold back, while he advanced towards us with his own. As soon as he came up with us he leaped on board the largest of our boats, and seated himself by the side of Captain Guy, pointing at the same time to the schooner, and repeating the words *Anamoo-moo!* and *Lama-Lama!* We now put back to the vessel, the four canoes following at a little distance.

Upon getting alongside the chief evinced symptoms of extreme surprise and delight, clapping his hands, slapping his thighs and breast, and laughing obstreperously. His followers behind joined in his merriment, and for some minutes the din was so excessive as to be absolutely deafening. Quiet being at length restored, Captain Guy ordered the boats to be hoisted up, as a necessary precaution, and gave the chief (whose name we soon found to be *Too-wit*) to understand that we could admit no more than twenty of his men on deck at one time. With this arrangement he appeared perfectly satisfied, and gave some directions to the canoes, when one of them approached, the rest remaining about fifty yards off. Twenty of the savages now got on board, and proceeded to ramble over every part of the deck, and scramble about among the rigging, making themselves much at home, and examining every article with great inquisitiveness.

It was quite evident that they had never before seen any of the white race—from whose complexion, indeed, they appeared to recoil. They believed the *Jane* to be a living creature, and seemed to be afraid of hurting it with the points of their spears, carefully turning them up. Our crew were much amused with the conduct of Too-wit in one instance. The cook was splitting some wood near the galley, and, by accident, struck his axe into the deck, making a gash of considerable depth. The chief immediately ran up, and pushing the cook on one side rather roughly, commenced a half whine, half howl, strongly indicative of sympathy in what he considered the sufferings of the schooner, patting and smoothing the gash with his hand, and washing it from a bucket of sea-water which stood by. This was a degree of ignorance for which we were not prepared, and for my part I could not help thinking some of it affected.

When the visitors had satisfied, as well as they could, their curiosity in regard to our upper works, they were admitted below, when their amazement exceeded all bounds. Their astonishment now appeared to be far too deep for words, for they roamed about in silence, broken only by low ejaculations. The arms afforded them much food for speculation, and they were suffered to handle and examine them at leisure. I do not believe that they had the least suspicion of their actual use, but rather took them for idols, seeing the care we had of them, and the attention with which we watched their movements while handling them. At the great guns their wonder was redoubled. They approached them with every mark of the profoundest reverence and awe, but forbore to examine them minutely. There were two large mirrors in the cabin, and here was the acme of their amazement. Too-wit was the first to approach them, and he had got in the middle of the cabin, with his face to one and his back to the other, before he fairly perceived them. Upon raising his eyes and seeing his reflected self in the glass, I thought the savage would go mad; but, upon turning short round to make a retreat, and beholding himself a second time in the opposite direction, I was afraid he would expire upon the spot. No persuasion could prevail upon him to take another look; but, throwing himself upon the floor, with his face buried in his hands, he remained thus until we were obliged to drag him upon deck.

The whole of the savages were admitted on board in this manner, twenty at a time, Too-wit being suffered to remain during the entire period. We saw no disposition to thievery among them, nor did we miss a single article after their departure. Throughout the whole of their visit they evinced the most friendly manner. There were, however, some points in their demeanour which we found it impossible to understand: for example, we could not get them to approach several very harmless objects—such as the schooner's sails, an egg, an open book, or a pan of flour. We endeavoured to ascertain if they had among them any articles which might be turned to account in the way of traffic, but found great difficulty in being comprehended. We made out, nevertheless, what greatly astonished us, that the islands abounded in the large tortoise of the Gallipagos, one of which we saw in the canoe of Too-wit. We saw also some *bêche de mer* in the hands of one of the savages, who was greedily devouring it in its natural state. These anomalies, for they were such when considered in regard to the latitude, induced Captain Guy to wish for a thorough investigation of the country, in the hope of making a profitable speculation in his discovery. . . . Too-wit himself remained on board, and, upon dropping our anchor, invited us to accompany him on shore, and visit his village in the interior. To this Captain Guy consented; and ten savages being left on board as hostages, a party of us, twelve in all, got in readiness to attend the chief. We took care to be well armed, yet without evincing any distrust. The schooner had her guns run out, her boarding-nettings up, and every other proper precaution was taken to guard against surprise. Directions were left with the chief mate to admit no person on board during our absence, and, in the event of our not appearing in twelve hours, to send the cutter, with a swivel, around the island in search of us. . . .

Chapter XIX

We were nearly three hours in reaching the village, it being more than nine miles in the interior, and the path lying through a rugged country. As we passed along, the party of Too-wit (the whole hundred and ten savages of the canoes) was momentarily strengthened by smaller detachments, of from two to six or seven, which joined us, as if by accident, at different turns of the road. There appeared so much of system in this that I could not help feeling distrust, and I spoke to Captain Guy of my apprehensions. It was now too late, however, to recede, and we concluded that our best security lay in evincing a perfect confidence in the good faith of Too-wit. We accordingly went on, keeping a wary eye upon the manœuvres of the savages, and not permitting them to divide our numbers by pushing in between. In this way, passing through a precipitous ravine, we at length reached what we were told was the only collection of habitations upon the island. As we came in sight of them, the chief set up a shout, and frequently repeated the word *Klock-klock*; which we supposed to be the name of the village, or perhaps the generic name for villages.

. . . . . .

As we approached the village with Too-wit and his party, a vast crowd of the people rushed out to meet us, with loud shouts, among which we could only distinguish the everlasting *Anamoo-moo!* and *Lama-Lama!* We were much surprised at perceiving that, with one or two exceptions, these newcomers were entirely naked, the skins being used only by the men of the canoes. All the weapons of the country seemed also to be in the possession of the latter, for there was no appearance of any among the villagers. There were a great many women and children, the former not altogether wanting in what might be termed personal beauty. They were straight, tall, and well formed, with a grace and freedom of carriage not to be found in civilized society. Their lips, however, like those of the men, were thick and clumsy, so that, even when laughing, the teeth were never disclosed. Their hair was of a finer texture than that of the males. Among these naked villagers there might have been ten or twelve who were clothed, like the party of Too-wit, in dresses of black skin, and armed with lances and heavy clubs. These appeared to have great influence among the rest, and were always addressed by the title *Wampoo*. These, too, were the tenants of the black skin palaces. That of Too-wit was situated in the centre of the village, and was much larger and somewhat better constructed than others of its kind. . . .

To this hut we were conducted with great solemnity, and as many of the natives crowded in after us as possible. Too-wit seated himself on the leaves, and made signs that we should follow his example. This we did, and presently found ourselves in a situation peculiarly uncomfortable, if not indeed critical. We were on the ground, twelve in number, with the savages, as many as forty, sitting on their hams so closely around us that, if any disturbance had arisen, we should have found it impossible to make use of our arms, or indeed to have risen on our feet. The pressure was not only inside the tent, but outside, where probably was every individual on the whole island, the crowd being prevented from trampling us to death only by the incessant exertions and vociferations of Too-wit. Our chief security lay, however, in the presence of Too-wit himself among us, and we resolved to stick by him closely, as the best chance of extricating ourselves from the dilemma, sacrificing him immediately upon the first appearance of hostile design.

After some trouble a certain degree of quiet was restored, when the chief addressed us in a speech of great length, and very nearly resembling the one delivered in the canoes, with the exception that the *Anamoo-moos!* were now somewhat more strenuously insisted upon than the *Lama-Lamas!* We listened in profound silence until the conclusion of his harangue, when Captain Guy replied by assuring the chief of his eternal friendship and goodwill, concluding what he had to say by a present of several strings of blue beads and a knife. At the former the monarch, much to our surprise, turned up his nose with some expression of contempt; but the knife gave him the most unlimited satisfaction, and he immediately ordered dinner. This was handed into the tent over the heads of the attendants, and consisted of the palpitating entrails of a species of unknown animal, probably one of the slim-legged hogs which we had observed in our approach to the village. Seeing us at a loss how to proceed, he began, by way of setting us an example, to devour yard after yard of the enticing food, until we could positively stand it no longer, and evinced such manifest symptoms of rebellion of stomach as inspired his majesty with a degree of astonishment only inferior to that brought about by the looking-glasses. We declined, however, partaking of the delicacies before us, and endeavoured to make him understand that we had no appetite whatever, having just finished a hearty *déjeuner*.

. . . . . .

Chapter XX

The chief was as good as his word, and we were soon plentifully supplied with fresh provision. We found the tortoises as fine as we had ever seen, and the ducks surpassed our best species of wild fowl, being exceedingly tender, juicy, and well-flavoured. Besides these, the savages brought us, upon our making them comprehend our wishes, a vast quantity of brown celery and scurvy grass, with a canoe-load of fresh fish and some dried. The celery was a treat indeed, and the scurvy grass proved of incalculable benefit in restoring those of our men who had shown symptoms of disease. In a very short time we had not a single person on the sick-list. We had also plenty of other kinds of fresh provisions, among which may be mentioned a species of shell-fish resembling the mussel in shape, but with the taste of an oyster. Shrimps, too, and prawns were abundant, and albatross and other birds' eggs with dark shells. We took in, too, a plentiful stock of the flesh of the hog which I have mentioned before. Most of the men found it a palatable food, but I thought it fishy and otherwise disagreeable. In return for these good things we presented the natives with blue beads, brass trinkets, nails, knives, and pieces of red cloth, they being fully delighted in the exchange. We established a regular market on shore, just under the guns of the schooner, where our barterings were carried on with every appearance of good faith, and a degree of order which their conduct at the village of Klock-klock had not led us to expect from the savages.

Matters went on thus very amicably for several days, during which parties of the natives were frequently on board the schooner, and parties of our men frequently on shore, making long excursions into the interior, and receiving no molestation whatever. Finding the ease with which the vessel might be loaded with *bêche de mer*, owing to the friendly disposition of the islanders, and the readiness with which they would render us assistance in collecting it, Captain Guy resolved to enter into negotiation with Too-wit for the erection of suitable houses in which to cure the article, and for the services of himself and tribe in gathering as much as possible, while he himself took advantage of the fine weather to prosecute his voyage to the southward. Upon mentioning this project to the chief he seemed very willing to enter into an agreement. A bargain was accordingly struck, perfectly satisfactory to both parties, by which it was arranged that, after making the necessary preparations such as laying off the proper grounds, erecting a portion of the buildings, and doing some other work in which the whole of our crew would be required, the schooner should proceed on her route, leaving three of her men on the island to superintend the fulfil-ment of the project, and instruct the natives in drying the *bêche de mer*. In regard to terms, these were made to depend upon the exertions of the savages in our absence. They were to receive a stipulated quantity of blue beads, knives, red cloth, and so forth, for every certain number of piculs of the *bêche de mer* which should be ready on our return.

. . . . . .

By the last of the month we had everything in readiness for departure. We had agreed, however, to pay a formal visit of leavestaking to the village, and Too-wit insisted so pertinaciously upon our keeping the promise, that we did not think it advisable to run the risk of offending him by a final refusal. I believe that not one of us had at this time the slightest suspicion of the good faith of the savages. They had uniformly behaved with the greatest decorum, aiding us with alacrity in our work, offering us their commodities, frequently without price, and never, in any instance, pilfering a single article, although the high value they set upon the goods we had with us was evident by the extravagant demonstrations of joy always manifested upon our making them a present. The women especially were most obliging in every respect, and, upon the whole, we should have been the most suspicious of human beings had we entertained a single thought of perfidy on the part of a people who treated us so well. A very short while sufficed to prove that this apparent kindness of disposition was only the result of a deeply-laid plan for our destruction, and that the islanders for whom we entertained such inordinate feelings of esteem, were among the most barbarous, subtle, and bloodthirsty wretches that ever contaminated the face of the globe.

It was on the first of February that we went on shore for the purpose of visiting the village. Although, as said before, we entertained not the slightest suspicion, still no proper precaution was neglected. Six men were left in the schooner with instructions to permit none of the savages to approach the vessel during our absence, under any pretence whatever, and to remain constantly on deck. The boarding-nettings were up, the guns double-shotted with grape and canister, and the swivels loaded with canisters of musket-balls. She lay, with her anchor apeak, about a mile from the shore, and no canoe could approach her in any direction without being distinctly seen and exposed to the full fire of our swivels immediately.

The six men being left on board, our shore-party consisted of thirty-two persons in all. We were armed to the teeth, having with us muskets, pistols, and cutlasses, besides, each had a long kind of seaman's knife, somewhat resembling the Bowie knife now so much used throughout our western and southern country. A hundred of the black-skin warriors met us at the landing for the purpose of accompanying us on our way. We noticed, however, with some surprise, that they were now entirely without arms; and, upon questioning Too-wit in relation to this circumstance, he merely answered that *Mattee non we pa pa si*—meaning that there was no need of arms where all were brothers. We took this in good part, and proceeded.

We had passed the spring and rivulet of which I before spoke, and were now entering upon a narrow gorge leading through the chain of soapstone hills among which the village was situated. This gorge was very rocky and uneven, so much so that it was with no little difficulty we scrambled through it on our first visit to Klock-klock. The whole length of the ravine might have been a mile and a half, or probably two miles. It wound in every possible direction through the hills (having apparently formed, at some remote period, the bed of a torrent), in no instance proceeding more than twenty yards without an abrupt turn. The sides of this dell would have averaged, I am sure, seventy or eighty feet in perpendicular altitude throughout the whole of their extent, and in some portions they arose to an astonishing height, overshadowing the pass so completely that but little of the light of day could penetrate. The general width was about forty feet, and occasionally it diminished so as not to allow the passage of more than five or six persons abreast. In short, there could be no place in the world better adapted for the consummation of an ambuscade, and it was no more than natural that we should look carefully to our arms as we entered upon it. When I now think of our egregious folly, the chief subject of astonishment seems to be, that we should have ever ventured, under any circumstances, so completely into the power of unknown savages as to permit them to march both before and behind us in our progress through this ravine. Yet such was the order we blindly took up, trusting foolishly to the force of our party, the unarmed condition of Too-wit and his men, the certain efficacy of our firearms (whose effect was yet a secret to the natives), and, more than all, to the long-sustained pretension of friendship kept up by these infamous wretches. Five or six of them went on before, as if to lead the way, ostentatiously busying themselves in removing the larger stones and rubbish from the path. Next came our own party. We walked closely together, taking care only to prevent separation. Behind followed the main body of the savages, observing unusual order and decorum.

Dirk Peters, a man named Wilson Allen, and myself were on the right of our companions, examining, as we went along, the singular stratification of the precipice which overhung us. A fissure in the soft rock attracted our attention. It was about wide enough for one person to enter without squeezing, and extended back into the hill some eighteen or twenty feet in a straight course, sloping afterward to the left. The height of the opening, as far as we could see into it from the main gorge, was perhaps sixty or seventy feet. There were one or two stunted shrubs growing from the crevices, bearing a species of filbert which I felt some curiosity to examine, and pushed in briskly for that purpose, gathering five or six of the nuts at a grasp, and then hastily retreating. As I turned, I found that Peters and Allen had followed me. I desired them to go back, as there was not room for two persons to pass, saying they should have some of my nuts. They accordingly turned, and were scrambling back, Allen being close to the mouth of the fissure, when I was suddenly aware of a concussion resembling nothing I had ever before experienced, and which impressed me with a vague conception, if indeed I then thought of anything, that the whole foundations of the solid globe were suddenly rent asunder, and that the day of universal dissolution was at hand.

Chapter XXI

As soon as I could collect my scattered senses, I found myself nearly suffocated, and grovelling in utter darkness among a quantity of loose earth, which was also falling upon me heavily in every direction, threatening to bury me entirely. Horribly alarmed at this idea, I struggled to gain my feet, and at last succeeded. I then remained motionless for some moments, endeavouring to conceive what had happened to me, and where I was. Presently I heard a deep groan just at my ear, and afterward the smothered voice of Peters calling to me for aid in the name of God. I scrambled one or two paces forward, when I fell directly over the head and shoulders of my companion, who, I soon discovered, was buried in a loose mass of earth as far as his middle, and struggling desperately to free himself from the pressure. I tore the dirt from around him with all the energy I could command, and at length succeeded in getting him out.

As soon as we sufficiently recovered from our fright and surprise to be capable of conversing rationally, we both came to the conclusion that the walls of the fissure in which we had ventured had, by some convulsion of nature, or probably from their own weight, caved in overhead, and that we were consequently lost for ever, being thus entombed alive. For a long time we gave up supinely to the most intense agony and despair, such as cannot be adequately imagined by those who have never been in a similar situation. I firmly believed that no incident ever occurring in the course of human events is more adapted to inspire the supremeness of mental and bodily distress than a case like our own, of living inhumation. The blackness of darkness which envelops the victim, the terrific oppression of lungs, the stifling fumes from the damp earth, unite with the ghastly considerations that we are beyond the remotest confines of hope, and that such is the allotted portion of *the dead*, to carry into the human heart a degree of appalling awe and horror not to be tolerated—never to be conceived.

At length Peters proposed that we should endeavour to ascertain precisely the extent of our calamity, and grope about our prison; it being barely possible, he observed, that some opening might yet be left us for escape. I caught eagerly at this hope, and, arousing myself to exertion, attempted to force my way through the loose earth. Hardly had I advanced a single step before a glimmer of light became perceptible, enough to convince me that, at all events, we should not immediately perish for want of air. We now took some degree of heart, and encouraged each other to hope for the best. Having scrambled over a bank of rubbish which impeded our farther progress in the direction of the light, we found less difficulty in advancing, and also experienced some relief from the excessive oppression of lungs which had tormented us. Presently we were enabled to obtain a glimpse of the objects around, and discovered that we were near the extremity of the straight portion of the fissure, where it made a turn to the left. A few struggles more, and we reached the bend, when, to our inexpressible joy, there appeared a long seam or crack extending upward a vast distance, generally at an angle of about forty-five degrees, although sometimes much more precipitous. We could not see through the whole extent of this opening; but, as a good deal of light came down it, we had little doubt of finding at the top of it (if we could by any means reach the top) a clear passage into the open air.

. . . . . .

After having reposed for about an hour, we pushed on slowly up the ravine, and had gone no great way before we heard a succession of tremendous yells. At length we reached what might be called the surface of the ground; for our path hitherto, since leaving the platform, had lain beneath an archway of high rock and foliage, at a vast distance overhead. With great caution we stole to a narrow opening, through which we had a clear sight of the surrounding country, when the whole dreadful secret of the concussion broke upon us in one moment and at one view.

The spot from which we looked was not far from the summit of the highest peak in the range of the soapstone hills. The gorge in which our party of thirty-two had entered ran within fifty feet to the left of us. But, for at least one hundred yards, the channel or bed of this gorge was entirely filled up with the chaotic ruins of more than a million tons of earth and stone that had been artificially tumbled within it. The means by which the vast mass had been precipitated were not more simple than evident, for sure traces of the murderous work were yet remaining. In several spots along the top of the eastern side of the gorge (we were now on the western) might be seen stakes of wood driven into the earth. In these spots the earth had not given way; but throughout the whole extent of the face of the precipice from which the mass *had* fallen, it was clear, from marks left in the soil resembling those made by the drill of the rock-blaster, that stakes similar to those we saw standing had been inserted, at not more than a yard apart, for the length of perhaps three hundred feet, and ranging at about ten feet back from the edge of the gulf. Strong cords of grape vine were attached to the stakes still remaining on the hill, and it was evident that such cords had also been attached to each of the other stakes. I have already spoken of the singular stratification of these soapstone hills; and the description just given of the narrow and deep fissure through which we effected our escape from inhumation will afford a further conception of its nature. This was such that almost every natural convulsion would be sure to split the soil into perpendicular layers or ridges running parallel with one another; and a very moderate exertion of art would be sufficient for effecting the same purpose. Of this stratification the savages had availed themselves to accomplish their treacherous ends. There can be no doubt that, by the continuous line of stakes, a partial rupture of the soil had been brought about, probably to the depth of one or two feet, when, by means of a savage pulling at the end of each of the cords (these cords being attached to the tops of the stakes, and extending back from the edge of the cliff), a vast leverage power was obtained, capable of hurling the whole face of the hill, upon a given signal, into the bosom of the abyss below. The fate of our poor companions was no longer a matter of uncertainty. We alone had escaped from the tempest of that overwhelming destruction. We were the only living white men upon the island.

Chapter XXII

Our situation, as it now appeared, was scarcely less dreadful than when we had conceived ourselves entombed forever. We saw before us no prospect but that of being put to death by the savages, or of dragging out a miserable existence in captivity among them. We might, to be sure, conceal ourselves for a time from their observation among the fastnesses of the hills, and, as a final resort, in the chasm from which we had just issued; but we must either perish in the long Polar winter through cold and famine, or be ultimately discovered in our efforts to obtain relief.

The whole country around us seemed to be swarming with savages, crowds of whom, we now perceived, had come over from the islands to the southward on flat rafts, doubtless with a view of lending their aid in the capture and plunder of the *Jane*. The vessel still lay calmly at anchor in the bay, those on board being apparently quite unconscious of any danger awaiting them. How we longed at that moment to be with them! either to aid in effecting their escape, or to perish with them in attempting a defence. We saw no chance even of warning them of their danger without bringing immediate destruction upon our own heads, with but a remote hope of benefit to them. A pistol fired might suffice to apprise them that something wrong had occurred; but the report could not possibly inform them that their only prospect of safety lay in getting out of the harbour forthwith—it could not tell them that no principles of honour now bound them to remain, that their companions were no longer among the living. Upon hearing the discharge they could not be more thoroughly prepared to meet the foe, who were now getting ready to attack, than they already were, and always had been. No good, therefore, and infinite harm, would result from our firing, and, after mature deliberation, we forbore.

Our next thought was to attempt to rush toward the vessel, to seize one of the four canoes which lay at the head of the bay, and endeavour to force a passage on board. But the utter impossibility of succeeding in this desperate task soon became evident. The country, as I said before, was literally swarming with the natives, skulking among the bushes and recesses of the hills, so as not to be observed from the schooner. In our immediate vicinity especially, and blockading the sole path by which we could hope to attain the shore at the proper point, were stationed the whole party of the black-skin warriors, with Too-wit at their head, and apparently only waiting for some re-enforcement to commence his onset upon the *Jane*. The canoes, too, which lay at the head of the bay, were manned with savages, unarmed, it is true, but who undoubtedly had arms within reach. We were forced, therefore, however unwillingly, to remain in our place of concealment, mere spectators of the conflict which presently ensued.

In about half an hour we saw some sixty or seventy rafts, or flatboats, with outriggers, filled with savages, and coming round the southern bight of the harbour. They appeared to have no arms except short clubs, and stones which lay in the bottom of the rafts. Immediately afterward another detachment, still larger, approached in an opposite direction, and with similar weapons. The four canoes, too, were now quickly filled with natives, starting up from the bushes at the head of the bay, and put off swiftly to join the other parties. Thus, in less time than I have taken to tell it, and as if by magic, the *Jane* saw herself surrounded by an immense multitude of desperadoes evidently bent upon capturing her at all hazards.

That they would succeed in so doing could not be doubted for an instant. The six men left in the vessel, however resolutely they might engage in her defence, were altogether unequal to the proper management of the guns, or in any manner to sustain a contest at such odds. I could hardly imagine that they would make resistance at all, but in this was deceived; for presently I saw them get springs upon the cable, and bring the vessel's starboard broadside to bear upon the canoes, which by this time were within pistol range, the rafts being nearly a quarter of a mile to windward. Owing to some cause unknown, but most probably to the agitation of our poor friends at seeing themselves in so hopeless a situation, the discharge was an entire failure. Not a canoe was hit or a single savage injured, the shot striking short and *ricocheting* over their heads. The only effect produced upon them was astonishment at the unexpected report and smoke, which was so excessive that for some moments I almost thought they would abandon their design entirely, and return to the shore. And this they would most likely have done had our men followed up their broadside by a discharge of small arms, in which, as the canoes were now so near at hand, they could not have failed in doing some execution, sufficient, at least, to deter this party from a farther advance, until they could have given the rafts also a broadside. But, in place of this, they left the canoe party to recover from their panic, and, by looking about them, to see that no injury had been sustained, while they flew to the larboard to get ready for the rafts.

The discharge to larboard produced the most terrible effect. The star and double-headed shot of the large guns cut seven or eight of the rafts completely asunder, and killed, perhaps, thirty or forty of the savages outright, while a hundred of them, at least, were thrown into the water, the most of them dreadfully wounded. The remainder, frightened out of their senses, commenced at once a precipitate retreat, not even waiting to pick up their maimed companions, who were swimming about in every direction, screaming and yelling for aid. This great success, however, came too late for the salvation of our devoted people. The canoe party were already on board the schooner to the number of more than a hundred and fifty, the most of them having succeeded in scrambling up the chains and over the boarding-nettings even before the matches had been applied to the larboard guns. Nothing now could withstand their brute rage. Our men were borne down at once, overwhelmed, trodden under foot, and absolutely torn to pieces in an instant.

Seeing this, the savages on the rafts got the better of their fears, and came up in shoals to the plunder. In five minutes the *Jane* was a pitiable scene indeed of havoc and tumultuous outrage. The decks were split open and ripped up; the cordage, sails, and everything movable on deck demolished as if by magic; while, by dint of pushing at the stern, towing with the canoes, and hauling at the sides, as they swam in thousands around the vessel, the wretches finally forced her on shore (the cable having been slipped), and delivered her over to the good offices of Too-wit, who, during the whole of the engagement, had remained, like a skilful general, his post of security and reconnoissance among the hills, but, now that the victory was completed to his satisfaction, condescended to scamper down with his warriors of the black skin, and became a partaker in the spoils.

. . . . . .

They had already made a complete wreck of the vessel, and were now preparing to set her on fire. In a little while we saw the smoke ascending in huge volumes from her main hatchway, and, shortly afterward, a dense mass of flame burst up from the forecastle. The rigging, masts, and what remained of the sails caught immediately, and the fire spread rapidly along the decks. Still a great many of the savages retained their stations about her, hammering with large stones, axes, and cannon-balls at the bolts and other copper and iron work. On the beach, and in canoes and rafts, there were not less, altogether, in the immediate vicinity of the schooner, than ten thousand natives, besides the shoals of them who, laden with booty, were making their way inland and over to the neighbouring islands. We now anticipated a catastrophe, and were not disappointed. First of all there came a smart shock (which we felt as distinctly where we were as if we had been slightly galvanized), but unattended with any visible signs of an explosion. The savages were evidently startled, and paused for an instant from their labours and yellings. They were upon the point of recommencing, when suddenly a mass of smoke puffed up from the decks, resembling a black and heavy thunder-cloud—then, as if from its bowels, arose a tall stream of vivid fire to the height, apparently, of a quarter of a mile—then there came a sudden circular expansion of the flame—then the whole atmosphere was magically crowded, in a single instant, with a wild chaos of wood, and metal, and human limbs—and, lastly, came the concussion in its fullest fury, which hurled us impetuously from our feet, while the hills echoed and re-echoed the tumult, and a dense shower of the minutest fragments of the ruins tumbled headlong in every direction around us.

The havoc among the savages far exceeded our utmost expectation, and they had now, indeed, reaped the full and perfect fruits of their treachery. Perhaps a thousand perished by the explosion, while at least an equal number were desperately mangled. The whole surface of the bay was literally strewn with the struggling and drowning wretches, and on shore matters were even worse. They seemed utterly appalled by the suddenness and completeness of their discomfiture, and made no efforts at assisting one another. At length we observed a total change in their demeanour. From absolute stupor, they appeared to be, all at once, aroused to the highest pitch of excitement, and rushed wildly about, going to and from a certain point on the beach, with the strangest expressions of mingled horror, rage, and intense curiosity depicted on their countenances, and shouting, at the top of their voices, "*Tekeli-li! Tekeli-li!*"

Presently we saw a large body go off into the hills, whence they returned in a short time, carrying stakes of wood. These they brought to the station where the crowd was the thickest, which now separated so as to afford us a view of the object of all this excitement. We perceived something white lying upon the ground, but could not immediately make out what it was. At length we saw that it was the carcass of the strange animal with the scarlet teeth and claws which the schooner had picked up at sea on the eighteenth of January. Captain Guy had had the body preserved for the purpose of stuffing the skin and taking it to England. I remember he had given some directions about it just before our making the island, and it had been brought into the cabin and stowed away in one of the lockers. It had now been thrown on shore by the explosion; but why it had occasioned so much concern among the savages was more than we could comprehend. Although they crowded around the carcass at a little distance, none of them seemed willing to approach it closely. By-and-by the men with the stakes drove them in a circle around it, and, no sooner was this arrangement completed, than the whole of the vast assemblage rushed into the interior of the island, with loud screams of "*Tekeli-li! Tekeli-li!*"

Chapter XXIII

. . . . . .

On the seventeenth we set out with the determination of examining more thoroughly the chasm of black granite into which we
had made our way in the first search. We remembered that one
of the fissures in the sides of this pit had been but partially looked
into, and we were anxious to explore it, although with no expectation of discovering here any opening.

. . . . . .

Chapter XXIV

On the twentieth of the month, finding it altogether impossible
to subsist any longer upon the filberts, the use of which occasioned
us the most excruciating torment, we resolved to make a desperate
attempt at descending the southern declivity of the hill. The face
of the precipice was here of the softest species of soapstone, although nearly perpendicular throughout its whole extent (a depth
of a hundred and fifty feet at the least), and in many places even
overarching. After a long search we discovered a narrow ledge about
twenty feet below the brink of the gulf; upon this Peters contrived
to leap, with what assistance I could render him by means of our
pocket-handkerchiefs tied together. With somewhat more difficulty
I also got down; and we then saw the possibility of descending the
whole way by the process in which we had clambered up from
the chasm when we had been buried by the fall of the hill—that
is, by cutting steps in the face of the soapstone with our knives.
The extreme hazard of the attempt can scarcely be conceived; but,
as there was no other resource, we determined to undertake it.

. . . . . .

We now found ourselves not far from the ravine which had
proved the tomb of our friends, and to the southward of the spot
where the hill had fallen. The place was one of singular wildness,
and its aspect brought to my mind the descriptions given by
travellers of those dreary regions marking the site of degraded
Babylon. Not to speak of the ruins of the disruptured cliff, which
formed a chaotic barrier in the vista to the northward, the surface

of the ground in every other direction was strewn with huge tumuli, apparently the wreck of some gigantic structures of art; although, in detail, no semblance of art could be detected. Scoria were abundant, and large shapeless blocks of the black granite, intermingled with others of marl,* and both granulated with metal. Of vegetation there were no traces whatsoever throughout the whole of the desolate area within sight. Several immense scorpions were seen, and various reptiles not elsewhere to be found in the high latitudes.

As food was our most immediate object, we resolved to make our way to the sea-coast, distant not more than half a mile, with a view of catching turtle, several of which we had observed from our place of concealment on the hill. We had proceeded some hundred yards, threading our route cautiously between the huge rocks and tumuli, when, upon turning a corner, five savages sprung upon us from a small cavern, felling Peters to the ground with a blow from a club. As he fell the whole party rushed upon him to secure their victim, leaving me time to recover from my astonishment. I still had the musket, but the barrel had received so much injury in being thrown from the precipice that I cast it aside as useless, preferring to trust my pistols, which had been carefully preserved in order. With these I advanced upon the assailants, firing one after the other in quick succession. Two savages fell, and one, who was in the act of thrusting a spear into Peters, sprung to his feet without accomplishing his purpose. My companion being thus released, we had no further difficulty. He had his pistols also, but prudently declined using them, confiding in his great personal strength, which far exceeded that of any person I have ever known. Seizing a club from one of the savages who had fallen, he dashed out the brains of the three who remained, killing each instantaneously with a single blow of the weapon, and leaving us completely masters of the field.

So rapidly had these events passed, that we could scarcely believe in their reality, and were standing over the bodies of the dead in a species of stupid contemplation, when we were brought to recollection by the sound of shouts in the distance. It was clear

* The marl was also black; indeed, we noticed no light-coloured substances of any kind upon the island. [Poe's note.]

that the savages had been alarmed by the firing, and that we had little chance of avoiding discovery. To regain the cliff, it would be necessary to proceed in the direction of the shouts; and even should we succeed in arriving at its base, we should never be able to ascend it without being seen. Our situation was one of the greatest peril, and we were hesitating in which path to commence a flight, when one of the savages whom I had shot, and supposed dead, sprang to his feet, and attempted to make his escape. We overtook him, however, before he had advanced many paces, and were about to put him to death, when Peters suggested that we might derive some benefit from forcing him to accompany us in our attempt to escape. We therefore dragged him with us, making him understand that we would shoot him if he offered resistance. In a few minutes he was perfectly submissive, and ran by our sides as we pushed in among the rocks, making for the seashore.

So far, the irregularities of the ground we had been traversing hid the sea, except at intervals, from our sight, and, when we first had it fairly in view, it was, perhaps, two hundred yards distant. As we emerged into the open beach we saw, to our great dismay, an immense crowd of the natives pouring from the village, and from all visible quarters of the island, making towards us with gesticulations of extreme fury, and howling like wild beasts. We were upon the point of turning upon our steps, and trying to secure a retreat among the fastnesses of the rougher ground, when I discovered the bows of two canoes projecting from behind a large rock which ran out into the water. Towards these we now ran with all speed, and, reaching them, found them unguarded, and without any other freight than three of the large Gallipago turtles and the usual supply of paddles for sixty rowers. We instantly took possession of one of them, and, forcing our captive on board, pushed out to sea with all the strength we could command.

We had not made, however, more than fifty yards from the shore before we became sufficiently calm to perceive the great oversight of which we had been guilty in leaving the other canoe in the power of the savages, who, by this time, were not more than twice as far from the beach as ourselves, and were rapidly advancing to the pursuit. No time was now to be lost. Our hope was, at best, a forlorn one, but we had none other. It was very doubtful whether, with the utmost exertion, we could get back in time to anticipate them in taking possession of the canoe; but yet there was a chance that we could. We might save ourselves if we succeeded, while not to make the attempt was to resign ourselves to inevitable butchery.

The canoe was modelled with the bow and stern alike, and, in place of turning it around, we merely changed our position in paddling. As soon as the savages perceived this they redoubled their yells, as well as their speed, and approached with inconceivable rapidity. We pulled, however, with all the energy of desperation, and arrived at the contested point before more than one of the natives had attained it. This man paid dearly for his superior agility, Peters shooting him through the head with a pistol as he approached the shore. The foremost among the rest of his party were probably some twenty or thirty paces distant as we seized upon the canoe. We at first endeavoured to pull her into the deep water, beyond the reach of the savages, but, finding her too firmly aground, and there being no time to spare, Peters, with one or two heavy strokes from the butt of the musket, succeeded in dashing out a large portion of the bow and of one side. We then pushed off. Two of the natives by this time had got hold of our boat, obstinately refusing to let go, until we were forced to dispatch them with our knives. We were now clear off, and making great way out to sea. The main body of the savages, upon reaching the broken canoe, set up the most tremendous yell of rage and disappointment conceivable. In truth, from everything I could see of these wretches, they appeared to be the most wicked, hypocritical, vindictive, bloodthirsty, and altogether fiendish race of men upon the face of the globe. It is clear we should have had no mercy had we fallen into their hands. They made a mad attempt at following us in the fractured canoe, but, finding it useless, again vented their rage in a series of hideous vociferations, and rushed up into the hills.

We were thus relieved from immediate danger, but our situation was still sufficiently gloomy. We knew that four canoes of the kind we had were at one time in the possession of the savages, and were not aware of the fact (afterward ascertained from our captive) that two of these had been blown to pieces in the explosion of the *Jane Guy*. We calculated, therefore, upon being yet pursued, as soon as our enemies could get round to the bay (distant about three miles) where the boats were usually laid up. Fearing this, we made every exertion to leave the island behind us, and went rapidly through the water, forcing the prisoner to take a paddle. In about half an hour, when we had gained, probably, five or six miles to the southward, a large fleet of the flat-bottomed canoes or rafts were seen to emerge from the bay evidently with the design of pursuit. Presently they put back, despairing to overtake us.

Chapter XXV

We now found ourselves in the wide and desolate Antarctic Ocean, in a latitude exceeding eighty-four degrees, in a frail canoe, and with no provision but the three turtles. The long Polar winter, too, could not be considered as far distant, and it became necessary that we should deliberate well upon the course to be pursued. There were six or seven islands in sight belonging to the same group, and distant from each other about five or six leagues; but upon neither of these had we any intention to venture. In coming from the northward in the *Jane Guy* we had been gradually leaving behind us the severest regions of ice—this, however little it may be in accordance with the generally received notions respecting the Antarctic, was a fact experience would not permit us to deny. To attempt, therefore, getting back, would be folly—especially at so late a period of the season. Only one course seemed to be left open for hope. We resolved to steer boldly to the southward, where there was at least a probability of discovering other lands, and more than a probability of finding a still milder climate.

So far we had found the Antarctic, like the Arctic Ocean, peculiarly free from violent storms or immoderately rough water; but our canoe was, at best, of frail structure, although large, and we set busily to work with a view of rendering her as safe as the limited means in our possession would admit. The body of the boat was of no better material than bark—the bark of a tree unknown. The ribs were of a tough osier, well adapted to the purpose for which it was used. We had fifty feet room from stem to stern, from four to six in breadth, and in depth throughout four feet and a half—the boats thus differing vastly in shape from those of any other inhabitants of the Southern Ocean with whom civilized nations are acquainted. We never did believe them the workmanship of the ignorant islanders who owned them; and some days after this period discovered, by questioning our captive, that they were in fact made by the natives of a group to the southwest of the country where we found them, having fallen accidentally into the hands of our barbarians. What we could do for the security of our boat was very little indeed. Several wide rents were discovered near both ends, and these we contrived to patch up with pieces of woollen jacket. With the help of the superfluous paddles, of which there were a great many, we erected a kind of framework about the bow, so as to break the force of any seas which might threaten to fill us in that quarter. We also set up two paddle-blades for masts, placing them opposite each other, one by each gunwale, thus saving the necessity of a yard. To these masts we attached a sail made of our shirts—doing this with some difficulty, as here we could get no assistance from our prisoner whatever, although he had been willing enough to labour in all the other operations. The sight of the linen seemed to affect him in a very singular manner. He could not be prevailed upon to touch it or go near it, shuddering when we attempted to force him, and shrieking out, "*Tekeli-li.*"

Having completed our arrangements in regard to the security of the canoe, we now set sail to the south-southeast for the present, with the view of weathering the most southerly of the group in sight. This being done, we turned the bow full to the southward. The weather could by no means be considered disagreeable. We had a prevailing and very gentle wind from the northward, a smooth sea, and continual daylight. No ice whatever was to be seen; *nor did I ever see one particle of this after leaving the parallel of Bennett's Islet.* Indeed, the temperature of the water was here far too warm for its existence in any quantity. Having killed the largest of our tortoises, and obtained from him not only food but a copious supply of water, we continued on our course, without any incident of moment, for perhaps seven or eight days, during which period we must have proceeded a vast distance to the southward, as the wind blew constantly with us, and a very strong current set continually in the direction we were pursuing.

March 1. Many unusual phenomena now indicated that we were entering upon a region of novelty and wonder. A high range of light gray vapour appeared constantly in the southern horizon, flaring up occasionally in lofty streaks, now darting from east to west, now from west to east, and again presenting a level and uniform summit—in short, having all the wild variations of the Aurora Borealis. The average height of this vapour, as apparent from our station, was about twenty-five degrees. The temperature of the sea seemed to be increasing momentarily, and there was a very perceptible alteration in its colour.

March 2. To-day, by repeated questioning of our captive, we came to the knowledge of many particulars in regard to the island of the massacre, its inhabitants, and customs—but with these how can I *now* detain the reader? I may say, however, that we learned there were eight islands in the group, that they were governed by a common king, named *Tsalemon* or *Psalemoun*, who resided in one of the smallest of the islands—that the black skins forming the dress of the warriors came from an animal of huge size to be found only in a valley near the court of the king—that the inhabitants of the group fabricated no other boats than the flat-bottomed rafts—the four canoes being all of the kind in their possession, and these having been obtained, by mere accident, from some large island in the southwest—that his own name was Nu-Nu—that he had no knowledge of Bennett's Islet—and that the appellation of the island we had left was *Tsalal*. The commencement of the words *Tsalemon* and *Tsalal* was given with a prolonged hissing sound, which we found it impossible to imitate, even after repeated endeavours, and which was precisely the same with the note of the black bittern we had eaten up on the summit of the hill.

March 3. The heat of the water was now truly remarkable, and in colour was undergoing a rapid change, being no longer transparent, but of a milky consistency and hue. In our immediate vicinity it was usually smooth, never so rough as to endanger the canoe—but we were frequently surprised at perceiving, to our right and left, at different distances, sudden and extensive agitations of the surface—these, we at length noticed, were always preceded by wild flickerings in the region of the vapour to the southward.

March 4. To-day, with the view of widening our sail, the breeze from the northward dying away perceptibly, I took from my coatpocket a white handkerchief. Nu-Nu was seated at my elbow, and the linen accidentally flaring in his face, he became violently affected with convulsions. These were succeeded by drowsiness and stupor, and low murmurings of *"Tekeli-li! Tekeli-li!"*

March 5. The wind had entirely ceased, but it was evident that we were still hurrying on to the southward, under the influence of a powerful current. And now, indeed, it would seem reasonable that we should experience some alarm at the turn events were taking—but we felt none. The countenance of Peters indicated nothing of this nature, although it wore at times an expression I could not fathom. The Polar winter appeared to be coming on—but coming without its terrors. I felt a *numbness* of body and mind—a dreaminess of sensation—but this was all.

March 6. The gray vapour had now arisen many more degrees above the horizon, and was gradually losing its grayness of tint. The heat of the water was extreme, even unpleasant to the touch, and its milky hue was more evident than ever. To-day a violent agitation of the water occurred very close to the canoe. It was attended, as usual, with a wild flaring up of the vapour at its summit, and a momentary division at its base. A fine white powder, resembling ashes—but certainly not such—fell over the canoe and over a large surface of the water, as the flickering died away among the vapour and the commotion subsided in the sea. Nu-Nu threw himself on his face in the bottom of the boat, and no persuasions could induce him to arise.

March 7. This day we questioned Nu-Nu concerning the motives of his countrymen in destroying our companions; but he appeared to be too utterly overcome by terror to afford us any rational reply. He still obstinately lay in the bottom of the boat; and, upon our reiterating the questions as to the motive made use only of idiotic gesticulations, such as raising with his forefinger the upper lip, and displaying the teeth which lay beneath it. These were black. We had never before seen the teeth of an inhabitant of Tsalal.

March 8. To-day there floated by us one of the white animals whose appearance upon the beach at Tsalal had occasioned so wild a commotion among the savages. I would have picked it up, but there came over me a sudden listlessness, and I forbore. The heat of the water still increased, and the hand could no longer be endured within it. Peters spoke little, and I knew not what to think of his apathy. Nu-Nu breathed, and no more.

March 9. The whole ashy material fell now continually around us, and in vast quantities. The range of vapour to the southward had arisen prodigiously in the horizon, and began to assume more distinctness of form. I can liken it to nothing but a limitless cataract, rolling silently into the sea from some immense and far-distant rampart in the heaven. The gigantic curtain ranged along the whole extent of the southern horizon. It emitted no sound.

March 21. A sullen darkness now hovered above us—but from out the milky depths of the ocean a luminous glare arose, and stole up along the bulwarks of the boat. We were nearly overwhelmed by the white ashy shower which settled upon us and upon the canoe, but melted into the water as it fell. The summit of the cataract was utterly lost in the dimness and the distance. Yet we were evidently approaching it with a hideous velocity. At intervals there were visible in it wide, yawning, but momentary rents, and from out these rents, within which was a chaos of flitting and indistinct images, there came rushing and mighty, but soundless winds, tearing up the enkindled ocean in their course.

March 22. The darkness had materially increased, relieved only by the glare of the water thrown back from the white curtain before us. Many gigantic and pallidly white birds flew continuously now from beyond the veil, and their scream was the eternal *Tekeli-li!* as they retreated from our vision. Hereupon Nu-Nu stirred in the bottom of the boat; but upon touching him, we found his spirit departed. And now we rushed into the embraces of the cataract, where a chasm threw itself open to receive us. But there arose in our pathway a shrouded human figure, very far larger in its proportions than any dweller among men. And the hue of the skin of the figure was of the perfect whiteness of the snow.

NOTE

The circumstances connected with the late sudden and distressing death of Mr. Pym are already well known to the public through the medium of the daily press. It is feared that the few remaining chapters which were to have completed his narrative, and which were retained by him, while the above were in type, for the purpose of revision, have been irrecoverably lost through the accident by which he perished himself. This, however, may prove not to be the case, and the papers, if ultimately found, will be given to the public.

. . . . . .

On one point in the narrative some remarks may well be offered; and it would afford the writer of this appendix much pleasure if what he may here observe should have a tendency to throw credit, in any degree, upon the very singular pages now published. We allude to the chasms found in the island of Tsalal . . .

Mr. Pym has given the figures of the chasms without comment, and speaks decidedly of the *indentures* found at the extremity of the most easterly of these chasms as having but a fanciful resemblance to alphabetical characters, and, in short, as being positively *not such*. This assertion is made in a manner so simple, and sustained by a species of demonstrations so conclusive, viz. (the fitting of the projections of the fragments found among the dust into the indentures upon the wall), that we are forced to believe the writer in earnest; and no reasonable reader should suppose otherwise. But as the facts in relation to *all* the figures are most singular (especially when taken in connection with statements made in the body of the narrative), it may be as well to say a word or two concerning them all—this, too, the more especially as the facts in question have, beyond doubt, escaped the attention of Mr. Poe.

Figure 1, then, figure 2, figure 3, and figure 5, when conjoined with one another in the precise order which the chasms themselves presented, and when deprived of the small lateral branches or arches (which, it will be remembered, served only as a means of communication between the main chambers, and were of totally distinct character), constitute an Ethiopian verbal root—the root

ᕮ ᕫ ᖇ, "To be shady"—whence all the inflections of shadow or darkness.

In regard to the "left or most northwardly" of the indentures in figure 4, it is more than probable that the opinion of Peters was correct, and that the hieroglyphical appearance was really the work of art, and intended as the representation of a human form. The delineation is before the reader,* and he may, or may not, perceive the resemblance suggested; but the rest of the indentures afford strong confirmation of Peters' idea. The upper range is evidently the Arabic verbal root ᓫᓬᒐᕭᒐ, "To be white," whence all the inflections of brilliancy and whiteness. The lower range is not so immediately perspicuous. The characters are somewhat broken and disjointed; nevertheless, it cannot be doubted that, in their perfect state, they formed the full Egyptian word Π&UΥPHC, "The region of the south." It should be observed that these interpretations confirm the opinion of Peters in regard to the "most northwardly" of the figures. The arm is outstretched towards the south.

Conclusions such as these open a wide field for speculation and exciting conjecture. They should be regarded, perhaps, in connection with some of the most faintly-detailed incidents of the narrative; although in no visible manner is this chain of connection complete. *Tekeli-li* was the cry of the affrighted natives of Tsalal upon discovering the carcass of the *white* animal picked up at sea. This also was the shuddering exclamation of the captive Tsalalian upon encountering the *white* materials in possession of Mr. Pym. This also was the shriek of the swift-flying, *white*, and gigantic birds which issued from the vapoury *white* curtain of the south. Nothing *white* was to be found at Tsalal, and nothing otherwise in the subsequent voyage to the region beyond. It is not impossible that "Tsalal," the appellation of the island of the chasms, may be found, upon minute philological scrutiny, to betray either some alliance with the chasms themselves, or some reference to the Ethiopian characters so mysteriously written in their windings.

"*I have graven it within the hills, and my vengeance upon the dust within the rock.*"

---

* Poe had presented these "figures of the chasm" in Chapter XXIII. [Ed.]

WILLIAM GILMORE SIMMS

(1806–1870)

Simms was a leading spokesman for the view that attempted to justify slavery by arguing that the South was a "Greek Democracy," a society which offered the white man unlimited opportunities for advancement and provided the black man with privileges not always available to the Northern "wage slave"—a guarantee of the elementary necessities of life and an acknowledgment of his brotherhood under God.

Born to humble parents in Charleston, South Carolina, Simms had little formal education but read voraciously. After early experience as an editor and an unsuccessful poet, he turned to writing novels and achieved success with such works as Guy Rivers (1834), an adventure tale set in the wilds of north Georgia; The Partisan (1835), a romance of the Revolutionary War; and The Yemassee (1835), a South Carolina "Border Romance" which dealt with Indian warfare and helped gain Simms a reputation as the "Southern Cooper." Following his second marriage, to the daughter of a prosperous planter, he resided at Woodlands, his wife's plantation, and became further involved in the role of defender of the South against such antislavery attacks as Harriet Martineau's Society in America and Harriet Beecher Stowe's Uncle Tom's Cabin.

"Caloya; or, The Loves of the Driver" appeared in a collection of stories entitled The Wigwam and the Cabin (1845–1846, see Bibliography) and deals with the attempts of a Negro slave, Mingo,

to seduce Caloya, a young Catawba Indian matron. Mingo represents one of the earliest appearances in American literature of the
stereotype of "the black stud." The story's open treatment of a
sexual theme in connection with the Negro caused it to be attacked for "coarseness" in both Northern and Southern reviews.
Although Simms presents Mingo as a not entirely unsympathetic
figure, Tremaine McDowell felt that elements in his characterization helped to establish such notions in fiction as "the black man's
pomposity, his overbearing nature, his untruthfulness, his violence,
his ungovernable temper, his liking for drink, and his lust." In the
following passage Colonel Gillison journeys to the slave quarter in
order to warn Mingo's termagant wife that the Indians plan her
husband's murder, a fate from which he is saved when the scolding
wife drives him home in disgrace.

Caloya; or, The Loves of the Driver

Meanwhile, the youthful master of the veteran Mingo meditated
in the silence of his hall the mode by which to save that amorous
personage from the threatened consequences of his impertinence.
Not that he felt any desire to screen the fellow from chastisement.
Had he been told that husband and wife had simply resolved to
scourge him with many stripes, he would have struck hands and
cried "cheer" as loudly as any more indifferent spectator. But the
vengeance of the Catawba Othello promised to be of a character
far too extreme, and, the inferior moral sense and sensibility of
both Indian and negro considered, too greatly disproportioned to
the offence. It was therefore necessary that what he proposed to do
should be done quickly; and, taking his hat, Colonel Gillison sallied
forth to the negro quarter, in the centre of which stood the superior habitation of the Driver. His object was simply to declare
to the unfaithful servant that his evil designs and deeds were discovered, as well by himself as by the Catawba—to promise him the
due consequences of his falsehood to himself, and to warn him of
what he had to fear, in the event of his again obtruding upon the
privacy of the squatters. To those who insist that the working
classes in the South should enjoy the good things of this world

in as bountiful a measure as the wealthy proprietors of the soil, it would be very shocking to see that they lived poorly, in dwellings which, though rather better than those of the Russian boor, are yet very mean in comparison with those built by Stephen Girard, John Jacob Astor, and persons of that calibre. Nay, it would be monstrous painful to perceive that the poor negroes are constantly subjected to the danger of ophthalmic and other diseases, from the continued smokes in which they live, the fruit of those liberal fires which they keep up at all seasons, and which the more fortunate condition of the poor in the free States, does not often compel them to endure at any. It would not greatly lessen the evil of this cruel destiny, to know that each had his house to himself, exclusively; that he had his little garden plat around it, and that his cabbages, turnips, corn and potatoes, not to speak of his celery, his salad, &c., are, in half the number of cases, quite as fine as those which appear on his master's table. Then, his poultry-yard, and pig-pen—are they not there also?—but then, it must be confessed that his stock is not quite so large as his owner's, and there, of course, the parallel must fail. He has one immunity, however, which is denied to the owner. The hawk (to whose unhappy door most disasters of the poultry yard are referred) seldom troubles his chickens—his hens lay more numerously than his master's, and the dogs always prefer to suck the eggs of a white rather than those of a black proprietor. These, it is confessed, are very curious facts, inscrutable, of course, to the uninitiated; and in which the irreverent and sceptical alone refuse to perceive any legitimate cause of wonder. You may see in his hovel and about it many little additaments which, among the poor of the South, are vulgarly considered comforts; with the poor of other countries, however, as they are seldom known to possess them, they are no doubt regarded as burthens, which it might be annoying to take care of and oppressive to endure. A negro slave not only has his own dwelling, but he keeps a plentiful fire within it for which he pays no taxes. That he lives upon the fat of the land you may readily believe, since he is proverbially much fatter himself than the people of any other class. He has his own grounds for cultivation, and, having a taste for field sports, he keeps his own dog for the chase— an animal always of very peculiar characteristics, some of which we shall endeavour one day to analyse and develop. He is as hardy and cheerful as he is fat, and, but for one thing, it might be concluded safely that his condition was very far before that of the North American Indian—his race is more prolific, and, by increasing rather than diminishing, multiply necessarily and unhappily the great sinfulness of mankind. This, it is true, is sometimes urged as a proof of improving civilization, but then, every justly-minded person must agree with Miss Martineau, that it is dreadfully immoral. We suspect we have been digressing.

Col. Gillison soon reached the negro quarter, and tapping at the door of the Driver's wigwam, was admitted, after a brief parley, by the legitimate spouse of that gallant. Mingo had been married to Diana by the Reverend Jonathan Buckthorn, a preacher of the Methodist persuasion, who rode a large circuit and had travelled, with praiseworthy charity, all the way from Savannah River, in all weathers and on a hard going nag, simply to unite this worthy couple in the holy bonds of wedlock. At that time, both the parties were devout members of the Church, but they suffered from frequent lapses; and Mingo, having been engaged in sundry *liaisons* —which however creditable to, and frequent among the French, Italian and English nobility, are highly censurable in a slave population, and a decisive proof of the demoralizing tendency of such an institution—was, at the formal complaint of the wife, "suspended" from the enjoyment of the Communion Table, and finally, on a continuance of this foreign and fashionable practice, fully expelled from all the privileges of the brotherhood. Diana had been something of a termagant, but Mingo had succeeded in outstorming her. For the first six months after marriage, the issue was considered very doubtful; but a decisive battle took place at the close of that period, in which the vigorous woman was compelled to give in and Mingo remained undisputed master of the field. But though overthrown and conquered, she was not quiescent; and her dissatisfaction at the result showed itself in repeated struggles, which, however, were too convulsive and transient to render necessary any very decided exercise of the husband's energies. She growled and grumbled still, without cessation, and though she did not dare to resent his frequent infidelities, she nevertheless pursued them with an avidity, and followed the movements of her treacherous lord with a jealous watchfulness, which proved that she did not the less keenly feel them. Absolute fear alone made her restrain the fury which was yet boiling and burning in her soul. When her master declared his desire to see Mingo, what was her answer? Not, certainly, that of a very dutiful or well satisfied spouse.

"Mingo, mossa? Whay him dey? Ha! mossa, you bes' ax ebbry woman on de plantation 'fore you come to he own wife. I bin marry to Mingo by Parson Buckthorn, and de Parson bin make Mingo promise for lub and 'bey me, but he forget all he promise tree day after we bin man and wife. He nebber bin lub 't all; and as for 'bey—lor' ha' massy 'pon me, mossa, I speak noting but de trute when I tell you—he 'bey ebbry woman from yer to town 'fore he 'bey he own dear wife. Der's not a woman, mossa, 'pon de tree plantation, he aint lub more dan Di. Sometime he gone to Misser Jacks place—he hab wife dere! Sometime he gone to Misser Gabeau—he hab wife dere! Nex' time, he gone to Squir' Collins—he hab wife dere! Whay he no hab wife, mossa? Who can tell? He hab wife ebbry which whay, and now, he no *sacrify*, he gone—you aint gwine to bleeb me, mossa, I know you aint— he gone and look for wife at Indian camp, whay down by de 'Red Gulley.' De trute is, mossa, Mingo is a mos' powerful black rascal of a nigger as ebber lib on gentleman plantation."

It was fortunate for young Gillison that he knew something of the nature of a termagant wife, and could make allowances for the injustice of a jealous one. He would otherwise have been persuaded by what he heard that his driver was one of the most uncomely of all the crow family. Though yielding no very credulous faith to the complaints of Diana, he still found it impossible to refuse to hear them; and all that he could do by dint of perseverance, was to diminish the long narratives upon which she was prepared to enter to prove her liege lord to be no better than he should be. . . .

HARRIET BEECHER STOWE

(1811–1896)

Uncle Tom's Cabin was one of the most influential novels in the history of American literature. It was the first American novel to sell over a million copies, it was translated into almost thirty languages, it ran for a year on the New York stage in a dramatic adaptation by George Aiken, and it won for Harriet Beecher Stowe an international reputation as a spokesman for human rights. Lincoln is said to have regarded the book as an important influence in instigating the Civil War, and Charles Sumner once remarked that "If Uncle Tom's Cabin had not been written Abraham Lincoln could not have been elected President of the United States."

Harriet Beecher, the daughter of Lyman Beecher and sister of Henry Ward Beecher, was born at Litchfield, Connecticut, into a family which belonged to the intellectual aristocracy of New England and was noted for its commitment to Calvinist orthodoxy and social improvement. In 1832 the family moved to Cincinnati, where her father became president of Lane Theological Seminary, and in 1836 she married the Rev. Calvin E. Stowe, a professor at the seminary. While living in Cincinnati she was influenced by the antislavery sentiment prevalent at her father's school and by a brief visit to Kentucky where she observed slavery first-hand.

Uncle Tom's Cabin was composed in Maine after Reverend Stowe had accepted an appointment at Bowdoin College in 1850, and it was serialized in the National Era from June 1851 to April

1852 before being published as a book in 1852. It was followed by A Key to Uncle Tom's Cabin (1853), a compilation of facts from newspapers, court records, and letters, which was designed to answer attacks on the novel's accuracy. Dred, A Tale of the Great Dismal Swamp (1856), her second antislavery novel, attempted to show the harmful effects of slavery on white slaveholders. In later years Mrs. Stowe wrote works of New England local color, such as The Minister's Wooing (1859), The Pearl of Orr's Island (1862), and Oldtown Folks (1869)—books generally regarded as having considerably more literary merit than her antislavery novels.

Despite the vehemence with which Uncle Tom's Cabin was denounced in the South, Mrs. Stowe took pains to avoid condemning that region. She found much to compliment in Southern character and society, and much to criticize in the North. She was incensed by the cooperation of Northern officials with the Fugitive Slave Act of 1850, which called for the return of escaped slaves to their owners; and the worst villain of her book, Simon Legree, is a Northerner by birth. Instead of assessing blame, though, she was chiefly interested in showing the horrible personal effects of slavery —the tearing apart of families on the auction block and the degradation of young Negro girls sold into concubinage.

Her approach to her novel is passionately religious. Tom, with his night of Gethsemane, his scourging, his martyrdom, and his benediction upon his tormentors, is clearly intended as a Christ figure. Mrs. Stowe once said that Tom's story had unfolded before her in a vision she experienced while participating in a communion service. At another time she claimed that God had written the novel and she was a mere amanuensis.

Though Tom is consistently patient, humble, and accepting, he does not entirely resemble the obsequious and servile figure his name has come to stand for in popular usage. He never conceals his desire for freedom; he steadfastly refuses to bend his will to Legree's; he advises two of Legree's slaves to escape; and the chief reason he does not make his own attempt at freedom is so that he may minister to the slaves who must remain in bondage at Legree's plantation. Yet the novel does contain many unconsciously condescending pronouncements on Negro character, and its most sensitive and intelligent Negroes are generally light-skinned.

Contrasting with Tom's patience and resignation is the militancy of George Harris, the victim of brutal treatment at the hands of a white master incensed by his own recognition of the moral and intellectual superiority of his slave. Harris's belief that "black is beautiful," his desire for a separate black nation, and his willingness to employ violence when necessary, including the shooting of a slave-catcher, make him a remarkably contemporary figure.

From Uncle Tom's Cabin

Topsy

One morning, while Miss Ophelia was busy in some of her domestic cares, St. Clare's voice was heard, calling her at the foot of the stairs.

"Come down here, Cousin; I've something to show you."

"What is it?" said Miss Ophelia, coming down, with her sewing in her hand.

"I've made a purchase for your department,—see here," said St. Clare; and, with the word, he pulled along a little Negro girl, about eight or nine years of age.

She was one of the blackest of her race; and her round, shining eyes, glittering as glass beads, moved with quick and restless glances over everything in the room. Her mouth, half open with astonishment at the wonders of the new Mas'r's parlor, displayed a white and brilliant set of teeth. Her woolly hair was braided in sundry little tails, which stuck out in every direction. The expression of her face was an odd mixture of shrewdness and cunning, over which was oddly drawn, like a kind of veil, an expression of the most doleful gravity and solemnity. She was dressed in a single filthy, ragged garment, made of bagging; and stood with her hands demurely folded before her. Altogether, there was something odd and goblin-like about her appearance—something, as Miss Ophelia afterwards said, "so heathenish," as to inspire that good lady with utter dismay; and, turning to St. Clare, she said,

"Augustine, what in the world have you brought that thing here for?"

"For you to educate, to be sure, and train in the way she should go. I thought she was rather a funny specimen in the Jim Crow line. Here, Topsy," he added, giving a whistle, as a man would to call the attention of a dog, "give us a song, now, and show us some of your dancing."

The black, glassy eyes glittered with a kind of wicked drollery, and the thing struck up, in a clear shrill voice, an odd Negro melody, to which she kept time with her hands and feet, spinning round, clapping her hands, knocking her knees together, in a wild, fantastic sort of time, and producing in her throat all those odd guttural sounds which distinguish the native music of her race; and finally, turning a summerset or two, and giving a prolonged closing note, as odd and unearthly as that of a steam-whistle, she came suddenly down on the carpet, and stood with her hands folded, and a most sanctimonious expression of meekness and so-lemnity over her face, only broken by the cunning glances which she shot askance from the corners of her eyes.

Miss Ophelia stood silent, perfectly paralyzed with amazement.

St. Clare, like a mischievous fellow as he was, appeared to enjoy her astonishment; and, addressing the child again, said,

"Topsy, this is your new mistress. I'm going to give you up to her; see now that you behave yourself."

"Yes, Mas'r," said Topsy, with sanctimonious gravity, her wicked eyes twinkling as she spoke.

"You're going to be good, Topsy, you understand," said St. Clare.

"O yes, Mas'r," said Topsy, with another twinkle, her hands still devoutly folded.

"Now, Augustine, what upon earth is this for?" said Miss Ophelia. "Your house is so full of these little plagues, now, that a body can't set down their foot without treading on 'em. I get up in the morning, and find one asleep behind the door, and see one black head poking out from under the table, one lying on the door-mat, —and they are mopping and mowing and grinning between all the railings, and tumbling over the kitchen floor! What on earth did you want to bring this one for?"

"For you to educate—didn't I tell you? You're always preaching about educating. I thought I would make you a present of a fresh-caught specimen, and let you try your hand on her, and bring her up in the way she should go."

"I don't want her, I am sure;—I have more to do with 'em now than I want to."

"That's you Christians, all over!—you'll get up a society, and get some poor missionary to spend all his days among just such heathen. But let me see one of you that would take one into your house with you, and take the labor of their conversion on your-selves! No; when it comes to that, they are dirty and disagreeable, and it's too much care, and so on."

"Augustine, you know I didn't think of it in that light," said Miss Ophelia, evidently softening. "Well, it might be a real mis-sionary work," said she, looking rather more favorably on the child.

St. Clare had touched the right string. Miss Ophelia's conscien-tiousness was ever on the alert. "But," she added, "I really didn't see the need of buying this one;—there are enough now, in your house, to take all my time and skill."

"Well, then, Cousin," said St. Clare, drawing her aside, "I ought to beg your pardon for my good-for-nothing speeches. You are so good, after all, that there's no sense in them. Why, the fact is, this concern belonged to a couple of drunken creatures that keep a low restaurant that I have to pass by every day, and I was tired of hearing her screaming, and them beating and swearing at her. She looked bright and funny, too, as if something might be made of her;—so I bought her, and I'll give her to you. Try, now, and give her a good orthodox New England bringing up, and see what it'll make of her. You know I haven't any gift that way; but I'd like you to try."

"Well, I'll do what I can," said Miss Ophelia; and she ap-proached her new subject very much as a person might be supposed to approach a black spider, supposing them to have benevolent designs toward it.

"She's dreadfully dirty, and half naked," she said.

"Well, take her down stairs, and make some of them clean and clothe her up."

Miss Ophelia carried her to the kitchen regions.

"Don't see what Mas'r St. Clare wants of 'nother nigger!" said

Dinah, surveying the new arrival with no friendly air. "Won't have her round under *my* feet, *I* know!"

"Pah!" said Rosa and Jane, with supreme disgust; "let her keep out of our way! What in the world Mas'r wanted another of these low niggers for, I can't see!"

"You go long! No more nigger dan you be, Miss Rosa," said Dinah, who felt this last remark a reflection on herself. "You seem to tink yourself white folks. You an't nerry one, black *nor* white. I'd like to be one or turrer."

Miss Ophelia saw that there was nobody in the camp that would undertake to oversee the cleansing and dressing of the new arrival; and so she was forced to do it herself, with some very ungracious and reluctant assistance from Jane.

It is not for ears polite to hear the particulars of the first toilet of a neglected, abused child. In fact, in this world, multitudes must live and die in a state that it would be too great a shock to the nerves of their fellow-mortals even to hear described. Miss Ophelia had a good, strong, practical deal of resolution; and she went through all the disgusting details with heroic thoroughness, though, it must be confessed, with no very gracious air,—for endurance was the utmost to which her principles could bring her. When she saw, on the back and shoulders of the child, great welts and calloused spots, ineffaceable marks of the system under which she had grown up thus far, her heart became pitiful within her.

"See there!" said Jane, pointing to the marks, "don't that show she's a limb? We'll have fine works with her, I reckon. I hate these nigger young uns! so disgusting! I wonder that Mas'r would buy her!"

The "young un" alluded to heard all these comments with the subdued and doleful air which seemed habitual to her, only scanning, with a keen and furtive glance of her flickering eyes, the ornaments which Jane wore in her ears. When arrayed at last in a suit of decent and whole clothing, her hair cropped short to her head, Miss Ophelia, with some satisfaction, said she looked more Christian-like than she did, and in her own mind began to mature some plans for her instruction.

Sitting down before her, she began to question her.

"How old are you, Topsy?"

"Dunno, Missis," said the image, with a grin that showed all her teeth.

"Don't know how old you are? Didn't anybody ever tell you? Who was your mother?"

"Never had none!" said the child, with another grin.

"Never had any mother? What do you mean? Where were you born?"

"Never was born!" persisted Topsy, with another grin, that looked so goblin-like, that, if Miss Ophelia had been at all nervous, she might have fancied that she had got hold of some sooty gnome from the land of Diablerie; but Miss Ophelia was not nervous, but plain and business-like, and she said, with some sternness,

"You musn't answer me in that way, child; I'm not playing with you. Tell me where you were born, and who your father and mother were."

"Never was born," reiterated the creature, more emphatically; "never had no father nor mother, nor nothin'. I was raised by a speculator, with lots of others. Old Aunt Sue used to take car on us."

The child was evidently sincere; and Jane, breaking into a short laugh, said,

"Laws, Missis, there's heaps of 'em. Speculators buys 'em up cheap, when they's little, and gets 'em raised for market."

"How long have you lived with your master and mistress?"

"Dunno, Missis."

"Is it a year, or more, or less?"

"Dunno, Missis."

"Laws, Missis, those low Negroes,—they can't tell; they don't know anything about time," said Jane; "they don't know what a year is; they don't know their own ages."

"Have you ever heard anything about God, Topsy?"

The child looked bewildered, but grinned as usual.

"Do you know who made you?"

"Nobody, as I knows on," said the child, with a short laugh.

The idea appeared to amuse her considerably; for her eyes twinkled, and she added,

"I spect I grow'd. Don't think nobody never made me."

"Do you know how to sew?" said Miss Ophelia, who thought she would turn her inquiries to something more tangible.

"No, Missis."

"What can you do?—what did you do for your master and mistress?"

"Fetch water, and wash dishes, and rub knives, and wait on folks."

"Were they good to you?"

"Spect they was," said the child, scanning Miss Ophelia cunningly.

Miss Ophelia rose from this encouraging colloquy; St. Clare was leaning over the back of her chair.

"You find virgin soil there, Cousin; put in your own ideas,—you won't find many to pull up."

Miss Ophelia's ideas of education, like all her other ideas, were very set and definite; and of the kind that prevailed in New England a century ago, and which are still preserved in some very retired and unsophisticated parts, where there are no railroads. As nearly as could be expressed, they could be comprised in very few words: to teach them to mind when they were spoken to; to teach them the catechism, sewing, and reading; and to whip them if they told lies. And though, of course, in the flood of light that is now poured on education, these are left far away in the rear, yet it is an undisputed fact that our grandmothers raised some tolerably fair men and women under this regime, as many of us can remember and testify. At all events, Miss Ophelia knew of nothing else to do; and, therefore, applied her mind to her heathen with the best diligence she could command.

The child was announced and considered in the family as Miss Ophelia's girl; and, as she was looked upon with no gracious eye in the kitchen, Miss Ophelia resolved to confine her sphere of operation and instruction chiefly to her own chamber. With a self-sacrifice which some of our readers will appreciate, she resolved, instead of comfortably making her own bed, sweeping and dusting her own chamber,—which she had hitherto done, in utter scorn of all offers of help from the chambermaids of the establishment, —to condemn herself to the martyrdom of instructing Topsy to perform these operations,—ah, woe the day! Did any of our readers ever do the same, they will appreciate the amount of her self-sacrifice.

Miss Ophelia began with Topsy by taking her into her chamber, the first morning, and solemnly commencing a course of instruction in the art and mystery of bed-making.

Behold, then, Topsy, washed and shorn of all the little braided tails wherein her heart had delighted, arrayed in a clean gown, with well-starched apron, standing reverently before Miss Ophelia, with an expression of solemnity well befitting a funeral.

"Now, Topsy, I'm going to show you just how my bed is to be made. I am very particular about my bed. You must learn exactly how to do it."

"Yes, ma'am," says Topsy, with a deep sigh, and a face of woful earnestness.

"Now, Topsy, look here;—this is the hem of the sheet;—this is the right side of the sheet, and this is the wrong;—will you remember?"

"Yes, ma'am," says Topsy, with another sigh.

"Well, now, the under sheet you must bring over the bolster,—so,—and tuck it clear down under the mattress nice and smooth,—so,—do you see?"

"Yes, ma'am," said Topsy, with profound attention.

"But the upper sheet," said Miss Ophelia, "must be brought down in this way, and tucked under firm and smooth at the foot,—so,—the narrow hem at the foot."

"Yes, ma'am," said Topsy, as before;—but we will add, what Miss Ophelia did not see, that, during the time when the good lady's back was turned, in the zeal of her manipulations, the young disciple had contrived to snatch a pair of gloves and a ribbon, which she had adroitly slipped into her sleeves, and stood with her hands dutifully folded, as before.

"Now, Topsy, let's see *you* do this," said Miss Ophelia, pulling off the clothes, and seating herself.

Topsy, with great gravity and adroitness, went through the exercise completely to Miss Ophelia's satisfaction; smoothing the sheets, patting out every wrinkle, and exhibiting, through the whole process, a gravity and seriousness with which her instructress was greatly edified. By an unlucky slip, however, a fluttering fragment of the ribbon hung out of one of her sleeves, just as she was finishing, and caught Miss Ophelia's attention. Instantly she pounced upon it. "What's this? You naughty, wicked child,—you've been stealing this!"

The ribbon was pulled out of Topsy's own sleeve, yet was she not in the least disconcerted; she only looked at it with an air of the most surprised and unconscious innocence.

"Laws! why, that ar's Miss Feely's ribbon, an't it? How could it a got caught in my sleeve?"

"Topsy, you naughty girl, don't you tell me a lie,—you stole that ribbon!"

"Missis, I declar for't, I didn't;—never seed it till dis yer blessed minnit."

"Topsy," said Miss Ophelia, "don't you know it's wicked to tell lies?"

"I never tells no lies, Miss Feely," said Topsy, with virtuous gravity; "it's jist the truth I've been a tellin now, and an't nothin else."

"Topsy, I shall have to whip you, if you tell lies so."

"Laws, Missis, if you's to whip all day, couldn't say no other way," said Topsy, beginning to blubber. "I never seed dat ar,—it must a got caught in my sleeve. Miss Feely must have left it on the bed, and it got caught in the clothes, and so got in my sleeve."

Miss Ophelia was so indignant at the barefaced lie, that she caught the child and shook her.

"Don't you tell me that again!"

The shake brought the gloves on to the floor, from the other sleeve.

"There, you!" said Miss Ophelia, "will you tell me now, you didn't steal the ribbon?"

Topsy now confessed to the gloves, but still persisted in denying the ribbon.

"Now, Topsy," said Miss Ophelia, "if you'll confess all about it, I won't whip you this time." Thus adjured, Topsy confessed to the ribbon and gloves, with woful protestations of penitence.

"Well, now, tell me. I know you must have taken other things since you have been in the house, for I let you run about all day yesterday. Now, tell me if you took anything, and I shan't whip you."

"Laws, Missis! I took Miss Eva's red thing she wars on her neck."

"You did, you naughty child!—Well, what else?"

"I took Rosa's yer-rings,—them red ones."

"Go bring them to me this minute, both of 'em."

"Laws, Missis! I can't,—they's burnt up!"

"Burnt up!—what a story! Go get 'em, or I'll whip you."

Topsy, with loud protestations, and tears, and groans, declared that she *could* not. "They's burnt up—they was."

"What did you burn 'em up for?" said Miss Ophelia.

"Cause I's wicked,—I is. I's mighty wicked, any how. I can't help it."

Just at this moment, Eva came innocently into the room, with the identical coral necklace on her neck.

"Why, Eva, where did you get your necklace?" said Miss Ophelia.

"Get it? Why, I've had it on all day," said Eva.

"Did you have it on yesterday?"

"Yes; and what is funny, Aunty, I had it on all night. I forgot to take it off when I went to bed."

Miss Ophelia looked perfectly bewildered; the more so, as Rosa, at that instant, came into the room, with a basket of newly-ironed linen poised on her head, and the coral ear-drops shaking in her ears!

"I'm sure I can't tell anything what to do with such a child!" she said, in despair. "What in the world did you tell me you took those things for, Topsy?"

"Why, Missis said I must 'fess; and I couldn't think of nothin' else to 'fess," said Topsy, rubbing her eyes.

"But, of course, I didn't want you to confess things you didn't do," said Miss Ophelia; "that's telling a lie, just as much as the other."

"Laws, now, is it?" said Topsy, with an air of innocent wonder.

"La, there an't any such thing as truth in that limb," said Rosa, looking indignantly at Topsy. "If I was Mas'r St. Clare, I'd whip her till the blood run. I would,—I'd let her catch it!"

"No, no, Rosa," said Eva, with an air of command, which the child could assume at times; "you mustn't talk so, Rosa. I can't bear to hear it."

"La sakes! Miss Eva, you's so good, you don't know nothing how to get along with niggers. There's no way but to cut 'em well up, I tell ye."

"Rosa!" said Eva, "hush! Don't you say another word of that sort!" and the eye of the child flashed, and her cheek deepened its color.

Rosa was cowed in a moment.

"Miss Eva has got the St. Clare blood in her, that's plain. She can speak, for all the world, just like her papa," she said, as she passed out of the room.

Eva stood looking at Topsy.

There stood the two children, representatives of the two extremes of society. The fair, high-bred child, with her golden head, her deep eyes, her spiritual, noble brow, and prince-like movements; and her black, keen, subtle, cringing, yet acute neighbor. They stood the representatives of their races. The Saxon, born of ages of cultivation, command, education, physical and moral eminence; the Afric, born of ages of oppression, submission, ignorance, toil, and vice!

. . . . . .

The Martyr

. . . The escape of Cassy and Emmeline irritated the before surly temper of Legree to the last degree; and his fury, as was to be expected, fell upon the defenceless head of Tom. When he hurriedly announced the tidings among his hands, there was a sudden light in Tom's eye, a sudden upraising of his hands, that did not escape him. He saw that he did not join the muster of the pursuers. He thought of forcing him to do it; but, having had, of old, experience of his inflexibility when commanded to take part in any deed of inhumanity, he would not, in his hurry, stop to enter into any conflict with him.

Tom, therefore, remained behind, with a few who had learned of him to pray, and offered up prayers for the escape of the fugitives.

When Legree returned, baffled and disappointed, all the long-working hatred of his soul towards his slave began to gather in a deadly and desperate form. Had not this man braved him,—steadily, powerfully, resistlessly,—ever since he bought him? Was there not a spirit in him which, silent as it was, burned on him like the fires of perdition?

"I *hate* him!" said Legree, that night, as he sat up in his bed; "I *hate* him! And isn't he MINE? Can't I do what I like with him? Who's to hinder, I wonder?" And Legree clenched his fist, and shook it, as if he had something in his hands that he could rend in pieces.

But, then, Tom was a faithful, valuable servant; and, although Legree hated him the more for that, yet the consideration was still somewhat of a restraint to him.

The next morning, he determined to say nothing, as yet; to assemble a party, from some neighboring plantations, with dogs and guns; to surround the swamp, and go about the hunt systematically. If it succeeded, well and good; if not, he would summon Tom before him, and—his teeth clenched and his blood boiled—*then* he would break that fellow down, or——there was a dire inward whisper, to which his soul assented.

· · · · · ·

The hunt was long, animated, and thorough, but unsuccessful; and, with grave, ironic exultation, Cassy looked down on Legree, as, weary and dispirited, he alighted from his horse.

"Now, Quimbo," said Legree, as he stretched himself down in the sitting-room, "you jest go and walk that Tom up here, right away! The old cuss is at the bottom of this yer whole matter; and I'll have it out of his old black hide, or I'll know the reason why!"

Sambo and Quimbo, both, though hating each other, were joined in one mind by a no less cordial hatred of Tom. Legree had told them, at first, that he had bought him for a general overseer, in his absence; and this had begun an ill will, on their part, which had increased, in their debased and servile natures, as they saw him becoming obnoxious to their master's displeasure. Quimbo, therefore, departed, with a will, to execute his orders.

Tom heard the message with a forewarning heart; for he knew all the plan of the fugitives' escape, and the place of their present concealment;—he knew the deadly character of the man he had to deal with, and his despotic power. But he felt strong in God to meet death, rather than betray the helpless.

He set his basket down by the row, and, looking up, said, "Into thy hands I commend my spirit! Thou hast redeemed me, oh Lord God of truth!" and then quietly yielded himself to the rough, brutal grasp with which Quimbo seized him.

"Ay, ay!" said the giant, as he dragged him along; "ye'll cotch it, now! I'll boun' Mas'r's back's up *high!* No sneaking out, now! Tell ye, ye'll get it, and no mistake! See how ye'll look, now, helpin' Mas'r's niggers to run away! See what ye'll get!"

The savage words none of them reached that ear!—a higher voice there was saying, "Fear not them that kill the body, and, after that, have no more that they can do." Nerve and bone of that poor man's body vibrated to those words, as if touched by the finger of God; and he felt the strength of a thousand souls in one. As he passed along, the trees and bushes, the huts of his servitude, the whole scene of his degradation, seemed to whirl by him as the landscape by the rushing car. His soul throbbed,—his home was in sight,—and the hour of release seemed at hand.

"Well, Tom!" said Legree, walking up, and seizing him grimly by the collar of his coat, and speaking through his teeth, in a paroxysm of determined rage, "do you know I've made up my mind to KILL you?"

"It's very likely, Mas'r," said Tom, calmly.

"I *have,*" said Legree, with grim, terrible calmness, "*done—just —that—thing,* Tom, unless you'll tell me what you know about these yer gals!"

Tom stood silent.

"D'ye hear!" said Legree, stamping, with a roar like that of an incensed lion. "Speak!"

"*I han't got nothing to tell, Mas'r,*" said Tom, with a slow, firm, deliberate utterance.

"Do you dare to tell me, ye old black Christian, ye don't *know?*" said Legree.

Tom was silent.

"Speak!" thundered Legree, striking him furiously. "Do you know anything?"

"I know, Mas'r; but I can't tell anything. *I can die!*"

Legree drew in a long breath; and, suppressing his rage, took Tom by the arm, and, approaching his face almost to his, said, in a terrible voice, "Hark 'e, Tom!—ye think, 'cause I've let you off before, I don't mean what I say; but, this time, I've *made up my mind,* and counted the cost. You've always stood it out agin' me: now, I'll *conquer ye, or kill ye!*—one or t'other. I'll count every drop of blood there is in you, and take 'em, one by one, till ye give up!"

Tom looked up to his master, and answered, "Mas'r, if you was sick, or in trouble, or dying, and I could save ye, I'd *give* ye my heart's blood; and if taking every drop of blood in this poor old body would save your precious soul, I'd give 'em freely, as the Lord gave his for me. O, Mas'r! don't bring this great sin on your soul! It will hurt you more than 'twill me! Do the worst you can, my troubles'll be over soon; but, if ye don't repent, yours won't *never* end!"

Like a strange snatch of heavenly music, heard in the lull of a tempest, this burst of feeling made a moment's blank pause. Legree stood aghast, and looked at Tom; and there was such a silence, that the tick of the old clock could be heard, measuring, with silent touch, the last moments of mercy and probation to that hardened heart.

It was but a moment. There was one hesitating pause,—one irresolute, relenting thrill,—and the spirit of evil came back, with seven-fold vehemence; and Legree, foaming with rage, smote his victim to the ground.

Scenes of blood and cruelty are shocking to our ear and heart. What man has nerve to do, man has not nerve to hear. What brother-man and brother-Christian must suffer, cannot be told us, even in our secret chamber, it so harrows up the soul! And yet, oh my country; these things are done under the shadow of thy laws! O, Christ! thy church sees them, almost in silence!

But, of old, there was One whose suffering changed an instrument of torture, degradation and shame, into a symbol of glory, honor, and immortal life; and, where His spirit is, neither degrading stripes, nor blood, nor insults, can make the Christian's last struggle less than glorious.

Was he alone, that long night, whose brave, loving spirit was bearing up, in that old shed, against buffeting and brutal stripes?

Nay! There stood by him ONE,—seen by him alone,—"like unto the Son of God."

The tempter stood by him, too,—blinded by furious, despotic will,—every moment pressing him to shun that agony by the betrayal of the innocent. But the brave, true heart was firm on the Eternal Rock. Like his Master, he knew that, if he saved others, himself he could not save; nor could utmost extremity wring from him words, save of prayer and holy trust.

"He's most gone, Mas'r," said Sambo, touched, in spite of himself, by the patience of his victim.

"Pay away, till he give up! Give it to him!—give it to him!" shouted Legree. "I'll take every drop of blood he has, unless he confesses!"

Tom opened his eyes, and looked upon his master. "Ye poor miserable crittur!" he said, "there an't no more ye can do! I forgive ye, with all my soul!" and he fainted entirely away.

"I b'lieve, my soul, he's done for, finally," said Legree, stepping forward, to look at him. "Yes, he is! Well, his mouth's shut up, at last,—that's one comfort!"

Yes, Legree; but who shall shut up that voice in thy soul? that soul, past repentance, past prayer, past hope, in whom the fire that never shall be quenched is already burning!

Yet Tom was not quite gone. His wondrous words and pious prayers had struck upon the hearts of the imbruted blacks, who had been the instruments of cruelty upon him; and, the instant Legree withdrew, they took him down, and, in their ignorance, sought to call him back to life,—as if *that* were any favor to him.

"Sartin, we's been doin' a drefful wicked thing!" said Sambo; "hopes Mas'r'll have to 'count for it, and not we."

They washed his wounds,—they provided a rude bed, of some refuse cotton, for him to lie down on; and one of them, stealing up to the house, begged a drink of brandy of Legree, pretending that he was tired, and wanted it for himself. He brought it back, and poured it down Tom's throat.

"O, Tom!" said Quimbo, "we's been awful wicked to ye!"

"I forgive ye, with all my heart!" said Tom, faintly.

"O, Tom! do tell us who is *Jesus*, anyhow?" said Sambo;—"Jesus, that's been a standin' by you so, all this night!—Who is he?"

The word roused the failing, fainting spirit. He poured forth a few energetic sentences of that wondrous One,—his life, his death, his everlasting presence, and power to save.

They wept,—both the two savage men.

"Why didn't I never hear this before?" said Sambo; "but I do believe!—I can't help it! Lord Jesus, have mercy on us!"

"Poor critturs!" said Tom, "I'd be willing to b'ar all I have, if it'll only bring ye to Christ! O, Lord! give me these two more souls, I pray!"

That prayer was answered!

[A Letter to a Friend]

. . . George remained four years at a French university, and, applying himself with an unintermittent zeal, obtained a very thorough education.

Political troubles in France, at last, led the family again to seek an asylum in this country.

George's feelings and views, as an educated man, may be best expressed in a letter to one of his friends.

"I feel somewhat at a loss, as to my future course. True, as you have said to me, I might mingle in the circles of the whites, in this country, my shade of color is so slight, and that of my wife and family scarce perceptible. Well, perhaps, on sufferance, I might. But, to tell you the truth, I have no wish to.

"My sympathies are not for my father's race, but for my mother's. To him I was no more than a fine dog or horse: to my poor heart-broken mother I was a *child*; and though I never saw her, after the cruel sale that separated us, till she died, yet I *know* she always loved me dearly. I know it by my own heart. When I think of all she suffered, of my own early sufferings, of the distresses and struggles of my heroic wife, of my sister, sold in the New Orleans slave-market,—though I hope to have no unchristian sentiments, yet I may be excused for saying, I have no wish to pass for an American, or to identify myself with them.

"It is with the oppressed, enslaved African race that I cast in my lot; and, if I wished anything, I would wish myself two shades darker, rather than one lighter.

"The desire and yearning of my soul is for an African *nationality*. I want a people that shall have a tangible, separate existence of its own; and where am I to look for it? Not in Hayti; for in Hayti they had nothing to start with. A stream cannot rise above its fountain. The race that formed the character of the Haytiens was a worn-out, effeminate one; and, of course, the subject race will be centuries in rising to anything.

"Where, then, shall I look? On the shores of Africa I see a republic,—a republic formed of picked men, who, by energy and self-educating force, have, in many cases, individually, raised themselves above a condition of slavery. Having gone through a preparatory stage of feebleness, this republic has, at last, become an acknowledged nation on the face of the earth,—acknowledged by both France and England. There it is my wish to go, and find myself a people.

"I am aware, now, that I shall have you all against me; but, before you strike, hear me. During my stay in France, I have followed up, with intense interest, the history of my people in America. I have noted the struggle between abolitionist and colonizationist, and have received some impressions, as a distant spectator, which could never have occurred to me as a participator.

"I grant that this Liberia may have subserved all sorts of purposes, by being played off, in the hands of our oppressors, against us. Doubtless the scheme may have been used, in unjustifiable ways, as a means of retarding our emancipation. But the question to me is, Is there not a God above all man's schemes? May He not have overruled their designs, and founded for us a nation by them?

"In these days, a nation is born in a day. A nation starts, now, with all the great problems of republican life and civilization wrought out to its hand;—it has not to discover, but only to apply. Let us, then, all take hold together, with all our might, and see what we can do with this new enterprise, and the whole splendid continent of Africa opens before us and our children. *Our nation* shall roll the tide of civilization and Christianity along its shores, and plant there mighty republics, that, growing with the rapidity of tropical vegetation, shall be for all coming ages.

"Do you say that I am deserting my enslaved brethren? I think not. If I forget them one hour, one moment of my life, so may God forget me! But, what can I do for them, here? Can I break their chains? No, not as an individual; but, let me go and form part of a nation, which shall have a voice in the councils of nations, and then we can speak. A nation has a right to argue, remonstrate, implore, and present the cause of its race,—which an individual has not.

"If Europe ever becomes a grand council of free nations,—as I trust in God it will,—if, there, serfdom, and all unjust and oppressive social inequalities, are done away; and if they, as France and England have done, acknowledge our position,—then, in the great congress of nations, we will make our appeal, and present the cause of our enslaved and suffering race; and it cannot be that free, enlightened America will not then desire to wipe from her escutcheon that bar sinister which disgraces her among nations, and is as truly a curse to her as to the enslaved.

"But, you will tell me, our race have equal rights to mingle in the American republic as the Irishman, the German, the Swede. Granted, they have. We *ought* to be free to meet and mingle,—to rise by our individual worth, without any consideration of caste or color; and they who deny us this right are false to their own professed principles of human equality. We ought, in particular, to be allowed *here*. We have *more* than the rights of common men;—we have the claim of an injured race for reparation. But, then, *I do not want it*; I want a country, a nation, of my own. I think that the African race has peculiarities, yet to be unfolded in the light of civilization and Christianity, which, if not the same with those of the Anglo-Saxon, may prove to be, morally, of even a higher type.

"To the Anglo-Saxon race has been intrusted the destinies of the world, during its pioneer period of struggle and conflict. To that mission its stern, inflexible, energetic elements, were well adapted; but, as a Christian, I look for another era to arise. On its borders I trust we stand; and the throes that now convulse the nations are, to my hope, but the birthpangs of an hour of universal peace and brotherhood.

"I trust that the development of Africa is to be essentially a Christian one. If not a dominant and commanding race, they are, at least, an affectionate, magnanimous, and forgiving one. Having been called in the furnace of injustice and oppression, they have need to bind closer to their hearts that sublime doctrine of love and forgiveness, through which alone they are to conquer, which it is to be their mission to spread over the continent of Africa.

"In myself, I confess, I am feeble for this,—full half the blood in my veins is the hot and hasty Saxon; but I have an eloquent preacher of the Gospel ever by my side, in the person of my beautiful wife. When I wander, her gentler spirit ever restores me, and keeps before my eyes the Christian calling and mission of our race. As a Christian patriot, as a teacher of Christianity, I go to *my country*,—my chosen, my glorious Africa!—and to her, in my heart, I sometimes apply those splendid words of prophecy: 'Whereas thou hast been forsaken and hated, so that no man went through thee; *I* will make thee an eternal excellence, a joy of many generations!'

"You will call me an enthusiast: you will tell me that I have not well considered what I am undertaking. But I have considered, and counted the cost. I go to *Liberia*, not as to an Elysium of romance, but as to a *field of work*. I expect to work with both hands,—to work *hard*; to work against all sorts of difficulties and discouragements; and to work till I die. This is what I go for; and in this I am quite sure I shall not be disappointed.

"Whatever you may think of my determination, do not divorce me from your confidence; and think that, in whatever I do, I act with a heart wholly given to my people.

"GEORGE HARRIS"

JOHN PENDLETON KENNEDY

(1795–1870)

————◆◆◆◆————

Kennedy was born in Baltimore, where he attended Baltimore College and became a lawyer. Related to prosperous Shenandoah Valley planters on his mother's side, he inherited a fortune in his mid-thirties and married the daughter of a successful Baltimore businessman. He was then able to devote more time to literature and the political career he had begun in 1820 by serving in the Maryland legislature. He was elected to Congress as a Whig in 1838 and served for three terms. His political writing, including Quodlibet, a satire on Jacksonian democracy, was immensely helpful to the Whigs, and in 1852 he was appointed Secretary of the Navy under President Fillmore.

His earliest writings were prose sketches in the manner of Washington Irving, and his admiration for Irving's style and spirit is further manifested in Swallow Barn (1832, revised 1851), a series of interrelated sketches of Virginia plantation life. In addition to Swallow Barn, Kennedy is remembered for Horse-Shoe Robinson (1835), a novel set against a Revolutionary War background in Virginia and the Carolinas. Kennedy was an associate of most of the leading American writers of his time and was a patron of Poe. In 1833 he had served on a committee which chose Poe's "MS. Found in a Bottle" for a prize, thus helping to launch the young author's career, and two years later he helped Poe attain a position on the Southern Literary Messenger. Kennedy was a friend

66

of William Makepeace Thackeray, whom he met during the English novelist's visit to America in 1855–56, and he supplied background information for Thackeray's novel The Virginians. G. P. R. James, the novelist and British consul at Norfolk, Virginia, was another literary friend, and James's The Old Dominion is dedicated to Kennedy.

Influenced by both Irving and Joseph Addison, Kennedy placed his emphasis in Swallow Barn, from which "The Quarter" is taken, on charm and graciousness. His white characters are aristocratic and his slaves picturesque, Kennedy apparently having decided that a realistic picture of the ugly side of slave life would be offensive to the cultivated reader whose taste for the genial had been developed by Irving. Despite his sentimental and aristocratic view of plantation life, which influenced scores of later white-column-and-magnolia novels, Kennedy sided with the North in the Civil War.

From Swallow Barn, or, A Sojourn in the Old Dominion

The Quarter

Having despatched these important matters at the stable, we left our horses in charge of the servants, and walked towards the cabins, which were not more than a few hundred paces distant. These hovels, with their appurtenances, formed an exceedingly picturesque landscape. They were scattered, without order, over the slope of a gentle hill; and many of them were embowered under old and majestic trees. The rudeness of their construction rather enhanced the attractiveness of the scene. Some few were built after the fashion of the better sort of cottages; but age had stamped its heavy traces upon their exterior: the green moss had gathered upon the roofs, and the coarse weatherboarding had broken, here and there, into chinks. But the more lowly of these structures, and the most numerous, were nothing more than plain log-cabins, compacted pretty much on the model by which boys build partridge-traps; being composed of the trunks of trees, still clothed with their bark, and knit together at the corners with so little regard to neatness that the timbers, being of unequal lengths, jutted beyond each other, sometimes to the length of a foot. Perhaps, none of these latter sort were more than twelve feet square, and not above seven in height. A door swung upon wooden hinges, and a small window of two narrow panes of glass were, in general, the only openings in the front. The intervals between the logs were filled with clay; and the roof, which was constructed of smaller timbers, laid lengthwise along it and projecting two or three feet beyond the side or gable walls, heightened, in a very marked degree, the rustic effect. The chimneys communicated even a droll expression to these habitations. They were, oddly enough, built of billets of wood, having a broad foundation of stone, and growing narrower as they rose, each receding gradually from the house to which it was attached, until it reached the height of the roof. These combustible materials were saved from the access of the fire by a thick coating of mud; and the whole structure, from its tapering form, might be said to bear some resemblance to the spout of a tea kettle; indeed, this domestic implement would furnish no unapt type of the complete cabin.

From this description, which may serve to illustrate a whole species of habitations very common in Virginia, it will be seen, that on the score of accommodation, the inmates of these dwellings were furnished according to a very primitive notion of comfort. Still, however, there were little garden-patches attached to each, where cymblings, cucumbers, sweet potatoes, water-melons and cabbage flourished in unrestrained luxuriance. Add to this, that there were abundance of poultry domesticated about the premises, and it may be perceived that, whatever might be the inconveniences of shelter, there was no want of what, in all countries, would be considered a reasonable supply of luxuries.

Nothing more attracted my observation than the swarms of little negroes that basked on the sunny sides of these cabins, and congregated to gaze at us as we surveyed their haunts. They were nearly all in that costume of the golden age which I have heretofore described; and showed their slim shanks and long heels in all varieties of their grotesque natures. Their predominant love of sunshine, and their lazy, listless postures, and apparent content to be silently looking abroad, might well afford a comparison to a set of terrapins luxuriating in the genial warmth of summer, on the logs of a mill-pond.

And there, too, were the prolific mothers of this redundant brood,—a number of stout negro-women who thronged the doors of the huts, full of idle curiosity to see us. And, when to these are added a few reverend, wrinkled, decrepit old men, with faces shortened as if with drawing-strings, noses that seemed to have run all to nostril, and with feet of the configuration of a mattock, my reader will have a tolerably correct idea of this negro-quarter, its population, buildings, external appearance, situation and extent.

Meriwether, I have said before, is a kind and considerate master. It is his custom frequently to visit his slaves, in order to inspect their condition, and, where it may be necessary, to add to their comforts or relieve their wants. His coming amongst them, therefore, is always hailed with pleasure. He has constituted himself into a high court of appeal, and makes it a rule to give all their petitions a patient hearing, and to do justice in the premises. This, he tells me, he considers as indispensably necessary;—he says, that no overseer is entirely to be trusted: that there are few men who have the temper to administer wholesome laws to any population, however small, without some omissions or irregularities; and that this is more emphatically true of those who administer them entirely at their own will. On the present occasion, in almost every house where Frank entered, there was some boon to be asked; and I observed, that in every case, the petitioner was either gratified or refused in such a tone as left no occasion or disposition to murmur. Most of the women had some bargains to offer, of fowls or eggs or other commodities of household use, and Meriwether generally referred them to his wife, who, I found, relied almost entirely on this resource, for the supply of such commodities; the negroes being regularly paid for whatever was offered in this way.

One old fellow had a special favour to ask,—a little money to get a new padding for his saddle, which, he said, "galled his cretur's back." Frank, after a few jocular passages with the veteran, gave him what he desired, and sent him off rejoicing.

"That, sir," said Meriwether, "is no less a personage than Jupiter. He is an old bachelor, and has his cabin here on the hill. He is now near seventy, and is a kind of King of the Quarter. He has a horse, which he extorted from me last Christmas; and I seldom come here without finding myself involved in some new demand, as a consequence of my donation. Now he wants a pair of spurs which, I suppose, I must give him. He is a preposterous coxcomb, and Ned has administered to his vanity by a present of a *chapeau de bras*—a relic of my military era, which he wears on Sundays with a conceit that has brought upon him as much envy as admiration—the usual condition of greatness."

The air of contentment and good humor and kind family attachment, which was apparent throughout this little community, and the familiar relations existing between them and the proprietor struck me very pleasantly. I came here a stranger, in great degree, to the negro character, knowing but little of the domestic history of these people, their duties, habits or temper, and somewhat disposed, indeed, from prepossessions, to look upon them as severely dealt with, and expecting to have my sympathies excited towards them as objects of commiseration. I have had, therefore, rather a special interest in observing them. The contrast between my preconceptions of their condition and the reality which I have witnessed, has brought me a most agreeable surprise. I will not say that, in a high state of cultivation and of such self-dependence as they might possibly attain in a separate national existence, they might not become a more respectable people; but I am quite sure they never could become a happier people than I find them here. Perhaps they are destined, ultimately, to that national existence, in the clime from which they derive their origin—that this is a transition state in which we see them in Virginia. If it be so, no tribe of people have ever passed from barbarism to civilization whose middle stage of progress has been more secure from harm, more genial to their character, or better supplied with mild and beneficent guardianship, adapted to the actual state of their intellectual feebleness, than the negroes of Swallow Barn. And, from what I can gather, it is pretty much the same on the other estates in this region. I hear of an unpleasant exception to this remark now and then; but under such conditions as warrant the opinion that the unfavorable case is not more common than that which may be found in a survey of any other department of society. The oppression of apprentices, of seamen, of soldiers, of subordinates, indeed, in every relation, may furnish elements for a bead-roll of social grievances quite as striking, if they were diligently noted and brought to view.

What the negro is finally capable of, in the way of civilization, I am not philosopher enough to determine. In the present stage of his existence, he presents himself to my mind as essentially parasitical in his nature. I mean that he is, in his moral constitution, a dependant upon the white race; dependant for guidance and direction even to the procurement of his most indispensable necessaries. Apart from this protection he has the helplessness of a child,—without foresight, without faculty of contrivance, without thrift of any kind. We have instances, in the neighborhood of this estate, of individuals of the tribe falling into the most deplorable destitution from the want of that constant supervision which the race seems to require. This helplessness may be the due and natural impression which two centuries of servitude have stamped upon the tribe. But it is not the less a present and insurmountable impediment to that most cruel of all projects—the direct, broad emancipation of these people;—an act of legislation in comparison with which the revocation of the edict of Nantes would be entitled to be ranked among political benefactions. Taking instruction from history, all organized slavery is inevitably but a temporary phase of human condition. Interest, necessity and instinct, all work to give progression to the relations of mankind, and finally to elevate each tribe or race to its maximum of refinement and power. We have no reason to suppose that the negro will be an exception to this law.

At present, I have said, he is parasitical. He grows upward, only as the vine to which nature has supplied the sturdy tree as a support. He is extravagantly imitative. The older negroes here have—with some spice of comic mixture in it—that formal, grave and ostentatious style of manners, which belonged to the gentlemen of former days; they are profuse of bows and compliments, and very aristocratic in their way. The younger ones are equally to be remarked for aping the style of the present time, and especially for such tags of dandyism in dress as come within their reach. Their fondness for music and dancing is a predominant passion. I never meet a negro man—unless he is quite old—that he is not whistling; and the women sing from morning till night. And as to dancing, the hardest day's work does not restrain their desire to indulge in such pastime. During the harvest, when their toil is pushed to its utmost—the time being one of recognized privileges—they dance almost the whole night. They are great sportsmen, too. They angle and haul the seine, and hunt and tend their traps, with a zest that never grows weary. Their gayety of heart is constitutional and perennial, and when they are together they are as voluble and noisy as so many blackbirds. In short, I think them the most good-natured, careless, light-hearted, and happily-constructed human beings I have ever seen. Having but few and simple wants, they seem to me to be provided with every comfort which falls within the ordinary compass of their wishes; and, I might say, that they find even more enjoyment,—as that word may be applied to express positive pleasures scattered through the course of daily occupation —than any other laboring people I am acquainted with.

I took occasion to express these opinions to Meriwether, and to tell him how much I was struck by the mild and kindly aspect of this society at the Quarter.

This, as I expected, brought him into a discourse.

"The world," said he, "has begun very seriously to discuss the evils of slavery, and the debate has sometimes, unfortunately, been levelled to the comprehension of our negroes, and pains have even been taken that it should reach them. I believe there are but few men who may not be persuaded that they suffer some wrong in the organization of society—for society has many wrongs, both accidental and contrived, in its structure. Extreme poverty is, perhaps, always a wrong done to the individual upon whom it is cast. Society can have no honest excuse for starving a human being. I dare say you can follow out that train of thought and find numerous evils to complain of. Ingenious men, some of them not very honest, have found in these topics themes for agitation and popular appeal in all ages. How likely are they to find, in this question of slavery, a theme for the highest excitement; and, especially, how easy is it to inflame the passions of these untutored and unreckoning people, our black population, with this subject! For slavery, as an original question, is wholly without justification or defence. It is theoretically and morally wrong—and fanatical and one-sided thinkers will call its continuance, even for a day, a wrong, under any modification of it. But, surely, if these people are consigned to our care by the accident, or, what is worse, the premeditated policy which has put them upon our commonwealth, the great duty that is left to us is, to shape our conduct, in reference to them, by a wise and beneficent consideration of the case as it exists, and to administer wholesome laws for their government, making their servitude as tolerable to them as we can consistently with our own safety and their ultimate good. We should not be justified in taking the hazard of internal convulsions to get rid of them; nor have we a right, in the desire to free ourselves, to whelm them in greater evils than their present bondage. A violent removal of them, or a general emancipation, would assuredly produce one or the other of these calamities. Has any sensible man, who takes a different view of this subject, ever reflected upon the consequences of committing two or three millions of persons, born and bred in a state so completely dependent as that of slavery—so unfurnished, so unintellectual, so utterly helpless, I may say—to all the responsibilities, cares and labors of a state of freedom? Must he not acknowledge, that the utmost we could give them would be but a nominal freedom, in doing which we should be guilty of a cruel desertion of our trust—inevitably leading them to progressive debasement, penury, oppression, and finally to extermination? I would not argue with that man whose bigotry to a sentiment was so blind and so fatal as to insist on this expedient. When the time comes, as I apprehend it will come,—and all the sooner, if it be not delayed by these efforts to arouse something like a vindictive feeling between the disputants on both sides—in which the roots of slavery will begin to lose their hold in our soil; and when we shall have the means for providing these people a proper asylum, I shall be glad to see the State devote her thoughts to that enterprise, and, if I am alive, will cheerfully and gratefully assist in it. In the meantime, we owe it to justice and humanity to treat these people with the most considerate kindness. As to what are ordinarily imagined to be the evils or sufferings of their condition, I do not believe in them. The evil is generally felt on the side of the master. Less work is exacted of them than voluntary laborers choose to perform: they have as many privileges as are compatible with the nature of their occupations: they are subsisted, in general, as comfortably— nay, in their estimation of comforts, more comfortably, than the rural population of other countries. And as to the severities that are alleged to be practised upon them, there is much more malice or invention than truth in the accusation. The slaveholders in this region are, in the main, men of kind and humane tempers—as pliant to the touch of compassion, and as sensible of its duties, as the best men in any community, and as little disposed to inflict injury upon their dependents. Indeed, the owner of slaves is less apt to be harsh in his requisitions of labor than those who toil much themselves. I suspect it is invariably characteristic of those who are in the habit of severely tasking themselves, that they are inclined to regulate their demands upon others by their own standard. Our slaves are punished for misdemeanors, pretty much as disorderly persons are punished in all societies; and I am quite of opinion that our statistics of crime and punishment will compare favorably with those of any other population. But the punishment, on our side, is remarked as the personal act of the master; whilst, elsewhere, it goes free of ill-natured comment, because it is set down to the course of justice. We, therefore, suffer a reproach which other polities escape, and the conclusion is made an item of complaint against slavery.

"It has not escaped the attention of our legislation to provide against the ill-treatment of our negro population. I heartily concur in all effective laws to punish cruelty in masters. Public opinion on that subject, however, is even stronger than law, and no man can hold up his head in this community who is chargeable with mal-treatment of his slaves.

"One thing I desire you specially to note: the question of eman-cipation is exclusively our own, and every intermeddling with it from abroad will but mar its chance of success. We cannot but regard such interference as an unwarrantable and mischievous design to do us injury, and, therefore, we resent it—sometimes, I am sorry to say, even to the point of involving the innocent negro in the rigor which it provokes. We think, and, indeed, we know, that we alone are able to deal properly with the subject; all others are misled by the feeling which the natural sentiment against slavery, in the abstract, excites. They act under imperfect knowledge and impulsive prejudices which are totally incompatible with wise action on any subject. We, on the contrary, have every motive to calm and prudent counsel. Our lives, fortunes, families—our commonwealth itself, are put at the hazard of this resolve. You gentlemen of the North greatly misapprehend us, if you suppose that we are in love with this slave institution—or that, for the most part, we even deem it profitable to us. There are amongst us, it is true, some persons who are inclined to be fanatical on this side of the question, and who bring themselves to adopt some bold dogmas tending to these extreme views—and it is not out of the course of events that the violence of the agitations against us may lead ultimately to a wide adoption of these dogmas amongst the slaveholding States. It is in the nature of men to recalcitrate against continual assault, and, through the zeal of such opposition, to run into ultraisms which cannot be defended. But at present, I am sure the Southern sentiment on this question is temperate and wise, and that we neither regard slavery as a good, nor account it, except in some favorable conditions, as profitable. The most we can say of it is that, as matters stand, it is the best auxiliary within our reach.

"Without troubling you with further reflections upon a dull subject, my conclusion is that the real friends of humanity should conspire to allay the ferments on this question, and, even at some cost, to endeavor to encourage the natural contentment of the slave himself, by arguments to reconcile him to a present destiny, which is, in fact, more free from sorrow and want than that of almost any other class of men occupying the same field of labor."

Meriwether was about to finish his discourse at this point, when a new vein of thought struck him:

"It has sometimes occurred to me," he continued, "that we might elevate our slave population, very advantageously to them and to us, by some reforms in our code. I think we are justly liable to reproach, for the neglect or omission of our laws to recognize and regulate marriages, and the relation of family amongst the negroes. We owe it to humanity and to the sacred obligation of Christian ordinances, to respect and secure the bonds of husband and wife, and parent and child. I am ashamed to acknowledge that I have no answer to make, in the way of justification of this neglect. We have no right to put man and wife asunder. The law should declare this, and forbid the separation under any contingency, except of crime. It should be equally peremptory in forbidding the coercive separation of children from the mother—at least during that period when the one requires the care of the other. A disregard of these attachments has brought more odium upon the conditions of servitude than all the rest of its imputed hardships; and a suitable provision for them would tend greatly to gratify the feelings of benevolent and conscientious slaveholders, whilst it would disarm all considerate and fair-minded men, of what they deem the strongest objection to the existing relations of master and slave.

"I have also another reform to propose," said Meriwether, smiling. "It is, to establish by law, an upper or privileged class of slaves —selecting them from the most deserving, above the age of forty-five years. These I would endue with something of a feudal character. They should be entitled to hold small tracts of land under their masters, rendering for it a certain rent, payable either in personal service or money. They should be elevated into this class through some order of court, founded on certificates of good conduct, and showing the assent of the master. And I think I would create legal jurisdictions, giving the masters or stewards civil and criminal judicial authority. I have some dream of a project of this kind in my head," he continued, "which I have not fully matured as yet. You will think, Mr. Littleton, that I am a man of schemes, if I go on much longer—but there is something in this notion which may be improved to advantage, and I should like, myself, to begin the experiment. Jupiter, here, shall be my first feudatory—my tenant in socage—my old villain!"

"I suspect," said I, "Jupiter considers that his dignity is not to be enhanced by any enlargement of privilege, as long as he is allowed to walk about in his military hat as King of the Quarter."

"Perhaps not," replied Meriwether, laughing; "then I shall be forced to make my commencement upon Carey."

"Carey," interrupted Hazard, "would think it small promotion to be allowed to hold land under you!"

"Faith! I shall be without a feudatory to begin with," said Meriwether. "But come with me; I have a visit to make to the cabin of old Lucy."

WALT WHITMAN

(1819–1892)

———◆◆◆◆———

Born on a Long Island farm, Whitman moved with his family to Brooklyn at an early age. Following experience as a typesetter, itinerant teacher, and editor of a minor Long Island newspaper, he became associated with several Brooklyn and New York newspapers during the 1840s and early 1850s. His most important journalistic post was the editorship of the Brooklyn Eagle (1846–48). Following a falling out with the Eagle owners, he served briefly as editor of the New Orleans Crescent.

In 1855 he published the first edition of Leaves of Grass, a book of poems which he revised and expanded throughout the remainder of his life and which ultimately contained such widely acclaimed pieces as "Song of Myself," "Out of the Cradle Endlessly Rocking," "When Lilacs Last in the Dooryard Bloom'd," and "Crossing Brooklyn Ferry." Though he had early affected a bohemian pose and was at one time fired from the post of clerk in the Bureau of Indian Affairs on the grounds that Leaves of Grass was an immoral book, by the end of his life he had come to be regarded as "the Good Gray Poet," a type of literary father-figure to the nation. Today he is remembered for his experiments in free verse, for his intense devotion to idealism and individualism, and for his introduction of the human body and sex as themes appropriate for poetry.

As editor of the Eagle, Whitman was a stanch supporter of the

Wilmot Proviso, a measure designed to prevent the extension of slavery into territory acquired as a result of the war with Mexico, but he was also severely critical of the "fanaticism" of abolitionists. His resignation from the Eagle resulted when he insisted on supporting the free-soil Democrats, who agreed with the principle of the Wilmot Proviso, whereas the paper's backers supported that wing of the Democratic party which was willing to compromise with the South.

In 1856 Whitman wrote "The Slave Trade," an article in Life Illustrated which exposed the ease with which ships engaged in the slave trade sailed from New York, though the trade was illegal and even carried a death penalty. Two years later he vigorously supported Judge E. D. Cullver in several editorials after the judge had been expelled from the First Baptist Church of Brooklyn for having stood up during a service one Sunday to take issue with the pastor's attempt to justify slavery from the pulpit. Yet, despite his opposition to slavery, Whitman consistently disagreed with the abolitionists' demand for compulsory freeing of slaves. Gay Wilson Allen has argued that Whitman was like Lincoln in that he was unwilling to sacrifice the Union for the sake of destroying slavery.

From Leaves of Grass

Song of Myself

. . . . .

The runaway slave came to my house and stopt outside,
I heard his motions crackling the twigs of the woodpile,
Through the swung half-door of the kitchen I saw him, limpsy and
    weak,
And went where he sat on a log and led him in and assured him,
And brought water and fill'd a tub for his sweated body and bruis'd
    feet,
And gave him a room that enter'd from my own, and gave him
    some coarse clean clothes,
And remembered perfectly well his revolving eyes and his awk-
    wardness,

And remembered putting plasters on the galls of his neck and
    ankles;
He staid with me a week before he was recuperated and pass'd
    north,
I had him sit next me at table, my fire-lock lean'd in the corner.

    . . . . . .

The negro holds firmly the reins of his four horses, the block swags
    underneath on its tied-over chain,
The negro that drives the long dray of the stone-yard, steady and
    tall he stands pois'd on one leg on the string-piece,
His blue shirt exposes his ample neck and breast and loosens over
    his hip-band,
His glance is calm and commanding, he tosses the slouch of his hat
    away from his forehead,
The sun falls on his crispy hair and mustache, falls on the black of
    his polish'd and perfect limbs.

I behold the picturesque giant and love him, and I do not stop
    there,
I go with the team also.

In me the caresser of life wherever moving, backward as well as
    forward sluing,
To niches aside and junior bending, not a person or object missing,
Absorbing all to myself and for this song.

    . . . . . .

The disdain and calmness of martyrs,
The mother of old, condemn'd for a witch, burnt with dry wood,
    her children gazing on,
The hounded slave that flags in the race, leans by the fence, blow-
    ing, cover'd with sweat,
The twinges that sting like needles his legs and neck, the murder-
    ous buckshot and the bullets,
All these I feel or am.

I am the hounded slave, I wince at the bite of the dogs,
Hell and despair are upon me, crack and again crack the marksmen,
I clutch the rails of the fence, my gore drips, thinn'd with the ooze
    of my skin,

I fall on the weeds and stones,
The riders spur their unwilling horses, haul close,
Taunt my dizzy ears and beat me violently over the head with
    whip-stocks.

. . . . . .

From *Children of Adam*

I Sing the Body Electric

. . . . . .

A man's body at auction,
(For before the war I often go to the slave-mart and watch the
    sale),
I help the auctioneer, the sloven does not half know his business.

Gentlemen look on this wonder,
Whatever the bids of the bidders they cannot be high enough
    for it,
For it the globe lay preparing quintillions of years without one
    animal or plant,
For it the revolving cycles truly and steadily roll'd.

In this head the all-baffling brain,
In it and below it the makings of heroes.

Examine these limbs, red, black, or white, they are cunning in
    tendon and nerve,
They shall be stript that you may see them.

Exquisite senses, life-lit eyes, pluck, volition,
Flakes of breast-muscle, pliant backbone and neck, flesh not flabby,
    good-sized arms and legs,
And wonders within there yet.

Within there runs blood,
The same old blood! the same red-running blood!

There swells and jets a heart, there all passions, desires, reachings, aspirations,
(Do you think they are not there because they are not express'd in parlors and lecture-rooms?)

This is not only one man, this the father of those who shall be fathers in their turns,
In him the start of populous states and rich republics,
Of him countless immortal lives with countless embodiments and enjoyments.

How do you know who shall come from the offspring of his offspring through the centuries?
(Who might you find you have come from yourself, if you could trace back through the centuries?)

A woman's body at auction,
She too is not only herself, she is the teeming mother of mothers,
She is the bearer of them that shall grow and be mates to the mothers.

Have you ever loved the body of a woman?
Have you ever loved the body of a man?
Do you not see that these are exactly the same to all in all nations and times all over the earth?

If any thing is sacred the human body is sacred,
And the glory and sweet of a man is the token of manhood untainted,
And in man or woman a clean, strong, firm-fibred body, is more beautiful than the most beautiful face.

Have you seen the fool that corrupted his own live body? or the fool that corrupted her own live body?
For they do not conceal themselves, and cannot conceal themselves.

. . . . . .

Ethiopia Saluting the Colors

Who are you dusky woman, so ancient hardly human,
With your wooly-white and turban'd head, and bare bony feet?
Why rising by the roadside here, do you the colors greet?

('Tis while our army lines Carolina's sands and pines,
Forth from thy hovel door thou Ethiopia com'st to me,
As under doughty Sherman I march toward the sea.)

Me master years a hundred since from my parents sunder'd,
A little child, they caught me as the savage beast is caught,
Then hither me across the sea the cruel slaver brought.

No further does she say, but lingering all the day,
Her high-borne turban'd head she wags, and rolls her darkling eye,
And courtesies to the regiments, the guidons moving by.

What is it fateful woman, so blear, hardly human?
Why wag your head with turban bound, yellow, red and green?
Are the things so strange and marvelous you see or have seen?

HERMAN MELVILLE

(1819–1891)

With the possible exception of Nathaniel Hawthorne, Herman Melville has received more attention from modern critics than any other American novelist. He was born to a wealthy New York City family, but by the time he was twelve his father had died bankrupt and his mother was left in desperate circumstances with seven other children. Following brief experiences as a clerk and a teacher, Melville went to sea at the age of nineteen, and in the following five years he served aboard merchantmen, whalers, and a United States Navy frigate, visiting the Marquesas Islands, Tahiti, and Central and South America. He spent at least a month living with Marquesan natives and for a time was held prisoner by a tribe of cannibals in the valley of Typee.

Having entered New York literary society, Melville published his first novel, Typee, in 1846. By 1850 he had written four more novels and gained a wide following. Moby Dick (1851), which was dedicated to his new friend Hawthorne, marked the beginning of Melville's decline in popularity with a literary public which preferred its South Sea adventure tales undiluted by metaphysical speculation. Piazza Tales (1856) included such classics of short fiction as "Benito Cereno" and "Bartleby the Scrivener." After 1857 Melville wrote no more prose in his remaining thirty-four years except for the novelette Billy Budd, on which he was still working at the time of his death. His last years were passed in obscurity as a customs inspector on a New York dock. The critical re-evaluation which has given him such an eminent place in American letters did not begin until 1920. It continues today.

"Benito Cereno" is based on a chapter in Captain Amasa Delano's A Narrative of Voyages and Travels (1817), which recorded an actual slave insurrection at sea. Many incidents in Melville's story were taken directly from this source, but several major changes were made, including the transformation of Benito from the scoundrel described in A Narrative to the sensitive, Hamlet-like figure of the novelette (the real Benito tried to besmirch Delano's character after the affair in order to avoid paying a promised reward); the change of the slave ship's name from the Tryal to the San Dominick; the transmutation of the American crew from an untrustworthy lot including several convicts to the collection of loyal New Englanders aboard the Bachelor's Delight; and the switch in dates from Delano's 1805 to Melville's 1799.

The question of whether Melville here adopts a pro- or anti-Negro attitude has been widely debated, some critics arguing that the story represents a reversal of the dignity and sympathy accorded Negro characters in such earlier Melville novels as Redburn (1849) and Moby Dick, while others contend that it is a subtle indictment of slavery and the manner in which it dehumanizes both master and bondsman. Some see "Benito Cereno" as an answer to the stereotype of the contented slave found in much Southern writing at the time, whereas others indict Melville for anti-Negro racism. Rarely noticed in the debate is the fact that Babo was held in slavery by both black and white masters. Joseph Schiffman has pointed to Melville's ambiguous view of slavery in Mardi (1849), which involves an allegorical trip through Vivenza, or the United States, and a debate over slavery between Yoomy, the poet, and Babbalannja, the philosopher. The poet cries out, "Were there no other way, and should their masters not relent, all honest hearts must cheer this tribe of Hamo on; though they cut their chains with blades thrice edged, and gory to the haft!" But the philosopher answers, "For these serfs you would cross spears; yet I would not. Better present woes for some, than future woes for all."

The year 1856, which also saw the publication of G. P. R. James's The Old Dominion, dealing with Nat Turner's insurrection, seems to have been a high point in popular concern over slave rebellions. Still remembered at the time Melville wrote "Benito Cereno" were two widely debated slave mutinies, one aboard the Spanish ship Amistad in 1839 and the other on the American brig Creole in 1841. In both cases the slaves had claimed their liberty after landing at a free port, and both incidents were followed by elaborate legal battles which divided the nation.

Benito Cereno

In the year 1799, Captain Amasa Delano, of Duxbury, in Massachusetts, commanding a large sealer and general trader, lay at anchor with a valuable cargo, in the harbor of St. Maria—a small, desert, uninhabited island toward the southern extremity of the long coast of Chili. There he had touched for water.

On the second day, not long after dawn, while lying in his berth, his mate came below, informing him that a strange sail was coming into the bay. Ships were then not so plenty in those waters as now. He rose, dressed, and went on deck.

The morning was one peculiar to that coast. Everything was mute and calm; everything gray. The sea, though undulated into long roods of swells, seemed fixed, and was sleeked at the surface like waved lead that has cooled and set in the smelter's mould. The sky seemed a gray surtout. Flights of troubled gray fowl, kith and kin with flights of troubled gray vapors among which they were mixed, skimmed low and fitfully over the waters, as swallows over meadows before storms. Shadows present, foreshadowing deeper shadows to come.

To Captain Delano's surprise, the stranger, viewed through the glass, showed no colors; though to do so upon entering a haven, however uninhabited in its shores, where but a single other ship might be lying, was the custom among peaceful seamen of all nations. Considering the lawlessness and loneliness of the spot, and the sort of stories, at that day, associated with those seas, Captain Delano's surprise might have deepened into some uneasiness had he not been a person of a singularly undistrustful good nature, not liable, except on extraordinary and repeated incentives, and hardly then, to indulge in personal alarms, any way involving the imputation of malign evil in man. Whether, in view of what humanity is capable, such a trait implies, along with a benevolent heart, more than ordinary quickness and accuracy of intellectual perception, may be left to the wise to determine.

But whatever misgivings might have obtruded on first seeing the stranger, would almost, in any seaman's mind, have been dissipated by observing that, the ship, in navigating into the harbor, was drawing too near the land; a sunken reef making out off her bow. This seemed to prove her a stranger, indeed, not only to the sealer, but the island; consequently, she could be no wonted freebooter on that ocean. With no small interest, Captain Delano continued to watch her—a proceeding not much facilitated by the vapors partly mantling the hull, through which the far matin light from her cabin streamed equivocally enough; much like the sun—by this time hemisphered on the rim of the horizon, and, apparently, in company with the strange ship entering the harbor—which, wimpled by the same low, creeping clouds, showed not unlike a Lima *intriguante*'s one sinister eye peering across the Plaza from the Indian loop-hole of her dusk *saya-y-manta*.

It might have been but a deception of the vapors, but, the longer the stranger was watched the more singular appeared her manœuvres. Ere long it seemed hard to decide whether she meant to come in or no—what she wanted, or what she was about. The wind, which had breezed up a little during the night, was now extremely light and baffling, which the more increased the apparent uncertainty of her movements.

Surmising, at last, that it might be a ship in distress, Captain Delano ordered his whale-boat to be dropped, and, much to the wary opposition of his mate, prepared to board her, and, at the least, pilot her in. On the night previous, a fishing-party of the seamen had gone a long distance to some detached rocks out of sight from the sealer, and, an hour or two before daybreak, had returned, having met with no small success. Presuming that the stranger might have been long off soundings, the good captain put several baskets of the fish, for presents, into his boat, and so pulled away. From her continuing too near the sunken reef, deeming her in danger, calling to his men, he made all haste to apprise those on board of their situation. But, some time ere the boat came up, the wind, light though it was, having shifted, had headed the vessel off, as well as partly broken the vapors from about her.

Upon gaining a less remote view, the ship, when made signally visible on the verge of the leaden-hued swells, with the shreds of fog here and there raggedly furring her, appeared like a white-washed monastery after a thunder-storm, seen perched upon some dun cliff among the Pyrenees. But it was no purely fanciful resemblance which now, for a moment, almost led Captain Delano to think that nothing less than a shipload of monks was before him. Peering over the bulwarks were what really seemed, in the hazy distance, throngs of dark cowls; while, fitfully revealed through the open port-holes, other dark moving figures were dimly described, as of Black Friars pacing the cloisters.

Upon a still nigher approach, this appearance was modified, and the true character of the vessel was plain—a Spanish merchantman of the first class, carrying negro slaves, amongst other valuable freight, from one colonial port to another. A very large, and, in its time, a very fine vessel, such as in those days were at intervals encountered along that main; sometimes superseded Acapulco treasure-ships, or retired frigates of the Spanish king's navy, which, like superannuated Italian palaces, still, under a decline of masters, preserved signs of former state.

As the whale-boat drew more and more nigh, the cause of the peculiar pipe-clayed aspect of the stranger was seen in the slovenly neglect pervading her. The spars, ropes, and great part of the bulwarks, looked woolly, from long unacquaintance with the scraper, tar, and the brush. Her keel seemed laid, her ribs put together, and she launched, from Ezekiel's Valley of Dry Bones.

In the present business in which she was engaged, the ship's general model and rig appeared to have undergone no material change from their original warlike and Froissart pattern. However, no guns were seen.

The tops were large, and were railed about with what had once been octagonal net-work, all now in sad disrepair. These tops hung overhead like three ruinous aviaries, in one of which was seen perched, on a ratlin, a white noddy, a strange fowl, so called from its lethargic, somnambulistic character, being frequently caught by hand at sea. Battered and mouldy, the castellated forecastle seemed some ancient turret, long ago taken by assault, and then left to decay. Toward the stern, two high-raised quarter galleries—the balustrades here and there covered with dry, tindery sea-moss—opening out from the unoccupied state-cabin, whose dead-lights, for all the mild weather, were hermetically closed and calked—these tenantless balconies hung over the sea as if it were the grand Venetian canal. But the principal relic of faded grandeur was the ample oval of the shield-like stern-piece, intricately carved with the arms of Castile and Leon, medallioned about by groups of myth-ological or symbolical devices; uppermost and central of which was a dark satyr in a mask, holding his foot on the prostrate neck of a writhing figure, likewise masked.

Whether the ship had a figure-head, or only a plain beak, was not quite certain, owing to canvas wrapped about that part, either to protect it while undergoing a re-furbishing, or else decently to hide its decay. Rudely painted or chalked, as in a sailor freak, along the forward side of a sort of pedestal below the canvas, was the sentence, "*Seguid vuestro jefe,*" (follow your leader); while upon the tarnished headboards, near by, appeared, in stately capitals, once gilt, the ship's name, "SAN DOMINICK," each letter streakingly corroded with tricklings of copper-spike rust; while, like mourning weeds, dark festoons of sea-grass slimily swept to and fro over the name, with every hearse-like roll of the hull.

As, at last, the boat was hooked from the bow along toward the gangway amidship, its keel, while yet some inches separated from the hull, harshly grated as on a sunken coral reef. It proved a huge bunch of conglobated barnacles adhering below the water to the side like a wen—a token of baffling airs and long calms passed somewhere in those seas.

Climbing the side, the visitor was at once surrounded by a clamorous throng of whites and blacks, but the latter outnumber-ing the former more than could have been expected, negro trans-portation-ship as the stranger in port was. But, in one language, and as with one voice, all poured out a common tale of suffering; in which the negresses, of whom there were not a few, exceeded the others in their dolorous vehemence. The scurvy, together with the fever, had swept off a great part of their number, more especially the Spaniards. Off Cape Horn they had narrowly escaped shipwreck; then, for days together, they had lain tranced without wind; their provisions were low; their water next to none; their lips that moment were baked.

While Captain Delano was thus made the mark of all eager tongues, his one eager glance took in all faces, with every other object about him.

Always upon first boarding a large and populous ship at sea, especially a foreign one, with a nondescript crew such as Lascars or Manilla men, the impression varies in a peculiar way from that produced by first entering a strange house with strange inmates in a strange land. Both house and ship—the one by its walls and blinds, the other by its high bulwarks like ramparts—hoard from view their interiors till the last moment: but in the case of the ship there is this addition; that the living spectacle it contains, upon its sudden and complete disclosure, has, in contrast with the blank ocean which zones it, something of the effect of enchantment. The ship seems unreal; these strange costumes, gestures, and faces, but a shadowy tableau just emerged from the deep, which directly must receive back what it gave.

Perhaps it was some such influence, as above is attempted to be described, which, in Captain Delano's mind, heightened whatever, upon a staid scrutiny, might have seemed unusual; especially the conspicuous figures of four elderly grizzled negroes, their heads like black, doddered willow tops, who, in venerable contrast to the tumult below them, were couched, sphynx-like, one on the starboard cat-head, another on the larboard, and the remaining pair face to face on the opposite bulwarks above the main-chains. They each had bits of unstranded old junk in their hands, and, with a sort of stoical self-content, were picking the junk into oakum, a small heap of which lay by their sides. They accompanied the task with a continuous, low, monotonous chant; droning and druling away like so many gray-headed bag-pipers playing a funeral march.

The quarter-deck rose into an ample elevated poop, upon the forward verge of which, lifted, like the oakum-pickers, some eight feet above the general throng, sat along in a row, separated by regular spaces, the cross-legged figures of six other blacks; each with a rusty hatchet in his hand, which, with a bit of brick and a rag, he was engaged like a scullion in scouring; while between each two was a small stack of hatchets, their rusted edges turned forward awaiting a like operation. Though occasionally the four oakum-pickers would briefly address some person or persons in the crowd below, yet the six hatchet-polishers neither spoke to others, nor breathed a whisper among themselves, but sat intent upon their task, except at intervals, when, with the peculiar love in negroes of uniting industry with pastime, two and two they sideways clashed their hatchets together, like cymbals, with a barbarous din. All six, unlike the generality, had the raw aspect of unsophisticated Africans.

But that first comprehensive glance which took in those ten figures, with scores less conspicuous, rested but an instant upon them, as, impatient of the hubbub of voices, the visitor turned in quest of whosoever it might be that commanded the ship.

But as if not unwilling to let nature make known her own case among his suffering charge, or else in despair of restraining it for the time, the Spanish captain, a gentlemanly, reserved-looking, and rather young man to a stranger's eye, dressed with singular richness, but bearing plain traces of recent sleepless cares and disquietudes, stood passively by, leaning against the main-mast, at one moment casting a dreary, spiritless look upon his excited people, at the next an unhappy glance toward his visitor. By his side stood a black of small stature, in whose rude face, as occasionally, like a shepherd's dog, he mutely turned it up into the Spaniard's, sorrow and affection were equally blended.

Struggling through the throng, the American advanced to the Spaniard, assuring him of his sympathies, and offering to render whatever assistance might be in his power. To which the Spaniard returned for the present but grave and ceremonious acknowledgments, his national formality dusked by the saturnine mood of ill-health.

But losing no time in mere compliments, Captain Delano, returning to the gangway, had his basket of fish brought up; and as the wind still continued light, so that some hours at least must elapse ere the ship could be brought to the anchorage, he bade his men return to the sealer, and fetch back as much water as the whale-boat could carry, with whatever soft bread the steward might have, all the remaining pumpkins on board, with a box of sugar, and a dozen of his private bottles of cider.

Not many minutes after the boat's pushing off, to the vexation of all, the wind entirely died away, and the tide turning, began drifting back the ship helplessly seaward. But trusting this would not long last, Captain Delano sought, with good hopes, to cheer up the strangers, feeling no small satisfaction that, with persons in their condition, he could—thanks to his frequent voyages along the Spanish Main—converse with some freedom in their native tongue.

While left alone with them, he was not long in observing some things tending to heighten his first impressions; but surprise was lost in pity, both for the Spaniards and blacks, alike evidently reduced from scarcity of water and provisions; while long-continued suffering seemed to have brought out the less good-natured qualities of the negroes, besides, at the same time, impairing the Spaniard's authority over them. But, under the circumstances, precisely this condition of things was to have been anticipated. In armies, navies, cities, or families, in nature herself, nothing more relaxes good order than misery. Still, Captain Delano was not without the idea, that had Benito Cereno been a man of greater energy, misrule would hardly have come to the present pass. But the debility, constitutional or induced by hardships, bodily and mental, of the Spanish captain, was too obvious to be overlooked. A prey to settled dejection, as if long mocked with hope he would not now indulge it, even when it had ceased to be a mock, the prospect of that day, or evening at furthest, lying at anchor, with plenty of water for his people, and a brother captain to counsel and befriend, seemed in no perceptible degree to encourage him. His mind appeared unstrung, if not still more seriously affected. Shut up in these oaken walls, chained to one dull round of command, whose unconditionality cloyed him, like some hypochondriac abbot he moved slowly about, at times suddenly pausing, starting, or staring, biting his lip, biting his fingernail, flushing, paling, twitching his beard, with other symptoms of an absent or moody mind. This distempered spirit was lodged, as before hinted, in as distempered a frame. He was rather tall, but seemed never to have been robust, and now with nervous suffering was almost worn to a skeleton. A tendency to some pulmonary complaint appeared to have been lately confirmed. His voice was like that of one with lungs half gone—hoarsely suppressed, a husky whisper. No wonder that, as in this state he tottered about, his private servant apprehensively followed him. Sometimes the negro gave his master his arm, or took his handkerchief out of his pocket for him; performing these and similar offices with that affectionate zeal which transmutes into something filial or fraternal acts in themselves but menial; and which has gained for the negro the repute of making the most pleasing body-servant in the world; one, too, whom a master need be on no stiffly superior terms with, but may treat with familiar trust; less a servant than a devoted companion.

Marking the noisy indocility of the blacks in general, as well as what seemed the sullen inefficiency of the whites, it was not without humane satisfaction that Captain Delano witnessed the steady good conduct of Babo.

But the good conduct of Babo, hardly more than the ill-behavior of others, seemed to withdraw the half-lunatic Don Benito from his cloudy languor. Not that such precisely was the impression made by the Spaniard on the mind of his visitor. The Spaniard's individual unrest was, for the present, but noted as a conspicuous feature in the ship's general affliction. Still, Captain Delano was not a little concerned at what he could not help taking for the time to be Don Benito's unfriendly indifference towards himself. The Spaniard's manner, too, conveyed a sort of sour and gloomy disdain, which he seemed at no pains to disguise. But this the American in charity ascribed to the harassing effects of sickness, since, in former instances, he had noted that there are peculiar natures on whom prolonged physical suffering seems to cancel every social instinct of kindness; as if, forced to black bread themselves, they deemed it but equity that each person coming nigh them should, indirectly, by some slight or affront, be made to partake of their fare.

But ere long Captain Delano bethought him that, indulgent as he was at the first, in judging the Spaniard, he might not, after all, have exercised charity enough. At bottom it was Don Benito's reserve which displeased him; but the same reserve was shown towards all but his faithful personal attendant. Even the formal reports which, according to sea-usage, were, at stated times, made to him by some petty underling, either a white, mulatto or black, he hardly had patience enough to listen to, without betraying contemptuous aversion. His manner upon such occasions was, in its degree, not unlike that which might be supposed to have been his imperial countryman's, Charles V, just previous to the anchoritish retirement of that monarch from the throne.

This splenetic disrelish of his place was evinced in almost every function pertaining to it. Proud as he was moody, he condescended to no personal mandate. Whatever special orders were necessary, their delivery was delegated to his body-servant, who in turn transferred them to their ultimate destination, through runners, alert Spanish boys or slave boys, like pages or pilot-fish within easy call continually hovering round Don Benito. So that to have beheld this undemonstrative invalid gliding about, apathetic and mute, no landsman could have dreamed that in him was lodged a dictatorship beyond which, while at sea, there was no earthly appeal.

Thus, the Spaniard, regarded in his reserve, seemed the involuntary victim of mental disorder. But, in fact, his reserve might, in some degree, have proceeded from design. If so, then here was evinced the unhealthy climax of that icy though conscientious policy, more or less adopted by all commanders of large ships, which, except in signal emergencies, obliterates alike the manifestation of sway with every trace of sociality; transforming the man into a block, or rather into a loaded cannon, which, until there is call for thunder, has nothing to say.

Viewing him in this light, it seemed but a natural token of the perverse habit induced by a long course of such hard self-restraint, that, notwithstanding the present condition of his ship, the Spaniard should still persist in a demeanor, which, however harmless, or, it may be, appropriate, in a well-appointed vessel, such as the *San Dominick* might have been at the outset of the voyage, was anything but judicious now. But the Spaniard, perhaps, thought that it was with captains as with gods: reserve, under all events, must still be their cue. But probably this appearance of slumbering dominion might have been but an attempted disguise to conscious imbecility—not deep policy, but shallow device. But be all this as it might, whether Don Benito's manner was designed or not, the more Captain Delano noted its pervading reserve, the less he felt uneasiness at any particular manifestation of that reserve towards himself.

Neither were his thoughts taken up by the captain alone. Wonted to the quiet orderliness of the sealer's comfortable family of a crew, the noisy confusion of the *San Dominick*'s suffering host repeatedly challenged his eye. Some prominent breaches, not only of discipline but of decency, were observed. These Captain Delano could not but ascribe, in the main, to the absence of those subordinate deck-officers to whom, along with higher duties, is intrusted what may be styled the police department of a populous ship. True, the old oakum-pickers appeared at times to act the part of monitorial constables to their countrymen, the blacks; but though occasionally succeeding in allaying trifling outbreaks now and then between man and man, they could do little or nothing toward establishing general quiet. The *San Dominick* was in the condition of a transatlantic emigrant ship, among whose multitude of living freight are some individuals, doubtless, as little troublesome as crates and bales; but the friendly remonstrances of such with their ruder companions are of not so much avail as the unfriendly arm of the mate. What the *San Dominick* wanted was, what the emigrant ship has, stern superior officers. But on these decks not so much as a fourth-mate was to be seen.

The visitor's curiosity was roused to learn the particulars of those mishaps which had brought about such absenteeism, with its consequences; because, though deriving some inkling of the voyage from the wails which at the first moment had greeted him, yet of the details no clear understanding had been had. The best account would, doubtless, be given by the captain. Yet at first the visitor was loth to ask it, unwilling to provoke some distant rebuff. But plucking up courage, he at last accosted Don Benito, renewing the expression of his benevolent interest, adding, that did he (Captain Delano) but know the particulars of the ship's misfortunes, he would, perhaps, be better able in the end to relieve them. Would Don Benito favor him with the whole story?

Don Benito faltered; then, like some somnambulist suddenly interfered with, vacantly stared at his visitor, and ended by looking down on the deck. He maintained this posture so long, that Captain Delano, almost equally disconcerted, and involuntarily almost as rude, turned suddenly from him, walking forward to accost one of the Spanish seamen for the desired information. But he had hardly gone five paces, when, with a sort of eagerness, Don Benito invited him back, regretting his momentary absence of mind, and professing readiness to gratify him.

While most part of the story was being given, the two captains stood on the after part of the main-deck, a privileged spot, no one being near but the servant.

"It is now a hundred and ninety days," began the Spaniard, in his husky whisper, "that this ship, well officered and well manned, with several cabin passengers—some fifty Spaniards in all—sailed from Buenos Ayres bound to Lima, with a general cargo, hardware, Paraguay tea and the like—and," pointing forward, "that parcel of negroes, now not more than a hundred and fifty, as you see, but then numbering over three hundred souls. Off Cape Horn we had heavy gales. In one moment, by night, three of my best officers, with fifteen sailors, were lost, with the main-yard; the spar snapping under them in the slings, as they sought, with heavers, to beat down the icy sail. To lighten the hull, the heavier sacks of mata were thrown into the sea, with most of the water-pipes lashed on deck at the time. And this last necessity it was, combined with the prolonged detentions afterwards experienced, which eventually brought about our chief causes of suffering. When——"

Here there was a sudden fainting attack of his cough, brought on, no doubt, by his mental distress. His servant sustained him, and drawing a cordial from his pocket placed it to his lips. He a little revived. But unwilling to leave him unsupported while yet imperfectly restored, the black with one arm still encircled his master, at the same time keeping his eye fixed on his face, as if to watch for the first sign of complete restoration, or relapse, as the event might prove.

The Spaniard proceeded, but brokenly and obscurely, as one in a dream.

—"Oh, my God! rather than pass through what I have, with joy I would have hailed the most terrible gales; but——"

His cough returned and with increased violence; this subsiding, with reddened lips and closed eyes he fell heavily against his supporter.

"His mind wanders. He was thinking of the plague that followed the gales," plaintively sighed the servant; "my poor, poor master!" wringing one hand, and with the other wiping the mouth. "But be patient, Señor," again turning to Captain Delano, "these fits do not last long; master will soon be himself."

Don Benito reviving, went on; but as this portion of the story was very brokenly delivered, the substance only will here be set down.

It appeared that after the ship had been many days tossed in storms off the Cape, the scurvy broke out, carrying off numbers of the whites and blacks. When at last they had worked round into the Pacific, their spars and sails were so damaged, and so inadequately handled by the surviving mariners, most of whom were become invalids, that, unable to lay her northerly course by the wind, which was powerful, the unmanageable ship, for successive days and nights, was blown northwestward, where the breeze suddenly deserted her, in unknown waters, to sultry calms. The absence of the water-pipes now proved as fatal to life as before their presence had menaced it. Induced, or at least aggravated, by the more than scanty allowance of water, a malignant fever followed the scurvy; with the excessive heat of the lengthened calm, making such short work of it as to sweep away, as by billows, whole families of the Africans, and a yet larger number, proportionably, of the Spaniards, including, by a luckless fatality, every remaining officer on board. Consequently, in the smart west winds eventually following the calm, the already rent sails, having to be simply dropped, not furled, at need, had been gradually reduced to the beggars' rags they were now. To procure substitutes for his lost sailors, as well as supplies of water and sails, the captain, at the earliest opportunity, had made for Baldivia, the southernmost civilized port of Chili and South America; but upon nearing the coast the thick weather had prevented him from so much as sighting that harbor. Since which period, almost without a crew, and almost without canvas and almost without water, and, at intervals, giving its added dead to the sea, the *San Dominick* had been battle-dored about by contrary winds, inveigled by currents, or grown weedy in calms. Like a man lost in woods, more than once she had doubled upon her own track.

"But throughout these calamities," huskily continued Don Benito, painfully turning in the half embrace of his servant, "I have to thank those negroes you see, who, though to your inexperienced eyes appearing unruly, have, indeed, conducted themselves with less of restlessness than even their owner could have thought possible under such circumstances."

Here he again fell faintly back. Again his mind wandered; but he rallied, and less obscurely proceeded.

"Yes, their owner was quite right in assuring me that no fetters would be needed with his blacks; so that while, as is wont in this transportation, those negroes have always remained upon deck—not thrust below, as in the Guineamen—they have, also, from the beginning, been freely permitted to range within given bounds at their pleasure."

Once more the faintness returned—his mind roved—but, recovering, he resumed:

"But it is Babo here to whom, under God, I owe not only my own preservation, but likewise to him, chiefly, the merit is due, of pacifying his more ignorant brethren, when at intervals tempted to murmurings."

"Ah, master," sighed the black, bowing his face, "don't speak of me; Babo is nothing; what Babo has done was but duty."

"Faithful fellow!" cried Captain Delano. "Don Benito, I envy you such a friend; slave I cannot call him."

As master and man stood before him, the black upholding the white, Captain Delano could not but bethink him of the beauty of that relationship which could present such a spectacle of fidelity on the one hand and confidence on the other. The scene was heightened by the contrast in dress, denoting their relative positions. The Spaniard wore a loose Chili jacket of dark velvet; white small-clothes and stockings, with silver buckles at the knee and instep; a high-crowned sombrero, of fine grass; a slender sword, silver mounted, hung from a knot in his sash—the last being an almost invariable adjunct, more for utility than ornament, of a South American gentleman's dress to this hour. Excepting when his occasional nervous contortions brought about disarray, there was a certain precision in his attire curiously at variance with the unsightly disorder around; especially in the belittered Ghetto, forward of the mainmast, wholly occupied by the blacks.

The servant wore nothing but wide trowsers, apparently, from their coarseness and patches, made out of some old topsail; they were clean, and confined at the waist by a bit of unstranded rope, which, with his composed, deprecatory air at times, made him look something like a begging friar of St. Francis.

However unsuitable for the time and place, at least in the blunt-thinking American's eyes, and however strangely surviving in the midst of all his afflictions, the toilette of Don Benito might not, in fashion at least, have gone beyond the style of the day among South Americans of his class. Though on the present voyage sailing from Buenos Ayres, he had avowed himself a native and resident of Chili, whose inhabitants had not so generally adopted the plain coat and once plebeian pantaloons; but, with a becoming modification, adhered to their provincial costume, picturesque as any in the world. Still, relatively to the pale history of the voyage, and his own pale face, there seemed something so incongruous in the Spaniard's apparel, as almost to suggest the image of an invalid courtier tottering about London streets in the time of the plague.

The portion of the narrative which, perhaps, most excited interest, as well as some surprise, considering the latitudes in question, was the long calms spoken of, and more particularly the ship's so long drifting about. Without communicating the opinion, of course, the American could not but impute at least part of the detentions both to clumsy seamanship and faulty navigation. Eyeing Don Benito's small, yellow hands, he easily inferred that the young captain had not got into command at the hawse-hole, but the cabin-window; and if so, why wonder at incompetence, in youth, sickness, and gentility united?

But drowning criticism in compassion, after a fresh repetition of his sympathies, Captain Delano, having heard out his story, not only engaged, as in the first place, to see Don Benito and his people supplied in their immediate bodily needs, but, also, now further promised to assist him in procuring a large permanent supply of water, as well as some sails and rigging; and, though it would involve no small embarrassment to himself, yet he would spare three of his best seamen for temporary deck officers; so that without delay the ship might proceed to Conception, there fully to refit for Lima, her destined port.

Such generosity was not without its effect, even upon the invalid. His face lighted up; eager and hectic, he met the honest glance of his visitor. With gratitude he seemed overcome.

"This excitement is bad for master," whispered the servant, taking his arm, and with soothing words gently drawing him aside.

When Don Benitó returned, the American was pained to observe that his hopefulness, like the sudden kindling in his cheek, was but febrile and transient.

Ere long, with a joyless mien, looking up towards the poop, the host invited his guest to accompany him there, for the benefit of what little breath of wind might be stirring.

As, during the telling of the story, Captain Delano had once or twice started at the occasional cymballing of the hatchet-polishers, wondering why such an interruption should be allowed, especially in that part of the ship, and in the ears of an invalid; and moreover, as the hatchets had anything but an attractive look, and the handlers of them still less so, it was, therefore, to tell the truth, not without some lurking reluctance, or even shrinking, it may be, that Captain Delano, with apparent complaisance, acquiesced in his host's invitation. The more so, since, with an untimely caprice of punctilio, rendered distressing by his cadaverous aspect, Don Benito, with Castilian bows, solemnly insisted upon his guest's preceding him up the ladder leading to the elevation; where, one on each side of the last step, sat for armorial supporters and sentries two of the ominous file. Gingerly enough stepped good Captain Delano between them, and in the instant of leaving them behind, like one running the gauntlet, he felt an apprehensive twitch in the calves of his legs.

But when, facing about, he saw the whole file, like so many organ-grinders, still stupidly intent on their work, unmindful of everything beside, he could not but smile at his late fidgety panic.

Presently, while standing with his host, looking forward upon the decks below, he was struck by one of those instances of insubordination previously alluded to. Three black boys, with two

Spanish boys, were sitting together on the hatches, scraping a rude wooden platter, in which some scanty mess had recently been cooked. Suddenly, one of the black boys, enraged at a word dropped by one of his white companions, seized a knife, and, though called to forbear by one of the oakum-pickers, struck the lad over the head, inflicting a gash from which blood flowed.

In amazement, Captain Delano inquired what this meant. To which the pale Don Benito dully muttered, that it was merely the sport of the lad.

"Pretty serious sport, truly," rejoined Captain Delano. "Had such a thing happened on board the *Bachelor's Delight*, instant punishment would have followed."

At these words the Spaniard turned upon the American one of his sudden, staring, half-lunatic looks; then, relapsing into his torpor, answered, "Doubtless, doubtless, Señor."

Is it, thought Captain Delano, that this hapless man is one of those paper captains I've known, who by policy wink at what by power they cannot put down? I know no sadder sight than a commander who has little of command but the name.

"I should think, Don Benito," he now said, glancing towards the oakum-picker who had sought to interfere with the boys, "that you would find it advantageous to keep all your blacks employed, especially the younger ones, no matter at what useless task, and no matter what happens to the ship. Why, even with my little band, I find such a course indispensable. I once kept a crew on my quarterdeck thrumming mats for my cabin, when, for three days, I had given up my ship—mats, men, and all—for a speedy loss, owing to the violence of a gale, in which we could do nothing but helplessly drive before it."

"Doubtless, doubtless," muttered Don Benito.

"But," continued Captain Delano, again glancing upon the oakum-pickers and then at the hatchet-polishers, near by, "I see you keep some, at least, of your host employed."

"Yes," was again the vacant response.

"Those old men there, shaking their pows from their pulpits," continued Captain Delano, pointing to the oakum-pickers, "seem to act the part of old dominies to the rest, little heeded as their admonitions are at times. Is this voluntary on their part, Don Benito, or have you appointed them shepherds to your flock of black sheep?"

"What posts they fill, I appointed them," rejoined the Spaniard, in an acrid tone, as if resenting some supposed satiric reflection.

"And these others, these Ashantee conjurors here," continued Captain Delano, rather uneasily eyeing the brandished steel of the hatchet-polishers, where, in spots, it had been brought to a shine, "this seems a curious business they are at, Don Benito?"

"In the gales we met," answered the Spaniard, "what of our general cargo was not thrown overboard was much damaged by the brine. Since coming into calm weather, I have had several cases of knives and hatchets daily brought up for overhauling and cleaning."

"A prudent idea, Don Benito. You are part owner of ship and cargo, I presume; but none of the slaves, perhaps?"

"I am owner of all you see," impatiently returned Don Benito, "except the main company of blacks, who belonged to my late friend, Alexandro Aranda."

As he mentioned this name, his air was heart-broken; his knees shook; his servant supported him.

Thinking he divined the cause of such unusual emotion, to confirm his surmise, Captain Delano, after a pause, said: "And may I ask, Don Benito, whether—since awhile ago you spoke of some cabin passengers—the friend, whose loss so afflicts you, at the outset of the voyage accompanied his blacks?"

"Yes."

"But died of the fever?"

"Died of the fever. Oh, could I but——"

Again quivering, the Spaniard paused.

"Pardon me," said Captain Delano, lowly, "but I think that, by a sympathetic experience, I conjecture, Don Benito, what it is that gives the keener edge to your grief. It was once my hard fortune to lose, at sea, a dear friend, my own brother, then supercargo. Assured of the welfare of his spirit, its departure I could have borne like a man; but that honest eye, that honest hand—both of which had so often met mine—and that warm heart; all, all—like scraps to the dogs—to throw all to the sharks! It was then I vowed never to have for fellow-voyager a man I loved, unless, unbeknown to him, I had provided every requisite, in case of a fatality, for embalming his mortal part for interment on shore. Were your friend's remains now on board this ship, Don Benito, not thus strangely would the mention of his name affect you."

"On board this ship?" echoed the Spaniard. Then, with horrified gestures, as directed against some spectre, he unconsciously fell into the ready arms of his attendant, who, with a silent appeal toward Captain Delano, seemed beseeching him not again to broach a theme so unspeakably distressing to his master.

This poor fellow now, thought the pained American, is the victim of that sad superstition which associates goblins with the deserted body of man, as ghosts with an abandoned house. How unlike are we made! What to me, in like case, would have been a solemn satisfaction, the bare suggestion, even, terrifies the Spaniard into this trance. Poor Alexandro Aranda! what would you say could you here see your friend—who, on former voyages, when you, for months, were left behind, has, I dare say, often longed, and longed, for one peep at you—now transported with terror at the least thought of having you anyway nigh him.

At this moment, with a dreary grave-yard toll, betokening a flaw, the ship's forecastle bell, smote by one of the grizzled oakum-pickers, proclaimed ten o'clock, through the leaden calm; when Captain Delano's attention was caught by the moving figure of a gigantic black, emerging from the general crowd below, and slowly advancing towards the elevated poop. An iron collar was about his neck, from which depended a chain, thrice wound round his body; the terminating links padlocked together at a broad band of iron, his girdle.

"How like a mute Atufal moves," murmured the servant.

The black mounted the steps of the poop, and, like a brave prisoner, brought up to receive sentence, stood in unquailing muteness before Don Benito, now recovered from his attack.

At the first glimpse of his approach, Don Benito had started, a resentful shadow swept over his face; and, as with the sudden memory of bootless rage, his white lips glued together.

This is some mulish mutineer, thought Captain Delano, surveying, not without a mixture of admiration, the colossal form of the negro.

"See, he waits your question, master," said the servant.

Thus reminded, Don Benito, nervously averting his glance, as if shunning, by anticipation, some rebellious response, in a disconcerted voice, thus spoke:—

"Atufal, will you ask my pardon, now?"

The black was silent.

"Again, master," murmured the servant, with bitter upbraiding eyeing his countryman. "Again, master; he will bend to master yet."

"Answer," said Don Benito, still averting his glance, "say but the one word, *pardon*, and your chains shall be off."

Upon this, the black, slowly raising both arms, let them lifelessly fall, his links clanking, his head bowed; as much as to say, "No, I am content."

"Go," said Don Benito, with inkept and unknown emotion.

Deliberately as he had come, the black obeyed.

"Excuse me, Don Benito," said Captain Delano, "but this scene surprises me; what means it, pray?"

"It means that that negro alone, of all the band, has given me peculiar cause of offense. I have put him in chains; I——"

Here he paused; his hand to his head, as if there were a swimming there, or a sudden bewilderment of memory had come over him; but meeting his servant's kindly glance seemed reassured, and proceeded:—

"I could not scourge such a form. But I told him he must ask my pardon. As yet he has not. At my command, every two hours he stands before me."

"And how long has this been?"

"Some sixty days."

"And obedient in all else? And respectful?"

"Yes."

"Upon my conscience, then," exclaimed Captain Delano, impulsively, "he has a royal spirit in him, this fellow."

"He may have some right to it," bitterly returned Don Benito, "he says he was king in his own land."

"Yes," said the servant, entering a word, "those slits in Atufal's ears once held wedges of gold; but poor Babo here, in his own land, was only a poor slave; a black man's slave was Babo, who now is the white's."

Somewhat annoyed by these conversational familiarities, Captain Delano turned curiously upon the attendant, then glanced inquiringly at his master; but, as if long wonted to these little informalities, neither master nor man seemed to understand him.

"What, pray, was Atufal's offense, Don Benito?" asked Captain Delano; "if it was not something very serious, take a fool's advice, and, in view of his general docility, as well as in some natural respect for his spirit, remit him his penalty."

"No, no, master never will do that," here murmured the servant to himself, "proud Atufal must first ask master's pardon. The slave there carries the padlock, but master here carries the key."

His attention thus directed, Captain Delano now noticed for the first, that, suspended by a slender silken cord, from Don Benito's neck, hung a key. At once, from the servant's muttered syllables, divining the key's purpose, he smiled and said:—"So, Don Benito—padlock and key—significant symbols, truly."

Biting his lip, Don Benito faltered.

Though the remark of Captain Delano, a man of such native simplicity as to be incapable of satire or irony, had been dropped in playful allusion to the Spaniard's singularly evidenced lordship over the black; yet the hypochondriac seemed some way to have taken it as a malicious reflection upon his confessed inability thus far to break down, at least, on a verbal summons, the entrenched will of the slave. Deploring this supposed misconception, yet despairing of correcting it, Captain Delano shifted the subject; but finding his companion more than ever withdrawn, as if still sourly digesting the lees of the presumed affront above-mentioned, by-and-by Captain Delano likewise became less talkative, oppressed, against his own will, by what seemed the secret vindictiveness of the morbidly sensitive Spaniard. But the good sailor, himself of a quite contrary disposition, refrained, on his part, alike from the appearance as from the feeling of resentment, and if silent, was only so from contagion.

Presently the Spaniard, assisted by his servant somewhat discourteously crossed over from his guest; a procedure which, sensibly enough, might have been allowed to pass for idle caprice of ill-humor, had not master and man, lingering round the corner of the elevated skylight, begun whispering together in low voices. This was unpleasing. And more; the moody air of the Spaniard, which at times had not been without a sort of valetudinarian stateliness, now seemed anything but dignified; while the menial familiarity of the servant lost its original charm of simple-hearted attachment.

In his embarrassment, the visitor turned his face to the other side of the ship. By so doing, his glance accidentally fell on a young Spanish sailor, a coil of rope in his hand, just stepped from the deck to the first round of the mizzen-rigging. Perhaps the man would not have been particularly noticed, were it not that, during his ascent to one of the yards, he, with a sort of covert intentness, kept his eye fixed on Captain Delano, from whom, presently, it passed, as if by a natural sequence, to the two whisperers.

His own attention thus redirected to that quarter, Captain Delano gave a slight start. From something in Don Benito's manner just then, it seemed as if the visitor had, at least partly, been the subject of the withdrawn consultation going on—a conjecture as little agreeable to the guest as it was little flattering to the host.

The singular alternations of courtesy and ill-breeding in the Spanish captain were unaccountable, except on one of two suppositions—innocent lunacy, or wicked imposture.

But the first idea, though it might naturally have occurred to an indifferent observer, and, in some respect, had not hitherto been wholly a stranger to Captain Delano's mind, yet, now that, in an incipient way, he began to regard the stranger's conduct something in the light of an intentional affront, of course the idea of lunacy was virtually vacated. But if not a lunatic, what then? Under the circumstances, would a gentleman, nay, any honest boor, act the part now acted by his host? The man was an impostor. Some low-born adventurer, masquerading as an oceanic grandee; yet so ignorant of the first requisites of mere gentleman-hood as to be betrayed into the present remarkable indecorum. That strange ceremoniousness, too, at other times evinced, seemed not uncharacteristic of one playing a part above his real level. Benito Cereno—Don Benito Cereno—a sounding name. One, too, at that period, not unknown, in the surname, to supercargoes and sea captains trading along the Spanish Main, as belonging to one of the most enterprising and extensive mercantile families in all those provinces; several members of it having titles; a sort of Castilian Rothschild, with a noble brother, or cousin, in every great trading town of South America. The alleged Don Benito was in early manhood, about twenty-nine or thirty. To assume a sort of roving cadetship in the maritime affairs of such a house, what more likely scheme for a young knave of talent and spirit? But the Spaniard was a pale invalid. Never mind. For even to the degree of simulating mortal disease, the craft of some tricksters had been known to attain. To think that, under the aspect of infantile weakness, the most savage energies might be couched—those velvets of the Spaniard but the silky paw of his fangs.

From no train of thought did these fancies come; not from within, but from without; suddenly, too, and in one throng, like hoar frost; yet as soon to vanish as the mild sun of Captain Delano's good-nature regained its meridian.

Glancing over once more towards his host—whose side-face, revealed above the skylight, was now turned towards him—he was struck by the profile, whose clearness of cut was refined by the thinness, incident to ill-health, as well as ennobled about the chin by the beard. Away with suspicion. He was a true off-shoot of a true hidalgo Cereno.

Relieved by these and other better thoughts, the visitor, lightly humming a tune, now began indifferently pacing the poop, so as not to betray to Don Benito that he had at all mistrusted incivility, much less duplicity; for such mistrust would yet be proved illusory, and by the event; though, for the present, the circumstance which had provoked that distrust remained unexplained. But when that little mystery should have been cleared up, Captain Delano thought he might extremely regret it, did he allow Don Benito to become aware that he had indulged in ungenerous surmises. In short, to the Spaniard's black-letter text, it was best, for awhile, to leave open margin.

Presently, his pale face twitching and overcast, the Spaniard, still supported by his attendant, moved over towards his guest, when, with even more than his usual embarrassment, and a strange sort of intriguing intonation in his husky whisper, the following conversation began:—

"Señor, may I ask how long you have lain at this isle?"

"Oh, but a day or two, Don Benito."

"And from what port are you last?"

"Canton."

"And there, Señor, you exchanged your sealskins for teas and silks, I think you said?"

"Yes. Silks, mostly."

"And the balance you took in specie, perhaps?"

Captain Delano, fidgeting a little, answered—

"Yes; some silver; not a very great deal, though."

"Ah—well. May I ask how many men have you, Señor?"

Captain Delano slightly started, but answered—

"About five-and-twenty, all told."

"And at present, Señor, all on board, I suppose?"

"All on board, Don Benito," replied the Captain, now with satisfaction.

"And will be to-night, Señor?"

At this last question, following so many pertinacious ones, for the soul of him Captain Delano could not but look very earnestly at the questioner, who, instead of meeting the glance, with every token of craven discomposure dropped his eyes to the deck; presenting an unworthy contrast to his servant, who, just then, was kneeling at his feet, adjusting a loose shoe-buckle; his disengaged face meantime, with humble curiosity, turned openly up into his master's downcast one.

The Spaniard, still with a guilty shuffle, repeated his question:

"And—and will be to-night, Señor?"

"Yes, for aught I know," returned Captain Delano—"but nay," rallying himself into fearless truth, "some of them talked of going off on another fishing party about midnight."

"Your ships generally go—go more or less armed, I believe, Señor?"

"Oh, a six-pounder or two, in case of emergency," was the intrepidly indifferent reply, "with a small stock of muskets, sealing-spears, and cutlasses, you know."

As he thus responded, Captain Delano again glanced at Don

Benito, but the latter's eyes were averted; while abruptly and awkwardly shifting the subject, he made some peevish allusion to the calm, and then, without apology, once more, with his attendant, withdrew to the opposite bulwarks, where the whispering was resumed.

At this moment, and ere Captain Delano could cast a cool thought upon what had just passed, the young Spanish sailor, before mentioned, was seen descending from the rigging. In act of stooping over to spring inboard to the deck, his voluminous, unconfined frock, or shirt, of coarse woolen, much spotted with tar, opened out far down the chest, revealing a soiled under-garment of what seemed the finest linen, edged, about the neck, with a narrow blue ribbon, sadly faded and worn. At this moment the young sailor's eye was again fixed on the whisperers, and Captain Delano thought he observed a lurking significance in it, as if silent signs, of some Freemason sort, had that instant been interchanged.

This once more impelled his own glance in the direction of Don Benito, and, as before, he could not but infer that himself formed the subject of the conference. He paused. The sound of the hatchet-polishing fell on his ears. He cast another swift side-look at the two. They had the air of conspirators. In connection with the late questionings, and the incident of the young sailor, these things now begat such return of involuntary suspicion, that the singular guilelessness of the American could not endure it. Plucking up a gay and humorous expression, he crossed over to the two rapidly, saying:—"Ha, Don Benito, your black here seems high in your trust; a sort of privy-counselor, in fact."

Upon this, the servant looked up with a good-natured grin, but the master started as from a venomous bite. It was a moment or two before the Spaniard sufficiently recovered himself to reply; which he did, at last, with cold constraint:—"Yes, Señor, I have trust in Babo."

Here Babo, changing his previous grin of mere animal humor into an intelligent smile, not ungratefully eyed his master.

Finding that the Spaniard now stood silent and reserved, as if involuntarily, or purposely giving hint that his guest's proximity was inconvenient just then, Captain Delano, unwilling to appear uncivil even to incivility itself, made some trivial remark and moved off; again and again turning over in his mind the mysterious demeanor of Don Benito Cereno.

He had descended from the poop, and, wrapped in thought, was passing near a dark hatchway, leading down into the steerage, when, perceiving motion there, he looked to see what moved. The same instant there was a sparkle in the shadowy hatchway, and he saw one of the Spanish sailors, prowling there, hurriedly placing his hand in the bosom of his frock, as if hiding something. Before the man could have been certain who it was that was passing, he slunk below out of sight. But enough was seen of him to make it sure that he was the same young sailor before noticed in the rigging.

What was that which so sparkled? thought Captain Delano. It was no lamp—no match—no live coal. Could it have been a jewel? But how come sailors with jewels?—or with silk-trimmed under-shirts either? Has he been robbing the trunks of the dead cabin-passengers? But if so, he would hardly wear one of the stolen articles on board ship here. Ah, ah—if, now, that was, indeed, a secret sign I saw passing between this suspicious fellow and his captain awhile since; if I could only be certain that, in my uneasi-ness, my senses did not deceive me, then——

Here, passing from one suspicious thing to another, his mind revolved the strange questions put to him concerning his ship.

By a curious coincidence, as each point was recalled, the black wizards of Ashantee would strike up with their hatchets, as in ominous comment on the white stranger's thoughts. Pressed by such enigmas and portents, it would have been almost against nature, had not, even into the least distrustful heart, some ugly misgivings obtruded.

Observing the ship, now helplessly fallen into a current, with enchanted sails, drifting with increased rapidity seaward; and noting that, from a lately intercepted projection of the land, the sealer was hidden, the stout mariner began to quake at thoughts which he barely durst confess to himself. Above all, he began to feel a ghostly dread of Don Benito. And yet, when he roused him-self, dilated his chest, felt himself strong on his legs, and coolly considered it—what did all these phantoms amount to?

Had the Spaniard any sinister scheme, it must have reference not so much to him (Captain Delano) as to his ship (the *Bachelor's Delight*). Hence the present drifting away of the one ship from the other, instead of favoring any such possible scheme, was, for the time, at least, opposed to it. Clearly any suspicion, combining such contradictions, must need be delusive. Besides, was it not absurd to think of a vessel in distress—a vessel by sickness almost dismanned of her crew—a vessel whose inmates were parched for water—was it not a thousand times absurd that such a craft should, at present, be of a piratical character; or her commander, either for himself or those under him, cherish any desire but for speedy relief and refreshment? But then, might not general distress, and thirst in particular, be affected? And might not that same undiminished Spanish crew, alleged to have perished off to a remnant, be at that very moment lurking in the hold? On heartbroken pretense of entreating a cup of cold water, fiends in human form had got into lonely dwellings, nor retired until a dark deed had been done. And among the Malay pirates, it was no unusual thing to lure ships after them into their treacherous harbors, or entice boarders from a declared enemy at sea, by the spectacle of thinly manned or vacant decks, beneath which prowled a hundred spears with yellow arms ready to upthrust them through the mats. Not that Captain Delano had entirely credited such things. He had heard of them—and now, as stories, they recurred. The present destination of the ship was the anchorage. There she would be near his own vessel. Upon gaining that vicinity, might not the *San Dominick*, like a slumbering volcano, suddenly let loose energies now hid?

He recalled the Spaniard's manner while telling his story. There was a gloomy hesitancy and subterfuge about it. It was just the manner of one making up his tale for evil purposes, as he goes. But if that story was not true, what was the truth? That the ship had unlawfully come into the Spaniard's possession? But in many of its details, especially in reference to the more calamitous parts, such as the fatalities among the seamen, the consequent prolonged beating about, the past sufferings from obstinate calms, and still continued suffering from thirst; in all these points, as well as others,

Don Benito's story had corroborated not only the wailing ejaculations of the indiscriminate multitude, white and black, but likewise—what seemed impossible to be counterfeit—by the very expression and play of every human feature, which Captain Delano
saw. If Don Benito's story was, throughout, an invention, then
every soul on board, down to the youngest negress, was his carefully drilled recruit in the plot: an incredible inference. And yet,
if there was ground for mistrusting his veracity, that inference was
a legitimate one.

But those questions of the Spaniard. There, indeed, one might
pause. Did they not seem put with much the same object with
which the burglar or assassin, by day-time, reconnoitres the walls
of a house? But, with ill purposes, to solicit such information
openly of the chief person endangered, and so, in effect, setting
him on his guard; how unlikely a procedure was that? Absurd,
then, to suppose that those questions had been prompted by evil
designs. Thus, the same conduct, which, in this instance, had raised
the alarm, served to dispel it. In short, scarce any suspicion or uneasiness, however apparently reasonable at the time, which was not
now, with equal apparent reason, dismissed.

At last he began to laugh at his former forebodings; and laugh
at the strange ship for, in its aspect, someway siding with them,
as it were; and laugh, too, at the odd-looking blacks, particularly
those old scissors-grinders, the Ashantees; and those bed-ridden
old knitting women, the oakum-pickers; and almost at the dark
Spaniard himself, the central hobgoblin of all.

For the rest, whatever in a serious way seemed enigmatical, was
now good-naturedly explained away by the thought that, for the
most part, the poor invalid scarcely knew what he was about;
either sulking in black vapors, or putting idle questions without
sense or object. Evidently, for the present, the man was not fit to
be intrusted with the ship. On some benevolent plea withdrawing
the command from him, Captain Delano would yet have to send
her to Conception, in charge of his second mate, a worthy person
and good navigator—a plan not more convenient for the *San
Dominick* than for Don Benito; for, relieved from all anxiety,
keeping wholly to his cabin, the sick man, under the good nursing
of his servant, would, probably, by the end of the passage, be in a

measure restored to health, and with that he should also be restored to authority.

Such were the American's thoughts. They were tranquilizing. There was a difference between the idea of Don Benito's darkly pre-ordaining Captain Delano's fate, and Captain Delano's lightly arranging Don Benito's. Nevertheless, it was not without something of relief that the good seaman presently perceived his whale-boat in the distance. Its absence had been prolonged by unexpected detention at the sealer's side, as well as its returning trip lengthened by the continual recession of the goal.

The advancing speck was observed by the blacks. Their shouts attracted the attention of Don Benito, who, with a return of courtesy, approaching Captain Delano, expressed satisfaction at the coming of some supplies, slight and temporary as they must necessarily prove.

Captain Delano responded; but while doing so, his attention was drawn to something passing on the deck below: among the crowd climbing the landward bulwarks, anxiously watching the coming boat, two blacks, to all appearances accidentally incommoded by one of the sailors, violently pushed him aside, which the sailor someway resenting, they dashed him to the deck, despite the earnest cries of the oakum-pickers.

"Don Benito," said Captain Delano quickly, "do you see what is going on there? Look!"

But, seized by his cough, the Spaniard staggered, with both hands to his face, on the point of falling. Captain Delano would have supported him, but the servant was more alert, who, with one hand sustaining his master, with the other applied the cordial. Don Benito restored, the black withdrew his support, slipping aside a little, but dutifully remaining within call of a whisper. Such discretion was here evinced as quite wiped away, in the visitor's eyes, any blemish of impropriety which might have attached to the attendant, from the indecorous conferences before mentioned; showing, too, that if the servant were to blame, it might be more the master's fault than his own, since, when left to himself, he could conduct thus well.

His glance called away from the spectacle of disorder to the more pleasing one before him, Captain Delano could not avoid again congratulating his host upon possessing such a servant, who, though perhaps a little too forward now and then, must upon the whole be invaluable to one in the invalid's situation.

"Tell me, Don Benito," he added, with a smile—"I should like to have your man here, myself—what will you take for him? Would fifty doubloons be any object?"

"Master wouldn't part with Babo for a thousand doubloons," murmured the black, overhearing the offer, and taking it in earnest, and, with the strange vanity of a faithful slave, appreciated by his master, scorning to hear so paltry a valuation put upon him by a stranger. But Don Benito, apparently hardly yet completely restored, and again interrupted by his cough, made but some broken reply.

Soon his physical distress became so great, affecting his mind, too, apparently, that, as if to screen the sad spectacle, the servant gently conducted his master below.

Left to himself, the American, to while away the time till his boat should arrive, would have pleasantly accosted some one of the few Spanish seamen he saw; but recalling something that Don Benito had said touching their ill conduct, he refrained; as a ship-master indisposed to countenance cowardice or unfaithfulness in seamen.

While, with these thoughts, standing with eye directed forward towards that handful of sailors, suddenly he thought that one or two of them returned the glance and with a sort of meaning. He rubbed his eyes, and looked again; but again seemed to see the same thing. Under a new form, but more obscure than any previous one, the old suspicions recurred, but, in the absence of Don Benito, with less of panic than before. Despite the bad account given of the sailors, Captain Delano resolved forthwith to accost one of them. Descending the poop, he made his way through the blacks, his movement drawing a queer cry from the oakum-pickers, prompted by whom, the negroes, twitching each other aside, divided before him; but, as if curious to see what was the object of this deliberate visit to their Ghetto, closing in behind, in tolerable order, followed the white stranger up. His progress thus proclaimed as by mounted kings-at-arms, and escorted as by a Caffre guard of honor, Captain Delano, assuming a good-humored, off-handed air, continued to advance; now and then saying a blithe word to the negroes, and his eye curiously surveying the white faces, here and there sparsely mixed in with the blacks, like stray white pawns venturously involved in the ranks of the chess-men opposed.

While thinking which of them to select for his purpose, he chanced to observe a sailor seated on the deck engaged in tarring the strap of a large block, a circle of blacks squatted round him inquisitively eyeing the process.

The mean employment of the man was in contrast with something superior in his figure. His hand, black with continually thrusting it into the tar-pot held for him by a negro, seemed not naturally allied to his face, a face which would have been a very fine one but for its haggardness. Whether this haggardness had aught to do with criminality, could not be determined; since, as intense heat and cold, though unlike, produce like sensations, so innocence and guilt, when, through casual association with mental pain, stamping any visible impress, use one seal—a hacked one.

Not again that this reflection occurred to Captain Delano at the time, charitable man as he was. Rather another idea. Because observing so singular a haggardness combined with a dark eye, averted as in trouble and shame, and then again recalling Don Benito's confessed ill opinion of his crew, insensibly he was operated upon by certain general notions which, while disconnecting pain and abashment from virtue, invariably link them with vice.

If, indeed, there be any wickedness on board this ship, thought Captain Delano, be sure that man there has fouled his hand in it, even as now he fouls it in the pitch. I don't like to accost him. I will speak to this other, this old Jack here on the windlass.

He advanced to an old Barcelona tar, in ragged red breeches and dirty night-cap, cheeks trenched and bronzed, whiskers dense as thorn hedges. Seated between two sleepy-looking Africans, this mariner, like his younger shipmate, was employed upon some rigging—splicing a cable—the sleepy-looking blacks performing the inferior function of holding the outer parts of the ropes for him.

Upon Captain Delano's approach, the man at once hung his head below its previous level; the one necessary for business. It appeared as if he desired to be thought absorbed, with more than common fidelity, in his task. Being addressed, he glanced up, but with what seemed a furtive, diffident air, which sat strangely enough on his weather-beaten visage, much as if a grizzly bear, instead of growling and biting, should simper and cast sheep's eyes. He was asked several questions concerning the voyage—questions purposely referring to several particulars in Don Benito's narrative, not previously corroborated by those impulsive cries greeting the visitor on first coming on board. The questions were briefly answered, confirming all that remained to be confirmed of the story. The negroes about the windlass joined in with the old sailor; but, as they became talkative, he by degrees became mute, and at length quite glum, seemed morosely unwilling to answer more questions, and yet, all the while, this ursine air was somewhat mixed with his sheepish one.

Despairing of getting into unembarrassed talk with such a centaur, Captain Delano, after glancing round for a more promising countenance, but seeing none, spoke pleasantly to the blacks to make way for him; and so, amid various grins and grimaces, returned to the poop, feeling a little strange at first, he could hardly tell why, but upon the whole with regained confidence in Benito Cereno.

How plainly, thought he, did that old whiskerando yonder betray a consciousness of ill desert. No doubt, when he saw me coming, he dreaded lest I, apprised by his Captain of the crew's general misbehavior, came with sharp words for him, and so down with his head. And yet—and yet, now that I think of it, that very old fellow, if I err not, was one of those who seemed so earnestly eyeing me here awhile since. Ah, these currents spin one's head round almost as much as they do the ship. Ha, there now's a pleasant sort of sunny sight; quite sociable, too.

His attention had been drawn to a slumbering negress, partly disclosed through the lace-work of some rigging, lying, with youthful limbs carelessly disposed, under the lee of the bulwarks, like a doe in the shade of a woodland rock. Sprawling at her lapped breasts, was her wide-awake fawn, stark naked, its black little body half lifted from the deck, crosswise with its dam's; its hands, like two paws, clambering upon her; its mouth and nose ineffectually rooting to get at the mark; and meantime giving a vexatious half-grunt, blending with the composed snore of the negress.

The uncommon vigor of the child at length roused the mother. She started up, at a distance facing Captain Delano. But as if not at all concerned at the attitude in which she had been caught, delightedly she caught the child up, with maternal transports, covering it with kisses.

There's naked nature, now; pure tenderness and love, thought Captain Delano, well pleased.

This incident prompted him to remark the other negresses more particularly than before. He was gratified with their manners: like most uncivilized women, they seemed at once tender of heart and tough of constitution; equally ready to die for their infants or fight for them. Unsophisticated as leopardesses; loving as doves. Ah! thought Captain Delano, these, perhaps, are some of the very women whom Ledyard saw in Africa, and gave such a noble account of.

These natural sights somehow insensibly deepened his confidence and ease. At last he looked to see how his boat was getting on; but it was still pretty remote. He turned to see if Don Benito had returned; but he had not.

To change the scene, as well as to please himself with a leisurely observation of the coming boat, stepping over into the mizzen-chains, he clambered his way into the starboard quarter-gallery—one of those abandoned Venetian-looking water-balconies previously mentioned—retreats cut off from the deck. As his foot pressed the half-damp, half-dry sea-mosses matting the place, and a chance phantom cats-paw—an islet of breeze, unheralded, unfolded—as this ghostly cats-paw came fanning his cheek; as his glance fell upon the row of small, round dead-lights—all closed like coppered eyes of the coffined—and the state-cabin door, once connecting with the gallery, even as the dead-lights had once looked out upon it, but now calked fast like a sarcophagus lid; and to a purple-black tarred-over, panel, threshold, and post; and he bethought him of the time when that state-cabin and this state-balcony had heard the voices of the Spanish king's officers, and the forms of the Lima viceroy's daughters had perhaps leaned where he stood—as these and other images flitted through his mind, as the cats-paw through the calm, gradually he felt rising a dreamy inquietude, like that of one who alone on the prairie feels unrest from the repose of the moon.

He leaned against the carved balustrade, again looking off toward his boat; but found his eye falling upon the ribbon grass, trailing along the ship's water-line, straight as a border of green box; and parterres of sea-weed, broad ovals and crescents, floating nigh and far, with what seemed long formal alleys between, crossing the terraces of swells, and sweeping round as if leading to the grottoes below. And overhanging all was the balustrade by his arm, which, partly stained with pitch and partly embossed with moss, seemed the charred ruin of some summer-house in a grand garden long running to waste.

Trying to break one charm, he was but becharmed anew. Though upon the wide sea, he seemed in some far inland country; prisoner in some deserted château, left to stare at empty grounds, and peer out at vague roads, where never wagon or wayfarer passed.

But these enchantments were a little disenchanted as his eye fell on the corroded main-chains. Of an ancient style, massy and rusty in link, shackle and bolt, they seemed even more fit for the ship's present business than the one for which she had been built.

Presently he thought something moved nigh the chains. He rubbed his eyes, and looked hard. Groves of rigging were about the chains; and there, peering from behind a great stay, like an Indian from behind a hemlock, a Spanish sailor, a marlingspike in his hand, was seen, who made what seemed an imperfect gesture towards the balcony, but immediately, as if alarmed by some advancing step along the deck within, vanished into the recesses of the hempen forest, like a poacher.

What meant this? Something the man had sought to communicate, unbeknown to any one, even to his captain. Did the secret involve aught unfavorable to his captain? Were those previous misgivings of Captain Delano's about to be verified? Or, in his haunted mood at the moment, had some random, unintentional motion of the man, while busy with the stay, as if repairing it, been mistaken for a significant beckoning?

Not unbewildered, again he gazed off for his boat. But it was temporarily hidden by a rocky spur of the isle. As with some eagerness he bent forward, watching for the first shooting view of its beak, the balustrade gave way before him like charcoal. Had he not clutched an outreaching rope he would have fallen into the sea.

The crash, though feeble, and the fall, though hollow, of the rotten fragments, must have been overheard. He glanced up. With sober curiosity peering down upon him was one of the old oakumpickers, slipped from his perch to an outside boom; while below the old negro, and, invisible to him, reconnoitering from a porthole like a fox from the mouth of its den, crouched the Spanish sailor again. From something suddenly suggested by the man's air, the mad idea now darted into Captain Delano's mind, that Don Benito's plea of indisposition, in withdrawing below, was but a pretense: that he was engaged there maturing his plot, of which the sailor, by some means gaining an inkling, had a mind to warn the stranger against; incited, it may be, by gratitude for a kind word on first boarding the ship. Was it from foreseeing some possible interference like this, that Don Benito had, beforehand, given such a bad character of his sailors, while praising the negroes; though, indeed, the former seemed as docile as the latter the contrary? The whites, too, by nature, were the shrewder race. A man with some evil design, would he not be likely to speak well of that stupidity which was blind to his depravity, and malign that intelligence from which it might be hidden? Not unlikely, perhaps. But if the whites had dark secrets concerning Don Benito, could then Don Benito be any way in complicity with the blacks? But they were too stupid. Besides, who ever heard of a white so far a renegade as to apostatize from his very species almost, by leaguing in against it with negroes? These difficulties recalled former ones. Lost in their mazes, Captain Delano, who had now regained the deck, was uneasily advancing along it, when he observed a new face; an aged sailor seated cross-legged near the main hatchway. His skin was shrunk up with wrinkles like a pelican's empty pouch; his hair frosted; his countenance grave and composed. His hands were full of ropes, which he was working into a large knot. Some blacks were about him obligingly dipping the strands for him, here and there, as the exigencies of the operation demanded.

Captain Delano crossed over to him, and stood in silence surveying the knot; his mind, by a not uncongenial transition, passing from its own entanglements to those of the hemp. For intricacy, such a knot he had never seen in an American ship, nor indeed any other. The old man looked like an Egyptian priest, making

Gordian knots for the temple of Ammon. The knot seemed a combination of double-bowline-knot, treble-crown-knot, back-handed-well-knot, knot-in-and-out-knot, and jamming-knot.

At last, puzzled to comprehend the meaning of such a knot, Captain Delano addressed the knotter:—

"What are you knotting there, my man?"

"The knot," was the brief reply, without looking up.

"So it seems; but what is it for?"

"For some one else to undo," muttered back the old man, plying his fingers harder than ever, the knot being now nearly completed.

While Captain Delano stood watching him, suddenly the old man threw the knot towards him, saying in broken English—the first heard in the ship—something to this effect: "Undo it, cut it, quick." It was said lowly, but with such condensation of rapidity, that the long, slow words in Spanish, which had preceded and followed, almost operated as covers to the brief English between.

For a moment, knot in hand, and knot in head, Captain Delano stood mute; while, without further heeding him, the old man was now intent upon other ropes. Presently there was a slight stir behind Captain Delano. Turning, he saw the chained negro, Atufal, standing quietly there. The next moment the old sailor rose, muttering, and, followed by his subordinate negroes, removed to the forward part of the ship, where in the crowd he disappeared.

An elderly negro, in a clout like an infant's, and with a pepper and salt head, and a kind of attorney air, now approached Captain Delano. In tolerable Spanish, and with a good-natured, knowing wink, he informed him that the old knotter was simple-witted, but harmless; often playing his odd tricks. The negro concluded by begging the knot, for of course the stranger would not care to be troubled with it. Unconsciously, it was handed to him. With a sort of congé, the negro received it, and, turning his back, ferreted into it like a detective custom-house office after smuggled laces. Soon, with some African word, equivalent to pshaw, he tossed the knot overboard.

All this is very queer now, thought Captain Delano, with a qualmish sort of emotion; but, as one feeling incipient seasickness, he strove, by ignoring the symptoms, to get rid of the malady.

Once more he looked off for his boat. To his delight, it was now again in view, leaving the rocky spur astern.

The sensation here experienced, after at first relieving his uneasiness, with unforeseen efficacy soon began to remove it. The less distant sight of that well-known boat—showing it, not as before, half blended with the haze, but with outline defined, so that its individuality, like a man's, was manifest; that boat, *Rover* by name, which, though now in strange seas, had often pressed the beach of Captain Delano's home, and, brought to its threshold for repairs, had familiarly lain there, as a Newfoundland dog; the sight of that household boat evoked a thousand trustful associations, which, contrasted with previous suspicions, filled him not only with lightsome confidence, but somehow with half humorous self-reproaches at his former lack of it.

"What, I, Amasa Delano—Jack of the Beach, as they called me when a lad—I, Amasa; the same that, duck-satchel in hand, used to paddle along the water-side to the schoolhouse made from the old hulk—I, little Jack of the Beach, that used to go berrying with cousin Nat and the rest; I to be murdered here at the ends of the earth, on board a haunted pirate-ship by a horrible Spaniard? Too nonsensical to think of! Who would murder Amasa Delano? His conscience is clean. There is some one above. Fie, fie, Jack of the Beach! you are a child indeed; a child of the second childhood, old boy; you are beginning to dote and drule, I'm afraid."

Light of heart and foot, he stepped aft, and there was met by Don Benito's servant, who, with a pleasing expression, responsive to his own present feelings, informed him that his master had recovered from the effects of his coughing fit, and had just ordered him to go present his compliments to his good guest, Don Amasa, and say that he (Don Benito) would soon have the happiness to rejoin him.

There now, do you mark that? again thought Captain Delano, walking the poop. What a donkey I was. This kind gentleman who here sends me his kind compliments, he, but ten minutes ago, dark-lantern in hand, was dodging round some old grind-stone in the hold, sharpening a hatchet for me, I thought. Well, well; these long calms have a morbid effect on the mind, I've often heard, though I never believed it before. Ha! glancing towards the boat; there's *Rover*; good dog; a white bone in her mouth. A pretty big bone though, seems to me.—What? Yes, she has fallen afoul of the bubbling tide-rip there. It sets her the other way, too, for the time. Patience.

It was now about noon, though, from the grayness of everything, it seemed to be getting towards dusk.

The calm was confirmed. In the far distance, away from the influence of land, the leaden ocean seemed laid out and leaded up, its course finished, soul gone, defunct. But the current from landward, where the ship was, increased; silently sweeping her further and further towards the tranced waters beyond.

Still, from his knowledge of those latitudes, cherishing hopes of a breeze, and a fair and fresh one, at any moment, Captain Delano, despite present prospects, buoyantly counted upon bringing the *San Dominick* safely to anchor ere night. The distance swept over was nothing; since, with a good wind, ten minutes' sailing would retrace more than sixty minutes, drifting. Meantime, one moment turning to mark *Rover* fighting the tide-rip, and the next to see Don Benito approaching, he continued walking the poop.

Gradually he felt a vexation arising from the delay of his boat; this soon merged into uneasiness; and at last—his eye falling continually, as from a stage-box into the pit, upon the strange crowd before and below him, and, by-and-by, recognizing there the face—now composed to indifference—of the Spanish sailor who had seemed to beckon from the main-chains—something of his old trepidations returned.

Ah, thought he—gravely enough—this is like the ague: because it went off, it follows not that it won't come back.

Though ashamed of the relapse, he could not altogether subdue it; and so, exerting his good-nature to the utmost, insensibly he came to a compromise.

Yes, this is a strange craft; a strange history, too, and strange folks on board. But—nothing more.

By way of keeping his mind out of mischief till the boat should arrive, he tried to occupy it with turning over and over, in a purely speculative sort of way, some lesser peculiarities of the captain and crew. Among others, four curious points recurred:

First, the affair of the Spanish lad assailed with a knife by the slave boy; an act winked at by Don Benito. Second, the tyranny in Don Benito's treatment of Atufal, the black; as if a child should lead a bull of the Nile by the ring in his nose. Third, the trampling of the sailor by the two negroes; a piece of insolence passed over without so much as a reprimand. Fourth, the cringing submission to their master, of all the ship's underlings, mostly blacks; as if by the least inadvertence they feared to draw down his despotic displeasure.

Coupling these points, they seemed somewhat contradictory. But what then, thought Captain Delano, glancing towards his now nearing boat—what then? Why, Don Benito is a very capricious commander. But he is not the first of the sort I have seen; though it's true he rather exceeds any other. But as a nation—continued he in his reveries—these Spaniards are all an odd set; the very word Spaniard has a curious, conspirator, Guy-Fawkish twang to it. And yet, I dare say, Spaniards in the main are as good folks as any in Duxbury, Massachusetts. Ah good! At last *Rover* has come.

As, with its welcome freight, the boat touched the side, the oakum-pickers, with venerable gestures, sought to restrain the blacks, who, at the sight of three gurried water-casks in its bottom, and a pile of wilted pumpkins in its bow, hung over the bulwarks in disorderly raptures.

Don Benito, with his servant, now appeared; his coming, perhaps, hastened by hearing the noise. Of him Captain Delano sought permission to serve out the water, so that all might share alike, and none injure themselves by unfair excess. But sensible, and, on Don Benito's account, kind as this offer was, it was received with what seemed impatience; as if aware that he lacked energy as a commander, Don Benito, with the true jealousy of weakness, resented as an affront any interference. So, at least, Captain Delano inferred.

In another moment the casks were being hoisted in, when some of the eager negroes accidentally jostled Captain Delano, where he stood by the gangway; so that, unmindful of Don Benito, yielding to the impulse of the moment, with good-natured authority he bade the blacks stand back; to enforce his words making use of a half-mirthful, half-menacing gesture. Instantly the blacks paused, just where they were, each negro and negress suspended in his or her posture, exactly as the word had found them—for a few seconds continuing so—while, as between the responsive posts of a telegraph, an unknown syllable ran from man to man among the perched oakum-pickers. While the visitor's attention was fixed by this scene, suddenly the hatchet-polishers half rose, and a rapid cry came from Don Benito.

Thinking that at the signal of the Spaniard he was about to be massacred, Captain Delano would have sprung for his boat, but paused, as the oakum-pickers, dropping down into the crowd with earnest exclamations, forced every white and every negro back, at the same moment, with gestures friendly and familiar, almost jocose, bidding him, in substance, not be a fool. Simultaneously the hatchet-polishers resumed their seats, quietly as so many tailors, and at once, as if nothing had happened, the work of hoisting in the casks was resumed, whites and blacks singing at the tackle.

Captain Delano glanced towards Don Benito. As he saw his meagre form in the act of recovering itself from reclining in the servant's arms, into which the agitated invalid had fallen, he could not but marvel at the panic by which himself had been surprised, on the darting supposition that such a commander, who, upon a legitimate occasion, so trivial, too, as it now appeared, could lose all self-command, was, with energetic iniquity, going to bring about his murder.

The casks being on deck, Captain Delano was handed a number of jars and cups by one of the steward's aids, who, in the name of his captain, entreated him to do as he had proposed—dole out the water. He complied, with republican impartiality as to this republican element, which always seeks one level, serving the oldest white no better than the youngest black; excepting, indeed, poor Don Benito, whose condition, if not rank, demanded an extra allowance. To him, in the first place, Captain Delano presented a fair pitcher of the fluid; but, thirsting as he was for it, the Spaniard quaffed not a drop until after several grave bows and salutes. A reciprocation of courtesies which the sight-loving Africans hailed with clapping of hands.

Two of the less wilted pumpkins being reserved for the cabin table, the residue were minced up on the spot for the general regalement. But the soft bread, sugar, and bottled cider, Captain Delano would have given the whites alone, and in chief Don Benito; but the latter objected; which disinterestedness not a little pleased the Americans; and so mouthfuls all around were given alike to whites and blacks; excepting one bottle of cider, which Babo insisted upon setting aside for his master.

Here it may be observed that as, on the first visit of the boat, the American had not permitted his men to board the ship, neither did he now; being unwilling to add to the confusion of the decks.

Not influenced by the peculiar good-humor at present prevailing, and for the time oblivious of any but benevolent thoughts, Captain Delano, who, from recent indications, counted upon a breeze within an hour or two at furthest, dispatched the boat back to the sealer, with orders for all the hands that could be spared immediately to set about rafting casks to the watering-place and filling them. Likewise he bade word be carried to his chief officer, that if, against present expectation, the ship was not brought to anchor by sunset, he need be under no concern; for as there was to be a full moon that night, he (Captain Delano) would remain on board ready to play the pilot, come the wind soon or late.

As the two captains stood together, observing the departing boat —the servant, as it happened, having just spied a spot on his master's velvet sleeve, and silently engaged rubbing it out—the American expressed his regrets that the *San Dominick* had no boats; none, at least, but the unseaworthy old hulk of the long-boat, which, warped as a camel's skeleton in the desert, and almost as bleached, lay pot-wise inverted amid-ships, one side a little tipped, furnishing a subterraneous sort of den for family groups of the blacks, mostly women and small children; who, squatting on old mats below, or perched above in the dark dome, on the elevated seats, were described, some distance within, like a social circle of bats, sheltering in some friendly cave; at intervals, ebon flights of naked boys and girls, three or four years old, darting in and out of the den's mouth.

"Had you three or four boats now, Don Benito," said Captain Delano, "I think that, by tugging at the oars, your negroes here might help along matters some. Did you sail from port without boats, Don Benito?"

"They were stove in the gales, Señor."

"That was bad. Many men, too, you lost then. Boats and men. Those must have been hard gales, Don Benito."

"Past all speech," cringed the Spaniard.

"Tell me, Don Benito," continued his companion with increased interest, "tell me, were these gales immediately off the pitch of Cape Horn?"

"Cape Horn?—who spoke of Cape Horn?"

"Yourself did, when giving me an account of your voyage," answered Captain Delano, with almost equal astonishment at this eating of his own words, even as he ever seemed eating his own heart, on the part of the Spaniard. "You yourself, Don Benito, spoke of Cape Horn," he emphatically repeated.

The Spaniard turned, in a sort of stooping posture, pausing an instant, as one about to make a plunging exchange of elements, as from air to water.

At this moment a messenger-boy, a white, hurried by, in the regular performance of his function carrying the last expired half-hour forward to the forecastle, from the cabin time-piece, to have it struck at the ship's large bell.

"Master," said the servant, discontinuing his work on the coat sleeve, and addressing the rapt Spaniard with a sort of timid apprehensiveness, as one charged with a duty, the discharge of which, it was foreseen, would prove irksome to the very person who had imposed it, and for whose benefit it was intended, "master told me never mind where he was, or how engaged, always to remind him, to a minute, when shaving-time comes. Miguel has gone to strike the half-hour afternoon. It is *now* master. Will master go into the cuddy?"

"Ah—yes," answered the Spaniard, starting, as from dreams into realities; then turning upon Captain Delano, he said that ere long he would resume the conversation.

"Then if master means to talk more to Don Amasa," said the servant, "why not let Don Amasa sit by master in the cuddy, and master can talk, and Don Amasa can listen, while Babo here lathers and strops."

"Yes," said Captain Delano, not unpleased with this sociable plan, "yes, Don Benito, unless you had rather not, I will go with you."

"Be it so, Señor."

As the three passed aft, the American could not but think it another strange instance of his host's capriciousness, this being shaved with such uncommon punctuality in the middle of the day. But he deemed it more than likely that the servant's anxious fidelity had something to do with the matter; inasmuch as the timely interruption served to rally his master from the mood which had evidently been coming upon him.

The place called the cuddy was a light deck-cabin formed by the poop, a sort of attic to the large cabin below. Part of it had formerly been the quarters of the officers; but since their death all the partitionings had been thrown down, and the whole interior converted into one spacious and airy marine hall; for absence of fine furniture and picturesque disarray of odd appurtenances, some-what answering to the wide, cluttered hall of some eccentric bachelor-squire in the country, who hangs his shooting-jacket and tobacco-pouch on deer antlers, and keeps his fishing-rod, tongs, and walking-stick in the same corner.

The similitude was heightened, if not originally suggested, by glimpses of the surrounding sea; since, in one aspect, the country and the ocean seem cousins-german.

The floor of the cuddy was matted. Overhead, four or five old muskets were stuck into horizontal holes along the beams. On one side was a claw-footed old table lashed to the deck; a thumbed missal on it, and over it a small, meagre crucifix attached to the bulk-head. Under the table lay a dented cutlass or two, with a hacked harpoon, among some melancholy old rigging, like a heap of poor friars' girdles. There were also two long, sharp-ribbed settees of Malacca cane, black with age, and uncomfortable to look at as inquisitors' racks, with a large, misshapen arm-chair, which, furnished with a rude barber's crotch at the back, working with a screw, seemed some grotesque engine of torment. A flag locker was in one corner, open, exposing various colored bunting, some rolled up, others half unrolled, still others tumbled. Opposite was a cumbrous washstand, of black mahogany, all of one block, with a pedestal, like a font, and over it a railed shelf, containing combs, brushes, and other implements of the toilet. A torn hammock of stained grass swung near; the sheets tossed, and the pillow wrinkled up like a brow, as if whoever slept here slept but illy, with alternate visitations of sad thoughts and bad dreams.

The further extremity of the cuddy, overhanging the ship's stern, was pierced with three openings, windows or port-holes, according as men or cannon might peer, socially or unsocially, out of them. At present neither men nor cannon were seen, though huge ring-bolts and other rusty iron fixtures of the wood-work hinted of twenty-four-pounders.

Glancing towards the hammock as he entered, Captain Delano said, "You sleep here, Don Benito?"

"Yes, Señor, since we got into mild weather."

"This seems a sort of dormitory, sitting-room, sail-loft, chapel, armory, and private closet all together, Don Benito," added Captain Delano, looking round.

"Yes, Señor; events have not been favorable to much order in my arrangements."

Here the servant, napkin on arm, made a motion as if waiting his master's good pleasure. Don Benito signified his readiness, when, seating him in the Malacca arm-chair, and for the guest's convenience drawing opposite one of the settees, the servant commenced operations by throwing back his master's collar and loosening his cravat.

There is something in the negro which, in a peculiar way, fits him for avocations about one's person. Most negroes are natural valets and hair-dressers; taking to the comb and brush congenially as to the castanets, and flourishing them apparently with almost equal satisfaction. There is, too, a smooth tact about them in this employment, with a marvelous, noiseless, gliding briskness, not ungraceful in its way, singularly pleasing to behold, and still more so to be the manipulated subject of. And above all is the great gift of good-humor. Not the mere grin or laugh is here meant. Those were unsuitable. But a certain easy cheerfulness, harmonious in every glance and gesture; as though God had set the whole negro to some pleasant tune.

When to this is added the docility arising from the unaspiring contentment of a limited mind, and that susceptibility of bland attachment sometimes inhering in indisputable inferiors, one readily perceives why those hypochondriacs, Johnson and Byron— it may be, something like the hypochondriac Benito Cereno—took to their hearts, almost to the exclusion of the entire white race, their serving men, the negroes, Barber and Fletcher. But if there be that in the negro which exempts him from the inflicted sourness of the morbid or cynical mind, how, in his most prepossessing aspects, must he appear to a benevolent one? When at ease with respect to exterior things, Captain Delano's nature was not only benign, but familiarly and humorously so. At home, he had often taken rare satisfaction in sitting in his door, watching some free man of color at his work or play. If on a voyage he chanced to have a black sailor, invariably he was on chatty and half-gamesome terms with him. In fact, like most men of a good, blithe heart, Captain Delano took to negroes, not philanthropically, but genially, just as other men to Newfoundland dogs.

Hitherto, the circumstances in which he found the *San Dominick* had repressed the tendency. But in the cuddy, relieved from his former uneasiness, and, for various reasons, more sociably inclined than at any previous period of the day, and seeing the colored servant, napkin on arm, so debonair about his master, in a business so familiar as that of shaving, too, all his old weakness for negroes returned.

Among other things, he was amused with an odd instance of the African love of bright colors and fine shows, in the black's informally taking from the flag-locker a great piece of bunting of all hues, and lavishly tucking it under his master's chin for an apron.

The mode of shaving among the Spaniards is a little different from what it is with other nations. They have a basin, specifically called a barber's basin, which on one side is scooped out, so as accurately to receive the chin, against which it is closely held in lathering; which is done, not with a brush, but with soap dipped in the water of the basin and rubbed on the face.

In the present instance salt-water was used for lack of better; and the parts lathered were only the upper lip, and low down under the throat, all the rest being cultivated beard.

The preliminaries being somewhat novel to Captain Delano, he sat curiously eyeing them, so that no conversation took place, nor, for the present, did Don Benito appear disposed to renew any.

Setting down his basin, the negro searched among the razors, as for the sharpest, and having found it, gave it an additional edge by expertly strapping it on the firm, smooth, oily skin of his open palm; he then made a gesture as if to begin, but midway stood suspended for an instant, one hand elevating the razor, the other professionally dabbling among the bubbling suds on the Spaniard's lank neck. Not unaffected by the close sight of the gleaming steel, Don Benito nervously shuddered; his usual ghastliness was heightened by the lather, which lather, again, was intensified in its hue by the contrasting sootiness of the negro's body. Altogether the scene was somewhat peculiar, at least to Captain Delano, nor, as he saw the two thus postured, could he resist the vagary, that in the black he saw a headsman, and in the white a man at the block. But this was one of those antic conceits, appearing and vanishing in a breath, from which, perhaps, the best regulated mind is not always free.

Meantime the agitation of the Spaniard had a little loosened the bunting from around him, so that one broad fold swept curtain-like over the chair-arm to the floor, revealing, amid a profusion of armorial bars and ground-colors—black, blue, and yellow—a closed castle in a blood-red field diagonal with a lion rampant in a white.

"The castle and the lion," exclaimed Captain Delano—"why, Don Benito, this is the flag of Spain you use here. It's well it's only I, and not the King, that sees this," he added, with a smile, "but" —turning towards the black—"it's all one, I suppose, so the colors be gay;" which playful remark did not fail somewhat to tickle the negro.

"Now, master," he said, readjusting the flag, and pressing the head gently further back into the crotch of the chair; "now, master," and the steel glanced nigh the throat.

Again Don Benito faintly shuddered.

"You must not shake so, master. See, Don Amasa, master always shakes when I shave him. And yet master knows I never yet have drawn blood, though it's true, if master will shake so, I may some of these times. Now master," he continued. "And now, Don Amasa, please go on with your talk about the gale, and all that; master can hear, and, between times, master can answer."

"Ah yes, these gales," said Captain Delano; "but the more I think of your voyage, Don Benito, the more I wonder, not at the gales, terrible as they must have been, but at the disastrous interval following them. For here, by your account, have you been these two months and more getting from Cape Horn to St. Maria, a distance which I myself, with a good wind, have sailed in a few days. True, you had calms, and long ones, but to be becalmed for two months, that is, at least, unusual. Why, Don Benito, had almost any other gentleman told me such a story, I should have been half disposed to a little incredulity."

Here an involuntary expression came over the Spaniard, similar to that just before on the deck, and whether it was the start he gave, or a sudden gawky roll of the hull in the calm, or a momentary unsteadiness of the servant's hand, however it was, just then the razor drew blood, spots of which stained the creamy lather under the throat: immediately the black barber drew back his steel, and, remaining in his professional attitude, back to Captain Delano, and face to Don Benito, held up the trickling razor, saying, with a sort of half humorous sorrow, "See, master—you shook so—here's Babo's first blood."

No sword drawn before James the First of England, no assassination in that timid King's presence, could have produced a more terrified aspect than was now presented by Don Benito.

Poor fellow, thought Captain Delano, so nervous he can't even bear the sight of barber's blood; and this unstrung, sick man, is it credible that I should have imagined he meant to spill all my blood, who can't endure the sight of one little drop of his own? Surely, Amasa Delano, you have been beside yourself this day. Tell it not when you get home, sappy Amasa. Well, well, he looks like a murderer, doesn't he? More like as if himself were to be done for. Well, well, this day's experience shall be a good lesson.

Meantime, while these things were running through the honest seaman's mind, the servant had taken the napkin from his arm, and to Don Benito had said—"But answer Don Amasa, please, master, while I wipe this ugly stuff off the razor, and strop it again."

As he said the words, his face was turned half round, so as to be alike visible to the Spaniard and the American, and seemed, by its expression, to hint, that he was desirous, by getting his master to go on with the conversation, considerately to withdraw his attention from the recent annoying accident. As if glad to snatch the offered relief, Don Benito resumed, rehearsing to Captain Delano, that not only were the calms of unusual duration, but the ship had fallen in with obstinate currents; and other things he added, some of which were but repetitions of former statements, to explain how it came to pass that the passage from Cape Horn to St. Maria had been so exceedingly long; now and then mingling with his words, incidental praises, less qualified than before, to the blacks, for their general good conduct. These particulars were not given consecutively, the servant, at convenient times, using his razor, and so, between the intervals of shaving, the story and panegyric went on with more than usual huskiness.

To Captain Delano's imagination, now again not wholly at rest, there was something so hollow in the Spaniard's manner, with apparently some reciprocal hollowness in the servant's dusky comment of silence, that the idea flashed across him, that possibly master and man, for some unknown purpose, were acting out, both in word and deed, nay, to the very tremor of Don Benito's limbs, some juggling play before him. Neither did the suspicion of collusion lack apparent support, from the fact of those whispered conferences before mentioned. But then, what could be the object of enacting this play of the barber before him? At last, regarding the notion as a whimsy, insensibly suggested, perhaps, by the theatrical aspect of Don Benito in his harlequin ensign, Captain Delano speedily banished it.

The shaving over, the servant bestirred himself with a small bottle of scented waters, pouring a few drops on the head, and then diligently rubbing; the vehemence of the exercise causing the muscles of his face to twitch rather strangely.

His next operation was with comb, scissors, and brush; going round and round, smoothing a curl here, clipping an unruly whisker-hair there, giving a graceful sweep to the temple-lock, with other impromptu touches evincing the hand of a master; while, like any resigned gentleman in barber's hands, Don Benito bore all, much less uneasily, at least, than he had done the razoring; indeed, he sat so pale and rigid now, that the negro seemed a Nubian sculptor finishing off a white statue-head.

All being over at last, the standard of Spain removed, tumbled up, and tossed back into the flag-locker, the negro's warm breath blowing away any stray hair which might have lodged down his master's neck; collar and cravat readjusted; a speck of lint whisked off the velvet lapel; all this being done; backing off a little space, and pausing with an expression of subdued self-complacency, the servant for a moment surveyed his master, as, in toilet at least, the creature of his own tasteful hands.

Captain Delano playfully complimented him upon his achievement; at the same time congratulating Don Benito.

But neither sweet waters, nor shampooing, nor fidelity, nor sociality, delighted the Spaniard. Seeing him relapsing into forbidding gloom, and still remaining seated, Captain Delano, thinking that his presence was undesired just then, withdrew, on pretense of seeing whether, as he had prophesied, any signs of a breeze were visible.

Walking forward to the main-mast, he stood awhile thinking over the scene, and not without some undefined misgivings, when he heard a noise near the cuddy, and turning, saw the negro, his hand to his cheek. Advancing, Captain Delano perceived that the cheek was bleeding. He was about to ask the cause, when the negro's wailing soliloquy enlightened him.

"Ah, when will master get better from his sickness; only the sour heart that sour sickness breeds made him serve Babo so; cutting Babo with the razor, because, only by accident, Babo had given master one little scratch; and for the first time in so many a day, too. Ah, ah, ah," holding his hand to his face.

Is it possible, thought Captain Delano; was it to wreak in private his Spanish spite against this poor friend of his, that Don Benito, by his sullen manner, impelled me to withdraw? Ah, this slavery breeds ugly passions in man.—Poor fellow!

He was about to speak in sympathy to the negro, but with a timid reluctance he now re-entered the cuddy.

Presently master and man came forth; Don Benito leaning on his servant as if nothing had happened.

But a sort of love-quarrel, after all, thought Captain Delano.

He accosted Don Benito, and they slowly walked together. They had gone but a few paces, when the steward—a tall, rajah-looking mulatto, orientally set off with a pagoda turban formed by three or four Madras handkerchiefs wound about his head, tier on tier—approaching with a saalam, announced lunch in the cabin.

On their way thither, the two captains were preceded by the mulatto, who, turning round as he advanced, with continual smiles and bows, ushered them on, a display of elegance which quite completed the insignificance of the small bare-headed Babo, who, as if not unconscious of inferiority, eyed askance the graceful steward. But in part, Captain Delano imputed his jealous watchfulness to that peculiar feeling which the full-blooded African entertains for the adulterated one. As for the steward, his manner, if not bespeaking much dignity or self-respect, yet evidenced his extreme desire to please; which is doubly meritorious, as at once Christian and Chesterfieldian.

Captain Delano observed with interest that while the complexion of the mulatto was hybrid, his physiognomy was European—classically so.

"Don Benito," whispered he, "I am glad to see this usher-of-the-golden-rod of yours; the sight refutes an ugly remark once made to me by a Barbados planter; that when a mulatto has a regular European face, look out for him; he is a devil. But see, your steward here has features more regular than King George's of England; and yet there he nods, and bows, and smiles; a king, indeed—the king of kind hearts and polite fellows. What a pleasant voice he has, too."

"He has, Señor."

"But tell me, has he not, so far as you have known him, always proved a good, worthy fellow?" said Captain Delano, pausing, while with a final genuflexion the steward disappeared into the cabin; "come, for the reason just mentioned, I am curious to know."

"Francesco is a good man," somewhat sluggishly responded Don

Benito, like a phlegmatic appreciator, who would neither find fault nor flatter.

"Ah, I thought so. For it were strange, indeed, and not very creditable to us white-skins, if a little of our blood mixed with the African's, should, far from improving the latter's quality, have the sad effect of pouring vitriolic acid into black broth; improving the hue, perhaps, but not the wholesomeness."

"Doubtless, doubtless, Señor, but"—glancing at Babo—"not to speak of negroes, your planter's remark I have heard applied to the Spanish and Indian intermixtures in our provinces. But I know nothing about the matter," he listlessly added.

And here they entered the cabin.

The lunch was a frugal one. Some of Captain Delano's fresh fish and pumpkins, biscuit and salt beef, the reserved bottle of cider, and the *San Dominick*'s last bottle of Canary.

As they entered, Francesco, with two or three colored aids, was hovering over the table giving the last adjustments. Upon perceiving their master they withdrew, Francesco making a smiling congé, and the Spaniard, without condescending to notice it, fastidiously remarking to his companion that he relished not superfluous attendance.

Without companions, host and guest sat down, like a childless married couple, at opposite ends of the table, Don Benito waving Captain Delano to his place, and, weak as he was, insisting upon that gentleman being seated before himself.

The negro placed a rug under Don Benito's feet, and a cushion behind his back, and then stood behind, not his master's chair, but Captain Delano's. At first, this a little surprised the latter. But it was soon evident that, in taking his position, the black was still true to his master; since by facing him he could the more readily anticipate his slightest want.

"This is an uncommonly intelligent fellow of yours, Don Benito," whispered Captain Delano across the table.

"You say true, Señor."

During the repast, the guest again reverted to parts of Don Benito's story, begging further particulars here and there. He inquired how it was that the scurvy and fever should have committed such wholesale havoc upon the whites, while destroying less than half of the blacks. As if this question reproduced the whole scene of plague before the Spaniard's eyes, miserably reminding him of his solitude in a cabin where before he had had so many friends and officers round him, his hand shook, his face became hueless, broken words escaped; but directly the sane memory of the past seemed replaced by insane terrors of the present. With starting eyes he stared before him at vacancy. For nothing was to be seen but the hand of his servant pushing the Canary over towards him. At length a few sips served partially to restore him. He made random reference to the different constitution of races, enabling one to offer more resistance to certain maladies than another. The thought was new to his companion.

Presently Captain Delano, intending to say something to his host concerning the pecuniary part of the business he had undertaken for him, especially—since he was strictly accountable to his owners—with reference to the new suit of sails, and other things of that sort; and naturally preferring to conduct such affairs in private, was desirous that the servant should withdraw; imagining that Don Benito for a few minutes could dispense with his attendance. He, however, waited awhile; thinking that, as the conversation proceeded, Don Benito, without being prompted, would perceive the propriety of the step.

But it was otherwise. At last catching his host's eye, Captain Delano, with a slight backward gesture of his thumb, whispered, "Don Benito, pardon me, but there is an interference with the full expression of what I have to say to you."

Upon this the Spaniard changed countenance; which was imputed to his resenting the hint, as in some way a reflection upon his servant. After a moment's pause, he assured his guest that the black's remaining with them could be of no disservice; because since losing his officers he had made Babo (whose original office, it now appeared, had been captain of the slaves) not only his constant attendant and companion, but in all things his confidant.

After this, nothing more could be said; though, indeed, Captain Delano could hardly avoid some little tinge of irritation upon being left ungratified in so inconsiderable a wish, by one, too, for whom he intended such solid services. But it is only his querulousness, thought he; and so filling his glass he proceeded to business.

The price of the sails and other matters was fixed upon. But while this was being done, the American observed that, though his original offer of assistance had been hailed with hectic animation, yet now when it was reduced to a business transaction, indifference and apathy were betrayed. Don Benito, in fact, appeared to submit to hearing the details more out of regard to common propriety, than from any impression that weighty benefit to himself and his voyage was involved.

Soon, his manner became still more reserved. The effort was vain to seek to draw him into social talk. Gnawed by his splenetic mood, he sat twitching his beard, while to little purpose the hand of his servant, mute as that on the wall, slowly pushed over the Canary.

Lunch being over, they sat down on the cushioned transom; the servant placing a pillow behind his master. The long continuance of the calm had now affected the atmosphere. Don Benito sighed heavily, as if for breath.

"Why not adjourn to the cuddy," said Captain Delano; "there is more air there." But the host sat silent and motionless.

Meantime his servant knelt before him, with a large fan of feathers. And Francesco coming in on tiptoes, handed the negro a little cup of aromatic waters, with which at intervals he chafed his master's brow; smoothing the hair along the temples as a nurse does a child's. He spoke no word. He only rested his eye on his master's, as if, amid all Don Benito's distress, a little to refresh his spirit by the silent sight of fidelity.

Presently the ship's bell sounded two o'clock; and through the cabin windows a slight rippling of the sea was discerned; and from the desired direction.

"There," exclaimed Captain Delano, "I told you so, Don Benito, look!"

He had risen to his feet, speaking in a very animated tone, with a view the more to rouse his companion. But though the crimson curtain of the stern-window near him that moment fluttered against his pale cheek, Don Benito seemed to have even less welcome for the breeze than the calm.

Poor fellow, thought Captain Delano, bitter experience has taught him that one ripple does not make a wind, any more than one swallow a summer. But he is mistaken for once. I will get his ship in for him, and prove it.

Briefly alluding to his weak condition, he urged his host to remain quietly where he was, since he (Captain Delano) would with pleasure takes upon himself the responsibility of making the best use of the wind.

Upon gaining the deck, Captain Delano started at the unexpected figure of Atufal, monumentally fixed at the threshold, like one of those sculptured porters of black marble guarding the porches of Egyptian tombs.

But this time the start was, perhaps, purely physical. Atufal's presence, singularly attesting docility even in sullenness, was contrasted with that of the hatchet-polishers, who in patience evinced their industry; while both spectacles showed, that lax as Don Benito's general authority might be, still, whenever he chose to exert it, no man so savage or colossal but must, more or less, bow.

Snatching a trumpet which hung from the bulwarks, with a free step Captain Delano advanced to the forward edge of the poop, issuing his orders in his best Spanish. The few sailors and many negroes, all equally pleased, obediently set about heading the ship towards the harbor.

While giving some directions about setting a lower stu'n'sail, suddenly Captain Delano heard a voice faithfully repeating his orders. Turning, he saw Babo, now for the time acting, under the pilot, his original part of captain of the slaves. This assistance proved valuable. Tattered sails and warped yards were soon brought into some trim. And no brace or halyard was pulled but to the blithe songs of the inspirited negroes.

Good fellows, thought Captain Delano, a little training would make fine sailors of them. Why see, the very women pull and sing too. These must be some of those Ashantee negresses that make such capital soldiers, I've heard. But who's at the helm? I must have a good hand there.

He went to see.

The *San Dominick* steered with a cumbrous tiller, with large horizontal pulleys attached. At each pulley-end stood a subordinate black, and between them, at the tiller-head, the responsible post, a Spanish seaman, whose countenance evinced his due share in the general hopefulness and confidence at the coming of the breeze.

He proved the same man who had behaved with so shame-faced an air on the windlass.

"Ah,—it is you, my man," exclaimed Captain Delano—"well, no more sheep's-eyes now;—look straight forward and keep the ship so. Good hand, I trust? And want to get into the harbor, don't you?"

The man assented with an inward chuckle, grasping the tiller-head firmly. Upon this, unperceived by the American, the two blacks eyed the sailor intently.

Finding all right at the helm, the pilot went forward to the forecastle, to see how matters stood there.

The ship now had way enough to breast the current. With the approach of evening, the breeze would be sure to freshen.

Having done all that was needed for the present, Captain Delano, giving his last orders to the sailors, turned aft to report affairs to Don Benito in the cabin; perhaps additionally incited to rejoin him by the hope of snatching a moment's private chat while the servant was engaged upon deck.

From opposite sides, there were, beneath the poop, two approaches to the cabin; one further forward than the other, and consequently communicating with a longer passage. Marking the servant still above, Captain Delano, taking the nighest entrance —the one last named, and at whose porch Atufal still stood— hurried on his way, till, arrived at the cabin threshold, he paused an instant, a little to recover from his eagerness. Then, with the words of his intended business upon his lips, he entered. As he advanced toward the seated Spaniard, he heard another footstep, keeping time with his. From the opposite door, a salver in hand, the servant was likewise advancing.

Confound the faithful fellow, thought Captain Delano; what a vexatious coincidence.

Possibly, the vexation might have been something different, were it not for the brisk confidence inspired by the breeze. But even as it was, he felt a slight twinge, from a sudden indefinite association in his mind of Babo with Atufal.

"Don Benito," said he, "I give you joy; the breeze will hold, and will increase. By the way, your tall man and time-piece, Atufal, stands without. By your order, of course?"

Don Benito recoiled, as if at some bland satirical touch, delivered with such adroit garnish of apparent good breeding as to present no handle for retort.

He is like one flayed alive, thought Captain Delano; where may one touch him without causing a shrink?

The servant moved before his master, adjusting a cushion; recalled to civility, the Spaniard stiffly replied: "You are right. The slave appears where you saw him, according to my command; which is, that if at the given hour I am below, he must take his stand and abide my coming."

"Ah now, pardon me, but that is treating the poor fellow like an ex-king indeed. Ah, Don Benito," smiling, "for all the license you permit in some things, I fear lest, at bottom, you are a bitter hard master."

Again Don Benito shrank; and this time, as the good sailor thought, from a genuine twinge of his conscience.

Again conversation became constrained. In vain Captain Delano called attention to the now perceptible motion of the keel gently cleaving the sea; with lack-lustre eye, Don Benito returned words few and reserved.

By-and-by, the wind, having steadily risen, and still blowing right into the harbor, bore the *San Dominick* swiftly on. Rounding a point of land, the sealer at distance came into open view.

Meantime Captain Delano had again repaired to the deck, remaining there some time. Having at last altered the ship's course, so as to give the reef a wide berth, he returned for a few moments below.

I will cheer up my poor friend, this time, thought he.

"Better and better, Don Benito," he cried as he blithely re-entered: "there will soon be an end to your cares, at least for awhile. For when, after a long, sad voyage, you know, the anchor drops into the haven, all its vast weight seems lifted from the captain's heart. We are getting on famously, Don Benito. My ship is in sight. Look through this side-light here; there she is; all a-taunt-o! The *Bachelor's Delight*, my good friend. Ah, how this wind braces one up. Come, you must take a cup of coffee with me this evening. My old steward will give you as fine a cup as ever any sultan tasted. What say you, Don Benito, will you?"

At first, the Spaniard glanced feverishly up, casting a longing look towards the sealer, while with mute concern his servant gazed into his face. Suddenly the old ague of coldness returned, and dropping back to his cushions he was silent.

"You do not answer. Come, all day you have been my host; would you have hospitality all on one side?"

"I cannot go," was the response.

"What? it will not fatigue you. The ships will lie together as near as they can, without swinging foul. It will be little more than stepping from deck to deck; which is but as from room to room. Come, come, you must not refuse me."

"I cannot go," decisively and repulsively repeated Don Benito.

Renouncing all but the last appearance of courtesy, with a sort of cadaverous sullenness, and biting his thin nails to the quick, he glanced, almost glared, at his guest, as if impatient that a stranger's presence should interfere with the full indulgence of his morbid hour. Meantime the sound of the parted waters came more and more gurglingly and merrily in at the windows; as reproaching him for his dark spleen; as telling him that, sulk as he might, and go mad with it, nature cared not a jot; since, whose fault was it, pray?

But the foul mood was now at its depth, as the fair wind at its height.

There was something in the man so far beyond any mere unsociality or sourness previously evinced, that even the forbearing good-nature of his guest could no longer endure it. Wholly at a loss to account for such demeanor, and deeming sickness with eccentricity, however extreme, no adequate excuse, well satisfied, too, that nothing in his own conduct could justify it, Captain Delano's pride began to be roused. Himself became reserved. But all seemed one to the Spaniard. Quitting him, therefore, Captain Delano once more went to the deck.

The ship was now within less than two miles of the sealer. The whale-boat was seen darting over the interval.

To be brief, the two vessels, thanks to the pilot's skill, ere long in neighborly style lay anchored together.

Before returning to his own vessel, Captain Delano had intended communicating to Don Benito the smaller details of the proposed services to be rendered. But, as it was, unwilling anew to subject himself to rebuffs, he resolved, now that he had seen the *San Dominick* safely moored, immediately to quit her, without further allusion to hospitality or business. Indefinitely postponing his ulterior plans, he would regulate his future actions according to future circumstances. His boat was ready to receive him; but his host still tarried below. Well, thought Captain Delano, if he has little breeding, the more need to show mine. He descended to the cabin to bid a ceremonious, and, it may be, tacitly rebukeful adieu. But to his great satisfaction, Don Benito, as if he began to feel the weight of that treatment with which his slighted guest had, not indecorously, retaliated upon him, now supported by his servant, rose to his feet, and grasping Captain Delano's hand, stood tremulous; too much agitated to speak. But the good augury hence drawn was suddenly dashed, by his resuming all his previous reserve, with augmented gloom, as, with half-averted eyes, he silently reseated himself on his cushions. With a corresponding return of his own chilled feelings, Captain Delano bowed and withdrew.

He was hardly midway in the narrow corridor, dim as a tunnel, leading from the cabin to the stairs, when a sound, as of the tolling for execution in some jail-yard, fell on his ears. It was the echo of the ship's flawed bell, striking the hour, drearily reverberated in this subterranean vault. Instantly, by a fatality not to be withstood, his mind, responsive to the portent, swarmed with superstitious suspicions. He paused. In images far swifter than these sentences, the minutest details of all his former distrusts swept through him.

Hitherto, credulous good-nature had been too ready to furnish excuses for reasonable fears. Why was the Spaniard, so superfluously punctilious at times, now heedless of common propriety in not accompanying to the side his departing guest? Did indisposition forbid? Indisposition had not forbidden more irksome exertion that day. His last equivocal demeanor recurred. He had risen to his feet, grasped his guest's hand, motioned toward his hat; then, in an instant, all was eclipsed in sinister muteness and gloom. Did this imply one brief, repentant relenting at the final moment, from some iniquitous plot, followed by remorseless return to it? His last glance seemed to express a calamitous, yet acquiescent farewell to Captain Delano forever. Why decline the invitation to visit the sealer that evening? Or was the Spaniard less hardened than the Jew, who refrained not from supping at the board of him whom the same night he meant to betray? What imported all those day-long enigmas and contradictions, except they were intended to mystify, preliminary to some stealthy blow? Atufal, the pretended rebel, but punctual shadow, that moment lurked by the threshold without. He seemed a sentry, and more. Who, by his own confession, had stationed him there? Was the negro now lying in wait?

The Spaniard behind—his creature before: to rush from darkness to light was the involuntary choice.

The next moment, with clenched jaw and hand, he passed Atufal, and stood unharmed in the light. As he saw his trim ship lying peacefully at anchor, and almost within ordinary call; as he saw his household boat, with familiar faces in it, patiently rising and falling on the short waves by the San Dominick's side; and then, glancing about the decks where he stood, saw the oakum-pickers still gravely plying their fingers; and heard the low, buzzing whistle and industrious hum of the hatchet-polishers, still bestirring themselves over their endless occupation; and more than all, as he saw the benign aspect of nature, taking her innocent repose in the evening; the screened sun in the quiet camp of the west shining out like the mild light from Abraham's tent; as charmed eye and ear took in all these, with the chained figure of the black, clenched jaw and hand relaxed. Once again he smiled at the phantoms which had mocked him, and felt something like a tinge of remorse, that, by harboring them even for a moment, he should, by implication, have betrayed an atheist doubt of the ever-watchful Providence above.

There was a few minutes' delay, while, in obedience to his orders, the boat was being hooked along to the gangway. During this interval, a sort of saddened satisfaction stole over Captain Delano, at thinking of the kindly offices he had that day discharged for a stranger. Ah, thought he, after good actions one's conscience is never ungrateful, however much so the benefited party may be.

Presently, his foot, in the first act of descent into the boat, pressed the first round of the side-ladder, his face presented inward upon the deck. In the same moment, he heard his name courteously sounded; and, to his pleased surprise, saw Don Benito advancing— an unwonted energy in his air, as if, at the last moment, intent upon making amends for his recent discourtesy. With instinctive good feeling, Captain Delano, withdrawing his foot, turned and reciprocally advanced. As he did so, the Spaniard's nervous eagerness increased, but his vital energy failed; so that, the better to support him, the servant, placing his master's hand on his naked shoulder, and gently holding it there, formed himself into a sort of crutch.

When the two captains met, the Spaniard again fervently took the hand of the American, at the same time casting an earnest glance into his eyes, but, as before, too much overcome to speak.

I have done him wrong, self-reproachfully thought Captain Delano; his apparent coldness has deceived me; in no instance has he meant to offend.

Meantime, as if fearful that the continuance of the scene might too much unstring his master, the servant seemed anxious to terminate it. And so, still presenting himself as a crutch, and walking between the two captains, he advanced with them towards the gangway; while still, as if full of kindly contrition, Don Benito would not let go the hand of Captain Delano, but retained it in his, across the black's body.

Soon they were standing by the side, looking over into the boat, whose crew turned up their curious eyes. Waiting a moment for the Spaniard to relinquish his hold, the now embarrassed Captain Delano lifted his foot, to overstep the threshold of the open gangway; but still Don Benito would not let go his hand. And yet, with an agitated tone, he said, "I can go no further; here I must bid you adieu, my dear, dear Don Amasa. Go—go!" suddenly tearing his hand loose, "go, and God guard you better than me, my best friend."

Not unaffected, Captain Delano would now have lingered; but

catching the meekly admonitory eye of the servant, with a hasty farewell he descended into his boat, followed by the continual adieus of Don Benito, standing rooted in the gangway.

Seating himself in the stern, Captain Delano, making a last salute, ordered the boat shoved off. The crew had their oars on end. The bowsmen pushed the boat a sufficient distance for the oars to be lengthwise dropped. The instant that was done, Don Benito sprang over the bulwarks, falling at the feet of Captain Delano; at the same time calling towards his ship, but in tones so frenzied, that none in the boat could understand him. But, as if not equally obtuse, three sailors, from three different and distant parts of the ship, splashed into the sea, swimming after their captain, as if intent upon his rescue.

The dismayed officer of the boat eagerly asked what this meant. To which, Captain Delano, turning a disdainful smile upon the unaccountable Spaniard, answered that, for his part, he neither knew nor cared; but it seemed as if Don Benito had taken it into his head to produce the impression among his people that the boat wanted to kidnap him. "Or else—give way for your lives," he wildly added, starting at a clattering hubbub in the ship, above which rang the tocsin of the hatchet-polishers; and seizing Don Benito by the throat he added, "this plotting pirate means murder!" Here, in apparent verification of the words, the servant, a dagger in his hand, was seen on the rail overhead, poised, in the act of leaping, as if with desperate fidelity to befriend his master to the last; while, seemingly to aid the black, the three white sailors were trying to clamber into the hampered bow. Meantime, the whole host of negroes, as if inflamed at the sight of their jeopardized captain, impended in one sooty avalanche over the bulwarks.

All this, with what preceded, and what followed, occurred with such involutions of rapidity, that past, present, and future seemed one.

Seeing the negro coming, Captain Delano had flung the Spaniard aside, almost in the very act of clutching him, and, by the unconscious recoil, shifting his place, with arms thrown up, so promptly grappled the servant in his descent, that with dagger presented at Captain Delano's heart, the black seemed of purpose to have leaped there as to his mark. But the weapon was wrenched away, and the assailant dashed down into the bottom of the boat, which now, with disentangled oars, began to speed through the sea.

At this juncture, the left hand of Captain Delano, on one side, again clutched the half-reclined Don Benito, heedless that he was in a speechless faint, while his right foot, on the other side, ground the prostrate negro; and his right arm pressed for added speed on the after oar, his eye bent forward, encouraging his men to their utmost.

But here, the officer of the boat, who had at last succeeded in beating off the towing sailors, and was now, with face turned aft, assisting the bowsman at his oar, suddenly called to Captain Delano, to see what the black was about; while a Portuguese oarsman shouted to him to give heed to what the Spaniard was saying.

Glancing down at his feet, Captain Delano saw the freed hand of the servant aiming with a second dagger—a small one, before concealed in his wool—with this he was snakishly writhing up from the boat's bottom, at the heart of his master, his countenance lividly vindictive, expressing the centred purpose of his soul; while the Spaniard, half-choked, was vainly shrinking away, with husky words, incoherent to all but the Portuguese.

That moment, across the long-benighted mind of Captain Delano, a flash of revelation swept, illuminating, in unanticipated clearness, his host's whole mysterious demeanor, with every enigmatic event of the day, as well as the entire past voyage of the *San Dominick*. He smote Babo's hand down, but his own heart smote him harder. With infinite pity he withdrew his hold from Don Benito. Not Captain Delano, but Don Benito, the black, in leaping into the boat, had intended to stab.

Both the black's hands were held, as, glancing up towards the *San Dominick*, Captain Delano, now with scales dropped from his eyes, saw the negroes, not in misrule, not in tumult, not as if frantically concerned for Don Benito, but with mask torn away, flourishing hatchets and knives, in ferocious piratical revolt. Like delirious black dervishes, the six Ashantees danced on the poop. Prevented by their foes from springing into the water, the Spanish boys were hurrying up to the topmost spars, while such of the few

Spanish sailors, not already in the sea, less alert, were described, helplessly mixed in, on deck, with the blacks.

Meantime Captain Delano hailed his own vessel, ordering the ports up, and the guns run out. But by this time the cable of the *San Dominick* had been cut; and the fag-end, in lashing out, whipped away the canvas shroud about the beak, suddenly revealing, as the bleached hull swung round towards the open ocean, death for the figure-head, in a human skeleton; chalky comment on the chalked words below, *"Follow your leader."*

At the sight, Don Benito, covering his face, wailed out: " 'Tis he, Aranda! my murdered, unburied friend!"

Upon reaching the sealer, calling for ropes, Captain Delano bound the negro, who made no resistance, and had him hoisted to the deck. He would then have assisted the now almost helpless Don Benito up the side; but Don Benito, wan as he was, refused to move, or be moved, until the negro should have been first put below out of view. When, presently assured that it was done, he no more shrank from the ascent.

The boat was immediately dispatched back to pick up the three swimming sailors. Meantime, the guns were in readiness, though, owing to the *San Dominick* having glided somewhat astern of the sealer, only the aftermost one could be brought to bear. With this, they fired six times; thinking to cripple the fugitive ship by bringing down her spars. But only a few inconsiderable ropes were shot away. Soon the ship was beyond the gun's range, steering broad out of the bay; the blacks thickly clustering round the bowsprit, one moment with taunting cries towards the whites, the next with up-thrown gestures hailing the now dusky moors of ocean—cawing crows escaped from the hand of the fowler.

The first impulse was to slip the cables and give chase. But, upon second thoughts, to pursue with whale-boat and yawl seemed more promising.

Upon inquiring of Don Benito what fire-arms they had on board the *San Dominick*, Captain Delano was answered that they had none that could be used; because, in the earlier stages of the mutiny, a cabin-passenger, since dead, had secretly put out of order the locks of what few muskets there were. But with all his remaining strength, Don Benito entreated the American not to give chase, either with ship or boat; for the negroes had already proved themselves such desperadoes, that, in case of a present assault, nothing but a total massacre of the whites could be looked for. But, regarding this warning as coming from one whose spirit had been crushed by misery, the American did not give up his design.

The boats were got ready and armed. Captain Delano ordered his men into them. He was going himself when Don Benito grasped his arm.

"What! have you saved my life, Señor, and are you now going to throw away your own?"

The officers also, for reasons connected with their interests and those of the voyage, and a duty owing to the owners, strongly objected against their commander's going. Weighing their remonstrances a moment, Captain Delano felt bound to remain; appointing his chief mate—an athletic and resolute man, who had been a privateer's-man—to head the party. The more to encourage the sailors, they were told, that the Spanish captain considered his ship good as lost; that she and her cargo, including some gold and silver, were worth more than a thousand dubloons. Take her, and no small part should be theirs. The sailors replied with a shout.

The fugitives had now almost gained an offing. It was nearly night; but the moon was rising. After hard, prolonged pulling, the boats came up on the ship's quarters, at a suitable distance laying upon their oars to discharge their muskets. Having no bullets to return, the negroes sent their yells. But, upon the second volley, Indian-like, they hurtled their hatchets. One took off a sailor's fingers. Another struck the whale-boat's bow, cutting off the rope there, and remaining stuck in the gunwale like a woodman's axe. Snatching it, quivering from its lodgement, the mate hurled it back. The returned gauntlet now stuck in the ship's broken quarter-gallery, and so remained.

The negroes giving too hot a reception, the whites kept a more respectful distance. Hovering now just out of reach of the hurtling hatchets, they, with a view to the close encounter which must soon come, sought to decoy the blacks into entirely disarming themselves of their most murderous weapons in a hand-to-hand fight, by foolishly flinging them, as missiles, short of the mark, into the sea. But, ere long, perceiving the stratagem, the negroes desisted, though not before many of them had to replace their lost hatchets with handspikes; an exchange which, as counted upon, proved, in the end, favorable to the assailants.

Meantime, with a strong wind, the ship still clove the water; the boats alternately falling behind, and pulling up, to discharge fresh volleys.

The fire was mostly directed towards the stern, since there, chiefly, the negroes, at present, were clustering. But to kill or maim the negroes was not the object. To take them, with the ship, was the object. To do it, the ship must be boarded; which could not be done by boats while she was sailing so fast.

A thought now struck the mate. Observing the Spanish boys still aloft, high as they could get, he called to them to descend to the yards, and cut adrift the sails. It was done. About this time, owing to causes hereafter to be shown, two Spaniards, in the dress of sailors, and conspicuously showing themselves, were killed; not by volleys, but by deliberate marksman's shots; while, as it afterwards appeared, by one of the general discharges, Atufal, the black, and the Spaniard at the helm likewise were killed. What now, with the loss of the sails, and loss of leaders, the ship became unmanageable to the negroes.

With creaking masts, she came heavily round to the wind; the prow slowly swinging into view of the boats, its skeleton gleaming in the horizontal moonlight, and casting a gigantic ribbed shadow upon the water. One extended arm of the ghost seemed beckoning the whites to avenge it.

"Follow your leader!" cried the mate; and, one on each bow, the boats boarded. Sealing-spears and cutlasses crossed hatchets and hand-spikes. Huddled upon the long-boat amidships, the negresses raised a wailing chant, whose chorus was the clash of the steel.

For a time, the attack wavered; the negroes wedging themselves to beat it back; the half-repelled sailors, as yet unable to gain a footing, fighting as troopers in the saddle, one leg sideways flung over the bulwarks, and one without, plying their cutlasses like carters' whips. But in vain. They were almost overborne, when, rallying themselves into a squad as one man, with a huzza, they sprang inboard, where, entangled, they involuntarily separated again. For a few breaths' space, there was a vague, muffled, inner sound, as of submerged sword-fish rushing hither and thither through shoals of black-fish. Soon, in a reunited band, and joined by the Spanish seamen, the whites came to the surface, irresistibly driving the negroes toward the stern. But a barricade of casks and sacks, from side to side, had been thrown up by the mainmast. Here the negroes faced about, and though scorning peace or truce, yet fain would have had respite. But, without pause, overleaping the barrier, the unflagging sailors again closed. Exhausted, the blacks now fought in despair. Their red tongues lolled, wolf-like, from their black mouths. But the pale sailors' teeth were set; not a word was spoken; and, in five minutes more, the ship was won.

Nearly a score of the negroes were killed. Exclusive of those by the balls, many were mangled; their wounds—mostly inflicted by the long-edged sealing-spears, resembling those shaven ones of the English at Preston Pans, made by the pooled scythes of the Highlanders. On the other side, none were killed, though several were wounded; some severely, including the mate. The surviving negroes were temporarily secured, and the ship, towed back into the harbor at midnight, once more lay anchored.

Omitting the incidents and arrangements ensuing, suffice it that, after two days spent in refitting, the ships sailed in company for Conception, in Chili, and thence for Lima, in Peru; where, before the vice-regal courts, the whole affair, from the beginning, underwent investigation.

Though, midway on the passage, the ill-fated Spaniard, relaxed from constraint, showed some signs of regaining health with free-will; yet, agreeably to his own foreboding, shortly before arriving at Lima, he relapsed, finally becoming so reduced as to be carried ashore in arms. Hearing of his story and plight, one of the many religious institutions of the City of Kings opened an hospitable refuge to him, where both physician and priest were his nurses, and a member of the order volunteered to be his one special guardian and consoler, by night and by day.

The following extracts, translated from one of the official Spanish documents, will, it is hoped, shed light on the preceding narrative, as well as, in the first place, reveal the true port of departure and true history of the *San Dominick*'s voyage, down to the time of her touching at the island of St. Maria.

But, ere the extracts come, it may be well to preface them with a remark.

The document selected, from among many others, for partial translation, contains the deposition of Benito Cereno; the first taken in the case. Some disclosures therein were, at the time, held dubious for both learned and natural reasons. The tribunal inclined to the opinion that the deponent, not undisturbed in his mind by recent events, raved of some things which could never have happened. But subsequent depositions of the surviving sailors, bearing out the revelations of their captain in several of the strangest particulars, gave credence to the rest. So that the tribunal, in its final decision, rested its capital sentences upon statements which, had they lacked confirmation, it would have deemed it but duty to reject.

———

I, DON JOSE DE ABOS AND PADILLA, His Majesty's Notary for the Royal Revenue, and Register of this Province, and Notary Public of the Holy Crusade of this Bishopric, etc.

Do certify and declare, as much as is requisite in law, that, in the criminal cause commenced the twenty-fourth of the month of September, in the year seventeen hundred and ninety-nine, against the negroes of the ship *San Dominick*, the following declaration before me was made:

Declaration of the first witness, DON BENITO CERENO.

The same day, and month, and year, His Honor, Doctor Juan Martinez de Rozas, Councilor of the Royal Audience of this Kingdom, and learned in the law of this Intendency, ordered the captain of the ship *San Dominick*, Don Benito Cereno, to appear; which he did in his litter, attended by the monk Infelez; of whom he received the oath, which he took by God, our Lord, and a sign of the Cross; under which he promised to tell the truth of whatever he should know and should be asked;—and being interrogated agreeably to the tenor of the act commencing the process, he said, that on the twentieth of May last, he set sail with his ship from the port of Valparaiso, bound to that of Callao; loaded with the produce of the country beside thirty cases of hardware and one hundred and sixty blacks, of both sexes, mostly belonging to Don Alexandro Aranda, gentleman, of the city of Mendoza; that the crew of the ship consisted of thirty-six men, beside the persons who went as passengers; that the negroes were in part as follows:

[*Here, in the original, follows a list of some fifty names, descriptions, and ages, compiled from certain recovered documents of Aranda's, and also from recollections of the deponent, from which portions only are extracted.*]

. . . One, from about eighteen to nineteen years, named José, and this was the man that waited upon his master, Don Alexandro, and who speaks well the Spanish, having served him four or five years; . . . a mulatto, named Francesco, the cabin steward, of a good person and voice, having sung in the Valparaiso churches, native of the province of Buenos Ayres, aged about thirty-five years. . . . A smart negro, named Dago, who had been for many years a grave-digger among the Spaniards, aged forty-six years . . . Four old negroes, born in Africa, from sixty to seventy, but sound, calkers by trade, whose names are as follows:—the first was named Muri, and he was killed (as was also his son named Diamelo); the second, Nacta; the third, Yola, likewise killed; the fourth, Ghofan; and six full-grown negroes, aged from thirty to forty-five, all raw, and born among the Ashantees—Matiluqui, Yan, Lecbe, Mapenda, Yambaio, Akim; four of whom were killed; . . . a powerful negro named Atufal, who being supposed to have been a chief in Africa, his owner set great store by him. . . . And a small negro of Senegal, but some years among the Spaniards, aged about thirty, which negro's name was Babo; . . . that he does not remember the names of the others, but that still expecting the residue of Don Alexandro's papers will be found, will then take due account of them all, and remit to the court; . . . and thirty-nine women and children of all ages.

[*The catalogue over, the deposition goes on.*]

. . . That all the negroes slept upon deck, as is customary in this navigation, and none wore fetters, because the owner, his friend Aranda, told him that they were all tractable; . . . that on the seventh day after leaving port, at three o'clock in the morning, all the Spaniards being asleep except the two officers on the watch, who were the boatswain, Juan Robles, and the carpenter, Juan Bautista Gayete, and the helmsman and his boy, the negroes revolted suddenly, wounded dangerously the boatswain and the carpenter, and successively killed eighteen men of those who were sleeping upon deck, some with hand-spikes and hatchets, and others by throwing them alive overboard, after tying them; that of the Spaniards upon deck, they left about seven, as he thinks, alive and tied, to manœuvre the ship, and three or four more, who hid themselves, remained also alive. Although in the act of revolt the negroes made themselves masters of the hatchway, six or seven wounded went through it to the cockpit, without any hindrance on their part; that during the act of revolt, the mate and another person, whose name he does not recollect, attempted to come up through the hatchway, but being quickly wounded, were obliged to return to the cabin; that the deponent resolved at break of day to come up the companion-way, where the negro Babo was, being the ringleader, and Atufal, who assisted him, and having spoken to them, exhorted them to cease committing such atrocities, asking them, at the same time, what they wanted and intended to do, offering, himself, to obey their commands; that notwithstanding this, they threw, in his presence, three men, alive and tied, overboard; that they told the deponent to come up, and that they would not kill him; which having done, the negro Babo asked him whether there were in those seas any negro countries where they might be carried, and he answered them, No; that the negro Babo afterwards told him to carry them to Senegal, or to the neighboring islands of St. Nicholas; and he answered, that this was impossible, on account of the great distance, the necessity involved of rounding Cape Horn, the bad condition of the vessel, the want of provisions, sails, and water; but that the negro Babo replied to him he must carry them in any way; that they would do and conform themselves to everything the deponent should require as to eating and drinking; that after a long conference, being absolutely compelled to please them, for they threatened to kill all the whites if they were not, at all events, carried to Senegal, he told them that what was most wanting for the voyage was water; that they would go near the coast to take it, and thence they would proceed on their course; that the negro Babo agreed to it; and the deponent

steered towards the intermediate ports, hoping to meet some
Spanish or foreign vessel that would save them; that within ten or
eleven days they saw the land, and continued their course by it in
the vicinity of Nasca; that the deponent observed that the negroes
were now restless and mutinous, because he did not effect the
taking in of water, the negro Babo having required, with threats,
that it should be done, without fail, the following day; he told
him he saw plainly that the coast was steep, and the rivers desig-
nated in the maps were not to be found, with other reasons suitable
to the circumstances; that the best way would be to go to the
island of Santa Maria, where they might water easily, it being a
solitary island, as the foreigners did; that the deponent did not go
to Pisco, that was near, nor make any other port of the coast,
because the negro Babo had intimated to him several times, that
he would kill all the whites the very moment he should perceive
any city, town, or settlement of any kind on the shores to which
they should be carried; that having determined to go to the island
of Santa Maria, as the deponent had planned, for the purpose of
trying whether, on the passage or near the island itself, they could
find any vessel that should favor them, or whether he could escape
from it in a boat to the neighboring coast of Arruco, to adopt
the necessary means he immediately changed his course, steering
for the island; that the negroes Babo and Atufal held daily conferences, in which they discussed what was necessary for their
design of returning to Senegal, whether they were to kill all the
Spaniards, and particularly the deponent; that eight days after
parting from the coast of Nasca, the deponent being on the watch
a little after day-break, and soon after the negroes had their meeting, the negro Babo came to the place where the deponent was,
and told him that he had determined to kill his master, Don
Alexandro Aranda, both because he and his companions could not
otherwise be sure of their liberty, and that to keep the seamen in
subjection, he wanted to prepare a warning of what road they
should be made to take did they or any of them oppose him; and
that, by means of the death of Don Alexandro, that warning would
best be given; but, that what this last meant, the deponent did not
at the time comprehend, nor could not, further than that the death
of Don Alexandro was intended; and moreover the negro Babo

proposed to the deponent to call the mate Raneds, who was sleeping in the cabin, before the thing was done, for fear, as the deponent understood it, that the mate, who was a good navigator, should be killed with Don Alexandro and the rest; that the deponent, who was the friend, from youth, of Don Alexandro, prayed and conjured, but all was useless; for the negro Babo answered him that the thing could not be prevented, and that all the Spaniards risked their death if they should attempt to frustrate his will in this matter, or any other; that, in this conflict, the deponent called the mate, Raneds, who was forced to go apart, and immediately the negro Babo commanded the Ashantee Martinqui and the Ashantee Lecbe to go and commit the murder; that those two went down with hatchets to the berth of Don Alexandro; that, yet half alive and mangled, they dragged him on deck; that they were going to throw him overboard in that state, but the negro Babo stopped them, bidding the murder be completed on the deck before him, which was done, when, by his orders, the body was carried below, forward; that nothing more was seen of it by the deponent for three days; . . . that Don Alonzo Sidonia, an old man, long resident at Valparaiso, and lately appointed to a civil office in Peru, whither he had taken passage, was at the time sleeping in the berth opposite Don Alexandro's; that awakening at his cries, surprised by them, and at the sight of the negroes with their bloody hatchets in their hands, he threw himself into the sea through a window which was near him, and was drowned, without it being in the power of the deponent to assist or take him up; . . . that a short time after killing Aranda, they brought upon deck his german-cousin, of middle-age, Don Francisco Masa, of Mendoza, and the young Don Joaquin, Marques de Aramboalaza, then lately from Spain, with his Spanish servant Ponce, and the three young clerks of Aranda, José Mozairi, Lorenzo Bargas, and Hermenegildo Gandix, all of Cadiz; that Don Joaquin and Hermenegildo Gandix, the negro Babo, for purposes hereafter to appear, preserved alive; but Don Francisco Masa, José Mozairi, and Lorenzo Bargas, with Ponce the servant, beside the boatswain, Juan Robles, the boatswain's mates, Manual Viscaya and Roderigo Hurta, and four of the sailors, the negro Babo ordered to be thrown alive into the sea, although they made no resistance, nor begged for anything else but mercy; that the boat-swain, Juan Robles, who knew how to swim, kept the longest above water, making acts of contrition, and, in the last words he uttered, charged this deponent to cause mass to be said for his soul to our Lady of Succor; . . . that, during the three days which followed, the deponent, uncertain what fate had befallen the remains of Don Alexandro, frequently asked the negro Babo where they were, and, if still on board, whether they were to be preserved for interment ashore, entreating him so to order it; that the negro Babo answered nothing till the fourth day, when at sunrise, the deponent coming on deck, the negro Babo showed him a skeleton, which had been substituted for the ship's proper figure-head—the image of Christopher Colon, the discoverer of the New World; that the negro Babo asked him whose skeleton that was, and whether, from its white-ness, he should not think it a white's; that, upon discovering his face, the negro Babo, coming close, said words to this effect: "Keep faith with the blacks from here to Senegal, or you shall in spirit, as now in body, follow your leader," pointing to the prow; . . . that the same morning the negro Babo took by succession each Span-iard forward, and asked him whose skeleton that was, and whether, from its whiteness, he should not think it a white's; that each Spaniard covered his face; that then to each the negro Babo re-peated the words in the first place said to the deponent; . . . that they (the Spaniards), being then assembled aft, the negro Babo harangued them, saying that he had now done all; that the de-ponent (as navigator for the negroes) might pursue his course, warning him and all of them that they should, soul and body, go the way of Don Alexandro, if he saw them (the Spaniards) speak or plot anything against them (the negroes)—a threat which was repeated every day; that, before the events last mentioned, they had tied the cook to throw him overboard, for it is not known what thing they heard him speak, but finally the negro Babo spared his life, at the request of the deponent; that a few days after, the deponent, endeavoring not to omit any means to preserve the lives of the remaining whites, spoke to the negroes of peace and tranquillity, and agreed to draw up a paper, signed by the deponent and the sailors who could write, as also by the negro Babo, for himself and all the blacks, in which the deponent obliged himself to carry them to Senegal, and they not to kill any more, and he formally to make over to them the ship, with the cargo, with which they were for that time satisfied and quieted. . . . But the next day, the more surely to guard against the sailors' escape, the negro Babo commanded all the boats to be destroyed but the long-boat, which was unseaworthy, and another, a cutter in good condition, which knowing it would yet be wanted for towing the water casks, he had it lowered down into the hold.

[*Various particulars of the prolonged and perplexed navigation ensuing here follow, with incidents of a calamitous calm, from which portion one passage is extracted, to wit:*]

. . . That on the fifth day of the calm, all on board suffering much from the heat, and want of water, and five having died in fits, and mad, the negroes became irritable, and for a chance gesture, which they deemed suspicious—though it was harmless— made by the mate, Raneds, to the deponent in the act of handing a quadrant, they killed him; but that for this they afterwards were sorry, the mate being the only remaining navigator on board, except the deponent.

. . . That omitting other events, which daily happened, and which can only serve uselessly to recall past misfortunes and conflicts, after seventy-three days' navigation, reckoned from the time they sailed from Nasca, during which they navigated under a scanty allowance of water, and were afflicted with the calms before mentioned, they at last arrived at the island of Santa Maria, on the seventeenth of the month of August, at about six o'clock in the afternoon, at which hour they cast anchor very near the American ship, *Bachelor's Delight*, which lay in the same bay, commanded by the generous Captain Amasa Delano; but at six o'clock in the morning, they had already described the port, and the negroes became uneasy, as soon as at distance they saw the ship, not having expected to see one there; that the negro Babo pacified them, assuring them that no fear need be had; that straightway he ordered the figure on the bow to be covered with canvas, as for repairs, and had the decks a little set in order; that for a time the negro Babo and the negro Atufal conferred; that the negro Atufal was for sailing away, but the negro Babo would not, and, by himself, cast about what to do; that at last he came to the deponent, proposing to him to say and do all that the deponent declares to have said and done to the American captain; . . . that the negro Babo warned him that if he varied in the least, or uttered any word, or gave any look that should give the least intimation of the past events or present state, he would instantly kill him, with all his companions, showing a dagger, which he carried hid, saying something which, as he understood it, meant that that dagger would be alert as his eyes; that the negro Babo then announced the plan to all his companions, which pleased them; that he then, the better to disguise the truth, devised many expedients, in some of them uniting deceit and defense; that of this sort was the device of the six Ashantees before named, who were his bravoes; that them he stationed on the break of the poop, as if to clean certain hatchets (in cases, which were part of the cargo), but in reality to use them, and distribute them at need, and at a given word he told them; that, among other devices, was the device of presenting Atufal, his right hand man, as chained, though in a moment the chains could be dropped; that in every particular he informed the deponent what part he was expected to enact in every device, and what story he was to tell on every occasion, always threatening him with instant death if he varied in the least: that, conscious that many of the negroes would be turbulent, the negro Babo appointed the four aged negroes, who were calkers, to keep what domestic order they could on the decks; that again and again he harangued the Spaniards and his companions, informing them of his intent, and of his devices, and of the invented story that this deponent was to tell; charging them lest any of them varied from that story; that these arrangements were made and matured during the interval of two or three hours, between their first sighting the ship and the arrival on board of Captain Amasa Delano; that this happened about half-past seven o'clock in the morning, Captain Amasa Delano coming in his boat, and all gladly receiving him; that the deponent, as well as he could force himself, acting then the part of principal owner, and a free captain of the ship, told Captain Amasa Delano, when called upon, that he came from Buenos Ayres, bound to Lima, with three hundred negroes; that off Cape Horn, and in a subsequent fever, many negroes had died; that also, by similar casualties, all the sea officers and the greatest part of the crew had died.

[*And so the deposition goes on, circumstantially recounting the fictitious story dictated to the deponent by Babo, and through the deponent imposed upon Captain Delano; and also recounting the friendly offers of Captain Delano, with other things, but all of which is here omitted. After the fictitious story, etc. the deposition proceeds:*]

. . . That the generous Captain Amasa Delano remained on board all the day, till he left the ship anchored at six o'clock in the evening, deponent speaking to him always of his pretended misfortunes, under the fore-mentioned principles, without having had it in his power to tell a single word, or give him the least hint, that he might know the truth and state of things; because the negro Babo, performing the office of an officious servant with all the appearance of submission of the humble slave, did not leave the deponent one moment; that this was in order to observe the deponent's actions and words, for the negro Babo understands well the Spanish; and besides, there were thereabout some others who were constantly on the watch, and likewise understood the Spanish; . . . that upon one occasion, while deponent was standing on the deck conversing with Amasa Delano, by a secret sign the negro Babo drew him (the deponent) aside, the act appearing as if originating with the deponent; that then, he being drawn aside, the negro Babo proposed to him to gain from Amasa Delano full particulars about his ship, and crew, and arms; that the deponent asked "For what?" that the negro Babo answered he might conceive; that, grieved at the prospect of what might overtake the generous Captain Amasa Delano, the deponent at first refused to ask the desired questions, and used every argument to induce the negro Babo to give up this new design; that the negro Babo showed the point of his dagger; that, after the information had been obtained the negro Babo again drew him aside, telling him that that very night he (the deponent) would be captain of two ships, instead of one, for that, great part of the American's ship's crew being to be absent fishing, the six Ashantees, without any one else, would easily take it; that at this time he said other things to the same purpose; that no entreaties availed; that before Amasa Delano's coming on board, no hint had been given touching the capture of the American ship; that to prevent this project the deponent was powerless; . . . that in some things his memory is confused, he cannot distinctly recall every event; . . . that as soon as they had cast anchor at six of the clock in the evening, as has before been stated, the American Captain took leave, to return to his vessel; that upon a sudden impulse, which the deponent believes to have come from God and his angels, he, after the farewell had been said, followed the generous Captain Amasa Delano as far as the gunwale, where he stayed, under pretense of taking leave, until Amasa Delano should have been seated in his boat; that on shoving off, the deponent sprang from the gunwale into the boat, and fell into it, he knows not how, God guarding him; that—

[*Here, in the original, follows the account of what further happened at the escape, and how the* San Dominick *was retaken, and of the passage to the coast; including in the recital many expressions of "eternal gratitude" to the "generous Captain Amasa Delano." The deposition then proceeds with recapitulatory remarks, and a partial renumeration of the negroes, making record of their individual part in the past events, with a view to furnishing, according to command of the court, the data whereon to found the criminal sentences to be pronounced. From this portion is the following.*]

—That he believes that all the negroes, though not in the first place knowing to the design of revolt, when it was accomplished, approved it. . . . That the negro José, eighteen years old, and in the personal service of Don Alexandro, was the one who communicated the information to the negro Babo, about the state of things in the cabin, before the revolt; that this is known, because, in the preceding midnight, he used to come from his berth, which was under his master's, in the cabin, to the deck where the ringleader and his associates were, and had secret conversations with the negro Babo, in which he was several times seen by the mate; that, one night, the mate drove him away twice; . . . that this same negro José was the one who, without being commanded to do so by the negro Babo, as Lecbe and Martinqui were, stabbed his master, Don Alexandro, after he had been dragged half-lifeless to the deck; . . . that the mulatto steward, Francesco, was of the first band of revolters, that he was, in all things, the creature and tool of the negro Babo; that, to make his court, he, just before a repast in the cabin, proposed, to the negro Babo, poisoning a dish for the generous Captain Amasa Delano; this is known and believed, because the negroes have said it; but that the negro Babo, having another design, forbade Francesco; . . . that the Ashantee Lecbe was one of the worst of them; for that, on the day the ship was retaken, he assisted in the defense of her, with a hatchet in each hand, with one of which he wounded, in the breast, the chief mate of Amasa Delano, in the first act of boarding; this all knew; that, in sight of the deponent, Lecbe struck, with a hatchet, Don Francisco Masa, when, by the negro Babo's orders, he was carrying him to throw him overboard, alive, besides participating in the murder, before mentioned, of Don Alexandro Aranda, and others of the cabin-passengers; that, owing to the fury with which the Ashantees fought in the engagement with the boats, but this Lecbe and Yan survived; that Yan was bad as Lecbe; that Yan was the man who, by Babo's command, willingly prepared the skeleton of Don Alexandro, in a way the negroes afterwards told the deponent, but which he, so long as reason is left him, can never divulge; that Yan and Lecbe were the two who, in a calm by night, riveted the skeleton to the bow; this also the negroes told him; that the negro Babo was he who traced the inscription below it; that the negro Babo was the plotter from first to last; he ordered every murder, and was the helm and keel of the revolt; that Atufal was his lieutenant in all; but Atufal, with his own hand, committed no murder; nor did the negro Babo; . . . that Atufal was shot, being killed in the fight with the boats, ere boarding; . . . that the negresses, of age, were knowing to the revolt, and testified themselves satisfied at the death of their master, Don Alexandro; that, had the negroes not restrained them, they would have tortured to death, instead of simply killing, the Spaniards slain by command of the negro Babo; that the negresses used their utmost influence to have the deponent made away with; that, in the various acts of murder, they sang songs and danced—not gaily, but solemnly; and before the engagement with the boats, as well as during the action, they sang melancholy songs to the negroes, and that this melancholy tone was more inflaming than a different one would have been, and was so intended; that all this is believed, because the negroes have said it.

—that of the thirty-six men of the crew, exclusive of the passengers (all of whom are now dead), which the deponent had knowledge of, six only remained alive, with four cabin-boys and ship-boys, not included with the crew; . . . that the negroes broke an arm of one of the cabin-boys and gave him strokes with hatchets.

[*Then follow various random disclosures referring to various periods of time. The following are extracted.*]

—That during the presence of Captain Amasa Delano on board, some attempts were made by the sailors, and one by Hermenegildo Gandix, to convey hints to him of the true state of affairs; but that these attempts were ineffectual, owing to fear of incurring death, and, furthermore, owing to the devices which offered contradictions to the true state of affairs, as well as owing to the generosity and piety of Amasa Delano incapable of sounding such wickedness; . . . that Luys Galgo, a sailor about sixty years of age, and formerly of the king's navy, was one of those who sought to convey tokens to Captain Amasa Delano; but his intent, though undiscovered, being suspected, he was, on a pretense, made to retire out of sight, and at last into the hold, and there was made away with. This the negroes have since said; . . . that one of the ship-boys feeling, from Captain Amasa Delano's presence, some hopes of release, and not having enough prudence, dropped some chance-word respecting his expectations, which being overheard and understood by a slave-boy with whom he was eating at the time, the latter struck him on the head with a knife, inflicting a bad wound, but of which the boy is now healing; that likewise, not long before the ship was brought to anchor, one of the seamen, steering at the time, endangered himself by letting the blacks remark some expression in his countenance, arising from a cause similar to the above; but this sailor, by his heedful after conduct, escaped; . . . that these statements are made to show the court that from the beginning to the end of the revolt, it was impossible for the deponent and his men to act otherwise than they did; . . .

—that the third clerk, Hermenegildo Gandix, who before had

been forced to live among the seamen, wearing a seaman's habit, and in all respects appearing to be one for the time; he, Gandix, was killed by a musket ball fired through mistake from the boats before boarding; having in his fright run up the mizzen-rigging, calling to the boats—"don't board," lest upon their boarding the negroes should kill him; that this inducing the Americans to believe he some way favored the cause of the negroes, they fired two balls at him, so that he fell wounded from the rigging, and was drowned in the sea; . . . —that the young Don Joaquin, Marques de Aramboalaza, like Hermenegildo Gandix, the third clerk, was degraded to the office and appearance of a common seaman; that upon one occasion when Don Joaquin shrank, the negro Babo commanded the Ashantee Lecbe to take tar and heat it, and pour it upon Don Joaquin's hands; . . . —that Don Joaquin was killed owing to another mistake of the Americans, but one impossible to be avoided, as upon the approach of the boats, Don Joaquin, with a hatchet tied edge out, and upright to his hand, was made by the negroes to appear on the bulwarks; whereupon, seen with arms in his hands and in a questionable attitude, he was shot for a renegade seaman; . . . —that on the person of Don Joaquin was found secreted a jewel, which, by papers that were discovered, proved to have been meant for the shrine of our Lady of Mercy in Lima; a votive offering, beforehand prepared and guarded, to attest his gratitude, when he should have landed in Peru, his last destination, for the safe conclusion of his entire voyage from Spain; . . . —that the jewel, with the other effects of the late Don Joaquin, is in the custody of the brethren of the Hospital de Sacerdotes, awaiting the disposition of the honorable court; . . . —that, owing to the condition of the deponent, as well as the haste in which the boats departed for the attack, the Americans were not forewarned that there were, among the apparent crew, a passenger and one of the clerks disguised by the negro Babo; . . . —that, beside the negroes killed in the action, some were killed after the capture and re-anchoring at night, when shackled to the ring-bolts on deck; that these deaths were committed by the sailors, ere they could be prevented. That so soon as informed of it, Captain Amasa Delano used all his authority, and, in particular with his own hand, struck down Martinez Gola, who, having found a razor in the pocket of an old jacket of his, which one of the shackled negroes had on, was aiming it at the negro's throat; that the noble Captain Amasa Delano also wrenched from the hand of Bartholomew Barlo a dagger, secreted at the time of the massacre of the whites, with which he was in the act of stabbing a shackled negro, who, the same day, with another negro, had thrown him down and jumped upon him; . . . —that, for all the events, befalling through so long a time, during which the ship was in the hands of the negro Babo, he cannot here give account; but that, what he has said is the most substantial of what occurs to him at present, and is the truth under the oath which he has taken; which declaration he affirmed and ratified, after hearing it read to him.

He said that he is twenty-nine years of age, and broken in body and mind; that when finally dismissed by the court, he shall not return home to Chili, but betake himself to the monastery on Mount Agonia without; and signed with his honor, and crossed himself, and, for the time, departed as he came, in his litter, with the monk Infelez, to the Hospital de Sacerdotes.

BENITO CERENO

DOCTOR ROZAS

If the Deposition have served as the key to fit into the lock of the complications which precede it, then, as a vault whose door has been flung back, the *San Dominick*'s hull lies open today.

Hitherto the nature of this narrative, besides rendering the intricacies in the beginning unavoidable, has more or less required that many things, instead of being set down in the order of occurrence, should be retrospectively, or irregularly given; this last is the case with the following passages, which will conclude the account:

During the long, mild voyage to Lima, there was, as before hinted, a period during which the sufferer a little recovered his health, or, at least in some degree, his tranquillity. Ere the decided relapse which came, the two captains had many cordial conversations—their fraternal unreserve in singular contrast with former withdrawments.

Again and again it was repeated, how hard it had been to enact the part forced on the Spaniard by Babo.

"Ah, my dear friend," Don Benito once said, "at those very

times when you thought me so morose and ungrateful, nay, when, as you now admit, you half thought me plotting your murder, at those very times my heart was frozen; I could not look at you, thinking of what, both on board this ship and your own, hung, from other hands, over my kind benefactor. And as God lives, Don Amasa, I know not whether desire for my own safety alone could have nerved me to that leap into your boat, had it not been for the thought that, did you, unenlightened, return to your ship, you, my best friend, with all who might be with you, stolen upon, that night, in your hammocks, would never in this world have wakened again. Do but think how you walked this deck, how you sat in this cabin, every inch of ground mined into honey-combs under you. Had I dropped the least hint, made the least advance towards an understanding between us, death, explosive death—yours as mine —would have ended the scene."

"True, true," cried Captain Delano, starting, "you have saved my life, Don Benito, more than I yours; saved it, too, against my knowledge and will."

"Nay, my friend," rejoined the Spaniard, courteous even to the point of religion, "God charmed your life, but you saved mine. To think of some things you did—those smilings and chattings, rash pointings and gesturings. For less than these, they slew my mate, Raneds; but you had the Prince of Heaven's safe-conduct through all ambuscades."

"Yes, all is owing to Providence, I know: but the temper of my mind that morning was more than commonly pleasant, while the sight of so much suffering, more apparent than real, added to my good-nature, compassion, and charity, happily interweaving the three. Had it been otherwise, doubtless, as you hint, some of my interferences might have ended unhappily enough. Besides, those feelings I spoke of enabled me to get the better of momentary distrust, at times when acuteness might have cost me my life, without saving another's. Only at the end did my suspicions get the better of me, and you know how wide of the mark they then proved."

"Wide, indeed," said Don Benito, sadly; "you were with me all day; stood with me, sat with me, talked with me, looked at me, ate with me, drank with me; and yet, your last act was to clutch for a monster, not only an innocent man, but the most pitiable of all men. To such degree may malign machinations and deceptions impose. So far may even the best man err, in judging the conduct of one with the recesses of whose condition he is not acquainted. But you were forced to it; and you were in time undeceived. Would that, in both respects, it was so ever, and with all men."

"You generalize, Don Benito; and mournfully enough. But the past is passed; why moralize upon it? Forget it. See, yon bright sun has forgotten it all, and the blue sea, and the blue sky; these have turned over new leaves."

"Because they have no memory," he dejectedly replied; "because they are not human."

"But these mild trades that now fan your cheek, do they not come with a human-like healing to you? Warm friends, steadfast friends are the trades."

"With their steadfastness they but waft me to my tomb, Señor," was the foreboding response.

"You are saved," cried Captain Delano, more and more astonished and pained; "you are saved: what has cast such a shadow upon you?"

"The negro."

There was silence, while the moody man sat, slowly and unconsciously gathering his mantle about him, as if it were a pall.

There was no more conversation that day.

But if the Spaniard's melancholy sometimes ended in muteness upon topics like the above, there were others upon which he never spoke at all; on which, indeed, all his old reserves were piled. Pass over the worst, and, only to elucidate, let an item or two of these be cited. The dress, so precise and costly, worn by him on the day whose events have been narrated, had not willingly been put on. And that silver-mounted sword, apparent symbol of despotic command, was not, indeed, a sword, but the ghost of one. The scabbard, artificially stiffened, was empty.

As for the black—whose brain, not body, had schemed and led the revolt, with the plot—his slight frame, inadequate to that which it held, had at once yielded to the superior muscular strength of his captor, in the boat. Seeing all was over, he uttered no sound, and could not be forced to. His aspect seemed to say, since I cannot do deeds, I will not speak words. Put in irons in the hold, with the rest, he was carried to Lima. During the passage, Don Benito did not visit him. Nor then, nor at any time after, would he look at him. Before the tribunal he refused. When pressed by the judges he fainted. On the testimony of the sailors alone rested the legal identity of Babo.

Some months after, dragged to the gibbet at the tail of a mule, the black met his voiceless end. The body was burned to ashes; but for many days, the head, that hive of subtlety, fixed on a pole in the Plaza, met, unabashed, the gaze of the whites; and across the Plaza looked towards St. Bartholomew's church, in whose vaults slept then, as now, the recovered bones of Aranda: and across the Rimac bridge looked towards the monastery, on Mount Agonia without; where, three months after being dismissed by the court, Benito Cereno, borne on the bier, did, indeed, follow his leader.

G. P. R. JAMES

(1799–1860)

Inspired by the historical romances of Sir Walter Scott and Washington Irving, George Payne Rainsford James was one of the most prolific English writers of the nineteenth century and produced more than a hundred novels. Born in London, the son of a physician and former naval officer, James traveled widely and read avidly as a youth. In addition to his novels, he was noted for biographies of such historical figures as Richelieu and Richard, the Lion Hearted. His interest in history led to an appointment as Historiographer Royal under William IV in 1839, and while occupying this post he produced several pamphlets, including A History of the United States Boundary Question (1839). In 1850 he was appointed British consul at Boston, and he served in the same post at Norfolk, Virginia, from 1852 to 1856. At the time of his death he was British consul at Venice.

Though his romances are often flimsy and melodramatic, they are noted for elaborate accuracy of historical setting. His style was parodied by Thackeray in "Barbazure, by G. P. R. Jeames, Esq.," which appeared in Novels by Eminent Hands, and he was again ridiculed in Thackeray's Book of Snobs.

The Old Dominion; or, The Southampton Massacre (1856) was dedicated to James Pendleton Kennedy, whose acquaintance James had made while living in America. The book consists of a series of letters written to his sister by Sir Richard Conway, an officer with the British Army in India who inherits a plantation in Virginia neighboring that on which Nat Turner is held a slave. Conway travels in Virginia incognito in order to observe first-hand the institution of slavery before deciding whether to free the slaves who were included in his inheritance. His observations on life in Virginia are somewhat reminiscent of Dickens's approach in Martin Chuzzlewit. In the course of his conversations with white Americans, Sir Richard acquires a view of the Negro as a happy, irresponsible child who fares much better than the British laboring man. His preconceptions are jarred when he meets the moody and intellectual Nat Turner.

In some ways the book is typical of the plantation literature turned out by Dion Boucicault, Thomas Nelson Page, Joel Chandler Harris, and James Pendleton Kennedy. Sir Richard falls in love with his cousin Bessy and encounters the usual complications of family rivalry and dirty work with the plantation deed. But accompanying the familiar plot involvements are observations on slavery, abolition, Negro character, and Nat Turner, as seen from a British point of view. After the slave rebellion breaks out, a large part of the book is given over to escape and chase sequences reminiscent of those in the novels of James Fenimore Cooper.

James seems unable to make up his mind about Nat Turner. Turner condones the murder of women and children, but he also resembles a romantic rebel chieftain straight out of a Scott novel of clan warfare on the Scottish border. The first person he kills is a Machiavellian Northern abolitionist preacher with the ticket-name M'Grubber, and he has sufficient sensibility to spare the lives of Bessy and Sir Richard, while preserving the papers which he knows will resolve the family feud and promote their marriage. Apparently unwilling to picture the slave leader's ultimate fate, James ends the novel with the rebellion crushed but Turner still free. Sir Richard decides to free his own slaves, but only after he has provided them with life incomes, since he feels they would be unable to fend for themselves in freedom.

From *The Old Dominion, or,*
The Southampton Massacre

[Sir Richard writes to his sister in England,
informing her of life in Virginia]

. . . Negro laughter! you may exclaim. Yes, my dear sister, whatever you may think, these poor, unhappy people, as we are taught
to believe them, laugh all day long with such merry and joyous
peals that it is impossible to believe that the iron we are told of
is pressing very deeply into their souls. At all events, I am quite
sure it does not affect their cheerfulness. I think I shall establish
it as a very good comparison to say, "As merry as a negro slave."

I hear you exclaim, my dear Kate, "You will, of course,
emancipate the slaves!" and you will be horrified when I reply,
"I do not know." But of this be assured: I will do what, on
mature reflection and personal observation, I judge to be the best
for them. No motive of sordid interest will have any effect upon
me, nor could ever induce me to keep my fellow-man in bondage.
I confess my preconceived opinions have been very much shaken
by what I myself have seen even during my short stay here, and by
the comparisons which my mind has been unconsciously insti-
tuting between the condition of the negro in the free states and in
the slaveholding communities. In the former he is decidedly a
sad, gloomy—ay, an ill-treated man, subject to more of the painful
restrictions of caste than I should have conceived possible. Here he
appears to be a cheerful, light-hearted, guileless, child-like creature,
treated with great familiarity, and as far as I have seen, with kindness. Whether this be a reality or merely a semblance, I shall
know hereafter; but, depend upon it, I will not act till . . .

[Mr. Wheatley, a Northerner sympathetic to the South,
tells Sir Richard about Negro character]

. . . "They are good creatures," said Mr. Wheatley, looking up
from his letter, "capable of strong affections and strong attachments, but child-like, and requiring constant supervision and care.
Now this very man, who has been so thoughtful on a matter in

which right notions have been drummed into him by long habit, would make the most egregious, the most absurd, and sometimes the most distressing blunders in regard to things out of his routine. There are two propensities, however, of which the race is rarely free—to pilfer and to lie. The pilfering is usually confined to petty articles, and it would really seem as if they reasoned with themselves upon the matter, judging that what they take will please and benefit them more than the loss will pain or injure you. The lie, too, has its bounds and restrictions. It is like the lie of a child, issuing from fear, or from the wish of giving pleasure or amusement."

"May not both habits," I said, "be naturally traced to the positions in which they are placed? Having no property themselves, not even in themselves, may not their pilfering be a just retribution upon those who are depriving them of all; and may not the lie from fear, or for the purpose of pleasing, be traced to an institution which deprives them of that manly dignity which knows not fear and scorns deception?"

His short, quick laugh broke in upon me again. "I think not," he said; "you must see more of them before you can judge. Then, perhaps, you may think that the pilfering is a mere proclivity of their vanity or their small appetites. What they take is generally a bright-colored ribbon, or a bit of lace, or a spoonful out of a pot of sweetmeats, or a glass out of a brandy-bottle. You can teach a dog to abstain from taking anything till it is given to him, but you can't teach them, do what you will. There is no race upon the face of the earth who should more frequently repeat the prayer, 'Lead us not into temptation,' for there is no race so little capable of withstanding it. Then, as to lying, it is mere childishness. First, they have what your authors call a *diabetes* of talk. Truth is a great deal too limited for them. They must speak about something, and when the lie proceeds from fear, it is, nine times out of ten, unreasonable fear; they are afraid of being blamed, of not being thought quick and ready at an answer, and consequently, when a question is asked them, rather than seem ignorant, they fabricate a falsehood. If any thing very important were at stake, a thousand to one they would tell the truth; but upon all these matters you must satisfy yourself, for of all the rusty, rickety, breakable commodities in this world, second-hand opinions are the worst, and yet nine men out of ten supply themselves at brokers' shops, when they could get them fresh and strong from the manufactory."

[Sir Richard meets Nat Turner]

. . . Everything had become dry except where the river, evidently greatly fallen since the preceding evening, wended quietly on its way, no longer hurried by the mass of waters pressed within its narrow banks. By the side sat a negro, fishing; and as this was the first human being I had seen since I set out, I thought I might as well go down and talk with him. When I came near I perceived he was one of the finest-formed men I had ever seen; tall and powerful, with none of the usual deformity of his race. He had indeed the thick lips, the nose flattened, though not very much, and the woolly hair of the negro; but there were no bowed shins, or large hands and feet; and yet, as far as I could judge from his color, he was of unmixed African blood. He did not condescend to lift his head when I came near, but continued his occupation, still gazing upon the glistening but somewhat turbid water.

"Have you had good sport?" said I.

"I have caught no fish," said he, abruptly, and then turning round for the first time, he looked to see who was the interrogator.

"Is not the water too muddy still?" I asked, somewhat struck by the man's manner and tone.

"Those who would catch large fish must fish in troubled waters," answered the man, gravely, casting in his line again. "I shall catch when the appointed time comes. Nothing happens, master, but at its appointed time, whether it be great or small."

I confess I was not a little surprised at such a reply from such a man. I had heard of negroes who display as great natural powers of mind as those of the white races, but I never yet had met with one. In all whom I had seen there was a certain lack of intellect. Quick comprehension there might be—often rapid combination, cunning seeming to supply the place of reasoning powers; but it was more like the comprehension, the cunning of a child, exercised only upon the objects near at hand, without the power of generalization or remote deduction. In fact, this man's words afforded the first attempt at any thing like a grasp of a wide and comprehensive idea which I had ever met with in his race, and they excited my curiosity greatly.

"I agree perfectly with you," I answered; "I am a full believer in a special Providence; but yet it would seem but a small and undignified exercise of that divine power to make you catch a fish at one moment more than at another."

"What is small and what is great to God Almighty?" asked the man, still keeping his eyes on the stream. "He made the insect as well as the biggest of beasts; he made the grain of sand as well as the mountain. How can you tell, master, how small events may affect great ones? My catching a fish now or then may, by giving food and comfort to a family, allay their discontent, and, putting off its outbreak, induce them to go on in quiet till some farther relief comes—in its due season also. Does not the Bible tell us that not a sparrow falls to the ground unnoticed? Every thing is by God's will; every thing is in God's time. What is small—what is great to him? In a universe, every thing has its proper place, every event its proper moment: the derangement of the least would destroy the order of the whole. My time will come too for whatever I have to do, and I am ready to do God's will, whatever it may be."

I never was more astonished in my life than by this man's discourse. I had heard Hindoos speak many a time in a somewhat similar way, but they are proverbially a thoughtful, speculative, I may almost say, a metaphysical race; but to hear such words from a poor despised negro—from one of a class to whom the higher ranges of thought seem forbidden as well by capability as by education, was very strange.

While he had been speaking he had only turned his face to me once, and when he ceased I went on musing for a minute or two, not jumping at a conclusion at once, but asking myself whether he had learned all this from some one else like a parrot, but rejecting that suspicion speedily as contradicted by his whole tone and manner, and then considering whether it was likely or unlikely that every faculty of the mind would be equally developed. Grasp of intellect, logical power he certainly possessed, but there are a good many (perhaps) subordinate qualities and faculties requisite to make such gifts available for man's conduct either toward his fellow-man or toward his God. I had almost come to the conclusion that he must possess them, when suddenly a laugh —the unmeaning, almost idiotic laugh of the negro race—broke from his lips, followed by "Ah, master, I've caught you!" and I saw him pulling a large fish toward the shore.

It seemed that this was all he wanted. He showed it to me with a sort of child-like triumph, and then, throwing away the pole with which he had been fishing, and rolling up his line, he walked some way by my side as I took my way homeward.

I was anxious to know more of this man, and tried to put him upon some of those tracks which I thought might bring forth the peculiarities of his mind. He seemed a little shy, however, in answering my inquiries and in following any train of thought which was placed before him. This was natural enough in one of an enslaved race, in whose bosom there must always be some feelings of wrong and oppression so long as there is vanity in the human heart, however kindly they may be treated, however incapable they may be of taking care of directing, and of providing for themselves. They will always feel an uncongeniality—a want of sympathy with the dominant race, and shrink into themselves more or less when brought into communication with their masters. He told me his name, which was Nathaniel Turner, and where he lived, which was not far distant; but only once was I able to bring from him a spark of that intellectual fire which he had previously displayed, and which was even now half smothered by that cunning which is common to savages and children. I told him I was an Englishman, and alluded to our having emancipated our slaves in the West India islands, and I could see the sort of eager light break forth from his eyes, but it was quenched the next moment, as if he still entertained some doubts and suspicions.

"Well, master," he said, "I can't tell whether you are right or wrong in freeing the slaves. I suppose you did it because you thought you had no right to make them slaves at first. But if you did think so, there was a great deal more to be done than merely to give them back their liberty. You had taken a great deal more from them than freedom; you had taken from them their country, their home, their habits, and I think you were bound either to restore to them all the things of their former state, or to take good care of them, and to fit them for the state into which you had brought them. However, I am a poor foolish man, and know nothing about these things. I have been a slave all my life, and have had very good masters. I doubt not it will all be brought right in the end, and perhaps we niggers are placed in the position proper for us. At all events, it is God's will, and we ought to be content. Now, it is possible this fish here in my hand would rather have been some great shark, or some beast, or some bird, or even perhaps a man, but God willed it otherwise; if not, he would never have been hanging on my hook. But should the pot say to the hand that fashioned it, 'Why madest thou me so?' I was born of a different color from you and your friends, and that difference of color is a great difference in this world. Content is every thing, good master, and I am very well content as I am, *so long as it is God's will I should be so.*"

[Uncle Jack, a "loyal" Negro preacher, debates with Nat Turner and M'Grubber, the abolitionist preacher]

. . . "It matters not to me when I eat or when I drink," answered Nat Turner, in what seemed to me to be a somewhat stilted tone. "The man who wishes to bring the body under the mind must not care about such things. I have often gone without food for three days."

"I should think that must require some practice and preparations," I answered, somewhat inclined to smile; "and unless it was done from necessity, I do not see the use of it."

"Nor I either," said Uncle Jack. "Food and drink are given to us for our natural support, and while we reverence God's blessings by using them moderately, we should show our thankfulness for them by using them as he wills."

"The use was very great," exclaimed Nat Turner, in a more excited tone than before; "and as to preparation, I have accustomed myself to abstinence from my childhood. I knew from my earliest years that I was born for great things. What placed that mark upon my forehead before my birth?" and he laid his finger upon a sort of scar on his brow resembling a cross; but before I could examine it accurately, he went on in the same tone: "Who taught me things which happened before I was born, and which were only known to my mother and my father? And if it was God did this, why did He do so but to show that He intended me to—to—do great things?"

I looked around to Uncle Jack, beginning to think that the man was going mad; and the old man, taking my glance as a question, answered, "All the people will tell you it is as he says, sir. But I think Nat lets his mind rest too much upon such things. I fear it may do him harm. He has got plenty of strong, good sense, and if he will but continually seek God's grace to use it right, he may indeed do great things among the poor people who surround him. But the quickest goes farthest wrong when he does not take the right way, and I fear that may be Nat's case."

"No fear, no fear," said the other; "God, who willed me to be what I am, will teach me to do what I have to do"; and then, dropping into an almost sepulchral tone, he added, "He will give me a sign; He has promised it."

Uncle Jack shook his head very gravely, and Bessy Davenport, who had not yet spoken, remarked, "We are often inclined, Nat, to misunderstand signs. Take care that you don't apply to yourself signs that may be intended for the whole world. Don't you remember, when there was an eclipse a little while ago, you said it was a sign sent to you?"

"I don't know what you mean by an eclipse," answered the man, gloomily, "but I know that there was a sign, and a terrible sign too. However," he continued, in a more cheerful tone, "every one must read such things by the lights he has got, and the Lord will not suffer those whom He favors to mistake. He will direct us," he added, with a sigh, and then seemed inclined to change the conversation. I tried to keep it in the same course, for I wanted to hear more of his views on such subjects; but, with a great deal of skill—I might almost say cunning—he avoided it, and I purposely brought up the subject of freedom and slavery. The old preacher spoke upon it frankly and freely enough, and with a degree of liberality toward the masters which greatly surprised me. He said that the great majority were excellent, good, and kind-hearted people, and that, if they were all such, his race would be much more happy under their management than they could be under their own. "The great evil of slavery, sir," he said, "is the possibility of any extent of ill treatment. Where such a possibility exists, the thing will occur. It is true, I have no opportunity of comparing any other state of society with this, and, for aught I know, there may be evils as great in all others. I can not remember my own country at all distinctly; some vague general notions I have about it, and, if they be correct, I was a great deal worse off there than I am here; but I can not be sure whether these notions came from my own recollections or from what I have read or heard. One thing, however, is certain; slavery has existed in all ages. The Hebrews had their bond-servants, and they themselves were hewers of wood and drawers of water to the King of Egypt."

"Ay, but they rose and delivered themselves, and God helped them," Nat Turner said, with a peculiar flash in his dark eye.

"He is a God of justice, and strong to deliver," said a voice at the door, speaking in a very nasal tone; and, turning round, to my great surprise I saw the lanky and extraordinary figure of the Rev. Mr. M'Grubber.

Nat Turner started forward and shook him by the hand, and Uncle Jack made him a formal and, I thought, a somewhat stiff bow. Bessy Davenport gave me a rueful and yet a merry glance, and, judging that we should not profit much by what was likely to follow, I prepared to take my departure.

Nat Turner, however, instantly began the conversation with his visitor, who was evidently an old acquaintance and friend, by calling upon him to tell Uncle Jack all that he had been telling him the day before. "You will convince him, but I can't," cried the man, not heeding a cloud that came over Mr. M'Grubber's brow, and a quick sign that he made to him to be silent; "his heart seems as hard as the nether mill-stone toward his own people."

"My heart is not hard, Nathaniel," answered Uncle Jack, "but I love my own people too well to try and make them discontented with a situation from which they can not escape, but which may be ameliorated if they show themselves peaceful, quiet, and faithful. It is my duty to preach peace and good-will, resignation to the will of God and dependence upon his mercy, and not to stimulate men's passions, either in a right or wrong cause, to conduct which may end—God only knows how."

While the two negroes had been speaking, Mr. M'Grubber had evidently been upon thorns, though at the end of Uncle Jack's reply he had put on a look of meek and pious resignation. "Far be it from me, brother," he said, "to stimulate men's passions, or induce them to act in any hasty or violent manner. God forbid that I should bring poor people into trouble, or do any thing which is not pointed out by calm reason and religion. But we are told that we must not spare to speak God's truth, and when I am asked what is right and what is wrong, must I not say what is right? Ay, if any poor soul demands of me, Has my fellow-man a right to keep me in bondage? wouldst thou have reply yea or nay? I preach the truth, brother, let the results be what they may. That is in God's hand, not mine."

Uncle Jack shook his head with a somewhat melancholy look, but merely said, "The apostle teaches us to be obedient to the powers that are; and again we are told that servants should obey their masters. He who teaches differently I can not look upon as speaking by the Holy Spirit, and I fear evil will come of it."

Thus saying, he left the cabin, and Bessy Davenport and I followed, after having taken leave of Nat Turner; and I thought, as I walked away, that I heard the voice of Mr. M'Grubber raised loud and harshly, and I doubted not that poor Nat was receiving a stout reproof for having betrayed to the ears of others the nature of the reverend gentleman's communications with himself.

On the whole, my visit had a good deal disappointed me. My first interview with Nat Turner had impressed me with the idea that he was very much more superior to the rest of his race than I found him upon farther acquaintance. That he was superior there could be no doubt, but I thought I had discovered traits in him that day of almost all the peculiar weaknesses of the African race. That he was cunning, superstitious, and conceited was very clear, and there was something in the expression of his face and the glance of his eye which inclined me to believe that there might be a certain degree of ruthless cruelty and fierce passion within, though now concealed, if not subdued, by the command he had acquired over himself.

. . . . . .

"It is a sad picture of human nature indeed," I said, "and, from what I see of the negro population, I am inclined to attribute less power to education and more to race than I once did."

"The more you see of them, the more you will think so," answered Bessy. "Good education might, and I have no doubt does, produce a great deal of improvement; but as no cosmetic that ever was tried will make a black man white, so I don't believe any education will make his mind and character those of a white man. And yet this good old preacher, Uncle Jack, seems an extraordinary exception."

[M'Grubber's abolitionist sermon]

. . . He subsequently took even a bolder strain, and, thrusting all religious topics aside, talked openly of slavery in its moral and political aspect. He did not at all conceal his opinions nor temper his terms, but denounced the peculiar institutions of the South as alike degrading to master and man, as evil in itself and all its consequences. One of the most powerful parts of his sermon, as it struck me, was that in which he justified not only slaves themselves in attempting to escape from bondage, but all who aided them in their efforts for that purpose. Breaking off in the midst of an argument, he suddenly began a sort of tale or apologue. He told them how a white man, an American, had been wrecked on the coast of Morocco; how he had been seized and exposed in the slave-market, sold to the highest bidder, carried up into the country, sold again and again, till at length he found himself working in a garden in the neighborhood of Tangier. Then he painted in glowing terms the misery of the man's situation; how he had thirsted, and panted, and pined for liberty; how he had cast his eyes over the blue sea, and longed for his native land, and his friends, and his family; how the very luxuries of the climate and the kindness of his master were disgusting and abhorrent to him in his state of slavery. He then told us that a friendly Moor, in whom he had created an interest, determined to assist him in escaping—that two Europeans who were in the port had entered into the scheme, and that a thousand difficulties and dangers, on which I will not dwell, were encountered and overcome, till at length the fugitive was placed safely on board an American ship. "Were these men wrong?" he exclaimed—"were these men criminal? Had he not a right to seek his liberty however he could find it? Did not the whole of these States ring with applause and admiration of those who enabled him to recover freedom, the best boon of life? Oh perverted moral sense, which can in one instance laud to the skies the same conduct which, in another precisely similar, it dooms to the prison or the gallows!"

While all this was going on, I felt some sort of apprehension as to the result, and I looked round from time to time to see what would be the impression upon the audience. The greater part of the listeners were white men, many of them slave-owners, generally men of strong passions but little subjected to control, and it would not at all have surprised me to see the preacher dragged from the platform and horsewhipped before the congregation. But I was mistaken: not a sound of disapprobation even met my ear. Some sighed and some shook the head, but nobody attempted to interrupt the preacher.

As soon as Mr. M'Grubber had done, I turned away with Mr. Wheatley, and we bent our steps toward Beavor, keeping silence till we had got beyond the limits of the meeting.

. . . . . .

"Although I judged it rash and most dangerous to preach such doctrines as we had heard to-night to a large crowd of negroes," I answered, "yet I could not help thinking many of Mr. M'Grubber's arguments were exceedingly specious, if not cogent; that little apologue of his, for instance, of the white slave in Barbary and his liberation. It struck me as a very happy illustration of his views."

"A cunning piece of rhetoric," answered my acute friend, "peculiarly illustrative of the rhetoric of fanatics. Do you not remark that whenever they have a point to carry, they employ a figure, and in that figure they presuppose a complete parity between two really dissimilar cases? Knock away the petitio principii, and what do you find? Here he places a white man always accustomed to freedom, and with all the intellectual qualities impliedly cultivated by a white man's education, with a white man's wants, wishes, habits, and feelings, exactly upon a par with a negro born upon a plantation, habituated from infancy to slavery, without a thought, a desire, or a notion beyond the state in which he was brought up, except such as may have been instilled into him by abolitionism. Is this fair, to begin with? Is there a parity between the two cases? Then, again, the white man is flying from the bonds which had been accidentally imposed upon him, returns to home, to his ancient habits, to the free use of faculties and endowments, which are sure, if rightly used, to lead to competence, if not to wealth, to independence, and to ease. The negro flying from his master, on the contrary, leaves family and friends, old habits and associations, food, care, and protection in sickness or old age, for a wide, unfriended, uncertain future, where there is nothing probably but long-protracted labor, unbefriended sickness, unpitied decrepitude, and death on a dunghill. His nominal independence is shackled by the continual necessity of seeking food by labor; and his freedom becomes a curse instead of a blessing, in consequence of the prejudices of color and caste. Is there any parity between these two cases? I declare I would a great deal rather be a slave to the hardest master I have ever seen in Virginia—and I have now been here many years—than I would be a free negro in an abolition state; but this was all rhetoric, mere rhetoric, the most cowardly and contemptible of all species of sophistry. Much better to say boldly, 'You have no right to reduce any man to slavery; you have no right to hold any man in slavery; you shall not do evil that good may come of it; the Declaration of Independence says that "all men are created equal; they are endowed by their Creator with certain inalienable rights; among these are life, liberty, and the pursuit of happiness." By holding any man in slavery, whatever be his color, you violate the first grand principle of the American Constitution, you break the solemn fact upon which this Union was founded, by which alone she claimed, maintained, and accomplished her independence of Great Britain.' Better to say this, and fight it out upon this ground, than go sneakingly to work to render the slaves discontented with their masters. I have come to the conclusion, my dear Sir Richard, that the abolitionists are the very worst enemies of the slaves themselves."

DION BOUCICAULT

(1 8 2 0 ? – 1 8 9 0)

Boucicault was born in Dublin, Ireland, attended London University, and broke away from an apprenticeship to a civil engineer to pursue a career in theater. After some success in London, he came to America in 1853, where his plays became tremendously popular. He was noted for his dramatizations of Dickens's novels and later achieved his greatest success with a series of comedies on Irish character that included The Colleen Bawn (1860). All told, he wrote one hundred thirty-two plays, some of the most popular with American audiences being The Poor of New York (1857), The Octoroon (1859), and Rip Van Winkle (1865).

The Octoroon; or, Life in Louisiana (1859) was adapted from Mayne Reid's novel, The Quadroon (1856). When the play opened in New York, Boucicault played the part of the Indian retainer, and his wife played the role of Zoe. Zoe became one of the most familiar examples in nineteenth-century literature of the "tragic mulatto" destined to an unhappy end because of her mixed blood. The machinations concerning the plantation deed, and the use of a lower-caste Irish villain, M'Closky, whose crudity stands in contrast to the elegant manners of the plantation aristocracy, are also familiar devices. Unusual, however, was M'Closky's being trapped through a time-exposure photograph which captured him in the very act of committing murder, a device Boucicault had borrowed from the English novel The Filibuster (1859) by Albany

Fonblanque. Boucicault succeeded in balancing criticisms of slavery against admiration for Southern character, and the play was popular with both Northern and Southern viewers. When it was performed before a London audience, though, Zoe was spared her life and allowed a happy ending.

As the following scene opens, George Peyton has just learned of the arrival of the sheriff to take possession of his widowed aunt's plantation, Terrebonne. Meanwhile Dora, an heiress, has made it clear that, should George marry her, her money will be available to save the estate. Later in the play M'Closky commits murder to prevent delivery of a bank draft which will save Terrebonne, and he is thus able to purchase Zoe at public auction when it is discovered that her father had neglected to make her legally free and she must be sold along with the plantation hands. M'Closky is eventually undone by the accidental photograph, but not before Zoe takes her life.

From The Octoroon; or, Life in Louisiana

. . . . . .

ZOE: They are gone! (*Glancing at George*) Poor fellow, he has lost all.

GEORGE: Poor child! how sad she looks now she has no resource.

ZOE: How shall I ask him to stay?

GEORGE: Zoe, will you remain here? I wish to speak to you.

ZOE (*aside*): Well, that saves trouble.

GEORGE: By our ruin you lose all.

ZOE: O, I'm nothing; think of yourself.

GEORGE: I can think of nothing but the image that remains face to face with me; so beautiful, so simple, so confiding, that I dare not express the feelings that have grown up so rapidly in my heart.

ZOE (*aside*): He means Dora.

GEORGE: If I dared to speak!

ZOE: That's just what you must do, and do it at once, or it will be too late.

GEORGE: Has my love been divined?

ZOE: It has been more than suspected.

GEORGE: Zoe, listen to me, then. I shall see this estate pass from me without a sigh, for it possesses no charm for me; the wealth I covet is the love of those around me—eyes that are rich in fond looks, lips that breathe endearing words; the only estate I value is the heart of one true woman, and the slaves I'd have are her thoughts.

ZOE: George, George, your words take away my breath!

GEORGE: The world, Zoe, the free struggle of minds and hands is before me; the education bestowed on me by my dear uncle is a noble heritage which no sheriff can seize; with that I can build up a fortune, spread a roof over the heads I love, and place before them the food I have earned; I will work—

ZOE: Work! I thought none but colored people worked.

GEORGE: Work, Zoe, is the salt that gives savor to life.

ZOE: Dora said you were slow; if she could hear you now—

GEORGE: Zoe, you are young; your mirror must have told you that you are beautiful. Is your heart free?

ZOE: Free? of course it is!

GEORGE: We have known each other but a few days, but to me those days have been worth all the rest of my life. Zoe, you have suspected the feeling that now commands an utterance— you have seen that I love you.

ZOE: Me! you love *me?*

GEORGE: As my wife—the sharer of my hopes, my ambitions, and my sorrows; under the shelter of your love I could watch the storms of fortune pass unheeded by.

ZOE: *My* love! *My* love? George, you know not what you say! *I* the sharer of your sorrows—your wife! Do you know what I am?

GEORGE: Your birth—I know it. Has not my dear aunt forgotten it—she who had the most right to remember it? You are illegitimate, but love knows no prejudice.

ZOE (*aside*): Alas! he does not know, he does not know! and will despise me, spurn me, loathe me, when he learns who, what, he has so loved. (*Aloud*) George, O, forgive me! Yes, I love you—I did not know it until your words showed me what has been in my heart; each of them awoke a new sense, and now I know how unhappy—how very unhappy I am.

GEORGE: Zoe, what have I said to wound you?

ZOE: Nothing; but you must learn what I thought you already knew. George, you cannot marry me; the laws forbid it!

GEORGE: Forbid it?

ZOE: There is a gulf between us, as wide as your love, as deep as my despair; but, O, tell me, say you will pity me! that you will not throw me from you like a poisoned thing!

GEORGE: Zoe, explain yourself—your language fills me with shapeless fears.

ZOE: And what shall I say? I—my mother was—no, no—not her! Why should I refer the blame to her? George, do you see that hand you hold? look at these fingers; do you see the nails are of a bluish tinge?

GEORGE: Yes, near the quick there is a faint blue mark.

ZOE: Look in my eyes; is not the same color in the white?

GEORGE: It is their beauty.

ZOE: Could you see the roots of my hair you would see the same dark, fatal mark. Do you know what that is?

GEORGE: No.

ZOE: That is the ineffaceable curse of Cain. Of the blood that feeds my heart, one drop in eight is black—bright red as the rest may be, that one drop poisons all the flood; those seven bright drops give me love like yours—hope like yours—ambition like yours—life hung with passions like dew-drops on the morning flowers; but the one black drop gives me despair, for I'm an unclean thing—forbidden by the laws—I'm an Octoroon!

GEORGE: Zoe, I love you none the less; this knowledge brings no revolt to my heart, and I can overcome the obstacle.

ZOE: But I cannot.

GEORGE: We can leave this country, and go far away where none can know.

ZOE: And your mother, she who from infancy treated me with such fondness, she who, as you said, has most reason to spurn me, can she forget what I am? Will she gladly see you wedded to the child of her husband's slave? No! she would revolt from it, as all but you would; and if I consented to hear the cries of my heart, if I did not crush out my infant love, what would she say to the poor girl on whom she had bestowed so much? No, no!

GEORGE. Zoe, must we immolate our lives on her prejudice?

ZOE: Yes, for I'd rather be black than ungrateful! Ah, George, our race has at least one virtue—it knows how to suffer!

GEORGE: Each word you utter makes my love sink deeper into my heart.

ZOE: And I remained here to induce you to offer that heart to Dora!

GEORGE: If you bid me do so I will obey you—

ZOE: No, no! if you cannot be mine, O, let me not blush when I think of you.

GEORGE: Dearest Zoe!

. . . . . .

GEORGE: My dear aunt, why do you not move from this painful scene? Go with Dora to Sunnyside.

MRS. P.: No, George; your uncle said to me with his dying breath, "Nellie, never leave Terrebonne," and I never *will* leave it, till the law compels me.

SCUD: Mr. George, I'm going to say somethin' that has been chokin' me for some time. I know you'll excuse it. Thar's Miss Dora—that girl's in love with you; yes, sir, her eyes are startin' out of her head with it: now her fortune would redeem a good part of this estate.

MRS. P.: Why, George, I never suspected this!

GEORGE: I did, aunt, I confess, but—

MRS. P.: And you hesitated from motives of delicacy?

SCUD: No, ma'am; here's the plan of it. Mr. George is in love with Zoe.

GEORGE: Scudder!

MRS. P.: George!

SCUD: Hold on, now! things have got so jammed in on top of us, we ain't got time to put kid gloves on to handle them. He loves Zoe, and has found out that she loves him. (*Sighing*) Well, that's all right; but as he can't marry her, and as Miss Dora would jump at him—

MRS. P.: Why didn't you mention this before?

SCUD: Why, because I love Zoe, too, and I couldn't take that young feller from her; and she's jist living on the sight of him, as I saw her do; and they so happy in spite of this yer misery around them, and they reproachin' themselves with not feeling as they ought. I've seen it, I tell you; and darn it, ma'am, can't you see that's what's been a hollowing me out so—I beg your pardon.

MRS. P.: O, George—my son, let me call you—I do not speak for my own sake, nor for the loss of the estate, but for the poor people here: they will be sold, divided, and taken away—they have been born here. Heaven has denied me children; so all the strings of my heart have grown around and amongst them, like the fibres and roots of an old tree in its native earth. O, let all go, but save them! With them around us, if we have not wealth, we shall at least have the home that they alone can make—

GEORGE. My dear mother—Mr. Scudder—you teach me what I ought to do; if Miss Sunnyside will accept me as I am, Terrebonne shall be saved: I will sell myself, but the slaves shall be protected.

MRS. P.: *Sell* yourself, George! Is not Dora worth any man's—

SCUD: Don't say that, ma'am; don't say that to a man that loves another gal. He's going to do an heroic act; don't spile it.

MRS. P.: But Zoe is only an Octoroon.

SCUD: She's won this race agin the white, anyhow; it's too late now to start her pedigree. (*As Dora enters*) Come, Mrs. Peyton, take my arm. Hush! here's the other one: she's a little too thoroughbred—too much of the greyhound; but the heart's there, I believe.

(*Exeunt Scudder and Mrs. Peyton*)

DORA: Poor Mrs. Peyton.

GEORGE: Miss Sunnyside, permit me a word: a feeling of delicacy has suspended upon my lips an avowal, which—

DORA (*aside*): O, dear, has he suddenly come to his senses?

(*Enter Zoe, stopping at back*)

GEORGE: In a word, I have seen and admired you!

DORA (*aside*): He has a strange way of showing it. European, I suppose.

GEORGE: If you would pardon the abruptness of the question, I would ask you, Do you think the sincere devotion of my life to make yours happy would succeed?

DORA (*aside*): Well, he has the oddest way of making love.

GEORGE: You are silent?

DORA: Mr. Peyton, I presume you have hesitated to make this avowal because you feared, in the present condition of affairs here, your object might be misconstrued, and that your attention was rather to my fortune than myself. (*A pause*) Why don't he speak?—I mean, you feared I might not give you credit for sincere and pure feelings. Well, you wrong me. I don't think you capable of anything else but—

GEORGE: No, I hesitated because an attachment I had formed before I had the pleasure of seeing you had not altogether died out.

DORA (*smiling*): Some of those sirens of Paris, I presume. (*Pausing*) I shall endeavor not to be jealous of the past; perhaps I have no right to be. (*Pausing*) But now that vagrant love is—eh, faded—is it not? Why don't you speak, sir?

GEORGE: Because, Miss Sunnyside, I have not learned to lie.

DORA: Good gracious—who wants you to?

GEORGE: I do, but I can't do it. No, the love I speak of is not such as you suppose—it is a passion that has grown up here since I arrived; but it is a hopeless, mad, wild feeling, that must perish.

DORA: Here! since you arrived! Impossible: you have seen no one; whom can you mean?

ZOE (*advancing*): Me.

GEORGE: Zoe!

DORA: You!

ZOE: Forgive him, Dora; for he knew no better until I told him. Dora, you are right. He is incapable of any but sincere and pure feelings—so are you. He loves me—what of that? You know you can't be jealous of a poor creature like me. If he caught the fever, were stung by a snake, or possessed of any other poisonous or unclean thing, you could pity, tend, love him through it, and for your gentle care he would love you in return. Well, is he not thus afflicted now? I am his love—he loves an Octoroon.

GEORGE: O, Zoe, you break my heart!

DORA: At college they said I was a fool—I must be. At New Orleans, they said, "She's pretty, very pretty, but no brains." I'm afraid they must be right; I can't understand a word of all this.

ZOE: Dear Dora, try to understand it with your heart. You love George; you love him dearly; I know it; and you deserve to be loved by him. He will love you—he must. His love for me will pass away—it shall. You heard him say it was hopeless. O, forgive him and me!

DORA (*weeping*): O, why did he speak to me at all then? You've made me cry, then, and I hate you both! (*Exit through room*)

(*Enter Mrs. Peyton and Scudder, M'Closky and Pointdexter*)

M'CLOSKY: I'm sorry to intrude, but the business I came upon will excuse me.

MRS. P.: Here is my nephew, sir.

ZOE: Perhaps I had better go.

M'CLOSKY: Wal, as it consarns you, perhaps you better had.

SCUD: Consarns Zoe?

M'CLOSKY: I don't know; she may as well hear the hull of it. Go on, Colonel—Colonel Pointdexter, ma'am—the mortgagee, auctioneer, and general agent.

POINT: Pardon me, madam, but do you know these papers?

(*He hands the papers to Mrs. Peyton*)

MRS. P.: (*taking them*): Yes, sir; they were the free papers of the girl Zoe; but they were in my husband's secretary. How came they in your possession?

M'CLOSKY: I—I found them.

GEORGE: And you purloined them?

M'CLOSKY: Hold on, you'll see. Go on, Colonel.

POINT: The list of your slaves is incomplete—it wants one.

SCUD: The boy Paul—we know it.

POINT: No, sir, you have omitted the Octoroon girl, Zoe.

MRS. P.: ⎫ Zoe!
ZOE: ⎭ Me!

POINT: At the time the judge executed those free papers to his infant slave, a judgment stood recorded against him; while that was on record he had no right to make away with his property. That judgment still exists: under it and others this estate is sold to-day. Those free papers ain't worth the sand that's on 'em.

MRS. P.: Zoe a slave! It is impossible!

POINT: It is certain, madam: the judge was negligent, and doubtless forgot this small formality.

SCUD: But the creditors will not claim the gal?

M'CLOSKY: Excuse me; one of the principal mortgagees has made the demand. (*Exeunt M'Closky and Pointdexter*)

. . . . . .

GEORGE: Zoe, they shall not take you from us while I live.

SCUD: Don't be a fool; they'd kill you, and then take her, just as soon as—stop: old Sunnyside, he'll buy her; that'll save her.

ZOE: No, it won't; we have confessed to Dora that we love each other. How can she then ask her father to free me?

SCUD: What in thunder made you do that?

ZOE: Because it was the truth, and I had rather be a slave with a free soul, than remain free with a slavish, deceitful heart. My father gives me freedom—at least he thought so. May Heaven bless him for the thought, bless him for the happiness he spread around my life. You say the proceeds of the sale will not cover his debts. Let me be sold then, that I may free his name. I give him back the liberty he bestowed upon me; for I can never repay him the love he bore his poor Octoroon child, on whose breast his last sigh was drawn, into whose eyes he looked with the last gaze of affection.

MRS. P.: O, my husband! I thank Heaven you have not lived to see this day.

ZOE: George, leave me! I would be alone a little while.

GEORGE: Zoe! (*Turning away overpowered*)

ZOE: Do not weep, George. Dear George, you now see what a miserable thing I am.

GEORGE: Zoe!

SCUD: I wish they could sell *me*! I brought half this ruin on this family, with my all-fired improvements. I deserve to be a nigger this day—I feel like one, inside. (*Exit Scudder*)

ZOE: Go now, George—leave me—take her with you. (*Exit Mrs. Peyton and George*) A slave! a slave! Is this a dream—for my brain reels with the blow? He said so. What! then I shall be sold!—sold! and my master—O! (*She falls on her knees, with her face in her hands*) No—no master but one. George—George —hush—they come! save me! No, (*looks off*) 'tis Pete and the servants—they come this way. (*Enters the inner room*)

(*Enter Pete, Grace, Minnie, Solon, Dido, and all Niggers*)

PETE: Cum yer now—stand round, 'cause I've got to talk to you darkies—keep dem chil'n quiet—don't make no noise, de missus up dar har us.

SOLON: Go on, Pete.

PETE: Gen'l'men, my colored frens and ladies, dar's mighty bad news gone round. Dis yer prop'ty to be sold—old Terrebonne —whar we all been raised, is gwine—dey's gwine to tak it away—can't stop here nohow.

OMNES: O-o!—O-o!

PETE: Hold quiet, you trash o' niggers! tink anybody wants you to cry? Who's you to set up screeching?—be quiet! But dis ain't all. Now, my cullud brethren, gird up your lines, and listen—hold on yer bref—it's a comin'. We tought dat de niggers would belong to de ole missus, and if she lost Terrebonne, we must live dere allers, and we would hire out, and bring our wages to old Missus Peyton.

OMNES: Ya! ya! Well—

PETE: Hush! I tell ye, 'tain't so—we can't do it—we've got to be sold—

OMNES: Sold!

PETE: Will you hush? she will har you. Yes! I listen dar jess now —dar was ole lady cryin'—Mas'r George—ah! you seen dem big tears in his eyes. O, Mas'r Scudder, he didn't cry zackly; both ob his eyes and cheek look like de bad Bayou in low season—so dry dat I cry for him. (*Raising his voice*) Den say de missus, " 'Tain't for de land I keer, but for dem poor niggers—dey'll be sold—dat wot stagger me." "No," say Mas'r George, "I'd rather sell myself fuss; but dey shan't suffer, nohow—I see 'em dam fuss."

OMNES: O, bless 'um! Bless Mas'r George.

PETE: Hole yer tongues. Yes, for you, for me, for dem little ones, dem folks cried. Now, den, if Grace dere wid her chil'n were all sold, she'll begin screechin' like a cat. She didn't mind how kind old judge was to her; and Solon, too, he'll holler, and break de ole lady's heart.

GRACE: No, Pete; no, I won't. I'll bear it.

PETE: I don't tink you will any more, but dis here will; 'cause de family spile Dido, dey has. She nebber was worth much a' dat nigger.

DIDO: How dar you say dat, you black nigger, you? I fetch as much as any odder cook in Louisiana.

PETE: What's the use of your takin' it kind, and comfortin' de missus' heart, if Minnie dere, and Louise, and Marie, and Julie is to spile it?

MINNIE: We won't, Pete; we won't.

PETE (to the men): Dar, do ye hear dat, ye mis'able darkies; dem gals is worth a boat load of kinder men dem is. Cum, for de pride of de family, let every darky look his best for the judge's sake— dat ole man so good to us, and dat ole woman—so dem strangers from New Orleans shall say, Dem's happy darkies, dem's a fine set of niggers; every one say when he's sold, "Lor' bless dis yer family I'm gwine out of, and send me as good a home."

OMNES: We'll do it, Pete; we'll do it.

PETE: Hush! hark! I tell ye dar's somebody in dar. Who is it?

GRACE: It's Missy Zoe. See! see!

PETE: Come along; she har what we say, and she's cryin' for us. None o' ye ign'rant niggers could cry for yerselves like dat. Come here quite: now quite. (*Exeunt Pete and all the Negroes, slowly*)

(*Enter Zoe who is supposed to have overheard the last scene*)

ZOE: O! must I learn from these poor wretches how much I owe, and how I ought to pay the debt? Have I slept upon the benefits I received, and never saw, never felt, never knew that I was forgetful and ungrateful? O, my father! my dear, dear father! forgive your poor child. You made her life too happy, and now these tears will flow. Let me hide them till I teach my heart. O, my—my heart! (*Exit, with a low, wailing, suffocating cry*)

PETE: Whar is she—whar is Miss Zoe?

SCUD: What's the matter?

PETE: Don't ax me. Whar's de gal? I say.

SCUD: Here she is—Zoe!—water—she faints.

PETE: No—no. 'Tain't no faint—she's a dying, sa: she got pizon from old Dido here, this mornin'.

GEORGE: Zoe!

SCUD: Zoe! is this true?—no, it ain't—darn it, say it ain't. Look here, you're free, you know; nary a master to hurt you now: you will stop here as long as you're a mind to, only don't look so.

DORA: Her eyes have changed color.

PETE: Dat's what her soul's gwine to do. It's going up dar, whar dere's no line atween folks.

GEORGE: She revives.

ZOE (*on the sofa*): George—where—where—

GEORGE: O, Zoe! what have you done?

ZOE: Last night I overheard you weeping in your room, and you said, "I'd rather see her dead than so!"

GEORGE: Have I then prompted you to this?

ZOE: No; but I loved you so, I could not bear my fate; and then I stood between your heart and hers. When I am dead she will not be jealous of your love for me, no laws will stand between us. Lift me; so—(*George raises her head*)—let me look at you, that your face may be the last I see of this world. O! George, you may, without a blush, confess your love for the Octoroon. (*She dies. George lowers her head gently and kneels beside her.*)

GEORGE WASHINGTON CABLE

(1844–1925)

Cable was "discovered" when Edward King visited New Orleans in 1872 while writing a series of articles on the "new South" for Scribner's Monthly. As a result of King's enthusiastic recommendation, Cable, a young bookkeeper with a passion for New Orleans history that manifested itself in the fiction he wrote in his spare time, published several stories in Scribner's during the 1870s. The Grandissimes appeared as a serial novel in the same magazine in 1878, and seven of Cable's tales were collected under the title Old Creole Days the following year. His reputation as a master of local color and a trenchant observer of Creole character was enhanced by the publication of several later novels and short-story collections, including the much-admired novelette, Madame Delphine (1881). In addition to writing, he joined Mark Twain on several lecture tours.

Cable, born in New Orleans, was descended from Virginia stock on his father's side, while his mother's family roots were in New England. He served in the Confederate cavalry and worked briefly as a reporter with the New Orleans Picayune before his appearance in Scribner's. Cable was one of the earliest writers to question the aristocratic tradition in Southern writing and to exploit the theme of decadence resulting from slavery. This theme, as well as his sensitive handling of the complex love-hate relationships between his black and white characters, has caused him to be viewed as a precursor of Faulkner. Sterling Brown wrote that "Cable gave shrewd, knowing interpretations of Negro character. The first genuine Southern liberal, Cable knew too much about slavery to idealize the old regime." Resentment over his liberal views apparently caused Cable's move from New Orleans to Northampton, Massachusetts, in 1885, though he denied that social pressures forced the move. Living in the North, he continued to express his social views in such works as The Silent South (1885) and The Negro Question (1890). These views unintentionally helped to launch the career of another New Orleans local-color writer, Grace King, who felt that Cable's slighting of Creoles while praising Negroes deserved to be answered in fiction.

The first group of excerpts here are intended as character sketches of Palmyre Philosophe, one of the most striking black women to be depicted in nineteenth-century literature and a principal character in The Grandissimes.

The following Bras-Coupé episode was originally composed as a short story under the title "Bibi," but the flogging and the hamstringing proved too violent for genteel tastes and the story was rejected by Scribner's as "unmitigatedly distressful." While acknowledging Cable's achievement as a realist, Newton Arvin felt that there was in his work a distasteful streak of "that peculiarly sweetish and effeminate sentimentality that throws one off in so much of the fiction of the period." Speaking of The Grandissimes (published as a book in 1880), Arvin wrote that "Even the great and terrible story of Bras-Coupé—the core around which the book grew—ends on a note of false and untrue feeling that for a moment seems almost to unman its power."

From The Grandissimes

[Palmyre Philosophe]

. . . On that lonely plantation at the Cannes Brulées, where Aurore Nancanou's childhood had been passed without brothers or sisters, there had been given her, according to the well-known custom of plantation life, a little quadroon slave-maid as her constant and only playmate. This maid began early to show herself in many ways remarkable. While yet a child she grew tall, lithe, agile; her eyes were large and black, and rolled and sparkled if she but turned to answer to her name. Her pale yellow forehead, low and shapely, with the jet hair above it, the heavily pencilled eyebrows and long lashes below, the faint red tinge that blushed with a kind of cold passion through the clear yellow skin of the cheek, the fullness of the red, voluptuous lips and the roundness of her perfect neck, gave her, even at fourteen, a barbaric and magnetic beauty, that startled the beholder like an unexpected drawing out of a jewelled sword. Such a type could have sprung only from high Latin ancestry on the one side and—we might venture—Jaloff African on the other. To these charms of person she added mental acuteness, conversational adroitness, concealed cunning, and noiseless but visible strength of will; and to these, that rarest of gifts in one of her tincture, the purity of true womanhood.

At fourteen a necessity which had been parleyed with for two years or more became imperative and Aurore's maid was taken from her. Explanation is almost superfluous. Aurore was to become a lady and her playmate a lady's maid; but not *her* maid, because the maid had become, of the two, the ruling spirit. It was a question of grave debate in the mind of M. De Grapion what disposition to make of her.

About this time the Grandissimes and De Grapions, through certain efforts of Honoré's father (since dead) were making some feeble pretences of mutual good feeling, and one of those Kentuckian dealers in corn and tobacco whose flat-boat fleets were always drifting down the Mississippi, becoming one day M. De Grapion's transient guest, accidentally mentioned a wish of Agricola Fusilier. Agricola, it appeared, had commissioned him to buy the most beautiful lady's maid that in his extended journeyings he might be able to find; he wanted to make her a gift to his niece, Honoré's sister. The Kentuckians saw the demand met in Aurore's playmate. M. De Grapion would not sell her. (Trade with a Grandissime? Let them suspect he needed money?) No; but he would ask Agricola to accept the services of the waiting-maid for, say, ten years. The Kentuckian accepted the proposition on the spot and it was by and by carried out. She was never recalled to the Cannes Brulées, but in subsequent years received her freedom from her master, and in New Orleans became Palmyre la Philosophe, as they say in the corrupt French of the old Creoles, or Palmyre Philosophe, noted for her taste and skill as a hairdresser, for the efficiency of her spells and the sagacity of her divinations, but most of all for the chaste austerity with which she practised the less baleful rites of the voudous.

. . . . . .

Doctor Keene, his ill-humor slept off, lay in bed in a quiescent state of great mental enjoyment. At times he would smile and close his eyes, open them again and murmur to himself, and turn his head languidly and smile again. And when the rain and wind, all tangled together, came against the window with a whirl and a slap, his smile broadened almost to laughter.

"He's in it," he murmured, "he's just reaching there. I would give fifty dollars to see him when he first gets into the house and sees where he is."

As this wish was finding expression on the lips of the little sick man, Joseph Frowenfeld was making room on a narrow door-step for the outward opening of a pair of small batten doors, upon which he had knocked with the vigorous haste of a man in the rain. As they parted, he hurriedly helped them open, darted within, heedless of the odd black shape which shuffled out of his way, wheeled and clapped them shut again, swung down the bar and then turned, and with the good-natured face that properly goes with a ducking, looked to see where he was.

One object—around which everything else instantly became nothing—set his gaze. On the high bed, whose hangings of blue we have already described, silently regarding the intruder with a pair of eyes that sent an icy thrill through him and fastened him where he stood, lay Palmyre Philosophe. Her dress was a long, snowy morning-gown, wound loosely about at the waist with a cord and tassel of scarlet silk; a bright-colored woollen shawl covered her from the waist down, and a necklace of red coral heightened to its utmost her untamable beauty.

An instantaneous indignation against Doctor Keene set the face of the speechless apothecary on fire, and this, being as instantaneously comprehended by the philosophe, was the best of introductions. Yet, her gaze did not change.

The Congo negress broke the spell with a bristling protest, all in African b's and k's, but hushed and drew off at a single word of command from her mistress.

In Frowenfeld's mind an angry determination was taking shape, to be neither trifled with nor contemned. And this again the quadroon discerned, before he was himself aware of it.

"Doctor Keene—" he began, but stopped, so uncomfortable were her eyes.

She did not stir or reply.

Then he bethought him with a start, and took off his dripping hat.

At this a perceptible sparkle of imperious approval shot along her glance; it gave the apothecary speech.

"The doctor is sick, and he asked me to dress your wound."

She made the slightest discernible motion of the head, remained for a moment silent, and then, still with the same eye, motioned her hand toward a chair near a comfortable fire.

He sat down. It would be well to dry himself. He drew near the hearth and let his gaze fall into the fire. When he presently lifted his eyes and looked full upon the woman with a steady, candid glance, she was regarding him with apparent coldness, but with secret diligence and scrutiny, and a yet more inward and secret surprise and admiration. Hard rubbing was bringing out the grain of the apothecary. But she presently suppressed the feeling. She hated men.

But Frowenfeld, even while his eyes met hers, could not resent her hostility. This monument of the shame of two races—this poisonous blossom of crime growing out of crime—this final, unanswerable white man's accuser—this would-be murderess— what ranks and companies would have to stand up in the Great Day with her and answer as accessory before the fact! He looked again into the fire.

The patient spoke:

"*Eh bi'n, Miché?*" Her look was severe, but less aggressive. The shuffle of the old negress's feet was heard and she appeared bearing warm and cold water and fresh bandages; after depositing them she tarried.

"Your fever is gone," said Frowenfeld, standing by the bed. He had laid his fingers on her wrist. She brushed them off and once more turned full upon him the cold hostility of her passionate eyes.

The apothecary, instead of blushing, turned pale.

"You—" he was going to say, "you insult me"; but his lips came tightly together. Two big cords appeared between his brows, and his blue eyes spoke for him. Then, as the returning blood rushed even to his forehead, he said, speaking his words one by one:

"Please understand that you must trust me."

She may not have understood his English, but she comprehended, nevertheless. She looked up fixedly for a moment, then passively closed her eyes. Then she turned, and Frowenfeld put out one strong arm, helped her to a sitting posture on the side of the bed and drew the shawl about her.

"Zizi," she said, and the negress, who had stood perfectly still since depositing the water and bandages, came forward and proceeded to bare the philosophe's superb shoulder. As Frowenfeld again put forward his hand, she lifted her own as if to prevent him, but he kindly and firmly put it away and addressed himself with silent diligence to his task; and by the time he had finished, his womanly touch, his commanding gentleness, his easy despatch, had inspired Palmyre not only with a sense of safety, comfort, and repose, but with a pleased wonder.

This woman had stood all her life with dagger drawn, on the defensive against what certainly was to her an unmerciful world. With possibly one exception, the man now before her was the only one she had ever encountered whose speech and gesture were clearly keyed to that profound respect which is woman's first, foundation claim on man. And yet by inexorable decree, she belonged to what we used to call "the happiest people under the sun." We ought to stop saying that.

So far as Palmyre knew, the entire masculine wing of the mighty and exalted race, three-fourths of whose blood bequeathed her none of its prerogatives, regarded her as legitimate prey. The man before her did not. There lay the fundamental difference that, in her sight, as soon as she discovered it, glorified him. Before this assurance the cold fierceness of her eyes gave way, and a friendlier light from them rewarded the apothecary's final touch. He called for more pillows, made a nest of them, and, as she let herself softly into it, directed his next consideration toward his hat and the door.

It was many an hour after he had backed out into the trivial remains of the rain-storm before he could replace with more tranquillizing images the vision of the philosophe reclining among her pillows, in the act of making that uneasy movement of her fingers upon the collar button of her robe, which women make when they are uncertain about the perfection of their dishabille, and giving her inaudible adieu with the majesty of an empress.

The Story of Bras-Coupé

. . . Bras-Coupé, they said, had been, in Africa and under another name, a prince among his people. In a certain war of conquest, to which he had been driven by *ennui*, he was captured, stripped of his royalty, marched down upon the beach of the Atlantic, and, attired as a true son of Adam, with two goodly arms intact, became a commodity. Passing out of first hands in barter for a looking-glass, he was shipped in good order and condition on board the good schooner *Egalité*, whereof Blank was master, to be delivered without delay at the port of Nouvelle Orléans (the dangers of fire and navigation excepted), unto Blank Blank. In witness whereof, He that made men's skins of different colors, but all blood of one, hath entered the same upon His book, and sealed it to the day of judgment.

Of the voyage little is recorded—here below; the less the better. Part of the living merchandise failed to keep; the weather was rough, the cargo large, the vessel small. However, the captain discovered there was room over the side, and there—all flesh is grass—from time to time during the voyage he jettisoned the unmerchantable.

Yet, when the reopened hatches let in the sweet smell of

the land, Bras-Coupé had come to the upper—the favored—the buttered side of the world; the anchor slid with a rumble of relief down through the muddy fathoms of the Mississippi, and the prince could hear through the schooner's side the savage current of the river, leaping and licking about the bows, and whimpering low welcomes home. A splended picture to the eyes of the royal captive, as his head came up out of the hatchway, was the little Franco-Spanish-American city that lay on the low, brimming bank. There were little forts that showed their white-washed teeth; there was a green parade-ground, and yellow bar-racks, and cabildo, and hospital, and cavalry stables, and custom-house, and a most inviting jail, convenient to the cathedral—all of dazzling white and yellow, with a black stripe marking the track of the conflagration of 1794, and here and there among the low roofs a lofty one with round-topped dormer windows and a breezy belvidere looking out upon the plantations of coffee and indigo beyond the town.

When Bras-Coupé staggered ashore, he stood but a moment among a drove of "likely boys," before Agricola Fusilier, managing the business adventures of the Grandissime estate, as well as the residents thereon, and struck with admiration for the physical beauties of the chieftain (a man may even fancy a negro—as a negro), bought the lot, and loth to resell him with the rest to some unappreciative 'Cadian, induced Don José Martinez' over-seer to become his purchaser.

Down in the rich parish of St. Bernard (whose boundary line now touches that of the distended city) lay the plantation, known, before Bras-Coupé passed away, as La Renaissance. Here it was that he entered at once upon a chapter of agreeable sur-prises. He was humanely met, presented with a clean garment, lifted into a cart drawn by oxen, taken to a whitewashed cabin of logs, finer than his palace at home, and made to comprehend that it was a free gift. He was also given some clean food, where-upon he fell sick. At home it would have been the part of piety for the magnate next the throne to launch him heavenward at once; but now, healing doses were administered, and to his amaze-ment he recovered. It reminded him that he was no longer king.

His name, he replied to an inquiry touching that subject, was

—— ——, something in the Jaloff tongue, which he by and by condescended to render into Congo: Mioko-Koanga, in French Bras-Coupé, the Arm Cut Off. Truly it would have been easy to admit, had this been his meaning, that his tribe, in losing him, had lost its strong right arm close off at the shoulder; not so easy for his high-paying purchaser to allow, if this other was his intent; that the arm which might no longer shake the spear or swing the wooden sword, was no better than a useless stump never to be lifted for aught else. But whether easy to allow or not, that was his meaning. He made himself a type of all Slavery, turning into flesh and blood the truth that all Slavery is maiming.

He beheld more luxury in a week than all his subjects had seen in a century. Here Congo girls were dressed in cottons and flannels worth, where he came from, an elephant's tusk apiece. Everybody wore clothes—children and lads alone excepted. Not a lion had invaded the settlement since his immigration. The serpents were as nothing; an occasional one coming up through the floor—that was all. True, there was more emaciation than unassisted conjecture could explain—a profusion of enlarged joints and diminished muscles, which, thank God, was even then confined to a narrow section and disappeared with Spanish rule. He had no experimental knowledge of it; nay, regular meals, on the contrary, gave him anxious concern, yet had the effect—spite of his apprehension that he was being fattened for a purpose—of restoring the herculean puissance which formerly in Africa had made him the terror of the battle.

When one day he had come to be quite himself, he was invited out into the sunshine, and escorted by the driver (a sort of foreman to the overseer), went forth dimly wondering. They reached a field where some men and women were hoeing. He had seen men and women—subjects of his—labor—a little—in Africa. The driver handed him a hoe; he examined it with silent interest—until by signs he was requested to join the pastime.

"What?"

He spoke, not with his lips, but with the recoil of his splendid frame and the ferocious expansion of his eyes. This invitation was a cataract of lightning leaping down an ink-black sky. In one instant of all-pervading clearness he read his sentence—WORK.

Bras-Coupé was six feet five. With a sweep as quick as instinct the back of the hoe smote the driver full in the head. Next, the prince lifted the nearest Congo crosswise, brought thirty-two teeth together in his wildly kicking leg and cast him away as a bad morsel; then throwing another into the branches of a willow, and a woman over his head into a draining-ditch, he made one bound for freedom, and fell to his knees, rocking from side to side under the effect of a pistol-ball from the overseer. It had struck him in the forehead, and, running around the skull in search of a penetrable spot, tradition—which sometimes jests— says came out despairingly, exactly where it had entered.

It so happened that, except the overseer, the whole company were black. Why should the trivial scandal be blabbed? A plaster or two made everything even in a short time, except in the driver's case—for the driver died. The woman whom Bras-Coupé had thrown over his head lived to sell calas to Joseph Frowenfeld.

Don José, young and austere, knew nothing about agriculture and cared as much about human nature. The overseer often thought this, but never said it; he would not trust even himself with the dangerous criticism. When he ventured to reveal the foregoing incidents to the Señor he laid all the blame possible upon the man whom death had removed beyond the reach of correction, and brought his account to a climax by hazarding the assertion that Bras-Coupé was an animal that could not be whipped.

"Caramba!" exclaimed the master, with gentle emphasis, "how so?"

"Perhaps Señor had better ride down to the quarters," replied the overseer.

It was a great sacrifice of dignity, but the master made it.

"Bring him out."

They brought him out—chains on his feet, chains on his wrists, an iron yoke on his neck. The Spanish-Creole master had often seen the bull, with his long, keen horns and blazing eye, standing in the arena; but this was as though he had come face to face with a rhinoceros.

"This man is not a Congo," he said.

"He is a Jaloff," replied the encouraged overseer. "See his fine, straight nose; moreover, he is a *candio*—a prince. If I whip him he will die."

The dauntless captive and fearless master stood looking into each other's eyes until each recognized in the other his peer in physical courage, and each was struck with an admiration for the other which no after difference was sufficient entirely to destroy. Had Bras-Coupé's eye quailed but once—just for one little instant —he would have got the lash; but, as it was—

"Get an interpreter," said Don José; then, more privately, "and come to an understanding. I shall require it of you."

Where might one find an interpreter—one not merely able to render a Jaloff's meaning into Creole French, or Spanish, but with such a turn for diplomatic correspondence as would bring about an "understanding" with this African buffalo? The overseer was left standing and thinking, and Clemence, who had not forgotten who threw her into the draining-ditch, cunningly passed by.

"Ah, Clemence—"

"*Mo pas capabe! Mo pas capabe!* (I cannot, I cannot!) *Ya, ya, ya! 'oir Miché Agricol' Fusilier! ouala yune bon monture, oui!*"— which was to signify that Agricola could interpret the very Papa Lébat.

"Agricola Fusilier! The last man on earth to make peace."

But there seemed to be no choice, and to Agricola the overseer went. It was but a little ride to the Grandissime place.

"I, Agricola Fusilier, stand as an interpreter to a negro? H-sir!"

"But I thought you might know of some person," said the weakening applicant, rubbing his ear with his hand.

"Ah!" replied Agricola, addressing the surrounding scenery, "if I did not—who would? You may take Palmyre."

The overseer softly smote his hands together at the happy thought.

"Yes," said Agricola, "take Palmyre; she has picked up as many negro dialects as I know European languages."

And she went to the don's plantation as interpretess, followed by Agricola's prayer to Fate that she might in some way be overtaken by disaster. The two hated each other with all the strength they had. He knew not only her pride, but her passion for the absent Honoré. He hated her, also, for her intelligence, for the high favor in which she stood with her mistress, and for her invincible spirit, which was more offensively patent to him than to others, since he was himself the chief object of her silent detestation.

It was Palmyre's habit to do nothing without painstaking. "When Mademoiselle comes to be Señora," thought she—she knew that her mistress and the don were affianced—"it will be well to have Señor's esteem. I shall endeavor to succeed." It was from this motive, then, that with the aid of her mistress she attired herself in a resplendence of scarlet and beads and feathers that could not fail the double purpose of connecting her with the children of Ethiopia and commanding the captive's instant admiration.

Alas for those who succeed too well! No sooner did the African turn his tiger glance upon her than the fire of his eyes died out; and when she spoke to him in the dear accents of his native tongue, the matter of strife vanished from his mind. He loved.

He sat down tamely in his irons and listened to Palmyre's argument as a wrecked mariner would listen to ghostly church-bells. He would give a short assent, feast his eyes, again assent, and feast his ears; but when at length she made bold to approach the actual issue, and finally uttered the loathed word, Work, he rose up, six feet five, a statue of indignation in black marble.

And then Palmyre, too, rose up, glorying in him, and went to explain to master and overseer. Bras-Coupé understood, she said, that he was a slave—it was the fortune of war, and he was a warrior; but, according to a generally recognized principle in African international law, he could not reasonably be expected to work.

"As Señor will remember I told him," remarked the overseer; "how can a man expect to plow with a zebra?"

Here he recalled a fact in his early experience. An African of this stripe had been found to answer admirably as a "driver" to make others work. A second and third parley, extending through two or three days, were held with the prince, looking to his appointment to the vacant office of driver; yet what was the master's amazement to learn at length that his Highness declined the proffered honor.

"Stop!" spoke the overseer again, detecting a look of alarm in Palmyre's face as she turned away, "he doesn't do any such thing. If Señor will let me take the man to Agricola—"

"No!" cried Palmyre, with an agonized look, "I will tell. He will take the place and fill it if you will give me to him for his own—but oh, messieurs, for the love of God—I do not want to be his wife!"

The overseer looked at the Señor, ready to approve whatever he should decide. Bras-Coupé's intrepid audacity took the Spaniard's heart by irresistible assault.

"I leave it entirely with Señor Fusilier," he said.

"But he is not my master; he has no right—"

"Silence!"

And she was silent; and so, sometimes, is fire in the wall.

Agricola's consent was given with malicious promptness, and as Bras-Coupé's fetters fell off it was decreed that, should he fill his office efficiently, there should be a wedding on the rear veranda of the Grandissime mansion simultaneously with the one already appointed to take place in the grand hall of the same house six months from that present day. In the meanwhile Palmyre should remain with Mademoiselle, who had promptly but quietly made up her mind that Palmyre should not be wed unless she wished to be. Bras-Coupé made no objection, was royally worthless for a time, but learned fast, mastered the "gumbo" dialect in a few weeks, and in six months was the most valuable man ever bought for gourde dollars. Nevertheless, there were but three persons within as many square miles who were not most vividly afraid of him.

The first was Palmyre. His bearing in her presence was ever one of solemn, exalted respect, which, whether from pure magnanimity in himself, or by reason of her magnetic eye, was something worth being there to see. "It was royal!" said the overseer.

The second was not that official. When Bras-Coupé said—as, at stated intervals, he did say—"*Mo courri c'ez Agricole Fusilier 'pou oir' n'amourouse* (I go to Agricola Fusilier to see my betrothed)," the overseer would sooner have intercepted a score of painted Chickasaws than that one lover. He would look after him and shake a prophetic head. "Trouble coming; better not deceive that fellow"; yet that was the very thing Palmyre dared do. Her admiration for Bras-Coupé was almost boundless. She rejoiced in his stature; she revelled in the contemplation of his untamable spirit; he seemed to her the gigantic embodiment of her own dark, fierce will, the expanded realization of her lifetime longing for terrible strength. But the single deficiency in all this impassioned regard was—what so many fairer loves have found impossible to explain to so many gentler lovers—an entire absence of preference; her heart she could not give him—she did not have it. Yet after her first prayer to the Spaniard and his overseer for deliverance, to the secret surprise and chagrin of her young mistress, she simulated content. It was artifice; she knew Agricola's power, and to seem to consent was her one chance with him. He might thus be beguiled into withdrawing his own consent. That failing, she had Mademoiselle's promise to come to the rescue, which she could use at the last moment; and that failing, there was a dirk in her bosom, for which a certain hard breast was not too hard. Another element of safety, of which she knew nothing, was a letter from the Cannes Brulées. The word had reached there that love had conquered— that, despite all hard words, and rancor, and positive injury, the Grandissime hand—the fairest of Grandissime hands—was about to be laid into that of one who without much stretch might be called a De Grapion; that there was, moreover, positive effort being made to induce a restitution of old gaming-table spoils. Honoré and Mademoiselle, his sister, one on each side of the Atlantic, were striving for this end. Don José sent this intelligence to his kinsman as glad tidings (a lover never imagines there are two sides to that which makes him happy), and, to add a touch of humor, told how Palmyre, also, was given to the chieftain. The letter that came back to the young Spaniard did not blame him so much: *he* was ignorant of all the facts; but a very formal one to Agricola begged to notify him that if Palmyre's union with Bras-Coupé should be completed, as sure as there was a God in heaven, the writer would have the life of the man who knowingly had thus endeavored to dishonor one who *shared the blood of the De Grapions*. Thereupon Agricola, contrary to his general character, began to drop hints to Don José that the engagement of Bras-Coupé and Palmyre need not be considered irreversible; but the don was not desirous of disappointing his terrible pet. Palmyre, unluckily, played her game a little too deeply. She thought the moment had come for herself to insist on the match, and thus provoke Agricola to forbid it. To her incalculable dismay she saw him a second time reconsider and become silent.

The second person who did not fear Bras-Coupé was Mademoiselle. On one of the giant's earliest visits to see Palmyre he obeyed the summons which she brought him, to appear before the lady. A more artificial man might have objected on the score of dress, his attire being a single gaudy garment tightly enveloping the waist and thighs. As his eyes fell upon the beautiful white lady he prostrated himself upon the ground, his arms outstretched before him. He would not move till she was gone. Then he arose like a hermit who has seen a vision. *"Bras-Coupé 'n pas oulé oir zombis* (Bras-Coupé dares not look upon a spirit).*"* From that hour he worshipped. He saw her often; every time, after one glance at her countenance, he would prostrate his gigantic length with his face in the dust.

The third person who did not fear him was—Agricola? Nay, it was the Spaniard—a man whose capability to fear anything in nature or beyond had never been discovered.

Long before the end of his probation Bras-Coupé would have slipped the entanglements of bondage, though as yet he felt them only as one feels a spider's web across the face, had not the master, according to a little affectation of the times, promoted him to be his game-keeper. Many a day did these two living magazines of wrath spend together in the dismal swamps and on the meagre intersecting ridges, making war upon deer and bear and wildcat; or on the Mississippi after wild goose and pelican; when even a word misplaced would have made either the slayer of the other. Yet the months ran smoothly round and the wedding night drew nigh.* A goodly company had assembled. All things were ready. The bride was dressed, the bridegroom had come. On the great back piazza, which had been inclosed with sail-cloth and lighted with lanterns, was Palmyre, full of a new and deep design and playing her deceit to the last, robed in costly garments to whose beauty was added the

* An over-zealous Franciscan once complained bitterly to the bishop of Havana, that people were being married in Louisiana in their own houses after dark and thinking nothing of it. It is not certain that he had reference to the Grandissime mansion; at any rate he was tittered down by the whole community. [Cable's note.]

charm of their having been worn once, and once only, by her be-
loved Mademoiselle.

But where was Bras-Coupé?

The question was asked of Palmyre by Agricola with a gaze that
meant in English, "No tricks, girl!"

Among the servants who huddled at the windows and door to see
the inner magnificence a frightened whisper was already going
round.

"We have made a sad discovery, Miché Fusilier," said the overseer. "Bras-Coupé is here; we have him in a room just yonder. But
—the truth is, sir, Bras-Coupé is a voudou."

"Well, and suppose he is; what of it? Only hush; do not let his
master know it. It is nothing; all the blacks are voudous, more or
less."

"But he declines to dress himself—has painted himself all rings
and stripes, antelope fashion."

"Tell him Agricola Fusilier says, 'dress immediately!' "

"Oh, Miché, we have said that five times already, and his answer
—you will pardon me—his answer is—spitting on the ground—
that you are a contemptible *dotchian* (white trash)."

There is nothing to do but privily to call the very bride—the
lady herself. She comes forth in all her glory, small, but oh, so
beautiful! Slam! Bras-Coupé is upon his face, his finger-tips touching the tips of her snowy slippers. She gently bids him go and dress,
and at once he goes.

Ah! now the question may be answered without whispering.
There is Bras-Coupé, towering above all heads, in ridiculous red
and blue regimentals, but with a look of savage dignity upon him
that keeps every one from laughing. The murmur of admiration
that passed along the thronged gallery leaped up into a shout in the
bosom of Palmyre. Oh, Bras-Coupé—heroic soul! She would not
falter. She would let the silly priest say his say—then her cunning
should help her *not to be* his wife, yet to show his mighty arm how
and when to strike.

"He is looking for Palmyre," said some, and at that moment he
saw her.

"Ho-o-o-o-o!"

Agricola's best roar was a penny trumpet to Bras-Coupé's note of joy. The whole masculine half of the in-door company flocked out to see what the matter was. Bras-Coupé was taking her hand in one of his and laying his other upon her head; and as some one made an unnecessary gesture for silence, he sang, beating slow and solemn time with his naked foot and with the hand that dropped hers to smite his breast:

> " 'En haut la montagne, zami,
>   Mo pé coupé canne, zami,
>   Pou' té' l' a' zen' zami,
>   Pou' mo baille Palmyre.
>   Ah! Palmyre, Palmyre mo c'ere,
>   Mo l'aimé' ou'—mo l'aimé ou'.' "

"Montagne?" asked one slave of another, "qui et çà, montagne? gnia pas quiç' ose comme çà dans la Louisiana? (What's a mountain? We haven't such things in Louisiana.)"

"Mein ye gagnein plein montagnes dans l'Afrique, listen!"

> " 'Ah! Palmyre, Palmyre, mo' piti zozo,
>   Mo l'aimé' ou'—mo l'aimé, l'aimé' ou'.' "

"Bravissimo!—" but just then a counter-attraction drew the white company back into the house. An old French priest with sandalled feet and a dirty face had arrived. There was a moment of hand-shaking with the good father, then a moment of palpitation and holding of the breath, and then—you would have known it by the turning away of two or three feminine heads in tears—the lily hand became the don's, to have and to hold, by authority of the Church and the Spanish king. And all was merry, save that outside there was coming up as villainous a night as ever cast black looks in through snug windows.

It was just as the newly wed Spaniard, with Agricola and all the guests, were concluding the by-play of marrying the darker couple, that the hurricane struck the dwelling. The holy and jovial father had made faint pretence of kissing this second bride; the ladies, colonels, dons, etc.—though the joke struck them as a trifle coarse —were beginning to laugh and clap hands again and the gowned jester to bow to right and left, when Bras-Coupé, tardily realizing the consummation of his hopes, stepped forward to embrace his wife.

"Bras-Coupé!"

The voice was that of Palmyre's mistress. She had not been able to comprehend her maid's behavior, but now Palmyre had darted upon her an appealing look.

The warrior stopped as if a javelin had flashed over his head and stuck in the wall.

"Bras-Coupé must wait till I give him his wife."

He sank, with hidden face, slowly to the floor.

"Bras-Coupé hears the voice of zombis; the voice is sweet, but the words are very strong; from the same sugar-cane comes *sirop* and *tafia*; Bras-Coupé says to zombis, 'Bras-Coupé will wait'; but if the *dotchians* deceive Bras-Coupé—" he rose to his feet with his eyes closed and his great black fist lifted over his head—"Bras-Coupé will call Voudou-Magnan!"

The crowd retreated and the storm fell like a burst of infernal applause. A whiff like fifty witches flouted up the canvas curtain of the gallery and a fierce black cloud, drawing the moon under its cloak, belched forth a stream of fire that seemed to flood the ground; a peal of thunder followed as if the sky had fallen in, the house quivered, the great oaks groaned, and every lesser thing bowed down before the awful blast. Every lip held its breath for a minute—or an hour, no one knew—there was a sudden lull of the wind, and the floods came down. Have you heard it thunder and rain in those Louisiana lowlands? Every clap seems to crack the world. It has rained a moment; you peer through the black pane —your house is an island, all the land is sea.

However, the supper was spread in the hall and in due time the guests were filled. Then a supper was spread in the big hall in the basement, below stairs, the sons and daughters of Ham came down like the fowls of the air upon a rice-field, and Bras-Coupé, throwing his heels about with the joyous carelessness of a smutted Mercury, for the first time in his life tasted the blood of the grape. A second, a fifth, a tenth time he tasted it, drinking more deeply each time, and would have taken it ten times more had not his bride cunningly concealed it. It was like stealing a tiger's kittens.

The moment quickly came when he wanted his eleventh

bumper. As he presented his request a silent shiver of consternation ran through the dark company; and when, in what the prince
meant as a remonstrative tone, he repeated the petition—splitting
the table with his fist by way of punctuation—there ensued a hus-
tling up staircases and a cramming into dim corners that left him
alone at the banquet.

Leaving the table, he strode upstairs and into the chirruping and
dancing of the grand salon. There was a halt in the cotillion and
a hush of amazement like the shutting off of steam. Bras-Coupé
strode straight to his master, laid his paw upon his fellow-bride-
groom's shoulder and in a thunder-tone demanded:

"More!"

The master swore a Spanish oath, lifted his hand and—fell,
beneath the terrific fist of his slave, with a bang that jingled the
candelabras. Dolorous stroke!—for the dealer of it. Given, apparently to him—poor, tipsy savage—in self-defence, punishable, in
a white offender, by a small fine or a few days' imprisonment, it
assured Bras-Coupé the death of a felon; such was the old *Code
Noir*. (We have a *Code Noir* now, but the new one is a mental
reservation, not an enactment.)

The guests stood for an instant as if frozen, smitten stiff with the
instant expectation of insurrection, conflagration and rapine (just
as we do to-day whenever some poor swaggering Pompey rolls up
his fist and gets a ball through his body), while, single-handed and
naked-fisted in a room full of swords, the giant stood over his master, making strange signs and passes and rolling out in wrathful
words of his mother tongue what it needed no interpreter to tell his
swarming enemies was a voudou malediction.

"*Nous sommes grigis!*" screamed two or three ladies, "we are
bewitched!"

"Look to your wives and daughters!" shouted a Brahmin-Man-
darin.

"Shoot the black devils without mercy!" cried a Mandarin-Fusi-
lier, unconsciously putting into a single outflash of words the whole
Creole treatment of race troubles.

With a single bound Bras-Coupé reached the drawing-room
door; his gaudy regimentals made a red and blue streak down the
hall; there was a rush of frilled and powdered gentlemen to the rear

veranda, an avalanche of lightning with Bras-Coupé in the midst making for the swamp, and then all without was blackness of darkness and all within was a wild commingled chatter of Creole, French, and Spanish tongues—in the midst of which the reluctant Agricola returned his dress-sword to its scabbard.

While the wet lanterns swung on crazily in the trees along the way by which the bridegroom was to have borne his bride; while Madame Grandissime prepared an impromptu bridal-chamber; while the Spaniard bathed his eye and the blue gash on his cheekbone; while Palmyre paced her room in a fever and wild tremor of conflicting emotions throughout the night and the guests splashed home after the storm as best they could, Bras-Coupé was practically declaring his independence on a slight rise of ground hardly sixty feet in circumference and lifted scarce above the water in the inmost depths of the swamp.

And what surroundings! Endless colonnades of cypresses; long, motionless drapings of gray moss; broad sheets of noisome waters, pitchy black, resting on bottomless ooze; cypress knees studding the surface; patches of floating green, gleaming brilliantly here and there; yonder where the sunbeams wedge themselves in, constellations of water-lilies, the many-hued iris, and a multitude of flowers that no man had named . . .

The pack of Cuban hounds that howl from Don José's kennels cannot snuff the trail of the stolen canoe that glides through the sombre blue vapors of the African's fastnesses. His arrows send no tell-tale reverberations to the distant clearing. Many a wretch in his native wilderness has Bras-Coupé himself, in palmier days, driven to just such an existence, to escape the chains and horrors of the barracoons; therefore not a whit broods he over man's inhumanity, but, taking the affair as a matter of course, casts about him for a future.

. . . . . .

One day at high noon the master was taken sick with fever.

The third noon after—the sad wife sitting by the bedside—suddenly, right in the centre of the room, with the open door behind him, stood the magnificent, half-nude form of Bras-Coupé. He did not fall down as the mistress's eyes met his, though all his flesh quivered. The master was lying with his eyes closed. The fever had done a fearful three days' work.

"*Mioko-koanga oulé so' femme.* (Bras-Coupé wants his wife.)"

The master started wildly and stared upon his slave.

"*Bras-Coupé oulé so' femme!*" repeated the black.

"Seize him!" cried the sick man, trying to rise.

But, though several servants had ventured in with frightened faces, none dared molest the giant. The master turned his entreating eyes upon his wife, but she seemed stunned, and only covered her face with her hands and sat as if paralyzed by a foreknowledge of what was coming.

Bras-Coupé lifted his great, black palm and commenced:

"*Mo cé voudrai que la maison ci là et tout ça qui pas femme' ici s'raient encore maudits!* (May this house and all in it who are not women be accursed.)"

The master fell back upon his pillow with a groan of helpless wrath.

The African pointed his finger through the open window.

"May its fields not know the plough nor nourish the cattle that overrun it."

The domestics, who had thus far stood their ground, suddenly rushed from the room like stampeded cattle, and at that moment appeared Palmyre.

"Speak to him," faintly cried the panting invalid.

She went firmly up to her husband and lifted her hand. With an easy motion, but quick as lightning, as a lion sets foot on a dog, he caught her by the arm.

"*Bras-Coupé oulé so' femme,*" he said, and just then Palmyre would have gone with him to the equator.

"You shall not have her!" gasped the master.

The African seemed to rise in height, and still holding his wife at arm's length, resumed his malediction:

"May weeds cover the ground until the air is full of their odor and the wild beasts of the forest come and lie down under their cover."

With a frantic effort the master lifted himself upon his elbow and extended his clenched fist in speechless defiance; but his brain reeled, his sight went out, and when again he saw, Palmyre and her mistress were bending over him, the overseer stood awkwardly by, and Bras-Coupé was gone.

The plantation became an invalid camp. The words of the voudou found fulfilment on every side. The plough went not out; the herds wandered through broken hedges from field to field and came up with staring bones and shrunken sides; a frenzied mob of weeds and thorns wrestled and throttled each other in a struggle for standing-room—rag-weed, smart-weed, sneeze-weed, bind-weed, iron-weed—until the burning skies of mid-summer checked their growth and crowned their unshorn tops with rank and dingy flowers.

"Why in the name of—St. Francis," asked the priest of the overseer, "didn't the Señora use her power over the black scoundrel when he stood and cursed, that day?"

"Why, to tell you the truth, father," said the overseer, in a discreet whisper, "I can only suppose she thought Bras-Coupé had half a right to do it."

"Ah, ah, I see; like her brother Honoré—looks at both sides of a question—a miserable practice; but why couldn't Palmyre use *her* eyes? They would have stopped him."

"Palmyre? Why Palmyre has become the best *monture* (Plutonian medium) in the parish. Agricola Fusilier himself is afraid of her. Sir, I think sometimes Bras-Coupé is dead and his spirit has gone into Palmyre. She would rather add to his curse than take from it."

"Ah!" said the jovial divine, with a fat smile, "castigation would help her case; the whip is a great sanctifier. I fancy it would even make a Christian of the inexpugnable Bras-Coupé."

But Bras-Coupé kept beyond the reach alike of the lash and of the Latin Bible.

. . . . . .

"The runaway slave," said the old French code, continued in force by the Spaniards, "the runaway slave who shall continue to be so for one month from the day of his being denounced to the officers of justice, shall have his ears cut off and shall be branded with the flower de luce on the shoulder; and on a second offence of the same nature, persisted in during one month of his being de-

nounced, he shall be hamstrung, and be marked with the flower
de luce on the other shoulder. On the third offence he shall die."
Bras-Coupé had run away only twice. "But," said Agricola, "these
'bossals' must be taught their place. Besides, there is Article 27 of
the same code: 'The slave who, having struck his master, shall have
produced a bruise, shall suffer capital punishment'—a very necessary law!" He concluded with a scowl upon Palmyre, who shot
back a glance which he never forgot.

The Spaniard showed himself very merciful—for a Spaniard; he
spared the captive's life. He might have been more merciful still;
but Honoré Grandissime said some indignant things in the African's favor, and as much to teach the Grandissimes a lesson as to
punish the runaway, he would have repented his clemency, as he
repented the momentary truce with Agricola, but for the tearful
pleading of the Señora and the hot, dry eyes of her maid. Because
of these he overlooked the offence against his person and estate,
and delivered Bras-Coupé to the law to suffer only the penalties
of the crime he had committed against society by attempting to be
a free man.

We repeat it for the credit of Palmyre, that she pleaded for
Bras-Coupé. But what it cost her to make that intercession, knowing that his death would leave her free, and that if he lived she
must be his wife, let us not attempt to say.

In the midst of the ancient town, in a part which is now crumbling away, stood the Calaboza, with its humid vaults, grated cells,
iron cages, and its whips; and there, soon enough, they strapped
Bras-Coupé face downward and laid on the lash. And yet not a
sound came from the mutilated but unconquered African to annoy
the ear of the sleeping city. . . .

He was brought at sunrise to the plantation. The air was sweet
with the smell of the weed-grown fields. The long-horned oxen that
drew him and the naked boy that drove the team stopped before
his cabin.

"You cannot put that creature in there," said the thoughtful
overseer. "He would suffocate under a roof—he has been too long
out-of-doors for that. Put him on my cottage porch." There, at
last, Palmyre burst into tears and sank down, while before her on
a soft bed of dry grass, rested the helpless form of the captive

giant, a cloth thrown over his galled back, his ears shorn from his head, and the tendons behind his knees severed. His eyes were dry, but there was in them that unspeakable despair that fills the eye of the charger when, fallen in battle, he gazes with sidewise-bended neck upon the ruin wrought upon him. His eye turned sometimes slowly to his wife. He need not demand her now—she was always by him.

There was much talk over him—much idle talk; no power or circumstance has ever been found that will keep a Creole from talking. He merely lay still under it with a fixed frown; but once some incautious tongue dropped the name of Agricola. The black man's eyes came so quickly round to Palmyre that she thought he would speak; but no; his words were all in his eyes. She answered their gleam with a fierce affirmative glance, whereupon he slowly bent his head and spat upon the floor.

There was yet one more trial of his wild nature. The mandate came from his master's sick-bed that he must lift the curse.

Bras-Coupé merely smiled. God keep thy enemy from such a smile!

The overseer, with a policy less Spanish than his master's, endeavored to use persuasion. But the fallen prince would not so much as turn one glance from his parted hamstrings. Palmyre was then besought to intercede. She made one poor attempt, but her husband was nearer doing her an unkindness than ever he had been before; he made a slow sign for silence—with his fist; and every mouth was stopped.

At midnight following, there came, on the breeze that blew from the mansion, a sound of running here and there, of wailing and sobbing—another Bridegroom was coming, and the Spaniard, with much such a lamp in hand as most of us shall be found with, neither burning brightly nor wholly gone out, went forth to meet Him.

"Bras-Coupé," said Palmyre, next evening, speaking low in his mangled ear, "the master is dead; he is just buried. As he was dying, Bras-Coupé, he asked that you would forgive him."

The maimed man looked steadfastly at his wife. He had not spoken since the lash struck him, and he spoke not now; but in those large, clear eyes, where his remaining strength seemed to have taken refuge as in a citadel, the old fierceness flared up for a moment, and then, like an expiring beacon, went out.

"Is your mistress well enough by this time to venture here?" whispered the overseer to Palmyre. "Let her come. Tell her not to fear, but to bring the babe—in her own arms, tell her—quickly!"

The lady came, her infant boy in her arms, knelt down beside the bed of sweet grass and set the child within the hollow of the African's arm. Bras-Coupé turned his gaze upon it; it smiled, its mother's smile, and put its hand upon the runaway's face, and the first tears of Bras-Coupé's life, the dying testimony of his humanity, gushed from his eyes and rolled down his cheek upon the infant's hand. He laid his own tenderly upon the babe's forehead, then removing it, waved it abroad, inaudibly moved his lips, dropped his arm, and closed his eyes. The curse was lifted.

"*Le pauv' dgiab'!*" said the overseer, wiping his eyes and looking fieldward. "Palmyre, you must get the priest."

The priest came, in the identical gown in which he had appeared the night of the two weddings. To the good father's many tender questions Bras-Coupé turned a failing eye that gave no answers; until, at length:

"Do you know where you are going?" asked the holy man.

"Yes," answered his eyes, brightening.

"Where?"

He did not reply; he was lost in contemplation, and seemed looking far away.

So the question was repeated.

"Do you know where you are going?"

And again the answer of the eyes. He knew.

"Where?"

The overseer at the edge of the porch, the widow with her babe, and Palmyre and the priest bending over the dying bed, turned an eager ear to catch the answer.

"To—" the voice failed a moment; the departing hero essayed again; again it failed; he tried once more, lifted his hand, and with an ecstatic, upward smile, whispered, "To—Africa"—and was gone.

[Clemence]

. . . "Oh," she resumed, as soon as she could be heard, "white folks is werry kine. Dey wants us to b'lieb we happy—dey *wants to b'lieb* we is. W'y, you know, dey 'bleeged to b'lieb it—fo' dey own cyumfut. 'Tis de sem weh wid de preache's; dey buil' we ow own sep'ate meet'n-houses; dey b'leebs us lak it de bess, an' dey *knows* dey lak it de bess."

The laugh at this was mostly her own. It is not a laughable sight to see the comfortable fractions of Christian communities everywhere striving, with sincere, pious, well-meant, criminal benevolence, to make their poor brethren contented with the ditch. Nor does it become so to see these efforts meet, or seem to meet, some degree of success. Happily man cannot so place his brother that his misery will continue unmitigated. You may dwarf a man to the mere stump of what he ought to be, and yet he will put out green leaves. "Free from care," we benignly observe of the dwarfed classes of society; but we forget, or have never thought, what a crime we commit when we rob men and women of their cares.

To Clemence the order of society was nothing. No upheaval could reach to the depth to which she was sunk. It is true, she was one of the population. She had certain affections toward people and places; but they were not of a consuming sort.

As for us, our feelings, our sentiments, affections, etc., are fine and keen, delicate and many; what we call refined. Why? Because we get them as we get our old swords and gems and laces—from our grandsires, mothers, and all. Refined they are—after centuries of refining. But the feelings handed down to Clemence had come through ages of African savagery; through fires that do not refine, but that blunt and blast and blacken and char; starvation, gluttony, drunkenness, thirst, drowning, nakedness, dirt, fetichism, debauchery, slaughter, pestilence and the rest—she was their heiress; they left her the cinders of human feelings. She remembered her mother. They had been separated in her childhood, in Virginia when it was a province. She remembered, with pride, the price her mother had brought at auction, and remarked, as an additional interesting item, that she had never seen or heard of her since. She had had children, assorted colors—had one with her now, the black boy that brought the basil to Joseph; the others were here and there, some in the Grandissime households or field-gangs, some elsewhere within occasional sight, some dead, some not accounted for. Husbands—like the Samaritan woman's. We know she was a constant singer and laugher. . . .

MARK TWAIN

(1835–1910)

Samuel Langhorne Clemens, or "Mark Twain," grew up in Hannibal, Missouri, the Mississippi River town immortalized in Tom Sawyer and Huckleberry Finn. After a few years as an itinerant newspaperman he set out in 1856 to seek his fortune in South America, but while traveling down the Mississippi he was overcome by the river's spell and decided to become a steamboat pilot. When the start of the Civil War put an end to river-boat operations, he volunteered for service in a Confederate militia unit, but soon deserted the war and traveled west to serve as assistant to his brother Orion, who had been appointed Secretary of the Nevada Territory. In 1863, while working on the Virginia City Territorial Enterprise, he adopted the pen name "Mark Twain," the Mississippi leadsman's cry for "safe water," and three years later he began a highly successful career as a public lecturer under the same pseudonym. Married in 1870 to Olivia Langdon, a wealthy woman from a genteel Eastern family, he settled in Hartford, Connecticut. Already known for several books of humorous stories and travel sketches, Twain soon produced his three masterpieces—The Adventures of Tom Sawyer (1876), Life on the Mississippi (1883), and The Adventures of Huckleberry Finn (1884). The bankruptcy which followed an unsuccessful investment in an early typesetting machine; the death of his daughter Susy in 1898 while he was engaged in a world-wide lecture tour to pay off his debts; and the death of his wife in 1904 all contributed to the increasingly bitter mood of his later works.

Despite his sympathy for the Confederacy, Twain was a consistent opponent of slavery and was once termed by his friend William Dean Howells "the most desouthernized Southerner I have ever known." While still a child he had seen a white master kill a slave, and one of the most disturbing memories of his youth was the sad faces of the slaves who lay stretched out on the streets of Hannibal, chained together to await shipment down the river. In later years he paid the way of a Negro student through Yale; he explained to Howells that he was doing so as "part of the reparation due from every white man to every black man."

Huckleberry Finn has long been hailed for what Ralph Ellison has termed its "great drama of interracial fraternity," its development of a relationship which begins with Huck's treatment of Nigger Jim as a minstrel darky and progresses to the point where Huck implicitly acknowledges Jim's humanity and cuts his ties to the conventional Southern morality which defined his fellow fugitive as a mere thing. Twain once more focused on slavery in Pudd'nhead Wilson (1894), in which the mulatto slave Roxana, fearful that the slave son she had borne a Virginia gentleman will be sold down the river, substitutes her own child for that of her white master, with the result that the white child is raised in slavery while the "black" receives a gentleman's education.

From The Adventures of Huckleberry Finn

Our Gang's Dark Oath

We went tiptoeing along a path amongst the trees back towards the end of the widow's garden, stooping down so as the branches wouldn't scrape our heads. When we was passing by the kitchen I fell over a root and made a noise. We scrouched down and laid still. Miss Watson's big nigger, named Jim, was setting in the kitchen door; we could see him pretty clear, because there was a light behind him. He got up and stretched his neck out about a minute, listening. Then he says:

"Who dah?"

He listened some more; then he came tiptoeing down and stood right between us; we could 'a' touched him, nearly: Well, likely it was minutes and minutes that there warn't a sound, and we all there so close together. There was a place on my ankle that got to itching, but I dasn't scratch it; and then my ear begun to itch; and next my back, right between my shoulders. Seemed like I'd die if I couldn't scratch. Well, I've noticed that thing plenty times since. If you are with the quality, or at a funeral, or trying to go to sleep when you ain't sleepy—if you are anywheres where it don't do for you to scratch, why you will itch all over in upward of a thousand places. Pretty soon Jim says:

"Say, who is you? Whar is you? Dog my cats ef I didn' hear sumf'n. Well, I know what I's gwyne to do: I's gwyne to set down here and listen tell I hears it ag'in."

So he set down on the ground betwixt me and Tom. He leaned his back up against a tree, and stretched his legs out till one of them most touched one of mine. My nose begun to itch. It itched till the tears come into my eyes. But I dasn't scratch. Then it begun to itch on the inside. Next I got to itching underneath. I didn't know how I was going to set still. This miserableness went on as much as six or seven minutes; but it seemed a sight longer than that. I was itching in eleven different places now. I reckoned I couldn't stand it more'n a minute longer, but I set my teeth hard and got ready to try. Just then Jim begun to breathe heavy; next he begun to snore—and then I was pretty soon comfortable again.

Tom he made a sign to me—kind of a little noise with his mouth—and we went creeping away on our hands and knees. When we was ten foot off Tom whispered to me, and wanted to tie Jim to the tree for fun. But I said no; he might wake and make a disturbance, and then they'd find out I warn't in. Then Tom said he hadn't got candles enough, and he would slip in the kitchen and get some more. I didn't want him to try. I said Jim might wake up and come. But Tom wanted to resk it; so we slid in there and got three candles, and Tom laid five cents on the table for pay. Then we got out, and I was in a sweat to get away; but nothing would do Tom but he must crawl to where Jim was, on his hands and knees, and play something on him. I waited, and it seemed a good while, everything was so still and lonesome.

As soon as Tom was back we cut along the path, around the garden fence, and by and by fetched up on the steep top of the hill the other side of the house. Tom said he slipped Jim's hat off of his head and hung it on a limb right over him, and Jim stirred a little, but he didn't wake. Afterward Jim said the witches bewitched him and put him in a trance, and rode him all over the state, and then set him under the trees again, and hung his hat on a limb to show who done it. And next time Jim told it he said they rode him down to New Orleans; and, after that, every time he told it he spread it more and more, till by and by he said they rode him all over the world, and tired him most to death, and his back was all over saddle-boils. Jim was monstrous proud about it, and he got so he wouldn't hardly notice the other niggers. Niggers would come miles to hear Jim tell about it, and he was more looked up to than any nigger in that country. Strange niggers would stand with their mouths open and look him all over, same as if he was a wonder. Niggers is always talking about witches in the dark by the kitchen fire; but whenever one was talking and letting on to know all about such things, Jim would happen in and say, "Hm! What you know 'bout witches?" and that nigger was corked up and had to take a back seat. Jim always kept that five-center piece round his neck with a string, and said it was a charm the devil give to him with his own hands, and told him he could cure anybody with it and fetch witches whenever he wanted to just by saying something to it; but he never told what it was he said to it. Niggers would come from all around there and give Jim anything they had, just for a sight of that five-center piece; but they wouldn't touch it, because the devil had had his hands on it. Jim was most ruined for a servant, because he got stuck up on account of having seen the devil and been rode by witches. . . .

Was Solomon Wise?

. . . I read considerable to Jim about kings and dukes and earls and such, and how gaudy they dressed, and how much style they put on, and called each other your majesty, and your grace, and your lordship, and so on, 'stead of mister; and Jim's eyes bugged out, and he was interested. He says:

"I didn't know dey was so many un um. I hain't hearn 'bout none un um, skasely, but ole King Sollermun, onless you counts dem kings dat's in a pack er k'yards. How much do a king git?"

"Get?" I says; "why, they get a thousand dollars a month if they want it; they can have just as much as they want; everything belongs to them."

"Ain' dat gay? En what dey got to do, Huck?"

"*They* don't do nothing! Why, how you talk! They just set around."

"No; is dat so?"

"Of course it is. They just set around—except, maybe, when there's a war; then they go to the war. But other times they just lazy around; or go hawking—just hawking and sp—Sh!—d'you hear a noise?"

We skipped out and looked; but it warn't nothing but the flutter of a steamboat's wheel away down, coming around the point; so we come back.

"Yes," says I, "and other times, when things is dull, they fuss with the parlment; and if everybody don't go just so he whacks their heads off. But mostly they hang round the harem."

"Roun' de which?"

"Harem."

"What's de harem?"

"The place where he keeps his wives. Don't you know about the harem? Solomon had one; he had about a million wives."

"Why, yes, dat's so; I—I'd done forgot it. A harem's a bo'd'n-house, I reck'n. Mos' likely dey has rackety times in de nussery. En I reck'n de wives quarrels considable; en dat 'crease de racket. Yit dey say Sollermun de wises' man dat ever liv'. I doan' take no stock in dat. Bekase why: would a wise man want to live in de mids' er sich a blim-blammin' all de time? No—'deed he wouldn't. A wise man 'ud take en buil' a biler-factry; en den he could shet *down* de biler-factry when he want to res'."

"Well, but he *was* the wisest man, anyway; because the widow she told me so, her own self."

"I doan' k'yer what de widder say, he *warn't* no wise man

nuther. He had some er de dad-fetchedes' ways I ever see. Does you know 'bout dat chile dat he 'uz gwyne to chop in two?"

"Yes, the widow told me all about it."

"*Well*, den! Warn' dat de beatenes' notion in de worl'? You jes' take en look at it a minute. Dah's de stump, dah—dat's one er de women; heah's you—dat's de yuther one; I's Sollermun; en dish yer dollar bill's de chile. Bofe un you claims it. What does I do? Does I shin aroun' mongs' de neighbors en fine out which un you de bill *do* b'long to, en han' it over to de right one, all safe en soun', de way dat anybody dat had any gumption would? No; I take en whack de bill in *two*, en give half un it to you, en de yuther half to de yuther woman. Dat's de way Sollermun was gwyne to do wid de chile. Now I want to ast you: what's de use er dat half a bill?—can't buy noth'n wid it. En what use is a half a chile? I wouldn' give a dern for a million un um."

"But hang it, Jim, you've clean missed the point—blame it, you've missed it a thousand mile."

"Who? Me? Go 'long. Doan' talk to *me* 'bout yo' pints. I reck'n I knows sense when I sees it; en day ain' no sense in sich doin's as dat. De 'spute warn't 'bout a half a chile, de 'spute was 'bout a whole chile; en de man dat think he kin settle a 'spute 'bout a whole chile wid a half a chile doan' know enough to come in out'n de rain. Doan' talk to me 'bout Sollermun, Huck, I knows him by de back."

"But I tell you you don't get the point."

"Blame de point! I reck'n I knows what I knows. En mine you, de *real* pint is down furder—it's down deeper. It lays in de way Sollermun was raised. You take a man dat's got on'y one or two chillen; is dat man gwyne to be wasteful o' chillen? No, he ain't; he can't 'ford it. *He* knows how to value 'em. But you take a man dat's got 'bout five million chillen runnin' roun' de house, en it's diffunt. *He* as soon chop a chile in two as a cat. Dey's plenty mo'. A chile er two, mo' er less, warn't no consekens to Sollermun, dad fetch him!"

I never see such a nigger. If he got a notion in his head once, there warn't no getting it out again. He was the most down on Solomon of any nigger I ever see. So I went to talking about other kings, and let Solomon slide. . . .

Fooling Poor Old Jim

. . . It was a monstrous big river here, with the tallest and the thickest kind of timber on both banks; just a solid wall, as well as I could see by the stars. I looked away down-stream, and seen a black speck on the water. I took after it; but when I got to it it warn't nothing but a couple of saw-logs made fast together. Then I see another speck, and chased that; then another, and this time I was right. It was the raft.

When I got to it Jim was setting there with his head down between his knees, asleep, with his right arm hanging over the steering-oar. The other oar was smashed off, and the raft was littered up with leaves and branches and dirt. So she'd had a rough time.

I made fast and laid down under Jim's nose on the raft, and begun to gap, and stretch my fists out against Jim, and says: "Hello, Jim, have I been asleep? Why didn't you stir me up?"

"Goodness gracious, is dat you, Huck? En you ain' dead—you ain' drownded—you's back ag'in? It's too good for true, honey, it's too good for true. Lemme look at you chile, lemme feel o' you. No, you ain' dead! you's back ag'in, 'live en soun', jis de same ole Huck—de same ole Huck, thanks to goodness!"

"What's the matter with you, Jim? You been a-drinking?"

"Drinkin'? Has I ben a-drinkin'? Has I had a chance to be a-drinkin'?"

"Well, then, what makes you talk so wild?"

"How does I talk wild?"

"*How?* Why, hain't you been talking about my coming back, and all that stuff, as if I'd been gone away?"

"Huck—Huck Finn, you look me in de eye; look me in de eye. *Hain't* you ben gone away?"

"Gone away? Why, what in the nation do you mean? I hain't been gone anywheres. Where would I go to?"

"Well, looky here, boss, dey's sumfn wrong, dey is. Is I *me*, or who *is* I? Is I heah, or whah *is* I? Now dat's what I wants to know."

"Well, I think you're here, plain enough, but I think you're a tangle-headed old fool, Jim."

"I is, is I? Well, you answer me dis: Didn't you tote out de line in de canoe fer to make fas' to de towhead?"

"No, I didn't. What towhead? I hain't seen no towhead."

"You hain't seen no towhead? Looky here, didn't de line pull loose en de raf' go a-hummin' down de river, en leave you en de canoe behine in de fog?"

"What fog?"

"Why, *de* fog!—de fog dat's been aroun' all night. En didn't you whoop, en didn't I whoop, tell we got mix' up in de islands en one un us got los' en t'other one was jis' as good as los', 'kase he didn' know whah he wuz? En didn't I bust up again a lot er dem islands en have a turrible time en mos' git drownded? Now ain't dat so, boss—ain't it so? You answer me dat."

"Well, this is too many for me, Jim. I hain't seen no fog, nor no islands, nor no troubles, nor nothing. I been setting here talking with you all night till you went to sleep about ten minutes ago, and I reckon I done the same. You couldn't 'a' got drunk in that time, so of course you've been dreaming."

"Dad fetch it, how is I gwyne to dream all dat in ten minutes?"

"Well, hang it all, you did dream it, because there didn't any of it happen."

"But, Huck, it's all jis' as plain to me as—"

"It don't make no difference how plain it is; there ain't nothing in it. I know, because I've been here all the time."

Jim didn't say nothing for about five minutes, but set there studying over it. Then he says:

"Well, den, I reck'n I did dream it, Huck; but dog my cats ef it ain't de powerfulest dream I ever see. En I hain't ever had no dream b'fo' dat's tired me like dis one."

"Oh, well, that's all right, because a dream does tire a body like everything sometimes. But this one was a staving dream; tell me all about it, Jim."

So Jim went to work and told me the whole thing right through, just as it happened, only he painted it up considerable. Then he said he must start in and " 'terpret" it, because it was sent for a warning. He said the first towhead stood for a man that would try to do us some good, but the current was another man that would get us away from him. The whoops was warnings that would come to us every now and then, and if we didn't try hard to make out to understand them they'd just take us into bad luck, 'stead of keeping us out of it. The lot of towheads was troubles we was going to get into with quarrelsome people and all kinds of mean folks, but if we minded our business and didn't talk back and aggravate them, we would pull through and get out of the fog and into the big clear river, which was the free states, and wouldn't have no more trouble.

It had clouded up pretty dark just after I got on to the raft, but it was clearing up again now.

"Oh, well, that's all interpreted well enough as far as it goes, Jim," I says; "but what does *these* things stand for?"

It was the leaves and rubbish on the raft and the smashed oar. You could see them first-rate now.

Jim looked at the trash, and then looked at me, and back at the trash again. He had got the dream fixed so strong in his head that he couldn't seem to shake it loose and get the facts back into its place again right away. But when he did get the thing straightened around he looked at me steady without ever smiling, and says:

"What do dey stan' for? I's gwyne to tell you. When I got all wore out wid work, en wid de callin' for you, en went to sleep, my heart wuz mos' broke bekase you wuz los', en I didn' k'yer no' mo' what become er me en de raf'. En when I wake up en find you back ag'in, all safe en soun', de tears come, en I could 'a' got down on my knees en kiss yo' foot, I's so thankful. En all you wuz thinkin' 'bout wuz how you could make a fool uv ole Jim wid a lie. Dat truck dah is *trash*; en trash is what people is dat puts dirt on de head er dey fren's en makes 'em ashamed."

Then he got up slow and walked to the wigwam, and went in there without saying anything but that. But that was enough. It made me feel so mean I could almost kissed *his* foot to get him to take it back.

It was fifteen minutes before I could work myself up to go and humble myself to a nigger; but I done it, and I warn't ever sorry for it afterward, neither. I didn't do him no more mean tricks, and I wouldn't done that one if I'd 'a' knowed it would make him feel that way.

The Rattlesnake-skin Does Its Work

. . . There warn't nothing to do now but to look out sharp for the town, and not pass it without seeing it. He said he'd be mighty sure to see it, because he'd be a free man the minute he seen it, but if he missed it he'd be in a slave country again and no more show for freedom. Every little while he jumps up and says:

"Dah she is?"

But it warn't. It was Jack-o'-lanterns, or lightning-bugs; so he set down again, and went to watching, same as before. Jim said it made him all over trembly and feverish to be so close to freedom. Well, I can tell you it made me all over trembly and feverish, too, to hear him, because I begun to get it through my head that he *was* most free—and who was to blame for it? Why, *me*. I couldn't get that out of my conscience, no how nor no way. It got to troubling me so I couldn't rest; I couldn't stay still in one place. It hadn't ever come home to me before, what this thing was that I was doing. But now it did; and it stayed with me, and scorched me more and more. I tried to make out to myself that *I* warn't to blame, because *I* didn't run Jim off from his rightful owner; but it warn't no use, conscience up and says, every time, "But you knowed he was running for his freedom, and you could 'a' paddled ashore and told somebody." That was so—I couldn't get around that no way. That was where it pinched. Conscience says to me, "What had poor Miss Watson done to you that you could see her nigger go off right under your eyes and never say one single word? What did that poor old woman do to you that you could treat her so mean? Why, she tried to learn you your book, she tried to learn you your manners, she tried to be good to you every way she knowed how. *That's* what she done."

I got to feeling so mean and so miserable I most wished I was dead. I fidgeted up and down the raft, abusing myself to myself, and Jim was fidgeting up and down past me. We neither of us could keep still. Every time he danced around and says, "Dah's Cairo!" it went through me like a shot, and I thought if it *was* Cairo I reckoned I would die of miserableness.

Jim talked out loud all the time while I was talking to myself. He was saying how the first thing he would do when he got to a free state he would go to saving up money and never spend a single cent, and when he got enough he would buy his wife, which was owned on a farm close to where Miss Watson lived; and then they would both work to buy the two children, and if their master wouldn't sell them, they'd get an Ab'litionist to go and steal them.

It most froze me to hear such talk. He wouldn't ever dared to talk such talk in his life before. Just see what a difference it made in him the minute he judged he was about free. It was according to the old saying, "Give a nigger an inch and he'll take an ell." Thinks I, this is what comes of my not thinking. Here was this nigger, which I had as good as helped to run away, coming right out flat-footed and saying he would steal his children—children that belonged to a man I didn't even know; a man that hadn't ever done me no harm.

I was sorry to hear Jim say that, it was such a lowering of him. My conscience got to stirring me up hotter than ever, until at last I says to it. "Let up on me—it ain't too late yet—I'll paddle ashore at the first light and tell." I felt easy and happy and light as a feather right off. All my troubles was gone. I went to looking out sharp for a light, and sort of singing to myself. By and by one showed. Jim sings out:

"We's safe, Huck, we's safe! Jump up and crack yo' heels! Dat's de good ole Cairo at las', I jis knows it!"

I says:

"I'll take the canoe and go and see, Jim. It mightn't be, you know."

He jumped and got the canoe ready, and put his old coat in the bottom for me to set on, and give me the paddle; and as I shoved off, he says:

"Pooty soon I'll be a-shout'n' for joy, en I'll say, it's all on accounts o' Huck; I's a free man, en I couldn't ever ben free ef it hadn't ben for Huck; Huck done it. Jim won't ever forget you, Huck; you's de bes' fren' Jim's ever had; en you's de *only* fren' ole Jim's got now."

I was paddling off, all in a sweat to tell on him; but when he says this, it seemed to kind of take the tuck all out of me. I went along slow then, and I warn't right down certain whether I was glad I started or whether I warn't. When I was fifty yards off, Jim says:

"Dah you goes, de ole true Huck; de on'y white genlman dat ever kep' his promise to ole Jim."

Well, I just felt sick. But I says, I *got* to do it—I can't get *out* of it. Right then along comes a skiff with two men in it with guns, and they stopped and I stopped. One of them says:

"What's that yonder?"

"A piece of raft," I says.

"Do you belong on it?"

"Yes, sir."

"Any men on it?"

"Only one, sir."

"Well, there's five niggers run off to-night up yonder, above the head of the bend. Is your man white or black?"

I didn't answer up promptly. I tried to, but the words wouldn't come. I tried for a second or two to brace up and out with it, but I warn't man enough—hadn't the spunk of a rabbit. I see I was weakening; so I just give up trying, and up and says:

"He's white." . . .

The Orneriness of Kings

. . . I went to sleep, and Jim didn't call me when it was my turn. He often done that. When I waked up just at daybreak he was sitting there with his head down betwixt his knees, moaning and mourning to himself. I didn't take notice nor let on. I knowed what it was about. He was thinking about his wife and his children, away up yonder, and he was low and homesick; because he hadn't ever been away from home before in his life; and I do believe he cared just as much for his people as white folks does for their'n. It don't seem natural, but I reckon it's so. He was often moaning and mourning that way nights, when he judged I was asleep, and saying, "Po' little 'Lizabeth! po' little Johnny! it's mighty hard; I spec' I ain't ever gwyne to see you no mo', no mo'!" He was a mighty good nigger, Jim was.

But this time I somehow got to talking to him about his wife and young ones; and by and by he says:

"What makes me feel so bad dis time 'uz bekase I hear sumpn over yonder on de bank like a whack, er a slam, while ago, en it mine me er de time I treat my little 'Lizabeth so ornery. She warn't on'y 'bout fo' year ole en she tuck de sk'yarlet fever, en had a powful rough spell; but she got well, en one day she was a-stannin' aroun', en I says to her, I says:

" 'Shet de do'.'

"She never done it; jis' stood dah, kiner smilin' up at me. It make me mad; en I says ag'in, mighty loud, I says:

" 'Doan' you hear me? Shet de do'!'

"She jis' stood de same way, kiner smilin' up. I was a-bilin'! I says:

" 'I lay I *make* you mine!'

"En wid dat I fetch' her a slap side de head dat sont her a-sprawlin'. Den I went into de yuther room, en 'uz gone 'bout ten minutes; en when I come back dah was dat do' a-stannin' open *yit*, en dat chile stannin' mos' right in it, a-lookin' down and mournin', en de tears runnin' down. My, but I *wuz* mad! I was a-gwyne for de chile, but jis' den—it was a do' dat open innerds—jis' den, 'long come de wind en slam it to, behine de chile, ker-*blam!*—en my lan', de chile never move'! My breff mos' hop outer me; en I feel so—so—I doan' know *how* I feel. I crope out, all a-tremblin', en crope aroun' en open de do' easy en slow, en poke my head in behine de chile, sof' en still, en all uv a sudden I says *pow!* jis' as loud as I could yell. *She never budge!* Oh, Huck, I bust out a-cryin' en grab her up in my arms, en say, 'Oh, de po' little thing! De Lord God Amighty fogive po' ole Jim, kaze he never gwyne to fogive hisself as long's he live!' Oh, she was plumb deef en dumb, Huck, plumb deef en dumb—en I'd ben a-treat'n her so!"

You Can't Pray a Lie

. . . Once I said to myself it would be a thousand times better for Jim to be a slave at home where his family was, as long as

he'd *got* to be a slave, and so I'd better write a letter to Tom
Sawyer and tell him to tell Miss Watson where he was. But I soon
give up that notion for two things: she'd be mad and disgusted
at his rascality and ungratefulness for leaving her, and so she'd
sell him straight down the river again; and if she didn't, everybody naturally despises an ungrateful nigger, and they'd make
Jim feel it all the time, and so he'd feel ornery and disgraced. And
then think of *me!* It would get all around that Huck Finn helped
a nigger to get his freedom; and if I was ever to see anybody from
that town again I'd be ready to get down and lick his boots for
shame. That's just the way: a person does a low-down thing, and
then he don't want to take no consequences of it. Thinks as long
as he can hide, it ain't no disgrace. That was my fix exactly. The
more I studied about this the more my conscience went to grinding
me, and the more wicked and low-down and ornery I got to feeling.
And at last, when it hit me all of a sudden that here was the plain
hand of Providence slapping me in the face and letting me know
my wickedness was being watched all the time from up there in
heaven, whilst I was stealing a poor old woman's nigger that hadn't
ever done me no harm, and now was showing me there's One that's
always on the lookout, and ain't a-going to allow no such miserable
doings to go only just so fur and no further, I most dropped in
my tracks I was so scared. Well, I tried the best I could to kinder
soften it up somehow for myself by saying I was brung up wicked,
and so I warn't so much to blame; but something inside of me
kept saying, "There was the Sunday-school, you could 'a' gone to
it; and if you'd 'a' done it they'd 'a' learnt you there that people
that acts as I'd been acting about that nigger goes to everlasting
fire."

It made me shiver. And I about made up my mind to pray, and
see if I couldn't try to quit being the kind of a boy I was and be
better. So I kneeled down. But the words wouldn't come. Why
wouldn't they? It warn't no use to try and hide it from Him.
Nor from *me*, neither. I knowed very well why they wouldn't
come. It was because my heart warn't right; it was because I warn't
square; it was because I was playing double. I was letting *on* to
give up sin, but away inside of me I was holding on to the biggest
one of all. I was trying to make my mouth *say* I would do the

right thing and the clean thing, and go and write to that nigger's owner and tell where he was; but deep down in me I knowed it was a lie, and He knowed it. You can't pray a lie—I found that out.

So I was full of trouble, full as I could be; and didn't know what to do. At last I had an idea; and I says, I'll go and write the letter —and *then* see if I can pray. Why, it was astonishing, the way I felt as light as a feather right straight off, and my troubles all gone. So I got a piece of paper and a pencil, all glad and excited, and set down and wrote:

Miss Watson, your runaway nigger Jim is down here two mile below Pikesville, and Mr. Phelps has got him and he will give him up for the reward if you send.

HUCK FINN.

I felt good and all washed clean of sin for the first time I had ever felt so in my life, and I knowed I could pray now. But I didn't do it straight off, but laid the paper down and set there thinking —thinking how good it was all this happened so, and how near I come to being lost and going to hell. And went on thinking. And got to thinking over our trip down the river; and I see Jim before me all the time: in the day and in the night-time, sometimes moonlight, sometimes storms, and we a-floating along, talking and singing and laughing. But somehow I couldn't seem to strike no places to harden me against him, but only the other kind. I'd see him standing my watch on top of his'n, 'stead of calling me, so I could go on sleeping; and see him how glad he was when I come back out of the fog; and when I come to him again in the swamp, up there where the feud was; and such-like times; and would always call me honey, and pet me, and do everything he could think of for me, and how good he always was; and at last I struck the time I saved him by telling the men we had smallpox aboard, and he was so grateful, and said I was the best friend old Jim ever had in the world, and the *only* one he's got now; and then I happened to look around and see that paper.

It was a close place. I took it up, and held it in my hand. I was a-trembling, because I'd got to decide, forever, betwixt two things, and I knowed it. I studied a minute, sort of holding my breath, and then says to myself:

"All right, then, I'll *go* to hell"—and tore it up.

It was awful thoughts and awful words, but they was said. And I let them stay said; and never thought no more about reforming. I shoved the whole thing out of my head, and said I would take up wickedness again, which was in my line, being brung up to it, and the other warn't. And for a starter I would go to work and steal Jim out of slavery again; and if I could think up anything worse, I would do that, too; because as long as I was in, and in for good, I might as well go the whole hog. . . .

IRWIN RUSSELL

(1853–1879)

In his introduction to Poems by Irwin Russell (1888), Joel Chandler Harris congratulated the poet for being one of the first Southern writers to perceive the literary possibilities in Negro character, and he praised the accuracy with which he thought Russell had detailed that character: "the Negro is there, the old-fashioned, unadulterated Negro, who is still dear to the Southern heart." Like other Southerners, Russell regarded the view of Negro life and character in Uncle Tom's Cabin as thoroughly inaccurate, and he thought of his poems as providing a corrective to Northern distortions.

Russell was born in Port Gibson, Mississippi, and was raised in St. Louis, Missouri, where he attended St. Louis University. After college he returned to Port Gibson to study law and was admitted to the Mississippi bar, but, finding law practice unrewarding and encouraged by Scribner's acceptance of some of his poems, he went to New York, hoping to make his living as a writer. Here too he was unsuccessful and he soon drifted to New Orleans. He died at the age of twenty-six while working as a reporter with the New Orleans Times.

Russell's poems were compiled by Harris in Poems by Irwin Russell, a posthumous edition of 1888, and in 1917 the book was enlarged and reissued under the title Christmas-Night in the Quarters. The poem from which the 1917 edition derived its title is an

adaptation of Robert Burns's "The Jolly Beggars" to a Southern
Negro background and is Russell's best-known work.

Christmas-Night in the Quarters

When merry Christmas-day is done,
And Christmas-night is just begun;
While clouds in slow procession drift,
To wish the moon-man "Christmas gift,"
Yet linger overhead, to know
What causes all the stir below;
At Uncle Johnny Booker's ball
The darkies hold high carnival.
From all the country-side they throng,
With laughter, shouts, and scraps of song—
Their whole deportment plainly showing
That to the Frolic they are going.
Some take the path with shoes in hand,
To traverse muddy bottom-land;
Aristocrats their steeds bestride—
Four on a mule, behold them ride!
And ten great oxen draw apace
The wagon from "de oder place,"
With forty guests, whose conversation
Betokens glad anticipation.
Not so with him who drives: old Jim
Is sagely solemn, hard, and grim,
And frolics have no joys for him.
He seldom speaks but to condemn—
Or utter some wise apothegm—
Or else, some crabbed thought pursuing,
Talk to his team, as now he's doing:

———

Come up heah, Star! Yee-bawee!
    You alluz is a-laggin'—

Mus' be you think I's dead,
   An' dis de huss you's draggin'—
You's 'mos' too lazy to draw yo' bref,
   Let 'lone drawin' de waggin.

Dis team—quit bel'rin', sah!
   De ladies don't submit 'at—
Dis team—you ol' fool ox,
   You heah me tell you quit 'at?
Dis team's des like de 'Nited States;
   Dat's what I's tryin' to git at!

De people rides behin',
   De pollytishners haulin'—
Sh'u'd be a well-bruk ox,
   To foller dat ar callin'—
An' sometimes nuffin won't do dem steers,
   But what dey mus' be stallin'!

Woo bahgh! Buck-kannon! Yes, sah,
   Sometimes dey will be stickin';
An' den, fus thing dey knows,
   Dey takes a rale good lickin'.
De folks gits down: an' den watch out
   For hommerin' an' kickin'.

Dey blows upon dey hands,
   Den flings 'em wid de nails up,
Jumps up an' cracks dey heels,
   An' pruzently dey sails up,
An' makes dem oxen hump deysef,
   By twistin' all dey tails up!

———

In this our age of printer's ink
'Tis books that show us how to think—
The rule reversed, and set at naught,
That held that books were born of thought.

We form our minds by pedants' rules,
And all we know is from the schools;
And when we work, or when we play,
We do it in an ordered way—
And Nature's self pronounce a ban on,
Whene'er she dares transgress a canon.
Untrammeled thus the simple race is
That "wuks the craps" on cotton places.
Original in act and thought,
Because unlearned and untaught.
Observe them at their Christmas party:
How unrestrained their mirth—how hearty!
How many things they say and do
That never would occur to you!
See Brudder Brown—whose saving grace
Would sanctify a quarter-race—
Out on the crowded floor advance,
To "beg a blessin' on dis dance."

———

O Mahsr! let dis gath'rin' fin' a blessin' in yo' sight!
Don't jedge us hard fur what we does—you knows it's Chrismus-
    night;
An' all de balunce ob de yeah we does as right's we kin.
Ef dancin's wrong, O Mahsr! let de time excuse de sin!

We labors in de vineya'd, wukin' hard an' wukin' true;
Now, shorely you won't notus, ef we eats a grape or two,
An' takes a leetle holiday,—a leetle restin'-spell,—
Bekase, nex' week, we'll start in fresh, an' labor twicet as well.

Remember, Mahsr,—min' dis, now,—de sinfulness ob sin
Is 'pendin' 'pon de sperret what we goes an' does it in:
An' in a righchis frame ob min' we's gwine to dance an' sing.
A-feelin' like King David, when he cut de pigeon-wing.

It seems to me—indeed it do—I mebbe mout be wrong—
That people raly *ought* to dance, when Chrismus comes along;

Des dance bekase dey's happy—like de birds hops in de trees,
De pine-top fiddle soundin' to de blowin' ob de breeze.

We has no ark to dance afore, like Isrul's prophet king;
We has no harp to soun' de cords, to holp us out to sing;
But 'cordin' to de gif's we has we does de bes' we knows,
An' folks don't 'spise de vi'let-flower bekase it ain't de rose.

You bless us, please, sah, eben ef we's doin' wrong to-night;
Kase den we'll need de blessin' more'n ef we's doin' right;
An' let de blessin' stay wid us, untel we comes to die,
An' goes to keep our Chrismus wid dem sheriffs in de sky!

Yes, tell dem preshis anguls we's a-gwine to jine 'em soon:
Our voices we's a-trainin' fur to sing de glory tune;
We's ready when you wants us, an' it ain't no matter when—
O Mahsr! call yo' chillen soon, an' take 'em home! Amen.

The rev'rend man is scarcely through,
When all the noise begins anew,
And with such force assaults the ears,
That through the din one hardly hears
Old fiddling Josey "sound his A,"
Correct the pitch, begin to play,
Stop, satisfied, then, with the bow,
Rap out the signal dancers know:

Git yo' pardners, fust kwattillion!
Stomp yo' feet, an' raise 'em high;
Tune is: "Oh! dat water-million!
Gwine to get to home bime-bye."
S'lute yo' pardners!—scrape perlitely—
Don't be bumpin' gin de res'—
Balance all!—now, step out rightly;
Alluz dance yo' lebbel bes'.
Fo'wa'd foah!—whoop up, niggers!

Back ag'in!—don't be so slow!—
Swing cornahs!—min' de figgers!
When I hollers, den yo' go.
Top ladies cross ober!
Hol' on, till I takes a dram—
Gemmen solo!—yes, *I's* sober—
Cain't say how de fiddle am.
Hands around!—hol' up yo' faces,
Don't be lookin' at yo' feet!
Swing yo' pardners to yo' places!
Dat's de way—dat's hard to beat.
Sides fo'w'd!—when you's ready—
Make a bow as low's you kin!
Swing acrost wid opp'site lady!
Now we'll let you swap ag'in:
Ladies change!—shet up dat talkin';
Do yo' talkin' arter while!
Right an' lef'!—don't want no walkin'—
Make yo' steps, an' show yo' style!

———

And so the "set" proceeds—its length
Determined by the dancers' strength;
And all agreed to yield the palm
For grace and skill to "Georgy Sam,"
Who stamps so hard, and leaps so high,
"Des watch him!" is the wond'ring cry—
"De nigger mus' be, for a fac',
Own cousin to a jumpin'-jack!"
On, on the restless fiddle sounds,
Still chorused by the curs and hounds;
Dance after dance succeeding fast,
Till supper is announced at last.
That scene—but why attempt to show it?
The most inventive modern poet,
In fine new words whose hope and trust is,
Could form no phrase to do it justice!
When supper ends—that is not soon—

The fiddle strikes the same old tune;
The dancers pound the floor again,
With all they have of might and main;
Old gossips, *almost* turning pale,
Attend Aunt Cassy's gruesome tale
Of conjurors, and ghosts, and devils,
That in the smoke-house hold their revels;
Each drowsy baby droops its head,
Yet scorns the very thought of bed:—
So wears the night, and wears so fast,
All wonder when they find it passed,
And hear the signal sound to go
From what few cocks are left to crow.
Then, one and all, you hear them shout:
"Hi! Booker! fotch de banjo out,
An' gib us *one* song 'fore we goes—
One ob de berry bes' you knows!"
Responding to the welcome call,
He takes the banjo from the wall,
And tunes the strings with skill and care,
Then strikes them with a master's air,
And tells, in melody and rhyme,
This legend of the olden time:

———

Go 'way, fiddle! folks is tired o' hearin' you a-squawkin'.
Keep silence fur yo' betters!—don't you heah de banjo talkin'?
About de 'possum's tail she's gwine to lecter—ladies, listen!—
About de ha'r whut isn't dar, an' why de ha'r is missin':

"Dar's gwine to be a' oberflow," said Noah, lookin' solemn—
Fur Noah tuk the "Herald," an' he read de ribber column—
An' so he sot his hands to wuk a-cl'arin' timber-patches,
An' 'lowed he's gwine to build a boat to beat de steamah *Natchez.*

Ol' Noah kep' a-nailin' an' a-chippin' an' a-sawin';
An' all de wicked neighbors kep' a-laughin' an' a-pshawin';

But Noah didn't min' 'em, knowin' whut wuz gwine to happen:
An' forty days an' forty nights de rain it kep' a-drappin'.

Now, Noah had done cotched a lot ob ebry sort o' beas'es—
Ob all de shows a-trabbelin', it beat 'em all to pieces!
He had a Morgan colt an' sebral head o' Jarsey cattle—
An' druv 'em 'board de Ark as soon's he heered de thunder rattle.

Den sech anoder fall ob rain!—it come so awful hebby,
De ribber riz immejitly, an' busted troo de lebbee;
De people all wuz drownded out—'cep' Noah an' de critters,
An' men he'd hired to work de boat—an' one to mix de bitters.

De Ark she kep' a-sailin' an' a-sailin' *an'* a-sailin';
De lion got his dander up, an' like to bruk de palin';
De sarpints hissed; de painters yelled; tell, whut wid all de fussin',
You c'u'dn't hardly heah de mate a-bossin' 'roun' an' cussin'.

Now, Ham, de only nigger whut wuz runnin' on de packet,
Got lonesome in de barber-shop, an' c'u'dn't stan' de racket;
An' so, fur to amuse he-se'f, he steamed some wood an' bent it,
An' soon he had a banjo made—de fust dat wuz invented.

He wet de ledder, stretched it on; made bridge an' screws an' apron;
An' fitted in a proper neck—'twuz berry long an' tap'rin';
He tuk some tin, an' twisted him a thimble fur to ring it;
An' den de mighty question riz: how wuz he gwine to string it?

De 'possum had as fine a tail as dis dat I's a-singin';
De ha'r's so long an' thick an' strong—des fit fur banjo-stringin';
Dat nigger shaved 'em off as short as wash-day-dinner graces;
An' sorted ob 'em by de size, f'om little E's to basses.

He strung her, tuned her, struck a jig—'twuz "Nebber min' de
        wedder"—
She soun' like forty-lebben bands a-playin' all togedder;
Some went to pattin'; some to dancin': Noah called de figgers;
An' Ham he sot an' knocked de tune, de happiest ob niggers!

Now, sence dat time—it's mighty strange—dere's not de slightes'
      showin'
Ob any ha'r at all upon the 'possum's tail a-growin';
An' curi's, too, dat nigger's ways: his people nebber los' 'em—
For whar you finds de nigger—dar's de banjo an' de 'possum!

> The night is spent; and as the day
> Throws up the first faint flash of gray,
> The guests pursue their homeward way;
> And through the field beyond the gin,
> Just as the stars are going in,
> See Santa Claus departing—grieving—
> His own dear Land of Cotton leaving.
> His work is done; he fain would rest
> Where people know and love him best.
> He pauses, listens, looks about;
> But go he must: his pass is out.
> So, coughing down the rising tears,
> He climbs the fence and disappears.
> And thus observes a colored youth
> (The common sentiment, in sooth):
> "Oh! what a blessin' 'tw'u'd ha' been,
> Ef Santa had been born a twin!
> We'd hab two Chrismuses a yeah—
> Or p'r'aps *one* brudder'd *settle* heah!"

JOEL CHANDLER HARRIS

(1848-1908)

◆◄◉►◆

Joel Chandler Harris is best known for his Uncle Remus tales, in which he employed Negro folk stories, proverbs, and plantation legends, and attempted to present Negro dialect accurately. Uncle Remus, the sage, kindly, and whimsical old ex-slave, who tells his tales to the son of his white employer, has become one of the most familiar figures in American writing, just as the animals endowed with human personalities who populate his fables—Brer Rabbit, Brer Fox, and Brer Wolf—have become known throughout the world.

Harris was born in Eatonton, Georgia, and had little formal education. He began his career as a printer, then held various editorial positions with several newspapers including the Atlanta Constitution, and eventually founded his own Uncle Remus's Magazine in 1900. His first Uncle Remus story appeared in the Constitution in 1879. His first collection, Uncle Remus: His Songs and His Sayings, was published in 1881 and was followed by more than half a dozen other Uncle Remus collections, including two published posthumously. Harris is also an important local colorist, and in such works as Mingo, and Other Sketches in Black and White (1884) and Free Joe, and Other Georgian Sketches (1887) he produced insightful portraits of Georgia aristocrats, poor whites, and former slaves.

Harris was an important contributor to the "Plantation Tradition" school of writing, which developed during the Reconstruction era and helped to glorify the "Lost Cause" while establishing the star-cross'd aristocrat and the humorous but sage Negro as familiar figures. According to Sterling Brown, the writers in this tradition "presented a glowing picture of the kindlier aspects of slavery. Their cardinal principles were mutual affection between the races; and the peculiar endowment of each race to occupy its role: one race the born master, one race the born slave. The road to reunion [with the North] was opening; tension was relaxing; the troubled past could be forgotten, the wrongs could be covered over, perhaps they had not been so bad, perhaps they could go away." One of the stereotyped characters that emerged from this literature is the wretched freedman who, like Free Joe, found his lot miserable when compared with that of the contented slave. But Harris was sympathetic toward his Negro characters, and Mingo, the former slave who renounces his own chance at a new life in order to care for the orphaned child of his late mistress, is one of the more noble figures to appear in Southern writing within this tradition. Even in Gabriel Tolliver (1902), a novel criticizing Republican Reconstruction policies, Harris deals with the Negroes who support the Union League not as contemptible figures but as the pitiful and misguided victims of carpetbaggers and scalawags.

From *Free Joe, and Other Georgian Sketches*

Free Joe and the Rest of the World

The name of Free Joe strikes humorously upon the ear of memory. It is impossible to say why, for he was the humblest, the simplest, and the most serious of all God's living creatures, sadly lacking in all those elements that suggest the humorous. It is certain, moreover, that in 1850 the sober-minded citizens of the little Georgian village of Hillsborough were not inclined to take a humorous view of Free Joe, and neither his name nor his presence provoked a smile. He was a black atom, drifting hither and thither without an owner, blown about by all the winds of circumstance, and given over to shiftlessness.

The problems of one generation are the paradoxes of a succeeding one, particularly if war, or some such incident, intervenes to clarify the atmosphere and strengthen the understanding. Thus, in 1850, Free Joe represented not only a problem of large concern, but, in the watchful eyes of Hillsborough, he was the embodiment of that vague and mysterious danger that seemed to be forever lurking on the outskirts of slavery, ready to sound a shrill and ghostly signal in the impenetrable swamps, and steal forth under the midnight stars to murder, rapine, and pillage,—a danger always threatening, and yet never assuming shape; intangible, and yet real; impossible, and yet not improbable. Across the serene and smiling front of safety, the pale outlines of the awful shadow of insurrection sometimes fell. With this invisible panorama as a background, it was natural that the figure of Free Joe, simple and humble as it was, should assume undue proportions. Go where he would, do what he might, he could not escape the finger of observation and the kindling eye of suspicion. His lightest words were noted, his slightest actions marked.

Under all the circumstances it was natural that his peculiar condition should reflect itself in his habits and manners. The slaves laughed loudly day by day, but Free Joe rarely laughed. The slaves sang at their work and danced at their frolics, but no one ever heard Free Joe sing or saw him dance. There was something painfully plaintive and appealing in his attitude, something touching in his anxiety to please. He was of the friendliest nature, and seemed to be delighted when he could amuse the little children who had made a playground of the public square. At times he would please them by making his little dog Dan perform all sorts of curious tricks, or he would tell them quaint stories of the beasts of the field and birds of the air; and frequently he was coaxed into relating the story of his own freedom. That story was brief, but tragical.

In the year of our Lord 1840, when a negro-speculator of a sportive turn of mind reached the little village of Hillsborough on his way to the Mississippi region, with a caravan of likely negroes of both sexes, he found much to interest him. In that day and at that time there were a number of young men in the village who had not bound themselves over to repentance for the various misdeeds of the flesh. To these young men the negro-speculator (Major Frampton was his name) proceeded to address himself. He was a Virginian, he declared; and, to prove the statement, he referred all the festively inclined young men of Hillsborough to a barrel of peach-brandy in one of his covered wagons. In the minds of these young men there was less doubt in regard to the age and quality of the brandy than there was in regard to the negro-trader's birthplace. Major Frampton might or might not have been born in the Old Dominion,—that was a matter for consideration and in-quiry,—but there could be no question as to the mellow pungency of the peach-brandy.

In his own estimation, Major Frampton was one of the most accomplished of men. He had summered at the Virginia Springs; he had been to Philadelphia, to Washington, to Richmond, to Lynchburg, and to Charleston, and had accumulated a great deal of experience which he found useful. Hillsborough was hid in the woods of Middle Georgia, and its general aspect of innocence im-pressed him. He looked on the young men who had shown their readiness to test his peach-brandy, as overgrown country boys who needed to be introduced to some of the arts and sciences he had at his command. Thereupon the major pitched his tents, figur-atively speaking, and became, for the time being, a part and parcel of the innocence that characterized Hillsborough. A wiser man would doubtless have made the same mistake.

The little village possessed advantages that seemed to be provi-dentially arranged to fit the various enterprises that Major Framp-ton had in view. There was the auction-block in front of the stuc-coed court-house, if he desired to dispose of a few of his negroes; there was a quarter-track, laid out to his hand and in excellent order, if he chose to enjoy the pleasures of horse-racing; there were secluded pine thickets within easy reach, if he desired to indulge in the exciting pastime of cock-fighting; and various lonely and unoccupied rooms in the second story of the tavern, if he cared to challenge the chances of dice or cards.

Major Frampton tried them all with varying luck, until he began his famous game of poker with Judge Alfred Wellington, a stately gentleman with a flowing white beard and mild blue eyes that gave him the appearance of a benevolent patriarch. The history of the game in which Major Frampton and Judge Alfred Wellington took part is something more than a tradition in Hillsborough, for there are still living three or four men who sat around the table and watched its progress. It is said that at various stages of the game Major Frampton would destroy the cards with which they were playing, and send for a new pack, but the result was always the same. The mild blue eyes of Judge Wellington, with few exceptions, continued to overlook "hands" that were invincible—a habit they had acquired during a long and arduous course of training from Saratoga to New Orleans. Major Frampton lost his money, his horses, his wagons, and all his negroes but one, his body-servant. When his misfortune had reached this limit, the major adjourned the game. The sun was shining brightly, and all nature was cheerful. It is said that the major also seemed to be cheerful. However this may be, he visited the court-house, and executed the papers that gave his body-servant his freedom. This being done, Major Frampton sauntered into a convenient pine thicket, and blew out his brains.

The negro thus freed came to be known as Free Joe. Compelled, under the law, to choose a guardian, he chose Judge Wellington, chiefly because his wife Lucinda was among the negroes won from Major Frampton. For several years Free Joe had what may be called a jovial time. His wife Lucinda was well provided for, and he found it a comparatively easy matter to provide for himself; so that, taking all the circumstances into consideration, it is not matter for astonishment that he became somewhat shiftless.

When Judge Wellington died, Free Joe's troubles began. The judge's negroes, including Lucinda, went to his half-brother, a man named Calderwood, who was a hard master and a rough customer generally,—a man of many eccentricities of mind and character. His neighbors had a habit of alluding to him as "Old Spite"; and the name seemed to fit him so completely, that he was known far and near as "Spite" Calderwood. He probably enjoyed the distinction the name gave him, at any rate, he never resented it, and it was not often that he missed an opportunity to show that he deserved it. Calderwood's place was two or three miles from the village of Hillsborough, and Free Joe visited his wife twice a week, Wednesday and Saturday nights.

One Sunday he was sitting in front of Lucinda's cabin, when Calderwood happened to pass that way.

"Howdy, marster?" said Free Joe, taking off his hat.

"Who are you?" exclaimed Calderwood abruptly, halting and staring at the negro.

"I'm name' Joe, marster. I'm Lucindy's ole man."

"Who do you belong to?"

"Marse John Evans is my gyardeen, marster."

"Big name—gyardeen. Show your pass."

Free Joe produced that document, and Calderwood read it aloud slowly, as if he found it difficult to get at the meaning:—

"To whom it may concern: This is to certify that the boy Joe Frampton has my permission to visit his wife Lucinda."

This was dated at Hillsborough, and signed *"John W. Evans."*

Calderwood read it twice, and then looked at Free Joe, elevating his eyebrows, and showing his discolored teeth.

"Some mighty big words in that there. Evans owns this place, I reckon. When's he comin' down to take hold?"

Free Joe fumbled with his hat. He was badly frightened.

"Lucindy say she speck you wouldn't min' my comin', long ez I behave, marster."

Calderwood tore the pass in pieces and flung it away.

"Don't want no free niggers 'round here," he exclaimed. "There's the big road. It'll carry you to town. Don't let me catch you here no more. Now, mind what I tell you."

Free Joe presented a shabby spectacle as he moved off with his little dog Dan slinking at his heels. It should be said in behalf of Dan, however, that his bristles were up, and that he looked back and growled. It may be that the dog had the advantage of insignificance, but it is difficult to conceive how a dog bold enough to raise his bristles under Calderwood's very eyes could be as insignificant as Free Joe. But both the negro and his little dog seemed to give a new and more dismal aspect to forlornness as they turned into the road and went toward Hillsborough.

After this incident Free Joe appeared to have clearer ideas concerning his peculiar condition. He realized the fact that though he was free he was more helpless than any slave. Having no owner, every man was his master. He knew that he was the object of suspicion, and therefore all his slender resources (ah! how pitifully slender they were!) were devoted to winning, not kindness and appreciation, but toleration; all his efforts were in the direction of mitigating the circumstances that tended to make his condition so much worse than that of the negroes around him,—negroes who had friends because they had masters.

So far as his own race was concerned, Free Joe was an exile. If the slaves secretly envied him his freedom (which is to be doubted, considering his miserable condition), they openly despised him, and lost no opportunity to treat him with contumely. Perhaps this was in some measure the result of the attitude which Free Joe chose to maintain toward them. No doubt his instinct taught him that to hold himself aloof from the slaves would be to invite from the whites the toleration which he coveted, and without which even his miserable condition would be rendered more miserable still.

His greatest trouble was the fact that he was not allowed to visit his wife; but he soon found a way out of this difficulty. After he had been ordered away from the Calderwood place, he was in the habit of wandering as far in that direction as prudence would permit. Near the Calderwood place, but not on Calderwood's land, lived an old man named Micajah Staley and his sister Becky Staley. These people were old and very poor. Old Micajah had a palsied arm and hand; but, in spite of this, he managed to earn a precarious living with his turning-lathe.

When he was a slave Free Joe would have scorned these representatives of a class known as poor white trash, but now he found them sympathetic and helpful in various ways. From the back door of their cabin he could hear the Calderwood negroes singing at night, and he sometimes fancied he could distinguish Lucinda's shrill treble rising above the other voices. A large poplar grew in the woods some distance from the Staley cabin, and at the foot of this tree Free Joe would sit for hours with his face turned toward Calderwood's. His little dog Dan would curl up in the leaves near by, and the two seemed to be as comfortable as possible.

One Saturday afternoon Free Joe, sitting at the foot of this friendly poplar, fell asleep. How long he slept, he could not tell; but when he awoke little Dan was licking his face, the moon was shining brightly, and Lucinda his wife stood before him laughing. The dog, seeing that Free Joe was asleep, had grown somewhat impatient, and he concluded to make an excursion to the Calderwood place on his own account. Lucinda was inclined to give the incident a twist in the direction of superstition.

"I 'uz settin' down front er de fireplace," she said, "cookin' me some meat, w'en all of a sudden I year sumpin at de do'—scratch, scratch. I tuck'n tu'n de meat over, en make out I aint year it. Bimeby it come dar 'gin—scratch, scratch. I up en open de do', I did, en, bless de Lord! dar wuz little Dan, en it look like ter me dat his ribs done grow tergeer. I gin 'im some bread, en den, w'en he start out, I tuck'n foller 'im, kaze, I say ter myse'f, maybe my nigger man mought be some'rs 'roun'. Dat ar little dog got sense, mon."

Free Joe laughed and dropped his hand lightly on Dan's head. For a long time after that he had no difficulty in seeing his wife. He had only to sit by the poplar-tree until little Dan could run and fetch her. But after a while the other negroes discovered that Lucinda was meeting Free Joe in the woods, and information of the fact soon reached Calderwood's ears. Calderwood was what is called a man of action. He said nothing; but one day he put Lucinda in his buggy, and carried her to Macon, sixty miles away. He carried her to Macon, and came back without her; and nobody in or around Hillsborough, or in that section, ever saw her again.

For many a night after that Free Joe sat in the woods and waited. Little Dan would run merrily off and be gone a long time, but he always came back without Lucinda. This happened over and over again. The "willis-whistlers" would call and call, like phantom huntsmen wandering on a far-off shore; the screech-owl would shake and shiver in the depths of the woods; the night-hawks, sweeping by on noiseless wings, would snap their beaks as though they enjoyed the huge joke of which Free Joe and little Dan were the victims; and the whip-poor-wills would cry to each other through the gloom. Each night seemed to be lonelier than the preceding, but Free Joe's patience was proof against loneliness. There came a time, however, when little Dan refused to go after Lucinda. When Free Joe motioned him in the direction of the Calderwood place, he would simply move about uneasily and whine; then he would curl up in the leaves and make himself comfortable.

One night, instead of going to the poplar-tree to wait for Lucinda, Free Joe went to the Staley cabin, and, in order to make his welcome good, as he expressed it, he carried with him an armful of fat-pine splinters. Miss Becky Staley had a great reputation in those parts as a fortune-teller, and the schoolgirls, as well as older people, often tested her powers in this direction, some in jest and some in earnest. Free Joe placed his humble offering of light-wood in the chimney-corner, and then seated himself on the steps, dropping his hat on the ground outside.

"Miss Becky," he said presently, "whar in de name er gracious you reckon Lucindy is?"

"Well, the Lord he'p the nigger!" exclaimed Miss Becky, in a tone that seemed to reproduce, by some curious agreement of sight with sound, her general aspect of peakedness. "Well, the Lord he'p the nigger! haint you been a-seein' her all this blessed time? She's over at old Spite Calderwood's, if she's anywheres, I reckon."

"No'm, dat I aint, Miss Becky. I aint seen Lucindy in now gwine on mighty nigh a mont'."

"Well, it haint a-gwine to hurt you," said Miss Becky, somewhat sharply. "In my day an' time it wuz allers took to be a bad sign when niggers got to honeyin' 'roun' an' gwine on."

"Yessum," said Free Joe, cheerfully assenting to the proposition —"yessum, dat's so, but me an' my ole 'oman, we 'uz raise tergeer, en dey aint bin many days w'en we 'uz 'way fum one 'n'er like we is now."

"Maybe she's up an' took up wi' some un else," said Micajah Staley from the corner. "You know what the sayin' is, 'New master, new nigger.' "

"Dat's so, dat's de sayin', but tain't wid my ole 'oman like 'tis wid yuther niggers. Me en her wuz des natally raise up tergeer. Dey's lots likelier niggers dan w'at I is," said Free Joe, viewing his shabbiness with a critical eye, "but I knows Lucindy mos' good ez I does little Dan dar—dat I does."

There was no reply to this, and Free Joe continued,—

"Miss Becky, I wish you please, ma'am, take en run yo' kyards en see sump'n n'er 'bout Lucindy; kaze ef she sick, I'm gwine dar. Dey ken take en take me up en gimme a stroppin', but I'm gwine dar."

Miss Becky got her cards, but first she picked up a cup, in the bottom of which were some coffee-grounds. These she whirled slowly round and round, ending finally by turning the cup upside down on the hearth and allowing it to remain in that position.

"I'll turn the cup first," said Miss Becky, "and then I'll run the cards and see what they say."

As she shuffled the cards the fire on the hearth burned low, and in its fitful light the gray-haired, thin-featured woman seemed to deserve the weird reputation which rumor and gossip had given her. She shuffled the cards for some moments, gazing intently in the dying fire; then, throwing a piece of pine on the coals, she made three divisions of the pack, disposing them about in her lap. Then she took the first pile, ran the cards slowly through her fingers, and studied them carefully. To the first she added the second pile. The study of these was evidently not satisfactory. She said nothing, but frowned heavily; and the frown deepened as she added the rest of the cards until the entire fifty-two had passed in review before her. Though she frowned, she seemed to be deeply interested. Without changing the relative position of the cards, she ran them all over again. Then she threw a larger piece of pine on the fire, shuffled the cards afresh, divided them into three piles, and subjected them to the same careful and critical examination.

"I can't tell the day when I've seed the cards run this a-way," she said after a while. "What is an' what aint, I'll never tell you; but I know what the cards sez."

"W'at does dey say, Miss Becky?" the negro inquired, in a tone the solemnity of which was heightened by its eagerness.

"They er runnin' quare. These here that I'm a-lookin' at," said Miss Becky, "they stan' for the past. Them there, they er the present; and the t'others, they er the future. Here's a bundle,"—tapping the ace of clubs with her thumb,—"an' here's a journey as plain as the nose on a man's face. Here's Lucinda"—

"Whar she, Miss Becky?"

"Here she is—the queen of spades."

Free Joe grinned. The idea seemed to please him immensely.

"Well, well, well!" he exclaimed. "Ef dat don't beat my time! De queen er spades! W'en Lucindy year dat hit'll tickle 'er, sho'!"

Miss Becky continued to run the cards back and forth through her fingers.

"Here's a bundle an' a journey, and here's Lucinda. An' here's ole Spite Calderwood."

She held the cards toward the negro and touched the king of clubs.

"De Lord he'p my soul!" exclaimed Free Joe with a chuckle. "De faver's dar. Yesser, dat's him! W'at de matter 'long wid all un um, Miss Becky?"

The old woman added the second pile of cards to the first, and then the third, still running them through her fingers slowly and critically. By this time the piece of pine in the fireplace had wrapped itself in a mantle of flame, illuminating the cabin and throwing into strange relief the figure of Miss Becky as she sat studying the cards. She frowned ominously at the cards and mumbled a few words to herself. Then she dropped her hands in her lap and gazed once more into the fire. Her shadow danced and capered on the wall and floor behind her, as if, looking over her shoulder into the future, it could behold a rare spectacle. After a while she picked up the cup that had been turned on the hearth. The coffee-grounds, shaken around, presented what seemed to be a most intricate map.

"Here's the journey," said Miss Becky, presently; "here's the big road, here's rivers to cross, here's the bundle to tote." She paused and sighed. "They haint no names writ here, an' what it all means I'll never tell you. Cajy, I wish you'd be so good as to han' me my pipe."

"I haint no hand wi' the kyards," said Cajy, as he handed the pipe, "but I reckon I can patch out your misinformation, Becky, bekaze the other day, whiles I was a-finishin' up Mizzers Perdue's rollin'-pin, I hearn a rattlin' in the road. I looked out, an' Spite

Calderwood was a-drivin' by in his buggy, an' thar sot Lucinda by him. It'd in-about drapt out er my min'.'"

Free Joe sat on the door-sill and fumbled at his hat, flinging it from one hand to the other.

"You aint see um gwine back, is you, Mars Cajy?" he asked after a while.

"Ef they went back by this road," said Mr. Staley, with the air of one who is accustomed to weigh well his words, "it must 'a' bin endurin' of the time whiles I was asleep, bekaze I haint bin no furder from my shop than to yon bed."

"Well, sir!" exclaimed Free Joe in an awed tone, which Mr. Staley seemed to regard as a tribute to his extraordinary powers of statement.

"Ef it's my beliefs you want," continued the old man, "I'll pitch 'em at you fair and free. My beliefs is that Spite Calderwood is gone an' took Lucindy outen the county. Bless your heart and soul! when Spite Calderwood meets the Old Boy in the road they'll be a turrible scuffle. You mark what I tell you."

Free Joe, still fumbling with his hat, rose and leaned against the door-facing. He seemed to be embarrassed. Presently he said,—

"I speck I better be gittin' 'long. Nex' time I see Lucindy, I'm gwine tell 'er w'at Miss Becky say 'bout de queen er spades—dat I is. Ef dat don't tickle 'er, dey ain't no nigger 'oman never bin tickle'."

He paused a moment, as though waiting for some remark or comment, some confirmation of misfortune, or, at the very least, some indorsement of his suggestion that Lucinda would be greatly pleased to know that she had figured as the queen of spades; but neither Miss Becky nor her brother said any thing.

"One minnit ridin' in the buggy 'longside er Mars Spite, en de nex' highfalutin' 'roun' playin' de queen er spades. Mon, deze yer nigger gals gittin' up in de pictur's; dey sholy is."

With a brief "Good-night, Miss Becky, Mars Cajy," Free Joe went out into the darkness, followed by little Dan. He made his way to the poplar, where Lucinda had been in the habit of meeting him, and sat down. He sat there a long time; he sat there until little Dan, growing restless, trotted off in the direction of the Calderwood place. Dozing against the poplar, in the gray dawn of the morning, Free Joe heard Spite Calderwood's fox-hounds in full cry a mile away.

"Shoo!" he exclaimed, scratching his head, and laughing to himself, "dem ar dogs is des a-warmin' dat old fox up."

But it was Dan the hounds were after, and the little dog came back no more. Free Joe waited and waited, until he grew tired of waiting. He went back the next night and waited, and for many nights thereafter. His waiting was in vain, and yet he never regarded it as in vain. Careless and shabby as he was, Free Joe was thoughtful enough to have his theory. He was convinced that little Dan had found Lucinda, and that some night when the moon was shining brightly through the trees, the dog would rouse him from his dreams as he sat sleeping at the foot of the poplar-tree, and he would open his eyes and behold Lucinda standing over him, laughing merrily as of old; and then he thought what fun they would have about the queen of spades.

How many long nights Free Joe waited at the foot of the poplar-tree for Lucinda and little Dan, no one can ever know. He kept no account of them, and they were not recorded by Micajah Staley nor by Miss Becky. The season ran into summer and then into fall. One night he went to the Staley cabin, cut the two old people an armful of wood, and seated himself on the door-steps, where he rested. He was always thankful—and proud, as it seemed—when Miss Becky gave him a cup of coffee, which she was sometimes thoughtful enough to do. He was especially thankful on this particular night.

"You er still layin' off for to strike up wi' Lucindy out thar in the woods, I reckon," said Micajah Staley, smiling grimly. The situation was not without its humorous aspects.

"Oh, dey er comin', Mars Cajy, dey er comin', sho," Free Joe replied. "I boun' you dey'll come; en w'en dey does come, I'll des take en fetch um yer, whar you kin see um wid you own eyes, you en Miss Becky."

"No," said Mr. Staley, with a quick and emphatic gesture of disapproval. "Don't! don't fetch 'em anywheres. Stay right wi' 'em as long as may be."

Free Joe chuckled, and slipped away into the night, while the two old people sat gazing in the fire. Finally Micajah spoke.

"Look at that nigger; look at 'im. He's pine-blank as happy now as a killdee by a mill-race. You can't 'faze 'em. I'd in-about give up my t'other hand ef I could stan' flat-footed, an' grin at trouble like that there nigger."

"Niggers is niggers," said Miss Becky, smiling grimly, "an' you can't rub it out; yit I lay I've seed a heap of white people lots meaner'n Free Joe. He grins,—an' that's nigger,—but I've ketched his under jaw a-trimblin' when Lucindy's name uz brung up. An' I tell you," she went on, bridling up a little, and speaking with almost fierce emphasis, "the Old Boy's done sharpened his claws for Spite Calderwood. You'll see it."

"Me, Rebecca?" said Mr. Staley, hugging his palsied arm; "me? I hope not."

"Well, you'll know it then," said Miss Becky, laughing heartily at her brother's look of alarm.

The next morning Micajah Staley had occasion to go into the woods after a piece of timber. He saw Free Joe sitting at the foot of the poplar, and the sight vexed him somewhat.

"Git up from there," he cried, "an' go an' arn your livin'. A mighty purty pass it's come to, when great big buck niggers can lie a-snorin' in the woods all day, when t'other folks is got to be up an' a-gwine. Git up from there!"

Receiving no response, Mr. Staley went to Free Joe, and shook him by the shoulder; but the negro made no response. He was dead. His hat was off, his head was bent, and a smile was on his face. It was as if he had bowed and smiled when death stood before him, humble to the last. His clothes were ragged; his hands were rough and callous; his shoes were literally tied together with strings; he was shabby in the extreme. A passer-by, glancing at him, could have no idea that such a humble creature had been summoned as a witness before the Lord God of Hosts.

From *Uncle Remus and His Friends* (1892)

Death and the Negro Man

One day Uncle Remus was grinding the axe with which he chopped kindling for the kitchen and the big house. The axe was very dull. It was full of "gaps," and the work of putting an edge on it was neither light nor agreeable. A Negro boy turned the grindstone, and the little boy poured on water when water was needed.

"Ef dis yer axe wuz a yard longer, it ud be a cross-cut saw, en den ef we had de lumber we could saw it up en build us a house," said the old man.

The Negro boy rolled his eyes and giggled, seeing which Uncle Remus bore so heavily on the axe that the grindstone could hardly be turned. The Negro boy ceased giggling, but he continued to roll his eyes.

"Turn it!" exclaimed the old man. "Turn it! Ef you don't turn it, I'll make you stan' dar plum' twel night gwine thoo de motions. I'll make you do like de nigger man done when he got tired er work."

The old man stopped talking, but the grinding went on. After a while, the little boy asked,—

"What did the man do when he got tired of work?"

"Dat's a tale, honey, en tellin' tales is playin'," replied Uncle Remus. He wiped the blade of the axe on the palm of his hand, and tried the edge with his thumb. "She won't shave," he said, by way of comment, "but I speck she'll do ter knock out kindlin'. Yit ef I had de time, I'd like ter stan' here en see how long dish yer triflin' vilyun would roll dem eyes at me."

In a little while the axe was supposed to be sharp enough, and then, dismissing the Negro boy, Uncle Remus seated himself on one end of the frame that supported the grindstone, wiped his forehead on his coat sleeve, and proceeded to enjoy what he called a breathing spell.

"Dat ar nigger man you hear me talk about," he remarked, "wuz a-gittin' sorter ole, en he got so he ain't want ter work nohow you kin fix it. When folks hangs back fum work what dey bin set ter do, hit natchully makes bad matters wuss, en dat de way 'twuz with dish yer nigger man. He helt back, en he hung back, en den de white folks got fretted wid 'im en sot 'im a task. Gentermens! dat nigger man wuz mad. He wuz one er deze yer Affiky niggers, en you know how dey is—bowlegged en bad-tempered. He quolled en he quolled when he 'uz by his own lone se'f, en he quolled when he 'uz wid tudder folks.

"He got so mad dat he say he hope ole Gran'sir Death 'll come take him off, en take his marster en de overseer 'long wid 'im. He talk so long en he talk so loud, dat de white folks hear what he say. Den de marster en de overseer make it up 'mongst deyse'f dat dey gwine ter play a prank on dat nigger man.

"So den, one night, a leetle atter midnight, de marster got'm a white counterpin, he did, en wrop hisse'f in it, en den he cut two eye-holes in a piller-case, en drawed it down over his head, en went down ter de house whar de nigger man stay. Nigger man ain't gone ter bed. He been fryin' meat en bakin' ashcake, en he sot dar in de cheer noddin', wid grease in his mouf en big hunk er ashcake in his han'. De do' wuz half-way open, en de fier burnin' low.

"De marster walk in, he did, en sorter cle'r up his th'oat. Nigger man ain't wake up. Ef he make any movement, it 'uz ter clinch de ashcake a leetle tighter. Den de marster knock on de do'—*blim-blim-blim!* Nigger man sorter fling his head back, but 'twa'n't long 'fo' hit drapt forrerd ag'in, en he went on wid his noddin' like nothin' ain't happen. De marster knock some mo'—*blam-blam-blam!* Dis time de nigger wake up en roll his eye-balls roun'. He see de big white thing, en he skeered ter move. His han' shake so he tu'n de ashcake loose.

"Nigger man 'low, 'Who dat?'

"De marster say: 'You call me, en I come.'

"Nigger man say: 'I ain't call you. What yo' name?'

"Marster 'low, 'Gran'sir Death.'

"Nigger man shake so he can't skacely set still. De col' sweat come out on 'im. He 'low, 'Marse Death, I ain't call you. Somebody been fool you.'

"De marster 'low, 'I been hear you call me p'intedly. I lissen at you terday, en yistiddy, en day 'fo' yistiddy. You say you want me ter take you en yo' marster en de overseer. Now I done come at yo' call.'

"Nigger man shake wuss. He say: 'Marse Death, go git de overseer fus'. He lots bigger en fatter dan what I is. You'll like him de bes'. Please, suh, don't take me dis time, en I won't bodder you no mo' long ez I live.'

"De marster 'low, 'I come fer de man dat call me! I'm in a hurry! Daylight mustn't ketch me here. Come on!'

"Well, suh, dat nigger man make a break for de winder, he did, en he went thoo it like a frog divin' in de mill pon'. He tuck ter de woods, en he 'uz gone mighty nigh a week. When he come back home he went ter work, en he work harder dan any er de res'. Somebody come 'long en try ter buy 'im, but his marster 'low he won't take lev'm hunder'd dollars for 'im,—cash money, paid down in his han'!"

PAUL LAURENCE DUNBAR

(1872–1906)

———— ◄◆►► ————

The first American Negro poet to be published in leading magazines and to gain a nationwide reputation, Paul Laurence Dunbar was the son of a former slave who had served in the Union army. He was born in Dayton, Ohio, where he achieved high honors at a predominantly white high school and worked as an elevator operator while composing his early poems. His first two volumes of poetry, Oak and Ivy (1893) and Majors and Minors (1895), were published privately. The latter was favorably reviewed by William Dean Howells, then an editor of the highly influential Harper's Monthly Magazine. Howells became a patron of Dunbar and wrote an introduction to his Lyrics of Lowly Life (1896), which helped establish the poet's wide acceptance among white readers. Other collections of Dunbar's poems are Lyrics of the Hearthside (1899), Lyrics of Love and Laughter (1903), and Lyrics of Sunshine and Shadows (1905). He also published several collections of short stories and four novels. The Sport of the Gods (1902), Dunbar's only novel focusing on Negro life, was the first novel to explore problems of city life experienced by Negroes who had migrated to New York from the South. Beset by tuberculosis, domestic problems, and debt, Dunbar died at the age of thirty-four.

Like Robert Burns, Dunbar wrote two types of poetry, one in dialect and the other in "literary" English. His "literary" poems, which he hoped to be remembered for, reflect popular taste of the "mauve decade" and are flawed by excessive sentimentality. Modern opinion follows Howells's estimate that Dunbar's most successful writings are his dialect poems on Negro plantation life, which were influenced by both James Whitcomb Riley's Hoosier dialect poetry and Joel Chandler Harris's Uncle Remus stories. Dunbar's dialect poems closely follow the traditional treatment of Negro character made popular by such white writers as Harris and Thomas Nelson Page. The mental outlook of Dunbar's jovial, childlike blacks is summed up in the concluding line of "Accountability": "Viney, go put on de kittle, I got one o' mastah's chickens." Indeed, Edward Margolies in Native Sons (see Bibliography) characterizes Dunbar as a Negro poet who merely reflected what whites wanted to read about Negroes. But Dunbar was also capable of such poems as "The Colored Soldiers," which reminded the nation of its debt to black Union veterans; "Black Sampson of Brandywine," an early assertion of black pride; and "We Wear the Mask," an anguished statement on the role-playing requisite for Negro survival in a white society.

Accountability

Folks ain't got no right to censuah othah folks about dey habits;
Him dat giv' de squir'ls de bushtails made de bobtails fu' de
    rabbits.
Him dat built de gread big mountains hollered out de little valleys,
Him dat made de streets an' driveways wasn't shamed to make de
    alleys.

We is all constructed diff'ent, d'ain't no two of us de same;
We cain't he'p ouah likes an' dislikes, ef we'se bad we ain't to
    blame.
Ef we'se good, we needn't show off, case you bet it ain't ouah doin'
We gits into su'ttain channels dat we jes' cain't he'p pu'suin'.

Paul Laurence Dunbar poems reprinted by permission of Dodd, Mead, & Company, Inc., from The Complete Poems of Paul Laurence Dunbar.

But we all fits into places dat no othah ones could fill,
An' we does the things we has to, big er little, good er ill.
John cain't tek de place o' Henry, Su an' Sally ain't alike;
Bass ain't nuthin' like a suckah, chub ain't nuthin' like a pike.

When you come to think about it, how it's all planned out it's
    splendid.
Nuthin's done er evah happens, 'dout hit's somefin' dat's intended;
Don't keer whut you does, you has to, an' hit sholy beats de
    dickens—
Viney, go put on de kittle, I got one o' mastah's chickens.

The Colored Soldiers

If the muse were mine to tempt it
    And my feeble voice were strong,
If my tongue were trained to measures,
    I would sing a stirring song.
I would sing a song heroic
    Of those noble sons of Ham,
Of the gallant colored soldiers
    Who fought for Uncle Sam!

In the early days you scorned them,
    And with many a flip and flout
Said "These battles are the white man's,
    And the whites will fight them out."
Up the hills you fought and faltered,
    In the vales you strove and bled,
While your ears still heard the thunder
    Of the foes' advancing tread.

Then distress fell on the nation,
    And the flag was drooping low;
Should the dust pollute your banner?
    No! the nation shouted, No!
So when War, in savage triumph,

Spread abroad his funeral pall—
Then you called the colored soldiers,
   And they answered to your call.

And like hounds unleashed and eager
   For the life blood of the prey,
Sprung they forth and bore them bravely
   In the thickest of the fray.
And where'er the fight was hottest,
   Where the bullets fastest fell,
There they pressed unblanched and fearless
   At the very mouth of hell.

Ah, they rallied to the standard
   To uphold it by their might;
None were stronger in the labors,
   None were braver in the fight.
From the blazing breach of Wagner
   To the plains of Olustee,
They were foremost in the fight
   Of the battles of the free.

And at Pillow! God have mercy
   On the deeds committed there,
And the souls of those poor victims
   Sent to Thee without a prayer.
Let the fulness of Thy pity
   O'er the hot wrought spirits sway
Of the gallant colored soldiers
   Who fell fighting on that day!

Yes, the Blacks enjoy their freedom,
   And they won it dearly, too;
For the life blood of their thousands
   Did the Southern fields bedew.
In the darkness of their bondage,
   In the depths of slavery's night,

Their muskets flashed the dawning,
    And they fought their way to light.

They were comrades then and brothers,
    Are they more or less to-day?
They were good to stop a bullet
    And to front the fearful fray.
They were citizens and soldiers,
    When rebellion raised its head;
And the traits that made them worthy—
    Ah! those virtues are not dead.

They have shared your nightly vigils,
    They have shared your daily toil;
And their blood with yours commingling
    Has enriched the Southern soil.
They have slept and marched and suffered
    'Neath the same dark skies as you,
They have met as fierce a foeman,
    And have been as brave and true.

And their deeds shall find a record
    In the registry of Fame;
For their blood has cleansed completely
    Every blot of Slavery's shame.
So all honor and all glory
    To those noble sons of Ham—
The gallant colored soldiers
    Who fought for Uncle Sam!

We Wear the Mask

We wear the mask that grins and lies,
It hides our cheeks and shades our eyes—
This debt we pay to human guile;
With torn and bleeding hearts we smile,
And mouth with myriad subtleties.

Why should the world be overwise,
In counting all our tears and sighs?
Nay, let them only see us, while
   We wear the mask.

We smile, but, O great Christ, our cries
To thee from tortured souls arise.
We sing, but oh the clay is vile
Beneath our feet, and long the mile;
But let the world dream otherwise,
   We wear the mask!

Why Fades a Dream?

Why fades a dream?
   An iridescent ray
Flecked in between the tryst
   Of night and day.
   Why fades a dream?—
Of consciousness the shade
Wrought out by lack of light and made
   Upon life's stream.
   Why fades a dream?

That thought may thrive,
   So fades the fleshless dream;
Lest men should learn to trust
   The things that seem.
   So fades a dream,
That living thought may grow
And like a waxing star-beam glow
   Upon life's stream—
   So fades a dream.

Sympathy

I know what the caged bird feels, alas!
    When the sun is bright on the upland slopes;
When the wind stirs soft through the springing grass,
And the river flows like a stream of glass;
    When the first bird sings and the first bud opes,
And the faint perfume from its chalice steals—
I know what the caged bird feels!

I know why the caged bird beats his wing
    Till its blood is red on the cruel bars;
For he must fly back to his perch and cling
When he fain would be on the bough a-swing;
    And a pain still throbs in the old, old scars
And they pulse again with a keener sting—
I know why he beats his wing!

I know why the caged bird sings, ah me,
    When his wing is bruised and his bosom sore—
When he beats his bars and he would be free;
It is not a carol of joy or glee,
    But a prayer that he sends from his heart's deep core,
But a plea, that upward to Heaven he flings—
I know why the caged bird sings!

The News

Whut dat you whisperin' keepin' f'om me?
Don't shut me out 'cause I's ol' an' can't see.
Somep'n's gone wrong dat's a-causin' you dread—
Don't be afeared to tell— Whut! mastah dead?

Somebody brung de news early to-day—
One of de sojers he led, do you say?
Didn't he foller whah ol' mastah lead?
How kin he live w'en his leadah is dead?

Let me lay down awhile, dah by his bed;
I wants to t'ink—hit ain't cleah in my head:—
Killed while a-leadin' his men into fight—
Dat's whut you said, ain't it, did I hyeah right?

Mastah, my mastah, dead dah in de fiel'?
Lif' me up some—dah, jes' so I kin kneel.
I was too weak to go wid him, dey said,
Well, now I'll—fin' him—so—mastah is dead.

Yes, suh, I's comin' ez fas' ez I kin—
'T was kin' o' da'k, but hit's lightah agin:
P'omised yo' pappy I'd allus tek keer
Of you—yes, mastah—I's follerin'—hyeah!

Chrismus on the Plantation

It was Chrismus Eve, I mind hit fu' a mighty gloomy day—
Bofe de weathah an' de people—not a one of us was gay;
Cose you'll t'ink dat's mighty funny 'twell I try to mek hit cleah,
Fu' a da'ky's allus happy when de holidays is neah.

But we wasn't, fu' dat mo'nin' Mastah'd tol' us we mus' go,
He'd been payin' us sence freedom, but he couldn't pay no mo';
He wa'n't nevah used to plannin' 'fo' he got so po' an' ol',
So he gwine to give up tryin', an' de homestead mus' be sol'.

I kin see him stan'in' now erpon de step ez cleah ez day,
Wid de win' a-kind o' fondlin' thoo his haih all thin an' gray;
An' I 'membah how he trimbled when he said, "It's ha'd fu' me,
Not to mek yo' Chrismus brightah, but I 'low it wa'n't to be."

All de women was a-cryin', an' de men, too, on de sly,
An' I noticed somep'n shinin' even in ol' Mastah's eye.
But we all stood still to listen ez ol' Ben come f'om de crowd
An' spoke up, a-try'n' to steady down his voice and mek it loud:—

"Look hyeah, Mastah, I's been servin' yo' fu' lo! dese many yeahs,
An' now, sence we's got freedom an' you's kind o' po', hit 'pears
Dat you want us all to leave you 'cause you don't t'ink you can pay.
Ef my membry hasn't fooled me, seem dat whut I hyead you say.

"Er in othah wo'ds, you wants us to fu'git dat you's been kin',
An' ez soon ez you is he'pless, we's to leave you hyeah behin'.
Well, ef dat's de way dis freedom ac's on people, white er black,
You kin jes' tell Mistah Lincum fu' to tek his freedom back.

"We gwine wo'k dis ol' plantation fu' whatevah we kin git,
Fu' I know hit did suppo't us, an' de place kin do it yit.
Now de land is yo's, de hands is ouahs, an' I reckon we'll be brave,
An' we'll bah ez much ez you do w'en we has to scrape an' save."

Ol' Mastah stood dah trimblin', but a-smilin' thoo his teahs,
An' den hit seemed jes' nachul-like, de place fah rung wid cheahs,
An' soon ez dey was quiet, some one sta'ted sof' an' low:
"Praise God," an' den we all jined in, "from whom all blessin's
flow!"

Well, dey wasn't no use tryin', ouah min's was sot to stay,
An' po' ol' Mastah couldn't plead ner baig, ner drive us 'way,
An' all at once, hit seemed to us, de day was bright agin,
So evahone was gay dat night, an' watched de Chrismus in.

At Candle-Lightin' Time

When I come in f'om de co'n-fiel' aftah wo'kin' ha'd all day,
It's amazin' nice to fin' my suppah all erpon de way;
An' it's nice to smell de coffee bubblin' ovah in de pot,
An' it's fine to see de meat a-sizzlin' teasin'-lak an' hot.

But when suppah-time is ovah, an' de t'ings is cleahed away;
Den de happy hours dat foller are de sweetes' of de day.
When my co'ncob pipe is sta'ted, an' de smoke is drawin' prime,
My ole 'ooman says, "I reckon, Ike, it's candle-lightin' time."

Den de chillun snuggle up to me, an' all commence to call,
"Oh, say, daddy, now it's time to mek de shadders on de wall."
So I puts my han's togethah—evah daddy knows de way—
An' de chillun snuggle closer 'roun' ez I begin to say:—

"Fus' thing, hyeah come Mistah Rabbit; don' you see him wo'k
    his eahs?
Huh, uh! dis mus' be a donkey—look, how innercent he 'pears!
Dah's de ole black swan a-swimmin'—ain't she got a' awful neck?
Who's dis feller dat's a-comin'? Why, dat's ole dog Tray, I 'spec'!"

Dat's de way I run on, tryin' fu' to please 'em all I can;
Den I hollahs, "Now be keerful—dis hyeah las' 's de buga-man!"
An' dey runs an' hides dey faces; dey ain't skeered—dey's lettin' on:
But de play ain't raaly ovah twell dat buga-man is gone.

So I jes' teks up my banjo, an' I plays a little chune,
An' you see dem haids come peepin' out to listen mighty soon.
Den my wife says, "Sich a pappy fu' to give you sich a fright!
Jes' you go to baid, an' leave him: say yo' prayers an' say good-
    night."

The Colored Band

W'en de colo'ed ban' comes ma'chin' down de street,
Don't you people stan' daih starin'; lif' yo' feet!
    Ain't dey playin'? Hip, hooray!
    Stir yo' stumps an' cleah de way,
Fu' de music dat dey mekin' can't be beat.

Oh, de major man's a-swingin' of his stick,
An' de pickaninnies crowdin' roun' him thick;
    In his go'geous uniform,
    He's de lightnin' of de sto'm,
An' de little clouds erroun' look mighty slick.

You kin hyeah a fine perfo'mance w'en de white ban's serenade,
    An' dey play dey high-toned music mighty sweet,

But hit's Sousa played in ragtime, an' hit's Rastus on Parade,
  W'en de colo'ed ban' comes ma'chin' down de street.

W'en de colo'ed ban' comes ma'chin' down de street
You kin hyeah de ladies all erroun' repeat:
  "Ain't dey handsome? Ain't dey gran'?
  Ain't dey splendid? Goodness, lan'!
W'y dey's pu'fect f'om dey fo'heads to dey feet!"

An' sich steppin' to de music down de line,
'T ain't de music by itself dat meks it fine,
  Hit's de walkin', step by step,
  An' de keepin' time wid "Hep,"
Dat it mek a common ditty soun' divine.

Oh, de white ban' play hits music, an' hit's mighty good to hyeah,
An' it sometimes leaves a ticklin' in yo' feet;
But de hea't goes into bus'ness fu' to he'p erlong de eah,
  W'en de colo'ed ban' goes ma'chin' down de street.

Black Samson of Brandywine

> "In the fight at Brandywine, Black Samson, a giant negro
> armed with a scythe, sweeps his way through the red ranks. . . ."
> C. M. Skinner's *Myths and Legends of Our Own Land*.

Gray are the pages of record,
  Dim are the volumes of eld;
Else had old Delaware told us
  More that her history held.
Told us with pride in the story,
  Honest and noble and fine,
More of the tale of my hero,
  Black Samson of Brandywine.

Sing of your chiefs and your nobles,
  Saxon and Celt and Gaul,
Breath of mine ever shall join you,
  Highly I honor them all.

Give to them all of their glory,
   But for this noble of mine,
Lend him a tithe of your tribute,
   Black Samson of Brandywine.

There in the heat of the battle,
   There in the stir of the fight,
Loomed he, an ebony giant,
   Black as the pinions of night.
Swinging his scythe like a mower
   Over a field of grain,
Needless the care of the gleaners,
   Where he had passed amain.

Straight through the human harvest,
   Cutting a bloody swath,
Woe to you, soldier of Briton!
   Death is abroad in his path.
Flee from the scythe of the reaper,
   Flee while the moment is thine,
None may with safety withstand him,
   Black Samson of Brandywine.

Was he a freeman or bondman?
   Was he a man or a thing?
What does it matter? His brav'ry
   Renders him royal—a king.
If he was only a chattel,
   Honor the ransom may pay
Of the royal, the loyal black giant
   Who fought for his country that day.

Noble and bright is the story,
   Worthy the touch of the lyre,
Sculptor or poet should find it
   Full of the stuff to inspire.
Beat it in brass and in copper,
   Tell it in storied line,

So that the world may remember
Black Samson of Brandywine.

On the Dedication of Dorothy Hall

Tuskegee, Ala., April 22, 1901

Not to the midnight of the gloomy past,
  Do we revert to-day; we look upon
The golden present and the future vast
  Whose vistas show us visions of the dawn.

Nor shall the sorrows of departed years
  The sweetness of our tranquil souls annoy,
The sunshine of our hopes dispels the tears,
  And clears our eyes to see this later joy.

Not ever in the years that God hath given
  Have we gone friendless down the thorny way,
Always the clouds of pregnant black were riven
  By flashes from His own eternal day.

The women of a race should be its pride;
  We glory in the strength our mothers had,
We glory that this strength was not denied
  To labor bravely, nobly, and be glad.

God give to these within this temple here,
  Clear vision of the dignity of toil,
That virtue in them may its blossoms rear
  Unspotted, fragrant, from the lowly soil.

God bless the givers for their noble deed,
  Shine on them with the mercy of Thy face,
Who come with open hearts to help and speed
  The striving women of a struggling race.

To the South

On Its New Slavery

Heart of the Southland, heed me pleading now,
Who bearest, unashamed, upon my brow
The long kiss of the loving tropic sun,
And yet, whose veins with thy red current run.

Borne on the bitter winds from every hand,
Strange tales are flying over all the land,
And Condemnation, with his pinions foul,
Glooms in the place where broods the midnight owl.

What art thou, that the world should point at thee,
And vaunt and chide the weakness that they see?
There was a time they were not wont to chide;
Where is thy old, uncompromising pride?

Blood-washed, thou shouldst lift up thine honored head,
White with the sorrow for thy loyal dead
Who lie on every plain, on every hill,
And whose high spirit walks the Southland still:

Whose infancy our mother's hands have nursed.
Thy manhood, gone to battle unaccursed,
Our fathers left to till th' reluctant field,
To rape the soil for what she would not yield;

Wooing for aye, the cold unam'rous sod,
Whose growth for them still meant a master's rod;
Tearing her bosom for the wealth that gave
The strength that made the toiler still a slave.

Too long we hear the deep impassioned cry
That echoes vainly to the heedless sky;
Too long, too long, the Macedonian call
Falls fainting far beyond the outward wall,

Within whose sweep, beneath the shadowing trees,
A slumbering nation takes its dangerous ease;
Too long the rumors of thy hatred go
For those who loved thee and thy children so.

Thou must arise forthwith, and strong, thou must
Throw off the smirching of this baser dust,
Lay by the practice of this later creed,
And be thine honest self again indeed.

There was a time when even slavery's chain
Held in some joys to alternate with pain,
Some little light to give the night relief,
Some little smiles to take the place of grief.

There was a time when, jocund as the day,
The toiler hoed his row and sung his lay,
Found something gleeful in the very air,
And solace for his toiling everywhere.

Now all is changed, within the rude stockade,
A bondsman whom the greed of men has made
Almost too brutish to deplore his plight,
Toils hopeless on from joyless morn till night.

For him no more the cabin's quiet rest,
The homely joys that gave to labor zest;
No more for him the merry banjo's sound,
Nor trip of lightsome dances footing round.

For him no more the lamp shall glow at eve,
Nor chubby children pluck him by the sleeve;
No more for him the master's eyes be bright—
He has nor freedom's nor a slave's delight.

What, was it all for naught, those awful years
That drenched a groaning land with blood and tears?

Was it to leave this sly convenient hell,
That brother fighting his own brother fell?

When that great struggle held the world in awe,
And all the nations blanched at what they saw,
Did Sanctioned Slavery bow its conquered head
That this unsanctioned crime might rise instead?

Is it for this we all have felt the flame—
This newer bondage and this deeper shame?
Nay, not for this, a nation's heroes bled,
And North and South with tears beheld their dead.

Oh, Mother South, hast thou forgot thy ways,
Forgot the glory of thine ancient days,
Forgot the honor that once made thee great,
And stooped to this unhallowèd estate?

It cannot last, thou wilt come forth in might,
A warrior queen full armored for the fight;
And thou wilt take, e'en with thy spear in rest,
Thy dusky children to thy saving breast.

Till then, no more, no more the gladsome song,
Strike only deeper chords, the notes of wrong;
Till then, the sigh, the tear, the oath, the moan,
Till thou, oh, South, and thine, come to thine own.

Compensation

Because I had loved so deeply,
    Because I had loved so long,
God in His great compassion
    Gave me the gift of song.

Because I have loved so vainly,
  And sung with such faltering breath,
The Master in infinite mercy
  Offers the boon of Death.

CHARLES W. CHESNUTT

(1858–1932)

Charles Waddell Chesnutt occupies a position in prose fiction analogous to that of Paul Laurence Dunbar in poetry. The first Negro short-story writer and novelist to attract a national audience, Chesnutt wrote stories for the prestigious Atlantic Monthly, and Houghton Mifflin published his collected stories and novels. Like Dunbar's reputation, which had been promoted by a white editor, William Dean Howells of Harper's Monthly, Chesnutt's popularity was widened by Walter Hines Page of The Atlantic Monthly. Chesnutt's editors, however, chose not to reveal his race until the stories had firmly established his position.

Chesnutt, born in Cleveland, moved at the age of eight with his family to Fayetteville, North Carolina, where he eventually taught school. Following a brief experience as a journalist in New York, he returned to Cleveland, where he was admitted to the bar and served as a court stenographer, having taught himself both law and stenography. His fiction began to appear in The Atlantic Monthly in 1887, and in 1899 two collections of his short stories were published, The Conjure Woman and The Wife of His Youth. Chesnutt then switched genre and produced three novels, none of which has been regarded with the critical favor that his stories received. The House behind the Cedars (1900) dealt with the unhappy attempt of a Negro girl to pass as white. The Marrow of Tradition (1901) was set against the background of the 1898 riots in Wilmington, North Carolina, which had prevented Negro voters from registering. It dealt with the struggle by a fictional Negro physician, whose son had been killed in the turmoil, to overcome an impulse toward violent retaliation and arrive at a moderate position. The Colonel's Dream (1905) presented the efforts of a white Southern colonel to eliminate the vestiges of slavery in the antebellum South through enlightened business practices in building cotton mills which would promote progress, prosperity, and harmony. Though he lived for another twenty-seven years, Chesnutt wrote little after 1905.

Like Dunbar, Chesnutt is sometimes accused of representing a bourgeois and accommodationist view, particularly in his novels. Unlike Dunbar, though, he gave the "Plantation Tradition" an ironic twist in his stories. While Uncle Julius, the Negro storyteller who appears in all the tales that comprise The Conjure Woman, seems at first to be a quaint and lovable "darky" straight out of white fiction of the "Plantation Tradition," all his stories establish some sort of advantage over his white employer. Underneath their humorous surface, the tales contain a bitter indictment of slavery. The stories collected in The Wife of His Youth present a more open attack on racist attitudes, in tones ranging from humorous to maudlin. Several stories satirize the pretensions of the "Blue Vein Society," a group of socially elite, light-skinned Negroes who despise their darker-skinned brothers, and two of them involve a Negro husband's return to a dark wife after unhappy experiences in white or light-skinned-Negro society. Countering the humor of "The Passing of Grandison" is the effusive sentimentality of "The Bouquet," in which a young black girl, barred from visiting a segregated cemetery, must employ the services of a dog to carry a bouquet of wilted flowers to the grave of her white schoolmistress.

From The Conjure Woman

Po' Sandy

On the northeast corner of my vineyard in central North Carolina, and fronting on the Lumberton plank-road, there stood a small frame house, of the simplest construction. It was built of pine lumber, and contained but one room, to which one window gave light and one door admission. Its weather-beaten sides revealed a virgin innocence of paint. Against one end of the house, and occupying half its width, there stood a huge brick chimney: the crumbling mortar had left large cracks between the bricks; the bricks themselves had begun to scale off in large flakes, leaving the chimney sprinkled with unsightly blotches. These evidences of decay were but partially concealed by a creeping vine, which extended its slender branches hither and thither in an ambitious but futile attempt to cover the whole chimney. The wooden shutter, which had once protected the unglazed window, had fallen from its hinges, and lay rotting in the rank grass and jimson weeds beneath. This building, I learned when I bought the place, had been used as a schoolhouse for several years prior to the breaking out of the war, since which time it had remained unoccupied, save when some stray cow or vagrant hog had sought shelter within its walls from the chill rains and nipping winds of winter.

One day my wife requested me to build her a new kitchen. The house erected by us, when we first came to live upon the vineyard, contained a very conveniently arranged kitchen; but for some occult reason my wife wanted a kitchen in the back yard, apart from the dwelling-house, after the usual Southern fashion. Of course I had to build it.

To save expense, I decided to tear down the old schoolhouse, and use the lumber, which was in a good state of preservation, in the construction of the new kitchen. Before demolishing the old house, however, I made an estimate of the amount of material contained in it, and found that I would have to buy several hundred feet of lumber additional, in order to build the new kitchen according to my wife's plan.

One morning old Julius McAdoo, our colored coachman, harnessed the gray mare to the rockaway, and drove my wife and me over to the sawmill from which I meant to order the new lumber. We drove down the long lane which led from our house to the plank-road; following the plank-road for about a mile, we turned into a road running through the forest and across the swamp to the sawmill beyond. Our carriage jolted over the half-rotted corduroy road which traversed the swamp, and then climbed the long hill leading to the sawmill. When we reached the mill, the foreman had gone over to a neighboring farmhouse, probably to smoke or gossip, and we were compelled to await his return before we could transact our business. We remained seated in the carriage, a few rods from the mill, and watched the leisurely movements of the mill-hands. We had not waited long before a huge pine log was placed in position, the machinery of the mill was set in motion, and the circular saw began to eat its way through the log, with a loud whir which resounded throughout the vicinity of the mill. The sound rose and fell in a sort of rhythmic cadence, which, heard from where we sat, was not unpleasing, and not loud enough to prevent conversation. When the saw started on its second journey through the log, Julius observed, in a lugubrious tone, and with a perceptible shudder:—

"Ugh! but dat des do cuddle my blood!"

"What's the matter, Uncle Julius?" inquired my wife, who is of a very sympathetic turn of mind. "Does the noise affect your nerves?"

"No, Mis' Annie," replied the old man, with emotion, "I ain' narvous; but dat saw, a-cuttin' en grindin' thoo dat stick er timber, en moanin', en groanin', en sweekin', kyars my 'memb'ance back ter ole times, en 'min's me er po' Sandy." The pathetic intonation with which he lengthened out the "po' Sandy" touched a responsive chord in our own hearts.

"And who was poor Sandy?" asked my wife, who takes a deep interest in the stories of plantation life which she hears from the lips of the older colored people. Some of these stories are quaintly humorous; others wildly extravagant, revealing the Oriental cast of the negro's imagination; while others, poured freely into the sympathetic ear of a Northern-bred woman, disclose many a tragic incident of the darker side of slavery.

"Sandy," said Julius, in reply to my wife's question, "was a nigger w'at useter b'long ter ole Mars Marrabo McSwayne. Mars Marrabo's place wuz on de yuther side'n de swamp, right nex' ter yo' place. Sandy wuz a monst'us good nigger, en could do so many things erbout a plantation, en alluz 'ten' ter his wuk so well, dat w'en Mars Marrabo's chilluns growed up en married off, dey all un 'em wanted dey daddy fer ter gin 'em Sandy fer a weddin' present. But Mars Marrabo knowed de res' would n' be satisfied ef he gin Sandy ter a'er one un 'em; so w'en dey wuz all done married, he fix it by 'lowin' one er his chilluns ter take Sandy fer a mont' er so, en den ernudder for a mont' er so, en so on dat erway tel day had all had 'im de same lenk er time; en den dey would all take him roun' ag'in, 'cep'n' oncet in a w'ile w'en Mars Marrabo would len' 'im ter some er his yuther kinfolks 'roun' de country, w'en dey wuz short er han's; tel bimeby it got so Sandy did n' hardly knowed whar he wuz gwine ter stay fum one week's een' ter de yuther.

"One time w'en Sandy wuz lent out ez yushal, a spekilater come erlong wid a lot er niggers, en Mars Marrabo swap' Sandy's wife off fer a noo 'oman. W'en Sandy come back, Mars Marrabo gin 'im a dollar, en 'lowed he wuz monst'us sorry fer ter break up de fambly, but de spekilater had gin 'im big boot, en times wuz hard en money skase, en so he wuz bleedst ter make de trade. Sandy tuk on some 'bout losin' his wife, but he soon seed dey want no use cryin' ober spilt merlasses; en bein' ez he lacked de looks er de noo 'oman, he tuk up wid her atter she'd be'n on de plantation a mont' er so.

"Sandy en his noo wife got on mighty well tergedder, en de niggers all 'mence' ter talk about how lovin' dey wuz. W'en Tenie wuz tuk sick oncet, Sandy useter set up all night wid' er, en den go ter wuk in de mawnin' des lack he had his reg'lar sleep; en Tenie would 'a' done anythin' in de worl' for her Sandy.

"Sandy en Tenie had n' be'n libbin' tergedder fer mo' d'n two mont's befo' Mars Marrabo's old uncle, w'at libbed down in Robeson County, sent up ter fin' out ef Mars Marrabo could n' len' 'im er hire 'im a good han' fer a mont' er so. Sandy's marster wuz one er dese yer easy-gwine folks w'at wanter please eve'ybody, en he says yas, he could len' 'im Sandy. En Mars Marrabo tol' Sandy fer ter git ready ter go down ter Robeson nex' day, fer ter stay a mont' er so.

"It wuz monst'us hard on Sandy fer ter take 'im 'way fum Tenie. It wuz so fur down ter Robeson dat he did n' hab no chance er comin' back ter see her tel de time wuz up; he would n' 'a' mine comin' ten er fifteen mile at night ter see Tenie, but Mars Marrabo's uncle's plantation wuz mo' d'n forty mile off. Sandy wuz

mighty sad en cas' down atter w'at Mars Marrabo tol' 'im, en he
says ter Tenie, sezee:—

" 'I'm gittin' monst'us ti'ed er dish yer gwine roun' so much.
Here I is lent ter Mars Jeems dis mont', en I got ter do so-en-so;
en ter Mars Archie de nex' mont', en I got ter do so-en-so; den I
got ter go ter Miss Jinnie's; en hit's Sandy dis en Sandy dat, en
Sandy yer en Sandy dere, tel it 'pears ter me I ain' got no home,
ner no marster, ner no mistiss, ner no nuffin. I can't eben keep
a wife: my yuther ole 'oman wuz sol' away widout my gittin' a
chance fer ter tell her good-by; en now I got ter go off en leab
you, Tenie, en I dunno whe'r I'm eber gwine ter see you ag'in er
no. I wisht I wuz a tree, er a stump, er a rock, er sump'n w'at could
stay on de plantation fer a w'ile.'

"Atter Sandy got thoo talkin', Tenie did n' say naer word, but
des sot dere by de fier, studyin' en studyin'. Bimeby she up'n'
says:—

" 'Sandy, is I eber tol' you I wuz a cunjuh 'oman?'

"Co'se Sandy had n' nebber dremp' er nuffin lack dat, en he
made a great 'miration w'en he hear w'at Tenie say. Bimeby Tenie
went on:—

" 'I ain' goophered nobody, ner done no cunjuh wuk, fer fifteen
year er mo'; en w'en I got religion I made up my mine I would n'
wuk no mo' goopher. But dey is some things I doan b'lieve it's no
sin fer ter do; en ef you doan wanter be sent roun' fum pillar ter
pos', en ef you doan wanter go down ter Robeson, I kin fix things
so you won't haf ter. Ef you'll des say de word, I kin turn you ter
w'ateber you wanter be, en you kin stay right whar you wanter, ez
long ez you mineter.'

"Sandy say he doan keer; he's willin' fer ter do anythin' fer ter
stay close ter Tenie. Den Tenie ax 'im ef he doan wanter be turnt
inter a rabbit.

"Sandy say, 'No, de dogs mought git atter me.'

" 'Shill I turn you ter a wolf?' sez Tenie.

" 'No, eve'ybody's skeered er a wolf, en I doan want nobody ter
be skeered er me.'

" 'Shill I turn you ter a mawkin'-bird?'

" 'No, a hawk mought ketch me. I wanter be turnt inter sump'n
w'at 'll stay in one place.'

" 'I kin turn you ter a tree,' sez Tenie. 'You won't hab no mouf ner years, but I kin turn you back oncet in a w'ile, so you kin git sump'n ter eat, en hear w'at 's gwine on.'

"Well, Sandy say dat 'll do. En so Tenie tuk 'im down by de aidge er de swamp, not fur fum de quarters, en turnt 'im inter a big pine-tree, en sot 'im out 'mongs' some yuther trees. En de nex' mawnin', ez some er de fiel' han's wuz gwine long dere, dey seed a tree w'at dey did n' 'member er habbin' seed befo'; it wuz monst'us quare, en dey wuz bleedst ter 'low dat dey had n' 'membered right, er e'se one er de saplin's had be'n growin' monst'us fas'.

"W'en Mars Marrabo 'skiver' dat Sandy wuz gone, he 'lowed Sandy had runned away. He got de dogs out, but de las' place dey could track Sandy ter wuz de foot er dat pine-tree. En dere de dogs stood en barked, en bayed, en pawed at de tree, en tried ter climb up on it; en w'en dey wuz tuk roun' thoo de swamp ter look fer de scent, dey broke loose en made fer dat tree ag'in. It wuz de beatenis' thing de w'ite folks eber hearn of, en Mars Marrabo 'lowed dat Sandy must 'a' clim' up on de tree en jump' off on a mule er sump'n, en rid fur ernuff fer ter spile de scent. Mars Marrabo wanted ter 'cuse some er de yuther niggers er heppin' Sandy off, but dey all 'nied it ter de las'; en eve'ybody knowed Tenie sot too much sto' by Sandy fer ter he'p 'im run away whar she could n' nebber see 'im no mo'.

"W'en Sandy had b'n gone long ernuff fer folks ter think he done got clean away, Tenie useter go down ter de woods at night en turn 'im back, en den dey'd slip up ter de cabin en set by de fire en talk. But dey ha' ter be monst'us keerful, er e'se somebody would 'a' seed 'em, en dat would 'a' spile' de whole thing; so Tenie alluz turnt Sandy back in de mawnin' early, befo' anybody wuz a-stirrin'.

"But Sandy did n' git erlong widout his trials en tribberlations. One day a woodpecker come erlong en 'mence' ter peck at de tree; en de nex' time Sandy wuz turnt back he had a little roun' hole in his arm, des lack a sharp stick be'n stuck in it. Atter dat Tenie sot a sparrer-hawk fer ter watch de tree; en w'en de wood-pecker come erlong nex' mawnin' fer ter finish his nes', he got gobble' up mos' fo' he stuck his bill in de bark.

"Nudder time, Mars Marrabo sent a nigger out in de woods fer ter chop tuppentime boxes. De man chop a box in dish yer tree, en hack' de bark up two er th'ee feet, fer ter let de tuppentime run. De nex' time Sandy wuz turnt back he had a big skyar on his lef' leg, des lack it be'n skunt; en it tuk Tenie nigh 'bout all night fer ter fix a mixtry ter kyo it up. Atter dat, Tenie sot a hawnet fer ter watch de tree; en w'en de nigger come back ag'in fer ter cut ernudder box on de yuther side'n de tree, de hawnet stun 'im so hard dat de ax slip en cut his foot nigh 'bout off.

"W'en Tenie see so many things happenin' ter de tree, she 'cluded she 'd ha' her turn Sandy ter sump'n e'se; en atter studyin' de matter ober, en talkin' wid Sandy one ebenin', she made up her mine fer ter fix up a goopher mixtry w'at would turn herse'f en Sandy ter foxes, er sump'n, so dey could run away en go some'rs whar dey could be free en lib lack w'ite folks.

"But dey ain' no tellin' w'at 's gwine ter happen in dis worl'. Tenie had got de night sot fer her en Sandy ter run away, w'en dat ve'y day one er Mars Marrabo's sons rid up ter de big house in his buggy, en say his wife wuz monst'us sick, en he want his mammy ter len' 'im a 'oman fer ter nuss his wife. Tenie's mistiss say sen' Tenie; she wuz a good nuss. Young mars wuz in a tarrible hurry fer ter git back home. Tenie wuz washin' at de big house dat day, en her mistiss say she should go right 'long wid her young marster. Tenie tried ter make some 'scuse fer ter git away en hide 'tel night, w'en she would have eve'ything fix' up fer her en Sandy; she say she wanter go ter her cabin fer ter git her bonnet. Her mistiss say it doan matter 'bout de bonnet; her head-hankcher wuz good ernuff. Den Tenie say she wanter git her bes' frock; her mistiss say no, she doan need no mo' frock, en w'en dat one got dirty she could git a clean one whar she wuz gwine. So Tenie had ter git in de buggy en go 'long wid young Mars Dunkin ter his plantation, w'ich wuz mo' d'n twenty mile away; en day wa'n't no chance er her seein' Sandy no mo' 'tel she come back home. De po' gal felt monst'us bad 'bout de way things wuz gwine on, en she knowed Sandy mus' be a wond'rin' why she did n' come en turn 'im back no mo'.

"W'iles Tenie wuz away nussin' young Mars Dunkin's wife, Mars Marrabo tuk a notion fer ter buil' 'im a noo kitchen; en bein' ez he had lots er timber on his place, he begun ter look 'roun' fer a tree ter hab de lumber sawed out'n. En I dunno how it come to be so, but he happen fer ter hit on de ve'y tree w'at Sandy wuz turnt inter. Tenie wuz gone, en dey wa'n't nobody ner nuffin fer ter watch de tree.

"De two men w'at cut de tree down say dey nebber had sech a time wid a tree befo': dey axes would glansh off, en did n' 'pear to make no progress thoo de wood; en of all de creakin', en shakin', en wobblin' you eber see, dat tree done it w'en it commence' ter fall. It wuz de beatenis' thing!

"W'en dey got de tree all trim' up, dey chain it up ter a timber waggin, en start fer de sawmill. But dey had a hard time gittin' de log dere: fus' dey got stuck in de mud w'en dey wuz gwine crosst de swamp, en it wuz two er th'ee hours befo' dey could git out. W'en dey start' on ag'in, de chain kep' a-comin' loose, en dey had ter keep a-stoppin' en a-stoppin' fer ter hitch de log up ag'in. W'en dey commence' ter climb de hill ter de sawmill, de log broke loose, en roll down de hill en in 'mongs' de trees, en hit tuk nigh 'bout half a day mo' ter git it haul' up ter de sawmill.

"De nex' mawnin' atter de day de tree wuz haul' ter de sawmill, Tenie come home. W'en she got back ter her cabin, de fus' thing she done wuz ter run down ter de woods en see how Sandy wuz gittin' on. W'en she seed de stump standin' dere, wid de sap runnin' out'n it, en de limbs layin' scattered roun', she nigh 'bout went out'n her min'. She run ter her cabin, en got her goopher mixtry, en den follered de track er de timber waggin ter de sawmill. She knowed Sandy could n' lib mo' d'n a minute er so ef she turnt him back, fer he wuz all chop' up so he'd 'a' be'n bleedst ter die. But she wanted ter turn 'im back long ernuff fer ter 'splain ter 'im dat she had n' went off a-purpose, en lef' 'im ter be chop' down en sawed up. She did n' want Sandy ter die wid no hard feelin's to'ds her.

"Da han's at de sawmill had des got de big log on de kerridge, en wuz startin' up de saw, w'en dey seed a 'oman runnin' up de hill, all out er bref, cryin' en gwine on des lack she wuz plumb 'stracted. It wuz Tenie; she come right inter de mill, en th'owed herse'f on de log, right in front er de saw, a-hollerin' en cryin' ter her Sandy ter fergib her, en not ter think hard er her, fer it wa'n't no fault er hern. Den Tenie 'membered de tree did n' hab no years, en she wuz gittin' ready fer ter wuk her goopher mixtry so ez ter turn Sandy back, w'en de mill-hands kotch holt er her en tied her arms wid a rope, en fasten' her to one er de posts in de saw-mill; en den dey started de saw up ag'in, en cut de log up inter bo'ds en scantlin's right befo' her eyes. But it wuz mighty hard wuk; fer of all de sweekin', en moanin', en groanin', dat log done it w'iles de saw wuz a-cuttin' thoo it. De saw wuz one er dese yer ole-timey, up-en-down saws, en hit tuk longer dem days ter saw a log 'en it do now. Dey greased de saw, but dat did n' stop de fuss; hit kep' right on, tel fin'ly dey got de log all sawed up.

"W'en de oberseah w'at run de sawmill come fum breakfas', de han's up en tell him 'bout de crazy 'oman—ez dey s'posed she wuz —w'at had come runnin' in de sawmill, a-hollerin' en gwine on, en tried ter th'ow herse'f befo' de saw. En de oberseah sent two er th'ee er de han's fer ter take Tenie back ter her marster's plantation.

"Tenie 'peared ter be out'n her min' fer a long time, en her marster ha' ter lock her up in de smoke-'ouse 'tel she got ober her spells. Mars Marrabo wuz monst'us mad, en hit would 'a' made yo' flesh crawl fer ter hear him cuss, 'caze he say de spekilater w'at he got Tenie fum had fooled 'im by wukkin' a crazy 'oman off on him. W'iles Tenie wuz lock up in de smoke-'ouse, Mars Marrabo tuk 'n' haul de lumber fum de sawmill, en put up his noo kitchen.

"W'en Tenie got quiet' down, so she could be 'lowed ter go 'roun' de plantation, she up'n' tole her marster all erbout Sandy en de pine-tree; en w'en Mars Marrabo hearn it, he 'lowed she wuz de wuss 'stracted nigger he eber hearn of. He did n' know w'at ter do wid Tenie: fus' he thought he'd put her in de po'house; but fin'ly, seein' ez she did n' do no harm ter nobody ner nuffin, but des went 'roun' moanin', en groanin', en shakin' her head, he 'cluded ter let her stay on de plantation en nuss de little nigger chilluns w'en dey mammies wuz ter wuk in de cotton-fiel'.

"De noo kitchen Mars Marrabo buil' wuz n' much use, fer it had n' be'n put up long befo' de niggers 'mence' ter notice quare things erbout it. Dey could hear sump'n moanin' en groanin' 'bout de kitchen in de night-time, en w'en de win' would blow dey could hear sump'n a-hollerin' en sweekin' lack it wuz in great pain en sufferin'. En it got so atter a w'ile dat it wuz all Mars Marrabo's wife could do ter git a 'oman ter stay in de kitchen in de daytime long ernuff ter do de cookin'; en dey wa'n't naer nigger on de plantation w'at would n' rudder take forty dan ter go 'bout dat kitchen atter dark,—dat is, 'cep'n' Tenie; she did n' 'pear ter min' de ha'nts. She useter slip 'roun' at night, en set on de kitchen steps, en lean up agin de do'-jamb, en run on ter herse'f wid some kine er foolishness w'at nobody could n' make out; fer Mars Marrabo had th'eaten' ter sen' her off'n de plantation ef she say anything ter any er de yuther niggers 'bout de pine-tree. But somehow er 'nudder de niggers foun' out all erbout it, en dey all knowed de kitchen wuz ha'nted by Sandy's sperrit. En bimeby hit got so Mars Marrabo's wife herse'f wuz skeered ter go out in de yard atter dark.

"W'en it come ter dat, Mars Marrabo tuk en to' de kitchen down, en use' de lumber fer ter buil' dat ole school'ouse w'at you er talkin' 'bout pullin' down. De school'ouse wuz n' use' 'cep'n' in de daytime, en on dark nights folks gwine 'long de road would hear quare soun's en see quare things. Po' ole Tenie useter go down dere at night, en wander 'roun' de school'ouse; en de niggers all 'lowed she went fer ter talk wid Sandy's sperrit. En one winter mawnin', w'en one er de boys went ter school early fer ter start de fire, w'at should he fin' but po' ole Tenie, layin' on de flo', stiff, en col', en dead. Dere did n' 'pear ter be nuffin pertickler de matter wid her,—she had des grieve' herse'f ter def fer her Sandy. Mars Marrabo did n' shed no tears. He thought Tenie wuz crazy, en dey wa'n't no tellin' w'at she mought do nex'; en dey ain' much room in dis worl' fer crazy w'ite folks, let 'lone a crazy nigger.

"Hit wa'n't long atter dat befo' Mars Marrabo sol' a piece er his track er lan' ter Mars Dugal' McAdoo,—*my* ole marster,—en dat's how de ole school'ouse happen to be on yo' place. W'en de wah broke out, de school stop', en de ole school'ouse be'n stannin' empty ever sence,—dat is, 'cep'n' fer de ha'nts. En folks sez dat de ole school'ouse, er any yuther house w'at got any er dat lumber in it w'at wuz sawed out'n de tree w'at Sandy wuz turnt inter, is gwine ter be ha'nted tel de las' piece er plank is rotted en crumble' inter dus'.'"

Annie had listened to this gruesome narrative with strained attention.

"What a system it was," she exclaimed, when Julius had finished, "under which such things were possible!"

"What things?" I asked, in amazement. "Are you seriously considering the possibility of a man's being turned into a tree?"

"Oh, no," she replied quickly, "not that;" and then she murmured absently, and with a dim look in her fine eyes, "Poor Tenie!"

We ordered the lumber, and returned home. That night, after we had gone to bed, and my wife had to all appearances been sound asleep for half an hour, she startled me out of an incipient doze by exclaiming suddenly,—

"John, I don't believe I want my new kitchen built out of the lumber in that old schoolhouse."

"You would n't for a moment allow yourself," I replied, with some asperity, "to be influenced by that absurdly impossible yarn which Julius was spinning to-day?"

"I know the story is absurd," she replied dreamily, "and I am not so silly as to believe it. But I don't think I should ever be able to take any pleasure in that kitchen if it were built out of that lumber. Besides, I think the kitchen would look better and last longer if the lumber were all new."

Of course she had her way. I bought the new lumber, though not without grumbling. A week or two later I was called away from home on business. On my return, after an absence of several days, my wife remarked to me,—

"John, there has been a split in the Sandy Run Colored Baptist Church, on the temperance question. About half the members have come out from the main body, and set up for themselves. Uncle Julius is one of the seceders, and he came to me yesterday and asked if they might not hold their meetings in the old schoolhouse for the present."

"I hope you did n't let the old rascal have it," I returned, with some warmth. I had just received a bill for the new lumber I had bought.

"Well," she replied, "I couldn't refuse him the use of the house for so good a purpose."

"And I'll venture to say," I continued, "that you subscribed something toward the support of the new church?"

She did not attempt to deny it.

"What are they going to do about the ghost?" I asked, somewhat curious to know how Julius would get around this obstacle.

"Oh," replied Annie, "Uncle Julius says that ghosts never disturb religious worship, but that if Sandy's spirit *should* happen to stray into meeting by mistake, no doubt the preaching would do it good."

From *The Wife of His Youth*

The Passing of Grandison

I

When it is said that it was done to please a woman, there ought perhaps to be enough said to explain anything; for what a man will not do to please a woman is yet to be discovered. Nevertheless, it might be well to state a few preliminary facts to make it clear why young Dick Owens tried to run one of his father's negro men off to Canada.

In the early fifties, when the growth of anti-slavery sentiment and the constant drain of fugitive slaves into the North had so alarmed the slaveholders of the border States as to lead to the passage of the Fugitive Slave Law, a young white man from Ohio, moved by compassion for the sufferings of a certain bondman who happened to have a "hard master," essayed to help the slave to freedom. The attempt was discovered and frustrated; the abductor was tried and convicted for slave-stealing, and sentenced to a term of imprisonment in the penitentiary. His death, after the expiration of only a small part of the sentence, from cholera contracted while nursing stricken fellow prisoners, lent to the case a melancholy interest that made it famous in anti-slavery annals.

Dick Owens had attended the trial. He was a youth of about twenty-two, intelligent, handsome, and amiable, but extremely indolent, in a graceful and gentlemanly way; or, as old Judge Fenderson put it more than once, he was lazy as the Devil,—a mere figure of speech, of course, and not one that did justice to the Enemy of Mankind. When asked why he never did anything serious, Dick would good-naturedly reply, with a well-modulated drawl, that he didn't have to. His father was rich; there was but one other child, an unmarried daughter, who because of poor health would probably never marry, and Dick was therefore heir presumptive to a large estate. Wealth or social position he did not need to seek, for he was born to both. Charity Lomax had shamed him into studying law, but notwithstanding an hour or so a day spent at old Judge Fenderson's office, he did not make remarkable headway in his legal studies.

"What Dick needs," said the judge, who was fond of tropes, as became a scholar, and of horses, as was befitting a Kentuckian, "is the whip of necessity, or the spur of ambition. If he had either, he would soon need the snaffle to hold him back."

But all Dick required, in fact, to prompt him to the most remarkable thing he accomplished before he was twenty-five, was a mere suggestion from Charity Lomax. The story was never really known to but two persons until after the war, when it came out because it was a good story and there was no particular reason for its concealment.

Young Owens had attended the trial of this slave-stealer, or martyr,—either or both,—and, when it was over, had gone to call on Charity Lomax, and, while they sat on the veranda after sundown, had told her all about the trial. He was a good talker, as his career in later years disclosed, and described the proceedings very graphically.

"I confess," he admitted, "that while my principles were against the prisoner, my sympathies were on his side. It appeared that he was of good family, and that he had an old father and mother, respectable people, dependent upon him for support and comfort in their declining years. He had been led into the matter by pity for a negro whose master ought to have been run out of the county long ago for abusing his slaves. If it had been merely a question of old Sam Briggs's negro, nobody would have cared anything about it. But Father and the rest of them stood on the principle of the thing, and told the judge so, and the fellow was sentenced to three years in the penitentiary."

Miss Lomax had listened with lively interest.

"I've always hated old Sam Briggs," she said emphatically, "ever since the time he broke a negro's leg with a piece of cordwood. When I hear of a cruel deed it makes the Quaker blood that came from my grandmother assert itself. Personally I wish that all Sam Briggs's negroes would run away. As for the young man, I regard him as a hero. He dared something for humanity. I could love a man who would take such chances for the sake of others."

"Could you love me, Charity, if I did something heroic?"

"You never will, Dick. You're too lazy for any use. You'll never do anything harder than playing cards or fox-hunting."

"Oh, come now, sweetheart! I've been courting you for a year, and it's the hardest work imaginable. Are you never going to love me?" he pleaded.

His hand sought hers, but she drew it back beyond his reach.

"I'll never love you, Dick Owens, until you have done something. When that time comes, I'll think about it."

"But it takes so long to do anything worth mentioning, and I don't want to wait. One must read two years to become a lawyer, and work five more to make a reputation. We shall both be gray by then."

"Oh, I don't know," she rejoined. "It does n't require a lifetime for a man to prove that he is a man. This one did something, or at least tried to."

"Well, I'm willing to attempt as much as any other man. What do you want me to do, sweetheart? Give me a test."

"Oh, dear me!" said Charity, "I don't care what you *do*, so you do *something*. Really, come to think of it, why should I care whether you do anything or not?"

"I'm sure I don't know why you should, Charity," rejoined Dick humbly, "for I'm aware that I'm not worthy of it."

"Except that I do hate," she added, relenting slightly, "to see a really clever man so utterly lazy and good for nothing."

"Thank you, my dear; a word of praise from you has sharpened my wits already. I have an idea! Will you love me if I run a negro off to Canada?"

"What nonsense!" said Charity scornfully. "You must be losing your wits. Steal another man's slave, indeed, while your father owns a hundred!"

"Oh, there 'll be no trouble about that," responded Dick lightly;

"I'll run off one of the old man's; we've got too many anyway. It may not be quite as difficult as the other man found it, but it will be just as unlawful, and will demonstrate what I am capable of."

"Seeing's believing," replied Charity. "Of course, what you are talking about now is merely absurd. I'm going away for three weeks, to visit my aunt in Tennessee. If you 're able to tell me, when I return, that you 've done something to prove your quality, I 'll—well, you may come and tell me about it."

II

Young Owens got up about nine o'clock next morning, and while making his toilet put some questions to his personal attendant, a rather bright looking young mulatto of about his own age.

"Tom," said Dick.

"Yas, Mars Dick," responded the servant.

"I 'm going on a trip North. Would you like to go with me?"

Now, if there was anything that Tom would have liked to make, it was a trip North. It was something he had long contemplated in the abstract, but had never been able to muster up sufficient courage to attempt in the concrete. He was prudent enough, however, to dissemble his feelings.

"I would n't min' it, Mars Dick, ez long ez you 'd take keer er me an' fetch me home all right."

Tom's eyes belied his words, however, and his young master felt well assured that Tom needed only a good opportunity to make him run away. Having a comfortable home, and a dismal prospect in case of failure, Tom was not likely to take any desperate chances; but young Owens was satisfied that in a free State but little persuasion would be required to lead Tom astray. With a very logical and characteristic desire to gain his end with the least necessary expenditure of effort, he decided to take Tom with him, if his father did not object.

Colonel Owens had left the house when Dick went to breakfast, so Dick did not see his father till luncheon.

"Father," he remarked casually to the colonel, over the fried chicken, "I'm feeling a trifle run down. I imagine my health would be improved somewhat by a little travel and change of scene."

"Why don't you take a trip North?" suggested his father. The colonel added to paternal affection a considerable respect for his son as the heir of a large estate. He himself had been "raised" in comparative poverty, and had laid the foundations of his fortune by hard work; and while he despised the ladder by which he had climbed, he could not entirely forget it, and unconsciously manifested, in his intercourse with his son, some of the poor man's deference toward the wealthy and well-born.

"I think I 'll adopt your suggestion, sir," replied the son, "and run up to New York; and after I 've been there awhile I may go on to Boston for a week or so. I 've never been there, you know."

"There are some matters you can talk over with my factor in New York," rejoined the colonel, "and while you are up there among the Yankees, I hope you 'll keep your eyes and ears open to find out what the rascally abolitionists are saying and doing. They 're becoming altogether too active for our comfort, and entirely too many ungrateful niggers are running away. I hope the conviction of that fellow yesterday may discourage the rest of the breed. I 'd just like to catch any one trying to run off one of my darkeys. He 'd get short shrift; I don't think any Court would have a chance to try him."

"They are a pestiferous lot," assented Dick, "and dangerous to our institutions. But say, father, if I go North I shall want to take Tom with me."

Now, the colonel, while a very indulgent father, had pronounced views on the subject of negroes, having studied them, as he often said, for a great many years, and, as he asserted oftener still, understanding them perfectly. It is scarcely worth while to say, either, that he valued more highly than if he had inherited them the slaves he had toiled and schemed for.

"I don't think it safe to take Tom up North," he declared, with promptness and decision. "He 's a good enough boy, but too smart to trust among those low-down abolitionists. I strongly suspect him of having learned to read, though I can't imagine how. I saw him with a newspaper the other day, and while he pretended to be looking at a woodcut, I 'm almost sure he was reading the paper. I think it by no means safe to take him."

Dick did not insist, because he knew it was useless. The colonel would have obliged his son in any other matter, but his negroes were the outward and visible sign of his wealth and station, and therefore sacred to him.

"Whom do you think it safe to take?" asked Dick. "I suppose I'll have to have a body-servant."

"What 's the matter with Grandison?" suggested the colonel. "He 's handy enough, and I reckon we can trust him. He 's too fond of good eating, to risk losing his regular meals; besides, he 's sweet on your mother's maid, Betty, and I 've promised to let 'em get married before long. I 'll have Grandison up, and we 'll talk to him. Here, you boy Jack," called the colonel to a yellow youth in the next room who was catching flies and pulling their wings off to pass the time, "go down to the barn and tell Grandison to come here."

"Grandison," said the colonel, when the negro stood before him, hat in hand.

"Yas, marster."

"Have n't I always treated you right?"

"Yas, marster."

"Have n't you always got all you wanted to eat?"

"Yas, marster."

"And as much whiskey and tobacco as was good for you, Grandison?"

"Y-a-s, marster."

"I should just like to know, Grandison, whether you don't think yourself a great deal better off than those poor free negroes down by the plank road, with no kind master to look after them and no mistress to give them medicine when they 're sick and—and"—

"Well, I sh'd jes' reckon I is better off, suh, dan dem low-down free niggers, suh! Ef anybody ax 'em who dey b'long ter, dey has ter say nobody, er e'se lie erbout it. Anybody ax me who I b'longs ter, I ain' got no 'casion ter be shame' ter tell 'em, no, suh, 'deed I ain', suh!"

The colonel was beaming. This was true gratitude, and his feudal heart thrilled at such appreciative homage. What cold-blooded, heartless monsters they were who would break up this blissful relationship of kindly protection on the one hand, of wise subordination and loyal dependence on the other! The colonel always became indignant at the mere thought of such wickedness.

"Grandison," the colonel continued, "your young master Dick is going North for a few weeks, and I am thinking of letting him take you along. I shall send you on this trip, Grandison, in order that you may take care of your young master. He will need some one to wait on him, and no one can ever do it so well as one of the boys brought up with him on the old plantation. I am going to trust him in your hands, and I 'm sure you 'll do your duty faithfully, and bring him back home safe and sound—to old Kentucky."

Grandison grinned. "Oh yas, marster, I 'll take keer er young Mars Dick."

"I want to warn you, though, Grandison," continued the colonel impressively, "against these cussed abolitionists, who try to entice servants from their comfortable homes and their indulgent masters, from the blue skies, the green fields, and the warm sunlight of their Southern home, and send them away off yonder to Canada, a dreary country, where the woods are full of wildcats and wolves and bears, where the snow lies up to the eaves of the houses for six months of the year, and the cold is so severe that it freezes your breath and curdles your blood; and where, when runaway niggers get sick and can't work, they are turned out to starve and die, unloved and uncared for. I reckon, Grandison, that you have too much sense to permit yourself to be led astray by any such foolish and wicked people."

" 'Deed, suh, I would n' 'low none er dem cussed, low-down abolitioners ter come nigh me, suh. I 'd—I 'd—would I be 'lowed ter hit 'em, suh?"

"Certainly, Grandison," replied the colonel, chuckling, "hit 'em as hard as you can. I reckon they 'd rather like it. Begad, I believe they would! It would serve 'em right to be hit by a nigger!"

"Er ef I did n't hit 'em, suh," continued Grandison reflectively, "I 'd tell Mars Dick, en he 'd fix 'em. He 'd smash de face off'n 'em, suh, I jes' knows he would."

"Oh yes, Grandison, your young master will protect you. You need fear no harm while he is near."

"Dey won't try ter steal me, will dey, marster?" asked the negro, with sudden alarm.

"I don't know, Grandison," replied the colonel, lighting a fresh cigar. "They 're a desperate set of lunatics, and there 's no telling what they may resort to. But if you stick close to your young master, and remember always that he is your best friend, and understands your real needs, and has your true interests at heart, and if you will be careful to avoid strangers who try to talk to you, you 'll stand a fair chance of getting back to your home and your friends. And if you please your master Dick, he 'll buy you a present, and a string of beads for Betty to wear when you and she get married in the fall."

"Thanky, marster, thanky, suh," replied Grandison, oozing gratitude at every pore; "you is a good marster, to be sho', suh; yas, 'deed you is. You kin jes' bet me and Mars Dick gwine git 'long jes' lack I wuz own boy ter Mars Dick. En it won't be my fault ef he don' want me fer his boy all de time, w'en we come back home ag'in."

"All right, Grandison, you may go now. You need n't work any more to-day, and here 's a piece of tobacco for you off my own plug."

"Thanky, marster, thanky, marster! You is de bes' marster any nigger ever had in dis worl'." And Grandison bowed and scraped and disappeared round the corner, his jaws closing around a large section of the colonel's best tobacco.

"You may take Grandison," said the colonel to his son. "I allow he 's abolitionist-proof."

III

Richard Owens, Esq., and servant, from Kentucky, registered at the fashionable New York hostelry for Southerners in those days, a hotel where an atmosphere congenial to Southern institutions was sedulously maintained. But there were negro waiters in the dining-room, and mulatto bell-boys, and Dick had no doubt that Grandison, with the native gregariousness and garrulousness of his race, would foregather and palaver with them sooner or later, and Dick hoped that they would speedily inoculate him with the virus of freedom. For it was not Dick's intention to say anything to his servant about his plan to free him, for obvious reasons. To mention one of them, if Grandison should go away, and by legal process be recaptured, his young master's part in the matter would doubtless become known, which would be embarrassing to Dick, to say the least. If, on the other hand, he should merely give Grandison sufficient latitude, he had no doubt he would eventually lose him. For while not exactly skeptical about Grandison's per-fervid loyalty, Dick had been a somewhat keen observer of human nature, in his own indolent way, and based his expectations upon the force of the example and argument that his servant could scarcely fail to encounter. Grandison should have a fair chance to become free by his own initiative; if it should become necessary to adopt other measures to get rid of him, it would be time enough to act when the necessity arose; and Dick Owens was not the youth to take needless trouble.

The young master renewed some acquaintances and made others, and spent a week or two very pleasantly in the best society of the metropolis, easily accessible to a wealthy, well-bred young South-erner, with proper introductions. Young women smiled on him, and young men of convivial habits pressed their hospitalities; but the memory of Charity's sweet, strong face and clear blue eyes made him proof against the blandishments of the one sex and the persuasions of the other. Meanwhile he kept Grandison supplied with pocket-money, and left him mainly to his own devices. Every night when Dick came in he hoped he might have to wait upon himself, and every morning he looked forward with pleasure to the prospect of making his toilet unaided. His hopes, however, were doomed to disappointment, for every night when he came in Grandison was on hand with a bootjack, and a nightcap mixed for his young master as the colonel had taught him to mix it, and every morning Grandison appeared with his master's boots blacked and his clothes brushed, and laid his linen out for the day.

"Grandison," said Dick one morning, after finishing his toilet, "this is the chance of your life to go around among your own people and see how they live. Have you met any of them?"

"Yas, suh, I 's seen some of 'em. But I don' keer nuffin fer 'em, suh. Dey 're diffe'nt f'm de niggers down ou' way. Dey 'lows dey 're free, but dey ain' got sense 'nuff ter know dey ain' half as well off as dey would be down Souf, whar dey 'd be 'preciated."

When two weeks had passed without any apparent effect of evil example upon Grandison, Dick resolved to go on to Boston, where he thought the atmosphere might prove more favorable to his ends. After he had been at the Revere House for a day or two without losing Grandison, he decided upon slightly different tactics.

Having ascertained from a city directory the addresses of several well-known abolitionists, he wrote them each a letter something like this:—

DEAR FRIEND AND BROTHER:—

A wicked slaveholder from Kentucky, stopping at the Revere House, has dared to insult the liberty-loving people of Boston by bringing his slave into their midst. Shall this be tolerated? Or shall steps be taken in the name of liberty to rescue a fellow-man from bondage? For obvious reasons I can only sign myself,

A FRIEND OF HUMANITY.

That his letter might have an opportunity to prove effective, Dick made it a point to send Grandison away from the hotel on various errands. On one of these occasions Dick watched him for quite a distance down the street. Grandison had scarcely left the hotel when a long-haired, sharp-featured man came out behind him, followed him, soon overtook him, and kept along beside him until they turned the next corner. Dick's hopes were roused by this spectacle, but sank correspondingly when Grandison returned to the hotel. As Grandison said nothing about the encounter, Dick hoped there might be some self-consciousness behind this unexpected reticence, the results of which might develop later on.

But Grandison was on hand again when his master came back to the hotel at night, and was in attendance again in the morning, with hot water, to assist at his master's toilet. Dick sent him on further errands from day to day, and upon one occasion came squarely up to him—inadvertently of course—while Grandison was engaged in conversation with a young white man in clerical garb. When Grandison saw Dick approaching, he edged away from the preacher and hastened toward his master, with a very evident expression of relief upon his countenance.

"Mars Dick," he said, "dese yer abolitioners is jes' pesterin' de life out er me tryin' ter git me ter run away. I don' pay no 'tention ter 'em, but dey riles me so sometimes dat I 'm feared I 'll hit some of 'em some er dese days, an' dat mought git me inter trouble. I ain' said nuffin' ter you 'bout it, Mars Dick, fer I did n' wanter 'sturb yo' min'; but I don' like it, suh; no, suh, I don'! Is we gwine back home 'fo' long, Mars Dick?"

"We 'll be going back soon enough," replied Dick somewhat shortly, while he inwardly cursed the stupidity of a slave who could be free and would not, and registered a secret vow that if he were unable to get rid of Grandison without assassinating him, and were therefore compelled to take him back to Kentucky, he would see that Grandison got a taste of an article of slavery that would make him regret his wasted opportunities. Meanwhile he determined to tempt his servant yet more strongly.

"Grandison," he said next morning, "I 'm going away for a day or two, but I shall leave you here. I shall lock up a hundred dollars in this drawer and give you the key. If you need any of it, use it and enjoy yourself,—spend it all if you like,—for this is probably the last chance you 'll have for some time to be in a free State, and you 'd better enjoy your liberty while you may."

When he came back a couple of days later and found the faithful Grandison at his post, and the hundred dollars intact, Dick felt seriously annoyed. His vexation was increased by the fact that he could not express his feelings adequately. He did not even scold Grandison; how could he, indeed, find fault with one who so sensibly recognized his true place in the economy of civilization, and kept it with such touching fidelity?

"I can't say a thing to him," groaned Dick. "He deserves a leather medal, made out of his own hide tanned. I reckon I 'll write to father and let him know what a model servant he has given me."

He wrote his father a letter which made the colonel swell with pride and pleasure. "I really think," the colonel observed to one of his friends, "that Dick ought to have the nigger interviewed by the Boston papers, so that they may see how contented and happy our darkeys really are."

Dick also wrote a long letter to Charity Lomax, in which he said, among other things, that if she knew how hard he was working, and under what difficulties, to accomplish something serious for her sake, she would no longer keep him in suspense, but overwhelm him with love and admiration.

Having thus exhausted without result the more obvious methods of getting rid of Grandison, and diplomacy having also proved a failure, Dick was forced to consider more radical measures. Of course he might run away himself, and abandon Grandison, but this would be merely to leave him in the United States, where he was still a slave, and where, with his notions of loyalty, he would speedily be reclaimed. It was necessary, in order to accomplish the purpose of his trip to the North, to leave Grandison permanently in Canada, where he would be legally free.

"I might extend my trip to Canada," he reflected, "but that would be too palpable. I have it! I 'll visit Niagara Falls on the way home, and lose him on the Canada side. When he once realizes that he is actually free, I 'll warrant that he 'll stay."

So the next day saw them westward bound, and in due course of time, by the somewhat slow conveyances of the period, they found themselves at Niagara. Dick walked and drove about the Falls for several days, taking Grandison along with him on most occasions. One morning they stood on the Canadian side, watching the wild whirl of the waters below them.

"Grandison," said Dick, raising his voice above the roar of the cataract, "do you know where you are now?"

"I 's wid you, Mars Dick; dat 's all I keers."

"You are now in Canada, Grandison, where your people go when they run away from their masters. If you wished, Grandison, you might walk away from me this very minute, and I could not lay my hand upon you to take you back."

Grandison looked around uneasily.

"Let 's go back ober de ribber, Mars Dick. I 's feared I 'll lose you ovuh heah, an' den I won' hab no marster, an' won't nebber be able to git back home no mo'."

Discouraged, but not yet hopeless, Dick said, a few minutes later,—

"Grandison, I 'm going up the road a bit, to the inn over yonder. You stay here until I return. I 'll not be gone a great while."

Grandison's eyes opened wide and he looked somewhat fearful.

"Is dey any er dem dadblasted abolitioners roun' heah, Mars Dick?"

"I don't imagine that there are," replied his master, hoping there might be. "But I 'm not afraid of *your* running away, Grandison. I only wish I were," he added to himself.

Dick walked leisurely down the road to where the whitewashed inn, built of stone, with true British solidity, loomed up through the trees by the roadside. Arrived there he ordered a glass of ale and a sandwich, and took a seat at a table by a window, from which he could see Grandison in the distance. For a while he hoped that the seed he had sown might have fallen on fertile ground, and that Grandison, relieved from the restraining power of a master's eye, and finding himself in a free country, might get up and walk away; but the hope was vain, for Grandison remained faithfully at his post, awaiting his master's return. He had seated himself on a broad flat stone, and, turning his eyes away from the grand and awe-inspiring spectacle that lay close at hand, was looking anxiously toward the inn where his master sat cursing his ill-timed fidelity.

By and by a girl came into the room to serve his order, and Dick very naturally glanced at her; and as she was young and pretty and remained in attendance, it was some minutes before he looked for Grandison. When he did so his faithful servant had disappeared.

To pay his reckoning and go away without the change was a matter quickly accomplished. Retracing his footsteps toward the Falls, he saw, to his great disgust, as he approached the spot where he had left Grandison, the familiar form of his servant stretched out on the ground, his face to the sun, his mouth open, sleeping the time away, oblivious alike to the grandeur of the scenery, the thunderous roar of the cataract, or the insidious voice of sentiment.

"Grandison," soliloquized his master, as he stood gazing down at his ebony encumbrance, "I do not deserve to be an American citizen; I ought not to have the advantages I possess over you; and I certainly am not worthy of Charity Lomax, if I am not smart enough to get rid of you. I have an idea! You shall yet be free, and I will be the instrument of your deliverance. Sleep on, faithful and affectionate servitor, and dream of the blue grass and the bright skies of old Kentucky, for it is only in your dreams that you will ever see them again!"

Dick retraced his footsteps towards the inn. The young woman chanced to look out of the window and saw the handsome young gentleman she had waited on a few minutes before, standing in the road a short distance away, apparently engaged in earnest conversation with a colored man employed as hostler for the inn. She thought she saw something pass from the white man to the other, but at that moment her duties called her away from the window, and when she looked out again the young gentleman had disappeared, and the hostler, with two other young men of the neighborhood, one white and one colored, were walking rapidly towards the Falls.

IV

Dick made the journey homeward alone, and as rapidly as the conveyances of the day would permit. As he drew near home his conduct in going back without Grandison took on a more serious aspect than it had borne at any previous time, and although he had prepared the colonel by a letter sent several days ahead, there was still the prospect of a bad quarter of an hour with him; not, indeed, that his father would upbraid him, but he was likely to make searching inquiries. And notwithstanding the vein of quiet recklessness that had carried Dick through his preposterous scheme, he was a very poor liar, having rarely had occasion or inclination to tell anything but the truth. Any reluctance to meet his father was more than offset, however, by a stronger force drawing him homeward, for Charity Lomax must long since have returned from her visit to her aunt in Tennessee.

Dick got off easier than he had expected. He told a straight story, and a truthful one, so far as it went.

The colonel raged at first, but rage soon subsided into anger, and anger moderated into annoyance, and annoyance into a sort of garrulous sense of injury. The colonel thought he had been hardly used; he had trusted this negro, and he had broken faith. Yet, after all, he did not blame Grandison so much as he did the abolitionists, who were undoubtedly at the bottom of it.

As for Charity Lomax, Dick told her, privately of course, that he had run his father's man, Grandison, off to Canada, and left him there.

"Oh, Dick," she had said with shuddering alarm, "what have you done? If they knew it they 'd send you to the penitentiary, like they did that Yankee."

"But they don't know it," he had replied seriously; adding, with an injured tone, "You don't seem to appreciate my heroism like you did that of the Yankee; perhaps it 's because I was n't caught and sent to the penitentiary. I thought you wanted me to do it."

"Why, Dick Owens!" she exclaimed. "You know I never dreamed of any such outrageous proceeding.

"But I presume I 'll have to marry you," she concluded, after some insistence on Dick's part, "if only to take care of you. You are too reckless for anything; and a man who goes chasing all over the North, being entertained by New York and Boston society and having negroes to throw away, needs some one to look after him."

"It 's a most remarkable thing," replied Dick fervently, "that your views correspond exactly with my profoundest convictions. It proves beyond question that we were made for one another."

They were married three weeks later. As each of them had just returned from a journey, they spent their honeymoon at home.

A week after the wedding they were seated, one afternoon, on the piazza of the colonel's house, where Dick had taken his bride, when a negro from the yard ran down the lane and threw open the big gate for the colonel's buggy to enter. The colonel was not alone. Beside him, ragged and travel-stained, bowed with weariness, and upon his face a haggard look that told of hardship and privation, sat the lost Grandison.

The colonel alighted at the steps.

"Take the lines, Tom," he said to the man who had opened the gate, "and drive round to the barn. Help Grandison down,—poor devil, he 's so stiff he can hardly move!—and get a tub of water and wash him and rub him down, and feed him, and give him a big drink of whiskey, and then let him come round and see his young master and his new mistress."

The colonel's face wore an expression compounded of joy and

indignation,—joy at the restoration of a valuable piece of property; indignation for reasons he proceeded to state.

"It 's astounding, the depths of depravity the human heart is capable of! I was coming along the road three miles away, when I heard some one call me from the roadside. I pulled up the mare, and who should come out of the woods but Grandison. The poor nigger could hardly crawl along, with the help of a broken limb. I was never more astonished in my life. You could have knocked me down with a feather. He seemed pretty far gone,—he could hardly talk above a whisper,—and I had to give him a mouthful of whiskey to brace him up so he could tell his story. It 's just as I thought from the beginning, Dick; Grandison had no notion of running away; he knew when he was well off, and where his friends were. All the persuasions of abolition liars and runaway niggers did not move him. But the desperation of those fanatics knew no bounds; their guilty consciences gave them no rest. They got the notion somehow that Grandison belonged to a nigger-catcher, and had been brought North as a spy to help capture ungrateful runaway servants. They actually kidnaped him—just think of it!—and gagged him and bound him and threw him rudely into a wagon, and carried him into the gloomy depths of a Canadian forest, and locked him in a lonely hut, and fed him on bread and water for three weeks. One of the scoundrels wanted to kill him, and persuaded the others that it ought to be done; but they got to quarreling about how they should do it, and before they had their minds made up Grandison escaped, and, keeping his back steadily to the North Star, made his way, after suffering incredible hardships, back to the old plantation, back to his master, his friends, and his home. Why, it 's as good as one of Scott's novels! Mr. Simms or some other one of our Southern authors ought to write it up."

"Don't you think, sir," suggested Dick, who had calmly smoked his cigar throughout the colonel's animated recital, "that that kidnaping yarn sounds a little improbable? Isn't there some more likely explanation?"

"Nonsense, Dick; it 's the gospel truth! Those infernal abolitionists are capable of anything—everything! Just think of their locking the poor, faithful nigger up, beating him, kicking him, depriving him of his liberty, keeping him on bread and water for three long, lonesome weeks, and he all the time pining for the old plantation!"

There were almost tears in the colonel's eyes at the picture of Grandison's sufferings that he conjured up. Dick still professed to be slightly skeptical, and met Charity's severely questioning eye with bland unconsciousness.

The colonel killed the fatted calf for Grandison, and for two or three weeks the returned wanderer's life was a slave's dream of pleasure. His fame spread throughout the county, and the colonel gave him a permanent place among the house servants, where he could always have him conveniently at hand to relate his adventures to admiring visitors.

About three weeks after Grandison's return the colonel's faith in sable humanity was rudely shaken, and its foundations almost broken up. He came near losing his belief in the fidelity of the negro to his master,—the servile virtue most highly prized and most sedulously cultivated by the colonel and his kind. One Monday morning Grandison was missing. And not only Grandison, but his wife, Betty the maid; his mother, aunt Eunice; his father, uncle Ike; his brothers, Tom and John, and his little sister Elsie, were likewise absent from the plantation; and a hurried search and inquiry in the neighborhood resulted in no information as to their whereabouts. So much valuable property could not be lost without an effort to recover it, and the wholesale nature of the transaction carried consternation to the hearts of those whose ledgers were chiefly bound in black. Extremely energetic measures were taken by the colonel and his friends. The fugitives were traced, and followed from point to point, on their northward run through Ohio. Several times the hunters were close upon their heels, but the magnitude of the escaping party begot unusual vigilance on the part of those who sympathized with the fugitives, and strangely enough, the underground railroad seemed to have had its tracks cleared and signals set for this particular train. Once, twice, the colonel thought he had them, but they slipped through his fingers.

One last glimpse he caught of his vanishing property, as he stood, accompanied by a United States marshal, on a wharf at a port on the south shore of Lake Erie. On the stern of a small steamboat which was receding rapidly from the wharf, with her nose pointing toward Canada, there stood a group of familiar dark faces, and the look they cast backward was not one of longing for the flesh-pots of Egypt. The colonel saw Grandison point him out to one of the crew of the vessel, who waved his hand derisively toward the colonel. The latter shook his fist impotently—and the incident was closed.

STEPHEN CRANE

(1 8 7 1 – 1 9 0 0)

———◆◄●►◆———

"The Knife" was among the last works written in Crane's brief life. It is one of the thirteen Whilomville Stories which first began appearing in Harper's in 1899 and were collected in 1900, shortly after their author's death. Crane modeled the township of "Whilomville" chiefly after Port Jervis, New York, where he lived from 1879 to 1882, although it also has elements of several New Jersey small towns in which he lived as a child.

The son of a Methodist minister, Crane was born in Newark, New Jersey. After brief periods of attendance at Lafayette College and Syracuse University, he turned to newspaper work in 1891 and soon became a free-lance journalist in New York, where, though he sold stories to the Herald and the Tribune, he experienced the life of poverty which influenced his naturalistic philosophy. His first novel, Maggie: A Girl of the Streets, was published at his own expense in 1893 and found few readers, but in 1895 his great novel of the Civil War, The Red Badge of Courage, became a best seller and resolved his financial difficulties. The same year also saw the publication of Black Riders, a book of free verse which showed the influence of Emily Dickinson. Crane spent most of his remaining years as a war correspondent, covering such conflicts as the Greco-Turkish War and the Spanish-American War. The hardships he endured while on these assignments contributed to his ill health and, seeking repose, he settled for a while in England, where he became acquainted with Joseph Conrad, Henry James, H. G. Wells, and others. Still plagued with tuberculosis, he moved to Germany for greater seclusion. He died there in 1900.

In The Monster (1899), a novelette also set in Whilomville, Crane dealt with the town's cruel reaction to an act of heroism by Henry Johnson, a Negro servant who had saved a white physician's son from fire but had been horribly disfigured and had lost his sanity in doing so. Johnson came to be shunned by the townspeople as "the Monster," while the doctor was ostracized for taking the Negro under his protection. Just as The Monster, with its faceless Negro, seems a precursor of Ellison's Invisible Man, so "The Knife," despite its play upon the stereotyped Negro's fondness for watermelon, seems to anticipate Richard Wright's and James Baldwin's explorations of the masks and role-playing forced upon the American black.

The Knife

I

Si Byrant's place was on the shore of the lake, and his garden patch, shielded from the north by a bold little promontory and a higher ridge inland, was accounted the most successful and surprising in all Whilomville township. One afternoon Si was working in the garden patch, when Doctor Trescott's man, Peter Washington, came trudging slowly along the road, observing nature. He scanned the white man's fine agricultural results. "Take your eye off them there melons, you rascal," said Si, placidly.

The negro's face widened in a grin of delight. "Well, Mist' Bryant, I raikon I ain't on'y make m'se'f covertous er-lookin' at dem yere mellums, sure 'nough. Dey suhtainly is grand."

"That's all right," responded Si, with affected bitterness of spirit. "That's all right. Just don't you admire 'em too much, that's all."

Peter chuckled and chuckled. "Ma Lode! Mist' Bryant, y-y-you don' think I'm gwine come prowlin' in dish yer gawden?"

"No, I know you hain't," said Si, with solemnity. "B'cause, if you did, I'd shoot you so full of holes you couldn't tell yourself from a sponge."

"Um—no, seh! No, seh! I don' raikon you'll get chance at Pete, Mist' Bryant. No, seh. I'll take an' run 'long an' rob er bank 'fore I'll come foolishin' 'roun *your* gawden, Mist' Bryant."

Bryant, gnarled and strong as an old tree, leaned on his hoe and laughed a Yankee laugh. His mouth remained tightly closed, but the sinister lines which ran from the sides of his nose to the meetings of his lips developed to form a comic oval, and he emitted a series of grunts, while his eyes gleamed merrily and his shoulders shook. Peter, on the contrary, threw back his head and guffawed thunderously. The effete joke in regard to an American negro's fondness for watermelons was still an admirable pleasantry to them, and this was not the first time they had engaged in badinage over it. In fact, this venerable survival had formed between them a friendship of casual roadside quality.

Afterward Peter went on up the road. He continued to chuckle until he was far away. He was going to pay a visit to old Alek Williams, a negro who lived with a large family in a hut clinging to the side of a mountain. The scattered colony of negroes which hovered near Whilomville was of interesting origin, being the result of some contrabands who had drifted as far north as Whilomville during the great civil war. The descendants of these adventurers were mainly conspicuous for their bewildering number and the facility which they possessed for adding even to this number. Speaking, for example, of the Jacksons—one couldn't hurl a stone into the hills about Whilomville without having it land on the roof of a hut full of Jacksons. The town reaped little in labour from these curious suburbs. There were a few men who came in regularly to work in gardens, to drive teams, to care for horses, and there were a few women who came in to cook or to wash. These latter had usually drunken husbands. In the main the colony loafed in high spirits, and the industrious minority gained no direct honour from their fellows, unless they spent their earnings on raiment, in which case they were naturally treated with distinction. On the whole, the hardships of these people were the wind, the rain, the snow, and any other physical difficulties which they could cultivate. About twice a year the lady philanthropists of Whilomville went up against them, and came away poorer in goods but rich in complacence. After one of these attacks the colony would preserve a comic air of rectitude for two days, and then relapse again to the genial irresponsibility of a crew of monkeys.

Peter Washington was one of the industrious class who occupied a position of distinction, for he surely spent his money on personal decoration. On occasion he would dress better than the Mayor of Whilomville himself, or at least in more colours, which was the main thing to the minds of his admirers. His ideal had been the late gallant Henry Johnson, whose conquests in Watermelon Alley, as well as in the hill shanties, had proved him the equal if not the superior of any Pullman car porter in the country. Perhaps Peter had too much Virginia laziness and humour in him to be a wholly adequate successor to the fastidious Henry Johnson, but, at any rate, he admired his memory so attentively as to be openly termed a dude by envious people.

On this afternoon he was going to call on old Alek Williams because Alek's eldest girl was just turned seventeen and, to Peter's mind, was a triumph of beauty. He was not wearing his best clothes, because on his last visit Alek's half-breed hound Susie had taken occasion to forcefully extract a quite large and valuable part of the visitor's trousers. When Peter arrived at the end of the rocky field which contained old Alek's shanty he stooped and provided himself with several large stones, weighing them carefully in his hand, and finally continuing his journey with three stones of about eight ounces each. When he was near the house, three gaunt hounds, Rover and Carlo and Susie, came sweeping down upon him. His impression was that they were going to climb him as if he were a tree, but at the critical moment they swerved and went growling and snapping around him, their heads low, their eyes malignant. The afternoon caller waited until Susie presented her side to him; then he heaved one of his eight-ounce rocks. When it landed, her hollow ribs gave forth a drum-like sound, and she was knocked sprawling, her legs in the air. The other hounds at once fled in horror, and she followed as soon as she was able, yelping at the top of her lungs. The afternoon caller resumed his march.

At the wild expressions of Susie's anguish old Alek had flung open the door and come hastily into the sunshine. "Yah, you Suse, come erlong outa dat now. What fer you— Oh, how do, how do, Mist' Wash'ton—how do?"

"How do, Mist' Willums? I done foun' it necessa'y fer ter damnearkill dish yer dawg a' yourn, Mist' Willums."

"Come in, come in, Mist' Wash'ton. Dawg no'count, Mist' Wash'ton." Then he turned to address the unfortunate animal. "Hu't, did it? Hu't? 'Pears like you gwine lun some saince by time somebody brek yer back. 'Pears like I gwine club yer inter er frazzle 'fore you fin' out some saince. G'w'on 'way f'm yah!"

As the old man and his guest entered the shanty a body of black children spread out in crescent-shape formation and observed Peter with awe. Fat old Mrs. Williams greeted him turbulently, while the eldest girl, Mollie, lurked in a corner and giggled with finished imbecility, gazing at the visitor with eyes that were shy and bold by turns. She seemed at times absurdly over-confident, at times foolishly afraid; but her giggle consistently endured. It was a giggle on which an irascible but right-minded judge would have ordered her forthwith to be buried alive.

Amid a great deal of hospitable gabbling, Peter was conducted to the best chair out of the three that the house contained. Enthroned therein, he made himself charming in talk to the old people, who beamed upon him joyously. As for Mollie, he affected to be unaware of her existence. This may have been a method for entrapping the sentimental interest of that young gazelle, or it may be that the giggle had worked upon him.

He was absolutely fascinating to the old people. They could talk like rotary snow-ploughs, and he gave them every chance, while his face was illumined with appreciation. They pressed him to stay for supper, and he consented, after a glance at the pot on the stove which was too furtive to be noted.

During the meal old Alek recounted the high state of Judge Hagenthorpe's kitchen garden, which Alek said was due to his unremitting industry and fine intelligence. Alek was a gardener, whenever impending starvation forced him to cease temporarily from being a lily of the field.

"Mist' Bryant he suhtainly got er grand gawden," observed Peter.

"Dat so, dat so, Mist' Wash'ton," assented Alek. "He got fine gawden."

"Seems like I nev' *did* see sech mellums, big as er bar'l, layin' dere. I don't raikon an'body in dish yer county kin hol' it with Mist' Bryant when comes ter mellums."

"Dat so, Mist' Wash'ton."

They did not talk of watermelons until their heads held nothing else, as the phrase goes. But they talked of watermelons until, when Peter started for home that night over a lonely road, they held a certain dominant position in his mind. Alek had come with him as far as the fence, in order to protect him from possible attack by the mongrels. There they had cheerfully parted, two honest men.

The night was dark, and heavy with moisture. Peter found it uncomfortable to walk rapidly. He merely loitered on the road. When opposite Si Bryant's place he paused and looked over the fence into the garden. He imagined he could see the form of a huge melon lying in dim stateliness not ten yards away. He looked at the Bryant house. Two windows, downstairs, were lighted. The Bryants kept no dog, old Si's favourite child having once been bitten by a dog, and having since died, within that year, of pneumonia.

Peering over the fence, Peter fancied that if any low-minded night prowler should happen to note the melon, he would not find it difficult to possess himself of it. This person would merely wait until the lights were out in the house, and the people presumably asleep. Then he would climb the fence, reach the melon in a few strides, sever the stem with his ready knife, and in a trice be back in the road with his prize. There need be no noise, and, after all, the house was some distance.

Selecting a smooth bit of turf, Peter took a seat by the roadside. From time to time he glanced at the lighted window.

II

When Peter and Alek had said good-bye, the old man turned back in the rocky field and shaped a slow course toward that high dim light which marked the little window of his shanty. It would be incorrect to say that Alek could think of nothing but watermelons. But it was true that Si Bryant's watermelon patch occupied a certain conspicuous position in his thoughts.

He sighed; he almost wished that he was again a conscienceless pickaninny, instead of being one of the most ornate, solemn, and look-at-me-sinner deacons that ever graced the handle of a collection basket. At this time it made him quite sad to reflect upon his granite integrity. A weaker man might perhaps bow his moral head to the temptation, but for him such a fall was impossible. He was a prince of the church, and if he had been nine princes of the church he could not have been more proud. In fact, religion was to the old man a sort of personal dignity. And he was on Sundays so obtrusively good that you could see his sanctity through a door. He forced it on you until you would have felt its influence even in a forecastle.

It was clear in his mind that he must put watermelon thoughts from him, and after a moment he told himself, with much ostentation, that he had done so. But it was cooler under the sky than in the shanty, and as he was not sleepy, he decided to take a stroll down to Si Bryant's place and look at the melons from a pinnacle of spotless innocence. Reaching the road, he paused to listen. It would not do to let Peter hear him, because that graceless rapscallion would probably misunderstand him. But, assuring himself that Peter was well on his way, he set out, walking briskly until he was within four hundred yards of Bryant's place. Here he went to the side of the road, and walked thereafter on the damp, yielding turf. He made no sound.

He did not go on to that point in the main road which was directly opposite the watermelon patch. He did not wish to have his ascetic contemplation disturbed by some chance wayfarer. He turned off along a short lane which led to Si Bryant's barn. Here he reached a place where he could see, over the fence, the faint shapes of the melons.

Alek was affected. The house was some distance away, there was no dog, and doubtless the Bryants would soon extinguish their lights and go to bed. Then some poor lost lamb of sin might come and scale the fence, reach a melon in a moment, sever the stem with his ready knife, and in a trice be back in the road with his prize. And this poor lost lamb of sin might even be a bishop, but no one would ever know it. Alek singled out with his eye a very large melon, and thought that the lamb would prove his judgment if he took that one.

He found a soft place in the grass, and arranged himself comfortably. He watched the lights in the windows.

III

It seemed to Peter Washington that the Bryants absolutely consulted their own wishes in regard to the time for retiring; but at last he saw the lighted windows fade briskly from left to right, and after a moment a window on the second floor blazed out against the darkness. Si was going to bed. In five minutes this window abruptly vanished, and all the world was night.

Peter spent the ensuing quarter-hour in no mental debate. His mind was fixed. He was here, and the melon was there. He would have it. But an idea of being caught appalled him. He thought of his position. He was the beau of his community, honoured right and left. He pictured the consternation of his friends and the cheers of his enemies if the hands of the redoubtable Si Bryant should grip him in his shame.

He arose and, going to the fence, listened. No sound broke the stillness, save the rhythmical incessant clicking of myriad insects and the guttural chanting of the frogs in the reeds at the lake-side. Moved by sudden decision, he climbed the fence and crept silently and swiftly down upon the melon. His open knife was in his hand. There was the melon, cool, fair to see, as pompous in its fatness as the cook in a monastery.

Peter put out a hand to steady it while he cut the stem. But at the instant he was aware that a black form had dropped over the fence lining the lane in front of him and was coming stealthily toward him. In a palsy of terror he dropped flat upon the ground, not having strength enough to run away. The next moment he was looking into the amazed and agonized face of old Alek Williams.

There was a moment of loaded silence, and then Peter was overcome by a mad inspiration. He suddenly dropped his knife and leaped upon Alek. "I got che!" he hissed. "I got che! I got che!" The old man sank down as limp as rags. "I got che! I got che! Steal Mist' Bryant's mellums, hey?"

Alek, in a low voice, began to beg. "Oh, Mist' Peter Wash'ton, don' go fer ter be too ha'd on er ole man! I nev' come yere fer ter steal 'em. 'Deed I didn't, Mist' Wash'ton! I come yere jes' fer ter *feel* 'em. Oh, please, Mist' Wash'ton—"

"Come erlong outa yere, you ol' rip," said Peter, "an' don' trumple on dese yer baids. I gwine put you w'ah you won' ketch col'."

Without difficulty he tumbled the whining Alek over the fence to the roadway and followed him with sheriff-like expedition. He took him by the scruff. "Come erlong, deacon. I raikon I gwine put you w'ah you kin pray, deacon. Come erlong, deacon."

The emphasis and reiteration of his layman's title in the church produced a deadly effect upon Alek. He felt to his marrow the heinous crime into which this treacherous night had betrayed him. As Peter marched his prisoner up the road toward the mouth of the lane, he continued his remarks: "Come erlong, deacon. Nev' see er man so anxious-like erbout er mellum-paitch, deacon. Seem like you jes' must see 'em er-growin' an' *feel* 'em, deacon. Mist' Bryant he'll be s'prised, deacon, findin' out you come fer ter *feel* his mellums. Come erlong, deacon. Mist' Bryant he expectin' some ole rip like you come soon."

They had almost reached the lane when Alek's cur Susie, who had followed her master, approached in the silence which attends dangerous dogs; and seeing indications of what she took to be war, she appended herself swiftly but firmly to the calf of Peter's left leg. The mêlée was short, but spirited. Alek had no wish to have his dog complicate his already serious misfortunes, and went manfully to the defence of his captor. He procured a large stone, and by beating this with both hands down upon the resounding skull of the animal, he induced her to quit her grip. Breathing heavily, Peter dropped into the long grass at the roadside. He said nothing.

"Mist' Wash'ton," said Alek at last, in a quavering voice, "I raikon I gwine wait yere see what you gwine do ter me."

Whereupon Peter passed into a spasmodic state, in which he rolled to and fro and shook.

"Mist' Wash'ton, I hope dish yer dog ain't gone an' give you fitses?"

Peter sat up suddenly. "No, she ain't," he answered; "but she gin me er big skeer; an' fer yer 'sistance with er cobblestone, Mist' Willums, I tell you what I gwine do—I tell you what I gwine do." He waited an impressive moment. "I gwine 'lease you!"

Old Alek trembled like a little bush in a wind. "Mist' Wash-'ton?"

Quoth Peter, deliberately, "I gwine 'lease you."

The old man was filled with a desire to negotiate this statement at once, but he felt the necessity of carrying off the event without an appearance of haste. "Yes, seh; thank 'e, seh; thank 'e, Mist' Wash'ton. I raikon I ramble home pressenly."

He waited an interval, and then dubiously said, "Good-evenin', Mist' Wash'ton."

"Good-evenin', deacon. Don' come foolin' roun' *feelin'* no mellums, and I say troof. Good-evenin', deacon."

Alek took off his hat and made three profound bows. "Thank 'e, seh. Thank 'e, seh. Thank 'e, seh."

Peter underwent another severe spasm, but the old man walked off toward his home with a humble and contrite heart.

IV

The next morning Alek proceeded from his shanty under the complete but customary illusion that he was going to work. He trudged manfully along until he reached the vicinity of Si Bryant's place. Then, by stages, he relapsed into a slink. He was passing the garden patch under full steam when, at some distance ahead of him, he saw Si Bryant leaning casually on the garden fence.

"Good-mornin', Alek."

"Good-mawnin', Mist' Bryant," answered Alek, with a new deference. He was marching on, when he was halted by a word— "Alek!"

He stopped. "Yes, seh."

"I found a knife this mornin' in th' road," drawled Si, "an' I thought maybe it was yourn."

Improved in mind by this divergence from the direct line of attack, Alek stepped up easily to look at the knife. "No, seh," he said, scanning it as it lay in Si's palm, while the cold steel-blue eyes of the white man looked down into his stomach, " 'tain't no knife er mine." But he knew the knife. He knew it as if it had been his mother. And at the same moment a spark flashed through his head and made wise his understanding. He knew everything. " 'Tain't much of er knife, Mist' Bryant," he said, deprecatingly.

" 'Tain't much of a knife, I know that," cried Si, in sudden heat, "but I found it this mornin' in my watermelon patch—hear?"

"Watahmellum paitch?" yelled Alek, not astounded.

"Yes, in my watermelon patch," sneered Si, "an' I think you know something about it, too!"

"Me?" cried Alek. "Me?"

"Yes—you!" said Si, with icy ferocity. "Yes—you!" He had become convinced that Alek was not in any way guilty, but he was certain that the old man knew the owner of the knife, and so he pressed him at first on criminal lines. "Alek, you might as well own up now. You've been meddlin' with my watermelons!"

"Me?" cried Alek again. "Yah's *ma* knife. I done cah'e it foh yeahs."

Bryant changed his ways. "Look here, Alek," he said, confidentially: "I know you and you know me, and there ain't no use in any more skirmishin'. *I* know that *you* know whose knife that is. Now whose is it?"

This challenge was so formidable in character that Alek temporarily quailed and began to stammer. "Er—now—Mist' Bryant— you—you—frien' er mine—"

"I know I'm a friend of yours, but," said Bryant, inexorably, "who owns this knife?"

Alek gathered unto himself some remnants of dignity and spoke with reproach: "Mist' Bryant, dish yer knife ain' mine."

"No," said Bryant, "it ain't. But you know who it belongs to, an' I want you to tell me—quick."

"Well, Mist' Bryant," answered Alek, scratching his wool, "I won't say 's I *do* know who b'longs ter dish yer knife, an' I won't say 's I *don't*."

Bryant again laughed his Yankee laugh, but this time there was little humour in it. It was dangerous.

Alek, seeing that he had got himself into hot water by the fine diplomacy of his last sentence, immediately began to flounder and totally submerge himself. "No, Mist' Bryant," he repeated, "I won't say 's I *do* know who b'longs ter dish yer knife, an' I won't say 's I *don't*." And he began to parrot this fatal sentence again and again. It seemed wound about his tongue. He could not rid himself of it. Its very power to make trouble for him seemed to originate the mysterious Afric reason for its repetition.

"Is he a very close friend of yourn?" said Bryant, softly.

"F-frien'?" stuttered Alek. He appeared to weigh this question with much care. "Well, seems like he *was* er frien', an' then agin, it seems like he—"

"It seems like he *wasn't?*" asked Bryant.

"Yes, seh, jest so, jest so," cried Alek. "Sometimes it seems like he *wasn't*. Then again—" He stopped for profound meditation.

The patience of the white man seemed inexhaustible. At length his low and oily voice broke the stillness. "Oh, well, of course if he's a friend of yourn, Alek! You know I wouldn't want to make no trouble for a friend of yourn."

"Yes, seh," cried the negro at once. "He's er frien' er mine. He is dat."

"Well, then, it seems as if about the only thing to do is for you to tell me his name so's I can send him his knife, and that's all there is to it."

Alek took off his hat, and in perplexity ran his hand over his wool. He studied the ground. But several times he raised his eyes to take a sly peep at the imperturbable visage of the white man. "Y-y-yes, Mist' Bryant.—I raikon dat's erbout all what kin be done. I gwine tell you who b'longs ter dish yer knife."

"Of course," said the smooth Bryant, "it ain't a very nice thing to have to do, but—"

"No, seh," cried Alek, brightly; "I'm gwine tell you, Mist' Bryant. I gwine tell you erbout dat knife. Mist' Bryant," he asked, solemnly, "does you know who b'longs ter dat knife?"

"No, I—"

"Well, I gwine tell. I gwine tell who. Mist' Bryant—" The old man drew himself to a stately pose and held forth his arm. "I gwine tell who. Mist' Bryant, *dish yer knife b'longs ter Sam Jackson!*"

Bryant was startled into indignation. "Who in hell is Sam Jackson?" he growled.

"He's a nigger," said Alek, impressively, "and he wuks in er lumber-yawd up yere in Hoswego."

VACHEL LINDSAY

(1879–1931)

Lindsay was born in Springfield, Illinois, to parents whose devout advocacy of the fundamentalist Campbellite sect influenced the mysticism and social Christianity which later characterized much of their son's poetry. He attended Hiram College in Ohio and later studied at the Chicago Art Institute. Having decided on a career as vagabond poet, he spent the years 1906 to 1912 on walking tours through the South, Midwest, and Southwest, trading poems for food and lodging. Rhymes to Be Traded for Bread was published in 1912, and the following year such poems as "General William Booth Enters into Heaven" and "The Congo" began to appear in Harriet Monroe's newly founded Poetry: A Magazine of Verse. His three most-admired collections of poems followed rapidly: General William Booth Enters into Heaven and Other Poems (1913), The Congo and Other Poems (1914), and The Chinese Nightingale and Other Poems (1917).

Widely hailed as an advocate of "the new poetry" and as a preacher of the gospel of beauty, Lindsay soon began a highly successful series of public readings of his own poems. He placed great emphasis on rhythm—he saw his poems as expressing such characteristic American rhythms as those of the Salvation Army rally, the Negro revival meeting, and the country dance—and this emphasis lent itself to the chanting, whispering, gesturing, and stomping platform style he called "the higher vaudeville." In 1925 Lindsay "discovered" Langston Hughes, who was then a bus boy at Washington's Wardman Park Hotel, and his reading of some of Hughes's work at a recital of his own poems helped to promote the young Negro's career. Lindsay's creative powers were already in decline, however, and in 1931, overcome with despair, he took his own life. "The Congo," one of Lindsay's most popular platform pieces, offers an interesting view of a white author's use of Negro materials on the eve of the Harlem Renaissance.

The Congo
A Study of the Negro Race

I. Their Basic Savagery

Fat black bucks in a wine-barrel room,
Barrel-house kings, with feet unstable,
Sagged and reeled and pounded on the table, *A deep rolling bass.*
Pounded on the table,
Beat an empty barrel with the handle of a broom,
Hard as they were able,
Boom, boom, Boom,
With a silk umbrella and the handle of a broom,
Boomlay, boomlay, boomlay, Boom.
THEN I had religion, THEN I had a vision.
I could not turn from their revel in derision.
THEN I SAW THE CONGO, CREEPING THROUGH THE *More*
    BLACK, *deliberate.*
CUTTING THROUGH THE FOREST WITH A GOLDEN TRACK. *Solemnly*
Then along that riverbank *chanted.*
A thousand miles
Tatooed cannibals danced in files;
Then I heard the boom of the blood-lust song
And a thigh-bone beating on a tin-pan gong.
And "BLOOD" screamed the whistles and the fifes of
        the warriors,

"BLOOD" screamed the skull-faced, lean witch-doc-
    tors,
Whirl ye the deadly voo-doo rattle,
Harry the uplands,
Steal all the cattle,
Rattle-rattle, rattle-rattle,
Bing.
Boomlay, boomlay, boomlay, BOOM,"

A rapidly piling cli-max of speed and racket.

A roaring, epic, rag-time tune
From the mouth of the Congo
To the Mountains of the Moon.

With a philosophic pause.

Death is an Elephant,
Torch-eyed and horrible,
Foam-flanked and terrible.
BOOM, steal the pygmies,
BOOM, kill the Arabs,
BOOM, kill the white men,
Hoo, Hoo, Hoo.

Shrilly and with a heavily accented metre.

Listen to the yell of Leopold's ghost
Burning in Hell for his hand-maimed host.
Hear how the demons chuckle and yell
Cutting his hands off, down in Hell.
Listen to the creepy proclamation,
Blown through the lairs of the forest-nation,
Blown past the white-ants' hill of clay,
Blown past the marsh where the butterflies play:
"Be careful what you do,
Or Mumbo-Jumbo, God of the Congo,
And all the other
Gods of the Congo,
Mumbo-Jumbo will hoo-doo you,
Mumbo-Jumbo will hoo-doo you,
Mumbo-Jumbo will hoo-doo you."

Like the wind in the chimney.

All the "o" sounds very golden.
Heavy accents very heavy. Light accents very light. Last line whispered.

II. Their Irrepressible High Spirits

Wild crap-shooters with a whoop and a call
Danced the juba in their gambling hall

Rather shrill and high

And laughed fit to kill, and shook the town,
And guyed the policemen and laughed them down
With a boomlay, boomlay, boomlay, BOOM.

THEN I SAW THE CONGO, CREEPING THROUGH THE
    BLACK,
CUTTING THROUGH THE FOREST WITH A GOLDEN TRACK.
A negro fairyland swung into view,
A minstrel river
Where dreams come true.
The ebony palace soared on high
Through the blossoming trees to the evening sky.
The inlaid porches and casements shone
With gold and ivory and elephant-bone.
And the black crowd laughed till their sides were sore
At the baboon butler in the agate door,
And the well-known tunes of the parrot band
That trilled on the bushes of that magic land.

Read exactly as in first section. Lay emphasis on the delicate ideas. Keep as light-footed as possible.

A troupe of skull-faced witch-men came
Through the agate doorway in suits of flame,
Yea, long-tailed coats with a gold-leaf crust
And hats that were covered with diamond-dust.
And the crowd in the court gave a whoop and a call
And danced the juba from wall to wall.
But the witch-men suddenly stilled the throng
With a stern cold glare, and a stern old
    song:—
"Mumbo-Jumbo will hoo-doo you." . . .
Just then from the doorway, as fat
    as shotes
Came the cake-walk princes in their long
    red coats,
Canes with a brilliant lacquer shine,
And tall silk hats that were red as wine.
And they pranced with their butterfly partners there,
Coal-black maidens with pearls in their hair,
Knee-skirts trimmed with the jassamine sweet,
And bells on their ankles and little black feet.

With pomposity.

With a great deliberation and ghostliness.

With overwhelming assurance, good cheer, and pomp.

With growing speed and sharply marked dance-rhythm.

And the couples railed at the chant and the frown
Of the witch-men lean, and laughed them down.
(Oh, rare was the revel, and well worth while
That made those glowering witch-men smile.)

The cake-walk royalty then began
To walk for a cake that was tall as a man
To the tune of "Boomlay, boomlay, BOOM,"
While the witch-men laughed, with a sinister air, *With a*
And sang with the scalawags prancing there:— *touch of*
"Walk with care, walk with care, *negro*
Or Mumbo-Jumbo, God of the Congo, *dialect, and*
And all of the other Gods of the Congo, *as rapidly*
Mumbo-Jumbo will hoo-doo you. *as possible*
Beware, beware, walk with care, *toward*
Boomlay, boomlay, boomlay, boom. *the end.*
Boomlay, boomlay, boomlay, boom.
Boomlay, boomlay, boomlay, boom.
Boomlay, boomlay, boomlay,
BOOM."
(Oh, rare was the revel, and well worth while *Slow philo-*
That made those glowering witch-men smile.) *sophic calm.*

III. The Hope of Their Religion

A good old negro in the slums of the town *Heavy bass.*
Preached at a sister for her velvet gown. *With a*
Howled at a brother for his low-down ways, *literal imi-*
His prowling, guzzling, sneak-thief days. *tation of*
Beat on the Bible till he wore it out *camp-meet-*
Starting the jubilee revival shout. *ing racket,*
And some had visions, as they stood on chairs, *and trance.*
And sang of Jacob, and the golden stairs,
And they all repented, a thousand strong,
From their stupor and savagery and sin and wrong,
And slammed with their hymn books till they shook
      the room
With "Glory, glory, glory,"
And "Boom, boom, BOOM."

THEN I SAW THE CONGO, CREEPING THROUGH THE
    BLACK,
CUTTING THROUGH THE JUNGLE WITH A GOLDEN
    TRACK.
And the gray sky opened like a new-rent veil
And showed the Apostles with their coats of mail.
In bright white steel they were seated round
And their fire-eyes watched where the Congo wound
And the twelve Apostles, from their thrones on high,
Thrilled all the forest with their heavenly cry:—
"Mumbo-Jumbo will die in the jungle;
Never again will he hoo-doo you,
Never again will he hoo-doo you."

*Exactly as
in the first
section.
Begin with
terror and
power, end
with joy.*

*Sung to the tune of
"Hark, ten thousand
harps and voices."*

Then along that river, a thousand miles,
The vine-snared trees fell down in files.
Pioneer angels cleared the way
For a Congo paradise, for babes at play,
For sacred capitals, for temples clean.
Gone were the skull-faced witch-men lean.
There, where the wild ghost-gods had wailed
A million boats of the angels sailed
With oars of silver, and prows of blue
And silken pennants that the sun shone through.
'Twas a land transfigured, 'twas a new creation.
Oh, a singing wind swept the negro nation
And on through the backwoods clearing flew:—
"Mumbo-Jumbo is dead in the jungle.
Never again will he hoo-doo you.
Never again will he hoo-doo you."

*With
growing
deliberation
and joy.*

*In a rather
high key—
as delicately
as possible.*

*To the tune of
"Hark, ten thousand
harps and voices."*

Redeemed were the forests, the beasts and the men,
And only the vulture dared again
By the far, lone mountains of the moon
To cry, in the silence, the Congo tune:—
"Mumbo-Jumbo will hoo-doo you,
Mumbo-Jumbo will hoo-doo you,
Mumbo . . . Jumbo . . . will . . .
    hoo-doo . . . you."

*Dying down into a
penetrating, terrified
whisper.*

W. E. B. DUBOIS

(1868–1963)

DuBois's The Souls of Black Folk (1903), which has had more than twenty printings, was for several decades perhaps the most significant examination of black consciousness by a Negro published in America. As John Hope Franklin has written, "It was several things at once: a deeply moving statement on the consciousness of color, a searching criticism of the philosophy of [Booker T.] Washington, a quite scholarly examination of certain phases of the history of the Negro, and an evaluation of some of the mainsprings of the culture of the Negro American."

William Edward Burghardt DuBois was born in Great Barrington, Massachusetts. He was graduated from Fisk University, received a Ph.D. from Harvard, and carried out further postgraduate studies at the University of Berlin. In 1896 he began teaching at Atlanta University, where he produced several sociological works, including The Philadelphia Negro (1899), which were among the first American books to reflect accurately Negro life and identity. Meanwhile, his doctoral dissertation, The Suppression of the African Slave Trade, had become the first volume in the Harvard Historical Studies series begun in 1896. In 1905 DuBois organized the Niagara Movement, which brought together Negro intellectuals dedicated to the establishment of racial equality, and a few years later he helped to establish the National Association for the Advancement of Colored People. By 1910 he had founded the

NAACP journal, Crisis, which he was to edit for several years. In The Souls of Black Folk and other works, DuBois became a strong opponent of the accommodationist viewpoint of Booker T. Washington, who was willing to restrain the Negro's quest for political power, civil rights, and higher education in order to achieve economic advances and conciliation with the South. As DuBois grew increasingly disillusioned with what he saw as the NAACP's "mere appeal based on the old liberalism," his interest in black consciousness throughout the world increased, and he helped organize the Pan African Congress of 1919 which met in Paris. His Color and Democracy: Colonies and Peace (1945) was a forceful argument against imperialism and in favor of independence for colonies.

In addition to many scholarly books and articles, DuBois wrote poetry, several novels, and an autobiography, and he founded and edited Phylon, "the Atlanta University Review of Race and Culture." One autobiographical work, Dusk of Dawn, appeared in 1940, and The Autobiography of W. E. B. DuBois was published posthumously in 1968. DuBois's thought moved steadily to the left, and he eventually joined the Communist Party. By the time of his death in 1963 he had renounced his American citizenship and went to Africa to become a citizen of Ghana, where he was a close associate of Premier Kwame Nkrumah.

"The Song of the Smoke" was first published in The Horizon in 1899.

The Song of the Smoke

I am the smoke king,
I am black.
I am swinging in the sky.
I am ringing worlds on high:
I am the thought of the throbbing mills,
I am the soul of the soul toil kills,
I am the ripple of trading rills,

Up I'm curling from the sod,
I am whirling home to God.

I am the smoke king,
I am black.

I am the smoke king,
I am black.
I am wreathing broken hearts,
I am sheathing devils' darts;
Dark inspiration of iron times,
Wedding the toil of toiling climes
Shedding the blood of bloodless crimes,

Down I lower in the blue,
Up I tower toward the true,
I am the smoke king,
I am black.

I am the smoke king,
I am black.
I am darkening with song,
I am hearkening to wrong;
I will be as black as blackness can,
The blacker the mantle the mightier the man,
My purpl'ing midnights no day dawn may ban.

I am carving God in night,
I am painting hell in white.
I am the smoke king,
I am black.

I am the smoke king,
I am black.
I am cursing ruddy morn,
I am nursing hearts unborn;
Souls unto me are as mists in the night,
I whiten my blackmen, I beckon my white,
What's the hue of a hide to a man in his might!
Hail, then, grilly, grimy hands,

Sweet Christ, pity toiling lands!
Hail to the smoke king,
Hail to the black!

From *The Souls of Black Folk*

Of Our Spiritual Strivings

O water, voice of my heart, crying in the sand,
   All night long crying with a mournful cry,
As I lie and listen, and cannot understand
      The voice of my heart in my side or the voice of the sea,
   O water, crying for rest, is it I, is it I?
   All night long the water is crying to me.

Unresting water, there shall never be rest
   Till the last moon droop and the last tide fail,
And the fire of the end begin to burn in the west;
      And the heart shall be weary and wonder and cry like the sea,
   All life long crying without avail,
      As the water all night long is crying to me.

—ARTHUR SYMONS

Between me and the other world there is ever an unasked question: unasked by some through feelings of delicacy; by others through the difficulty of rightly framing it. All, nevertheless, flutter round it. They approach me in a half-hesitant sort of way, eye me curiously or compassionately, and then, instead of saying directly, How does it feel to be a problem? they say, I know an excellent colored man in my town; or, I fought at Mechanicsville; or, Do not these Southern outrages make your blood boil? At these I smile, or am interested, or reduce the boiling to a simmer, as the occasion may require. To the real question, How does it feel to be a problem? I answer seldom a word.

And yet, being a problem is a strange experience,—peculiar even for one who has never been anything else, save perhaps in babyhood and in Europe. It is in the early days of rollicking boyhood that the revelation first bursts upon one, all in a day, as it were. I remember well when the shadow swept across me. I was a little

thing, away up in the hills of New England, where the dark Housa-
tonic winds between Hoosac and Taghkanic to the sea. In a wee
wooden schoolhouse, something put it into the boys' and girls'
heads to buy gorgeous visiting-cards—ten cents a package—and
exchange. The exchange was merry, till one girl, a tall newcomer,
refused my card,—refused it peremptorily, with a glance. Then it
dawned upon me with a certain suddenness that I was different
from the others; or like, mayhap, in heart and life and longing, but
shut out from their world by a vast veil. I had thereafter no desire
to tear down that veil, to creep through; I held all beyond it in
common contempt, and lived above it in a region of blue sky and
great wandering shadows. That sky was bluest when I could beat
my mates at examination-time, or beat them at a foot-race, or even
beat their stringy heads. Alas, with the years all this fine contempt
began to fade; for the worlds I longed for, and all their dazzling
opportunities, were theirs, not mine. But they should not keep
these prizes, I said; some, all, I would wrest from them. Just how
I would do it I could never decide: by reading law, by healing the
sick, by telling the wonderful tales that swam in my head,—some
way. With other black boys the strife was not so fiercely sunny:
their youth shrunk into tasteless sycophancy, or into silent hatred
of the pale world about them and mocking distrust of everything
white; or wasted itself in a bitter cry, Why did God make me an
outcast and a stranger in mine own house? The shades of the
prison-house closed round about us all: walls strait and stubborn
to the whitest, but relentlessly narrow, tall, and unscalable to sons
of night who must plod darkly on in resignation, or beat unavailing
palms against the stone, or steadily, half hopelessly, watch the
streak of blue above.

After the Egyptian and Indian, the Greek and Roman, the Teu-
ton and Mongolian, the Negro is a sort of seventh son, born with
a veil, and gifted with second-sight in this American world,—a
world which yields him no true self-consciousness, but only lets him
see himself through the revelation of the other world. It is a peculiar sensation, this double-consciousness, this sense of always looking
at one's self through the eyes of others, of measuring one's soul by
the tape of a world that looks on in amused contempt and pity.
One ever feels his twoness,—an American, a Negro; two souls, two

thoughts, two unreconciled strivings; two warring ideals in one dark body, whose dogged strength alone keeps it from being torn asunder.

The history of the American Negro is the history of this strife,—this longing to attain self-conscious manhood, to merge his double self into a better and truer self. In this merging he wishes neither of the older selves to be lost. He would not Africanize America, for America has too much to teach the world and Africa. He would not bleach his Negro soul in a flood of white Americanism, for he knows that Negro blood has a message for the world. He simply wishes to make it possible for a man to be both a Negro and an American, without being cursed and spit upon by his fellows, without having the doors of Opportunity closed roughly in his face.

This, then, is the end of his striving; to be a co-worker in the kingdom of culture, to escape both death and isolation, to husband and use his best powers and his latent genius. These powers of body and mind have in the past been strangely wasted, dispersed, or forgotten. The shadow of a mighty Negro past flits through the tale of Ethiopia the Shadowy and of Egypt the Sphinx. Throughout history, the powers of single black men flash here and there like falling stars, and die sometimes before the world has rightly gauged their brightness. Here in America, in the few days since Emancipation, the black man's turning hither and thither in hesitant and doubtful striving has often made his very strength to lose effectiveness, to seem like absence of power, like weakness. And yet it is not weakness,—it is the contradiction of double aims. The double-aimed struggle of the black artisan,—on the one hand to escape white contempt for a nation of mere hewers of wood and drawers of water, and on the other hand to plough and nail and dig for a poverty-stricken horde,—could only result in making him a poor craftsman, for he had but half a heart in either cause. By the poverty and ignorance of his people, the Negro minister or doctor was tempted toward quackery and demagogy; and by the criticism of the other world, toward ideals that made him ashamed of his lowly tasks. The would-be black *savant* was confronted by the paradox that the knowledge his people needed was a twice-told tale to his white neighbors, while the knowledge which would teach the white world was Greek to his own flesh and blood. The innate love of harmony and beauty that set the ruder souls of his people a-dancing and a-singing raised but confusion and doubt in the soul of the black artist; for the beauty revealed to him was the soul-beauty of a race which his larger audience despised, and he could not articulate the message of another people. This waste of double aims, this seeking to satisfy two unreconciled ideals, has wrought sad havoc with the courage and faith and deeds of ten thousand thousand people,—has sent them often wooing false gods and invoking false means of salvation, and at times has even seemed about to make them ashamed of themselves.

Away back in the days of bondage they thought to see in one divine event the end of all doubt and disappointment; few men ever worshipped Freedom with half such unquestioning faith as did the American Negro for two centuries. To him, so far as he thought and dreamed, slavery was indeed the sum of all villainies, the cause of all sorrow, the root of all prejudice; Emancipation was the key to a promised land of sweeter beauty than ever stretched before the eyes of wearied Israelites. In song and exhortation swelled one refrain—Liberty; in his tears and curses the God he implored had Freedom in his right hand. At last it came,—suddenly, fearfully, like a dream. With one wild carnival of blood and passion came the message in his own plaintive cadences:—

> "Shout, O children!
> Shout, you're free!
> For God has bought your liberty!"

Years have passed away since then,—ten, twenty, forty; forty years of national life, forty years of renewal and development, and yet the swarthy spectre sits in its accustomed seat at the Nation's feast. In vain do we cry to this our vastest social problem:—

> "Take any shape but that, and my firm nerves
> Shall never tremble!"

The Nation has not yet found peace from its sins; the freedman has not yet found in freedom his promised land. Whatever of good may have come in these years of change, the shadow of a deep disappointment rests upon the Negro people,—a disappointment all the more bitter because the unattained ideal was unbounded save by the simple ignorance of a lowly people.

The first decade was merely a prolongation of the vain search for freedom, the boon that seemed ever barely to elude their grasp,—like a tantalizing will-o'-the-wisp, maddening and misleading the headless host. The holocaust of war, the terrors of the Ku Klux Klan, the lies of carpet-baggers, the disorganization of industry, and the contradictory advice of friends and foes, left the bewildered serf with no new watchword beyond the old cry for freedom. As the time flew, however, he began to grasp a new idea. The ideal of liberty demanded for its attainment powerful means, and these the Fifteenth Amendment gave him. The ballot, which before he had looked upon as a visible sign of freedom, he now regarded as the chief means of gaining and perfecting the liberty with which war had partially endowed him. And why not? Had not votes made war and emancipated millions? Had not votes enfranchised the freedmen? Was anything impossible to a power that had done all this? A million black men started with renewed zeal to vote themselves into the kingdom. So the decade flew away, the revolution of 1876 came, and left the half-free serf weary, wondering but still inspired. Slowly but steadily, in the following years, a new vision began gradually to replace the dream of political power,—a powerful movement, the rise of another ideal to guide the unguided, another pillar of fire by night after a clouded day. It was the ideal of "book-learning"; the curiosity, born of compulsory ignorance, to know and test the power of the cabalistic letters of the white man, the longing to know. Here at last seemed to have been discovered the mountain path to Canaan; longer than the highway of Emancipation and law, steep and rugged, but straight, leading to heights high enough to overlook life.

Up the new path the advance guard toiled, slowly, heavily, doggedly; only those who have watched and guided the faltering feet, the misty minds, the dull understandings, of the dark pupils of these schools know how faithfully, how piteously, this people strove to learn. It was weary work. The cold statistician wrote down the inches of progress here and there, noted also where here and there a foot had slipped or some one had fallen. To the tired climbers, the horizon was ever dark, the mists were often cold, the Canaan was always dim and far away. If, however, the vistas disclosed as yet no goal, no resting-place, little but flattery and criticism, the journey at least gave leisure for reflection and self-examination; it changed the child of Emancipation to the youth with dawning self-consciousness, self-realization, self-respect. In those sombre forests of his striving his own soul rose before him, and he saw himself,—darkly as through a veil; and yet he saw in himself some faint revelation of his power, of his mission. He began to have a dim feeling that, to attain his place in the world, he must be himself, and not another. For the first time he sought to analyze the burden he bore upon his back, that deadweight of social degradation partially masked behind a half-named Negro problem. He felt his poverty; without a cent, without a home, without land, tools, or savings, he had entered into competition with rich, landed, skilled neighbors. To be a poor man is hard, but to be a poor race in a land of dollars is the very bottom of hardships. He felt the weight of his ignorance,—not simply of letters, but of life, of business, of the humanities; the accumulated sloth and shirking and awkwardness of decades and centuries shackled his hands and feet. Nor was his burden all poverty and ignorance. The red stain of bastardy, which two centuries of systemic legal defilement of Negro women had stamped upon his race, meant not only the loss of ancient African chastity, but also the hereditary weight of a mass of corruption from white adulterers, threatening almost the obliteration of the Negro home.

A people thus handicapped ought not to be asked to race with the world, but rather allowed to give all its time and thought to its own social problems. But alas! while sociologists gleefully count his bastards and his prostitutes, the very soul of the toiling, sweating black man is darkened by the shadow of a vast despair. Men call the shadow prejudice, and learnedly explain it as the natural defence of culture against barbarism, learning against ignorance, purity against crime, the "higher" against the "lower" races. To which the Negro cries Amen! and swears that to so much of this strange prejudice as is founded on just homage to civilization, culture, righteousness, and progress, he humbly bows and meekly does obeisance. But before that nameless prejudice that leaps beyond all this he stands helpless, dismayed, and well-nigh speechless; before that personal disrespect and mockery, the ridicule and systematic humiliation, the distortion of fact and wanton license of fancy, the cynical ignoring of the better and the boisterous welcoming of the worse, the all-pervading desire to inculcate disdain for everything black, from Toussaint to the devil,—before this there rises a sickening despair that would disarm and discourage any nation save that black host to whom "discouragement" is an unwritten word.

But the facing of so vast a prejudice could not but bring the inevitable self-questioning, self-disparagement, and lowering of ideals which ever accompany repression and breed in an atmosphere of contempt and hate. Whispering and portents came borne upon the four winds: Lo! we are diseased and dying, cried the dark hosts; we cannot write, our voting is vain; what need of education, since we must always cook and serve? And the Nation echoed and enforced this self-criticism, saying: Be content to be servants, and nothing more; what need of higher culture for half-men? Away with the black man's ballot, by force or fraud,—and behold the suicide of a race! Nevertheless, out of the evil came something of good,—the more careful adjustment of education to real life, the clearer perception of the Negroes' social responsibilities, and the sobering realization of the meaning of progress.

So dawned the time of *Sturm und Drang*: storm and stress to-day rocks our little boat on the mad waters of the world-sea; there is within and without the sound of conflict, the burning of body and rending of soul; inspiration strives with doubt, and faith with vain questionings. The bright ideals of the past,—physical freedom, political power, the training of brains and the training of hands,—all these in turn have waxed and waned, until even the last grows dim and overcast. Are they all wrong,—all false? No, not that, but each alone was over-simple and incomplete,—the dreams of a credulous race-childhood, or the fond imaginings of the other world which does not know and does not want to know our power. To be really true, all these ideals must be melted and welded into one. The training of the schools we need to-day more than ever,—the training of deft hands, quick eyes and ears, and above all the broader, deeper, higher culture of gifted minds and pure hearts.

The power of the ballot we need in sheer self-defence,—else what shall save us from a second slavery? Freedom, too, the long-sought, we still seek,—the freedom of life and limb, the freedom to work and think, the freedom to love and aspire. Work, culture, liberty,—all these we need, not singly but together, not successively but together, each growing and aiding each, and all striving toward that vaster ideal that swims before the Negro people, the ideal of human brotherhood, gained through the unifying ideal of Race; the ideal of fostering and developing the traits and talents of the Negro, not in opposition to or contempt for other races, but rather in large conformity to the greater ideals of the American Republic, in order that some day on American soil two world-races may give each to each those characteristics both so sadly lack. We the darker ones come even now not altogether empty-handed: there are to-day no truer exponents of the pure human spirit of the Declaration of Independence than the American Negroes; there is no true American music but the wild sweet melodies of the Negro slave; the American fairy tales and folk-lore are Indian and African; and, all in all, we black men seem the sole oasis of simple faith and reverence in a dusty desert of dollars and smartness. Will America be poorer if she replace her brutal dyspeptic blundering with light-hearted but determined Negro humility? or her coarse and cruel wit with loving jovial good-humor? or her vulgar music with the soul of the Sorrow Songs?

Merely a concrete test of the underlying principles of the great republic is the Negro Problem, and the spiritual striving of the freedmen's sons is the travail of souls whose burden is almost beyond the measure of their strength, but who bear it in the name of an historic race, in the name of this the land of their fathers' fathers, and in the name of human opportunity. . . .

THEODORE DREISER

(1871–1945)

<hr>

Dreiser was a leading American exponent of naturalism, the late-nineteenth-century school of thought which, viewing man as devoid of free will and victimized by social, economic, and biological forces beyond his control, demanded of the artist scientific detachment in his treatment of human predicaments. Dreiser usually thought of his stories and novels as "case studies" rather than literary inventions, and his works typically take their titles from the names of his main characters. Despite his naturalistic attention to fact and detail, he was rarely detached about his characters and often lavished pity on the victims who populate his fiction.

Dreiser was born in Sullivan, Indiana, to a German immigrant father of fiercely pious Catholic conviction and a gentle Mennonite mother. Self-conscious about his family's immigrant status (a feeling which was to be intensified by anti-German feeling in the country during World War I, when he wrote "Nigger Jeff") and engulfed by poverty and his father's intolerance, Dreiser in his early years hungered for affluence. He developed a view of American society as cruel and chaotic, one in which the individual is justified in grabbing whatever money and power he can in order to compensate for the impossibility of finding spiritual satisfaction in his society. In 1892 he began a journalistic career with the Chicago Globe and eventually worked on newspapers in St. Louis, Pittsburgh, and New York. His first novel, Sister Carrie (1900), was at first withheld from circulation because it failed to moralize about Carrie's sins, but Jennie Gerhardt (1911), The Financier (1912), The Titan (1914), The Genius (1915), and An American Tragedy (1925) reached wide audiences. After An American Tragedy, probably Dreiser's best-written and best-known work, his literary powers declined and he turned increasingly to social commentary in such books as Dreiser Looks at Russia (1928) and Tragic America (1931). In his last years he was increasingly involved in communist causes, though at the same time he became interested in the mystical and quietist tradition of his mother's religion. At his death in 1945 he left his entire estate to his wife but requested that on her death the remainder should go to a home for Negro orphans.

Dreiser's works have sometimes been criticized as heavy, rambling, verbose, clumsy, and overburdened with minute detail. "Yet in all these stories," wrote Alfred Kazin, ". . . what stands out most is Dreiser's ability to bring home to us the profound and yet incommunicable feelings that human beings experience in solitude. No one else in our recent literature has known so well how to dramatize what the individual feels when he is alone entirely with himself." Robert A. Bone, in The Negro Novel in America (see Bibliography), describes Dreiser as an important influence on Richard Wright and sees a direct line of descent, through Native Son, from Dreiser to the "Wright School" of Negro writers, among whose members Bone includes Chester Himes.

"Nigger Jeff" was published in Free and Other Stories (1918).

Nigger Jeff

The city editor was waiting for one of his best reporters, Elmer Davies by name, a vain and rather self-sufficient youth who was inclined to be of that turn of mind which sees in life only a fixed and ordered process of rewards and punishments. If one did not do exactly right, one did not get along well. On the contrary, if one did, one did. Only the so-called evil were really punished, only the good truly rewarded—or Mr. Davies had heard this so long in his youth that he had come nearly to believe it. Presently he appeared. He was dressed in a new spring suit, a new hat and new shoes. In the lapel of his coat was a small bunch of violets. It was one o'clock of a sunny spring afternoon, and he was feeling exceedingly well and good-natured—quite fit, indeed. The world was going unusually well with him. It seemed worth singing about.

"Read that, Davies," said the city editor, handing him the clipping. "I'll tell you afterward what I want you to do."

The reporter stood by the editorial chair and read:

> Pleasant Valley, Ko., April 16.
> A most dastardly crime has just been reported here. Jeff Ingalls, a negro, this morning assaulted Ada Whitaker, the nineteen-year-old daughter of Morgan Whitaker, a well-to-do farmer, whose home is four miles south of this place. A posse, headed by Sheriff Mathews, has started in pursuit. If he is caught, it is thought he will be lynched.

The reporter raised his eyes as he finished. What a terrible crime! What evil people there were in the world! No doubt such a creature ought to be lynched, and that quickly.

"You had better go out there, Davies," said the city editor. "It looks as if something might come of that. A lynching up here would be a big thing. There's never been one in this state."

Davies smiled. He was always pleased to be sent out of town. It was a mark of appreciation. The city editor rarely sent any of the other men on these big stories. What a nice ride he would have!

As he went along, however, a few minutes later he began to meditate on this. Perhaps, as the city editor had suggested, he might be compelled to witness an actual lynching. That was by no means so pleasant in itself. In his fixed code of rewards and punishments he had no particular place for lynchings, even for crimes of the nature described, especially if he had to witness the lynching. It was too horrible a kind of reward or punishment. Once, in line of duty, he had been compelled to witness a hanging, and that had made him sick—deathly so—even though carried out as a part of the due process of law of his day and place. Now, as he looked at this fine day and his excellent clothes, he was not so sure that this was a worthwhile assignment. Why should he always be selected for such things—just because he could write? There were others—lots of men on the staff. He began to hope as he went along that nothing really serious would come of it, that they would catch the man before he got there and put him in jail—or, if the worst had to be—painful thought! that it would be all over by the time he got there. Let's see—the telegram had been filed at nine A.M. It was now one-thirty and would be three by the time he got out there, all of that. That would give them time enough, and then, if all were well, or ill, as it were, he could just gather the details of the crime and the—aftermath—and return. The mere thought of an approaching lynching troubled him greatly, and the farther he went the less he liked it.

He found the village of Pleasant Valley a very small affair indeed, just a few dozen houses nestling between green slopes of low hills, with one small business corner and a rambling array of lanes. One or two merchants of K——, the city from which he had just arrived, lived out here, but otherwise it was very rural. He took notes of the whiteness of the little houses, the shimmering beauty of the small stream one had to cross in going from the depot. At the one main corner a few men were gathered about a typical village barroom. Davies headed for this as being the most likely source of information.

In mingling with this company at first he said nothing about his being a newspaper man, being very doubtful as to its effect upon them, their freedom of speech and manner.

The whole company was apparently tense with interest in the crime, which still remained unpunished, seemingly craving excitement and desirous of seeing something done about it. No such opportunity to work up wrath and vent their stored-up animal propensities had probably occurred here in years. He took this occasion to inquire into the exact details of the attack, where it had occurred, where the Whitakers lived. Then, seeing that mere talk prevailed here, he went away thinking that he had best find out for himself how the victim was. As yet she had not been described, and it was necessary to know a little something about her. Accordingly, he sought an old man who kept a stable in the village, and procured a horse. No carriage was to be had. Davies was not an excellent rider, but he made a shift of it. The Whitaker home was not so very far away—about four miles out—and before long he was knocking at its front door, set back a hundred feet from the rough country road.

"I'm from the *Times*," he said to the tall, raw-boned woman who opened the door, with an attempt at being impressive. His position as reporter in this matter was a little dubious; he might be welcome, and he might not. Then he asked if this were Mrs. Whitaker, and how Miss Whitaker was by now.

"She's doing very well," answered the woman, who seemed decidedly stern, if repressed and nervous, a Spartan type. "Won't you come in? She's rather feverish, but the doctor says she'll probably be all right later on." She said no more.

Davies acknowledged the invitation by entering. He was very anxious to see the girl, but she was sleeping under the influence of an opiate, and he did not care to press the matter at once.

"When did this happen?" he asked.

"About eight o'clock this morning," said the woman. "She started to go over to our next door neighbor here, Mr. Edmonds, and this negro met her. We didn't know anything about it until she came crying through the gate and dropped down in here."

"Were you the first one to meet her?" asked Davies.

"Yes, I was the only one," said Mrs. Whitaker. "The men had all gone to the fields."

Davies listened to more of the details, the type and history of the man, and then rose to go. Before doing so he was allowed to have a look at the girl, who was still sleeping. She was young and rather pretty. In the yard he met a country man who was just coming to get home news. The latter imparted more information.

"They're lookin' all around south of here," he said, speaking of a crowd which was supposed to be searching. "I expect they'll make short work of him if they get him. He can't get away very well, for he's on foot, wherever he is. The sheriff's after him too, with a deputy or two, I believe. He'll be tryin' to save him an' take him over to Clayton, but I don't believe he'll be able to do it, not if the crowd catches him first."

So, thought Davies, he would probably have to witness a lynching after all. The prospect was most unhappy.

"Does any one know where this negro lived?" he asked heavily, a growing sense of his duty weighing upon him.

"Oh, right down here a little way," replied the farmer. "Jeff Ingalls was his name. We all know him around here. He worked for one and another of the farmers hereabouts, and don't appear to have had such a bad record, either, except for drinkin' a little now and then. Miss Ada recognized him, all right. You follow this road to the next crossing and turn to the right. It's a little log house that sets back off the road—something like that one you see down the lane there, only it's got lots o' chips scattered about."

Davies decided to go there first, but changed his mind. It was growing late, and he thought he had better return to the village. Perhaps by now developments in connection with the sheriff or the posse were to be learned.

Accordingly, he rode back and put the horse in the hands of its owner, hoping that all had been concluded and that he might learn of it here. At the principal corner much the same company was still present, arguing, fomenting, gesticulating. They seemed parts of different companies that earlier in the day had been out searching. He wondered what they had been doing since, and then decided to ingratiate himself by telling them he had just come from the Whitakers and what he had learned there of the present condition of the girl and the movements of the sheriff.

Just then a young farmer came galloping up. He was coatless, hatless, breathless.

"They've got him!" he shouted excitedly. "They've got him!"

A chorus of "whos," "wheres" and "whens" greeted this information as the crowd gathered about the rider.

"Why, Mathews caught him up here at his own house!" exclaimed the latter, pulling out a handkerchief and wiping his face. "He must 'a' gone back there for something. Mathews's takin' him over to Clayton, so they think, but they don't project he'll ever get there. They're after him now, but Mathews says he'll shoot the first man that tries to take him away."

"Which way'd he go?" exclaimed the men in chorus, stirring as if to make an attack.

" 'Cross Sellers' Lane," said the rider. "The boys think he's goin' by way of Baldwin."

"Whoopee!" yelled one of the listeners. "We'll get him away from him, all right! Are you goin', Sam?"

"You bet!" said the latter. "Wait'll I get my horse!"

"Lord!" thought Davies. "To think of being (perforce) one of a lynching party—a hired spectator!"

He delayed no longer, however, but hastened to secure his horse again. He saw that the crowd would be off in a minute to catch up with the sheriff. There would be information in that quarter, drama very likely.

"What's doin'?" inquired the liveryman as he noted Davies' excited appearance.

"They're after him," replied the latter nervously. "The sheriff's caught him. They're going now to try to take him away from him, or that's what they say. The sheriff is taking him over to Clayton, by way of Baldwin. I wanted to get over there if I can. Give me the horse again, and I'll give you a couple of dollars more."

The liveryman led the horse out, but not without many provisionary cautions as to the care which was to be taken of him, the damages which would ensue if it were not. He was not to be ridden beyond midnight. If one were wanted for longer than that Davies must get him elsewhere or come and get another, to all of which Davies promptly agreed. He then mounted and rode away.

When he reached the corner again several of the men who had gone for their horses were already there, ready to start. The young man who had brought the news had long since dashed off to other parts.

Davies waited to see which road this new company would take. Then through as pleasant a country as one would wish to see, up hill and down dale, with charming vistas breaking upon the gaze at every turn, he did the riding of his life. So disturbed was the reporter by the grim turn things had taken that he scarcely noted the beauty that was stretched before him, save to note that it was so. Death! Death! The proximity of involuntary and enforced death was what weighed upon him now.

In about an hour the company had come in sight of the sheriff, who, with two other men, was driving a wagon he had borrowed along a lone country road. The latter was sitting at the back, a revolver in each hand, his face toward the group, which at sight of him trailed after at a respectful distance. Excited as every one was, there was no disposition, for the time being at least, to halt the progress of the law.

"He's in that wagon," Davies heard one man say. "Don't you see they've got him in there tied and laid down?"

Davies looked.

"That's right," said another. "I see him now."

"What we ought to do," said a third, who was riding near the front, "is to take him away and hang him. That's just what he deserves, and that's what he'll get before we're through to-day."

"Yes!" called the sheriff, who seemed to have heard this. "You're not goin' to do any hangin' this day, so you just might as well go on back." He did not appear to be much troubled by the appearance of the crowd.

"Where's old man Whitaker?" asked one of the men who seemed to feel that they needed a leader. "He'd get him quick enough!"

"He's with the other crowd, down below Olney," was the reply.

"Somebody ought to go an' tell him."

"Clark's gone," assured another, who hoped for the worst.

Davies rode among the company a prey to mingled and singular feelings. He was very much excited and yet depressed by the character of the crowd which, in so far as he could see, was largely impelled to its jaunt by curiosity and yet also able under sufficient motivation on the part of some one—any one, really—to kill too. There was not so much daring as a desire to gain daring from others, an unconscious wish or impulse to organize the total strength or will of those present into one strength or one will, sufficient to overcome the sheriff and inflict death upon his charge. It was strange—almost intellectually incomprehensible—and yet so it was. The men were plainly afraid of the determined sheriff. They thought something ought to be done, but they did not feel like getting into trouble.

Mathews, a large solemn, sage, brown man in worn clothes and a faded brown hat, contemplated the recent addition to his trailers with apparent indifference. Seemingly he was determined to protect his man and avoid mob justice, come what may. A mob should not have him if he had to shoot, and if he shot it would be to kill. Finally, since the company thus added to did not dash upon him, he seemingly decided to scare them off. Apparently he thought he could do this, since they trailed like calves.

"Stop a minute!" he called to his driver.

The latter pulled up. So did the crowd behind. Then the sheriff stood over the prostrate body of the negro, who lay in the jolting wagon beneath him, and called back:

"Go 'way from here, you people! Go on, now! I won't have you follerin' after me!"

"Give us the nigger!" yelled one in a half-bantering, half-derisive tone of voice.

"I'll give ye just two minutes to go on back out o' this road," returned the sheriff grimly, pulling out his watch and looking at it. They were about a hundred feet apart. "If you don't, I'll clear you out!"

"Give us the nigger!"

"I know you, Scott," answered Mathews, recognizing the voice. "I'll arrest every last one of ye tomorrow. Mark my word!"

The company listened in silence, the horses champing and twisting.

"We've got a right to foller," answered one of the men.

"I give ye fair warning," said the sheriff, jumping from his wagon and leveling his pistols as he approached. "When I count five I'll begin to shoot!"

He was a serious and stalwart figure as he approached, and the crowd fell back a little.

"Git out o' this now!" he yelled. "One—Two—"

The company turned completely and retreated, Davies among them.

"We'll foller him when he gits further on," said one of the men in explanation.

"He's got to do it," said another. "Let him git a little ways ahead."

The sheriff returned to his wagon and drove on. He seemed, however, to realize that he would not be obeyed and that safety lay in haste alone. His wagon was traveling fast. If only he could lose them or get a good start he might possibly get to Clayton and the strong county jail by morning. His followers, however, trailed him swiftly as might be, determined not to be left behind.

"He's goin' to Baldwin," said one of the company of which Davies was a member.

"Where's that?" asked Davies.

"Over west o' here, about four miles."

"Why is he going there?"

"That's where he lives. I guess he thinks if he kin git 'im over there he kin purtect 'im till he kin git more help from Clayton. I calc'late he'll try an' take 'im over yet to-night, or early in the mornin' shore."

Davies smiled at the man's English. This countryside lingo always fascinated him.

Yet the men lagged, hesitating as to what to do. They did not want to lose sight of Mathews, and yet cowardice controlled them. They did not want to get into direct altercation with the law. It wasn't their place to hang the man, although plainly they felt that he ought to be hanged, and that it would be a stirring and exciting thing if he were. Consequently they desired to watch and be on hand—to get old Whitaker and his son Jake, if they could, who were out looking elsewhere. They wanted to see what the father and brother would do.

The quandary was solved by one of the men, who suggested that they could get to Baldwin by going back to Pleasant Valley and taking the Sand River pike, and that in the meantime they might come upon Whitaker and his son en route, or leave word at his house. It was a shorter cut than this the sheriff was taking, although he would get there first now. Possibly they could beat him at least to Clayton, if he attempted to go on. The Clayton road was back via Pleasant Valley, or near it, and easily intercepted. Therefore, while one or two remained to trail the sheriff and give the alarm in case he did attempt to go on to Clayton, the rest, followed by Davies, set off at a gallop to Pleasant Valley. It was nearly dusk now when they arrived and stopped at the corner store —supper time. The fires of evening meals were marked by upcurling smoke from chimneys. Here, somehow, the zest to follow seemed to depart. Evidently the sheriff had worsted them for the night. Morg Whitaker, the father, had not been found; neither had Jake. Perhaps they had better eat. Two or three had already secretly fallen away.

They were telling the news of what had occurred so far to one of the two storekeepers who kept the place, when suddenly Jake Whitaker, the girl's brother, and several companions came riding up. They had been scouring the territory to the north of the town, and were hot and tired. Plainly they were unaware of the developments of which the crowd had been a part.

"The sheriff's got 'im!" exclaimed one of the company, with that blatance which always accompanies the telling of great news in small rural companies. "He taken him over to Baldwin in a wagon a coupla hours ago."

"Which way did he go?" asked the son, whose hardy figure, worn, hand-me-down clothes and rakish hat showed up picturesquely as he turned here and there on his horse.

"'Cross Sellers' Lane. You won't git 'em that-a-way, though, Jake. He's already over there by now. Better take the short cut."

A babble of voices now made the scene more interesting. One told how the negro had been caught, another that the sheriff was defiant, a third that men were still tracking him or over there watching, until all the chief points of the drama had been spoken if not heard.

Instantly suppers were forgotten. The whole customary order of the evening was overturned once more. The company started off on another excited jaunt, up hill and down dale, through the lovely country that lay between Baldwin and Pleasant Valley.

By now Davies was very weary of this procedure and of his saddle. He wondered when, if ever, this story was to culminate, let alone he write it. Tragic as it might prove, he could not nevertheless spend an indefinite period trailing a possibility, and yet, so great was the potentiality of the present situation, he dared not leave. By contrast with the horror impending, as he now noted, the night was so beautiful that it was all but poignant. Stars were already beginning to shine. Distant lamps twinkled like yellow eyes from the cottages in the valleys and on the hillsides. The air was fresh and tender. Some peafowls were crying afar off, and the east promised a golden moon.

Silently the assembled company trotted on—no more than a score in all. In the dusk, and with Jake ahead, it seemed too grim a pilgrimage for joking. Young Jake, riding silently toward the front, looked as if tragedy were all he craved. His friends seemed considerately to withdraw from him, seeing that he was the aggrieved.

After an hour's riding Baldwin came into view, lying in a sheltering cup of low hills. Already its lights were twinkling softly and there was still an air of honest firesides and cheery suppers about it which appealed to Davies in his hungry state. Still, he had no thought now of anything save this pursuit.

Once in the village, the company was greeted by calls of recognition. Everybody seemed to know what they had come for. The sheriff and his charge were still there, so a dozen citizens volunteered. The local storekeepers and loungers followed the cavalcade up the street to the sheriff's house, for the riders had now fallen into a solemn walk.

"You won't get him though, boys," said one whom Davies later learned was Seavey, the village postmaster and telegraph operator, a rather youthful person of between twenty-five and thirty, as they passed his door. "He's got two deputies in there with him, or did have, and they say he's going to take him over to Clayton."

At the first street corner they were joined by the several men who had followed the sheriff.

"He tried to give us the slip," they volunteered excitedly, "but he's got the nigger in the house, there, down in the cellar. The deputies ain't with him. They've gone somewhere for help—Clayton, maybe."

"How do you know?"

"We saw 'em go out that back way. We think we did, anyhow."

A hundred feet from the sheriff's little white cottage, which backed up against a sloping field, the men parleyed. Then Jake announced that he proposed to go boldly up to the sheriff's door and demand the negro.

"If he don't turn him out I'll break in the door an' take him!" he said.

"That's right! We'll stand by you, Whitaker," commented several.

By now the throng of unmounted natives had gathered. The whole village was up and about, its one street alive and running with people. Heads appeared at doors and windows. Riders pranced up and down, hallooing. A few revolver shots were heard. Presently the mob gathered even closer to the sheriff's gate, and Jake stepped forward as leader. Instead, however, of going boldly up to the door as at first it appeared he would, he stopped at the gate, calling to the sheriff.

"Hello, Mathews!"

"Eh, eh, eh!" bellowed the crowd.

The call was repeated. Still no answer. Apparently to the sheriff delay appeared to be his one best weapon.

Their coming, however, was not as unexpected as some might have thought. The figure of the sheriff was plainly to be seen close to one of the front windows. He appeared to be holding a double-barreled shotgun. The negro, as it developed later, was cowering and chattering in the darkest corner of the cellar, hearkening no doubt to the voices and firing of the revolvers outside.

Suddenly, and just as Jake was about to go forward, the front door of the house flew open, and in the glow of a single lamp inside appeared first the double-barreled end of the gun, followed immediately by the form of Mathews, who held the weapon poised ready for a quick throw to the shoulder. All except Jake fell back.

"Mr. Mathews," he called deliberately, "we want that nigger!"

"Well, you can't git 'im!" replied the sheriff. "He's not here."

"Then what you got that gun fer?" yelled a voice.

Mathews made no answer.

"Better give him up, Mathews," called another, who was safe in the crowd, "or we'll come in an' take him!"

"No you won't," said the sheriff defiantly. "I said the man wasn't here. I say it ag'in. You couldn't have him if he was, an' you can't come in my house! Now if you people don't want trouble you'd better go on away."

"He's down in the cellar!" yelled another.

"Why don't you let us see?" asked another.

Mathews waved his gun slightly.

"You'd better go away from here now," cautioned the sheriff. "I'm tellin' ye! I'll have warrants out for the lot o' ye, if ye don't mind!"

The crowd continued to simmer and stew, while Jake stood as before. He was very pale and tense, but lacked initiative.

"He won't shoot," called some one at the back of the crowd. "Why don't you go in, Jake, an' git him?"

"Sure! Rush in. That's it!" observed a second.

"He won't, eh?" replied the sheriff softly. Then he added in a lower tone, "The first man that comes inside that gate takes the consequences."

No one ventured inside the gate; many even fell back. It seemed as if the planned assault had come to nothing.

"Why not go around the back way?" called some one else.

"Try it!" replied the sheriff. "See what you find on that side! I told you you couldn't come inside. You'd better go away from here now before ye git into trouble," he repeated. "You can't come in, an' it'll only mean bloodshed."

There was more chattering and jesting while the sheriff stood on guard. He, however, said no more. Nor did he allow the banter, turmoil and lust for tragedy to disturb him. Only, he kept his eye on Jake, on whose movements the crowd seemed to hang.

Time passed, and still nothing was done. The truth was that young Jake, put to the test, was not sufficiently courageous himself, for all his daring, and felt the weakness of the crowd behind him. To all intents and purposes he was alone, for he did not inspire confidence. He finally fell back a little, observing, "I'll git 'im before mornin', all right," and now the crowd itself began to disperse, returning to its stores and homes or standing about the postoffice and the one village drugstore. Finally, Davies smiled and came away. He was sure he had the story of a defeated mob. The sheriff was to be his great hero. He proposed to interview him later. For the present, he meant to seek out Seavey, the telegraph operator, and arrange to file a message, then see if something to eat was not to be had somewhere.

After a time he found the operator and told him what he wanted —to write and file a story as he wrote it. The latter indicated a table in the little postoffice and telegraph station which he could use. He became very much interested in the reporter when he learned he was from the *Times*, and when Davies asked where he could get something to eat said he would run across the street and tell the proprietor of the only boarding house to fix him something which he could consume as he wrote. He appeared to be interested in how a newspaper man would go about telling a story of this kind over a wire.

"You start your story," he said, "and I'll come back and see if I can get the *Times* on the wire."

Davies sat down and began his account. He was intent on describing things to date, the uncertainty and turmoil, the apparent victory of the sheriff. Plainly the courage of the latter had won, and it was all so picturesque. "A foiled lynching," he began, and as he wrote, the obliging postmaster, who had by now returned, picked up the pages and carefully deciphered them for himself.

"That's all right. I'll see if I can get the *Times* now," he commented.

"Very obliging postmaster," thought Davies as he wrote, but he had so often encountered pleasant and obliging people on his rounds that he soon dropped that thought.

The food was brought, and still Davies wrote on, munching as he did so. In a little while the *Times* answered an often-repeated call.

"Davies at Baldwin," ticked the postmaster, "get ready for quite a story!"

"Let 'er go!" answered the operator at the *Times*, who had been expecting this dispatch.

As the events of the day formulated themselves in his mind, Davies wrote and turned over page after page. Between whiles he looked out through the small window before him where afar off he could see a lonely light twinkling against a hillside. Not infrequently he stopped his work to see if anything new was happening, whether the situation was in any danger of changing, but apparently it was not. He then proposed to remain until all possibility of a tragedy, this night anyhow, was eliminated. The operator also wandered about, waiting for an accumulation of pages upon which he could work but making sure to keep up with the writer. The two became quite friendly.

Finally, his dispatch nearly finished, he asked the postmaster to caution the night editor at K—— to the effect, that if anything more happened before one in the morning he would file it, but not to expect anything more as nothing might happen. The reply came that he was to remain and await developments. Then he and the postmaster sat down to talk.

About eleven o'clock, when both had about convinced themselves that all was over for this night anyhow, and the lights in the village had all but vanished, a stillness of the purest, summery-est, country-est quality having settled down, a faint beating of hoofs, which seemed to suggest the approach of a large cavalcade, could be heard out on the Sand River pike as Davies by now had come to learn it was, back or northwest of the postoffice. At the sound the postmaster got up, as did Davies, both stepping outside and listening. On it came, and as the volume increased, the former said, "Might be help for the sheriff, but I doubt it. I telegraphed Clayton six times to-day. They wouldn't come that way, though. It's the wrong road." Now, thought Davies nervously, after all there might be something to add to his story, and he had so wished that it was all over! Lynchings, as he now felt, were horrible things. He wished people wouldn't do such things—take the law, which now more than ever he respected, into their own hands. It was too brutal, cruel. That negro cowering there in the dark probably, and the sheriff all taut and tense, worrying over his charge and his duty, were not happy things to contemplate in the face of such a thing as this. It was true that the crime which had been committed was dreadful, but still why couldn't people allow the law to take its course? It was so much better. The law was powerful enough to deal with cases of this kind.

"They're comin' back, all right," said the postmaster solemnly, as he and Davies stared in the direction of the sound which grew louder from moment to moment.

"It's not any help from Clayton, I'm afraid."

"By George, I think you're right!" answered the reporter, something telling him that more trouble was at hand. "Here they come!"

As he spoke there was a clattering of hoofs and crunching of saddle girths as a large company of men dashed up the road and

turned into the narrow street of the village, the figure of Jake
Whitaker and an older bearded man in a wide black hat riding
side by side in front.

"There's Jake," said the postmaster, "and that's his father riding
beside him there. The old man's a terror when he gets his dander
up. Sompin's sure to happen now."

Davies realized that in his absence writing, a new turn had been
given to things. Evidently the son had returned to Pleasant Valley
and organized a new posse or gone out to meet his father.

Instantly the place was astir again. Lights appeared in doorways
and windows, and both were thrown open. People were leaning or
gazing out to see what new movement was afoot. Davies noted at
once that there was none of the brash enthusiasm about this company such as had characterized the previous descent. There was
grimness everywhere, and he now began to feel that this was the
beginning of the end. After the cavalcade had passed down the
street toward the sheriff's house, which was quite dark now, he ran
after it, arriving a few moments after the former, which was already
in part dismounted. The townspeople followed. The sheriff, as it
now developed, had not relaxed any of his vigilance, however; he
was not sleeping, and as the crowd reappeared the light inside reappeared.

By the light of the moon, which was almost overhead, Davies was
able to make out several of his companions of the afternoon, and
Jake, the son. There were many more, though, now, whom he did
not know, and foremost among them this old man.

The latter was strong, iron-gray, and wore a full beard. He looked
very much like a blacksmith.

"Keep your eye on the old man," advised the postmaster, who
had by now come up and was standing by.

While they were still looking, the old man went boldly forward
to the little front porch of the house and knocked at the door.
Some one lifted a curtain at the window and peeped out.

"Hello, in there!" cried the old man, knocking again.

"What do you want?" asked a voice.

"I want that nigger!"

"Well, you can't have him! I've told you people that once."

"Bring him out or I'll break down the door!" said the old man.

"If you do it's at your own risk. I know you, Whitaker, an' you know me. I'll give ye two minutes to get off that porch!"

"I want that nigger, I tell ye!"

"If ye don't git off that porch I'll fire through the door," said the voice solemnly. "One—Two—"

The old man backed cautiously away.

"Come out, Mathews!" yelled the crowd. "You've got to give him up this time. We ain't goin' back without him."

Slowly the door opened, as if the individual within were very well satisfied as to his power to handle the mob. He had done it once before this night, why not again? It revealed his tall form, armed with his shotgun. He looked around very stolidly, and then addressed the old man as one would a friend.

"Ye can't have him, Morgan," he said. "It's ag'in' the law. You know that as well as I do."

"Law or no law," said the old man, "I want that nigger!"

"I tell you I can't let you have him, Morgan. It's ag'in' the law. You know you oughtn't to be comin' around here at this time o' night actin' so."

"Well, I'll take him then," said the old man, making a move.

"Stand back!" shouted the sheriff, leveling his gun on the instant. "I'll blow ye into kingdom come, sure as hell!"

A noticeable movement on the part of the crowd ceased. The sheriff lowered his weapon as if he thought the danger were once more over.

"You-all ought to be ashamed of yerselves," he went on, his voice sinking to a gentle neighborly reproof, "tryin' to upset the law this way."

"The nigger didn't upset no law, did he?" asked one derisively.

"Well, the law's goin' to take care of the nigger now," Mathews made answer.

"Give us that scoundrel, Mathews; you'd better do it," said the old man. "It'll save a heap o' trouble."

"I'll not argue with ye, Morgan. I said ye couldn't have him, an' ye can't. If ye want bloodshed, all right. But don't blame me. I'll kill the first man that tries to make a move this way."

He shifted his gun handily and waited. The crowd stood outside his little fence murmuring.

Presently the old man retired and spoke to several others. There was more murmuring, and then he came back to the dead line.

"We don't want to cause trouble, Mathews," he began explanatively, moving his hand oratorically, "but we think you ought to see that it won't do any good to stand out. We think that—"

Davies and the postmaster were watching young Jake, whose peculiar attitude attracted their attention. The latter was standing poised at the edge of the crowd, evidently seeking to remain unobserved. His eyes were on the sheriff, who was hearkening to the old man. Suddenly, as the father talked and when the sheriff seemed for a moment mollified and unsuspecting, he made a quick run for the porch. There was an intense movement all along the line as the life and death of the deed became apparent. Quickly the sheriff drew his gun to his shoulder. Both triggers were pressed at the same time, and the gun spoke, but not before Jake was in and under him. The latter had been in sufficient time to knock the gun barrel upward and fall upon his man. Both shots blazed harmlessly over the heads of the crowd in red puffs, and then followed a general onslaught. Men leaped the fence by tens and crowded upon the little cottage. They swarmed about every side of the house and crowded upon the porch, where four men were scuffling with the sheriff. The latter soon gave up, vowing vengeance and the law. Torches were brought, and a rope. A wagon drove up and was backed into the yard. Then began the calls for the negro.

As Davies contemplated all this he could not help thinking of the negro who during all this turmoil must have been crouching in his corner in the cellar, trembling for his fate. Now indeed he must realize that his end was near. He could not have dozed or lost consciousness during the intervening hours, but must have been cowering there, wondering and praying. All the while he must have been terrified lest the sheriff might not get him away in time. Now, at the sound of horses' feet and the new murmurs of contention, how must his body quake and his teeth chatter!

"I'd hate to be that nigger," commented the postmaster grimly, "but you can't do anything with 'em. The county oughta sent help."

"It's horrible, horrible!" was all Davies could say.

He moved closer to the house, with the crowd, eager to observe every detail of the procedure. Now it was that a number of the men, as eager in their search as bloodhounds, appeared at a low cellar entryway at the side of the house carrying a rope. Others followed with torches. Headed by father and son they began to descend into the dark hole. With impressive daring, Davies, who was by no means sure that he would be allowed but who was also determined if possible to see, followed.

Suddenly, in the farthest corner, he espied Ingalls. The latter in his fear and agony had worked himself into a crouching position, as if he were about to spring. His nails were apparently forced into the earth. His eyes were rolling, his mouth foaming.

"Oh, my Lawd, boss," he moaned, gazing almost as one blind, at the lights, "oh, my Lawd, boss, don't kill me! I won't do it no mo'. I didn't go to do it. I didn't mean to dis time. I was just drunk, boss. Oh, my Lawd! My Lawd!" His teeth chattered the while his mouth seemed to gape open. He was no longer sane really, but kept repeating monotonously, "Oh, my Lawd!"

"Here he is, boys! Pull him out," cried the father.

The negro now gave one yell of terror and collapsed, falling prone. He quite bounded as he did so, coming down with a dead chug on the earthen floor. Reason had forsaken him. He was by now a groveling, foaming brute. The last gleam of intelligence was that which notified him of the set eyes of his pursuers.

Davies, who by now had retreated to the grass outside before this sight, was standing but ten feet back when they began to reappear after seizing and binding him. Although shaken to the roots of his being, he still had all the cool observing powers of the trained and relentless reporter. Even now he noted the color values of the scene, the red, smoky heads of the torches, the disheveled appearance of the men, the scuffling and pulling. Then all at once he clapped his hands over his mouth, almost unconscious of what he was doing.

"Oh, my God!" he whispered, his voice losing power.

The sickening sight was that of the negro, foaming at the mouth, bloodshot as to his eyes, his hands working convulsively, being dragged up the cellar steps feet foremost. They had tied a rope about his waist and feet, and so had hauled him out, leaving his head to hang and drag. The black face was distorted beyond all human semblance.

"Oh, my God!" said Davies again, biting his fingers unconsciously.

The crowd gathered about now more closely than ever, more horror-stricken than gleeful at their own work. None apparently had either the courage or the charity to gainsay what was being done. With a kind of mechanical deftness now the negro was rudely lifted and like a sack of wheat thrown into the wagon. Father and son now mounted in front to drive and the crowd took to their horses, content to clatter, a silent cavalcade, behind. As Davies afterwards concluded, they were not so much hardened lynchers perhaps as curious spectators, the majority of them, eager for any variation—any excuse for one—to the dreary commonplaces of their existences. The task to most—all indeed—was entirely new. Wide-eyed and nerve-racked, Davies ran for his own horse and mounting followed. He was so excited he scarcely knew what he was doing.

Slowly the silent company now took its way up the Sand River pike whence it had come. The moon was still high, pouring down a wash of silvery light. As Davies rode he wondered how he was to complete his telegram, but decided that he could not. When this was over there would be no time. How long would it be before they would really hang him? And would they? The whole procedure seemed so unreal, so barbaric that he could scarcely believe it —that he was a part of it. Still they rode on.

"Are they really going to hang him? " he asked of one who rode beside him, a total stranger who seemed however not to resent his presence.

"That's what they got 'im fer," answered the stranger.

And think, he thought to himself, to-morrow night he would be resting in his own good bed back in K——!

Davies dropped behind again and into silence and tried to recover his nerves. He could scarcely realize that he, ordinarily accustomed to the routine of the city, its humdrum and at least outward social regularity, was a part of this. The night was so soft, the air so refreshing. The shadowy trees were stirring with a cool night wind. Why should any one have to die this way? Why couldn't the people of Baldwin or elsewhere have bestirred themselves on the side of the law before this, just let it take its course? Both father and son now seemed brutal, the injury to the daughter and sister not so vital as all this. Still, also, custom seemed to require death in this way for this. It was like some axiomatic, mathematic law— hard, but custom. The silent company, an articulated, mechanical and therefore terrible thing, moved on. It also was axiomatic, mathematic. After a time he drew near to the wagon and looked at the negro again.

The latter, as Davies was glad to note, seemed still out of his senses. He was breathing heavily and groaning, but probably not with any conscious pain. His eyes were fixed and staring, his face and hands bleeding as if they had been scratched or trampled upon. He was crumpled limply.

But Davies could stand it no longer now. He fell back, sick at heart, content to see no more. It seemed a ghastly, murderous thing to do. Still the company moved on and he followed, past fields lit white by the moon, under dark, silent groups of trees, through which the moonlight fell in patches, up low hills and down into valleys, until at last a little stream came into view, the same little stream, as it proved, which he had seen earlier to-day and for a bridge over which they were heading. Here it ran now, sparkling like electricity in the night. After a time the road drew closer to the water and then crossed directly over the bridge, which could be seen a little way ahead.

Up to this the company now rode and then halted. The wagon was driven up on the bridge, and father and son got out. All the riders, including Davies, dismounted, and a full score of them gathered about the wagon from which the negro was lifted, quite as one might a bag. Fortunately, as Davies now told himself, he was still unconscious, an accidental mercy. Nevertheless he decided now that he could not witness the end, and went down by the water-side slightly above the bridge. He was not, after all, the utterly relentless reporter. From where he stood, however, he could see long beams of iron projecting out over the water, where the bridge was braced, and some of the men fastening a rope to a beam, and then he could see that they were fixing the other end around the negro's neck.

Finally the curious company stood back, and he turned his face away.

"Have you anything to say?" a voice demanded.

There was no answer. The negro was probably lolling and groaning, quite as unconscious as he was before.

Then came the concerted action of a dozen men, the lifting of the black mass into the air, and then Davies saw the limp form plunge down and pull up with a creaking sound of rope. In the weak moonlight it seemed as if the body were struggling, but he could not tell. He watched, wide-mouthed and silent, and then the body ceased moving. Then after a time he heard the company making ready to depart, and finally it did so, leaving him quite indifferently to himself and his thoughts. Only the black mass swaying in the pale light over the glimmering water seemed human and alive, his sole companion.

He sat down upon the bank and gazed in silence. Now the horror was gone. The suffering was ended. He was no longer afraid. Everything was summery and beautiful. The whole cavalcade had disappeared; the moon finally sank. His horse, tethered to a sapling beyond the bridge, waited patiently. Still he sat. He might now have hurried back to the small postoffice in Baldwin and attempted to file additional details of this story, providing he could find Seavey, but it would have done no good. It was quite too late, and anyhow what did it matter? No other reporter had been present, and he could write a fuller, sadder, more colorful story on the morrow. He wondered idly what had become of Seavey? Why had he not followed? Life seemed so sad, so strange, so mysterious, so inexplicable.

As he still sat there the light of morning broke, a tender lavender and gray in the east. Then came the roseate hues of dawn, all the wondrous coloring of celestial halls, to which the waters of the stream responded. The white pebbles shone pinkily at the bottom, the grass and sedges first black now gleamed a translucent green. Still the body hung there black and limp against the sky, and now a light breeze sprang up and stirred it visibly. At last he arose, mounted his horse and made his way back to Pleasant Valley, too full of the late tragedy to be much interested in anything else. Rousing his liveryman, he adjusted his difficulties with him by telling him the whole story, assuring him of his horse's care and handing him a five-dollar bill. Then he left, to walk and think again.

Since there was no train before noon and his duty plainly called him to a portion of another day's work here, he decided to make a day of it, idling about and getting additional details as to what further might be done. Who would cut the body down? What about arresting the lynchers—the father and son, for instance? What about the sheriff now? Would he act as he threatened? If he telegraphed the main fact of the lynching his city editor would not mind, he knew, his coming late, and the day here was so beautiful. He proceeded to talk with citizens and officials, rode out to the injured girl's home, rode to Baldwin to see the sheriff. There was a singular silence and placidity in that corner. The latter assured him that he knew nearly all of those who had taken part, and proposed to swear out warrants for them, but just the same Davies noted that he took his defeat as he did his danger, philosophically. There was no real activity in that corner later. He wished to remain a popular sheriff, no doubt.

It was sundown again before he remembered that he had not discovered whether the body had been removed. Nor had he heard why the negro came back, nor exactly how he was caught. A nine o'clock evening train to the city giving him a little more time for investigation, he decided to avail himself of it. The negro's cabin was two miles out along a pine-shaded road, but so pleasant was the evening that he decided to walk. En route, the last rays of the sinking sun stretched long shadows of budding trees across his path. It was not long before he came upon the cabin, a one-story affair set well back from the road and surrounded with a few scattered trees. By now it was quite dark. The ground between the cabin and the road was open, and strewn with the chips of a woodpile. The roof was sagged, and the windows patched in places, but for all that it had the glow of a home. Through the front door, which stood open, the blaze of a wood-fire might be seen, its yellow light filling the interior with a golden glow.

Hesitating before the door, Davies finally knocked. Receiving no answer he looked in on the battered cane chairs and aged furniture with considerable interest. It was a typical negro cabin, poor beyond the need of description. After a time a door in the rear of the room opened and a little negro girl entered carrying a battered tin lamp without any chimney. She had not heard his knock and started perceptibly at the sight of his figure in the doorway. Then she raised her smoking lamp above her head in order to see better, and approached.

There was something ridiculous about her unformed figure and loose gingham dress, as he noted. Her feet and hands were so large. Her black head was strongly emphasized by little pigtails of hair done up in white twine, which stood out all over her head. Her dark skin was made apparently more so by contrast with her white teeth and the whites of her eyes.

Davies looked at her for a moment but little moved now by the oddity which ordinarily would have amused him, and asked, "Is this where Ingalls lived?"

The girl nodded her head. She was exceedingly subdued, and looked as if she might have been crying.

"Has the body been brought here?"

"Yes, suh," she answered, with a soft negro accent.

"When did they bring it?"

"Dis moanin'."

"Are you his sister?"

"Yes, suh."

"Well, can you tell me how they caught him? When did he come back, and what for?" He was feeling slightly ashamed to intrude thus.

"In de afternoon, about two."

"And what for?" repeated Davies.

"To see us," answered the girl. "To see my motha'."

"Well, did he want anything? He didn't come just to see her, did he?"

"Yes, suh," said the girl, "he come to say good-by. We doan know when dey caught him." Her voice wavered.

"Well, didn't he know he might get caught?" asked Davies sympathetically, seeing that the girl was so moved.

"Yes, suh, I think he did."

She still stood very quietly holding the poor battered lamp up, and looking down.

"Well, what did he have to say?" asked Davies.

"He didn' have nothin' much to say, suh. He said he wanted to see motha'. He was a-goin' away."

The girl seemed to regard Davies as an official of some sort, and he knew it.

"Can I have a look at the body?" he asked.

The girl did not answer, but started as if to lead the way.

"When is the funeral?" he asked.

"Tomorra'."

The girl then led him through several bare sheds of rooms strung in a row to the furthermost one of the line. This last seemed a sort of storage shed for odds and ends. It had several windows, but they were quite bare of glass and open to the moonlight save for a few wooden boards nailed across from the outside. Davies had been wondering all the while where the body was and at the lonely and forsaken air of the place. No one but this little pig-tailed girl seemed about. If they had any colored neighbors they were probably afraid to be seen here.

Now, as he stepped into this cool, dark, exposed outer room, the desolation seemed quite complete. It was very bare, a mere shed or wash-room. There was the body in the middle of the room, stretched upon an ironing board which rested on a box and a chair, and covered with a white sheet. All the corners of the room were quite dark. Only its middle was brightened by splotches of silvery light.

Davies came forward, the while the girl left him, still carrying her lamp. Evidently she thought the moon lighted up the room sufficiently, and she did not feel equal to remaining. He lifted the sheet quite boldly, for he could see well enough, and looked at the still, black form. The face was extremely distorted, even in death, and he could see where the rope had tightened. A bar of cool moonlight lay just across the face and breast. He was still looking, thinking soon to restore the covering, when a sound, half sigh, half groan, reached his ears.

At it he started as if a ghost had made it. It was so eerie and unexpected in this dark place. His muscles tightened. Instantly his heart went hammering like mad. His first impression was that it must have come from the dead.

"Oo-o-ohh!" came the sound again, this time whimpering, as if some one were crying.

Instantly he turned, for now it seemed to come from a corner of the room, the extreme corner to his right, back of him. Greatly disturbed, he approached, and then as his eyes strained he seemed to catch the shadow of something, the figure of a woman, perhaps, crouching against the walls, huddled up, dark, almost indistinguishable.

"Oh, oh, oh!" the sound now repeated itself, even more plaintively than before.

Davies began to understand. He approached slowly, then more swiftly desired to withdraw, for he was in the presence of an old black mammy, doubled up and weeping. She was in the very niche of the two walls, her head sunk on her knees, her body quite still. "Oh, oh, oh!" she repeated, as he stood there near her.

Davies drew silently back. Before such grief his intrusion seemed cold and unwarranted. The guiltlessness of the mother—her love—how could one balance that against the other? The sensation of tears came to his eyes. He instantly covered the dead and withdrew.

Out in the moonlight he struck a brisk pace, but soon stopped and looked back. The whole dreary cabin, with its one golden eye, the door, seemed such a pitiful thing. The weeping mammy, alone in her corner—and he had come back to say "Good-by!" Davies swelled with feeling. The night, the tragedy, the grief, he saw it all. But also with the cruel instinct of the budding artist that he already was, he was beginning to meditate on the character of story it would make—the color, the pathos. The knowledge now that it was not always exact justice that was meted out to all and that it was not so much the business of the writer to indict as to interpret was borne in on him with distinctness by the cruel sorrow of the mother, whose blame, if any, was infinitesimal.

"I'll get it all in!" he exclaimed feelingly, if triumphantly at last. "I'll get it all in!"

JAMES WELDON JOHNSON

(1871–1938)

As a literary figure, James Weldon Johnson was an elder statesman
and theoretician in the Harlem Renaissance of the 1920s. As a
dedicated social reformer, he served as Field Secretary and General
Secretary of the National Association for the Advancement of
Colored People, and led a campaign in behalf of the Dyer Anti-
Lynching Bill, which, though passed by the House in 1922, was
blocked in the Senate.

Johnson was born into middle-class Negro society in Jacksonville, Florida, where his father was a waiter in a fashionable hotel
and his mother taught school. He attended Atlanta University and
returned to Jacksonville, where he served as a teacher and school
principal, became the first Negro in post-Reconstruction times to
be admitted to the Florida bar, and started a short-lived Negro
newspaper. With his brother, Rosamond, he then enjoyed a highly
successful career as a Tin Pan Alley song writer and toured Paris
and London. While still writing popular songs he studied English
literature under Brander Matthews at Columbia University.

In 1904 he turned to politics and worked with a New York City
Colored Republican Club for the election of Theodore Roosevelt.
Next, as a diplomat, he served as United States Consul in Vene-
zuela and Nicaragua, and came to oppose the occupation of Nicaragua in particular and American paternalism in Latin America in
general. In 1912 he published the novel Autobiography of an Ex-
Colored Man anonymously, but the book went unnoticed until
reissued under Johnson's name in 1927 with an introduction by

Carl Van Vechten. The novel, which was a major influence on later Harlem Renaissance writers, describes a life in many ways the opposite of Johnson's own. It presents a young light-skinned Negro who, overwhelmed by having witnessed a lynching, abandons his dreams of writing great music based on Negro folk themes and passes into the white world, where he becomes a successful businessman.

In God's Trombones (1927), a collection of Negro folk sermons, and in various poems such as "O Black and Unknown Bards" (1917), Johnson broke with Dunbar's dialect poetry, which he saw as perpetuating the "Black Sambo" stereotype, and treated the heritage of the inspirational sermon with a seriousness and dignity it had rarely been accorded before. While these poems and his many critical essays were contributing to the Harlem Renaissance, Johnson continued his work as a NAACP official and a lobbyist for various reform bills. In 1931 he became professor of Creative Literature at Fisk University, and he was still active in this post at the time of his death in an auto accident in 1938. Among his other important works are The Books of American Negro Spirituals (1925) and his autobiography, Along This Way (1933). In The Roots of Negro Racial Consciousness, a study of Harlem Renaissance authors (see Bibliography), Stephen Bronz notes: "Johnson was incensed by injustices to the Negro, but rarely expressed his anger beyond the bounds of carefully controlled, urbanely phrased protest. Though proud of the Negro, and even somewhat chauvinistic, he felt friendly towards and at ease with sympathetic whites."

O Black and Unknown Bards

O black and unknown bards of long ago,
How came your lips to touch the sacred fire?
How, in your darkness, did you come to know
The power and beauty of the minstrel's lyre?

Who first from midst his bonds lifted his eyes?
Who first from out the still watch, lone and long,
Feeling the ancient faith of prophets rise
Within his dark-kept soul, burst into song?

Heart of what slave poured out such melody
As "Steal away to Jesus"? On its strains
His spirit must have nightly floated free,
Though still about his hands he felt his chains.
Who heard great "Jordan roll"? Whose starward eye
Saw chariot "swing low"? And who was he
That breathed that comforting, melodic sigh,
"Nobody knows de trouble I see"?

What merely living clod, what captive thing,
Could up toward God through all its darkness grope,
And find within its deadened heart to sing
These songs of sorrow, love and faith, and hope?
How did it catch that subtle undertone,
That note in music heard not with the ears?
How sound the elusive reed so seldom blown,
Which stirs the soul or melts the heart to tears?

Not that great German master in his dream
Of harmonies that thundered amongst the stars
At the creation, ever heard a theme
Nobler than "Go down, Moses." Mark its bars
How like a mighty trumpet-call they stir
The blood. Such are the notes that men have sung
Going to valorous deeds; such tones there were
That helped make history when Time was young.

There is a wide, wide wonder in it all,
That from degraded rest and servile toil
The fiery spirit of the seer should call
These simple children of the sun and soil.
O black slave singers, gone, forgot, unfamed,

You—you alone, of all the long, long line
Of those who've sung untaught, unknown, unnamed,
Have stretched out upward, seeking the divine.

You sang not deeds of heroes or of kings;
No chant of bloody war, no exulting paean
Of arms-won triumphs; but your humble strings
You touched in chord with music empyrean.
You sang far better than you knew; the songs
That for your listeners' hungry hearts sufficed
Still live—but more than this to you belongs:
You sang a race from wood and stone to Christ.

Go Down Death: a Funeral Sermon

Weep not, weep not,
She is not dead;
She's resting in the bosom of Jesus.
Heart-broken husband—weep no more;
Grief-stricken son—weep no more;
Left-lonesome daughter—weep no more;
She's only just gone home.

Day before yesterday morning,
God was looking down from his great, high heaven,
Looking down on all his children,
And his eye fell on Sister Caroline,
Tossing on her bed of pain.
And God's big heart was touched with pity,
With the everlasting pity.

And God sat back on his throne,
And he commanded that tall, bright angel standing at his right
    hand:
Call me Death!
And that tall, bright angel cried in a voice
That broke like a clap of thunder:

Call Death!—Call Death!
And the echo sounded down the streets of heaven
Till it reached away back to that shadowy place,
Where Death waits with his pale, white horses.

And Death heard the summons,
And he leaped on his fastest horse,
Pale as a sheet in the moonlight.
Up the golden street Death galloped,
And the hoofs of his horse struck fire from the gold,
But they didn't make no sound.
Up Death rode to the Great White Throne,
And waited for God's command.

And God said: Go down, Death, go down,
Go down to Savannah, Georgia,
Down in Yamacraw,
And find Sister Caroline.
She's borne the burden and heat of the day,
She's labored long in my vineyard,
And she's tired—
She's weary—
Go down, Death, and bring her to me.

And Death didn't say a word,
But he loosed the reins on his pale, white horse,
And he clamped the spurs to his bloodless sides,
And out and down he rode,
Through heaven's pearly gates,
Past suns and moons and stars;
On Death rode,
And the foam from his horse was like a comet in the sky;
On Death rode,
Leaving the lightning's flash behind;
Straight on down he came.

While we were watching round her bed,
She turned her eyes and looked away,

She saw what we couldn't see;
She saw Old Death. She saw Old Death
Coming like a falling star.
But Death didn't frighten Sister Caroline;
He looked to her like a welcome friend.
And she whispered to us: I'm going home,
And she smiled and closed her eyes.

And Death took her up like a baby,
And she lay in his icy arms,
But she didn't feel no chill.
And Death began to ride again—
Up beyond the evening star,
Out beyond the morning star,
Into the glittering light of glory,
On to the Great White Throne.
And there he laid Sister Caroline
On the loving breast of Jesus.

And Jesus took his own hand and wiped away her tears,
And he smoothed the furrows from her face,
And the angels sang a little song,
And Jesus rocked her in his arms,
And kept a-saying: Take your rest,
Take your rest, take your rest.

Weep not—weep not,
She is not dead;
She's resting in the bosom of Jesus.

CLAUDE McKAY

(1891–1948)

————————◆◀◉▶◆————————

Claude McKay was a major figure in the Harlem Renaissance of the 1920s, a period described by Stephen Bronz (see Bibliography) in these terms: "Harlem Renaissance books were reviewed in leading white newspapers and magazines, and the authors, centered in Harlem, were lionized at white literary parties. At the same time, plays by Negroes, such as Shuffle Along, and plays about Negroes, such as Emperor Jones and Green Pastures, packed Broadway theaters. And Harlem became a fad, as whites ventured uptown in search of the exotic, Negro women, and jazz."

McKay, born the son of a farmer on the island of Jamaica, had already been hailed as "the Bobby Burns of Jamaica" for a volume of poems, Songs of Jamaica (1912), before coming to the United States in 1912. After studying at Tuskegee Institute and Kansas State University, he moved to Harlem and supported himself with various menial jobs while writing poetry. In 1919 he moved to Europe and lived in London for a year, where he published Spring in New Hampshire (1920), another collection of poems. Back in New York in 1921, he became an editor for two radical publications, The Masses and The Liberator, and the next year he published Harlem Shadows, perhaps his finest collection of poems. Attracted to communism, he visited Russia in 1922, delivering an address to the Third International, and then, following extensive travel in Europe and Africa, he settled in France for several years.

Home to Harlem (1928), his first novel, was a best seller, but it incurred the wrath of some Negro critics because of its candid picture of Harlem low-life. In addition to two more novels, Mc-Kay wrote Gingertown (1932), a collection of short stories; A Long Way from Home (1937), an autobiography; and Harlem: Negro Metropolis (1940), a sociological study. In 1944 he converted to Catholicism.

Despite the popularity of Home to Harlem, McKay is best known for his poems, particularly his sonnets. Although his nature poems in Songs of Jamaica and Spring in New Hampshire are quite successful, his militant sonnets, such as "If We Must Die," have come to be his most admired works. His ability to play restraining form against impassioned content has reminded some readers of the sonnets of social comment by Milton and Wordsworth. Perhaps an important factor in McKay's militant stance was a legend handed down in his family which held that his ancestors, carried in chains from Madagascar, had avoided the fragmented family life so characteristic of slavery by publicly vowing to kill themselves should they be sold to separate masters.

Summer Morn in New Hampshire

All yesterday it poured, and all night long
    I could not sleep; the rain unceasing beat
Upon the shingled roof like a weird song,
    Upon the grass like running children's feet.
And down the mountains by the dark cloud kissed,
    Like a strange shape in filmy veiling dressed,
Slid slowly, silently, the wraith-like mist,
    And nestled soft against the earth's wet breast.

But lo, there was a miracle at dawn!
    The still air stirred at touch of the faint breeze,
The sun a sheet of gold bequeathed the lawn,
    The songsters twittered in the rustling trees.

And all things were transfigured in the day,
But me whom radiant beauty could not move;
For you, more wonderful, were far away,
And I was blind with hunger for your love.

Home Thoughts

Oh something just now must be happening there!
That suddenly and quiveringly here,
Amid the city's noises, I must think
Of mangoes leaning to the river's brink,
And dexterous Davie climbing high above,
The gold fruits ebon-speckled to remove,
And toss them quickly in the tangled mass
Of wis-wis twisted round the guinea grass.
And Cyril coming through the bramble-track
A prize bunch of bananas on his back;
And Georgie—none could ever dive like him—
Throwing his scanty clothes off for a swim;
And schoolboys, from Bridge-tunnel going home,
Watching the waters downward dash and foam.
This is no daytime dream, there's something in it,
Oh something's happening there this very minute!

Baptism

Into the furnace let me go alone;
Stay you without in terror of the heat.
I will go naked in—for thus 'tis sweet—
Into the weird depths of the hottest zone.
I will not quiver in the frailest bone,
You will not note a flicker of defeat;
My heart shall tremble not its fate to meet,
My mouth give utterance to any moan.
The yawning oven spits forth fiery spears;
Red aspish tongues shout wordlessly my name.

Desire destroys, consumes my mortal fears,
Transforming me into a shape of flame.
I will come out, back to your world of tears,
A stronger soul within a finer frame.

If We Must Die

If we must die, let it not be like hogs
Hunted and penned in an inglorious spot,
While round us bark the mad and hungry dogs,
Making their mock at our accursed lot.
If we must die, O let us nobly die,
So that our precious blood may not be shed
In vain; then even the monsters we defy
Shall be constrained to honor us though dead!
O kinsmen! we must meet the common foe!
Though far outnumbered let us show us brave,
And for their thousand blows deal one deathblow!
What though before us lies the open grave?
Like men we'll face the murderous, cowardly pack,
Pressed to the wall, dying, but fighting back!

The Lynching

His spirit in smoke ascended to high heaven.
His father, by the cruelest way of pain,
Had bidden him to his bosom once again;
The awful sin remained still unforgiven.
All night a bright and solitary star
(Perchance the one that ever guided him,
Yet gave him up at last to Fate's wild whim)
Hung pitifully o'er the swinging char.
Day dawned, and soon the mixed crowds came to view
The ghastly body swaying in the sun:
The women thronged to look, but never a one
Showed sorrow in her eyes of steely blue.

And little lads, lynchers that were to be,
Danced round the dreadful thing in fiendish glee.

Outcast

For the dim regions whence my fathers came
My spirit, bondaged by the body, longs.
Words felt, but never heard, my lips would frame;
My soul would sing forgotten jungle songs.
I would go back to darkness and to peace,
But the great western world holds me in fee,
And I may never hope for full release
While to its alien gods I bend my knee.
Something in me is lost, forever lost,
Some vital thing has gone out of my heart,
And I must walk the way of life a ghost
Among the sons of earth, a thing apart.

For I was born, far from my native clime,
Under the white man's menace, out of time.

The Negro's Tragedy

It is the Negro's tragedy I feel
Which binds me like a heavy iron chain,
It is the Negro's wounds I want to heal
Because I know the keenness of his pain.
Only a thorn-crowned Negro and no white
Can penetrate into the Negro's ken,
Or feel the thickness of the shroud of night
Which hides and buries him from other men.

So what I write is urged out of my blood.
There is no white man who could write my book,
Though many think their story should be told
Of what the Negro people ought to brook.

Our statesmen roam the world to set things right.
This Negro laughs and prays to God for Light!

America

Although she feeds me bread of bitterness,
And sinks into my throat her tiger's tooth,
Stealing my breath of life, I will confess
I love this cultured hell that tests my youth!
Her vigor flows like tides into my blood,
Giving me strength erect against her hate.
Her bigness sweeps my being like a flood.
Yet as a rebel fronts a king in state,
I stand within her walls with not a shred
Of terror, malice, not a word of jeer.
Darkly I gaze into the days ahead,
And see her might and granite wonders there,
Beneath the touch of Time's unerring hand,
Like priceless treasures sinking in the sand.

Harlem Shadows

I hear the halting footsteps of a lass
    In Negro Harlem when the night lets fall
Its veil. I see the shapes of girls who pass
    To bend and barter at desire's call.
Ah, little dark girls who in slippered feet
Go prowling through the night from street to street!

Through the long night until the silver break
    Of day the little gray feet know no rest;
Through the lone night until the last snow-flake
    Has dropped from heaven upon the earth's
            white breast,
The dusky, half-clad girls of tired feet
Are trudging, thinly shod, from street to street.

Ah, stern harsh world, that in the wretched way
    Of poverty, dishonor and disgrace,
Has pushed the timid little feet of clay,
    The sacred brown feet of my fallen race!
Ah, heart of me, the weary, weary feet
In Harlem wandering from street to street.

The White House*

Your door is shut against my tightened face,
And I am sharp as steel with discontent;
But I possess the courage and the grace
To bear my anger proudly and unbent.
The pavement slabs burn loose beneath my feet,
A chafing savage, down the decent street;
And passion rends my vitals as I pass,
Where boldly shines your shuttered door of glass.
Oh, I must search for wisdom every hour,
Deep in my wrathful bosom sore and raw,
And find in it the superhuman power
To hold me to the letter of your law!
Oh, I must keep my heart inviolate
Against the potent poison of your hate.

* "My title was symbolic . . . it had no reference to the official residence of
the President of the United States. . . . The title 'White Houses' changed
the whole symbolic intent and meaning of the poem, making it appear as if
the burning ambition of the black malcontent was to enter white houses in
general." [Claude McKay: A Long Way from Home (1937), pp. 313–314.]

COUNTEE CULLEN

(1903–1946)

As Countee Cullen's poem "Yet Do I Marvel" suggests, he saw an inherent conflict between blackness and lyricism. Although he was an important figure in fermenting black consciousness during the Harlem Renaissance through his editorship of Opportunity, and although he became sufficiently involved in social protest to support the Communist Party in the 1932 presidential election, he felt uncomfortable in the role of racial spokesman and regarded himself as primarily a romantic and lyric poet. He looked to John Keats for his own poetic inspiration, and in the introduction to Caroling Dusk, an anthology of Negro verse he edited in 1927, he urged Negro poets to seek models not in African heritage but in English and American poetic tradition.

Adopted at the age of thirteen by Rev. Frederick A. Cullen, a Methodist minister in Harlem, Countee Cullen was raised in the secure and conservative environment of a parsonage. He was graduated from New York University, where he was elected to Phi Beta Kappa, and received an M.A. from Harvard, where he studied poetry with Robert Hillyer. Cullen's first collection of poems, Color (1925), which included many of his best works, was published while he was still an undergraduate. Later collections of poetry include Copper Sun (1927), The Ballad of the Brown Girl (1928), The Black Christ (1929), The Medea and Other Poems (1935), and The Lost Zoo (1940). One Way to Heaven, a novel, was published in 1932, and in 1946 Cullen collaborated with Arna Bontemps on the musical play St. Louis Woman. On These I Stand, a selection by the poet of his best poems, was published posthumously in 1947.

Cullen's post as assistant editor of Opportunity, Journal of Negro Life, brought him into contact with leading figures of the Negro Renaissance of the 1920s. He won a Guggenheim Fellowship in 1928 and lived in France for two years. In 1934 he took a position as a French teacher at a Harlem junior high school, and he remained a teacher in Harlem until his death in 1946. During his last years he produced several children's books.

Although his foster father was president of a local NAACP chapter and helped to found the National Urban League, Countee Cullen once claimed that he had never been interested in politics, and, when interviewed in 1939 in connection with Gunnar Myrdal's study of race in America, he stated, "I have met with very few instances of discrimination during my life." He wanted to be regarded as a poet rather than as a Negro poet, and his wide study of poetic theory and tradition is manifested in the variety of verse forms he employed, including ballad stanzas, heroic couplets, blank verse, and Spenserian stanzas. Ironically, despite his hesitancy about dealing with racial matters in poetry, he is best remembered for poems such as "Yet Do I Marvel" and "Heritage," which draw directly upon his experience as a black man in America.

Yet Do I Marvel

I doubt not God is good, well-meaning, kind,
And did He stoop to quibble could tell why
The little buried mole continues blind,
Why flesh that mirrors Him must some day die,

Make plain the reason tortured Tantalus
Is baited by the fickle fruit, declare
If merely brute caprice dooms Sisyphus
To struggle up a never-ending stair.
Inscrutable His ways are, and immune
To catechism by a mind too strewn
With petty cares to slightly understand
What awful brain compels His awful hand.
Yet do I marvel at this curious thing:
To make a poet black, and bid him sing!

A Song of Praise

(For one who praised his lady's being fair)

You have not heard my love's dark throat,
    Slow-fluting like a reed,
Release the perfect golden note
    She caged there for my need.

Her walk is like the replica
    Of some barbaric dance
Wherein the soul of Africa
    Is winged with arrogance.

And yet so light she steps across
    The ways her sure feet pass,
She does not dent the smoothest moss
    Or bend the thinnest grass.

My love is dark as yours is fair,
    Yet lovelier I hold her
Than listless maids with pallid hair,
    And blood that's thin and colder.

You-proud-and-to-be-pitied one,
    Gaze on her and despair;
Then seal your lips until the sun
    Discovers one as fair.

Incident

(For Eric Walrond)

Once riding in old Baltimore,
   Heart-filled, head-filled with glee,
I saw a Baltimorean
   Keep looking straight at me.

Now I was eight and very small,
   And he was no whit bigger,
And so I smiled, but he poked out
   His tongue, and called me, "Nigger."

I saw the whole of Baltimore
   From May until December;
Of all the things that happened there
   That's all that I remember.

Heritage

(For Harold Jackman)

What is Africa to me:
Copper sun or scarlet sea,
Jungle star or jungle track,
Strong bronzed men, or regal black
Women from whose loins I sprang
When the birds of Eden sang?
One three centuries removed
From the scenes his fathers loved,
Spicy grove, cinnamon tree,
What is Africa to me?

So I lie, who all day long
Want no sound except the song
Sung by wild barbaric birds
Goading massive jungle herds,
Juggernauts of flesh that pass

Trampling tall defiant grass
Where young forest lovers lie,
Plighting troth beneath the sky.
So I lie, who always hear,
Though I cram against my ear
Both my thumbs, and keep them there,
Great drums throbbing through the air.
So I lie, whose fount of pride,
Dear distress, and joy allied,
Is my somber flesh and skin,
With the dark blood dammed within
Like great pulsing tides of wine
That, I fear, must burst the fine
Channels of the chafing net
Where they surge and foam and fret.

Africa? A book one thumbs
Listlessly, till slumber comes.
Unremembered are her bats
Circling through the night, her cats
Crouching in the river reeds,
Stalking gentle flesh that feeds
By the river brink; no more
Does the bugle-throated roar
Cry that monarch claws have leapt
From the scabbards where they slept.
Silver snakes that once a year
Doff the lovely coats you wear,
Seek no covert in your fear
Lest a mortal eye should see;
What's your nakedness to me?
Here no leprous flowers rear
Fierce corollas in the air;
Here no bodies sleek and wet,
Dripping mingled rain and sweat,
Tread the savage measures of
Jungle boys and girls in love.
What is last year's snow to me,

Last year's anything? The tree
Budding yearly must forget
How its past arose or set—
Bough and blossom, flower, fruit,
Even what shy bird with mute
Wonder at her travail there,
Meekly labored in its hair.
One three centuries removed
From the scenes his fathers loved,
Spicy grove, cinnamon tree,
What is Africa to me?

So I lie, who find no peace
Night or day, no slight release
From the unremittant beat
Made by cruel padded feet
Walking through my body's street.
Up and down they go, and back,
Treading out a jungle track.
So I lie, who never quite
Safely sleep from rain at night—
I can never rest at all
When the rain begins to fall;
Like a soul gone mad with pain
I must match its weird refrain;
Ever must I twist and squirm,
Writhing like a baited worm,
While its primal measures drip
Through my body, crying, "Strip!
Doff this new exuberance.
Come and dance the Lover's Dance!"
In an old remembered way
Rain works on me night and day.

Quaint, outlandish heathen gods
Black men fashion out of rods,
Clay, and brittle bits of stone,

In a likeness like their own,
My conversion came high-priced;
I belong to Jesus Christ,
Preacher of humility;
Heathen gods are naught to me.

Father, Son, and Holy Ghost,
So I make an idle boast;
Jesus of the twice-turned cheek,
Lamb of God, although I speak
With my mouth thus, in my heart
Do I play a double part.
Ever at Thy glowing altar
Must my heart grow sick and falter,
Wishing He I served were black,
Thinking then it would not lack
Precedent of pain to guide it,
Let who would or might deride it;
Surely then this flesh would know
Yours had borne a kindred woe.
Lord, I fashion dark gods, too,
Daring even to give You
Dark despairing features where,
Crowned with dark rebellious hair,
Patience wavers just so much as
Mortal grief compels, while touches
Quick and hot, of anger, rise
To smitten cheek and weary eyes.
Lord, forgive me if my need
Sometimes shapes a human creed.
All day long and all night through,
One thing only must I do:
Quench my pride and cool my blood,
Lest I perish in the flood.
Lest a hidden ember set
Timber that I thought was wet
Burning like the dryest flax,

Melting like the merest wax,
Lest the grave restore its dead.
Not yet has my heart or head
In the least way realized
They and I are civilized.

From the Dark Tower

(*To Charles S. Johnson*)

We shall not always plant while others reap
The golden increment of bursting fruit,
Not always countenance, abject and mute,
That lesser men should hold their brothers cheap;
Not everlastingly while others sleep
Shall we beguile their limbs with mellow flute,
Not always bend to some more subtle brute;
We were not made eternally to weep.

The night whose sable breast relieves the stark,
White stars is no less lovely being dark,
And there are buds that cannot bloom at all
In light, but crumple, piteous, and fall;
So in the dark we hide the heart that bleeds,
And wait, and tend our agonizing seeds.

Black Majesty

(*After reading John W. Vandercook's chronicle of sable glory*)

These men were kings, albeit they were black,
Christophe and Dessalines and L'Ouverture;
Their majesty has made me turn my back
Upon a plaint I once shaped to endure.
These men were black, I say, but they were crowned
And purple-clad, however brief their time.
Stifle your agony; let grief be drowned;
We know joy had a day once and a clime.

Dark gutter-snipe, black sprawler-in-the-mud,
A thing men did a man may do again.
What answers filter through your sluggish blood
To these dark ghosts who knew so bright a reign?
"Lo, I am dark, but comely," Sheba sings.
"And we were black," three shades reply, "but kings."

ARNA BONTEMPS

(1902–   )

Arna Bontemps has been a central figure in American Negro literary circles since the 1920s. Besides editing several anthologies, he has written poetry, short stories, novels, a play, children's books, and numerous critical essays.

He was born in Alexandria, Louisiana, and was raised in California, where he attended Pacific Union College. He later studied at Columbia University and the University of Chicago. He arrived in New York during the Harlem Renaissance, and his poems published in Opportunity and The Crisis were an important contribution to the movement. In 1943 he became Head Librarian at Fisk University, a post he was to hold for over twenty years. He now teaches English at the University of Illinois at Chicago Circle. His first novel, God Sends Sunday, appeared in 1931 and later provided the basis for a musical play. Another novel, Black Thunder (1935), dealt with a slave rebellion in Virginia and has been favorably compared to William Styron's The Confessions of Nat Turner. His anthologies include The Poetry of the Negro (1949, edited with Langston Hughes) and American Negro Poetry (1963). Among his other books are Drums at Dusk (1939), Frederick Douglass (1958), Story of the Negro (1958), and 100 Years of Negro Freedom (1961).

A Black Man Talks of Reaping

I have sown beside all waters in my day.
I planted deep, within my heart the fear
That wind or fowl would take the grain away.
I planted safe against this stark, lean year.

I scattered seed enough to plant the land
In rows from Canada to Mexico,
But for my reaping only what the hand
Can hold at once is all that I can show.

Yet what I sowed and what the orchard yields
My brother's sons are gathering stalk and root,
Small wonder then my children glean in fields
They have not sown, and feed on bitter fruit.

The Day-Breakers

We are not come to wage a strife
    With swords upon this hill.
It is not wise to waste the life
    Against a stubborn will.
Yet would we die as some have done,
Beating a way for the rising sun.

Southern Mansion

Poplars are standing there still as death
And ghosts of dead men
Meet their ladies walking
Two by two beneath the shade
And standing on the marble steps.

There is a sound of music echoing
Through the open door
And in the field there is
Another sound tinkling in the cotton:
Chains of bondmen dragging on the ground.

The years go back with an iron clank,
A hand is on the gate,
A dry leaf trembles on the wall.
Ghosts are walking.
They have broken roses down
And poplars stand there still as death.

SHERWOOD ANDERSON

(1876–1941)

Sherwood Anderson's "The Man Who Became a Woman," which
appeared in a collection of stories entitled Horses and Men (1923),
was written during the era of the Harlem Renaissance and, like
many white writings of that time, celebrates Negro primitivism.
Works such as Eugene O'Neill's The Emperor Jones and All God's
Chillun Got Wings, Waldo Frank's Holiday, Carl Van Vechten's
Nigger Heaven, DuBose Heyward's Porgy and Mamba's Daughters,
Julia Peterkin's Scarlet Sister Mary, and Anderson's Dark Laughter
idealized the Negro as an exotic, often noble primitive whose
simplicity, spontaneity, and uninhibited sexuality stood in sharp
contrast with the neuroses and repression of a white world bound
by Puritan ethics and the worship of the dollar. The Twenties was
also the time when America discovered psychoanalysis, and a significant element of Freudianism often characterizes these works,
particularly those by Anderson, who was sometimes labeled "the
American Freudian." But Frederick J. Hoffman, in Freudianism
and the Literary Mind (see Bibliography), offers us this caution:
"If you have been unable to follow with me into the lives of these
characters, Anderson seems to be saying; if they still seem queer to
you—if their acts are merely violent and inexplicably so—Dr.
Freud has studied these matters calmly and scientifically, and he
will aid you. But if you do go to him, you will have failed to understand much of what I wish to say to you . . ."

Anderson was raised in Clyde, Ohio, the small town upon which much of his major work, Winesburg, Ohio (1919), is based. The son of a harness-maker, Anderson received little formal education and as a youth held a variety of odd jobs, including several which brought him into contact with Negroes, stable boys, and race-horse trainers. After serving with the army in the Spanish-American War, he became an advertising copy writer in Chicago and then bought a paint factory in Elyria, Ohio. Despite financial success, he grew increasingly unhappy with commercial values, and in 1913 he left his wife and business to move to Chicago, where he again supported himself in advertising while he worked on two novels. In Chicago he became a friend of Floyd Dell, who introduced him to such writers as Ben Hecht, Carl Sandburg, and Theodore Dreiser and found a publisher for his first novel, Windy McPherson's Son (1916). Winesburg, Ohio (1919), which won a wide audience, explored the drabness of American small-town life through sketches of the fictional town's quietly desperate inhabitants. Overwhelmed by conventional propriety and by the depersonalization of the machine age, Anderson's characters were frustrated in their attempts to discover meaning in life and could find escape only in a type of mystical sexual experience. Dark Laughter (1925), a novel, contrasted natural and unrepressed Negroes with neurotic white victims of the machine age. Anderson was more successful with short fiction than with the novel, however, and his best writing appeared in such story collections as Winesburg, Ohio, The Triumph of the Egg (1923), and Horses and Men (1923). In 1927 he retired to Marion, Virginia, where he edited two newspapers and continued to write fiction, though he never attained the critical success of his earlier work. He died in 1941 while on a trip to South America.

From **The Man Who Became a Woman**

. . . And so you see, after Tom left, I hadn't much to do evenings and then the new stallion, the three-year-old, came on with a Negro swipe named Burt.

I liked him fine and he liked me but not the same as Tom and me. We got to be friends all right and I suppose Burt would have done things for me, and maybe me for him, that Tom and me wouldn't have done for each other.

But with a Negro you couldn't be close friends like you can with another white man. There's some reason you can't understand but it's true. There's been too much talk about the difference between whites and blacks and you're both shy, and anyway no use trying and I suppose Burt and I both knew it and so I was pretty lonesome.

. . . . . .

Burt was pretty good to me. He always helped me cool Pick-it-boy out after a race and he did the things himself that take the most skill and quickness, like getting the bandages on a horse's leg smooth, and seeing that every strap is setting just right, and every buckle drawn up to just the right hole, before your horse goes out on the track for a heat.

Burt knew there was something wrong with me and put himself out not to let the boss know. When the boss was around he was always bragging about me. "The brightest kid I've ever worked with around the tracks," he would say and grin, and that at a time when I wasn't worth my salt.

When you go out with the horses there is one job that always takes a lot of time. In the late afternoon, after your horse has been in a race and after you have washed him and rubbed him out, he has to be walked slowly, sometimes for hours and hours, so he'll cool out slowly and won't get musclebound. I got so I did that job for both our horses and Burt did the more important things. It left him free to go talk or shoot dice with the other niggers and I didn't mind. I rather liked it and after a hard race even the stallion, O My Man, was tame enough, even when there were mares about.

You walk and walk and walk, around a little circle, and your horse's head is right by your shoulder, and all around you the life of the place you are in is going on, and in a queer way you get so you aren't really a part of it at all. Perhaps no one ever gets as I was then, except boys that aren't quite men yet and who like me have never been with girls or women—to really be with them, up to the hilt, I mean. I used to wonder if young girls got that way too before they married or did what we used to call "go on the town."

If I remember it right though, I didn't do much thinking then. Often I would have forgotten supper if Burt hadn't shouted at me and reminded me, and sometimes he forgot and went off to town with one of the other niggers and I did forget.

There I was with the horse, going slow slow slow, around a circle that way. The people were leaving the fair grounds now, some afoot, some driving away to the farms in wagons and fords. Clouds of dust floated in the air and over to the west, where the town was, maybe the sun was going down, a red ball of fire through the dust. Only a few hours before the crowd had been all filled with excitement and everyone shouting. Let us suppose my horse had been in a race that afternoon and I had stood in front of the grandstand with my horse blanket over my shoulder, alongside of Burt perhaps, and when they came into the stretch my owner began to call, in that queer high voice of his that seemed to float over the top of all the shouting up in the grandstand. And his voice was saying over and over, "Go, pick it boy, pick it boy, pick it boy," the way he always did, and my heart was thumping so I could hardly breathe, and Burt was leaning over and snapping his fingers and muttering, "Come, little sweet. Come on home. Your Mama wants you. Come get your 'lasses and bread, little Pick-it-boy."

Well, all that was over now and the voices of the people left around were all low. And Pick-it-boy—I was leading him slowly around the little ring, to cool him out slowly, as I've said—he was different too. Maybe he had pretty nearly broken his heart trying to get down to the wire in front, or getting down there in front, and now everything inside him was quiet and tired, as it was nearly all the time these days in me, except in me tired but not quiet.

You remember I've told you we always walked in a circle, round and round. I guess something inside me got to going round and round and round too. The sun did sometimes and the trees and the clouds of dust. I had to think sometimes about putting down my feet so they went down in the right place and I didn't get to staggering like a drunken man.

And a funny feeling came that it is going to be hard to describe. It had something to do with the life in the horse and in me. Sometimes, these late years, I've thought maybe Negroes would understand what I'm trying to talk about now better than any white man ever will. I mean something about men and animals, something between them, something that can perhaps only happen to a white man when he has slipped off his base a little, as I suppose I had then. I think maybe a lot of horsey people feel it sometimes though. It's something like this, maybe—do you suppose it could be that something we whites have got, and think such a lot of, and are so proud about, isn't much of any good after all?

It's something in us that wants to be big and grand and important maybe and won't let us just be, like a horse or a dog or a bird can. Let's say Pick-it-boy had won his race that day. He did that pretty often that summer. Well, he was neither proud, like I would have been in his place, or mean in one part of the inside of him either. He was just himself, doing with a kind of simplicity. That's what Pick-it-boy was like and I got to feeling it in him as I walked with him slowly in the gathering darkness. I got inside him in some way I can't explain and he got inside me. Often we would stop walking for no cause and he would put his nose up against my face.

. . . . . .

Then I was sound asleep and dreaming and—bang like being hit with a club by someone who has sneaked up behind you—I got another wallop.

What I suppose is that, being upset the way I was, I had forgotten to bolt the door to Pick-it-boy's stall down below and two Negro men had come in there, thinking they were in their own place, and had climbed up through the hole where I was. They were half lit-up but not what you might call dead drunk, and I suppose they were up against something a couple of white swipes, who had some money in their pockets, wouldn't have been up against.

What I mean is that a couple of white swipes, having liquored themselves up and being down there in the town on a bat, if they wanted a woman or a couple of women would have been able to find them. There is always a few women of that kind can be found around any town I've ever seen or heard of, and of course a bartender would have given them the tip where to go.

But a Negro, up there in that country, where there aren't any, or anyway mighty few Negro women, wouldn't know what to do when he felt that way and would be up against it.

It's so always. Burt and several other Negroes I've known pretty well have talked to me about it, lots of times. You take now a young Negro man—not a race track swipe or a tramp or any other low-down kind of a fellow—but, let us say, one who has been to college, and has behaved himself and tried to be a good man, the best he could, and be clean, as they say. He isn't any better off, is he? If he has made himself some money and wants to go sit in a swell restaurant, or go to hear some good music, or see a good play at the theater, he gets what we used to call on the tracks, "the messy end of the dung fork," doesn't he?

And even in such a low-down place as what people call a "bad house" it's the same way. The white swipes and others can go into a place where they have Negro women fast enough, and they do it too, but you let a Negro swipe try it the other way around and see how he comes out.

You see, I can think this whole thing out fairly now, sitting here in my own house and writing, and with my wife Jessie in the kitchen making a pie or something, and I can show just how the two Negro men who came into that loft, where I was asleep, were justified in what they did, and I can preach about how the Negroes are up against it in this country, like a daisy, but I tell you what, I didn't think things out that way that night.

For, you understand, what they thought, they being half liquored-up, and when one of them had jerked the blankets off me, was that I was a woman. One of them carried a lantern but it was smoky and dirty and didn't give out much light. So they must have figured it out—my body being pretty white and slender then, like a young girl's body I suppose—that some white swipe had brought me up there. The kind of girls around a town that will come with a swipe to a race track on a rainy night aren't very fancy females but you'll find that kind in the towns all right. I've seen many a one in my day.

And so, I figure, these two big buck niggers, being piped that way, just made up their minds they would snatch me away from the white swipe who had brought me out there, and who had left me lying carelessly around.

"Jes' you lie still honey. We ain't gwine hurt you none," one of them said, with a little chuckling laugh that had something in it besides a laugh, too. It was the kind of laugh that gives you the shivers.

The devil of it was I couldn't say anything, not even a word. Why I couldn't yell out and say "What the hell," and just kid them a little and shoo them out of there I don't know, but I couldn't. I tried and tried so that my throat hurt but I didn't say a word. I just lay there staring at them.

It was a mixed-up night. I've never gone through another night like it.

Was I scared? Lord Almighty, I'll tell you what, I was scared.

Because the two black faces were leaning right over me now, and I could feel their liquored-up breaths on my cheeks, and their eyes were shining in the dim light from that smoky lantern, and right in the center of their eyes was that dancing flickering light I've told you about your seeing in the eyes of wild animals, when you were carrying a lantern through the woods at night.

It was a puzzler! All my life, you see—me never having had any sisters, and at that time never having had a sweetheart either—I had been dreaming and thinking about women, and I suppose I'd always been dreaming about a pure innocent one, for myself, made for me by God, maybe. Men are that way. No matter how big they talk about "let the women go hang," they've always got that notion tucked away inside themselves, somewhere. It's a kind of chesty man's notion, I suppose, but they've got it and the kind of up-and-coming women we have nowadays who are always saying, "I'm as good as a man and will do what the men do," are on the wrong trail if they really ever want to, what you might say "hog-tie" a fellow of their own.

So I had invented a kind of princess, with black hair and a slender willowy body to dream about. And I thought of her as being shy and afraid to ever tell any thing she really felt to anyone but just me. I suppose I fancied that if I ever found such a woman in the flesh I would be the strong sure one and she the timid shrinking one.

And now I was that woman, or something like her, myself.

I gave a kind of wriggle, like a fish you have just taken off the hook. What I did next wasn't a thought-out thing. I was caught and I squirmed, that's all.

The two niggers both jumped at me but somehow—the lantern having been kicked over and having gone out the first move they made—well in some way, when they both lunged at me they missed.

As good luck would have it my feet found the hole, where you put hay down to the horse in the stall below, and through which we crawled up when it was time to go to bed in our blankets up in the hay, and down I slid, not bothering to try to find the ladder with my feet but just letting myself go.

In less than a second I was out of doors in the dark and the rain and the two blacks were down the hole and out the door of the stall after me.

How long or how far they really followed me I suppose I'll never know. It was black dark and raining hard now and a roaring wind had begun to blow. Of course, my body being white, it must have made some kind of a faint streak in the darkness as I ran, and anyway I thought they could see me and I knew I couldn't see them and that made my terror ten times worse. Every minute I thought they would grab me.

You know how it is when a person is all upset and full of terror as I was. I suppose maybe the two niggers followed me for a while, running across the muddy race track and into the grove of trees that grew in the oval inside the track, but likely enough, after just a few minutes, they gave up the chase and went back, found their own place and went to sleep. They were liquored-up, as I've said, and maybe partly funning too.

But I didn't know that, if they were. As I ran I kept hearing sounds, sounds made by the rain coming down through the dead old leaves left on the trees and by the wind blowing, and it may be that the sound that scared me most of all was my own bare feet stepping on a dead branch and breaking it or something like that.

There was something strange and scary, a steady sound, like a heavy man running and breathing hard, right at my shoulder. It may have been my own breath, coming quick and fast. And I thought I heard that chuckling laugh I'd heard up in the loft, the laugh that sent the shivers right down through me. Of course every tree I came close to looked like a man standing there, ready to grab me, and I kept dodging and going—bang—into other trees. My shoulders kept knocking against trees in that way and the skin was all knocked off, and every time it happened I thought a big black hand had come down and clutched at me and was tearing my flesh.

How long it went on I don't know, maybe an hour, maybe five minutes. But anyway the darkness didn't let up, and the terror didn't let up, and I couldn't, to save my life, scream or make any sound.

Just why I couldn't I don't know. Could it be because at the time I was a woman, while at the same time I wasn't a woman? It may be that I was too ashamed of having turned into a girl and being afraid of a man to make any sound. I don't know about that. It's over my head.

But anyway I couldn't make a sound. I tried and tried and my throat hurt from trying and no sound came.

And then, after a long time, or what seemed like a long time, I got out from among the trees inside the track and was on the track itself again. I thought the two black men were still after me, you understand, and I ran like a madman.

Of course, running along the track that way, it must have been up the back stretch, I came after a time to where the old slaughterhouse stood, in that field, beside the track. I knew it by its ungodly smell, scared as I was. Then, in some way, I managed to get over the high old fair ground fence and was in the field, where the slaughterhouse was.

All the time I was trying to yell or scream, or be sensible and tell those two black men that I was a man and not a woman, but I couldn't make it. And then I heard a sound like a board cracking or breaking in the fence and thought they were still after me.

So I kept on running like a crazy man, in the field, and just then I stumbled and fell over something. I've told you how the old slaughterhouse field was filled with bones, that had been lying there a long time and had all been washed white. There were heads of sheep and cows and all kinds of things.

And when I fell and pitched forward I fell right into the midst of something, still and cold and white.

It was probably the skeleton of a horse lying there. In small towns like that, they take an old worn-out horse, that has died, and haul him off to some field outside of town and skin him for the hide, that they can sell for a dollar or two. It doesn't make any difference what the horse has been, that's the way he usually ends up. Maybe even Pick-it-boy, or O My Man, or a lot of other good fast ones I've seen and known have ended that way by this time.

And so I think it was the bones of a horse lying there and he must have been lying on his back. The birds and wild animals had picked all his flesh away and the rain had washed his bones clean.

Anyway I fell and pitched forward and my side got cut pretty deep and my hands clutched at something. I had fallen right in between the ribs of the horse and they seemed to wrap themselves around me close. And my hands, clutching upwards, had got hold of the cheeks of that dead horse and the bones of his cheeks were cold as ice with the rain washing over them. White bones wrapped around me and white bones in my hands.

There was a new terror now that seemed to go down to the very bottom of me, to the bottom of the inside of me, I mean. It shook me like I have seen a rat in a barn shaken by a dog. It was a terror like a big wave that hits you when you are walking on a seashore, maybe. You see it coming and you try to run and get away but when you start to run inshore there is a stone cliff you can't climb. So the wave comes high as a mountain, and there it is, right in front of you and nothing in all this world can stop it. And now it had knocked you down and rolled and tumbled you over and over and washed you clean, clean, but dead maybe.

And that's the way I felt—I seemed to myself dead with blind terror. It was a feeling like the finger of God running down your back and burning you clean, I mean.

It burned all that silly nonsense about being a girl right out of me.

I screamed at last and the spell that was on me was broken. I'll bet the scream I let out of me could have been heard a mile and a half.

Right away I felt better and crawled out from among the pile of bones, and then I stood on my own feet again and I wasn't a woman, or a young girl any more but a man and my own self, and as far as I know I've been that way ever since. Even the black night seemed warm and alive now, like a mother might be to a kid in the dark.

Only I couldn't go back to the race track because I was blubbering and crying and was ashamed of myself and of what a fool I had made of myself. Someone might see me and I couldn't stand that, not at that moment.

So I went across the field, walking now, not running like a crazy man, and pretty soon I came to a fence and crawled over and got into another field, in which there was a straw stack, I just happened to find in the pitch darkness.

The straw stack had been there a long time and some sheep had nibbled away at it until they had made a pretty deep hole, like a cave, in the side of it. I found the hole and crawled in and there were some sheep in there, about a dozen of them.

When I came in, creeping on my hands and knees, they didn't make much fuss, just stirred around a little and then settled down.

So I settled down amongst them too. They were warm and gentle and kind, like Pick-it-boy, and being in there with them made me feel better than I would have felt being with any human person I knew at that time.

So I settled down and slept after a while, and when I woke up it was daylight and not very cold and the rain was over. The clouds were breaking away from the sky now and maybe there would be a fair the next week but if there was I knew I wouldn't be there to see it.

Because what I expected to happen did happen. I had to go back across the fields and the fair ground to the place where my clothes were, right in the broad daylight, and me stark naked, and of course I knew someone would be up and would raise a shout, and every swipe and every driver would stick his head out and would whoop with laughter.

And there would be a thousand questions asked, and I would be too mad and too ashamed to answer, and would perhaps begin to blubber, and that would make me more ashamed than ever.

It all turned out just as I expected, except that when the noise and the shouts of laughter were going it the loudest, Burt came out of the stall where O My Man was kept, and when he saw me he didn't know what was the matter but he knew something was up that wasn't on the square and for which I wasn't to blame.

So he got so all-fired mad he couldn't speak for a minute, and then he grabbed a pitchfork and began prancing up and down before the other stalls, giving that gang of swipes and drivers such a royal old dressing-down as you never heard. You should have heard him sling language. It was grand to hear.

And while he was doing it I sneaked up into the loft, blubbering because I was so pleased and happy to hear him swear that way, and I got my wet clothes on quick and got down, and gave Pick-it-boy a good-bye kiss on the cheek and lit out.

The last I saw of all that part of my life was Burt, still going it, and yelling out for the man who had put up a trick on me to come out and get what was coming to him. He had the pitchfork in his hand and was swinging it around, and every now and then he would make a kind of lunge at a tree or something, he was so mad through, and there was no one else in sight at all. And Burt didn't even see me cutting out along the fence through a gate and down the hill and out of the race-horse and the tramp life for the rest of my days.

JEAN TOOMER

(1894–1967)

―――――◆◄■►◆――――

"By far the most impressive product of the Negro Renaissance,"
Robert A. Bone said of Jean Toomer's Cane (1923), "it ranks with
Richard Wright's Native Son and Ralph Ellison's Invisible Man
as a measure of the Negro novelist's highest achievement. Jean
Toomer belongs to that first rank of writers who use words almost
as a plastic medium, shaping new meanings from an original and
highly personal style."

Born in Washington, D.C., the grandson of P. B. S. Pinch-
back, who had been acting governor of Louisiana during the
Reconstruction, Toomer studied at the University of Wisconsin
and at New York's City College. He contributed to several of the
"lost generation" journals, including Broom, Dial, and The Little
Review, and became associated with such writers as Hart Crane,
Kenneth Burke, and Waldo Frank. Cane was published in 1923,
but despite praise from Sherwood Anderson, Allen Tate, and a few
other perceptive writers, the book was largely ignored. Influenced
by the mystical philosophy of Ouspensky's Tertium Organum,
Toomer then went to France to study briefly under the Russian
mystic Georges Ivanovich Gurdjieff and later attempted to preach
Gurdjieff's views in New York. Increasingly discouraged by publishers' rejections, Toomer gradually drifted into obscurity, and by
the early 1930s he had ceased to be a practicing writer. A light-

skinned man, Toomer married twice, both times to white women, and he seems to have struggled with the problem of whether to call himself a white or a Negro. He apparently spent part of his life passing as a white man, and it is said that he once denied permission for James Weldon Johnson to include his work in an anthology of Negro authors. In his last years he settled in Bucks County, Pennsylvania, where he engaged in various Quaker activities and wrote for the Friends Intelligencer.

Cane is a miscellany of poems, short stories, character sketches, and dramatic passages. Impressionistic and mystical, the book presents a series of sketches of Negroes living in rural Georgia and Washington, D.C. The device of interweaving a collection of "grotesques" with a sense of locality clearly reflects the influence of Sherwood Anderson's Winesburg, Ohio, which had been published four years earlier. Impressions for the book were gathered when Toomer went to Georgia to teach in a country school and learn something of his racial heritage. Several of the book's sketches, such as that of Fern with her Jewish father and Negro mother, involve the theme of mixed blood, and the book tends to idealize primitivism and passion. Toomer's ambivalent emotions about his own identity are reflected in his feeling about the South. As Edward Margolies noted in Native Sons, "No Negro writer has written of the South with so much sense of pain and beauty inextricably linked."

Fern

Face flowed into her eyes. Flowed in soft cream foam and plaintive ripples, in such a way that wherever your glance may momentarily have rested, it immediately thereafter wavered in the direction of her eyes. The soft suggestion of down slightly darkened, like the shadow of a bird's wing might, the creamy brown color of her upper lip. Why, after noticing it, you sought her eyes, I cannot tell you. Her nose was aquiline, Semitic. If you have heard a Jewish cantor sing, if he has touched you and made your own sorrow seem trivial when compared with his, you will know my feeling when I follow the curves of her profile, like mobile rivers, to their common delta. They were strange eyes. In this, that they sought nothing—that is, nothing that was obvious and tangible and that one could see, and they gave the impression that nothing was to be denied. When a woman seeks, you will have observed, her eyes deny. Fern's eyes desired nothing that you could give her; there was no reason why they should withhold. Men saw her eyes and fooled themselves. Fern's eyes said to them that she was easy. When she was young, a few men took her, but got no joy from it. And then, once done, they felt bound to her (quite unlike their hit and run with other girls), felt as though it would take them a lifetime to fulfill an obligation which they could find no name for. They became attached to her, and hungered after finding the barest trace of what she might desire. As she grew up, new men who came to town felt as almost everyone did who ever saw her: that they would not be denied. Men were everlastingly bringing her their bodies. Something inside of her got tired of them, I guess, for I am certain that for the life of her she could not tell why or how she began to turn them off. A man in fever is no trifling thing to send away. They began to leave her, baffled and ashamed, yet vowing to themselves that some day they would do some fine thing for her: send her candy every week and not let her know whom it came from, watch out for her wedding-day and give her a magnificent something with no name on it, buy a house and deed it to her, rescue her from some unworthy fellow who had tricked her into marrying him. As you know, men are apt to idolize or fear that which they cannot understand, especially if it be a woman. She did not deny them, yet the fact was that they were denied. A sort of superstition crept into their consciousness of her being somehow above them. Being above them meant that she was not to be approached by anyone. She became a virgin. Now a virgin in a small Southern town is by no means the usual thing, if you will believe me. That the sexes were made to mate is the practice of the South. Particularly, black folks were made to mate. And it is black folks whom I have been talking about thus far. What white men thought of Fern I can arrive at only by analogy. They let her alone.

Anyone, of course, could see her, could see her eyes. If you walked up the Dixie Pike most any time of day, you'd be most like to see her resting listless-like on the railing of her porch, back propped against a post, head tilted a little forward because there was a nail in the porch post just where her head came which for some reason or other she never took the trouble to pull out. Her eyes, if it were sunset, rested idly where the sun, molten and glorious, was pouring down between the fringe of pines. Or maybe they gazed at the gray cabin on the knoll from which an evening folk-song was coming. Perhaps they followed a cow that had been turned loose to roam and feed on cotton-stalks and corn leaves. Like as not they'd settle on some vague spot above the horizon, though hardly a trace of wistfulness would come to them. If it were dusk, then they'd wait for the search-light of the evening train which you could see miles up the track before it flared across the Dixie Pike, close to her home. Wherever they looked, you'd follow them and then waver back. Like her face, the whole country-side seemed to flow into her eyes. Flowed into them with the soft listless cadence of Georgia's South. A young Negro, once, was looking at her, spellbound, from the road. A white man passing in a buggy had to flick him with his whip if he was to get by without running him over. I first saw her on her porch. I was passing with a fellow whose crusty numbness (I was from the North and suspected of being prejudiced and stuck-up) was melting as he found me warm. I asked him who she was. "That's Fern," was all that I could get from him. Some folks already thought that I was given to nosing around; I let it go at that, so far as questions were concerned. But at first sight of her I felt as if I heard a Jewish cantor sing. As if his singing rose above the unheard chorus of a folk-song. And I felt bound to her. I too had my dreams: something I would do for her. I have knocked about from town to town too much not to know the futility of mere change of place. Besides, picture if you can, this cream-colored solitary girl sitting at a tenement window looking down on the indifferent throngs of Harlem. Better that she listen to folk-songs at dusk in Georgia, you would say, and so would I. Or, suppose she came up North and married. Even a doctor or a lawyer, say, one who would be sure to get along—that is, make money. You and I know, who have had experience in such things, that love is not a thing like prejudice which can be bettered by changes of town. Could men in Washington, Chicago, or New York, more than the men of Georgia, bring her something left vacant by the bestowal of their bodies? You and I who know men in these cities will have to say, they could not. See her out and out a prostitute along State Street in Chicago. See her move into a Southern town where white men are more aggressive. See her become a white man's concubine. . . . Something I must do for her. There was myself. What could I do for her? Talk, of course. Push back the fringe of pines upon new horizons. To what purpose? and what for? Her? Myself? Men in her case seem to lose their selfishness. I lost mine before I touched her. I ask you, friend (it makes no difference if you sit in the Pullman or the Jim Crow as the train crosses her road), what thoughts would come to you—that is, after you'd finished with the thoughts that leap into men's minds at the sight of a pretty woman who will not deny them; what thoughts would come to you, had you seen her in a quick flash, keen and intuitively, as she sat there on her porch when your train thundered by? Would you have got off at the next station and come back for her to take her where? Would you have completely forgotten her as soon as you reached Macon, Atlanta, Augusta, Pasadena, Madison, Chicago, Boston, or New Orleans? Would you tell your wife or sweetheart about a girl you saw? Your thoughts can help me, and I would like to know. Something I would do for her. . . .

One evening I walked up the Pike on purpose, and stopped to say hello. Some of her family were about, but they moved away to make room for me. Damn if I knew how to begin. Would you? Mr. and Miss So-and-So, people, the weather, the crops, the new preacher, the frolic, the church benefit, rabbit and possum hunting, the new soft drink they had at old Pap's store, the schedule of the trains, what kind of town Macon was, Negro's migration north, boll-weevils, syrup, the Bible—to all these things she gave a yassur or nassur, without further comment. I began to wonder if perhaps my own emotional sensibility had played one of its tricks on me. "Let's take a walk," I at last ventured. The suggestion, coming after so long an isolation, was novel enough, I guess, to surprise. But it wasn't that. Something told me that men before me had said just that as a prelude to the offering of their bodies. I tried to tell her with my eyes. I think she understood. The thing from her that made my throat catch, vanished. Its passing left her visible in a way I'd thought, but never seen. We walked down the Pike with people on all the porches gaping at us. "Doesn't it make you mad?" She meant the row of petty gossiping people. She meant the world. Through a canebrake that was ripe for cutting, the branch was reached. Under a sweet-gum tree, and where reddish leaves had dammed the creek a little, we sat down. Dusk, suggesting the almost imperceptible procession of giant trees, settled with a purple haze about the cane. I felt strange, as I always do in Georgia, particularly at dusk. I felt that things unseen to men were tangibly immediate. It would not have surprised me had I had vision. People have them in Georgia more often than you would suppose. A black woman once saw the mother of Christ and drew her in charcoal on the courthouse wall. . . . When one is on the soil of one's ancestors, most anything can come to one. . . . From force of habit, I suppose, I held Fern in my arms —that is, without at first noticing it. Then my mind came back to her. Her eyes, unusually weird and open, held me. Held God. He flowed in as I've seen the countryside flow in. Seen men. I must have done something—what, I don't know, in the confusion of my emotion. She sprang up. Rushed some distance from me. Fell to her knees, and began swaying, swaying. Her body was tortured with something it could not let out. Like boiling sap it flooded arms and fingers till she shook them as if they burned her. It found her throat, and spattered inarticulately in plaintive, convulsive sounds, mingled with calls to Christ Jesus. And then she sang, brokenly. A Jewish cantor singing with a broken voice. A child's voice, uncertain, or an old man's. Dusk hid her; I could hear only her song. It seemed to me as though she were pounding her head in anguish upon the ground. I rushed to her. She fainted in my arms.

There was talk about her fainting with me in the canefield. And I got one or two ugly looks from town men who'd set themselves up to protect her. In fact, there was talk of making me leave town. But they never did. They kept a watch-out for me, though. Shortly after, I came back north. From the train window I saw her as I crossed her road. Saw her on her porch, head tilted a little forward where the nail was, eyes vaguely focused on the sunset. Saw her face flow into them, the countryside and something that I call God, flowing into them. . . . Nothing ever really happened. Nothing ever came to Fern, not even I. Something I would do for her. Some fine unnamed thing. . . . And, friend, you? She is still living, I have reason to know. Her name, against the chance that you might happen down that way, is Fernie May Rosen.

WILLIAM CARLOS WILLIAMS

(1883–1963)

William Carlos Williams, the son of an English father and a
Puerto Rican mother, was born and raised in Rutherford, New
Jersey, close to Paterson, the town he memorialized in one of his
best-known works. He studied medicine at the University of Pennsylvania, interned in New York City, and went on to study pedi-
atrics at the University of Leipzig. While at Pennsylvania he
became a friend of Ezra Pound, then a graduate student in romance languages, and it was under Pound's influence that he
studied the theories of the Imagist poets and developed his own
notion of "objectivism" in poetry. Poems, his first collection of
verse, was published in 1909. The following year he returned to
Rutherford, where he practiced medicine for most of his remaining
years. Throughout the 1920s he contributed to many "little magazines" and for a time edited the journal Contact. Paterson, which
appeared in five parts from 1946 to 1958, is a long epic poem
tracing the history and mythic meaning of the New Jersey city
from Indian times to the present. Although involved throughout
his life in a highly demanding medical career, Williams produced
over twenty-five books, including novels, an autobiography, and
collections of his poetry, short stories, and essays.

"Advent of the Slaves" is taken from In the American Grain
(1925), a collection of poetic and impressionistic essays on American history, which Horace Gregory described as "a source book of

*highly individual and radical discoveries." The book had a strong
influence on Hart Crane, whose The Bridge echoed several of
Williams's observations. Like Anderson's "The Man Who Became
a Woman" and Toomer's Cane, "Advent of the Slaves" reflects
the equation of blackness and primitivism made by both black and
white writers in the Twenties.*

Advent of the Slaves

The colored men and women whom I know intimately add a
quality, that is delightful, to the life about me.

There is little use, after all—save in a title—of speaking of the
advent of the slaves; these were just men of a certain mettle who
came to America in ships, like the rest. The minor differences of
condition were of no importance—the mere condition of their
coming is of no importance—

The colored men and women whom I have known intimately
have a racial character which has impressed me. I have not much
bothered to know why, exactly, this has been so—

The one thing that never seems to occur to anybody is that the
negroes have a quality which they have brought to America. It
is not important that it is available or not to us for any special
use—

Poised against the *Mayflower* is the slave ship—manned by
Yankees and Englishmen—bringing another race to try upon the
New World, that will prove its tenacity and ability to thrive by
seizing upon the Christian religion—a thing to replace their own
elephant-, snake- and gorilla-filled jungles—on which to fasten for
stability, blowing into it the soul of their own darkness, where, as
were the Aztecs in their bloody chapels, they are founded—

They helped to build "a society that was rich and in some
ways sumptuous and curiously oriental." "Puritan Massachusetts,
unable to rid itself of the idea of man's essential wickedness, could
not envision this earthly paradise, Georgia—" "In many families

every child had his individual slave: great gentlemen almost openly kept their concubines: great ladies half dozed through the long summer afternoons on their shaded piazzas mollified by the slow fanning of their black attendants, and by the laving of their feet in water periodically fetched anew from the spring house"—it is a sunken quality, or it is a living quality—it is no matter which.

All the rest is to keep from having to say anything more—like a nigger: it is their beauty. When they try to make their race an issue—it is nothing. In a chorus singing *Trovatore*, they are nothing. But saying *nothing*, dancing *nothing*, "NOBODY," it is a quality—

Bert Williams, author of a Russian ballet, *The Kiss*; that's worse than nothin'. But "Somewhere the sun am shinin'—for ME . . ." That's SOMETHIN'. Taking his shoes off; that's SOMETHIN'. . . . dancing, singing with the wild abandon of being close, closer, closest together; waggin', wavin', weavin', shakin'; or alone, in a cabin, at night, in the stillness, in the moonlight—bein' nothin'—with gravity, with tenderness—they arrive and "walk all over God's heaven—"

There is a solidity, a racial irreducible minimum, which gives them poise in a world where they have no authority—

Or a ramshackle "castle," peaked with doll's house gables, all awry, by the railroad; where the boys came with their "brides" in those good days JUST before the war; old shoes and a shambling independence: a tigerish life, lived in defiance over a worthless son, by virtue of fierce courage, a heavy fearless voice and a desperate determination to be let alone—with two reminiscent, shrewd, remembering eyes stamping authenticity upon her words —and long gorilla arms to deal a heavy blow upon man or woman who may threaten her, with a shouted threat of knife-thrust or hatchet stroke if that fails. She was knocked down, bellowing like a buffalo, maltreated—by whom? You wouldn't get it out of her. But she announced to whoever has ears, in this place or the next, that it wouldn't happen another time—and it hasn't. On a Saturday night shuffling along absorbed, with slow, swinging gait, or staring into odd corners, or settling back on her heels with a belligerent scowl if greeted—ready to talk: "Why how are ya?"—anywhere. "Go ahead, kill me, I ain't afraid of ya."

I remember with thrilling pleasure and deep satisfaction E. K. Means' tale, *Diada Daughter of Discord*, an outstanding story of a wild nigger wench, billeted upon a friend's family by her owner while he went for a short boat trip without her. Read *Diada*— cutting cane stalks, sharpening them with lightning speed and driving them through the attacking hounds.

> "faces like
> old Florentine oak.
>
> Also
>
> the set pieces
> of your faces stir me—
> leading citizens—
> but not
> in the same way."

Nothin' makes much difference—to Otie: Butcher knife, butcher knife, Mr. Gould wants you.

It's a quality, the same as "Sweet everlasting voices be still."

Of the colored men and women whom I have known intimately, the most loquacious is M.—who can't eat eggs because it gives him the hives. Language grows in the original from his laughing lips, "You know that bloom of youth stuff," his shy crooked smile, weary, slow, topping his svelte figure, his straight, slim six feet of willowy grace, drooping from the shoulders, smiling sleepy eyes. "White blood and colored blood don't mix," said he nursing his injury, "Doc, I got a hemorrhage of the FLUTE," he said. "Cocaine for horses, cocaine for mules, IN THE *TRENCHES!*" he yelled as I removed the bandage. "I'm going to feed this to the ducks," he said. The relief is never ending, never failing. It is water from a spring to talk with him—it is a quality. I wish I might write a book of his improvisations in slang. I wish I might write a play in collaboration with him.

His old man is a different sort: I once made several pages of notes upon his conversation—but I lost them; he was an able fisherman along the North Atlantic shore, resistant as an eel. In the hold of the vessel when they were packing porgies, ice and fish filling the hold of the schooner in heavy layers, it was he who could stay down there at work longest—

For sheer sordidness we never touch them, the desperate drunkenness, upon foul stuff, in which they nearly die in a heap of rags under the eaves in the attic of some revolting, disease-ridden female's dump—fly-covered, dazed—

For purity of religious devotion, in the simplicity of their manoeuvres, they exceed our greatest application. Personal cleanliness becomes them with an oriental grace before which our ablutions pale to insignificance.

They wear the BEST fabrics that money can buy, man and woman alike.

It is nothing, nothing.

There was Georgie Anderson whom I remember as some female who walked upon air and light—in her wild girlhood.

And there was "Dudu," gentle as the dew or rain in April— but I knew she had a temper for those who offended her—

And there are many others.

Put them on a ship, under any circumstances you may fancy and you have them coming, coming. Why for?

Nothin'—

As old man Hemby said to me at the door: "I'm here. I come after you yesterday but I couldn't find you. Doctor, I'm in a bad fix; I want you to do something for me."

WILLIAM FAULKNER

(1897–1962)

Faulkner was born in New Albany, Mississippi, and grew up in Oxford, home of the University of Mississippi. In 1918 he enlisted in the British Royal Air Force, and following the war he returned to Oxford and attended the University for two years. After a series of odd jobs he went to New Orleans in 1924 to seek newspaper work, and there he met Sherwood Anderson, under whose influence he wrote criticism and poetry for The Double-Dealer, an avant-garde magazine. In the same year he published a book of poetry, The Marble Faun, and began work on his first novel, Soldier's Pay, which was published two years later. By 1925 he had settled again in Oxford, where he lived for most of his remaining years, and in 1929 he published Sartoris and The Sound and the Fury, the two novels which initiated his "Yoknapatawpha cycle." Centered in Yoknapatawpha County, his fictional name for Lafayette County in northern Mississippi, these books dealt with the decay of aristo-cratic old families such as the Compsons and the Sartorises, the endurance of Negroes, and the rise of Flem Snopes and the ma-terialistic "new South."

Among the novels Faulkner wrote after 1929 are As I Lay Dying (1930), Light in August (1932), Absalom, Absalom! (1936), The Wild Palms (1939), The Hamlet (1940), Intruder in the Dust (1948), Requiem for a Nun (1951), A Fable (1954), and The Reivers (1962). His short-story collections include These Thirteen

(1931), The Unvanquished (1938), Go Down Moses (1942), Knight's Gambit (1949), Collected Stories (1950), and Big Woods (1955). Although most of Faulkner's books were out of print by the mid-1940s, a Faulkner revival began in 1946 with the publication of The Viking Portable Faulkner edited by Malcolm Cowley. The object of little favorable criticism before 1945, Faulkner rapidly became recognized as a major writer, and in 1950 he received the Nobel Prize. Among honors which followed were a National Book Award for Collected Stories, another National Book Award and a Pulitzer Prize for A Fable, and a posthumous Pulitzer Prize for The Reivers. In 1955 he was a visiting writer in Japan, and in 1957 and 1958 he was writer-in-residence at the University of Virginia.

Faulkner's view of the Negro—compounded of fear and hope, condescension and admiration—is as complex as it is central to his works. Although in The Wild Palms he described the "indelible mark of ten thousand Southern deputy sheriffs, urban and suburban—the snapped hat-brim, the sadist's eyes, the slightly and unmistakably bulged coat, the air not swaggering exactly but of a formally pre-absolved brutality," he later stated in an interview that, if a struggle ever developed between the federal government and Mississippi, he would fight on Mississippi's side, "even if it meant going out into the streets and shooting Negroes." Yet Faulkner had a profound ability to deal with his Negro characters as human beings. As Ralph Ellison noted in "Twentieth-Century Fiction and the Black Mask of Humanity," "[Faulkner] has been more willing perhaps than any other artist to start with the stereotype, accept it as true, and then seek out the human truth which it hides." And Irving Howe adds, "We witness in Faulkner's novels a quick and steep ascent: from benevolence to recognition of injustice, from amusement over idiosyncrasies to a principled concern with status, from cozy familiarity to a discovery of the estrangement of the races."

Faulkner's conception of the Negro plays a part in many of his works, but it is a central concern in The Sound and the Fury, Light in August, Go Down Moses, and Intruder in the Dust. Faulkner stories that deal importantly with Negroes are "Centaur in Brass," "Dry September," "Red Leaves," "That Evening Sun," and Part

Four of "The Bear." His chief Negro characters are Dilsey, the Negro cook in The Sound and the Fury who provides a center of reality and warmth in the crumbling Compson family and has been seen as a symbol of Christian resignation and endurance; Joe Christmas, the hero of Light in August who believes himself to be a Negro and who tries to find an identity and escape it at the same time; and Lucas Beauchamp, the Negro patriarch in "The Fire and the Hearth" and Intruder in the Dust, who refuses to "act like a nigger." One of the most compelling figures in all of Faulkner's fiction, Beauchamp was described by Charles H. Nilon, in Faulkner and the Negro (see Bibliography), thus: "He has pride and humility, honor and dignity. The favorite Faulkner adjectives may be applied to him: impervious, impenetrable, imponderable." Yet it is characteristic of Faulkner's complicated view that Intruder in the Dust, the very book that ennobles Beauchamp, is also a propaganda novel which argues against intervention in the South by federal "outsiders" bent on securing civil rights for Negroes.

"Red Leaves" was first published in The Saturday Evening Post in 1930 and was reprinted in These Thirteen and Collected Stories.

Red Leaves

I

The two Indians crossed the plantation toward the slave quarters. Neat with whitewash, of baked soft brick, the two rows of houses in which lived the slaves belonging to the clan, faced one another across the mild shade of the lane marked and scored with naked feet and with a few homemade toys mute in the dust. There was no sign of life.

"I know what we will find," the first Indian said.

"What we will not find," the second said. Although it was noon, the lane was vacant, the doors of the cabins empty and quiet; no cooking smoke rose from any of the chinked and plastered chimneys.

"Yes. It happened like this when the father of him who is now the Man, died."

"You mean, of him who was the Man."

"Yao."

The first Indian's name was Three Basket. He was perhaps sixty. They were both squat men, a little solid, burgher-like; paunchy, with big heads, big, broad, dust-colored faces of a certain blurred serenity like carved heads on a ruined wall in Siam or Sumatra, looming out of a mist. The sun had done it, the violent sun, the violent shade. Their hair looked like sedge grass on burnt-over land. Clamped through one ear Three Basket wore an enameled snuffbox.

"I have said all the time that this is not the good way. In the old days there were no quarters, no Negroes. A man's time was his own then. He had time. Now he must spend most of it finding work for them who prefer sweating to do."

"They are like horses and dogs."

"They are like nothing in this sensible world. Nothing contents them save sweat. They are worse than the white people."

"It is not as though the Man himself had to find work for them to do."

"You said it. I do not like slavery. It is not the good way. In the old days, there was the good way. But not now."

"You do not remember the old way either."

"I have listened to them who do. And I have tried this way. Man was not made to sweat."

"That's so. See what it has done to their flesh."

"Yes. Black. It has a bitter taste, too."

"You have eaten of it?"

"Once. I was young then, and more hardy in the appetite than now. Now it is different with me."

"Yes. They are too valuable to eat now."

"There is a bitter taste to the flesh which I do not like."

"They are too valuable to eat, anyway, when the white men will give horses for them."

They entered the lane. The mute, meager toys—the fetish-shaped objects made of wood and rags and feathers—lay in the dust about the patinaed doorsteps, among bones and broken gourd dishes. But there was no sound from any cabin, no face in any door; had not been since yesterday, when Issetibbeha died. But they already knew what they would find.

It was in the central cabin, a house a little larger than the others, where at certain phases of the moon the Negroes would gather to begin their ceremonies before removing after nightfall to the creek bottom, where they kept the drums. In this room they kept the minor accessories, the cryptic ornaments, the ceremonial records which consisted of sticks daubed with red clay in symbols. It had a hearth in the center of the floor, beneath a hole in the roof, with a few cold wood ashes and a suspended iron pot. The window shutters were closed; when the two Indians entered, after the abashless sunlight they could distinguish nothing with the eyes save a movement, shadow, out of which eyeballs rolled, so that the place appeared to be full of Negroes. The two Indians stood in the doorway.

"Yao," Basket said. "I said this is not the good way."

"I don't think I want to be here," the second said.

"That is black man's fear which you smell. It does not smell as ours does."

"I don't think I want to be here."

"Your fear has an odor too."

"Maybe it is Issetibbeha which we smell."

"Yao. He knows. He knows what we will find here. He knew when he died what we should find here today." Out of the rank twilight of the room the eyes, the smell, of Negroes rolled about them. "I am Three Basket, whom you know," Basket said into the room. "We are come from the Man. He whom we seek is gone?" The Negroes said nothing. The smell of them, of their bodies, seemed to ebb and flux in the still hot air. They seemed to be musing as one upon something remote, inscrutable. They were like a single octopus. They were like the roots of a huge tree uncovered, the earth broken momentarily upon the writhen, thick, fetid tangle of its lightless and outraged life. "Come," Basket said. "You know our errand. Is he whom we seek gone?"

"They are thinking something," the second said. "I do not want to be here."

"They are knowing something," Basket said.

"They are hiding him, you think?"

"No. He is gone. He has been gone since last night. It happened like this before, when the grandfather of him who is now the Man died. It took us three days to catch him. For three days Doom lay above the ground, saying 'I see my horse and my dog. But I do not see my slave. What have you done with him that you will not permit me to lie quiet?' "

"They do not like to die."

"Yao. They cling. It makes trouble for us, always. A people without honor and without decorum. Always a trouble."

"I do not like it here."

"Nor do I. But then, they are savages; they cannot be expected to regard usage. That is why I say that this way is a bad way."

"Yao. They cling. They would even rather work in the sun than to enter the earth with a chief. But he is gone."

The Negroes had said nothing, made no sound. The white eyeballs rolled, wild, subdued; the smell was rank, violent. "Yes, they fear," the second said. "What shall we do now?"

"Let us go and talk with the Man."

"Will Moketubbe listen?"

"What can he do? He will not like to. But he is the Man now."

"Yao. He is the Man. He can wear the shoes with the red heels all the time now." They turned and went out. There was no door in the door frame. There were no doors in any of the cabins.

"He did that anyway," Basket said.

"Behind Issetibbeha's back. But now they are his shoes, since he is the Man."

"Yao. Issetibbeha did not like it. I have heard. I know that he said to Moketubbe: 'When you are the Man, the shoes will be yours. But until then, they are my shoes.' But now Moketubbe is the Man; he can wear them."

"Yao," the second said. "He is the Man now. He used to wear the shoes behind Issetibbeha's back, and it was not known if Issetibbeha knew this or not. And then Issetibbeha became dead, who was not old, and the shoes are Moketubbe's, since he is the Man now. What do you think of that?"

"I don't think about it," Basket said. "Do you?"

"No," the second said.

"Good," Basket said. "You are wise."

II

The house sat on a knoll, surrounded by oak trees. The front of it was one story in height, composed of the deck house of a steamboat which had gone ashore and which Doom, Issetibbeha's father, had dismantled with his slaves and hauled on cypress rollers twelve miles home overland. It took them five months. His house consisted at the time of one brick wall. He set the steamboat broadside on to the wall, where now the chipped and flaked gilding of the rococo cornices arched in faint splendor above the gilt lettering of the stateroom names above the jalousied doors.

Doom had been born merely a subchief, a Mingo, one of three children on the mother's side of the family. He made a journey— he was a young man then and New Orleans was a European city —from north Mississippi to New Orleans by keel boat, where he met the Chevalier Sœur Blonde de Vitry, a man whose social position, on its face, was as equivocal as Doom's own. In New Orleans, among the gamblers and cutthroats of the river front, Doom, under the tutelage of his patron, passed as the chief, the Man, the hereditary owner of that land which belonged to the male side of the family; it was the Chevalier de Vitry who called him *du homme*, and hence Doom.

They were seen everywhere together—the Indian, the squat man with a bold, inscrutable, underbred face, and the Parisian, the expatriate, the friend, it was said, of Carondelet and the intimate of General Wilkinson. Then they disappeared, the two of them, vanishing from their old equivocal haunts and leaving behind them the legend of the sums which Doom was believed to have won, and some tale about a young woman, daughter of a fairly well-to-do West Indian family, the son and brother of whom sought Doom with a pistol about his old haunts for some time after his disappearance.

Six months later the young woman herself disappeared, boarding the St. Louis packet, which put in one night at a wood landing on the north Mississippi side, where the woman, accompanied by a Negro maid, got off. Four Indians met her with a horse and wagon, and they traveled for three days, slowly, since she was already big with child, to the plantation, where she found that Doom was now chief. He never told her how he accomplished it, save that his uncle and his cousin had died suddenly. At that time the house consisted of a brick wall built by shiftless slaves, against which was propped a thatched lean-to divided into rooms and littered with bones and refuse, set in the center of ten thousand acres of matchless parklike forest where deer grazed like domestic cattle. Doom and the woman were married there a short time before Issetibbeha was born, by a combination itinerant minister and slave trader who arrived on a mule, to the saddle of which was lashed a cotton umbrella and a three-gallon demijohn of whiskey. After that, Doom began to acquire more slaves and to cultivate some of his land, as the white people did. But he never had enough for them to do. In utter idleness the majority of them led lives transplanted whole out of African jungles, save on the occasions when, entertaining guests, Doom coursed them with dogs.

When Doom died, Issetibbeha, his son, was nineteen. He became proprietor of the land and of the quintupled herd of blacks for which he had no use at all. Though the title of Man rested with him, there was a hierarchy of cousins and uncles who ruled the clan and who finally gathered in squatting conclave over the Negro question, squatting profoundly beneath the golden names above the doors of the steamboat.

"We cannot eat them," one said.

"Why not?"

"There are too many of them."

"That's true," a third said. "Once we started, we should have to eat them all. And that much flesh diet is not good for man."

"Perhaps they will be like deer flesh. That cannot hurt you."

"We might kill a few of them and not eat them," Issetibbeha said.

They looked at him for a while. "What for?" one said.

"That is true," a second said. "We cannot do that. They are too valuable; remember all the bother they have caused us, finding things for them to do. We must do as the white men do."

"How is that?" Issetibbeha said.

"Raise more Negroes by clearing more land to make corn to feed them, then sell them. We will clear the land and plant it with food and raise Negroes and sell them to the white men for money."

"But what will we do with this money?" a third said.

They thought for a while.

"We will see," the first said. They squatted, profound, grave.

"It means work," the third said.

"Let the Negroes do it," the first said.

"Yao. Let them. To sweat is bad. It is damp. It opens the pores."

"And then the night air enters."

"Yao. Let the Negroes do it. They appear to like sweating."

So they cleared the land with the Negroes and planted it in grain. Up to that time the slaves had lived in a huge pen with a lean-to roof over one corner, like a pen for pigs. But now they began to build quarters, cabins, putting the young Negroes in the cabins in pairs to mate; five years later Issetibbeha sold forty head to a Memphis trader, and he took the money and went abroad upon it, his maternal uncle from New Orleans conducting the trip. At that time the Chevalier Sœur Blonde de Vitry was an old man in Paris, in a toupee and a corset, with a careful toothless old face fixed in a grimace quizzical and profoundly tragic. He borrowed three hundred dollars from Issetibbeha and in return he introduced him into certain circles; a year later Issetibbeha returned home with a gilt bed, a pair of girandoles by whose light it was said that Pompadour arranged her hair while Louis smirked at his mirrored face across her powdered shoulder, and a pair of slippers with red heels. They were too small for him, since he had not worn shoes at all until he reached New Orleans on his way abroad.

He brought the slippers home in tissue paper and kept them in the remaining pocket of a pair of saddlebags filled with cedar shavings, save when he took them out on occasion for his son, Moketubbe, to play with. At three years of age Moketubbe had a broad, flat, Mongolian face that appeared to exist in a complete and unfathomable lethargy, until confronted by the slippers.

Moketubbe's mother was a comely girl whom Issetibbeha had

seen one day working in her shift in a melon patch. He stopped and watched her for a while—the broad, solid thighs, the sound back, the serene face. He was on his way to the creek to fish that day, but he didn't go any farther; perhaps while he stood there watching the unaware girl he may have remembered his own mother, the city woman, the fugitive with her fans and laces and her Negro blood, and all the tawdry shabbiness of that sorry affair. Within the year Moketubbe was born; even at three he could not get his feet into the slippers. Watching him in the still, hot afternoons as he struggled with the slippers with a certain monstrous repudiation of fact, Issetibbeha laughed quietly to himself. He laughed at Moketubbe and the shoes for several years, because Moketubbe did not give up trying to put them on until he was sixteen. Then he quit. Or Issetibbeha thought he had. But he had merely quit trying in Issetibbeha's presence. Issetibbeha's newest wife told him that Moketubbe had stolen and hidden the shoes. Issetibbeha quit laughing then, and he sent the woman away, so that he was alone. "Yao," he said. "I too like being alive, it seems." He sent for Moketubbe. "I give them to you," he said.

Moketubbe was twenty-five then, unmarried. Issetibbeha was not tall, but he was taller by six inches than his son and almost a hundred pounds lighter. Moketubbe was already diseased with flesh, with a pale, broad, inert face and dropsical hands and feet. "They are yours now," Issetibbeha said, watching him. Moketubbe had looked at him once when he entered, a glance brief, discreet, veiled.

"Thanks," he said.

Issetibbeha looked at him. He could never tell if Moketubbe saw anything, looked at anything. "Why will it not be the same if I give the slippers to you?"

"Thanks," Moketubbe said. Issetibbeha was using snuff at the time; a white man had shown him how to put the powder into his lip and scour it against his teeth with a twig of gum or of alphea.

"Well," he said, "a man cannot live forever." He looked at his son, then his gaze went blank in turn, unseeing, and he mused for an instant. You could not tell what he was thinking, save that he said half aloud: "Yao. But Doom's uncle had no shoes with red heels." He looked at his son again, fat, inert. "Beneath all that, a man might think of doing anything and it not be known until too late." He sat in a splint chair hammocked with deer thongs. "He cannot even get them on; he and I are both frustrated by the same gross meat which he wears. He cannot even get them on. But is that my fault?"

He lived for five years longer, then he died. He was sick one night, and though the doctor came in a skunk-skin vest and burned sticks, he died before noon.

That was yesterday; the grave was dug, and for twelve hours now the People had been coming in wagons and carriages and on horseback and afoot, to eat the baked dog and the succotash and the yams cooked in ashes and to attend the funeral.

III

"It will be three days," Basket said, as he and the other Indian returned to the house. "It will be three days and the food will not be enough; I have seen it before."

The second Indian's name was Louis Berry. "He will smell too, in this weather."

"Yao. They are nothing but a trouble and a care."

"Maybe it will not take three days."

"They run far. Yao. We will smell this Man before he enters the earth. You watch and see if I am not right."

They approached the house.

"He can wear the shoes now," Berry said. "He can wear them now in man's sight."

"He cannot wear them for a while yet," Basket said. Berry looked at him. "He will lead the hunt."

"Moketubbe?" Berry said. "Do you think he will? A man to whom even talking is travail?"

"What else can he do? It is his own father who will soon begin to smell."

"That is true," Berry said. "There is even yet a price he must pay for the shoes. Yao. He has truly bought them. What do you think?"

"What do you think?"

"What do you think?"

"I think nothing."

"Nor do I. Issetibbeha will not need the shoes now. Let Moke-tubbe have them; Issetibbeha will not care."

"Yao. Man must die."

"Yao. Let him; there is still the Man."

The bark roof of the porch was supported by peeled cypress poles, high above the texas of the steamboat, shading an unfloored banquette where on the trodden earth mules and horses were tethered in bad weather. On the forward end of the steamboat's deck sat an old man and two women. One of the women was dressing a fowl, the other was shelling corn. The old man was talking. He was barefoot, in a long linen frock coat and a beaver hat.

"This world is going to the dogs," he said. "It is being ruined by white men. We got along fine for years and years, before the white men foisted their Negroes upon us. In the old days the old men sat in the shade and ate stewed deer's flesh and corn and smoked tobacco and talked of honor and grave affairs; now what do we do? Even the old wear themselves into the grave taking care of them that like sweating." When Basket and Berry crossed the deck he ceased and looked up at them. His eyes were querulous, bleared; his face was myriad with tiny wrinkles. "He is fled also," he said.

"Yes," Berry said, "he is gone."

"I knew it. I told them so. It will take three weeks, like when Doom died. You watch and see."

"It was three days, not three weeks," Berry said.

"Were you there?"

"No," Berry said. "But I have heard."

"Well, I was there," the old man said. "For three whole weeks, through the swamps and the briers—" They went on and left him talking.

What had been the saloon of the steamboat was now a shell, rotting slowly; the polished mahogany, the carving glinting momentarily and fading through the mold in figures cabalistic and profound; the gutted windows were like cataracted eyes. It contained a few sacks of seed or grain, and the fore part of the running gear of a barouche, to the axle of which two C-springs rusted in graceful curves, supporting nothing. In one corner a fox cub ran steadily and soundlessly up and down a willow cage; three scrawny gamecocks moved in the dust, and the place was pocked and marked with their dried droppings.

They passed through the brick wall and entered a big room of chinked logs. It contained the hinder part of the barouche, and the dismantled body lying on its side, the window slatted over with willow withes, through which protruded the heads, the still, beady, outraged eyes and frayed combs of still more game chickens. It was floored with packed clay; in one corner leaned a crude plow and two hand-hewn boat paddles. From the ceiling, suspended by four deer thongs, hung the gilt bed which Issetibbeha had fetched from Paris. It had neither mattress nor springs, the frame crisscrossed now by a neat hammocking of thongs.

Issetibbeha had tried to have his newest wife, the young one, sleep in the bed. He was congenitally short of breath himself, and he passed the nights half reclining in his splint chair. He would see her to bed and, later, wakeful, sleeping as he did but three or four hours a night, he would sit in the darkness and simulate slumber and listen to her sneak infinitesimally from the gilt and ribboned bed, to lie on a quilt pallet on the floor until just before daylight. Then she would enter the bed quietly again and in turn simulate slumber, while in the darkness beside her Issetibbeha quietly laughed and laughed.

The girandoles were lashed by thongs to two sticks propped in a corner where a ten-gallon whisky keg lay also. There was a clay hearth; facing it, in the splint chair, Moketubbe sat. He was maybe an inch better than five feet tall, and he weighed two hundred and fifty pounds. He wore a broadcloth coat and no shirt, his round, smooth copper balloon of belly swelling above the bottom piece of a suit of linen underwear. On his feet were the slippers with the red heels. Behind his chair stood a stripling with a punkah-like fan made of fringed paper. Moketubbe sat motionless, with his broad, yellow face with its closed eyes and flat nostrils, his flipper-like arms extended. On his face was an expression profound, tragic, and inert. He did not open his eyes when Basket and Berry came in.

"He has worn them since daylight?" Basket said.

"Since daylight," the stripling said. The fan did not cease. "You can see."

"Yao," Basket said. "We can see." Moketubbe did not move. He looked like an effigy, like a Malay god in frock coat, drawers, naked chest, the trivial scarlet-heeled shoes.

"I wouldn't disturb him, if I were you," the stripling said.

"Not if I were you," Basket said. He and Berry squatted. The stripling moved the fan steadily. "O Man," Basket said, "listen." Moketubbe did not move. "He is gone," Basket said.

"I told you so," the stripling said. "I knew he would flee. I told you."

"Yao," Basket said. "You are not the first to tell us afterward what we should have known before. Why is it that some of you wise men took no steps yesterday to prevent this?"

"He does not wish to die," Berry said.

"Why should he not wish it?" Basket said.

"Because he must die some day is no reason," the stripling said. "That would not convince me either, old man."

"Hold your tongue," Berry said.

"For twenty years," Basket said, "while others of his race sweat in the fields, he served the Man in the shade. Why should he not wish to die, since he did not wish to sweat?"

"And it will be quick," Berry said. "It will not take long."

"Catch him and tell him that," the stripling said.

"Hush," Berry said. They squatted, watching Moketubbe's face. He might have been dead himself. It was as though he were cased so in flesh that even breathing took place too deep within him to show.

"Listen, O Man," Basket said. "Issetibbeha is dead. He waits. His dog and his horse we have. But his slave has fled. The one who held the pot for him, who ate of his food, from his dish, is fled. Issetibbeha waits."

"Yao," Berry said.

"This is not the first time," Basket said. "This happened when Doom, thy grandfather, lay waiting at the door of the earth. He lay waiting three days, saying, 'Where is my Negro?' And Issetibbeha, thy father, answered, 'I will find him. Rest; I will bring him to you so that you may begin the journey.' "

"Yao," Berry said.

Moketubbe had not moved, had not opened his eyes.

"For three days Issetibbeha hunted in the bottom," Basket said. "He did not even return home for food, until the Negro was with him; then he said to Doom, his father, 'Here is thy dog, thy horse, thy Negro; rest.' Issetibbeha, who is dead since yesterday, said it. And now Issetibbeha's Negro is fled. His horse and his dog wait with him, but his Negro is fled."

"Yao," Berry said.

Moketubbe had not moved. His eyes were closed; upon his supine monstrous shape there was a colossal inertia, something profoundly immobile, beyond and impervious to flesh. They watched his face, squatting.

"When thy father was newly the Man, this happened," Basket said. "And it was Issetibbeha who brought back the slave to where his father waited to enter the earth." Moketubbe's face had not moved, his eyes had not moved. After a while Basket said, "Remove the shoes."

The stripling removed the shoes. Moketubbe began to pant, his bare chest moving deep, as though he were rising from beyond his unfathomed flesh back into life, like up from the water, the sea. But his eyes had not opened yet.

Berry said, "He will lead the hunt."

"Yao," Basket said. "He is the Man. He will lead the hunt."

IV

All that day the Negro, Issetibbeha's body servant, hidden in the barn, watched Issetibbeha's dying. He was forty, a Guinea man. He had a flat nose, a close, small head; the inside corners of his eyes showed red a little, and his prominent gums were a pale bluish red above his square, broad teeth. He had been taken at fourteen by a trader off Kamerun, before his teeth had been filed. He had been Issetibbeha's body servant for twenty-three years.

On the day before, the day on which Issetibbeha lay sick, he returned to the quarters at dusk. In that unhurried hour the smoke of the cooking fires blew slowly across the street from door to door, carrying into the opposite one the smell of the identical meat and bread. The women tended them; the men were gathered at the head of the lane, watching him as he came down the slope from the house, putting his naked feet down carefully in a strange dusk. To the waiting men his eyeballs were a little luminous.

"Issetibbeha is not dead yet," the headman said.

"Not dead," the body servant said. "Who not dead?"

In the dusk they had faces like his, the different ages, the thoughts sealed inscrutable behind faces like the death masks of apes. The smell of the fires, the cooking, blew sharp and slow across the strange dusk, as from another world, above the lane and the pickaninnies naked in the dust.

"If he lives past sundown, he will live until daybreak," one said.

"Who says?"

"Talk says."

"Yao. Talk says. We know but one thing." They looked at the body servant as he stood among them, his eyeballs a little luminous. He was breathing slow and deep. His chest was bare; he was sweating a little. "He knows. He knows it."

"Let us let the drums talk."

"Yao. Let the drums tell it."

The drums began after dark. They kept them hidden in the creek bottom. They were made of hollowed cypress knees, and the Negroes kept them hidden; why, none knew. They were buried in the mud on the bank of a slough; a lad of fourteen guarded them. He was undersized, and a mute; he squatted in the mud there all day, clouded over with mosquitoes, naked save for the mud with which he coated himself against the mosquitoes, and about his neck a fiber bag containing a pig's rib to which black shreds of flesh still adhered, and two scaly barks on a wire. He slobbered onto his clutched knees, drooling; now and then Indians came noiselessly out of the bushes behind him and stood there and contemplated him for a while and went away, and he never knew it.

From the loft of the stable where he lay hidden until dark and after, the Negro could hear the drums. They were three miles away, but he could hear them as though they were in the barn itself below him, thudding and thudding. It was as though he could see the fire too, and the black limbs turning into and out of the flames in copper gleams. Only there would be no fire. There would be no more light there than where he lay in the dusty loft, with the whispering arpeggios of rat feet along the warm and immemorial ax-squared rafters. The only fire there would be the smudge against mosquitoes where the women with nursing children crouched, their heavy sluggish breasts nippled full and smooth into the mouths of men children; contemplative, oblivious of the drumming, since a fire would signify life.

There was a fire in the steamboat, where Issetibbeha lay dying among his wives, beneath the lashed girandoles and the suspended bed. He could see the smoke, and just before sunset he saw the doctor come out, in a waistcoat made of skunk skins, and set fire to two clay-daubed sticks at the bows of the boat deck. "So he is not dead yet," the Negro said into the whispering gloom of the loft, answering himself; he could hear the two voices, himself and himself:

"Who not dead?"

"You are dead."

"Yao, I am dead," he said quietly. He wished to be where the drums were. He imagined himself springing out of the bushes, leaping among the drums on his bare, lean, greasy, invisible limbs. But he could not do that, because man leaped past life, into where death was; he dashed into death and did not die, because when death took a man, it took him just this side of the end of living. It was when death overran him from behind, still in life. The thin whisper of rat feet died in fainting gusts along the rafters. Once he had eaten rat. He was a boy then, but just come to America. They had lived ninety days in a three-foot-high 'tween-deck in tropic latitudes, hearing from topside the drunken New England captain intoning aloud from a book which he did not recognize for ten years afterward to be the Bible. Squatting in the stable so, he had watched the rat, civilized, by association with man reft of its inherent cunning of limb and eye; he had caught it without difficulty, with scarce a movement of his hand, and he ate it slowly, wondering how any of the rats had escaped so long. At that time he was still wearing the single white garment which the trader, a deacon in the Unitarian church, had given him, and he spoke then only his native tongue.

He was naked now, save for a pair of dungaree pants bought by Indians from white men, and an amulet slung on a thong about his hips. The amulet consisted of one half of a mother-of-pearl lorgnon which Issetibbeha had brought back from Paris, and the skull of a cottonmouth moccasin. He had killed the snake himself and eaten it, save the poison head. He lay in the loft, watching the house, the steamboat, listening to the drums, thinking of himself among the drums.

He lay there all night. The next morning he saw the doctor come out, in his skunk vest, and get on his mule and ride away, and he became quite still and watched the final dust from beneath the mule's delicate feet die away, and then he found that he was still breathing and it seemed strange to him that he still breathed air, still needed air. Then he lay and watched quietly, waiting to move, his eyeballs a little luminous, but with a quiet light, and his breathing light and regular, and saw Louis Berry come out and look at the sky. It was good light then, and already five Indians squatted in their Sunday clothes along the steamboat deck; by noon there were twenty-five there. That afternoon they dug the trench in which the meat would be baked, and the yams; by that time there were almost a hundred guests—decorous, quiet, patient in their stiff European finery—and he watched Berry lead Issetibbeha's mare from the stable and tie her to a tree, and then he watched Berry emerge from the house with the old hound which lay beside Issetibbeha's chair. He tied the hound to the tree too, and it sat there, looking gravely about at the faces. Then it began to howl. It was still howling at sundown, when the Negro climbed down the back wall of the barn and entered the spring branch, where it was already dusk. He began to run then. He could hear the hound howling behind him, and near the spring, already running, he passed another Negro. The two men, the one motionless and the other running, looked for an instant at each other as though across an actual boundary between two different worlds.

He ran on into full darkness, mouth closed, fists doubled, his broad nostrils bellowing steadily.

He ran on in the darkness. He knew the country well, because he had hunted it often with Issetibbeha, following on his mule the course of the fox or the cat beside Issetibbeha's mare; he knew it as well as did the men who would pursue him. He saw them for the first time shortly before sunset of the second day. He had run thirty miles then, up the creek bottom, before doubling back; lying in a pawpaw thicket he saw the pursuit for the first time. There were two of them, in shirts and straw hats, carrying their neatly rolled trousers under their arms, and they had no weapons. They were middle-aged, paunchy, and they could not have moved very fast anyway; it would be twelve hours before they could return to where he lay watching them. "So I will have until midnight to rest," he said. He was near enough to the plantation to smell the cooking fires, and he thought how he ought to be hungry, since he had not eaten in thirty hours. "But it is more important to rest," he told himself. He continued to tell himself that, lying in the pawpaw thicket, because the effort of resting, the need and the haste to rest, made his heart thud the same as the running had done. It was as though he had forgot how to rest, as though the six hours were not long enough to do it in, to remember again how to do it.

As soon as dark came he moved again. He had thought to keep going steadily and quietly through the night, since there was nowhere for him to go, but as soon as he moved he began to run at top speed, breasting his panting chest, his broad-flaring nostrils through the choked and whipping darkness. He ran for an hour, lost by then, without direction, when suddenly he stopped, and after a time his thudding heart unraveled from the sound of the drums. By the sound they were not two miles away; he followed the sound until he could smell the smudge fire and taste the acrid smoke. When he stood among them the drums did not cease, only the headman came to him where he stood in the drifting smudge, panting, his nostrils flaring and pulsing, the hushed glare of his ceaseless eyeballs in his mud-daubed face as though they were worked from lungs.

"We have expected thee," the headman said. "Go, now."

"Go?"

"Eat, and go. The dead may not consort with the living; thou knowest that."

"Yao. I know that." They did not look at one another. The drums had not ceased.

"Wilt thou eat?" the headman said.

"I am not hungry. I caught a rabbit this afternoon, and ate while I lay hidden."

"Take some cooked meat with thee, then."

He accepted the cooked meat, wrapped in leaves, and entered the creek bottom again; after a while the sound of the drums ceased. He walked steadily until daybreak. "I have twelve hours," he said. "Maybe more, since the trail was followed by night." He squatted and ate the meat and wiped his hands on his thighs. Then he rose and removed the dungaree pants and squatted again beside a slough and coated himself with mud—face, arms, body and legs—and squatted again, clasping his knees, his head bowed. When it was light enough to see, he moved back into the swamp and squatted again and went to sleep so. He did not dream at all. It was well that he moved, for, waking suddenly in broad daylight and the high sun, he saw the two Indians. They still carried their neatly rolled trousers; they stood opposite the place where he lay hidden, paunchy, thick, soft-looking, a little ludicrous in their straw hats and shirt tails.

"This is wearying work," one said.

"I'd rather be at home in the shade myself," the other said. "But there is the Man waiting at the door to the earth."

"Yao." They looked quietly about; stooping, one of them removed from his shirt tail a clot of cockleburs. "Damn that Negro," he said.

"Yao. When have they ever been anything but a trial and a care to us?"

In the early afternoon, from the top of a tree, the Negro looked down into the plantation. He could see Issetibbeha's body in a hammock between the two trees where the horse and the dog were tethered, and the concourse about the steamboat was filled with wagons and horses and mules, with carts and saddle-horses, while in bright clumps the women and the smaller children and the old men squatted about the long trench where the smoke from the barbecuing meat blew slow and thick. The men and the big boys would all be down there in the creek bottom behind him, on the trail, their Sunday clothes rolled carefully up and wedged into tree crotches. There was a clump of men near the door to the house, to the saloon of the steamboat, though, and he watched them, and after a while he saw them bring Moketubbe out in a litter made of buckskin and persimmon poles; high hidden in his leafed nook the Negro, the quarry, looked quietly down upon his irrevocable doom with an expression as profound as Moketubbe's own. "Yao," he said quietly. "He will go then. That man whose body had been dead for fifteen years, he will go also."

In the middle of the afternoon he came face to face with an Indian. They were both on a footlog across a slough—the Negro gaunt, lean, hard, tireless and desperate; the Indian thick, soft-looking, the apparent embodiment of the ultimate and the supreme reluctance and inertia. The Indian made no move, no sound; he stood on the log and watched the Negro plunge into the slough and swim ashore and crash away into the undergrowth.

Just before sunset he lay behind a down log. Up the log in slow procession moved a line of ants. He caught them and ate them slowly, with a kind of detachment, like that of a dinner guest eating salted nuts from a dish. They too had a salt taste, engendering a salivary reaction out of all proportion. He ate them slowly, watching the unbroken line move up the log and into oblivious doom with a steady and terrific undeviation. He had eaten nothing else all day; in his caked mud mask his eyes rolled in reddened rims. At sunset, creeping along the creek bank toward where he had spotted a frog, a cottonmouth moccasin slashed him suddenly across the forearm with a thick, sluggish blow. It struck clumsily, leaving two long slashes across his arm like two razor slashes, and half sprawled with its own momentum and rage, it appeared for the moment utterly helpless with its own awkwardness and choleric anger. "Olé, grandfather," the Negro said. He touched its head and watched it slash him again across his arm, and again, with thick, raking, awkward blows. "It's that I do not wish to die," he said. Then he said it again—"It's that I do not wish to die"—in a quiet tone, of slow and low amaze, as

though it were something that, until the words had said themselves, he found that he had not known, or had not known the
depth and extent of his desire.

V

Moketubbe took the slippers with him. He could not wear them
very long while in motion, not even in the litter where he was
slung reclining, so they rested upon a square of fawnskin upon his
lap—the cracked, frail slippers a little shapeless now, with their
scaled patent-leather surfaces and buckleless tongues and scarlet
heels, lying upon the supine obese shape just barely alive, carried
through swamp and brier by swinging relays of men who bore
steadily all day long the crime and its object, on the business of the
slain. To Moketubbe it must have been as though, himself immortal, he were being carried rapidly through hell by doomed
spirits which, alive, had contemplated his disaster, and, dead, were
oblivious partners to his damnation.

After resting for a while, the litter propped in the center of the
squatting circle and Moketubbe motionless in it, with closed eyes
and his face at once peaceful for the instant and filled with inescapable foreknowledge, he could wear the slippers for a while.
The stripling put them on him, forcing his big, tender, dropsical
feet into them; whereupon into his face came again that expression
tragic, passive and profoundly attentive, which dyspeptics wear.
Then they went on. He made no move, no sound, inert in the
rhythmic litter out of some reserve of inertia, or maybe of some
kingly virtue such as courage or fortitude. After a time they set
the litter down and looked at him, at the yellow face like that of
an idol, beaded over with sweat. Then Three Basket or Had-Two-
Fathers would say: "Take them off. Honor has been served." They
would remove the shoes. Moketubbe's face would not alter, but
only then would his breathing become perceptible, going in and
out of his pale lips with a faint ah-ah-ah sound, and they would
squat again while the couriers and the runners came up.

"Not yet?"

"Not yet. He is going east. By sunset he will reach Mouth of
Tippah. Then he will turn back. We may take him tomorrow."

"Let us hope so. It will not be too soon."

"Yao. It has been three days now."

"When Doom died, it took only three days."

"But that was an old man. This one is young."

"Yao. A good race. If he is taken tomorrow, I will win a horse."

"May you win it."

"Yao. This work is not pleasant."

That was the day on which the food gave out at the plantation. The guests returned home and came back the next day with more food, enough for a week longer. On that day Issetibbeha began to smell; they could smell him for a long way up and down the bottom when it got hot toward noon and the wind blew. But they didn't capture the Negro on that day, nor on the next. It was about dusk on the sixth day when the couriers came up to the litter; they had found blood. "He has injured himself."

"Not bad, I hope," Basket said. "We cannot send with Issetibbeha one who will be of no service to him."

"Not whom Issetibbeha himself will have to nurse and care for," Berry said.

"We do not know," the courier said. "He has hidden himself. He has crept back into the swamp. We have left pickets."

They trotted with the litter now. The place where the Negro had crept into the swamp was an hour away. In the hurry and excitement they had forgotten that Moketubbe still wore the slippers; when they reached the place Moketubbe had fainted. They removed the slippers and brought him to.

With dark, they formed a circle about the swamp. They squatted, clouded over with gnats and mosquitoes; the evening star burned low and close down the west, and the constellations began to wheel overhead. "We will give him time," they said. "Tomorrow is just another name for today."

"Yao. Let him have time." Then they ceased, and gazed as one into the darkness where the swamp lay. After a while the noise ceased, and soon the courier came out of the darkness.

"He tried to break out."

"But you turned him back?"

"He turned back. We feared for a moment, the three of us. We could smell him creeping in the darkness, and we could smell something else, which we did not know. That was why we feared, until he told us. He said to slay him there, since it would be dark and he would not have to see the face when it came. But it was not that which we smelled; he told us what it was. A snake had struck him. That was two days ago. The arm swelled, and it smelled bad. But it was not that which we smelled then, because the swelling had gone down and his arm was no larger than that of a child. He showed us. We felt the arm, all of us did; it was no larger than that of a child. He said to give him a hatchet so he could chop the arm off. But tomorrow is today also."

"Yao. Tomorrow is today."

"We feared for a while. Then he went back into the swamp."

"That is good."

"Yao. We feared. Shall I tell the Man?"

"I will see," Basket said. He went away. The courier squatted, telling again about the Negro. Basket returned. "The Man says that it is good. Return to your post."

The courier crept away. They squatted about the litter; now and then they slept. Sometime after midnight the Negro waked them. He began to shout and talk to himself, his voice coming sharp and sudden out of the darkness, then he fell silent. Dawn came; a white crane flapped slowly across the jonquil sky. Basket was awake. "Let us go now," he said. "It is today."

Two Indians entered the swamp, their movements noisy. Before they reached the Negro they stopped, because he began to sing. They could see him, naked and mud-caked, sitting on a log, singing. They squatted silently a short distance away, until he finished. He was chanting something in his own language, his face lifted to the rising sun. His voice was clear, full, with a quality wild and sad. "Let him have time," the Indians said, squatting, patient, waiting. He ceased and they approached. He looked back and up at them through the cracked mud mask. His eyes were bloodshot, his lips cracked upon his square short teeth. The mask of mud appeared to be loose on his face, as if he might have lost flesh since he put it there; he held his left arm close to his breast. From the elbow down it was caked and shapeless with black mud. They could smell him, a rank smell. He watched them quietly until one touched him on the arm. "Come," the Indian said. "You ran well. Do not be ashamed."

VI

As they neared the plantation in the tainted bright morning, the Negro's eyes began to roll a little, like those of a horse. The smoke from the cooking pit blew low along the earth and upon the squatting and waiting guests about the yard and upon the steamboat deck, in their bright, stiff, harsh finery; the women, the children, the old men. They had sent couriers along the bottom, and another on ahead, and Issetibbeha's body had already been removed to where the grave waited, along with the horse and the dog, though they could still smell him in death about the house where he had lived in life. The guests were beginning to move toward the grave when the bearers of Moketubbe's litter mounted the slope.

The Negro was the tallest there, his high, close, mud-caked head looming above them all. He was breathing hard, as though the desperate effort of the six suspended and desperate days had catapulted upon him at once; although they walked slowly, his naked scarred chest rose and fell above the close-clutched left arm. He looked this way and that continuously, as if he were not seeing, as though sight never quite caught up with the looking. His mouth was open a little upon his big white teeth; he began to pant. The already moving guests halted, pausing, looking back, some with pieces of meat in their hands, as the Negro looked about at their faces with his wild, restrained, unceasing eyes.

"Will you eat first?" Basket said. He had to say it twice.

"Yes," the Negro said. "That's it. I want to eat."

The throng had begun to press back toward the center; the word passed to the outermost: "He will eat first."

They reached the steamboat. "Sit down," Basket said. The Negro sat on the edge of the deck. He was still panting, his chest rising and falling, his head ceaseless with its white eyeballs, turning from side to side. It was as if the inability to see came from within, from hopelessness, not from absence of vision. They brought food and watched quietly as he tried to eat it. He put the food into his mouth and chewed it, but chewing, the half-masticated matter began to emerge from the corners of his mouth and to drool down his chin, onto his chest, and after a while he stopped chewing and sat there, naked, covered with dried mud, the plate on his knees, and his mouth filled with a mass of chewed food, open, his eyes wide and unceasing, panting and panting. They watched him, patient, implacable, waiting.

"Come," Basket said at last.

"It's water I want," the Negro said. "I want water."

The well was a little way down the slope toward the quarters. The slope lay dappled with the shadows of noon, of that peaceful hour when, Issetibbeha napping in his chair and waiting for the noon meal and the long afternoon to sleep in, the Negro, the body servant, would be free. He would sit in the kitchen door then, talking with the women who prepared the food. Beyond the kitchen the lane between the quarters would be quiet, peaceful, with the women talking to one another across the lane and the smoke of the dinner fires blowing upon the pickaninnies like ebony toys in the dust.

"Come," Basket said.

The Negro walked among them, taller than any. The guests were moving on toward where Issetibbeha and the horse and the dog waited. The Negro walked with his high ceaseless head, his panting chest. "Come," Basket said. "You wanted water."

"Yes," the Negro said. "Yes." He looked back at the house, then down to the quarters, where today no fire burned, no face showed in any door, no pickaninny in the dust, panting. "It struck me here, raking me across this arm; once, twice, three times. I said, 'Olé, Grandfather.' "

"Come now," Basket said. The Negro was still going through the motion of walking, his knee action high, his head high, as though he were on a treadmill. His eyeballs had a wild, restrained glare, like those of a horse. "You wanted water," Basket said. "Here it is."

There was a gourd in the well. They dipped it full and gave it to the Negro, and they watched him try to drink. His eyes had not ceased as he tilted the gourd slowly against his caked face. They could watch his throat working and the bright water cascading from either side of the gourd, down his chin and breast. Then the water stopped. "Come," Basket said.

"Wait," the Negro said. He dipped the gourd again and tilted it against his face, beneath his ceaseless eyes. Again they watched his throat working and the unswallowed water sheathing broken and myriad down his chin, channeling his caked chest. They waited, patient, grave, decorous, implacable; clansman and guest and kin. Then the water ceased, though still the empty gourd tilted higher and higher, and still his black throat aped the vain motion of his frustrated swallowing. A piece of water-loosened mud carried away from his chest and broke at his muddy feet, and in the empty gourd they could hear his breath: ah-ah-ah.

"Come," Basket said, taking the gourd from the Negro and hanging it back in the well.

JAMES THURBER

(1894–1961)

━━━━━◆◗●◖◆━━━━━

James Thurber was born and raised in Columbus, Ohio, and attended Ohio State University for three years. He served as a State Department code clerk in Washington and New York, and then turned to journalism, working with the Columbus Dispatch, the Paris edition of the Chicago Tribune, and the New York Evening Post. In 1926 he became a contributing editor on The New Yorker, which had been founded a year earlier, and thus began Thurber's life-long association with that magazine.

One of the most distinguished satirists of modern times, Thurber turned his attention to various aspects of the human comedy, including popular psychology, pseudo-scientific sex literature, modern war, government authority, and the battle of the sexes. Though his characters are often battered by an incredibly malign or absurd fate, they carry on doggedly, sustained by a sense of the irony of it all. Anything but bitter, Thurber's satiric outlook is gentle and whimsical, and at times even melancholy. He was noted not only for his fiction but also for his humorous drawings of overbearing women, timid men, and mournful dogs.

His many books of stories, essays, and fables include Is Sex Necessary? (1929), The Owl in the Attic and Other Perplexities (1931), My Life and Hard Times (1933), Let Your Mind Alone (1937), Fables for Our Time (1940), The Thurber Carnival

(1945), The Thurber Album (1952), Further Fables for Our Times (1956), and Lanterns and Lances (1961). The Male Animal (1940) is a comedy about academic freedom written in collaboration with Elliott Nugent; Men, Women, and Dogs (1943) is a collection of his drawings; and The Years with Ross (1959) is an affectionate reminiscence of experiences on The New Yorker with his friend, editor Harold Ross.

Despite its delightful absurdity, "A Sequence of Servants," which appeared in My Life and Hard Times (1933), raises questions about the propriety of ethnic humor, always a thorny subject in America. But if the sketch's Negro servants are not presented in a flattering manner, neither are the whites—Thurber's people do not usually emerge with a great deal of decorum from their eccentric bouts with life. Moreover, it is worth noting that exaggerated Negro dialect, fantastic characters, and absurd situations have become the stock-in-trade of contemporary black comedians such as Godfrey Cambridge and Flip Wilson. Negro servants are presented humorously in several Thurber sketches, and "The Tree on the Diamond," an autobiographical sketch in The Thurber Album (1952), presents some real-life Negroes Thurber knew during his boyhood in Columbus.

A Sequence of Servants

When I look back on the long line of servants my mother hired during the years I lived at home, I remember clearly ten or twelve of them (we had about a hundred and sixty-two, all told, but few of them were memorable). There was, among the immortals, Dora Gedd, a quiet, mousy girl of thirty-two who one night shot at a man in her room, throwing our household into an uproar that was equalled perhaps only by the goings-on the night the ghost got in. Nobody knew how her lover, a morose garage man, got into the house, but everybody for two blocks knew how he got out. Dora had dressed up in a lavender evening gown for the occasion and she wore a mass of jewelry, some of which was my mother's. She kept shouting something from Shakespeare after the shooting—I forget just what—and pursued the gentleman downstairs from her attic room. When he got to the second floor he rushed into my father's room. It was this entrance, and not the shot or the shouting, that aroused father, a deep sleeper always. "Get me out of here!" shouted the victim. This situation rapidly developed, from then on, into one of those bewildering involvements for which my family had, I am afraid, a kind of unhappy genius. When the cops arrived Dora was shooting out the Welsbach gas mantles in the living room, and her gentleman friend had fled. By dawn everything was quiet once more.

There were others. Gertie Straub: big, genial, and ruddy, a collector of pints of rye (we learned after she was gone), who came in after two o'clock one night from a dancing party at Buckeye Lake and awakened us by bumping into and knocking over furniture. "Who's down there?" called mother from upstairs. "It's me, dearie," said Gertie, "Gertie Straub." "What are you *doing?*" demanded mother. "Dusting," said Gertie.

Juanemma Kramer was one of my favorites. Her mother loved the name Juanita so dearly that she had worked the first part of it into the names of all her daughters—they were (in addition to a Juanita) Juanemma, Juanhelen, and Juangrace. Juanemma was a thin, nervous maid who lived in constant dread of being hypnotized. Nor were her fears unfounded, for she was so extremely susceptible to hypnotic suggestion that one evening at B. F. Keith's theatre when a man on the stage was hypnotized, Juanemma, in the audience, was hypnotized too and floundered out into the aisle making the same cheeping sound that the subject on the stage, who had been told he was a chicken, was making. The act was abandoned and some xylophone players were brought on to restore order. One night, when our house was deep in quiet slumber, Juanemma became hypnotized in her sleep. She dreamed that a man "put her under" and then disappeared without "bringing her out." This was explained when, at last, a police surgeon whom we called in—he was the only doctor we could persuade to come out at three in the morning—slapped her into consciousness. It got so finally that any buzzing or whirling sound or any flashing object would put Juanemma under, and we had to let her go. I was reminded of her recently when, at a performance of the movie *Rasputin and the Empress*, there came the scene in which Lionel Barrymore as the unholy priest hypnotizes the Czarevitch by spinning before his eyes a glittering watch. If Juanemma sat in any theatre and witnessed that scene she must, I am sure, have gone under instantly. Happily, she seems to have missed the picture, for otherwise Mr. Barrymore might have had to dress up again as Rasputin (which God forbid) and journey across the country to get her out of it—excellent publicity but a great bother.

Before I go on to Vashti, whose last name I forget, I will look in passing at another of our white maids (Vashti was colored). Belle Giddin distinguished herself by one gesture which fortunately did not result in the bedlam occasioned by Juanemma's hypnotic states or Dora Gedd's shooting spree. Bella burned her finger grievously, and purposely, one afternoon in the steam of a boiling kettle so that she could find out whether the pain-killer she had bought one night at a tent-show for fifty cents was any good. It was only fair.

Vashti turned out, in the end, to be partly legendary. She was a comely and sombre negress who was always able to find things my mother lost. "I don't know what's become of my garnet brooch," my mother said one day. "Yassum," said Vashti. In half an hour she had found it. "Where in the world was it?" asked mother. "In de yahd," said Vashti. "De dog mussa drug it out."

Vashti was in love with a young colored chauffeur named Charley, but she was also desired by her stepfather, whom none of us had ever seen but who was, she said, a handsome but messin' round gentleman from Georgia who had come north and married Vashti's mother just so he could be near Vashti. Charley, her fiancé, was for killing the stepfather but we counselled flight to another city. Vashti, however, would burst into tears and hymns and vow she'd never leave us; she got a certain pleasure out of bearing her cross. Thus we all lived in jeopardy, for the possibility that Vashti, Charley, and her stepfather might fight it out some night in our kitchen did not, at times, seem remote. Once I went into the kitchen at midnight to make some coffee. Charley was standing at a window looking out into the back yard; Vashti was rolling her eyes. "Heah he come! Heah he come!" she moaned. The stepfather didn't show up, however.

Charley finally saved up twenty-seven dollars toward taking Vashti away but one day he impulsively bought a .22 revolver with a mother-of-pearl handle and demanded that Vashti tell him where her mother and step-father lived. "Doan go up dere, doan go *up* dere!" said Vashti. "Mah mothah is just as rarin' as he is!" Charley, however, insisted. It came out then that Vashti didn't have any stepfather; there was no such person. Charley threw her over for a yellow gal named Nancy: he never forgave Vashti for the vanishing from his life of a menace that had come to mean more to him than Vashti herself. Afterwards, if you asked Vashti about her stepfather or about Charley she would say, proudly, and with a woman-of-the-world air, "Neither one ob 'em is messin' round *me* any mo'."

Mrs. Doody, a huge, middle-aged woman with a religious taint, came into and went out of our house like a comet. The second night she was there she went berserk while doing the dishes and, under the impression that father was the Antichrist, pursued him several times up the back stairs and down the front. He had been sitting quietly over his coffee in the living room when she burst in from the kitchen waving a bread knife. My brother Herman finally felled her with a piece of Libby's cut glass that had been a wedding present of mother's. Mother, I remember, was in the attic at the time, trying to find some old things, and, appearing on the scene in the midst of it all, got the quick and mistaken impression that father was chasing Mrs. Doody.

Mrs. Robertson, a fat and mumbly old colored woman, who might have been sixty and who might have been a hundred, gave us more than one turn during the many years that she did our washing. She had been a slave down South and she remembered "having seen the troops marching—a mess o' blue, den a mass o' gray." "What," my mother asked her once, "were they fighting about?" "Dat," said Mrs. Robertson, "Ah don't know." She had a feeling, at all times, that something was going to happen. I can see her now, staggering up from the basement with a basketful of clothes and coming abruptly to a halt in the middle of the kitchen. "Hahk!" she would say, in a deep, guttural voice. We would all hark; there was never anything to be heard. Neither, when she shouted "Look yondah!" and pointed a trembling hand at a window, was there ever anything to be seen. Father protested time and again that he couldn't stand Mrs. Robertson around, but mother always refused to let her go. It seems that she was a jewel. Once she walked unbidden, a dishpan full of wrung-out clothes under her arm, into father's study, where he was engrossed in some figures. Father looked up. She regarded him for a moment in silence. Then—"Look out!" she said, and withdrew. Another time, a murky winter afternoon, she came flubbering up the cellar stairs and bounced, out of breath, into the kitchen. Father was in the kitchen sipping some black coffee; he was in a jittery state of nerves from the effects of having had a tooth out, and had been in bed most of the day. "Dey is a death watch downstaihs!" rumbled the old colored lady. It developed that she had heard a strange "chipping" noise back of the furnace. "That was a cricket," said father. "Um-*hm*," said Mrs. Robertson. "Dat was uh death watch!" With that she put on her hat and went home, poising just long enough at the back door to observe darkly to father, "*Dey ain't no way!*" It upset him for days.

Mrs. Robertson had only one great hour that I can think of —Jack Johnson's victory over Mistah Jeffries on the Fourth of July, 1910. She took a prominent part in the colored parade through the South End that night, playing a Spanish fandango on a banjo. The procession was led by the pastor of her church who, Mrs. Robertson later told us, had 'splained that the victory of Jack over Mistah Jeffries proved "de 'speriority ob de race." "What," asked my mother, "did he mean by that?" "Dat," said Mrs. Robertson, "Ah don't know."

Our other servants I don't remember so clearly, except the one who set the house on fire (her name eludes me), and Edda Millmoss. Edda was always slightly morose but she had gone along for months, all the time she was with us, quietly and efficiently attending to her work, until the night we had Carson Blair and F. R.

Gardiner to dinner—both men of importance to my father's ambitions. Then suddenly, while serving the entrée, Edda dropped everything and, pointing a quivering finger at father, accused him in a long rigamarole of having done her out of her rights to the land on which Trinity Church in New York stands. Mr. Gardiner had one of his "attacks" and the whole evening turned out miserably.

RICHARD WRIGHT

(1908–1960)

————————◆◆◆◆◆————————

Richard Wright is often called the first major black writer in America. His Native Son, published in 1940, was a significant event not only in the history of Negro letters but also in the development of the American naturalistic novel. It illustrated the manner in which brutal environment produces brutal character as well as offering disturbing insight into the psychological aberrations brought about by life in the urban ghetto.

Wright was born on a plantation near Natchez, Mississippi, and spent his early years drifting with his family from town to town in Mississippi, Tennessee, and Arkansas. His father abandoned the family, and his mother was later stricken with paralysis, which forced her to send her two sons to an orphanage. Removed from the orphanage, Wright was handed along from relative to relative. Rootless, alienated, and angry, he resisted his relatives' religious preaching and grew contemptuous of schools and formal education. He set off on his own at fifteen and worked in Memphis before setting out for Chicago in 1927. Meanwhile, he had "developed the habit of reading everything that fell into my hands." Like many young men in the 1920s, he fell under the spell of H. L. Mencken, whose criticisms of American life not only helped Wright formulate his own views but also gave him insight into the social uses of literature.

After holding the assortment of menial jobs described in "The Man Who Went to Chicago," he was put out of work by the depression. By 1934 he had joined the Communist Party, and soon he was writing for New Masses and other left-wing journals. In 1937 he moved to New York, where he became Harlem editor for the Daily Worker. His first book, Uncle Tom's Children (1938), pictured the plight of rural Southern Negroes, and in Native Son (1940) he turned to the urban Negro ghetto. In the first book Wright attempted to evoke sympathy for black victims of injustice, but with Bigger Thomas, the now legendary protagonist of Native Son, he risked confirming the white man's stereotyped image of the brutality of Negroes in order to show the social forces which turn a man into an animal and make violence the only possible expression of individuality. Black Boy, a biography of Wright's life to the age of seventeen, was published in 1945. At the end of World War II, Wright moved to Paris, where he lived until his death in 1960. Wright had withdrawn from the Communist Party in 1942, unwilling to submit to the requisite dogma and discipline, and now, living in France, he turned to existentialism and the writings of Sartre and Camus. During his residence in France he produced several novels, including The Outsider (1953) and The Long Dream (1958), and he wrote volumes of social commentary, such as Black Power (1954) and White Man, Listen! (1957).

"The Man Who Went to Chicago" originally appeared under the title "Early Days in Chicago" in 1945 and was published under its new title in Eight Men (1961), a volume bringing together character sketches published at various stages of Wright's career.

The Man Who Went to Chicago

When I rose in the morning the temperature had dropped below zero. The house was as cold to me as the Southern streets had been in winter. I dressed, doubling my clothing. I ate in a restaurant,

caught a streetcar, and rode south, rode until I could see no more
black faces on the sidewalks. I had now crossed the boundary line
of the Black Belt and had entered the territory where jobs were
perhaps to be had from white folks. I walked the streets and looked
into shop windows until I saw a sign in a delicatessen: PORTER
WANTED.

I went in and a stout white woman came to me.

"Vat do you vant?" she asked.

The voice jarred me. She's Jewish, I thought, remembering
with shame the obscenities I used to shout at Jewish storekeepers
in Arkansas.

"I thought maybe you needed a porter," I said.

"Meester 'Offman, he eesn't here yet," she said. "Vill you vait?"

"Yes, ma'am."

"Seet down."

"No, ma'am, I'll wait outside."

"But eet's cold out zhere," she said.

"That's all right," I said.

She shrugged. I went to the sidewalk. I waited for half an hour
in the bitter cold, regretting that I had not remained in the warm
store, but unable to go back inside. A bald, stoutish white man
went into the store and pulled off his coat. Yes, he was the boss
man . . .

"Zo you vant a job?" he asked.

"Yes, sir," I answered, guessing at the meaning of his words.

"Vhere you vork before?"

"In Memphis, Tennessee."

"My brudder-in-law vorked in Tennessee vonce," he said.

I was hired. The work was easy, but I found to my dismay
that I could not understand a third of what was said to me. My
slow Southern ears were baffled by their clouded, thick accents.
One morning Mrs. Hoffman asked me to go to a neighboring
store—it was owned by a cousin of hers—and get a can of chicken
à la king. I had never heard the phrase before and I asked her to
repeat it.

"Don't you know nosing?" she demanded of me.

"If you would write it down for me, I'd know what to get," I
ventured timidly.

"I can't vite!" she shouted in a sudden fury. "Vat kinda boy iss you?"

I memorized the separate sounds that she had uttered and went to the neighboring store.

"Mrs. Hoffman wants a can Cheek Keeng Awr Lar Keeng," I said slowly, hoping he would not think I was being offensive.

"All vite," he said, after staring at me a moment.

He put a can into a paper bag and gave it to me; outside in the street I opened the bag and read the label: Chicken à la King. I cursed, disgusted with myself. I knew those words. It had been her thick accent that had thrown me off. Yet I was not angry with her for speaking broken English; my English, too, was broken. But why could she not have taken more patience? Only one answer came to my mind. I was black and she did not care. Or so I thought . . . I was persisting in reading my present environment in the light of my old one. I reasoned thus: though English was my native tongue and America my native land, she, an alien, could operate a store and earn a living in a neighborhood where I could not even live. I reasoned further that she was aware of this and was trying to protect her position against me.

It was not until I had left the delicatessen job that I saw how grossly I had misread the motives and attitudes of Mr. Hoffman and his wife. I had not yet learned anything that would have helped me to thread my way through these perplexing racial relations. Accepting my environment at its face value, trapped by my own emotions, I kept asking myself what had black people done to bring this crazy world upon them?

The fact of the separation of white and black was clear to me; it was its effect upon the personalities of people that stumped and dismayed me. I did not feel that I was a threat to anybody; yet, as soon as I had grown old enough to think, I had learned that my entire personality, my aspirations, had long ago been discounted; that, in a measure, the very meaning of the words I spoke could not be fully understood.

And when I contemplated the area of No Man's Land into which the Negro mind in America had been shunted I wondered if there had ever been in all human history a more corroding and devastating attack upon the personalities of men than the idea of racial discrimination. In order to escape the racial attack that went to the roots of my life, I would have gladly accepted any way of life but the one in which I found myself. I would have agreed to live under a system of feudal oppression, not because I preferred feudalism but because I felt that feudalism made use of a limited part of a man, defined man, his rank, his function in society. I would have consented to live under the most rigid type of dictatorship, for I felt that dictatorships, too, defined the use of men, however degrading that use might be.

While working as a porter in Memphis I had often stood aghast as a friend of mine had offered himself to be kicked by the white men; but now, while working in Chicago, I was learning that perhaps even a kick was better than uncertainty . . . I had elected, in my fevered search for honorable adjustment to the American scene, not to submit and in doing so I had embraced the daily horror of anxiety, of tension, of eternal disquiet. I could now sympathize with—though I could never bring myself to approve—those tortured blacks who had given up and had gone to their white tormentors and had said: "Kick me, if that's all there is for me; kick me and let me feel at home, let me have peace!"

Color hate defined the place of black life as below that of white life; and the black man, responding to the same dreams as the white man, strove to bury within his heart his awareness of this difference because it made him lonely and afraid. Hated by whites and being an organic part of the culture that hated him, the black man grew in turn to hate in himself that which others hated in him. But pride would make him hate his self-hate, for he would not want whites to know that he was so thoroughly conquered by them that his total life was conditioned by their attitude; but in the act of hiding his self-hate, he could not help but hate those who evoked his self-hate in him. So each part of his day would be consumed in a war with himself, a good part of his energy would be spent in keeping control of his unruly emotions, emotions which he had not wished to have, but could not help having. Held at bay by the hate of others, preoccupied with his own feelings, he was continuously at war with reality. He became inefficient, less able to see and judge the objective world. And when he reached that state, the white people looked at him and laughed and said:

"Look, didn't I tell you niggers were that way?"

To solve this tangle of balked emotion, I loaded the empty part of the ship of my personality with fantasies of ambition to keep it from toppling over into the sea of senselessness. Like any other American, I dreamed of going into business and making money; I dreamed of working for a firm that would allow me to advance until I reached an important position; I even dreamed of organizing secret groups of blacks to fight all whites . . . And if the blacks would not agree to organize, then they would have to be fought. I would end up again with self-hate, but it was now a self-hate that was projected outward upon other blacks. Yet I knew—with that part of my mind that the whites had given me—that none of my dreams were possible. Then I would hate myself for allowing my mind to dwell upon the unattainable. Thus the circle would complete itself.

Slowly I began to forge in the depths of my mind a mechanism that repressed all the dreams and desires that the Chicago streets, the newspapers, the movies were evoking in me. I was going through a second childhood; a new sense of the limit of the possible was being born in me. What could I dream of that had the barest possibility of coming true? I could think of nothing. And, slowly, it was upon exactly that nothingness that my mind began to dwell, that constant sense of wanting without having, of being hated without reason. A dim notion of what life meant to a Negro in America was coming to consciousness in me, not in terms of external events, lynchings, Jim Crowism, and the endless brutalities, but in terms of crossed-up feeling, of emotional tension. I sensed that Negro life was a sprawling land of unconscious suffering, and there were but few Negroes who knew the meaning of their lives, who could tell their story.

Word reached me that an examination for postal clerk was impending and at once I filed an application and waited. As the date for the examination drew near, I was faced with another problem. How could I get a free day without losing my job? In the South it would have been an unwise policy for a Negro to have gone to his white boss and asked for time to take an examination for another job. It would have implied that the Negro did not like to work for the white boss, that he felt he was not receiving just consideration and, inasmuch as most jobs that Negroes held in the South involved a personal, paternalistic relationship, he would have been risking an argument that might have led to violence.

I now began to speculate about what kind of man Mr. Hoffman was, and I found that I did not know him; that is, I did not know his basic attitude toward Negroes. If I asked him, would he be sympathetic enough to allow me time off with pay? I needed the money. Perhaps he would say: "Go home and stay home if you don't like this job!" I was not sure of him. I decided, therefore, that I had better not risk it. I would forfeit the money and stay away without telling him.

The examination was scheduled to take place on a Monday; I had been working steadily and I would be too tired to do my best if I took the examination without benefit of rest. I decided to stay away from the shop Saturday, Sunday, and Monday. But what could I tell Mr. Hoffman? Yes, I would tell him that I had been ill. No, that was too thin. I would tell him that my mother had died in Memphis and that I had gone down to bury her. That lie might work.

I took the examination and when I came to the store on Tuesday, Mr. Hoffman was astonished, of course.

"I didn't sink you vould ever come back," he said.

"I'm awfully sorry, Mr. Hoffman."

"Vat happened?"

"My mother died in Memphis and I had to go down and bury her," I lied.

He looked at me, then shook his head.

"Rich, you lie," he said.

"I'm not lying," I lied stoutly.

"You vanted to do somesink, zo you zayed ervay," he said, shrugging.

"No, sir. I'm telling you the truth," I piled another lie upon the first one.

"No. You lie. You disappoint me," he said.

"Well, all I can do is tell you the truth," I lied indignantly.

"Vy didn't you use the phone?"

"I didn't think of it," I told a fresh lie.

"Rich, if your mudder die, you vould tell me," he said.

"I didn't have time. Had to catch the train," I lied yet again.

"Vhere did you get the money?"

"My aunt gave it to me," I said, disgusted that I had to lie and lie again.

"I don't vant a boy vat tells lies," he said.

"I don't lie," I lied passionately to protect my lies.

Mrs. Hoffman joined in and both of them hammered at me.

"Ve know. You come from ze Zouth. You feel you can't tell us ze truth. But ve don't bother you. Ve don't feel like people in ze Zouth. Ve treat you nice, don't ve?" they asked.

"Yes, ma'am," I mumbled.

"Zen vy lie?"

"I'm not lying," I cried with all my strength.

I became angry because I knew that they knew that I was lying. I had lied to protect myself, and then I had to lie to protect my lie. I had met so many white faces that would have violently disapproved of my taking the examination that I could not have risked telling Mr. Hoffman the truth. But how could I tell him that I had lied because I was so unsure of myself? Lying was bad, but revealing my own sense of insecurity would have been worse. It would have been shameful, and I did not like to feel ashamed.

Their attitudes had proved utterly amazing. They were taking time out from their duties in the store to talk to me, and I had never encountered anything like that from whites before. A Southern white man would have said: "Get to hell out of here!" or "All right, nigger. Get to work." But no white people had ever stood their ground and probed at me, questioned me at such length. It dawned upon me that they were trying to treat me as an equal, which made it even more impossible for me ever to tell them that I had lied, why I had lied. I felt that if I confessed I would be giving them a moral advantage over me that would have been unbearable.

"All vight, zay and vork," Mr. Hoffman said. "I know you're lying, but I don't care, Rich."

I wanted to quit. He had insulted me. But I liked him in spite of myself. Yes, I had done wrong; but how on earth could I have known the kind of people I was working for? Perhaps Mr. Hoffman would have gladly consented for me to take the examination; but my hopes had been far weaker than my powerful fears.

Working with them from day to day and knowing that they knew I had lied from fear crushed me. I knew that they pitied me and pitied the fear in me. I resolved to quit and risk hunger rather than stay with them. I left the job that following Saturday, not telling them that I would not be back, not possessing the heart to say good-by. I just wanted to go quickly and have them forget that I had ever worked for them.

After an idle week, I got a job as a dishwasher in a North Side café that had just opened. My boss, a white woman, directed me in unpacking barrels of dishes, setting up new tables, painting, and so on. I had charge of serving breakfast; in the late afternoon I carted trays of food to patrons in the hotel who did not want to come down to eat. My wages were fifteen dollars a week; the hours were long, but I ate my meals on the job.

The cook was an elderly Finnish woman with a sharp, bony face. There were several white waitresses. I was the only Negro in the café. The waitresses were a hard, brisk lot, and I was keenly aware of how their attitudes contrasted with those of Southern white girls. They had not been taught to keep a gulf between me and themselves; they were relatively free of the heritage of racial hate.

One morning as I was making coffee, Cora came forward with a tray loaded with food and squeezed against me to draw a cup of coffee.

"Pardon me, Richard," she said.

"Oh, that's all right," I said in an even tone.

But I was aware that she was a white girl and that her body was pressed closely against mine, an incident that had never happened to me before in my life, an incident charged with the memory of dread. But she was not conscious of my blackness or of what her actions would have meant in the South. And had I not been born in the South, her trivial act would have been as unnoticed by me as it was by her. As she stood close to me, I could not help thinking that if a Southern white girl had wanted to draw a cup of coffee, she would have commanded me to step aside so that she might not come in contact with me. The work of the hot and busy kitchen would have had to cease for the moment so that I could have taken my tainted body far enough away to allow the Southern white girl a chance to get a cup of coffee. There lay a deep, emotional safety in knowing that the white girl who was now leaning carelessly against me was not thinking of me, had no deep, vague, irrational fright that made her feel that I was a creature to be avoided at all costs.

One summer morning a white girl came late to work and rushed into the pantry where I was busy. She went into the women's room and changed her clothes; I heard the door open and a second later I was surprised to hear her voice:

"Richard, quick! Tie my apron!"

She was standing with her back to me and the strings of her apron dangled loose. There was a moment of indecision on my part, then I took the two loose strings and carried them around her body and brought them again to her back and tied them in a clumsy knot.

"Thanks a million," she said, grasping my hand for a split second, and was gone.

I continued my work, filled with all the possible meanings that that tiny, simple, human event could have meant to any Negro in the South where I had spent most of my hungry days.

I did not feel any admiration or any hate for the girls. My attitude was one of abiding and friendly wonder. For the most part I was silent with them, though I knew that I had a firmer grasp of life than most of them. As I worked I listened to their talk and perceived its puzzled, wandering, superficial fumbling with the problems and facts of life. There were many things they wondered about that I could have explained to them, but I never dared.

During my lunch hour, which I spent on a bench in a nearby park, the waitresses would come and sit beside me, talking at random, laughing, joking, smoking cigarettes. I learned about their tawdry dreams, their simple hopes, their home lives, their fear of feeling anything deeply, their sex problems, their husbands. They were an eager, restless, talkative, ignorant bunch, but casually kind and impersonal for all that. They knew nothing of hate and fear, and strove instinctively to avoid all passion.

I often wondered what they were trying to get out of life, but I never stumbled upon a clue, and I doubt if they themselves had any notion. They lived on the surface of their days; their smiles were surface smiles, and their tears were surface tears. Negroes lived a truer and deeper life than they, but I wished that Negroes, too, could live as thoughtlessly, serenely, as they. The girls never talked of their feelings; none of them possessed the insight or the emotional equipment to understand themselves or others. How far apart in culture we stood! All my life I had done nothing but feel and cultivate my feelings; all their lives they had done nothing but strive for petty goals, the trivial material prizes of American life. We shared a common tongue, but my language was a different language from theirs.

It was in the psychological distance that separated the races that the deepest meaning of the problem of the Negro lay for me. For these poor, ignorant white girls to have understood my life would have meant nothing short of a vast revolution in theirs. And I was convinced that what they needed to make them complete and grown-up in their living was the inclusion in their personalities of a knowledge of lives such as I lived and suffered containedly.

As I, in memory, think back now upon those girls and their lives I feel that for white America to understand the significance of the problem of the Negro will take a bigger and tougher America than any we have yet known. I feel that America's past is too shallow, her national character too superficially optimistic, her very morality too suffused with color hate for her to accomplish so vast and complex a task. Culturally the Negro represents a paradox: Though he is an organic part of the nation, he is excluded by the entire tide and direction of American culture. Frankly, it is felt to be right to exclude him, and it is felt to be wrong to admit him freely. Therefore if, within the confines of its present culture, the nation ever seeks to purge itself of its color hate, it will find itself at war with itself, convulsed by a spasm of emotional and moral confusion. If the nation ever finds itself examining its real relation to the Negro, it will find itself doing infinitely more than that; for the anti-Negro attitude of whites represents but a tiny part—though a symbolically significant one—of the moral attitude of the nation. Our too-young and too-new America, lusty because it is lonely, aggressive because it is afraid, insists upon seeing the world in terms of good and bad, the holy and the evil, the high and the low, the white and the black; our America is frightened by fact, by history, by processes, by necessity. It hugs the easy way of damning those whom it cannot understand, of excluding those who look different; and it salves its conscience with a self-draped cloak of righteousness. Am I damning my native land? No; for I, too, share these faults of character! And I really do not think that America, adolescent and cocksure, a stranger to suffering and travail, an enemy of passion and sacrifice, is ready to probe into its most fundamental beliefs.

I knew that not race alone, not color alone, but the daily values that gave meaning to life stood between me and those white girls with whom I worked. Their constant outward-looking, their mania for radios, cars, and a thousand other trinkets, made them dream and fix their eyes upon the trash of life, made it impossible for them to learn a language that could have taught them to speak of what was in their or others' hearts. The words of their souls were the syllables of popular songs.

The essence of the irony of the plight of the Negro in America, to me, is that he is doomed to live in isolation, while those who condemn him seek the basest goals of any people on the face of the earth. Perhaps it would be possible for the Negro to become reconciled to his plight if he could be made to believe that his sufferings were for some remote, high, sacrificial end; but sharing the culture that condemns him, and seeing that a lust for trash is what blinds the nation to his claims, is what sets storms to roiling in his soul.

Though I had fled the pressure of the South, my outward conduct had not changed. I had been schooled to present an unalteringly smiling face and I continued to do so despite the fact that my environment allowed more open expression. I hid my feelings and avoided all relationships with whites that might cause me to reveal them.

Tillie, the Finnish cook, was a tall, ageless, red-faced, raw-boned woman with long snow-white hair, which she balled in a knot at the nape of her neck. She cooked expertly and was superbly efficient. One morning as I passed the sizzling stove, I thought I heard Tillie cough and spit, but I saw nothing; her face, obscured by steam, was bent over a big pot. My senses told me that Tillie had coughed and spat into that pot, but my heart told me that no human being could possibly be so filthy. I decided to watch her. An hour or so later I heard Tillie clear her throat with a grunt, saw her cough and spit into the boiling soup. I held my breath; I did not want to believe what I had seen.

Should I tell the boss lady? Would she believe me? I watched Tillie for another day to make sure that she was spitting into the food. She was; there was no doubt of it. But who would believe me if I told them what was happening? I was the only black person in the café. Perhaps they would think that I hated the cook. I stopped eating my meals there and bided my time.

The business of the café was growing rapidly and a Negro girl was hired to make salads. I went to her at once.

"Look, can I trust you?" I asked.

"What are you talking about?" she asked.

"I want you to say nothing, but watch that cook."

"For what?"

"Now, don't get scared. Just watch the cook."

She looked at me as though she thought I was crazy; and, frankly, I felt that perhaps I ought not to say anything to anybody.

"What do you mean?" she demanded.

"All right," I said. "I'll tell you. That cook spits in the food."

"What are you saying?" she asked aloud.

"Keep quiet," I said.

"Spitting?" she asked me in a whisper. "Why would she do that?"

"I don't know. But watch her."

She walked away from me with a funny look in her eyes. But half an hour later she came rushing to me, looking ill, sinking into a chair.

"Oh, God, I feel awful!"

"Did you see it?"

"She *is* spitting in the food!"

"What ought we do?" I asked.

"Tell the lady," she said.

"She wouldn't believe me," I said.

She widened her eyes as she understood. We were black and the cook was white.

"But I can't work here if she's going to do that," she said.

"Then you tell her," I said.

"She wouldn't believe me either," she said.

She rose and ran to the women's room. When she returned she stared at me. We were two Negroes and we were silently asking ourselves if the white boss lady would believe us if we told her that her expert white cook was spitting in the food all day long as it cooked on the stove.

"I don't know," she wailed, in a whisper, and walked away.

I thought of telling the waitresses about the cook, but I could not get up enough nerve. Many of the girls were friendly with Tillie. Yet I could not let the cook spit in the food all day. That was wrong by any human standard of conduct. I washed dishes, thinking, wondering; I served breakfast, thinking, wondering; I served meals in the apartments of patrons upstairs, thinking, wondering. Each time I picked up a tray of food I felt like retching. Finally the Negro salad girl came to me and handed me her purse and hat.

"I'm going to tell her and quit, goddamn," she said.

"I'll quit too, if she doesn't fire her," I said.

"Oh, she won't believe me," she wailed, in agony.

"You tell her. You're a woman. She might believe you."

Her eyes welled with tears and she sat for a long time; then she rose and went abruptly into the dining room. I went to the door and peered. Yes, she was at the desk, talking to the boss lady. She returned to the kitchen and went into the pantry; I followed her.

"Did you tell her?" I asked.

"Yes."

"What did she say?"

"She said I was crazy."

"Oh, God!" I said.

"She just looked at me with those gray eyes of hers," the girl said. "Why would Tillie do that?"

"I don't know," I said.

The boss lady came to the door and called the girl; both of them went into the dining room. Tillie came over to me; a hard cold look was in her eyes.

"What's happening here?" she asked.

"I don't know," I said, wanting to slap her across the mouth.

She muttered something and went back to the stove, coughed, and spat into a bubbling pot. I left the kitchen and went into the back areaway to breathe. The boss lady came out.

"Richard," she said.

Her face was pale. I was smoking a cigarette and I did not look at her.

"Is this true?"

"Yes, ma'am."

"It couldn't be. Do you know what you're saying?"

"Just watch her," I said.

"I don't know," she moaned.

She looked crushed. She went back into the dining room, but I saw her watching the cook through the doors. I watched both of them, the boss lady and the cook, praying that the cook would spit again. She did. The boss lady came into the kitchen and stared at Tillie, but she did not utter a word. She burst into tears and ran back into the dining room.

"What's happening here?" Tillie demanded.

No one answered. The boss lady came out and tossed Tillie her hat, coat, and money.

"Now, get out of here, you dirty dog!" she said.

Tillie stared, then slowly picked up her hat, coat, and the money; she stood a moment, wiped sweat from her forehead with her hand, then spat—this time on the floor. She left.

Nobody was ever able to fathom why Tillie liked to spit into the food.

Brooding over Tillie, I recalled the time when the boss man in Mississippi had come to me and had tossed my wages to me and said:

"Get out, nigger! I don't like your looks."

And I wondered if a Negro who did not smile and grin was as morally loathsome to whites as a cook who spat into the food.

The following summer I was called for temporary duty in the post office, and the work lasted into the winter. Aunt Cleo succumbed to a severe cardiac condition and, hard on the heels of her illness, my brother developed stomach ulcers. To rush my worries to a climax, my mother also became ill. I felt that I was maintaining a private hospital. Finally, the post-office work ceased altogether and I haunted the city for jobs. But when I went into the streets in the morning I saw sights that killed my hope for the rest of the day. Unemployed men loitered in doorways with blank looks in their eyes, sat dejectedly on front steps in shabby clothing, congregated in sullen groups on street corners, and filled all the empty benches in the parks of Chicago's South Side.

Luck of a sort came when a distant cousin of mine, who was a superintendent for a Negro burial society, offered me a position on his staff as an agent. The thought of selling insurance polices to ignorant Negroes disgusted me.

"Well, if you don't sell them, somebody else will," my cousin told me. "You've got to eat, haven't you?"

During that year I worked for several burial and insurance societies that operated among Negroes, and I received a new kind of education. I found that the burial societies, with some exceptions, were mostly "rackets." Some of them conducted their business legitimately, but there were many that exploited the ignorance of their black customers.

I was paid under a system that netted me fifteen dollars for every dollar's worth of new premiums that I placed upon the company's books, and for every dollar's worth of old premiums that lapsed I was penalized fifteen dollars. In addition, I was paid a commission of ten per cent on total premiums collected, but during the Depression it was extremely difficult to persuade a black family to buy a policy carrying even a dime premium. I considered myself lucky if, after subtracting lapses from new business, there remained fifteen dollars that I could call my own.

This "gambling" method of remuneration was practiced by some of the burial companies because of the tremendous "turnover" in policyholders, and the companies had to have a constant stream of new business to keep afloat. Whenever a black family moved or suffered a slight reverse in fortune, it usually let its policy lapse and later bought another policy from some other company.

Each day now I saw how the Negro in Chicago lived, for I visited hundreds of dingy flats filled with rickety furniture and ill-clad children. Most of the policyholders were illiterate and did not know that their policies carried clauses severely restricting their benefit payments, and, as an insurance agent, it was not my duty to tell them.

After tramping the streets and pounding on doors to collect premiums, I was dry, strained, too tired to read or write. I hungered for relief and, as a salesman in insurance to many young black girls, I found it. There were many comely black housewives who, trying desperately to keep up their insurance payments, were willing to make bargains to escape paying a ten-cent premium. I had a long, tortured affair with one girl by paying her ten-cent premium each week. She was an illiterate black child with a baby whose father she did not know. During the entire period of my relationship with her, she had but one demand to make of me: she wanted me to take her to a circus. Just what significance circuses had for her, I was never able to learn.

After I had been with her one morning—in exchange for the dime premium—I sat on the sofa in the front room and began to read a book I had with me. She came over shyly.

"Lemme see that," she said.

"What?" I asked.

"That book," she said.

I gave her the book; she looked at it intently. I saw that she was holding it upside down.

"What's in here you keep reading?" she asked.

"Can't you really read?" I asked.

"Naw," she giggled. "You know I can't read."

"You can read *some*," I said.

"Naw," she said.

I stared at her and wondered just what a life like hers meant in the scheme of things, and I came to the conclusion that it meant absolutely nothing. And neither did my life mean anything.

"How come you looking at me that way for?"

"Nothing."

"You don't talk much."

"There isn't much to say."

"I wished Jim was here," she sighed.

"Who's Jim?" I asked, jealous. I knew that she had other men, but I resented her mentioning them in my presence.

"Just a friend," she said.

I hated her then, then hated myself for coming to her.

"Do you like Jim better than you like me?" I asked.

"Naw. Jim just likes to talk."

"Then why do you be with me, if you like Jim better?" I asked, trying to make an issue and feeling a wave of disgust because I wanted to.

"You all right," she said, giggling. "I like you."

"I could kill you," I said.

"What?" she exclaimed.

"Nothing," I said, ashamed.

"Kill me, you said? You crazy, man," she said.

"Maybe I am," I muttered, angry that I was sitting beside a human being to whom I could not talk, angry with myself for coming to her, hating my wild and restless loneliness.

"You oughta go home and sleep," she said. "You tired."

"What do you ever think about?" I demanded harshly.

"Lotta things."

"What, for example?"

"You," she said, smiling.

"You know I mean just one dime to you each week," I said.

"Naw, I thinka lotta you."

"Then what do you think?"

" 'Bout how you talk when you talk. I wished I could talk like you," she said seriously.

"Why?" I taunted her.

"When you gonna take me to a circus?" she demanded suddenly.

"You ought to be in a circus," I said.

"I'd like it," she said, her eyes shining.

I wanted to laugh, but her words sounded so sincere that I could not.

"There's no circus in town," I said.

"I bet there is and you won't tell me 'cause you don't wanna take me," she said, pouting.

"But there's no circus in town, I tell you!"

"When will one come?"

"I don't know."

"Can't you read it in the papers?" she asked.

"There's nothing in the papers about a circus."

"There is," she said. "If I could read, I'd find it."

I laughed, and she was hurt.

"There *is* a circus in town," she said stoutly.

"There's no circus in town," I said. "But if you want to learn to read, then I'll teach you."

She nestled at my side, giggling.

"See that word?" I said, pointing.

"Yeah."

"That's an 'and,' " I said.

She doubled, giggling.

"What's the matter?" I asked.

She rolled on the floor, giggling.

"What's so funny?" I demanded.

"You," she giggled. "You so funny."

I rose.

"The hell with you," I said.

"Don't you go and cuss me now," she said. "I don't cuss you."

"I'm sorry," I said.

I got my hat and went to the door.

"I'll see you next week?" she asked.

"Maybe," I said.

When I was on the sidewalk, she called to me from a window.

"You promised to take me to a circus, remember?"

"Yes." I walked close to the window. "What is it you like about a circus?"

"The animals," she said simply.

I felt that there was a hidden meaning, perhaps, in what she had said, but I could not find it. She laughed and slammed the window shut.

Each time I left her I resolved not to visit her again. I could not talk to her; I merely listened to her passionate desire to see a circus. She was not calculating; if she liked a man, she just liked him. Sex relations were the only relations she had ever had; no others were possible with her, so limited was her intelligence.

Most of the other agents also had their bought girls and they were extremely anxious to keep other agents from tampering with them. One day a new section of the South Side was given to me as a part of my collection area, and the agent from whom the territory had been taken suddenly became very friendly with me.

"Say, Wright," he asked, "did you collect from Ewing on Champlain Avenue yet?"

"Yes," I answered, after consulting my book.

"How did you like her?" he asked, staring at me.

"She's a good-looking number," I said.

"You had anything to do with her yet?" he asked.

"No, but I'd like to," I said laughing.

"Look," he said. "I'm a friend of yours."

"Since when?" I countered.

"No, I'm really a friend," he said.

"What's on your mind?"

"Listen, that gal's sick," he said seriously.

"What do you mean?"

"She's got the clap," he said. "Keep away from her. She'll lay with anybody."

"Gee, I'm glad you told me," I said.

"You had your eye on her, didn't you?" he asked.

"Yes, I did," I said.

"Leave her alone," he said. "She'll get you down."

That night I told my cousin what the agent had said about Miss Ewing. My cousin laughed.

"That gal's all right," he said. "That agent's been fooling around with her. He told you she had a disease so that you'd be scared to bother her. He was protecting her from you."

That was the way the black women were regarded by the black agents. Some of the agents were vicious; if they had claims to pay to a sick black woman and if the woman was able to have sex relations with them, they would insist upon it, using the claims money as a bribe. If the woman refused, they would report to the office that the woman was a malingerer. The average black woman would submit because she needed the money badly.

As an insurance agent, it was necessary for me to take part in one swindle. It appears that the burial society had originally issued a policy that was—from their point of view—too liberal in its provisions, and the officials decided to exchange the policies then in the hands of their clients for other policies carrying stricter clauses. Of course, this had to be done in a manner that would not allow the policyholder to know that his policy was being switched—that he was being swindled. I did not like it, but there was only one thing I could do to keep from being a party to it: I could quit and starve. But I did not feel that being honest was worth the price of starvation.

The swindle worked in this way. In my visits to the homes of the policyholders to collect premiums, I was accompanied by the superintendent who claimed to the policyholder that he was making a routine inspection. The policyholder, usually an illiterate black woman, would dig up her policy from the bottom of a trunk or chest and hand it to the superintendent. Meanwhile I would be marking the woman's premium book, an act which would distract her from what the superintendent was doing. The superintendent would exchange the old policy for a new one which was identical in color, serial number, and beneficiary, but which carried smaller payments. It was dirty work and I wondered how I could stop it. And when I could think of no safe way I would curse myself and the victims and forget about it. (The black owners of the burial societies were leaders in the Negro communities and were respected by whites.)

When I reached the relief station, I felt that I was making a public confession of my hunger. I sat waiting for hours, resentful of the mass of hungry people about me. My turn finally came and I was questioned by a middle-class Negro woman who asked me for a short history of my life. As I waited, I became aware of something happening in the room. The black men and women were mumbling quietly among themselves; they had not known one another before they had come here, but now their timidity and shame were wearing off and they were exchanging experiences. Before this they had lived as individuals, each somewhat afraid of the other, each seeking his own pleasure, each stanch in that degree of Americanism that had been allowed him. But now life had tossed them together, and they were learning to know the sentiments of their neighbors for the first time; their talking was enabling them to sense the collectivity of their lives, and some of their fear was passing.

Did the relief officials realize what was happening? No. If they had, they would have stopped it. But they saw their "clients" through the eyes of their profession, saw only what their "science" allowed them to see. As I listened to the talk, I could see black minds shedding many illusions. These people now knew that the past had betrayed them, had cast them out; but they did not know what the future would be like, did not know what they wanted. Yes, some of the things that the Communists said were true; they maintained that there came times in history when a ruling class could no longer rule. And now I sat looking at the beginnings of anarchy. To permit the birth of this new consciousness in these people was proof that those who ruled did not quite know what they were doing, assuming that they were trying to save themselves and their class. Had they understood what was happening, they would never have allowed millions of perplexed and defeated people to sit together for long hours and talk, for out of their talk was rising a new realization of life. And once this new conception of themselves had formed, no power on earth could alter it.

I left the relief station with the promise that food would be sent to me, but I also left with a knowledge that the relief officials had not wanted to give to me. I had felt the possibility of creating a new understanding of life in the minds of people rejected by the society in which they lived, people to whom the Chicago *Tribune* referred contemptuously as the "idle" ones, as though these people had deliberately sought their present state of helplessness.

Who would give these people a meaningful way of life? Communist theory defined these people as the molders of the future of mankind, but the Communist speeches I had heard in the park had mocked that definition. These people, of course, were not ready for a revolution; they had not abandoned their past lives by choice, but because they simply could not live the old way any longer. Now, what new faith would they embrace? The day I begged bread from the city officials was the day that showed me I was not alone in my loneliness; society had cast millions of others with me. But how could I be with them? How many understood what was happening? My mind swam with questions that I could not answer.

I was slowly beginning to comprehend the meaning of my environment; a sense of direction was beginning to emerge from the conditions of my life. I began to feel something more powerful than I could express. My speech and manner changed. My cynicism slid from me. I grew open and questioning. I wanted to know.

If I were a member of the class that rules, I would post men in all the neighborhoods of the nation, not to spy upon or club rebellious workers, not to break strikes or disrupt unions, but to ferret out those who no longer respond to the system under which they live. I would make it known that the real danger does not stem from those who seek to grab their share of wealth through force, or from those who try to defend their property through violence, for both of these groups, by their affirmative acts, support the values of the system under which they live. The millions that I would fear are those who do not dream of the prizes that the nation holds forth, for it is in them, though they may not know it, that a revolution has taken place and is biding its time to translate itself into a new and strange way of life.

I feel that the Negroes' relation to America is symbolically peculiar, and from the Negroes' ultimate reactions to their trapped state a lesson can be learned about America's future. Negroes are told in a language they cannot possibly misunderstand that their native land is not their own; and when, acting upon impulses which they share with whites, they try to assert a claim to their birthright, whites retaliate with terror, never pausing to consider the consequences should the Negroes give up completely. The whites never dream that they would face a situation far more terrifying if they were confronted by Negroes who made no claims at all than by those who are buoyed up by social aggressiveness.

My knowledge of how Negroes react to their plight makes me declare than no man can possibly be individually guilty of treason, that an insurgent act is but a man's desperate answer to those who twist his environment so that he cannot fully share the spirit of his native land. Treason is a crime of the State.

Christmas came and I was once more called to the post office for temporary work. This time I met many young white men and we discussed world happenings, the vast armies of unemployed, the rising tide of radical action. I now detected a change in the attitudes of the whites I met; their privations were making them regard Negroes with new eyes, and, for the first time, I was invited to their homes.

When the work in the post office ended, I was assigned by the relief system as an orderly to a medical research institute in one of the largest and wealthiest hospitals in Chicago. I cleaned operating rooms, dog, rat, mice, cat, and rabbit pens, and fed guinea pigs. Four of us Negroes worked there and we occupied an underworld position, remembering that we must restrict ourselves—when not engaged upon some task—to the basement corridors, so that we would not mingle with white nurses, doctors, or visitors.

The sharp line of racial division drawn by the hospital authorities came to me the first morning when I walked along an underground corridor and saw two long lines of women coming toward me. A line of white girls marched past, clad in starched uniforms that gleamed white; their faces were alert, their step quick, their bodies lean and shapely, their shoulders erect, their faces lit with the light of purpose. And after them came a line of black girls, old, fat, dressed in ragged gingham, walking loosely, carrying tin cans of soap powder, rags, mops, brooms . . . I wondered what law of the universe kept them from being mixed? The sun would not have stopped shining had there been a few black girls in the first line, and the earth would not have stopped whirling on its axis had there been a few white girls in the second line. But the two lines I saw graded social status in purely racial terms.

Of the three Negroes who worked with me, one was a boy about my own age, Bill, who was either sleepy or drunk most of the time. Bill straightened his hair and I suspected that he kept a bottle hidden somewhere in the piles of hay which we fed to the guinea pigs. He did not like me and I did not like him, though I tried harder than he to conceal my dislike. We had nothing in common except that we were both black and lost. While I contained my frustration, he drank to drown his. Often I tried to talk to him, tried in simple words to convey to him some of my ideas, and he would listen in sullen silence. Then one day he came to me with an angry look on his face.

"I got it," he said.

"You've got what?" I asked.

"This old race problem you keep talking about," he said.

"What about it?"

"Well, it's this way," he explained seriously. "Let the government give every man a gun and five bullets, then let us all start over again. Make it just like it was in the beginning. The ones who come out on top, white or black, let them rule."

His simplicity terrified me. I had never met a Negro who was so irredeemably brutalized. I stopped pumping my ideas into Bill's brain for fear that the fumes of alcohol might send him reeling toward some fantastic fate.

The two other Negroes were elderly and had been employed in the institute for fifteen years or more. One was Brand, a short, black, morose bachelor; the other was Cooke, a tall, yellow, spectacled fellow who spent his spare time keeping track of world events through the Chicago *Tribune*. Brand and Cooke hated each other for a reason that I was never able to determine, and they spent a good part of each day quarreling.

When I began working at the institute, I recalled my adolescent dream of wanting to be a medical research worker. Daily I saw young Jewish boys and girls receiving instruction in chemistry and medicine that the average black boy or girl could never receive. When I was alone, I wandered and poked my fingers into strange chemicals, watched intricate machines trace red and black lines on ruled paper. At times I paused and stared at the walls of the rooms, at the floor, at the wide desks at which the white doctors sat; and I realized—with a feeling that I could never quite get used to—that I was looking at the world of another race.

My interest in what was happening in the institute amused

the three other Negroes with whom I worked. They had no curiosity about "white folks' things," while I wanted to know if the dogs being treated for diabetes were getting well; if the rats and mice in which cancer had been induced showed any signs of responding to treatment. I wanted to know the principle that lay behind the Aschheim-Zondek tests that were made with rabbits, the Wassermann tests that were made with guinea pigs. But when I asked a timid question I found that even Jewish doctors had learned to imitate the sadistic method of humbling a Negro that the others had cultivated.

"If you know too much, boy, your brains might explode," a doctor said one day.

Each Saturday morning I assisted a young Jewish doctor in slitting the vocal cords of a fresh batch of dogs from the city pound. The object was to devocalize the dogs so that their howls would not disturb the patients in the other parts of the hospital. I held each dog as the doctor injected Nembutal into its veins to make it unconscious; then I held the dog's jaws open as the doctor inserted the scalpel and severed the vocal cords. Later, when the dogs came to, they would lift their heads to the ceiling and gape in a soundless wail. The sight became lodged in my imagination as a symbol of silent suffering.

To me Nembutal was a powerful and mysterious liquid, but when I asked questions about its properties I could not obtain a single intelligent answer. The doctor simply ignored me with:

"Come on. Bring me the next dog. I haven't got all day."

One Saturday morning, after I had held the dogs for their vocal cords to be slit, the doctor left the Nembutal on a bench. I picked it up, uncorked it, and smelled it. It was odorless. Suddenly Brand ran to me with a stricken face.

"What're you doing?" he asked.

"I was smelling this stuff to see if it had any odor," I said.

"Did you really smell it?" he asked me.

"Yes."

"Oh, God!" he exclaimed.

"What's the matter?" I asked.

"You shouldn't've done that!" he shouted.

"Why?"

He grabbed my arm and jerked me across the room.

"Come on!" he yelled, snatching open the door.

"What's the matter?" I asked.

"I gotta get you to a doctor 'fore it's too late," he gasped.

Had my foolish curiosity made me inhale something danger-ous?

"But— Is it poisonous?"

"Run, boy!" he said, pulling me. "You'll fall dead."

Filled with fear, with Brand pulling my arm, I rushed out of the room, raced across a rear areaway, into another room, then down a long corridor. I wanted to ask Brand what symptoms I must expect, but we were running too fast. Brand finally stopped, gasping for breath. My heart beat wildly and my blood pounded in my head. Brand then dropped to the concrete floor, stretched out on his back, and yelled with laughter, shaking all over. He beat his fists against the concrete; he moaned, giggled, he kicked.

I tried to master my outrage, wondering if some of the white doctors had told him to play the joke. He rose and wiped tears from his eyes, still laughing. I walked away from him. He knew that I was angry and he followed me.

"Don't get mad," he gasped through his laughter.

"Go to hell," I said.

"I couldn't help it," he giggled. "You looked at me like you'd believe anything I said. Man, you was scared."

He leaned against the wall, laughing again, stomping his feet. I was angry, for I felt that he would spread the story. I knew that Bill and Cooke never ventured beyond the safe bounds of Negro living, and they would never blunder into anything like this. And if they heard about this, they would laugh for months.

"Brand, if you mention this, I'll kill you," I swore.

"You ain't mad?" he asked, laughing, staring at me through tears.

Sniffing, Brand walked ahead of me. I followed him back into the room that housed the dogs. All day, while at some task, he would pause and giggle, then smother the giggling with his hand, looking at me out of the corner of his eyes, shaking his head. He laughed at me for a week. I kept my temper and let him amuse himself. I finally found out the properties of Nembutal by consulting medical books; but I never told Brand.

One summer morning, just as I began work, a young Jewish boy came to me with a stop watch in his hand.

"Dr. ———— wants me to time you when you clean a room," he said. "We're trying to make the institute more efficient."

"I'm doing my work, and getting through on time," I said.

"This is the boss's order," he said.

"Why don't you work for a change?" I blurted, angry.

"Now, look," he said. "*This* is my work. Now *you* work."

I got a mop and pail, sprayed a room with disinfectant, and scrubbed at coagulated blood and hardened dog, rat, and rabbit feces. The normal temperature of a room was ninety, but, as the sun beat down upon the skylights, the temperature rose above a hundred. Stripped to my waist, I slung the mop, moving steadily like a machine, hearing the boy press the button on the stop watch as I finished cleaning a room.

"Well, how is it?" I asked.

"It took you seventeen minutes to clean that last room," he said. "That ought to be the time for each room."

"But that room was not very dirty," I said.

"You have seventeen rooms to clean," he went on as though I had not spoken. "Seventeen times seventeen make four hours and forty-nine minutes." He wrote upon a little pad. "After lunch, clean the five flights of stone stairs. I timed a boy who scrubbed one step and multiplied that time by the number of steps. You ought to be through by six."

"Suppose I want relief?" I asked.

"You'll manage," he said and left.

Never had I felt so much the slave as when I scoured those stone steps each afternoon. Working against time, I would wet five steps, sprinkle soap powder, and then a white doctor or a nurse would come along and, instead of avoiding the soapy steps, would walk on them and track the dirty water onto the steps that I had already cleaned. To obviate this, I cleaned but two steps at a time, a distance over which a ten-year-old child could step. But it did no good. The white people still plopped their feet down into the dirty water and muddied the other clean steps. If I ever really hotly hated unthinking whites, it was then. Not once during my entire stay at the institute did a single white person show enough courtesy to avoid a wet step. I would be on my knees, scrubbing, sweating, pouring out what limited energy my body could wring from my meager diet, and I would hear feet approaching. I would pause and curse with tense lips:

"These sonofabitches are going to dirty these steps again, goddamn their souls to hell!"

Sometimes a sadistically observant white man would notice that he had tracked dirty water up the steps, and he would look back down at me and smile and say:

"Boy, we sure keep you busy, don't we?"

And I would not be able to answer.

The feud that went on between Brand and Cooke continued. Although they were working daily in a building where scientific history was being made, the light of curiosity was never in their eyes. They were conditioned to their racial "place," had learned to see only a part of the whites and the white world; and the whites, too, had learned to see only a part of the lives of the blacks and their world.

Perhaps Brand and Cooke, lacking interests that could absorb them, fuming like children over trifles, simply invented their hate of each other in order to have something to feel deeply about. Or perhaps there was in them a vague tension stemming from their chronically frustrating way of life, a pain whose cause they did not know; and, like those devocalized dogs, they would whirl and snap at the air when their old pain struck them. Anyway, they argued about the weather, sports, sex, war, race, politics, and religion; neither of them knew much about the subjects they debated, but it seemed that the less they knew the better they could argue.

The tug of war between the two elderly men reached a climax one winter day at noon. It was incredibly cold and an icy gale swept up and down the Chicago streets with blizzard force. The door of the animal-filled room was locked, for we always insisted that we be allowed one hour in which to eat and rest. Bill and I were sitting on wooden boxes, eating our lunches out of paper bags. Brand was washing his hands at the sink. Cooke was sitting on a rickety stool, munching an apple and reading the Chicago *Tribune*.

Now and then a devocalized dog lifted his nose to the ceiling and howled soundlessly. The room was filled with many rows of high steel tiers. Perched upon each of these tiers were layers of steel cages containing the dogs, rats, mice, rabbits, and guinea pigs. Each cage was labeled in some indecipherable scientific jargon. Along the walls of the room were long charts with zigzagging red and black lines that traced the success or failure of some experiment. The lonely piping of guinea pigs floated unheeded about us. Hay rustled as a rabbit leaped restlessly about in its pen. A rat scampered around in its steel prison. Cooke tapped the newspaper for attention.

"It says here," Cooke mumbled through a mouthful of apple, "that this is the coldest day since 1888."

Bill and I sat unconcerned. Brand chuckled softly.

"What in hell you laughing about?" Cooke demanded of Brand.

"You can't believe what that damn *Tribune* says," Brand said.

"How come I can't?" Cooke demanded. "It's the world's greatest newspaper."

Brand did not reply; he shook his head pityingly and chuckled again.

"Stop that damn laughing at me!" Cooke said angrily.

"I laugh as much as I wanna," Brand said. "You don't know what you talking about. The *Herald-Examiner* says it's the coldest day since 1873."

"But the *Trib* oughta know," Cooke countered. "It's older'n that *Examiner*."

"That damn *Trib* don't know nothing!" Brand drowned out Cooke's voice.

"How in hell you know?" Cooke asked with rising anger.

The argument waxed until Cooke shouted that if Brand did not shut up he was going to "cut his black throat."

Brand whirled from the sink, his hands dripping soapy water, his eyes blazing.

"Take that back," Brand said.

"I take nothing back! What you wanna do about it?" Cooke taunted.

The two elderly Negroes glared at each other. I wondered if the quarrel was really serious, or if it would turn out harmlessly as so many others had done.

Suddenly Cooke dropped the Chicago *Tribune* and pulled a long knife from his pocket; his thumb pressed a button and a gleaming steel blade leaped out. Brand stepped back quickly and seized an ice pick that was stuck in a wooden board above the sink.

"Put that knife down," Brand said.

"Stay 'way from me, or I'll cut your throat," Cooke warned.

Brand lunged with the ice pick. Cooke dodged out of range. They circled each other like fighters in a prize ring. The cancerous and tubercular rats and mice leaped about in their cages. The guinea pigs whistled in fright. The diabetic dogs bared their teeth and barked soundlessly in our direction. The Aschheim-Zondek rabbits flopped their ears and tried to hide in the corners of their pens. Cooke now crouched and sprang forward with the knife. Bill and I jumped to our feet, speechless with surprise. Brand retreated. The eyes of both men were hard and unblinking; they were breathing deeply.

"Say, cut it out!" I called in alarm.

"Them damn fools is really fighting," Bill said in amazement.

Slashing at each other, Brand and Cooke surged up and down the aisles of steel tiers. Suddenly Brand uttered a bellow and charged into Cooke and swept him violently backward. Cooke grasped Brand's hand to keep the ice pick from sinking into his chest. Brand broke free and charged Cooke again, sweeping him into an animal-filled steel tier. The tier balanced itself on its edge for an indecisive moment, then toppled.

Like kingpins, one steel tier lammed into another, then they all crashed to the floor with a sound as of the roof falling. The whole aspect of the room altered quicker than the eye could follow. Brand and Cooke stood stock-still, their eyes fastened upon each other, their pointed weapons raised; but they were dimly aware of the havoc that churned about them.

The steel tiers lay jumbled; the doors of the cages swung open. Rats and mice and dogs and rabbits moved over the floor in wild panic. The Wassermann guinea pigs were squealing as though judgment day had come. Here and there an animal had been crushed beneath a cage.

All four of us looked at one another. We knew what this meant. We might lose our jobs. We were already regarded as black dunces; and if the doctors saw this mess they would take it as final proof. Bill rushed to the door to make sure that it was locked. I glanced at the clock and saw that it was 12:30. We had one half-hour of grace.

"Come on," Bill said uneasily. "We got to get this place cleaned."

Brand and Cooke stared at each other, both doubting.

"Give me your knife, Cooke," I said.

"Naw! Take Brand's ice pick *first*," Cooke said.

"The hell you say!" Brand said. "Take his knife *first!*"

A knock sounded at the door.

"Sssssh," Bill said.

We waited. We heard footsteps going away. We'll all lose our jobs, I thought.

Persuading the fighters to surrender their weapons was a difficult task, but at last it was done and we could begin to set things right. Slowly Brand stooped and tugged at one end of a steel tier. Cooke stooped to help him. Both men seemed to be acting in a dream. Soon, however, all four of us were working frantically, watching the clock.

As we labored we conspired to keep the fight a secret; we agreed to tell the doctors—if any should ask—that we had not been in the room during our lunch hour; we felt that that lie would explain why no one had unlocked the door when the knock had come.

We righted the tiers and replaced the cages; then we were faced with the impossible task of sorting the cancerous rats and mice, the diabetic dogs, the Aschheim-Zondek rabbits, and the Wassermann guinea pigs. Whether we kept our jobs or not depended up how shrewdly we could cover up all evidence of the fight. It was pure guesswork, but we had to try to put the animals back into the correct cages. We knew that certain rats or mice went into certain cages, but we did not know *what* rat or mouse went into *what* cage. We did not know a tubercular mouse from a cancerous mouse—the white doctors had made sure that we would not know. They had never taken time to answer a single question; though we worked in the institute, we were as remote from the meaning of the experiments as if we lived in the moon. The doctors had laughed at what they felt was our childlike interest in the fate of the animals.

First we sorted the dogs; that was fairly easy, for we could remember the size and color of most of them. But the rats and mice and guinea pigs baffled us completely.

We put our heads together and pondered, down in the underworld of the great scientific institute. It was a strange scientific conference; the fate of the entire medical research institute rested in our ignorant, black hands.

We remembered the number of rats, mice, or guinea pigs—we had to handle them several times a day—that went into a given cage, and we supplied the number helter-skelter from those animals that we could catch running loose on the floor. We discovered that many rats, mice, and guinea pigs were missing—they had been killed in the scuffle. We solved that problem by taking healthy stock from other cages and putting them into cages with sick animals. We repeated this process until we were certain that, numerically at least, all the animals with which the doctors were experimenting were accounted for.

The rabbits came last. We broke the rabbits down into two general groups; those that had fur on their bellies and those that did not. We knew that all those rabbits that had shaven bellies— our scientific knowledge adequately covered this point because it was our job to shave the rabbits—were undergoing the Aschheim-Zondek tests. But in what pen did a given rabbit belong? We did not know. I solved the problem very simply. I counted the shaven rabbits; they numbered seventeen. I counted the pens labeled "Aschheim-Zondek," then proceeded to drop a shaven rabbit into each pen at random. And again we were numerically successful. At least white America had taught us how to count. . . .

Lastly we carefully wrapped all the dead animals in newspapers and hid their bodies in a garbage can.

At a few minutes to one the room was in order; that is, the kind of order that we four Negroes could figure out. I unlocked the door and we sat waiting, whispering, vowing secrecy, wondering what the reaction of the doctors would be.

Finally a doctor came, gray-haired, white-coated, spectacled, efficient, serious, taciturn, bearing a tray upon which sat a bottle of mysterious fluid and a hypodermic needle.

"My rats, please."

Cooke shuffled forward to serve him. We held our breath. Cooke got the cage which he knew the doctor always called for at that hour and brought it forward. One by one, Cooke took out the rats and held them as the doctor solemnly injected the mysterious fluid under their skins.

"Thank you, Cooke," the doctor murmured.

"Not at all, sir," Cooke mumbled with a suppressed gasp.

When the doctor had gone we looked at one another, hardly daring to believe that our secret would be kept. We were so anxious that we did not know whether to curse or laugh. Another doctor came.

"Give me A-Z rabbit number 14."

"Yes, sir," I said.

I brought him the rabbit and he took it upstairs to the operating room. We waited for repercussions. None came.

All that afternoon the doctors came and went. I would run into the room—stealing a few seconds from my step-scrubbing—and ask what progress was being made and would learn that the doctors had detected nothing. At quitting time we felt triumphant.

"They won't ever know," Cooke boasted in a whisper.

I saw Brand stiffen. I knew that he was aching to dispute Cooke's optimism, but the memory of the fight he had just had was so fresh in his mind that he could not speak.

Another day went by and nothing happened. Then another day. The doctors examined the animals and wrote in their little black books, in their big black books, and continued to trace red and black lines upon the charts.

A week passed and we felt out of danger. Not one question had been asked.

Of course, we four black men were much too modest to make our contribution known, but we often wondered what went on in the laboratories after that secret disaster. Was some scientific hypothesis, well on its way to validation and ultimate public use, discarded because of unexpected findings on that cold winter day? Was some tested principle given a new and strange refinement because of fresh, remarkable evidence? Did some brooding research worker—those who held stop watches and slopped their feet carelessly in the water of the steps I tried so hard to keep clean—get a wild, if brief, glimpse of a new scientific truth? Well, we never heard . . .

I brooded upon whether I should have gone to the director's office and told him what had happened, but each time I thought of it I remembered that the director had been the man who had ordered the boy to stand over me while I was working and time my movements with a stop watch. He did not regard me as a human being. I did not share his world. I earned thirteen dollars a week and I had to support four people with it, and should I risk that thirteen dollars by acting idealistically? Brand and Cooke would have hated me and would have eventually driven me from the job had I "told" on them. The hospital kept us four Negroes as though we were close kin to the animals we tended, huddled together down in the underworld corridors of the hospital, separated by a vast psychological distance from the significant processes of the rest of the hospital—just as America had kept us locked in the dark underworld of American life for three hundred years—and we had made our own code of ethics, values, loyalty.

EUDORA WELTY

(1909-)

The daughter of an insurance-company president, Eudora Welty was born in Jackson, Mississippi, where she has spent most of her life. She attended Mississippi State College for Women for a year, received a B.A. from the University of Wisconsin, and spent another year at Columbia University's School of Advertising. She received a Guggenheim fellowship in 1942 and in 1955 was awarded the William Dean Howells medal of the American Academy of Arts and Sciences for The Ponder Heart, a comic monologue on small-town Mississippi life. Having published her first works in little magazines such as Manuscript and Southern Review, she was soon writing for Atlantic Monthly, Harper's Bazaar, and The New Yorker. Her collections of short stories include A Curtain of Green (1941), The Wide Net (1943), The Golden Apples (1949), and The Bride of the Innisfallen (1955). Her novels are The Robber Bridegroom (1942), Delta Wedding (1946), and The Ponder Heart (1954).

Many critics have noted the paradoxical combination in her work of structural simplicity and stylistic precision on the one hand with an element of myth or fantasy on the other. Alun R. Jones praises Miss Welty's exceptional ability to sustain a mood, and he notes that she is always aware of "mythical and imaginative reality impinging on and informing the trivial and the banal." Katherine

Anne Porter describes "A Worn Path" as the kind of story in which "external act and the internal voiceless life of the human imagination almost meet and mingle on the mysterious threshold between dream and waking, one reality refusing to admit or confirm the existence of the other, yet both conspiring toward the same end."

Despite her upper-middle-class Mississippi background, Miss Welty consistently stresses the individual humanity of her black characters. John Edward Hardy writes, "As clearly as any other white American author, including among the others Twain and Faulkner, she has penetrated the clichés of social stereotype in the creation of her Negro characters. She is intensely aware of the clichés, and often deliberately sets them up as a foil to the final, intuitive recognition of the human person." Of "A Worn Path" Hardy declares, "There is nowhere in modern literature a more scathing indictment of the fool's pride of the white man in the superiority of his civilization, of his fool's confidence in the virtue of the 'soothing medicine' he offers to heal the hurts of that 'stubborn case,' black mankind."

A Worn Path

It was December—a bright frozen day in the early morning. Far out in the country there was an old Negro woman with her head tied in a red rag, coming along a path through the pinewoods. Her name was Phoenix Jackson. She was very old and small and she walked slowly in the dark pine shadows, moving a little from side to side in her steps, with the balanced heaviness and lightness of a pendulum in a grandfather clock. She carried a thin, small cane made from an umbrella, and with this she kept tapping the frozen earth in front of her. This made a grave and persistent noise in the still air, that seemed meditative like the chirping of a solitary little bird.

She wore a dark striped dress reaching down to her shoe tops, and an equally long apron of bleached sugar sacks, with a full pocket: all neat and tidy, but every time she took a step she might have fallen over her shoelaces, which dragged from her unlaced shoes. She looked straight ahead. Her eyes were blue with age. Her skin had a pattern all its own of numberless branching wrinkles and as though a whole little tree stood in the middle of her forehead, but a golden color ran underneath, and the two knobs of her cheeks were illumined by a yellow burning under the dark. Under the red rag her hair came down on her neck in the frailest of ringlets, still black, and with an odor like copper.

Now and then there was a quivering in the thicket. Old Phoenix said, "Out of my way, all you foxes, owls, beetles, jack rabbits, coons and wild animals! . . . Keep out from under these feet, little bobwhites. . . . Keep the big wild hogs out of my path. Don't let none of those come running my direction. I got a long way." Under her small black-freckled hand her cane, limber as a buggy whip, would switch at the brush as if to rouse up any hiding things.

On she went. The woods were deep and still. The sun made the pine needles almost too bright to look at, up where the wind rocked. The cones dropped as light as feathers. Down in the hollow was the mourning dove—it was not too late for him.

The path ran up a hill. "Seem like there is chains about my feet, time I get this far," she said, in the voice of argument old people keep to use with themselves. "Something always take a hold of me on this hill—pleads I should stay."

After she got to the top she turned and gave a full, severe look behind her where she had come. "Up through pines," she said at length. "Now down through oaks."

Her eyes opened their widest, and she started down gently. But before she got to the bottom of the hill a bush caught her dress.

Her fingers were busy and intent, but her skirts were full and long, so that before she could pull them free in one place they were caught in another. It was not possible to allow the dress to tear. "I in the thorny bush," she said. "Thorns, you doing your appointed work. Never want to let folks pass, no sir. Old eyes thought you was a pretty little *green* bush."

Finally, trembling all over, she stood free, and after a moment dared to stoop for her cane.

"Sun so high!" she cried, leaning back and looking, while the thick tears went over her eyes. "The time getting all gone here."

At the foot of this hill was a place where a log was laid across the creek.

"Now comes the trial," said Phoenix.

Putting her right foot out, she mounted the log and shut her eyes. Lifting her skirt, leveling her cane fiercely before her, like a festival figure in some parade, she began to march across. Then she opened her eyes and she was safe on the other side.

"I wasn't as old as I thought," she said.

But she sat down to rest. She spread her skirts on the bank around her and folded her hands over her knees. Up above her was a tree in a pearly cloud of mistletoe. She did not dare to close her eyes, and when a little boy brought her a plate with a slice of marble-cake on it she spoke to him. "That would be acceptable," she said. But when she went to take it there was just her own hand in the air.

So she left that tree, and had to go through a barbed-wire fence. There she had to creep and crawl, spreading her knees and stretching her fingers like a baby trying to climb the steps. But she talked loudly to herself: she could not let her dress be torn now, so late in the day, and she could not pay for having her arm or her leg sawed off if she got caught fast where she was.

At last she was safe through the fence and risen up out in the clearing. Big dead trees, like black men with one arm, were standing in the purple stalks of the withered cotton field. There sat a buzzard.

"Who you watching?"

In the furrow she made her way along.

"Glad this not the season for bulls," she said, looking sideways, "and the good Lord made his snakes to curl up and sleep in the winter. A pleasure I don't see no two-headed snake coming around that tree, where it come once. It took a while to get by him, back in the summer."

She passed through the old cotton and went into a field of dead corn. It whispered and shook and was taller than her head. "Through the maze now," she said, for there was no path.

Then there was something tall, black, and skinny there, moving before her.

At first she took it for a man. It could have been a man dancing in the field. But she stood still and listened, and it did not make a sound. It was as silent as a ghost.

"Ghost," she said sharply, "who be you the ghost of? For I have heard of nary death close by."

But there was no answer—only the ragged dancing in the wind.

She shut her eyes, reached out her hand, and touched a sleeve. She found a coat and inside that an emptiness, cold as ice.

"You scarecrow," she said. Her face lighted. "I ought to be shut up for good," she said with laughter. "My senses is gone. I too old. I the oldest people I ever know. Dance, old scarecrow," she said, "while I dancing with you."

She kicked her foot over the furrow, and with mouth drawn down, shook her head once or twice in a little strutting way. Some husks blew down and whirled in streamers about her skirts.

Then she went on, parting her way from side to side with the cane, through the whispering field. At last she came to the end, to a wagon track where the silver grass blew between the red ruts. The quail were walking around like pullets, seeming all dainty and unseen.

"Walk pretty," she said. "This the easy place. This the easy going."

She followed the track, swaying through the quiet bare fields, through the little strings of trees silver in their dead leaves, past cabins silver from weather, with the doors and windows boarded shut, all like old women under a spell sitting there. "I walking in their sleep," she said, nodding her head vigorously.

In a ravine she went where a spring was silently flowing through a hollow log. Old Phoenix bent and drank. "Sweet-gum makes the water sweet," she said, and drank more. "Nobody know who made this well, for it was here when I was born."

The track crossed a swampy part where the moss hung as white as lace from every limb. "Sleep on, alligators, and blow your bubbles." Then the track went into the road.

Deep, deep the road went down between the high green-colored banks. Overhead the live-oaks met, and it was as dark as a cave.

A black dog with a lolling tongue came up out of the weeds by the ditch. She was meditating, and not ready, and when he came at her she only hit him a little with her cane. Over she went in the ditch, like a little puff of milkweed.

Down there, her senses drifted away. A dream visited her, and she reached her hand up, but nothing reached down and gave her a pull. So she lay there and presently went to talking. "Old woman," she said to herself, "that black dog come up out of the weeds to stall you off, and now there he sitting on his fine tail, smiling at you."

A white man finally came along and found her—a hunter, a young man, with his dog on a chain.

"Well, Granny!" he laughed. "What are you doing there?"

"Lying on my back like a June-bug waiting to be turned over, mister," she said, reaching up her hand.

He lifted her up, gave her a swing in the air, and set her down. "Anything broken, Granny?"

"No sir, them old dead weeds is springy enough," said Phoenix, when she had got her breath. "I thank you for your trouble."

"Where do you live, Granny?" he asked, while the two dogs were growling at each other.

"Away back yonder, sir, behind the ridge. You can't even see it from here."

"On your way home?"

"No sir, I going to town."

"Why, that's too far! That's as far as I walk when I come out myself, and I get something for my trouble." He patted the stuffed bag he carried, and there hung down a little closed claw. It was one of the bobwhites, with its beak hooked bitterly to show it was dead. "Now you go on home, Granny!"

"I bound to go to town, mister," said Phoenix. "The time come around."

He gave another laugh, filling the whole landscape. "I know you old colored people! Wouldn't miss going to town to see Santa Claus!"

But something held old Phoenix very still. The deep lines in her face went into a fierce and different radiation. Without warning, she had seen with her own eyes a flashing nickel fall out of the man's pocket onto the ground.

"How old are you, Granny?" he was saying.

"There is no telling, mister," she said, "no telling."

Then she gave a little cry and clapped her hands and said, "Git on away from here, dog! Look! Look at that dog!" She laughed as if in admiration. "He ain't scared of nobody. He a big black dog." She whispered, "Sic him!"

"Watch me get rid of that cur," said the man. "Sic him, Pete! Sic him!"

Phoenix heard the dogs fighting, and heard the man running and throwing sticks. She even heard a gunshot. But she was slowly bending forward by that time, further and further forward, the lids stretched down over her eyes, as if she were doing this in her sleep. Her chin was lowered almost to her knees. The yellow palm of her hand came out from the fold of her apron. Her fingers slid down and along the ground under the piece of money with the grace and care they would have in lifting an egg from under a setting hen. Then she slowly straightened up, she stood erect, and the nickel was in her apron pocket. A bird flew by. Her lips moved. "God watching me the whole time. I come to stealing."

The man came back, and his own dog panted about them. "Well, I scared him off that time," he said, and then he laughed and lifted his gun and pointed it at Phoenix.

She stood straight and faced him.

"Doesn't the gun scare you?" he said, still pointing it.

"No, sir, I seen plenty go off closer by, in my day, and for less than what I done," she said, holding utterly still.

He smiled, and shouldered the gun. "Well, Granny," he said, "you must be a hundred years old, and scared of nothing. I'd give you a dime if I had any money with me. But you take my advice and stay home, and nothing will happen to you."

"I bound to go on my way, mister," said Phoenix. She inclined her head in the red rag. Then they went in different directions, but she could hear the gun shooting again and again over the hill.

She walked on. The shadows hung from the oak trees to the

road like curtains. Then she smelled wood-smoke, and smelled the river, and she saw a steeple and the cabins on their steep steps. Dozens of little black children whirled around her. There ahead was Natchez shining. Bells were ringing. She walked on.

In the paved city it was Christmas time. There were red and green electric lights strung and crisscrossed everywhere, and all turned on in the daytime. Old Phoenix would have been lost if she had not distrusted her eyesight and depended on her feet to know where to take her.

She paused quietly on the sidewalk where people were passing by. A lady came along in the crowd, carrying an armful of red-, green- and silver-wrapped presents; she gave off perfume like the red roses in hot summer, and Phoenix stopped her.

"Please, missy, will you lace up my shoe?" She held up her foot.

"What do you want, Grandma?"

"See my shoe," said Phoenix. "Do all right for out in the country, but wouldn't look right to go in a big building."

"Stand still then, Grandma," said the lady. She put her packages down on the sidewalk beside her and laced and tied both shoes tightly.

"Can't lace 'em with a cane," said Phoenix. "Thank you, missy. I doesn't mind asking a nice lady to tie up my shoe, when I gets out on the street."

Moving slowly and from side to side, she went into the big building, and into a tower of steps, where she walked up and around and around until her feet knew to stop.

She entered a door, and there she saw nailed up on the wall the document that had been stamped with the gold seal and framed in the gold frame, which matched the dream that was hung up in her head.

"Here I be," she said. There was a fixed and ceremonial stiffness over her body.

"A charity case, I suppose," said an attendant who sat at the desk before her.

But Phoenix only looked above her head. There was sweat on her face, the wrinkles in her skin shone like a bright net.

"Speak up, Grandma," the woman said. "What's your name?

We must have your history, you know. Have you been here before? What seems to be the trouble with you?"

Old Phoenix only gave a twitch to her face as if a fly were bothering her.

"Are you deaf?" cried the attendant.

But then the nurse came in.

"Oh, that's just old Aunt Phoenix," she said. "She doesn't come for herself—she has a little grandson. She makes these trips just as regular as clockwork. She lives away back off the Old Natchez Trace." She bent down. "Well, Aunt Phoenix, why don't you just take a seat? We won't keep you standing after your long trip." She pointed.

The old woman sat down, bolt upright in the chair.

"Now, how is the boy?" asked the nurse.

Old Phoenix did not speak.

"I said, how is the boy?"

But Phoenix only waited and stared straight ahead, her face very solemn and withdrawn into rigidity.

"Is his throat any better?" asked the nurse. "Aunt Phoenix, don't you hear me? Is your grandson's throat any better since the last time you came for the medicine?"

With her hands on her knees, the old woman waited, silent, erect and motionless, just as if she were in armor.

"You mustn't take up our time this way, Aunt Phoenix," the nurse said. "Tell us quickly about your grandson, and get it over. He isn't dead, is he?"

At last there came a flicker and then a flame of comprehension across her face, and she spoke.

"My grandson. It was my memory had left me. There I sat and forgot why I made my long trip."

"Forgot?" The nurse frowned. "After you came so far?"

Then Phoenix was like an old woman begging a dignified forgiveness for waking up frightened in the night. "I never did go to school, I was too old at the Surrender," she said in a soft voice. "I'm an old woman without an education. It was my memory fail me. My little grandson, he is just the same, and I forgot it in the coming."

"Throat never heals, does it?" said the nurse, speaking in a loud, sure voice to old Phoenix. By now she had a card with something written on it, a little list. "Yes. Swallowed lye. When was it?—January—two-three years ago—"

Phoenix spoke unasked now. "No, missy, he not dead, he just the same. Every little while his throat begin to close up again, and he not able to swallow. He not get his breath. He not able to help himself. So the time come around, and I go on another trip for the soothing medicine."

"All right. The doctor said as long as you came to get it, you could have it," said the nurse. "But it's an obstinate case."

"My little grandson, he sit up there in the house all wrapped up, waiting by himself," Phoenix went on. "We is the only two left in the world. He suffer and it don't seem to put him back at all. He got a sweet look. He going to last. He wear a little patch quilt and peep out holding his mouth open like a little bird. I remembers so plain now. I not going to forget him again, no, the whole enduring time. I could tell him from all the others in creation."

"All right." The nurse was trying to hush her now. She brought her a bottle of medicine. "Charity," she said, making a check mark in a book.

Old Phoenix held the bottle close to her eyes, and then carefully put it into her pocket.

"I thank you," she said.

"It's Christmas time, Grandma," said the attendant. "Could I give you a few pennies out of my purse?"

"Five pennies is a nickel," said Phoenix stiffly.

"Here's a nickel," said the attendant.

Phoenix rose carefully and held out her hand. She received the nickel and then fished the other nickel out of her pocket and laid it beside the new one. She stared at her palm closely, with her head on one side.

Then she gave a tap with her cane on the floor.

"This is what come to me to do," she said. "I going to the store and buy my child a little windmill they sells, made out of paper. He going to find it hard to believe there such a thing in the world.

I'll march myself back where he waiting, holding it straight up in this hand."

She lifted her free hand, gave a little nod, turned around, and walked out of the doctor's office. Then her slow step began on the stairs, going down.

MARGARET WALKER

(1915-   )

------◆◆◆◆------

The daughter of a Negro Methodist minister, Margaret Walker was
born in Birmingham, Alabama, and studied at Northwestern University and later at the University of Iowa, from which she received
a Ph.D. in creative writing in 1965 for her novel Jubilee. She has
taught English at Jackson State College in Mississippi since 1949;
prior to that she taught at Livingstone College in North Carolina
and at West Virginia State College. Before becoming a teacher
she was a social worker, newspaper reporter, and magazine editor.

"For My People" (1937) is a social-protest poem in the tradition of W. E. B. DuBois and Fenton Johnson. Expressing bitterness not only with racial injustice but also with the effects of the
depression, it is similar in theme to Richard Wright's essays and
fiction of about the same time. Originally published in Poetry
Magazine in 1937, "For My People" became the title poem for
Miss Walker's first book of poems, published in the Yale University Series of Younger Poets in 1942 as the selection of the year.
In 1944 she received a Rosenwald Fellowship, but, having married
and become the mother of four children, she wrote little between
For My People (1942) and Jubilee, the historical novel which
received a Houghton Mifflin Literary Fellowship in 1966 and
became the first novel about the Civil War written from the slave's
point of view.

For My People

For my people everywhere singing their slave songs repeatedly: their dirges and their ditties and their blues and jubilees, praying their prayers nightly to an unknown god, bending their knees humbly to an unseen power;

For my people lending their strength to the years: to the gone years and the now years and the maybe years, washing ironing cooking scrubbing sewing mending hoeing plowing digging planting pruning patching dragging along never gaining never reaping never knowing and never understanding;

For my playmates in the clay and dust and sand of Alabama backyards playing baptizing and preaching, and doctor and jail and soldier and school and mama and cooking and playhouse and concert and store and Miss Choomby and hair and company;

For the cramped bewildered years we went to school to learn to know the reasons why and the answers to and the people who and the places where and the days when, in memory of the bitter hours when we discovered we were black and poor and small and different and nobody wondered and nobody understood;

For the boys and girls who grew in spite of these things to be Man and Woman, to laugh and dance and sing and play and drink their wine and religion and success, to marry their playmates and bear children and then die of consumption and anemia and lynching;

For my people thronging 47th Street in Chicago and Lenox Avenue in New York and Rampart Street in New Orleans, lost disinherited dispossessed and HAPPY people filling the cabarets and taverns and other people's pockets needing bread and shoes and milk and land and money and Something—Something all our own;

For my people walking blindly, spreading joy, losing time being lazy, sleeping when hungry, shouting when burdened, drinking when hopeless, tied and shackled and tangled among ourselves by the unseen creatures who tower over us omnisciently and laugh;

For my people blundering and groping and floundering in the dark of churches and schools and clubs and societies, associations and councils and committees and conventions, distressed and disturbed and deceived and devoured by money-hungry glory-craving leeches, preyed on by facile force of state and fad and novelty by false prophet and holy believer;

For my people standing staring trying to fashion a better way from confusion from hypocrisy and misunderstanding, trying to fashion a world that will hold all the people all the faces all the adams and eves and their countless generations;

Let a new earth rise. Let another world be born. Let a bloody peace be written in the sky. Let a second generation full of courage issue forth, let a people loving freedom come to growth, let a beauty full of healing and a strength of final clenching be the pulsing in our spirits and our blood. Let the martial songs be written, let the dirges disappear. Let a race of men now rise and take control!

MELVIN B. TOLSON

(1898–1966)

––––––◂◆▸––––––

Tolson was born in Moberly, Missouri, and attended Fisk and Lincoln Universities before receiving an M.A. at Columbia for a thesis about Harlem Renaissance writers. He taught at Langston University in Oklahoma, where he also served four terms as mayor of Langston. He was on the faculty of Tuskegee Institute at the time of his death.

Commissioned Poet Laureate of Liberia in 1947, he wrote the verse drama Libretto for the Republic of Liberia to mark the Liberian Centennial and International Exposition. When it was published in 1953, some critics compared the Libretto to Crane's The Bridge, Eliot's The Waste Land, and Pound's Cantos. In a preface to the poem Allen Tate wrote, "For the first time, it seems to me, a Negro poet has assimilated completely the full poetic language of his time and, by implication, the language of the Anglo-American poetic tradition." This very assimilation of modern Anglo-American poetic language and tradition has been criticized by those contemporary Negro critics who champion a black aesthetic or a cultural black nationalism. The poem required copious notes to explain its recondite allusions, and in an interview published in Herbert Hill's Anger, and Beyond, Tolson wryly noted, "the Libretto is very literary, to say the least. I thought the Establishment, the Academy, would like it."

Tolson's next book of poetry, Harlem Gallery (1965), presented its learned references in a context of convincingly detailed Harlem life. The poems offered an extraordinary collection of portraits, including Hideho Heights, "the Redskin beatnik bard of Lenox Avenue"; Kilroy, "the president of Afro-American Freedom, Inc."; and Black Diamond, "the kingpin of Harlem rackets." In his introduction to the book Karl Shapiro declared that "a great poet has been living in our midst for decades and is almost totally unknown, even by the literati, even by poets."

"Dark Symphony," one of Tolson's earlier, more lyric works, won the National Poetry Contest conducted by the American Negro Exposition in Chicago and was published in his first collection of poems, Rendezvous with America (1944).

Dark Symphony

I

Allegro Moderato

Black Crispus Attucks taught
   Us how to die
Before white Patrick Henry's bugle breath
Uttered the vertical
   Transmitting cry:
"Yea, give me liberty or give me death."

Waifs of the auction block,
   Men black and strong
The juggernauts of despotism withstood,
Loin-girt with faith that worms
   Equate the wrong
And dust is purged to create brotherhood.

No Banquo's ghost can rise
   Against us now,

Aver we hobnailed Man beneath the brute,
Squeezed down the thorns of greed
        On Labor's brow,
Garroted lands and carted off the loot.

II

Lento Grave

The centuries-old pathos in our voices
Saddens the great white world,
And the wizardry of our dusky rhythms
Conjures up shadow-shapes of ante-bellum years:

Black slaves singing *One More River to Cross*
In the torture tombs of slave-ships,
Black slaves singing *Steal Away to Jesus*
In jungle swamps,
Black slaves singing *The Crucifixion*
In slave-pens at midnight,
Black slaves singing *Swing Low, Sweet Chariot*
In cabins of death,
Black slaves singing *Go Down, Moses*
In the canebrakes of the Southern Pharaohs.

III

Andante Sostenuto

They tell us to forget
The Golgotha we tread . . .
We who are scourged with hate,
A price upon our head.
They who have shackled us
Require of us a song,
They who have wasted us
Bid us condone the wrong.

They tell us to forget
Democracy is spurned.

They tell us to forget
The Bill of Rights is burned.
Three hundred years we slaved,
We slave and suffer yet:
Though flesh and bone rebel,
They tell us to forget!

Oh, how can we forget
Our human rights denied?
Oh, how can we forget
Our manhood crucified?
When Justice is profaned
And plea with curse is met,
When Freedom's gates are barred,
Oh, how can we forget?

IV

Tempo Primo

The New Negro strides upon the continent
In seven-league boots . . .
The New Negro
Who sprang from the vigor-stout loins
Of Nat Turner, gallows-martyr for Freedom,
Of Joseph Cinquez, Black Moses of the Amistad Mutiny,
Of Frederick Douglass, oracle of the Catholic Man,
Of Sojourner Truth, eye and ear of Lincoln's legions,
Of Harriet Tubman, Saint Bernard of the Underground Railroad.

The New Negro
Breaks the icons of his detractors,
Wipes out the conspiracy of silence,
Speaks to *his* America:
"My history-moulding ancestors
Planted the first crops of wheat on these shores,
Built ships to conquer the seven seas,
Erected the Cotton Empire,
Flung railroads across a hemisphere,

Disemboweled the earth's iron and coal,
Tunneled the mountains and bridged rivers,
Harvested the grain and hewed forests,
Sentineled the Thirteen Colonies,
Unfurled Old Glory at the North Pole,
Fought a hundred battles for the Republic."

The New Negro:
His giant hands fling murals upon high chambers,
His drama teaches a world to laugh and weep,
His music leads continents captive,
His voice thunders the Brotherhood of Labor,
His science creates seven wonders,
His Republic of Letters challenges the Negro-baiters.

The New Negro,
Hard-muscled, Fascist-hating, Democracy-ensouled,
Strides in seven-league boots
Along the Highway of Today
Toward the Promised Land of Tomorrow!

V

Larghetto

None in the Land can say
To us black men Today:
You send the tractors on their bloody path,
And create Okies for *The Grapes of Wrath*.
You breed the slum that breeds a *Native Son*
To damn the good earth Pilgrim Fathers won.

None in the Land can say
To us black men Today:
You dupe the poor with rags-to-riches tales,
And leave the workers empty dinner pails.
You stuff the ballot box, and honest men
Are muzzled by your demagogic din.

None in the Land can say
To us black men Today:
You smash stock markets with your coined blitzkriegs,
And make a hundred million guinea pigs.
You counterfeit our Christianity,
And bring contempt upon Democracy.

None in the Land can say
To us black men Today:
You prowl when citizens are fast asleep,
And hatch Fifth Column plots to blast the deep
Foundations of the State and leave the Land
A vast Sahara with a Fascist brand.

VI

Tempo di Marcia

Out of abysses of Illiteracy,
Through labyrinths of Lies,
Across waste lands of Disease . . .
We advance!

Out of dead-ends of Poverty,
Through wildernesses of Superstition,
Across barricades of Jim Crowism . . .
We advance!

With the Peoples of the World . . .
We advance!

LIONEL TRILLING

(1905–   )

━━━━━━◆●◆◆━━━━━━

Critic, novelist, and short-story writer, Lionel Trilling is George
Edward Woodberry Professor of Literature and Criticism at Columbia University. He was born in New York City and received his
B.A., M.A., and Ph.D. at Columbia, where he began teaching in
1931 after service on the faculties at the University of Wisconsin
and Hunter College. A founder, along with John Crowe Ransom
and F. O. Matthiessen, of the Kenyon School of Letters at Kenyon
College, he has been a Visiting Professor at Oxford University and
holds honorary degrees from Trinity College (Connecticut), Harvard, and Northwestern. His works include two critical biographies,
Matthew Arnold (1939) and E. M. Forster (1943); a novel, Middle of the Journey (1947); and several essay collections: The
Liberal Imagination (1950), The Opposing Self (1955), A Gathering of Fugitives (1956), and Beyond Culture (1965).

Centered on a child's concomitant discovery of evil and initiation
into adulthood, "The Other Margaret" also raises discomforting
questions about conventional liberal attitudes toward race relations.
The story appears to have been influenced at several points by
Gerard Manley Hopkins' poem "Spring and Fall: To a Young
Child."

The Other Margaret

Mark Jennings stood the picture up on the wide counter and he and Stephen Elwin stepped back and looked at it. It was one of Rouault's kings. A person looking at it for the first time might find it repellent, even brutal or cruel. It was full of rude blacks that might seem barbarically untidy.

But the two men knew the picture well. They looked at it in silence. The admiration they were sharing made a community between them which at their age was rare, for they had both passed forty. Jennings waited for Elwin to speak first—they were friends but Elwin was the customer. Besides, the frame had been designed by Jennings and in buying a reproduced picture the frame is of great importance, accounting for more than half the cost. Elwin had bought the picture some weeks before but he was seeing it framed for the first time.

Elwin said, "The frame is very good, Mark. It's perfect." He was a rather tall man with an attractive, competent face. He touched the frame curiously with the tip of his forefinger.

Jennings replied in a judicious tone, as if it were not his own good taste but that of a very gifted apprentice of his. "I think so," he said. And he too touched the frame, but intimately, rubbing briskly up and down one moulding with an artisan's possessive thumb, putting an unneeded last touch. He explained what considerations of color and proportion made the frame right for the picture. He spoke as if these were simple rules anyone might find in a book.

The king, blackbearded and crowned, faced in profile to the left. He had a fierce quality that had modulated, but not softened, to authority. One could feel of him—it was the reason why Elwin had bought the picture—that he had passed beyond ordinary matters of personality and was worthy of the crown he was wearing. Yet he was human and tragic. He was not unlike the sculptured kings of Chartres. In his right hand he held a spray of flowers.

"Is he a favorite of yours?" Elwin said. He did not know

whether he meant the king or the king's painter. Indeed, as he asked the question, it seemed to him that he had assumed that the painter was this archaic personage himself. He had never imagined the painter painting the canvas with a brush. It was the beginning of a new thought about the picture.

Jennings answered with a modified version of the Latin gesture of esteem, a single decisive shake of his lifted hand, thumb and forefinger touching in a circle.

Elwin acknowledged the answer with a nod but said nothing. He did not want Jenning's admiration, even though he had asked for it. Jennings would naturally give as much admiration to most of the fine pictures in fine reproduction with which his shop was filled. At that moment, Elwin was not interested in admiration or in art. But he liked what Jennings said next.

"It will give you a lot of satisfaction," Jennings said. It was exactly as if he had just sold Elwin a suit or a pair of shoes.

Elwin said, "Yes," a little hesitatingly, only politely agreeing, not committing himself in the matter of his money's worth until it should be proved.

From behind the partition that made Jennings' little office they had been hearing a man talking on the telephone. Now the conversation ended and a young soldier, a second lieutenant, came out into the shop. Jennings said to him, "Did the call get through?" and the young man said, "Oh yes, after some difficulty. It was eighty-five cents. Let me pay you for it." "Oh nonsense," said Jennings, and took him by the arm and quickly introduced him to Elwin as a cousin of his wife's. The young man offered Elwin the hand that had been reaching into his pocket and said, "I'm glad to meet you, sir."

He said it very nicely, with the niceness that new young officers are likely to have. Pleased with themselves, they are certain that everyone will be nice to them. This young man's gold bar did a good deal for him, did perhaps more than rank ought to have to do for a man. He was not really much of a person. Yet Elwin, meeting him, felt the familiar emotion in which he could not distinguish guilt from envy. He knew it well, knew how to control it and it did not diminish, not much, the sense of holiday he was having. The holiday was made by his leaving his office a little early. He published scientific books in a small but successful way and the war had made a great pressure of work for him, but he had left his office early when Jennings phoned that the picture was back from the framer's.

The young lieutenant was looking at the picture. He so clearly did not like it that Jennings said quickly, "Mr. Elwin's just bought it."

The lieutenant regarded the picture thoughtfully. "Very nice," he said, with an enthusiastic and insincere shake of his head. He did not want to spoil things for Jennings by undermining the confidence of the customer. Elwin looked from the king to the lieutenant and back to the king. It was perfectly polite, only as if he had looked at the young man to hear his opinion more clearly and then had examined again the thing they were talking about.

But Jennings understood the movement of Elwin's glance, for when the lieutenant had shaken hands and left the shop, Jennings said stoutly, "He's a good kid."

"Yes he is," Elwin said serenely.

"It's funny seeing him an officer. He used to be against anything like that. But he was glad to go—he said he did not want to miss sharing the experience of his generation."

"A lot of them say that." Elwin had heard it often from the young men, the clever ones. Someone had started it and all the young men with the semi-political views said it. Their reasons for saying it were various. Elwin liked some of the reasons and disliked others, but whether he liked the reasons or not, he never heard the phrase without a twinge of envy. Now it comforted him to think that this man with the black beard and the flower had done his fighting without any remarks about experience and generations.

The idea of age and death did not present itself to Elwin in any horrifying way. It had first come to him in the form of a sentence from one of Hazlitt's essays. The sentence was, "No young man believes he shall ever die," and the words had come to him suddenly from the past, part of an elaborate recollection of a scene at high school. When he looked up the quotation, he found that he had remembered it with perfect accuracy, down to that very *shall* which struck his modern ear as odd and even ungrammatical. The memory had begun with the winter sunlight coming through the dirty windows of the classroom. Then there was the color, texture and smell of varnished wood. But these details were only pointing to the teacher himself and what he was saying. He was a Mr. Baxter, a heron-like man, esteemed as brilliant and eccentric, what some students called "a real person." Suddenly Mr. Baxter in a loud voice had uttered that sentence of Hazlitt's. He held the book in his hand but did not read from it. "No young man believes he shall ever die," he said, just as if he had thought of it himself.

It had been very startling to hear him say that, and this effect was of course just what the teacher wanted. It was the opening sentence of an essay called "On the Feeling of Immortality in Youth," and to Baxter it was important that the class should see what a bold and captivating way it was to begin an essay, how it was exactly as if someone had suddenly said the words, not written them after thought.

The chalky familiar classroom had been glorified by this moment of Mr. Baxter's. So many things had been said in the room, but here was one thing that had been said which was true. It was true in two ways. For Mr. Baxter it was true that no *young* man believes he shall ever die, but Mr. Baxter was not exactly a young man. For Stephen Elwin it was true that he would never die—he was scarcely even a young man yet, still only a boy. Between the student and the teacher the great difference was that the student would never die. Stephen Elwin had pitied Mr. Baxter and had been proud of himself. And mixed with the boy's feeling of immortality was a boy's pleasure at being involved with ideas which were not only solemn but complicated, for Mr. Baxter's mortality should have denied, but actually did not deny, the immortality that Stephen felt.

The Hazlitt sentence, once it had been remembered, had not left Elwin. Every now and then, sometimes just as he was falling asleep, sometimes just as he was waking up, sometimes right in the middle of anything at all, the sentence and the full awareness of what it meant would come to him. It felt like an internal explosion. It was not, however, an explosion of force but rather an explosion of light. It was not without pain but it was not wholly painful.

With the picture neatly wrapped in heavy brown paper, Elwin walked down Madison Avenue. It was still early. On a sudden impulse he walked west at 60th Street. Usually he came home by taxi, but this evening he thought of the Fifth Avenue bus, for some reason remembering that it was officially called a "coach" and that his father had spoken of it so, and had sometimes even referred to it as a "stage." The "coach" that he signaled was of the old kind, open wooden deck, platform at the rear, stairs connecting platform and deck with a big architectural curve. He saw it with surprise and affection. He had supposed that this model of bus had long been out of service and as he hailed it his mind sought for and found a word long unused. "DeDion," he said, pleased at having found it. "DeDion Bouton."

He pronounced it *Deedeeon*, the way he and his friends had said it in 1917 when they had discussed the fine and powerful motors from Europe that were then being used for the buses. Some of them had been Fiats, but the most powerful of all were said to be the DeDions from France. No one knew the authority for this superlative judgment, but boys finding a pleasure in firm opinions did not care. Elwin remembered the special note in his friends' voices as they spoke of the DeDions. They talked about the great Mediterranean motors with a respect that was not only technical but historical. There had never been more than a few of the DeDions in America. Even in 1917 they were no longer being imported and the boys thought of them as old and rare.

Elwin took his seat inside the bus, at the rear. As suddenly as the name DeDion, it came to him how the open deck had once been a deck indeed—how, as sometimes the only passenger braving the weather up there, he had been the captain of the adventure, facing into the cold wind, even into the snow or rain, stoic, assailed but unmoved by the elements, inhaling health, fortitude and growth, for he had a boy's certainty that the more he endured, the stronger he would become. And when he had learned to board the bus and alight from it while it was still moving—"board" and "alight" were words the company used in its notices—how far advanced in life he had felt. So many landmarks of Elwin's boyhood in the city had vanished but this shabby bus had endured since the days when it had taken him daily to school.

At 82nd Street the bus stopped for a red light. A boy stood at the curb near the iron stanchion that bore the bus-stop sign. He clutched something in his hand. It must have been a coin, for he said to the conductor, "Mister, how much does it cost to ride on this bus?"

Elwin could not be sure of the boy's age, but he was perhaps twelve, Elwin's own age when he had been touched by his friends' elegiac discussions of the DeDions. The boy was not alone, he had a friend with him, and to see this friend, clearly a follower, was to understand the quality of the chief. The subaltern was a boy like any other, but the face of his leader was alight with the power of mind and a great urgency. Perhaps he was only late and in a hurry, but in any case the urgency illuminated his remarkable face.

The conductor did not answer the question.

"Mister," the boy said again, "how much does it cost to ride on this bus?"

His friend stood by, sharing passively in the question but saying nothing. They did not dare "board" until they knew whether or not their resources were sufficient.

The boy was dressed sturdily enough, perhaps for a boy of his age he was even well dressed. But he had been on the town or in the park most of the afternoon, or perhaps he had been one of those boys who, half in awe, half in rowdy levity, troop incessantly through the Egyptian rooms of the Museum, repeatedly entering and emerging from and entering again the narrow slits of the grave vaults. His knickerbockers were sliding at the knees and his effort to control a drop at his nose further compromised but by no means destroyed his dignity. He had the clear cheeks and well-shaped head of a carefully reared child, but he seemed too far from home at this hour quite to be the child of very careful parents. There was an air about him which suggested that he had learned to expect at least a little resistance from the world and that he was ready to meet it.

The conductor did not reply to the second question. He had taken a large black wallet of imitation leather from some cranny of the rear platform and was making marks with a pencil on the cardboard trip-sheet it contained. He was an old man.

"Mister," said the boy again, and his voice, though tense, was reasonable. It was the very spirit of reasonableness. "Mister, how much does it cost to ride on this bus? A nickel or a dime?"

The conductor elaborately lifted his eyes from his record. He looked at the boy not hostilely nor yet quite facetiously, but with a certain quiet air of settled satisfaction. "What do you want to know for?" he said.

Elwin wanted to lower the window to tell the boy it was a dime. But he had waited too long. The conductor put his hand on the bell-button and gave the driver the signal. The light changed and the bus began to move.

"Mister!" the boy shouted. He may have been late to his supper but it was not this urgency that made his voice go up so loud and high. "For God's sake, mister!"

He of course did not bring in God by way of appeal. There was no longer any hope of his getting an answer. It was rather an expostulation with the unreasonable, the most passionate thing imaginable. Elwin looked back and saw the boy's hatred still following the conductor and, naturally, not only the conductor but the whole bus.

The conductor had now the modest look of a person who has just delivered a rebuke which was not only deserved but witty.

Well, Elwin thought, he is an old man and his pride is somewhere involved. Perhaps it was only that he could not at the moment bring himself to answer a question.

But he believed that in the past it could have happened. When he was a boy the conductor might have said, "What do you want to know for?"—boys must always be teased a little by men. But the teasing would have stopped in time for him to board the bus. The bus was peculiarly safe. The people who rode in it and paid a dime after they had taken their seats were known to be nicer than the people who rode in the subway for a nickel which they paid before admission. It was the first public conveyance to which "nervous" parents entrusted their children—the conductors were known for their almost paternal kindness. For example, if you found on your trip to school that you had forgotten your money, the conductor would not fail to quiet the fear of authority that clutched your guilty heart. But this old man had outlived his fatherhood, which had once extended to all the bus-world of children. His own sons and daughters by now would have grown and gone and given him the usual causes for bitterness.

The old man's foolish triumph was something that must be understood. Elwin tried to know the weariness and sense of final loss that moved the old conductor to stand on that small dignity of his. He at once brought into consideration the conditions of life of the old man, especially the lack of all the advantages that he himself had had—the gentle rearing and the good education that made a man like Stephen Elwin answerable for all his actions. It had long been the habit of Elwin's mind to raise considerations of just this sort whenever he had reason to be annoyed with anyone who was not more powerful than himself.

But now, strangely, although the habit was in force, it did not check his anger. It was bewildering that he should feel anger at a poor ignorant man, a working man. It was the first time in his life that he had ever felt so. It shamed him. And he was the more bewildered and ashamed when he understood, as he did, that he was just as angry at the boy as at the old man. He was seeing the boy full grown and the self-pity and hatred taking root beside the urgency and power. The conductor and the boy were links in the great chain of the world's rage.

Clearly it was an unreasoning thing to feel. It was not what a wise man would feel. At this time in his life Stephen Elwin had the wish to be wise. He had never known a wise man. The very word sounded like something in a tale read to children. But the occasion for courage had passed. By courage Elwin meant something very simple, an unbending resistance of spirit under extreme physical difficulties. It was a boy's notion, but it had stayed with Elwin through most of his life, through his business and his pleasure, and nothing that he had ever done had given him the proof that he wanted. And now that the chance for that was gone—he was forty-one years old—it seemed to him that perhaps to be wise was almost as manly a thing as to be brave.

Two wars had passed Elwin by. For one he was too young, for the other too old, though by no means, of course, old. Had it not been for the war, and the consideration of age it so ruthlessly raised, the recollection of the sentence from Hazlitt would no doubt have been delayed by several years, and so too would the impulse to which it had given rise, the desire to have "wisdom." More and more in the last few months, Elwin had been able to experience the sensation of being wise, for it was indeed a sensation, a feeling of stamina, poise and illumination.

He was puzzled and unhappy as he "alighted" from the bus at 92nd Street. It seemed to him a great failure that his knowledge of death and his having reached the years of wisdom—they were the same thing—had not prevented him from feeling anger at an old man and a boy. It then occurred to him to think that perhaps he had felt his anger not in despite of wisdom but because of it. It was a disturbing, even a horrifying, fancy. Yet as he walked the two blocks to his home, he could not help recurring to it, with what was, as he had to see, a certain gratification.

In his pleasant living room, in his comfortable chair, Stephen Elwin watched his daughter as she mixed the drink he usually had before dinner. She was thirteen. About a month ago she had made this her job, almost her duty, and she performed it with an unspeakable seriousness. She measured out the whiskey and poured it into the tumbler. With the ice-tongs she reached the ice gently into the bottom of the glass so that there would not be the least splash of whiskey. She opened the bottle of soda. Holding up the glass for her father's inspection, she poured the soda slowly, ready to stop at her father's word. Elwin cried "Whoa!" and at the word he thought that his daughter had reached the stage of her growth where she did indeed look like a well-bred pony.

Now Margaret was searching for the stirring-spoon. But she had forgotten to put it on the tray with all the other paraphernalia and she gave a little cry of vexation and went to fetch it. Elwin did not tell her not to bother, that it did not matter if the drink was not stirred. He understood that this business had to proceed with a ceremonial completeness.

Margaret returned with the stirring-spoon. She stirred the highball and the soda foamed up. She waited until it subsided, meanwhile shaking the spoon dry over the glass with three precise little shakes. She handed her father the drink and put a coaster on the table by his chair. She watched while he took his first sip. He had taken the whole responsibility for the proportion of soda to whiskey. Still, she wanted to be told that she had made the drink just right. Elwin said, "Fine. Just right," and Margaret tried not to show the absurd pleasure she felt.

For this ritual of Margaret's there were, as Elwin guessed, several motives. The honor of her home required that her father not make his own highball in the pantry and bring it out to drink in his chair, not after she had begun to take notice that in the homes of some of her schoolmates, every evening and not only at dinner-parties, a servant brought in, quite as a matter of course, a large tray of drinking equipment. But Margaret had other reasons than snobbishness—Elwin thought that she needed to establish a "custom," not only for now but for the future, against the time when she could say to her children, "And every night before dinner it was the *custom* in our family for me to make my father a drink." He supposed that this ritual of the drink was Margaret's first traffic with the future. It seemed to him that to know a thing like this about his daughter was one of the products of what could be called wisdom and he thought with irony but also with pleasure of his becoming a dim but necessary figure in Margaret's story of the past.

"I bought a picture today," Elwin said.

Margaret cocked an eye at him, as if to say, "Are you on the loose again?" She said, "What is it? Did you bring it home?"

"Oh, just a reproduction, a Rouault."

"Rouault?" she said. She shook her head decisively. "Don't know him." It quite settled Rouault for the moment.

"Don't know him?"

"Never heard of him."

"Well, take a look at it—it's over there."

She untied the string and took off the paper and sat there on the big hassock, her feet far out in front of her, holding the great king at arm's length. It was to Elwin strange and funny, this confrontation of the black, calm, tragic king and this blonde child in her sweater and skirt, in her moccasin shoes. She became abstracted and withdrawn in her scrutiny of the picture. Then Elwin, seeing the breadth and brightness of her brow, the steady intelligence of her gaze, understood that there was really no comic disproportion.

What was funny was the equality. The young lieutenant had been quite neutralized by the picture. Even Mark Jennings had been a little diminished by it. But Margaret, with her grave, luminous brow, was able to meet it head on. And not in agreement either.

"You don't like it?" Elwin said.

She looked from the picture to him and said, "I don't think so."

She said it softly but it was pretty positive. She herself painted and she was in a very simple relation to pictures. She rose and placed the picture on the sofa as if to give it another chance in a different position and a better light. She stood at a distance and looked at it and Elwin stood behind her to get the same view of it that she had. He put his hand on her shoulder. After a moment she looked up at him and smiled. "I don't really *like* it," she said. The modulation of her voice was not apology, but simply a gesture of making room for another opinion. She did not think it was important whether she liked or disliked the picture. It said something to her that was not in her experience or that she did not want in her experience. Liking the picture would have given her pleasure. She got no pleasure from not liking it. It seemed to Elwin that in the little shake of her head, in her tone and smile, there was a quality, really monumental, by which he could explain his anger at the old conductor and the boy and forgive himself for having had it.

When Lucy Elwin came in, her face was flushed from the stove and she had a look of triumphant anticipation. She shamelessly communicated this to her family. "It's going to be ve-ry good," she said, not as if she were promising them a fine dinner, rather as if she were threatening them with a grim fate. She meant that her dinner was going to be so very good that if they did not extravagantly admire it, if they merely took it for granted, they would be made to feel sorry. "It will be ready in about ten minutes," she said. "Are you very hungry?"

"Just enough," Elwin said. "Are you tired?" For his wife had stretched out in the armchair and put back her head. She slouched with her long legs at full length, her skirt a little disordered, one ankle laid on the other. Her eyes being closed made her complicated face look simple and she seemed young and self-indulgent, like a girl who escapes from the embarrassment of herself into a broody trance. It was an attitude that had lately become frequent with Margaret.

Lucy Elwin said, "Yes, a little tired. But really, you know, I'd almost rather do the work myself than have that Margaret around."

She spoke with her eyes still closed, and so she did not see her daughter stiffen. But Elwin did. He knew that it was not because Margaret thought that her mother meant her but because of the feelings she had for the other Margaret, the maid. The other Margaret, as so often, had not come to work that day.

Margaret had mixed a drink for her mother and now she was standing beside Lucy's chair, waiting with exaggerated patience for Lucy to open her eyes. She said, "Here's your drink, mother!"

She said it as if she had waited quite long enough, using the lumpish, martyred, unsuccessful irony of thirteen, her eyebrows very weary, the expression of her mouth very dry. Lucy opened her eyes and sat up straight in her chair. She took the drink from Margaret and smiled. "Thank you, dear," she said. For the moment it was as if Margaret were the mother, full of rectitude and manners, and Lucy the careless daughter.

That Lucy was being careless even her husband felt. No one could say of their Negro maid, the other Margaret, that she was a pleasant person. Even Elwin would have to admit to a sense of strain in her presence. But surely Lucy took too passionate a notice of her. Elwin felt that this was not in keeping with his wife's nature. But no, that was really not so. It was often disquieting to Elwin, the willingness that Lucy had to get angry even with simple people when she thought they were not behaving well. And lately she had been full of stories about the nasty and insulted temper that was being shown by the people one daily dealt with. Only yesterday, for example, there had been her story of the soda-fountain man who made a point of mopping and puttering and changing the position of pieces of pie and only after he had shown his indifference and independence would take your order. Elwin had to balance against the notice his wife took of such things the deep, literal, almost childish way she spoke of them, the innocence of her passion. But this particular story of the soda-fountain clerk had really distressed him, actually embarrassing him for Lucy, and he had pointed out to her how frequent such stories had become. She had simply stared at him, the fact was so very clear. "Why, it's the war," she said. "People are just much meaner since the war." And when his rebuke had moved on to the matter of the maid Margaret, Lucy had said in the most matter-of-fact way, "Why, she just hates us." And she had shocked Elwin by giving, just like any middle-class housewife, a list of all the precious things Margaret had broken. "And observe," Lucy had said, "that never once has she broken anything cheap or ordinary, only the things I've pointed out to her that needed care."

Elwin had to admit that the list made a case. Still, even if the number of the green Wedgwood coffee cups had been much diminished, cups for which Elwin himself had a special fondness, and even if the Persian bowl had been dropped and the glass urn they had brought from Sweden had been cracked in the sink, they must surely not talk of such things. The very costliness of the objects which proved Margaret's animosity, the very affection which the Elwins felt for them, made the whole situation impossible to consider.

Lucy must indeed have been unaware of how deeply her husband resisted her carelessness in these matters and of what her daughter was now feeling. Otherwise she would not have begun her story, her eyes narrowing in anger at the recollection, "Oh, such a rotten thing happened on the way home on the bus."

It was Elwin who had had the thing happen on the bus, not quite "rotten" but sufficiently disturbing, and he was startled, as if his wife's consciousness had in some way become mixed up with his own in a clairvoyant experience. And this feeling was not diminished as Lucy told her story about a young woman who had asked the conductor a question. It was a simple, ordinary question, Lucy said, about what street one transferred at. The conductor at first had not answered, and then, when he came around again and the question was asked again, he had looked at the young woman —"looked her straight in the face," Lucy said—and had replied in a loud voice, "Vot deed you shay?"

"*Mother!*" cried Margaret. Her voice was all absolute childish horror.

Elwin at once saw what was happening, but Lucy, absorbed in what she had experienced, only said mildly, "What's the matter, dear?"

"Mother!" Margaret grieved, "you mustn't do that." Her face was quite aghast and she was standing stiff with actual fright.

"Why, do what, Margaret?" said Lucy. She was troubled for her daughter but entirely bewildered.

"Make fun of—fun of—" But Margaret could not say it.

"Of Jews?" said Elwin in a loud, firm, downright voice.

Margaret nodded miserably. Elwin said with enough sharpness, "Margaret, whatever makes you think that Lucy is making fun of Jews? She is simply repeating—"

"Oh," Margaret cried, her face a silly little moon of gratitude and relief. "Oh," she said happily, "what the woman said to the conductor!"

"No, Margaret. How absurd!" Lucy cried. "*Not* what the woman said to the conductor. What the conductor said to the woman."

Margaret just sat there glowering with silence and anger.

Elwin said to Margaret with a pedagogic clearness and patience, "The conductor was making fun of the woman for being Jewish."

"Not at all," Lucy said, beginning to be a little tried by so much misunderstanding. "Not at all, she wasn't Jewish at all. He was insulting her by pretending that she was Jewish."

Margaret had only one question to ask. "The *conductor?*" she cried with desperate emphasis.

And when Lucy said that it was indeed the conductor, Margaret said nothing, but shrugged her shoulders in an elaborate way and made with her hands a large grimace of despairing incomprehension. She was dismissing the grownups by this pantomime, appealing beyond all their sad nonsense to her own world of sure right reason. In that world one knew where one was, one knew that to say things about Jews was bad and that working men were good. And *therefore*.

Elwin, whose awareness was all aroused, wondered in tender amusement what his daughter would have felt if she had known that her gesture, which she had drawn from the large available stock of the folk-culture of children, had originally been a satiric mimicry of a puzzled shrugging Jew. The Margaret who stood there in sullenness was so very different from the Margaret who, only a few minutes before, had looked at the picture with him and had seemed, almost, to be teaching him something. Now he had to teach her. "That isn't a very pretty gesture," he said. "And what, please, is so difficult about Lucy's story? Don't you believe it?"

A mistake, as he saw at once. Margaret was standing there trapped—no, she did not believe it, but she did not dare say so. Elwin corrected himself and gave her her chance. "Do you think Lucy didn't hear right?"

Margaret nodded eagerly, humbly glad to take the way out that was being offered her.

"We studied the transit system," she said by way of explanation. "We made a study of it." She stopped. Elwin knew how her argument ran, but she herself was not entirely sure of it. She said tentatively, by way of a beginning, "They are underpaid."

Lucy was being really irresponsible, Elwin thought, for she said in an abstracted tone, as if she were musing on the early clues of an interesting scientific generalization, "They hate *women*—it's women they're always rude to. Never the men." Margaret's face flushed, and her eyes darkened at this new expression of her mother's moral obtuseness, and Elwin felt a quick impatience with his daughter's sensitivity—it seemed suddenly to have taken on a pedantic air. But he was annoyed with Lucy too, who ought surely be more aware of what her daughter was feeling. No doubt he was the more annoyed because his own incident of the bus was untold and would remain untold. But it was Lucy who saved the situation she had created. She suddenly remembered the kitchen. She hurried out, then came back, caught Margaret by the arm in a bustle of haste and said, "Come and hurl the salad." This was a famous new joke in the family. Elwin had made it, Margaret loved it. It had reference to a "tossed green salad" on a pretentious restaurant menu. Of the salad, when it was served to them in all its wiltedness, Elwin had said that apparently it needed to be more than tossed, it needed to be hurled.

And so all at once the family was restored, a family with a family joke. Margaret stood there grinning in the embarrassment of the voluptuous pleasure she felt at happiness returned. But she must have been very angry with her mother, for she came back and pulled Elwin's head down and whispered into his ear where he would be able to find and inspect the presents she had for Lucy's birthday next week.

He was to look for two things. In the top left-hand drawer of Margaret's desk he would find the "bought present" and on the shelf in the clothes closet he would find the "made present." The bought present was a wallet, a beautiful green wallet, so clearly expensive that Elwin understood why his daughter had had to tease him for money to supplement her savings, and so adult in its expensiveness that he had to understand how inexorably she was growing up.

The made present was also green, a green lamb, large enough to have to be held in two hands, with black feet and wide black eyes. The eyes stared out with a great charming question to the world, expressing the comic grace of the lamb's awkwardness. Elwin wondered if Margaret had been at all aware of how much the lamb was a self-portrait. When Elwin, some two years before, had listened to his daughter playing her first full piece on the recorder, he had thought that nothing could be more wonderful than the impervious gravity of her face as her eyes focused on the bell of the instrument and on the music-book while she blew her tune in a daze of concentration; yet only a few months later, when she had progressed so far as to be up to airs from Mozart, she had been able, in the very midst of a roulade, with her fingers moving fast, to glance up at him with a twinkling, sidelong look, her mouth puckering in a smile as she kept her lips pursed, amused by the music, amused by the frank excess of its ornamentation and by her own virtuosity. For Elwin the smile was the expression of gay and conscious life, of life innocently aware of itself and fond of itself, and, although there was something painful in having to make the admission, it was even more endearing than Margaret's earlier gravity. Life aware of itself seemed so much more life.

His daughter's room was full of life. His own old microscope stood on Margaret's desk and around it was a litter of slides and of the various objects from which she had been cutting sections, a prune and a dried apricot, a sliver of wood, a piece of cheese and what seemed to be a cockroach. There were tools for carving wood and for cutting linoleum blocks. The books were beginning to be too many for the small bookshelf, starting with *The Little Family* and going on to his own soiled copy of *The Light That Failed* that Margaret had unearthed. There was her easel and on one wall was a print of Picasso's trapeze people in flight, like fierce flames, and on another wall one of Benton's righteous stylizations, both at home, knowing nothing of their antagonism to each other. The dolls were no longer so much to the fore as they once were, but they were still about, and so was the elaborate doll's house which contained in precise miniature, accumulated over years, almost every object of daily living, tiny skillets, lamps, cups, kettles, packaged groceries. Surrounded by all that his daughter made and did and read, Elwin could not understand how she found the time. And then, on the thought of what time could be to a child, there came to him with more painful illumination than usual, the recurrent sentence. "No young man believes he shall ever die." And he stood contemplating the room with a kind of desolation of love for it.

Margaret burst in suddenly as if she were running away from something—as indeed she was, for her eyes blazed with the anger she was fleeing. She flung herself on the bed, ignoring her father's presence.

"Margaret, what's the matter?" Elwin said.

But she did not answer.

"Margaret!" There was the note of discipline in his voice. "Tell me what the matter is."

She was not crying, but her face, when she lifted it from the pillow, was red and swollen. "It's mother," she said. "The way she talked to Margaret."

"To Margaret? Has Margaret come?"

"Yes, she came." The tone implied: through flood and fire. "And mother—oh!" She broke off and shook her head in a rather histrionic expression of how impossible it was to tell what her mother had done.

"What did she say that was so terrible?"

"She said—she said, 'Look here—'" But Margaret could not go on.

Lucy strode into the room with quite as much impulse as Margaret had and with eyes blazing quite as fiercely as her daughter's. "Look here, Margaret," she said. "I've quite enough trouble with that Margaret without your nonsense. Nobody is being exploited in this house and nobody is being bullied and I'm not going to have you making situations about nothing. I'm sure your Miss Hoxie is very sweet and nice, but you seem to have got your ideas from her all mixed up. You weren't that way about Millie when she was with us. As a matter of fact," Lucy said with remorseless irony, "you were often not at all nice to her."

Margaret had not heard the end of Lucy's speech. At the mention of Miss Hoxie in the tone that Lucy had used—"your Miss Hoxie"—at the sacred name of her teacher blasphemously uttered, she looked at her mother with the horror of seeing her now in her true terrible colors. The last bond between them had snapped at this attack upon her heart's best loyalty.

But Lucy was taking no account of finer feelings. She closed the door and said firmly, "Now look here, the simple fact is that that Margaret is a thoroughly disagreeable person, a nasty, mean person."

"Oh, she is not," Margaret wailed. And then, despite all her passion, the simple fact broke in upon her irresistibly. Elwin's heart quite melted as he saw her confront the fact and struggle with it. For the fact was as Lucy had stated it, and he himself at that moment had to realize it. And it was wonderful to see that Margaret's mind, whatever the inclination of her will, was unable to resist a fact. But the mind that had momentarily deserted her will, came quickly again to its help. "She's not responsible," she said desperately. "It's not her fault. She couldn't help it. Society—" But at that big word she halted, unable to handle it. "We can't blame her," she said defiantly but a little lamely.

At that moment Lucy saw the green clay lamb that Elwin was still holding. She rushed to it and took it and cried, "Margaret, is this yours? I've never seen it, why didn't you show it to me?"

It was, of course, a decided point for Margaret that her birthday surprise was spoiled. She sat there looking dry and indifferent amid the ruins of family custom. Elwin said, "It's a birthday present for you, Lucy. You weren't supposed to see it," and their glances met briefly. He had been a little treacherous, for he could have managed to put the lamb out of sight, but some craftiness, not entirely conscious, had suggested its usefulness for peace.

"It's so *lovely*," Lucy said. "Is it really for me?"

Margaret had to acknowledge that it was, but with an elaborate ungraciousness from her bruised and empty heart. Her mother might have the gift, meaningless as it now was. But Lucy was in a flood of thanks and praise impossible to withstand—it was lovely, she said, to have a gift in advance of her birthday, it was something she had always wanted as a child and had never been able to induce her parents to allow, that she should have one, just one, of her presents before the others, and the lamb itself was simply beautiful, quite the nicest thing Margaret had ever made. "Oh, I love it," she said, stroking its face and then its rump. "Why darling!" she cried, "it looks exactly like you!" And Margaret had to submit to the child's pain at seeing the eminence of grief and grievance swept away. But at last, carried beyond the vacant moment when the forgiving and forgiven feeling had not yet come, she sat there in an embarrassed glow, beaming shyly as her mother kissed her and said quietly and finally, "Thank you."

When they were in the dining room, all three of them feeling chastened and purged, Lucy said, "I must have it here by my place." And she put the lamb by her at the table, touching its cheek affectionately.

The dinner that Lucy had cooked was served by the other Margaret. She was a tall, rather light colored girl, with a genteel manner and eyebrows that were now kept very high. As she presented the casserole to Lucy, she looked far off into a distance and stood a little too far away for convenience. Lucy sat there with the serving spoon and fork in her hand and then said, "Come a little closer, Margaret." Margaret Elwin sat rigid, watching. Margaret the maid edged a little closer and continued her gaze. She moved to serve Elwin but Lucy said, "It's Margaret you serve next." Her tone was a little dry. Margaret Elwin flushed and looked mortified. It had been a matter of some satisfaction that she was now of an age to be served at table just after her mother, but she hated to have a point made of it if Margaret objected, and Margaret did seem to object and would not accept the reassuring smile that was being offered her over the casserole.

In the interval between the serving of the casserole and the serving of the salad that had once that evening made the family peace, Margaret held her parents with a stern and desperate eye. But she was unable to suppress a glance her mother sent to her father, a glance that had in it a touch of mild triumph. And her father did not this time fortify himself against it. The odds were terribly against her and she looked from one to the other and said in an intense whisper, "It's not her fault. She's not responsible."

"Why not?" Elwin asked.

It was his voice that made the question baffling to Margaret. She did not answer, or try to. It was not merely that the question was, for the moment, beyond her powers. Nor was it that she was puzzled because her father had seemed to change sides. But she was touched by the sense, so little formulated, so fleeting as scarcely to establish itself in her memory, that something other than the question, or the problem itself, was involved here. She barely perceived, yet she did perceive, her mother's quick glance at her father under lowered lids. It was something more than a glance of surprise. Neither Margaret nor Lucy, of course, knew anything about the sentence from Hazlitt. But this was one of the moments when the sentence had occurred to Elwin and with it the explosion of light. And his wife and daughter had heard the event in his voice. For Elwin an illumination, but a dark illumination, was thrown around the matter that concerned them. It seemed to him—not suddenly, for it had been advancing in his mind for some hours now—that in the aspect of his knowledge of death, all men were equal in their responsibility. The two bus conductors, Lucy's and his own, the boy with his face contorted in rational rage against the injustice he suffered, Margaret the maid with her genteel malice—all of them, quite as much as he himself, bore their own blame. Exemption was not given by age or youth, or sex, or color, or condition of life. It was the sense of this that made his voice so strange at his own dinner-table, as if it came not merely from another place but another time.

"Why not?" he said again. "Why not, Margaret?"

Margaret looked at her father's face and tried to answer. She seriously marshaled her thoughts and, as always, the sight of his daughter actually thinking touched Elwin profoundly. "It's because —because society didn't give her a chance," she said slowly. "She has a handicap. Because she's colored. She has to struggle so hard —against prejudice. It's so *hard* for her."

"It's true," Elwin said. "It's very hard for her. But it's hard for Millie too." Millie had been with the Elwins for nearly seven years. Some months ago she had left them to nurse a dying sister in the South.

Margaret of course knew what her father meant, that Millie, despite "society," was warm and good and capable. Her answer was quick, too quick. "Oh, Millie has a slave-psychology," she said loftily.

Really, Elwin thought, Miss Hoxie went too far. He felt a kind of disgust that a child should have been given such a phrase to use. It was a good school, he approved of its theory; but it must not give Margaret such things to say. He wondered if Margaret had submitted the question of Millie to Miss Hoxie. If she had, and if this was the answer she had been given, his daughter had been, yes, corrupted. He said, "You should not say such things about Millie. She is a good loyal person and you haven't any right to say she is not."

"Loyal!" said Margaret in triumph. "Loyal!"

"Why yes. To her sister in Alabama, Margaret, just as much as to us. Is it what you call slave-psychology to be loyal to your own sister?"

But Margaret was not to be put down. She kept in mind the main point, which was not Millie but the other Margaret.

"I notice," she said defiantly, "that when Millie sends you parts of the money you lent her, you take it all right."

Poor child, she had fumbled, and Elwin laid his hand on hers on the table. "But Margaret! Of course I do," he said. "If I didn't, wouldn't that be slave-psychology? Millie would feel very lowered if I didn't take it."

"But she can't afford it," Margaret insisted.

"No, she can't afford it."

"Well then!" and she confronted the oppressor in her father.

"But she can't afford not to. She needs it for her pride. She needs to think of herself as a person who pays her debts, as a responsible person."

"I wonder," Lucy said, "I wonder how Millie is. Poor thing!" She was not being irrelevant. She was successful in bringing her husband up short. Yes, all that his "wisdom" had done was to lead him to defeat his daughter in argument. And defeat made Margaret stupid and obstinate. She said, "Well, anyway, it's not Margaret's fault," and sat sulking.

Had he been truly the wise man he wanted to be, he would have been able to explain, to Margaret and himself, the nature of the double truth. As much as Margaret, he believed that "society is responsible." He believed the other truth too. He felt rather tired, as if the little debate with Margaret had been more momentous than he understood. Yet wisdom, a small measure of it, did seem to come. It came suddenly, as no doubt was the way of moments of wisdom, and he perceived what stupidly he had not understood earlier, that it was not the other Margaret but herself that his Margaret was grieving for, that in her foolish and passionate argument, with the foolish phrases derived from the admired Miss Hoxie, she was defending herself from her own impending responsibility. Poor thing, she saw it moving toward her through the air at a great rate, and she did not want it. Naturally enough, she did not want it. And he, for what reason he did not know, was forcing it upon her.

He understood why Lucy, when they had risen from the table, made quiet haste to put her arm around Margaret's shoulders as they went into the living room.

They were sitting in the living room, a rather silent family for the moment, when the other Margaret stood in the doorway. "You may as well know," she said, "that I'm through here." And she added, "I've had enough."

There was a little cry, as of horror, from Margaret. She looked at her parents with a bitter and tragic triumph. Lucy said shortly, "Very well, Margaret. Just finish up and I'll pay you." The quick acceptance took the maid aback. Angrier than before, she turned abruptly back into the dining room.

For the third time that evening, Margaret Elwin sat in wretched isolation. Her father did not watch her, but he knew what she felt.

She had been told *she* might go, never to return. She saw the great and frightening world before her. It was after all possible so to offend her parents that this expulsion would follow. Elwin rose to get a cigarette from the table near the sofa on which Margaret sat and he passed his hand over her bright hair. The picture of the king with the flower in his hand was in the other corner of the sofa.

It was as Elwin's hand was on his daughter's head that they heard the crash, and Elwin felt under his hand how Margaret's body experienced a kind of convulsion. He turned and saw Lucy already at the door of the dining room, while there on the floor, in many pieces, as if it had fallen with force, lay the smashed green lamb, more white clay showing than green glaze. Lucy stooped down to the fragments, examining them, delicately turning them over one by one, as if already estimating the possibility of mending.

The maid Margaret stood there, a napkin in her hand clutched to her breast. All the genteel contempt had left her face. She looked only frightened, as if something was now, at last, going to be done to her. For her, almost more than for his own Margaret, Elwin felt sad. He said, "It's all right, Margaret. Don't worry, it's all right." It was a foolish and weak thing to say. It was not all right, and Lucy was still crouching, heartbroken, over the pieces. But he had had to say it, weak and foolish as it was.

"Ah, darling, don't feel too bad," Lucy said to her daughter as she came back into the living room, tenderly holding the smashed thing in her hand.

But Margaret did not answer or even hear. She was staring into the dining room with wide, fixed eyes. "She meant to do it," she said. "She *meant* to do it."

"Oh, no," Lucy said in her most matter-of-fact voice. "Oh, no, dear. It was just an accident."

"She meant to do it, she meant to do it." And then Margaret said, "I *saw* her." She alone had been facing into the dining room and could have seen. "I saw her—with the napkin. She made a movement," and Margaret made a movement, "like this . . ."

Over her head her parents' eyes met. They knew that they could only offer the feeble lying of parents to a child. But they were determined to continue. "Oh, no," Elwin said, "it just happened." And he wondered if the king, within his line of vision as he stood there trying to comfort his daughter, would ever return to the old, fine, tragic power, for at the moment he seemed only quaint, extravagant and beside the point.

"She meant to. She didn't like me. She hated me," and the great sobs began to come. But Elwin knew that it was not because the other Margaret hated her that his Margaret wept, but because she had with her own eyes seen the actual possibility of what she herself might do, the insupportable fact of her own moral life. She was weeping bitterly now, her whole body shaking with the deepest of sobs, and she found refuge in a corner of the sofa, hiding her head from her parents. She had drawn up her knees, making herself as tight and inaccessible as she could, and Elwin, to comfort her, sat on what little space she allowed him on the sofa beside her, stroking her burrowing head and her heaving back, quite unable, whatever he might have hoped and wanted, to give her any better help than that.

LANGSTON HUGHES

(1902–1967)

◆━◆◾◆━◆

Langston Hughes, the most popular writer produced by the Harlem Renaissance of the 1920s, was also America's most prolific Negro author, having produced over forty books, including collections of poems and short stories, a novel, histories, and children's fiction.

Hughes was born in Joplin, Missouri, and spent his youth in Lawrence, Kansas; Lincoln, Illinois; and Cleveland, Ohio. His grandmother, with whom he lived for several years at Lawrence, was the widow of one of the five Negroes who had fought with John Brown at Harper's Ferry. After he was graduated from high school in Cleveland, he spent fifteen months in Mexico visiting with his father and then went on to a year's study at Columbia University. Bored with college, he took a job as a seaman and sailed to West Africa and northern Europe. After living in Italy and France and working as a dishwasher in Paris night clubs, he returned to America and was soon employed as a bus boy in Washington's Wardman Park Hotel. He was "discovered" in 1925 by Vachel Lindsay, who brought public attention to the young Negro poet by reciting some of his verses at a reading of his own poems. That same year Hughes won Opportunity's poetry prize, and within a short time his first two books of poems, The Weary Blues and Fine Clothes to the Jew (both 1926), established him as a leading figure in the Harlem Renaissance.

Heeding Lindsay's advice, Hughes returned to college, and in

1929 he was graduated from Lincoln University, where in his senior year he had written his first novel, Not Without Laughter (1930). In the meantime he had begun the first of the public poetry readings which continued throughout his life. By the early 1930s Hughes had become a member of the Communist Party, and in 1932 he began an extended trip to Russia, where he worked as adviser on a film about Negro life in America. His first Broadway play, Mulatto, was produced in 1935, and in later years he wrote many other dramas and helped to establish Negro theatrical groups in Harlem, Chicago, and Los Angeles.

But Hughes is known chiefly as a poet. He produced ten volumes of verse, including The Negro Mother (1931), Scottsboro Limited (1932), The Dream Keeper (1932), Shakespeare in Harlem (1942), Montage of a Dream Deferred (1951), Selected Poems (1959), and The Panther and the Lash (1967). His poems follow Lindsay and Carl Sandburg in their social realism. Like Lindsay, he was interested in jazz and folk rhythms, and many of his poems were designed for oral interpretation. Like Sandburg, he showed an abiding interest in the "little people," an affection which won him such titles as "Poet Laureate of the Negro People" and "Poet Laureate of Harlem."

Hughes is also celebrated for his series of "Simple" sketches, which he began to write for the Chicago Defender, a Negro newspaper, in the early 1940s. Ultimately published in several volumes, including Simple Speaks His Mind (1950), Simple Takes a Wife (1953), and Simple Stakes a Claim (1957), these sketches presented a type of Harlem Everyman, Jess B. Semple ("just be simple"), who offered humorous but biting observations on subjects ranging from segregated motels to Negro sex magazines. Hughes's technique of attacking racial injustice with comic irony in the Simple sketches and in his poems has been rejected as irrelevant by more militant spokesmen, but he never lost his faith in the efficacy of laughter as a means to social reform. His last poems, particularly some of those in the posthumously published Panther and the Lash, show a growing impatience with the pace of the rights movement, but even here he spoke of the Black Panthers as "motivated by the truest of the oldest lies."

Among Hughes's other works are two autobiographies, The Big

Sea (1940) and I Wonder as I Wander (1956); *several historical works, such as* Fight for Freedom: The Story of the NAACP (1962) *and* Black Magic: A Pictorial History of the Negro in American Entertainment (*with Melton Meltzer, 1967); and collections of short stories, including* The Ways of White Folks (1940) *and* Something in Common (1963). *He also translated the poems of Federico García Lorca and edited anthologies such as* Poems from Black Africa (1963) *and* The Best Short Stories by Negro Writers (1967). *Hughes taught at Atlanta University and was poet-in-residence at the University of Chicago's Laboratory School. His awards included Guggenheim and Rosenwald Fellowships, an honorary doctorate from Lincoln University, and a grant from the American Academy of Arts and Letters.*

"Lenox Avenue Bar" *appeared in* The Panther and the Lash; *all the other following poems were published in* Selected Poems (1959). *The Simple pieces are from* The Best of Simple (1961).

Daybreak in Alabama

When I get to be a composer
I'm gonna write me some music about
Daybreak in Alabama
And I'm gonna put the purtiest songs in it
Rising out of the ground like a swamp mist
And falling out of heaven like soft dew.
I'm gonna put some tall tall trees in it
And the scent of pine needles
And the smell of red clay after rain
And long red necks

And poppy colored faces
And big brown arms
And the field daisy eyes
Of black and white black white black people
And I'm gonna put white hands
And black hands and brown and yellow hands
And red clay earth hands in it
Touching everybody with kind fingers
And touching each other natural as dew
In that dawn of music when I
Get to be a composer
And write about daybreak
In Alabama.

Roland Hayes Beaten (Georgia: 1942)

Negroes,
Sweet and docile,
Meek, humble, and kind:
Beware the day
They change their minds!

Wind
In the cotton fields,
Gentle breeze:
Beware the hour
It uproots trees!

Railroad Avenue

Dusk dark
On Railroad Avenue.
Lights in the fish joints,
Lights in the pool rooms.
A box-car some train
Has forgotten
In the middle of the
Block.

A player piano,
A victrola.
    942
    Was the number.

A boy
Lounging on a corner.
A passing girl
With purple powdered skin.
        Laughter
        Suddenly
        Like a taut drum.
        Laughter
        Suddenly
        Neither truth nor lie.
        Laughter
Hardening the dusk dark evening.
        Laughter
Shaking the lights in the fish joints,
Rolling white balls in the pool rooms,
And leaving untouched the box-car
Some train has forgotten.

Theme for English B

The instructor said,

> *Go home and write*
> *a page tonight.*
> *And let that page come out of you—*
> *Then, it will be true.*

I wonder if it's that simple?
I am twenty-two, colored, born in Winston-Salem.
I went to school there, then Durham, then here
to this college on the hill above Harlem.
I am the only colored student in my class.
The steps from the hill lead down into Harlem,
through a park, then I cross St. Nicholas,

Eighth Avenue, Seventh, and I come to the Y,
the Harlem Branch Y, where I take the elevator
up to my room, sit down, and write this page:

It's not easy to know what is true for you or me
at twenty-two, my age. But I guess I'm what
I feel and see and hear, Harlem, I hear you:
hear you, hear me—we two—you, me, talk on this page.
(I hear New York, too.) Me—who?
Well, I like to eat, sleep, drink, and be in love.
I like to work, read, learn, and understand life.
I like a pipe for a Christmas present,
or records—Bessie, bop, or Bach.
I guess being colored doesn't make me *not* like
the same things other folks like who are other races.
So will my page be colored that I write?
Being me, it will not be white.
But it will be
a part of you, instructor.
You are white—
yet a part of me, as I am a part of you.
That's American.
Sometimes perhaps you don't want to be a part of me.
Nor do I often want to be a part of you.
But we are, that's true!
As I learn from you,
I guess you learn from me—
although you're older—and white—
and somewhat more free.

This is my page for English B.

High to Low

God knows
We have our troubles, too—
One trouble is you:
you talk too loud,
cuss too loud,

look too black,
don't get anywhere,
and sometimes it seems
you don't even care.
The way you send your kids to school
stockings down,
(not Ethical Culture)
the way you shout out loud in church,
(not St. Philips)
and the way you lounge on doorsteps
just as if you were down South,
(not at 409) *
the way you clown—
the way, in other words,
you let me down—
me, trying to uphold the race
and you—
well, you can see,
we have our problems,
too, with you.

Subway Rush Hour

Mingled
breath and smell
so close
mingled
black and white
so near
no room for fear.

Harlem

What happens to a dream deferred?

Does it dry up
like a raisin in the sun?

* 409 Edgecombe Avenue, a fashionable Harlem address. [Ed.]

Or fester like a sore—
And then run?
Does it stink like rotten meat?
Or crust and sugar over—
like a syrupy sweet?

Maybe it just sags
like a heavy load.

Or does it explode?

A Toast to Harlem

Quiet can seem unduly loud at times. Since nobody at the bar was saying a word during a lull in the bright blues-blare of the Wishing Well's usually overworked juke box, I addressed my friend Simple.

"Since you told me last night you are an Indian, explain to me how it is you find yourself living in a furnished room in Harlem, my brave buck, instead of on a reservation?"

"I am a colored Indian," said Simple.

"In other words, a Negro."

"A Black Foot Indian, daddy-o, not a red one. Anyhow, Harlem is the place I always did want to be. And if it wasn't for landladies, I would be happy. That's a fact! I love Harlem."

"What is it you love about Harlem?"

"It's so full of Negroes," said Simple. "I feel like I got protection."

"From what?"

"From white folks," said Simple. "Furthermore, I like Harlem because it belongs to me."

"Harlem does not belong to you. You don't own the houses in Harlem. They belong to white folks."

"I might not own 'em," said Simple, "but I live in 'em. It would take an atom bomb to get me out."

"Or a depression," I said.

"I would not move for no depression. No, I would not go back down South, not even to Baltimore. I am in Harlem to stay! You say the houses ain't mine. Well, the sidewalk is—and don't nobody push me off. The cops don't even say, 'Move on,' hardly no more. They learned something from them Harlem riots. They used to beat your head right in public, but now they only beat it after they get you down to the stationhouse. And they don't beat it then if they think you know a colored congressman."

"Harlem has a few Negro leaders," I said.

"Elected by my *own* vote," said Simple. "Here I ain't scared to vote—that's another thing I like about Harlem. I also like it because we've got subways and it does not take all day to get downtown, neither are you Jim Crowed on the way. Why, Negroes is running some of these subway trains. This morning I rode the A Train down to 34th Street. There were a Negro driving it, making ninety miles a hour. That cat *were really driving* that train! Every time he flew by one of them local stations looks like he was saying, 'Look at me! This train is mine!' That cat were gone, ole man. Which is another reason why I like Harlem! Sometimes I run into Duke Ellington on 125th Street and I say, 'What you know there, Duke?' Duke says, 'Solid, ole man.' He does not know me from Adam, but he speaks. One day I saw Lena Horne coming out of the Hotel Theresa and I said, 'Hubba! Hubba!' Lena smiled. Folks is friendly in Harlem. I feel like I got the world in a jug and the stopper in my hand! So drink a toast to Harlem!"

Simple lifted his glass of beer:

> "Here's to Harlem!
> They say Heaven is Paradise.
> If Harlem ain't Heaven,
> Then a mouse ain't mice!"

"Heaven is a state of mind," I commented.

"It sure is *mine*," said Simple, draining his glass. "From Central Park to 179th, from river to river, Harlem is mine! Lots of white folks is scared to come up here, too, after dark."

"That is nothing to be proud of," I said.

"I am sorry white folks is scared to come to Harlem, but I am scared to go around some of *them*. Why, for instant, in my home town once before I came North to live, I was walking down the street when a white woman jumped out of her door and said, 'Boy, get away from here because I am scared of you.'

"I said, 'Why?'

"She said, 'Because you are black.'

"I said, 'Lady, I am scared of you because you are white.' I went on down the street, but I kept wishing I was blacker—so I could of scared that lady to death. So help me, I did. Imagine somebody talking about they is scared of me because I am black! I got more reason to be scared of white folks than they have of me."

"Right," I said.

"The white race drug me over here from Africa, slaved me, freed me, lynched me, starved me during the depression, Jim Crowed me during the war—then they come talking about they is scared of me! Which is why I am glad I have got one spot to call my own where I hold sway—Harlem. Harlem, where I can thumb my nose at the world!"

"You talk just like a Negro nationalist," I said.

"What's that?"

"Someone who wants Negroes to be on top."

"When everybody else keeps me on the *bottom*, I don't see why I shouldn't want to be on top. I will, too, someday."

"That's the spirit that causes wars," I said.

"I would not mind a war if I could win it. White folks fight, lynch, and enjoy themselves."

"There you go," I said. "That old *race-against-race* jargon. There'll never be peace that way. The world tomorrow ought to be a world where everybody gets along together. The least we can do is extend a friendly hand."

"Every time I extend my hand I get put back in my place. You know them poetries about the black cat that tried to be friendly with the white one:

> "The black cat said to the white cat,
> 'Let's sport around the town.'
> The white cat said to the black cat,
> 'You better set your black self down!' "

"Unfriendliness of that nature should not exist," I said. "Folks ought to live like neighbors."

"You're talking about what ought to be. But as long as what *is* is —and Georgia is Georgia—I will take Harlem for mine. At least, if trouble comes, I will have *my own window* to shoot from."

"I refuse to argue with you any more," I said. "What Harlem ought to hold out to the world from its windows is a friendly hand, not a belligerent attitude."

"It will not be my attitude I will have out my window," said Simple.

Temptation

"When the Lord said, 'Let there be light,' and there was light, what I want to know is where was us colored people?"

"What do you mean, 'Where were we colored people?' " I said.

"We must *not* of been there," said Simple, "because we are still dark. Either He did not include me or else I were not there."

"The Lord was not referring to people when He said, 'Let there be light.' He was referring to the elements, the atmosphere, the air."

"He must have included some people," said Simple, "because white people are light, in fact, *white*, whilst I am dark. How come? I say, we were not there."

"Then where do you think we were?"

"Late as usual," said Simple, "old C. P. Time. We must have been down the road a piece and did not get back on time."

"There was no C. P. Time in those days," I said. "In fact, no people were created—so there couldn't be any Colored People's Time. The Lord God had not yet breathed the breath of life into anyone."

"No?" said Simple.

"No," said I, "because it wasn't until Genesis 2 and 7 that God 'formed man of the dust of the earth and breathed into his nostrils the breath of life and man became a living soul.' His name was Adam. Then He took one of Adam's ribs and made a woman."

"Then trouble began," said Simple. "Thank God, they was both white."

"How do you know Adam and Eve were white?" I asked.

"When I was a kid I seen them on the Sunday school cards," said Simple. "Ever since I been seeing a Sunday school card, they was white. That is why I want to know where was us Negroes when the Lord said, 'Let there be light'?"

"Oh, man, you have a color complex so bad you want to trace it back to the Bible."

"No, I don't. I just want to know how come Adam and Eve was white. If they had started out black, this world might not be in the fix it is today. Eve might not of paid that serpent no attention. I never did know a Negro yet that liked a snake."

"That snake is a symbol," I said, "a symbol of temptation and sin. And that symbol would be the same, no matter what the race."

"I am not talking about no symbol," said Simple. "I am talking about the day when Eve took that apple and Adam et. From then on the human race has been in trouble. There ain't a colored woman living what would take no apple from a snake—and she better not give no snake-apples to her husband!"

"Adam and Eve are symbols, too," I said.

"You are simple yourself," said Simple. "But I just wish we colored folks had been somewhere around at the start. I do not know where we was when Eden was a garden, but we sure didn't get in on none of the crops. If we had, we would not be so poor today. White folks started out ahead and they are still ahead. Look at me!"

"I am looking," I said.

"Made in the image of God," said Simple, "but I never did see anybody like me on a Sunday school card."

"Probably nobody looked like you in Biblical days," I said. "The American Negro did not exist in B.C. You're a product of Caucasia and Africa, Harlem and Dixie. You've been conditioned entirely by our environment, our modern times."

"Times have been hard," said Simple, "but still I am a child of God."

"In the cosmic sense, we are all children of God."

"I have been baptized," said Simple, "also anointed with oil. When I were a child I come through at the mourners' bench. I was converted. I have listened to Daddy Grace and et with Father Divine, moaned with Elder Lawson and prayed with Adam Powell.

Also I have been to the Episcopalians with Joyce. But if a snake were to come up to me and offer *me* an apple, I would say, 'Varmint, be on your way! No fruit today! Bud, you got the wrong stud now, so get along somehow, be off down the road because you're lower than a toad!' Then that serpent would respect me as a wise man—and this world would not be where it is—all on account of an apple. That apple has turned into an atom now."

"To hear you talk, if you had been in the Garden of Eden, the world would still be a Paradise," I said. "Man would not have fallen into sin."

"Not *this* man," said Simple. "I would have stayed in that garden making grape wine, singing like Crosby, and feeling fine! I would not be scuffling out in this rough world, neither would I be in Harlem. If I was Adam I would just stay in Eden in that garden with no rent to pay, no landladies to dodge, no time clock to punch—and *my* picture on a Sunday school card. I'd be a *real gone guy* even if I didn't have but one name—Adam—and no initials."

"You would be *real gone* all right. But you were not there. So, my dear fellow, I trust you will not let your rather late arrival on our contemporary stage distort your perspective."

"No," said Simple.

Lenox Avenue Bar

Weaving
between assorted terrors
is the Jew
who owns the place—
one Jew,
fifty Negroes:
embroideries
(heirloomed
from ancient evenings)
tattered
in this neon
place.

GWENDOLYN BROOKS

(1917-   )

Gwendolyn Brooks, in private life Mrs. Henry L. Blakely, was born in Topeka, Kansas, and was raised in Chicago, where she attended Wilson Junior College and has lived most of her life. The mother of two children, she has always seen herself primarily as a wife and mother and only secondarily as a poet.

Her first volume of poems, A Street in Bronzeville, appeared in 1945. In 1950 she became the first Negro poet to receive the Pulitzer Prize, awarded for her second book of poems, Annie Allen (1949). She has published other volumes of poetry, The Bean Eaters (1960), Selected Poems (1963), and In the Mecca (1968), and a novel, Maud Martha (1953). Miss Brooks has taught at four Illinois colleges (Elmhurst, Columbia, Northeastern State, and Chicago Teachers) and has given poetry readings at the Library of Congress and on National Educational Television. In addition to the Pulitzer Prize, she has received an American Academy of Arts and Letters award, a Guggenheim Fellowship, and Poetry Magazine's Eunice Tietjens Memorial Award. An adept practitioner of the sonnet, Miss Brooks once claimed that her poetic intent was "to vivify the universal fact . . . but the universal wears contemporary clothing very well."

the preacher: ruminates behind the sermon

I think it must be lonely to be God.
Nobody loves a master. No. Despite
The bright hosannas, bright dear-Lords, and bright
Determined reverence of Sunday eyes.

Picture Jehovah striding through the hall
Of His importance, creatures running out
From servant-corners to acclaim, to shout
Appreciation of His merit's glare.

But who walks with Him?—dares to take His arm,
To slap Him on the shoulder, tweak His ear,
Buy Him a Coca-Cola or a beer,
Pooh-pooh His politics, call Him a fool?

Perhaps—who knows?—He tires of looking down.
Those eyes are never lifted. Never straight.
Perhaps sometimes He tires of being great
In solitude. Without a hand to hold.

People Who Have No Children Can Be Hard

People who have no children can be hard:
Attain a mail of ice and insolence:
Need not pause in the fire, and in no sense
Hesitate in the hurricane to guard.
And when wide world is bitten and bewarred
They perish purely, waving their spirits hence
Without a trace of grace or of offense

To laugh or fail, diffident, wonder-starred.
While through a throttling dark we others hear
The little lifting helplessness, the queer
Whimper-whine; whose unridiculous
Lost softness softly makes a trap for us.
And makes a curse. And makes a sugar of
The malocclusions, the inconditions of love.

The Bean Eaters

They eat beans mostly, this old yellow pair.
Dinner is a casual affair.
Plain chipware on a plain and creaking wood,
Tin flatware.

Two who are Mostly Good.
Two who have lived their day,
But keep on putting on their clothes
And putting things away.

And remembering . . .
Remembering, with twinklings and twinges,
As they lean over the beans in their rented back room that is full of
beads and receipts and dolls and cloths, tobacco crumbs, vases
and fringes.

The *Chicago Defender* Sends a Man to Little Rock

Fall, 1957

In Little Rock the people bear
Babes, and comb and part their hair
And watch the want ads, put repair
To roof and latch. While wheat toast burns
A woman waters multiferns.

Time upholds or overturns
The many, tight, and small concerns.

In Little Rock the people sing
Sunday hymns like anything,
Through Sunday pomp and polishing.

And after testament and tunes,
Some soften Sunday afternoons
With lemon tea and Lorna Doones.

I forecast
And I believe
Come Christmas Little Rock will cleave
To Christmas tree and trifle, weave,
From laugh and tinsel, texture fast.

In Little Rock is baseball; Barcarolle.
That hotness in July . . . the uniformed figures raw and implacable
And not intellectual,
Batting the hotness or clawing the suffering dust.
The Open Air Concert, on the special twilight green. . . .
When Beethoven is brutal or whispers to lady-like air.
Blanket-sitters are solemn, as Johann troubles to lean
To tell them what to mean. . . .

There is love, too, in Little Rock. Soft women softly
Opening themselves in kindness,
Or, pitying one's blindness,
Awaiting one's pleasure
In azure
Glory with anguished rose at the root. . . .
To wash away old semi-discomfitures.
They re-teach purple and unsullen blue.
The wispy soils go. And uncertain
Half-havings have they clarified to sures.

In Little Rock they know
Not answering the telephone is a way of rejecting life,
That it is our business to be bothered, is our business
To cherish bores or boredom, be polite
To lies and love and many-faceted fuzziness.

I scratch my head, massage the hate-I-had.
I blink across my prim and pencilled pad.
The saga I was sent for is not down.
Because there is a puzzle in this town.
The biggest News I do not dare
Telegraph to the Editor's chair:
"They are like people everywhere."

The angry Editor would reply
In hundred harryings of Why.

And true, they are hurling spittle, rock,
Garbage and fruit in Little Rock.
And I saw coiling storm a-writhe
On bright madonnas. And a scythe
Of men harassing brownish girls.
(The bows and barrettes in the curls
And braids declined away from joy.)

I saw a bleeding brownish boy. . . .

The lariat lynch-wish I deplored.

The loveliest lynchee was our Lord.

Medgar Evers

For Charles Evers

The man whose height his fear improved he
arranged to fear no further. The raw
intoxicated time was time for better birth or
a final death.

Old styles, old tempos, all the engagement of
the day—the sedate, the regulated fray—
the antique light, the Moral rose, old gusts,
tight whistlings from the past, the mothballs
in the Love at last our man forswore.

Medgar Evers annoyed confetti and assorted
brands of businessmen's eyes.

The shows came down: to maxims and surprise.
And palsy.

Roaring no rapt arise-ye to the dead, he
leaned across tomorrow. People said that
he was holding clean globes in his hands.

RALPH ELLISON

(1914-   )

Ralph Ellison's Invisible Man (1952), winner of the National Book Award in 1952 and voted the most distinguished novel of the previous twenty years in a 1965 poll of two hundred writers, editors, and critics conducted by the New York Herald Tribune's Book Week, has been the subject of more critical discussion than any other work by a black American. Indeed, F. W. Dupee recognized the book's potential status as an American classic when he termed it "a veritable Moby Dick of the racial crisis."

Ralph Waldo Ellison was born in Oklahoma City, Oklahoma, in 1914. When his father, a construction worker, died three years later, his mother supported the family through domestic work. After three years at Tuskegee Institute, where he studied music, Ellison went to New York in 1936 intending to become a sculptor, but his interests soon turned to literature. In New York he met Langston Hughes and Richard Wright while working for the Federal Writers Project. Wright, who became a close friend, encouraged his interest in literature, urging him to study Conrad, Henry James, and Dostoevski, and soon Ellison's stories, essays, and reviews were appearing in such journals as New Masses and Antioch Review. Under Wright's influence he also developed an interest in radical politics, but, unlike Wright, he remained aloof from political organizations and did not join the Communist Party. He was briefly editor of Negro Quarterly. Aided by a Rosenwald Fellowship after the war, during which he had served in the Merchant Marine, Ellison worked for several years on Invisible Man and published the novel in 1952 to widespread critical acclaim. The book traces the childhood and college experiences of an idealistic young Negro in the South and follows him to his ultimate disillusionment in New York, where he retreats as an "invisible man" into a subterranean Harlem chamber, although he hopes to return to the world some day with a positive Negro identity. The episodic book, which explores various ideological approaches to racial problems, is grim and often despairing, but at all times it is informed by a profound sense of comic irony.

Since the publication of Invisible Man Ellison has held various academic posts at Bard College, the University of Chicago, Rutgers University, and Yale University. He has also delivered guest lectures at many American schools and has been awarded the Rome Fellowship of the American Academy of Arts and Letters, an honorary doctorate at Tuskegee, and membership in the American Institute of Arts and Letters. In 1964 he published Shadow and Act, a collection of essays and reviews dealing mainly with literature and music. He has been at work for several years on a second novel.

Ellison has consistently argued for the primacy of the writer's fidelity to his craft. Although he writes from the point of view of the black experience, he has always measured himself against writers such as James and Conrad, seeing the function of the novelist as "learning to conceive of human values in the ways which have been established by the great writers who have developed and extended the art." Inevitably, he has been attacked (by Irving Howe and other critics) for failing to adopt an activist stance in his writings, but Ellison, who insists on his membership in the freedom movement, answers, "To think that a writer must think about his Negroness is to fall into a trap."

Unlike Wright, Chester Himes, and LeRoi Jones, Ellison has maintained a confident and positive attitude about the possibilities of life in America. As the narrator of Invisible Man says at the novel's end, "I've overstayed my hibernation, since there's a possibility that even an invisible man has a socially responsible role to play." Though Marcus Klein terms this conclusion "desperate, empty, unreasonable, and programmatic optimism," Ellison's idealism appears to have become even more pronounced in several essays in Shadow and Act.

"The Art of Fiction: An Interview," by Alfred Chester and Vilma Howard, which was published in Shadow and Act, appeared originally in the Spring 1955 Paris Review, with the following introductory note.

The Art of Fiction: an Interview
By Alfred Chester and Vilma Howard

When Invisible Man, Ralph Ellison's first novel, received the National Book award for 1952, the author in his acceptance speech noted with dismay and gratification the conferring of the award to what he called "an attempt at a major novel." His gratification was understandable, so too his dismay when one considers the amount of objectivity Mr. Ellison can display toward his own work. He felt the state of United States fiction to be so unhappy that it was an "attempt" rather than an achievement which received the important award.

Many of us will disagree with Mr. Ellison's evaluation of his own work. Its crackling, brilliant, sometimes wild, but always controlled prose warrants this; so does the care and logic with which its form is revealed, and not least its theme: that of a young Negro who emerges from the South and—in the tradition of James's Hyacinth Robinson and Stendhal's Julien Sorel—moves into the adventure of life at large.

In the summer of 1954, Mr. Ellison came abroad to travel and lecture. His visit ended with Paris where for a very few weeks he mingled with the American expatriate group to whom his work was known and of much interest. The day before he left he talked to us in the Café de la Mairie du VIᵉ about art and the novel.

Ralph Ellison takes both art and the novel seriously. And the Café de la Mairie has a tradition of seriousness behind it, for *here was written Djuna Barnes's spectacular novel,* Nightwood. *There is a tradition, too, of speech and eloquence, for Miss Barnes's hero, Dr. O'Connor, often drew a crowd of listeners to his mighty rhetoric. So here gravity is in the air and rhetoric too. While Mr. Ellison speaks, he rarely pauses, and although the strain of organizing his thought is sometimes evident, his phraseology and the quiet steady flow and development of ideas are overwhelming. To listen to him is rather like sitting in the back of a huge hall and feeling the lecturer's faraway eyes staring directly into your own. The highly emphatic, almost professorial intonations, startle with their distance, self-confidence, and warm undertones of humor.*

ELLISON: Let me say right now that my book is not an autobiographical work.

INTERVIEWERS: You weren't thrown out of school like the boy in your novel?

ELLISON: No. Though, like him, I went from one job to another.

INTERVIEWERS: Why did you give up music and begin writing?

ELLISON: I didn't give up music, but I became interested in writing through incessant reading. In 1935 I discovered Eliot's *The Waste Land* which moved and intrigued me but defied my powers of analysis—such as they were—and I wondered why I had never read anything of equal intensity and sensibility by an American Negro writer. Later on, in New York, I read a poem by Richard Wright, who, as luck would have it, came to town the next week. He was editing a magazine called *New Challenge* and asked me to try a book review of E. Waters Turpin's *These Low Grounds.* On the basis of this review Wright suggested that I try a short story, which I did. I tried to use my knowledge of riding freight trains. He liked the story well enough to accept it and it got as far as the galley proofs when it was bumped from the issue because there was too much material. Just after that the magazine failed.

INTERVIEWERS: But you went on writing—

ELLISON: With difficulty, because this was the Recession of 1937. I went to Dayton, Ohio, where my brother and I hunted and sold game to earn a living. At night I practiced writing and studied Joyce, Dostoevski, Stein, and Hemingway. Especially Hemingway;

I read him to learn his sentence structure and how to organize a story. I guess many young writers were doing this, but I also used his description of hunting when I went into the fields the next day. I had been hunting since I was eleven, but no one had broken down the process of wing-shooting for me, and it was from reading Hemingway that I learned to lead a bird. When he describes something in print, believe him; believe him even when he describes the process of art in terms of baseball or boxing; he's been there.

INTERVIEWERS: Were you affected by the social realism of the period?

ELLISON: I was seeking to learn and social realism was a highly regarded theory, though I didn't think too much of the so-called proletarian fiction even when I was most impressed by Marxism. I was intrigued by Malraux, who at that time was being claimed by the Communists. I noticed, however, that whenever the heroes of *Man's Fate* regarded their condition during moments of heightened self-consciousness, their thinking was something other than Marxist. Actually they were more profoundly intellectual than their real-life counterparts. Of course, Malraux was more of a humanist than most of the Marxist writers of that period—and also much more of an artist. He was the artist-revolutionary rather than a politician when he wrote *Man's Fate*, and the book lives not because of a political position embraced at the time but because of its larger concern with the tragic struggle of humanity. Most of the social realists of the period were concerned less with tragedy than with injustice. I wasn't, and am not, *primarily* concerned with injustice, but with art.

INTERVIEWERS: Then you consider your novel a purely literary work as opposed to one in the tradition of social protest.

ELLISON: Now, mind, I recognize no dichotomy between art and protest. Dostoevski's *Notes from Underground* is, among other things, a protest against the limitations of nineteenth-century rationalism; *Don Quixote, Man's Fate, Oedipus Rex, The Trial* —all these embody protest, even against the limitation of human life itself. If social protest is antithetical to art, what then shall we make of Goya, Dickens, and Twain? One hears a lot of complaints about the so-called "protest novel," especially when written by Negroes; but it seems to me that the critics could more accurately complain about the lack of craftsmanship and the provincialism which is typical of such works.

INTERVIEWERS: But isn't it going to be difficult for the Negro writer to escape provincialism when his literature is concerned with a minority?

ELLISON: All novels are about certain minorities: the individual is a minority. The universal in the novel—and isn't that what we're all clamoring for these days?—is reached only through the depiction of the specific man in a specific circumstance.

INTERVIEWERS: But still, how is the Negro writer, in terms of what is expected of him by critics and readers, going to escape his particular need for social protest and reach the "universal" you speak of?

ELLISON: If the Negro, or any other writer, is going to do what is expected of him, he's lost the battle before he takes the field. I suspect that all the agony that goes into writing is borne precisely because the writer longs for acceptance—but it must be acceptance on his own terms. Perhaps, though, this thing cuts both ways: the Negro novelist draws his blackness too tightly around him when he sits down to write—that's what the anti-protest critics believe —but perhaps the white reader draws his whiteness around himself when he sits down to read. He doesn't want to identify himself with Negro characters in terms of our immediate racial and social situation, though on the deeper human level identification can become compelling when the situation is revealed artistically. The white reader doesn't want to get too close, not even in an imaginary re-creation of society. Negro writers have felt this, and it has led to much of our failure.

Too many books by Negro writers are addressed to a white audience. By doing this the authors run the risk of limiting themselves to the audience's presumptions of what a Negro is or should be; the tendency is to become involved in polemics, to plead the Negro's humanity. You know, many white people question that humanity, but I don't think that Negroes can afford to indulge in such a false issue. For us the question should be, what are the specific *forms* of that humanity, and what in our background is worth preserving or abandoning. The clue to this can be found in folklore, which offers the first drawings of any group's character.

It preserves mainly those situations which have repeated themselves again and again in the history of any given group. It describes those rites, manners, customs, and so forth, which insure the good life, or destroy it; and it describes those boundaries of feeling, thought, and action which that particular group has found to be the limitation of the human condition. It projects this wisdom in symbols which express the group's will to survive; it embodies those values by which the group lives and dies. These drawings may be crude but they are nonetheless profound in that they represent the group's attempt to humanize the world. It's no accident that great literature, the product of individual artists, is erected upon this humble base. The hero of Dostoevski's *Notes from Underground* and the hero of Gogol's "The Overcoat" appear in their rudimentary forms far back in Russian folklore. French literature has never ceased exploring the nature of the Frenchman. Or take Picasso—

INTERVIEWERS: How does Picasso fit into all this?

ELLISON: Why, he's the greatest wrestler with forms and techniques of them all. Just the same, he's never abandoned the old symbolic forms of Spanish art: the guitar, the bull, daggers, women, shawls, veils, mirrors. Such symbols serve a dual function: they allow the artist to speak of complex experiences and to annihilate time with simple lines and curves; and they allow the viewer an orientation, both emotional and associative, which goes so deep that a total culture may resound in a simple rhythm, an image. It has been said that Escudero could recapitulate the history and spirit of the Spanish dance with a simple arabesque of his fingers.

INTERVIEWERS: But these are examples from homogeneous cultures. How representative of the American nation would you say Negro folklore is?

ELLISON: The history of the American Negro is a most intimate part of American history. Through the very process of slavery came the building of the United States. Negro folklore, evolving within a larger culture which regarded it as inferior, was an especially courageous expression. It announced the Negro's willingness to trust his own experience, his own sensibilities as to the definition of reality, rather than allow his masters to define these crucial matters for him. His experience is that of America and the West, and is as rich a body of experience as one would find anywhere. We can view it narrowly as something exotic, folksy, or "low-down," or we may identify ourselves with it and recognize it as an important segment of the larger American experience—not lying at the bottom of it, but intertwined, diffused in its very texture. I can't take this lightly or be impressed by those who cannot see its importance; it is important to *me*. One ironic witness to the beauty and the universality of this art is the fact that the descendants of the very men who enslaved us can now sing the spirituals and find in the singing an exaltation of their own humanity. Just take a look at some of the slave songs, blues, folk ballads; their possibilities for the writer are infinitely suggestive. Some of them have named human situations so well that a whole corps of writers could not exhaust their universality. For instance, here's an old slave verse:

> Ole Aunt Dinah, she's just like me
> She work so hard she want to be free
> But ole Aunt Dinah's gittin' kinda ole
> She's afraid to go to Canada on account of the cold.

> Ole Uncle Jack, now he's a mighty "good nigger"
> You tell him that you want to be free for a fac'
> Next thing you know they done stripped the skin off your back.

> Now ole Uncle Ned, he want to be free
> He found his way north by the moss on the tree
> He cross that river floating in a tub
> The patateroller* give him a mighty close rub.

It's crude, but in it you have three universal attitudes toward the problem of freedom. You can refine it and sketch in the psychological subtleties and historical and philosophical allusions, action and whatnot, but I don't think its basic definition can be exhausted. Perhaps some genius could do as much with it as Mann has done with the Joseph story.

INTERVIEWERS: Can you give us an example of the use of folklore in your own novel?

* Patroller.

ELLISON: Well, there are certain themes, symbols, and images which are based on folk material. For example, there is the old saying among Negroes: If you're black, stay back; if you're brown, stick around; if you're white, you're right. And there is the joke Negroes tell on themselves about their being so black they can't be seen in the dark. In my book this sort of thing was merged with the meanings which blackness and light have long had in Western mythology: evil and goodness, ignorance and knowledge, and so on. In my novel the narrator's development is one through blackness to light; that is, from ignorance to enlightenment: invisibility to visibility. He leaves the South and goes North; this, as you will notice in reading Negro folk tales, is always the road to freedom—the movement upward. You have the same thing again when he leaves his underground cave for the open.

It took me a long time to learn how to adapt such examples of myth into my work—also ritual. The use of ritual is equally a vital part of the creative process. I learned a few things from Eliot, Joyce and Hemingway, but not how to adapt them. When I started writing, I knew that in both *The Waste Land* and *Ulysses* ancient myth and ritual were used to give form and significance to the material; but it took me a few years to realize that the myths and rites which we find functioning in our everyday lives could be used in the same way. In my first attempt at a novel —which I was unable to complete—I began by trying to manipulate the simple structural unities of *beginning, middle,* and *end,* but when I attempted to deal with the psychological strata—the images, symbols, and emotional configurations—of the experience at hand, I discovered that the unities were simply cool points of stability on which one could suspend the narrative line—but beneath the surface of apparently rational human relationships there seethed a chaos before which I was helpless. People rationalize what they shun or are incapable of dealing with; these superstitions and their rationalizations become ritual as they govern behavior. The rituals become social forms, and it is one of the functions of the artist to recognize them and raise them to the level of art.

I don't know whether I'm getting this over or not. Let's put it this way: Take the "Battle Royal" passage in my novel, where the boys are blindfolded and forced to fight each other for the amusement of the white observers. This is a vital part of behavior pattern in the South, which both Negroes and whites thoughtlessly accept. It is a ritual in preservation of caste lines, a keeping of taboo to appease the gods and ward off bad luck. It is also the initiation ritual to which all greenhorns are subjected. This passage states what Negroes will see I did not have to invent; the patterns were already there in society so that all I had to do was present them in a broader context of meaning. In any society there are many rituals of situation which, for the most part, go unquestioned. They can be simple or elaborate, but they are the connective tissue between the work of art and the audience.

INTERVIEWERS: Do you think a reader unacquainted with this folklore can properly understand your work?

ELLISON: Yes, I think so. It's like Jazz; there's no inherent problem which prohibits understanding but the assumptions brought to it. We don't all dig Shakespeare uniformly, or even "Little Red Riding Hood." The understanding of art depends finally upon one's willingness to extend one's humanity and one's knowledge of human life. I noticed, incidentally, that the Germans, having no special caste assumptions concerning American Negroes, dealt with my work simply as a novel. I think the Americans will come to view it that way in twenty years—if it's around that long.

INTERVIEWERS: Don't you think it will be?

ELLISON: I doubt it. It's not an important novel. I failed of eloquence and many of the immediate issues are rapidly fading away. If it does last, it will be simply because there are things going on in its depth that are of more permanent interest than on its surface. I hope so, anyway.

INTERVIEWERS: Have the critics given you any constructive help in your writing, or changed in any way your aims in fiction?

ELLISON: No, except that I have a better idea of how the critics react, of what they see and fail to see, of how their sense of life differs with mine and mine with theirs. In some instances they were nice for the wrong reasons. In the U.S.—and I don't want this to sound like an apology for my own failures—some reviewers did not see what was before them because of this nonsense about protest.

INTERVIEWERS: Did the critics change your view of yourself as a writer?

ELLISON: I can't say that they did. I've been seeing by my own candle too long for that. The critics did give me a sharper sense of a larger audience, yes; and some convinced me that they were willing to judge me in terms of my writing rather than in terms of my racial identity. But there is one widely syndicated critical bankrupt who made liberal noises during the thirties and has been frightened ever since. He attacked my book as a "literary race riot." By and large, the critics and readers gave me an affirmed sense of my identity as a writer. You might know this within yourself, but to have it affirmed by others is of utmost importance. Writing is, after all, a form of communication.

INTERVIEWERS: When did you begin *Invisible Man*?

ELLISON: In the summer of 1945. I had returned from the sea, ill, with advice to get some rest. Part of my illness was due, no doubt, to the fact that I had not been able to write a novel for which I'd received a Rosenwald Fellowship the previous winter. So on a farm in Vermont where I was reading *The Hero* by Lord Ragland and speculating on the nature of Negro leadership in the U.S., I wrote the first paragraph of *Invisible Man*, and was soon involved in the struggle of creating the novel.

INTERVIEWERS: How long did it take you to write it?

ELLISON: Five years with one year out for a short novel which was unsatisfactory, ill-conceived, and never submitted for publication.

INTERVIEWERS: Did you have everything thought out before you began to write *Invisible Man*?

ELLISON: The symbols and their connections were known to me. I began it with a chart of the three-part division. It was a conceptual frame with most of the ideas and some incidents indicated. The three parts represent the narrator's movement from, using Kenneth Burke's terms, purpose to passion to perception. These three major sections are built up of smaller units of three which mark the course of the action and which depend for their development upon what I hoped was a consistent and developing motivation. However, you'll note that the maximum insight on the hero's part isn't reached until the final section. After all, it's a novel about innocence and human error, a struggle through illusion to reality. Each section begins with a sheet of paper; each piece of paper is exchanged for another and contains a definition of his identity, or the social role he is to play as defined for him by others. But all say essentially the same thing: "Keep this nigger boy running." Before he could have some voice in his own destiny he had to discard these old identities and illusions; his enlightenment couldn't come until then. Once he recognizes the hole of darkness into which these papers put him, he has to burn them. That's the plan and the intention; whether I achieved this is something else.

INTERVIEWERS: Would you say that the search for identity is primarily an American theme?

ELLISON: It is *the* American theme. The nature of our society is such that we are prevented from knowing who we are. It is still a young society, and this is an integral part of its development.

INTERVIEWERS: A common criticism of "first novels" is that the central incident is either omitted or weak. *Invisible Man* seems to suffer here; shouldn't we have been present at the scenes which are the dividing lines in the book—namely, when the Brotherhood organization moves the narrator downtown, then back uptown?

ELLISON: I think you missed the point. The major flaw in the hero's character is his unquestioning willingness to do what is required of him by others as a way to success, and this was the specific form of his "innocence." He goes where he is told to go; he does what he is told to do; he does not even choose his Brotherhood name. It is chosen for him and he accepts it. He has accepted party discipline and thus cannot be present at the scene since it is not the will of the Brotherhood leaders. What is important is not the scene but his failure to question their decision. There is also the fact that no single person can be everywhere at once, nor can a single consciousness be aware of all the nuances of a large social action. What happens uptown while he is downtown is part of his darkness, both symbolic and actual. No; I don't feel that any vital scenes have been left out.

INTERVIEWERS: Why did you find it necessary to shift styles throughout the book; particularly in the Prologue and Epilogue?

ELLISON: The Prologue was written afterwards, really—in terms of a shift in the hero's point of view. I wanted to throw the reader off balance—make him accept certain non-naturalistic effects. It was really a memoir written underground, and I wanted a foreshadowing through which I hoped the reader would view the actions which took place in the main body of the book. For another thing, the styles of life presented are different. In the South, where he was trying to fit into a traditional pattern and where his sense of certainty had not yet been challenged, I felt a more naturalistic treatment was adequate. The college trustee's speech to the students is really an echo of a certain kind of Southern rhetoric and I enjoyed trying to re-create it. As the hero passes from the South to the North, from the relatively stable to the swiftly changing, his sense of certainty is lost and the style becomes expressionistic. Later on during his fall from grace in the Brotherhood it becomes somewhat surrealistic. The styles try to express both his state of consciousness and the state of society. The Epilogue was necessary to complete the action begun when he set out to write his memoirs.

INTERVIEWERS: After four hundred pages you still felt the Epilogue was necessary?

ELLISON: Yes. Look at it this way. The book is a series of reversals. It is the portrait of the artist as a rabble-rouser, thus the various mediums of expression. In the Epilogue the hero discovers what he had not discovered throughout the book: you have to make your own decisions; you have to think for yourself. The hero comes up from underground because the act of writing and thinking necessitated it. He could not stay down there.

INTERVIEWERS: You say that the book is "a series of reversals." It seemed to us that this was a weakness, that it was built on a series of provocative situations which were canceled by the calling up of conventional emotions.

ELLISON: I don't quite see what you mean.

INTERVIEWERS: Well, for one thing, you begin with a provocative situation of the American Negro's status in society. The responsibility for this is that of the white American citizen; that's where the guilt lies. Then you cancel it by introducing the Communist Party, or the Brotherhood, so that the reader tends to say to himself, "Ah, they're the guilty ones. They're the ones who mistreat him; not us."

ELLISON: I think that's a case of misreading. And I didn't identify the Brotherhood as the C.P., but since you do I'll remind you that they too are white. The hero's invisibility is not a matter of being seen, but a refusal to run the risk of his own humanity, which involves guilt. This is not an attack upon white society! It is what the hero refuses to do in each section which leads to further action. He must assert and achieve his own humanity; he cannot run with the pack and do this—this is the reason for all the reversals. The Epilogue is the most final reversal of all; therefore it is a necessary statement.

INTERVIEWERS: And the love affairs—or almost-love-affairs—

ELLISON: [Laughing] I'm glad you put it that way. The point is that when thrown into a situation which he thinks he wants, the hero is sometimes thrown at a loss; he doesn't know how to act. After he had made this speech about the Place of the Woman in Our Society, for example, and was approached by one of the women in the audience, he thought she wanted to talk about the Brotherhood and found that she wanted to talk about brother-and-sisterhood. Look, didn't you find the book at all funny? I felt that such a man as this character would have been incapable of a love affair; it would have been inconsistent with his personality.

INTERVIEWERS: Do you have any difficulty controlling your characters? E. M. Forster says that he sometimes finds a character running away with him.

ELLISON: No, because I find that a sense of the ritual understructure of the fiction helps to guide the creation of characters. Action is the thing. We are what we do and not do. The problem for me is to get from A to B to C. My anxiety about transitions greatly prolonged the writing of my book. The naturalists stick to case histories and sociology and are willing to compete with the camera and the tape recorder. I despise concreteness in writing, but when reality is deranged in fiction, one must worry about the seams.

INTERVIEWERS: Do you have difficulty turning real characters into fiction?

ELLISON: Real characters are just a limitation. It's like turning your own life into fiction: you have to be hindered by chronology and fact. A number of the characters just jumped out, like Rinehart and Ras.

INTERVIEWERS: Isn't Ras based on Marcus Garvey? *

ELLISON: No. In 1950 my wife and I were staying at a vacation spot where we met some white liberals who thought the best way to be friendly was to tell us what it was like to be Negro. I got mad at hearing this from people who otherwise seemed very intelligent. I had already sketched Ras, but the passion of his statement came out after I went upstairs that night feeling that we needed to have this thing out once and for all and get it done with; then we could go on living like people and individuals. No conscious reference to Garvey is intended.

INTERVIEWERS: What about Rinehart? Is he related to Rinehart in the blues tradition, or Django Rheinhardt, the jazz musician?

ELLISON: There is a peculiar set of circumstances connected with my choice of that name. My old Oklahoma friend, Jimmy Rushing, the blues singer, used to sing one with a refrain that went:

> Rinehart, Rinehart,
> It's so lonesome up here
> On Beacon Hill,

which haunted me, and as I was thinking of a character who was a master of disguise, of coincidence, this name with its suggestion of inner and outer came to my mind. Later I learned that it was a call used by Harvard students when they prepared to riot, a call to chaos. Which is very interesting, because it is not long after Rinehart appears in my novel that the riot breaks out in Harlem. Rinehart is my name for the personification of chaos. He is also intended to represent America and change. He has lived so long with chaos that he knows how to manipulate it. It is the old theme of *The Confidence Man*. He is a figure in a country with no solid past or stable class lines; therefore he is able to move about easily from one to the other. . . .

You know, I'm still thinking of your question about the use of Negro experience as material for fiction. One function of serious literature is to deal with the moral core of a given society. Well,

* Marcus Garvey: Negro nationalist and founder of a "Back to Africa" movement in the United States during the early 1900s. [Interviewers' note.]

in the United States the Negro and his status have always stood for that moral concern. He symbolizes among other things the human and social possibility of equality. This is the moral question raised in our two great nineteenth-century novels, *Moby Dick* and *Huckleberry Finn*. The very center of Twain's book revolves finally around the boy's relations with Nigger Jim and the question of what Huck should do about getting Jim free after the two scoundrels had sold him. There is a magic here worth conjuring, and that reaches to the very nerve of the American consciousness—so why should I abandon it? Our so-called race problem has now lined up with the world problems of colonialism and the struggle of the West to gain the allegiance of the remaining non-white people who have thus far remained outside the Communist sphere; thus its possibilities for art have increased rather than lessened. Looking at the novelist as manipulator and depicter of moral problems, I ask myself how much of the achievement of democratic ideals in the U.S. has been affected by the steady pressure of Negroes and those whites who were sensitive to the implications of our condition; and I know that without that pressure the position of our country before the world would be much more serious than it is even now. Here is part of the social dynamics of a great society. Perhaps the discomfort about protest in books by Negro authors comes because since the nineteenth century American literature has avoided profound moral searching. It was too painful and besides there were specific problems of language and form to which the writers could address themselves. They did wonderful things, but perhaps they left the real problems untouched. There are exceptions, of course, like Faulkner who has been working the great moral theme all along, taking it up where Mark Twain put it down.

I feel that with my decision to devote myself to the novel I took on one of the responsibilities inherited by those who practice the craft in the U.S.: that of describing for all that fragment of the huge diverse American experience which I know best, and which offers me the possibility of contributing not only to the growth of the literature but to the shaping of the culture as I should like it to be. The American novel is in this sense a conquest of the frontier; as it describes our experience, it creates it.

JAMES BALDWIN

(1 9 2 4 –   )

<hr/>

Generally regarded as the most important black writer to emerge in the last fifteen years, James Baldwin has attained a stature achieved previously among American Negro writers only by Richard Wright and Ralph Ellison. Baldwin was born in Harlem, the first in a family of nine children, to a father who was a factory worker and a lay preacher in a store-front church. At fourteen Baldwin himself became a preacher, but he rankled under his father's severe discipline and by the time of his graduation from DeWitt Clinton High School in 1942 he had rejected both his father and his church. In 1944 he met Richard Wright; the latter's death in 1960, according to Robert A. Bone in The Negro Novel in America, was an important turning point in Baldwin's career. Up to that time, according to Bone, Baldwin had defined himself in opposition to a father figure and had rejected Wright's use of fiction as a vehicle for social protest, but since Wright's death he has increasingly turned to protest and adopted a prophetic strain.

Although aided by Saxton and Rosenwald fellowships, Baldwin made little headway as a writer until he began a nine-year residence in France in 1948, hoping that physical disengagement from the American racial dilemma would help him find his own identity and maturity as an artist. In 1953 he published Go Tell It on the Mountain, which was based on his experiences in his father's Harlem church and is usually considered his best novel. His second novel, Giovanni's Room (1956), employs white characters and is concerned with the discovery by an American expatriate living in France of his homosexuality. Another Country (1962), which dealt with several characters' quests for identity in a series of inter-racial love affairs, both homosexual and heterosexual, was viewed by most critics as a disappointment. But the novel is interesting for its assertion of his growing anger at America and a new tone of militancy. In his latest novel, Tell Me How Long the Train's Been Gone (1968), the tone of angry protest is even more pronounced.

Beginning with a lonely protagonist isolated by blackness and homosexuality and deeply enmeshed in conflict with father and church, Baldwin's novels have moved through acceptance of race and sexual condition, to pronouncement of a Negro and a homo-sexual strength achieved through suffering. Baldwin once ac-knowledged his indebtedness to Dostoevski, Proust, and James, and in an early essay he wrote that "social affairs are not generally speaking the writer's prime concern, whether they ought to be or not; it is absolutely necessary that he establish between himself and these affairs a distance that will allow, at least, for clarity." But in later works, particularly the play Blues for Mr. Charlie (1964) and the story "Going to Meet the Man" (1965), he has increas-ingly tended to make his characters function as social types rather than as individuals in quest of personal identity. Negro author Albert Murray writes that "Baldwin has relied more and more on the abstract categories of academic research and less and less on the poetic insights of the creative artist," and critic Bone adds, "Some-thing like good works and politics have been the recent bent of his career. Unable to grow as an artist, he has fallen back upon a tradition of protest writing which he formerly denounced."

Although he regards himself as chiefly a novelist, Baldwin's high critical reputation is based largely on his essays, which have ap-peared in three volumes, Notes of a Native Son (1955), Nobody Knows My Name (1961), and The Fire Next Time (1963). Robert F. Sayre summed up widely held critical opinion when he wrote that Baldwin "has learned the art of the novel but taught the art of the essay." As with his novels, Baldwin's later essays have tended to move from the personal to the social, from interrogation to exhortation. The Fire Next Time, with its prophetic prediction of future urban violence and Negro unwillingness to participate in foreign wars, shocked many whites by providing their first insight into the growing bitterness in the black ghettos. Baldwin has also published a collection of short stories, Going to Meet the Man (1965), and in 1964 he collaborated with Richard Avedon on Nothing Personal, writing an essay bitterly critical of the sterility of American life to accompany Avedon's photographs. He has also written two plays, Amen Corner (1955) and Blues for Mr. Charlie (1964), the latter described by Robert Bone as an "unspeakably bad propaganda piece."

Despite his denunciation of contemporary American society, Baldwin is no darling of the new wave of black militants. Eldridge Cleaver, in a scathingly personal attack in Soul on Ice, rejects Baldwin for still "embodying in his art the self-flagellating policy of Martin Luther King." "There is in James Baldwin's work," Cleaver concludes, "the most grueling, agonizing, total hatred of the blacks, particularly of himself, and the most shameful, fanatical, fawning, sycophantic love of the whites that one can find in the writings of any black American writer of note in our time."

"Stranger in the Village" was published in Notes of a Native Son (1955).

From Notes of a Native Son

Stranger in the Village

From all available evidence no black man had ever set foot in this tiny Swiss village before I came. I was told before arriving that I would probably be a "sight" for the village; I took this to mean that people of my complexion were rarely seen in Switzerland, and also that city people are always something of a "sight" outside of the city. It did not occur to me—possibly because I am an American—that there could be people anywhere who had never seen a Negro.

It is a fact that cannot be explained on the basis of the inaccessibility of the village. The village is very high, but it is only four hours from Milan and three hours from Lausanne. It is true that it is virtually unknown. Few people making plans for a holiday would elect to come here. On the other hand, the villagers are able, presumably, to come and go as they please—which they do: to another town at the foot of the mountain, with a population of approximately five thousand, the nearest place to see a movie or go to the bank. In the village there is no movie house, no bank, no library, no theater; very few radios, one jeep, one station wagon; and, at the moment, one typewriter, mine, an invention which the woman next door to me here had never seen. There are about six hundred people living here, all Catholic—I conclude this from the fact that the Catholic church is open all year round, whereas the Protestant chapel, set off on a hill a little removed from the village, is open only in the summertime when the tourists arrive. There are four or five hotels, all closed now, and four or five *bistros*, of which, however, only two do any business during the winter. These two do not do a great deal, for life in the village seems to end around nine or ten o'clock. There are a few stores, butcher, baker, *épicerie*, a hardware store, and a money-changer—who cannot change travelers' checks, but must send them down to the bank, an operation which takes two or three days. There is something called the *Ballet Haus*, closed in the winter and used for God knows what, certainly not ballet, during the summer. There seems to be only one schoolhouse in the village, and this for the quite young children; I suppose this to mean that their older brothers and sisters at some point descend from these mountains in order to complete their education—possibly, again, to the town just below. The landscape is absolutely forbidding, mountains towering on all four sides, ice and snow as far as the eye can reach. In this white wilderness, men and women and children move all day, carrying washing, wood, buckets of milk or water, sometimes skiing on Sunday afternoons. All week long boys and young men are to be seen shoveling snow off the rooftops, or dragging wood down from the forest in sleds.

The village's only real attraction, which explains the tourist season, is the hot spring water. A disquietingly high proportion of these tourists are cripples, or semicripples, who come year after year—from other parts of Switzerland, usually—to take the waters. This lends the village, at the height of the season, a rather terrifying air of sanctity, as though it were a lesser Lourdes. There is often something beautiful, there is always something awful, in the spectacle of a person who has lost one of his faculties, a faculty he never questioned until it was gone, and who struggles to recover it. Yet people remain people, on crutches or indeed on deathbeds; and wherever I passed, the first summer I was here, among the native villagers or among the lame, a wind passed with me—of astonishment, curiosity, amusement, and outrage. That first summer I stayed two weeks and never intended to return. But I did return in the winter, to work; the village offers, obviously, no distractions whatever and has the further advantage of being extremely cheap. Now it is winter again, a year later, and I am here again. Everyone in the village knows my name, though they scarcely ever use it, knows that I come from America—though, this, apparently, they will never really believe: black men come from Africa—and everyone knows that I am the friend of the son of a woman who was born here, and that I am staying in their chalet. But I remain as much a stranger today as I was the first day I arrived, and the children shout *Neger! Neger!* as I walk along the streets.

It must be admitted that in the beginning I was far too shocked to have any real reaction. In so far as I reacted at all, I reacted by trying to be pleasant—it being a great part of the American Negro's education (long before he goes to school) that he must make people "like" him. This smile-and-the-world-smiles-with-you routine worked about as well in this situation as it had in the situation for which it was designed, which is to say that it did not work at all. No one, after all, can be liked whose human weight and complexity cannot be, or has not been, admitted. My smile was simply another unheard-of phenomenon which allowed them to see my teeth—they did not, really, see my smile and I began to think that, should I take to snarling, no one would notice any difference. All of the physical characteristics of the Negro which had caused me, in America, a very different and almost forgotten pain were nothing less than miraculous—or infernal—in the eyes of the village people. Some thought my hair was the color of tar, that it had the texture of wire, or the texture of cotton. It was jocularly suggested that I might let it all grow long and make myself a winter coat. If I sat in the sun for more than five minutes some daring creature was certain to come along and gingerly put his fingers on my hair, as though he were afraid of an electric shock, or put his hand on my hand, astonished that the color did not rub off. In all of this, in which it must be conceded there was the charm of genuine wonder and in which there was certainly no element of intentional unkindness, there was yet no suggestion that I was human: I was simply a living wonder.

I knew that they did not mean to be unkind, and I know it now; it is necessary, nevertheless, for me to repeat this to myself each time that I walk out of the chalet. The children who shout *Neger!* have no way of knowing the echoes this sound raises in me. They are brimming with good humor and the more daring swell with pride when I stop to speak with them. Just the same, there are days when I cannot pause and smile, when I have no heart to play with them; when, indeed, I mutter sourly to myself, exactly as I muttered on the streets of a city these children have never seen, when I was no bigger than these children are now: *Your* mother *was a nigger*. Joyce is right about history being a nightmare—but it may be the nightmare from which no one *can* awaken. People are trapped in history and history is trapped in them.

There is a custom in the village—I am told it is repeated in many villages—of "buying" African natives for the purpose of converting them to Christianity. There stands in the church all year round a small box with a slot for money, decorated with a black figurine, and into this box the villagers drop their francs. During the *carnaval* which precedes Lent, two village children have their faces blackened—out of which bloodless darkness their blue eyes shine like ice—and fantastic horsehair wigs are placed on their blond heads; thus disguised, they solicit among the villagers for money for the missionaries in Africa. Between the box in the church and the blackened children, the village "bought" last year six or eight African natives. This was reported to me with pride by the wife of one of the *bistro* owners and I was careful to express astonishment and pleasure at the solicitude shown by the village for the souls of black folk. The *bistro* owner's wife beamed with a pleasure far more genuine than my own and seemed to feel that I might now breathe more easily concerning the souls of at least six of my kinsmen.

I tried not to think of these so lately baptized kinsmen, of the price paid for them, or the peculiar price they themselves would pay, and said nothing about my father, who having taking his own conversion too literally never, at bottom, forgave the white world (which he described as heathen) for having saddled him with a Christ in whom, to judge at least from their treatment of him, they themselves no longer believed. I thought of white men arriving for the first time in an African village, strangers there, as I am a stranger here, and tried to imagine the astounded populace touching their hair and marveling at the color of their skin. But there is a great difference between being the first white man to be seen by Africans and being the first black man to be seen by whites. The white man takes the astonishment as tribute, for he arrives to conquer and to convert the natives, whose inferiority in relation to himself is not even to be questioned; whereas I, without a thought of conquest, find myself among a people whose culture controls me, has even, in a sense, created me, people who have cost me more in anguish and rage than they will ever know, who yet do not even know of my existence. The astonishment with which I might have greeted them, should they have stumbled into my African village a few hundred years ago, might have rejoiced their hearts. But the astonishment with which they greet me today can only poison mine.

And this is so despite everything I may do to feel differently, despite my friendly conversations with the *bistro* owner's wife, despite their three-year-old son who has at last become my friend, despite the *saluts* and *bonsoirs* which I exchange with people as I walk, despite the fact that I know that no individual can be taken to task for what history is doing, or has done. I say that the culture of these people controls me—but they can scarcely be held responsible for European culture. America comes out of Europe, but these people have never seen America, nor have most of them seen more of Europe than the hamlet at the foot of their mountain. Yet they move with an authority which I shall never have; and they regard me, quite rightly, not only as a stranger in their village but as a suspect latecomer, bearing no credentials, to everything they have—however unconsciously—inherited.

For this village, even were it incomparably more remote and incredibly more primitive, is the West, the West onto which I have been so strangely grafted. These people cannot be, from the point of view of power, strangers anywhere in the world; they have made the modern world, in effect, even if they do not know it. The most illiterate among them is related, in a way that I am not, to Dante, Shakespeare, Michelangelo, Aeschylus, Da Vinci, Rembrandt, and Racine; the cathedral at Chartres says something to them which it cannot say to me, as indeed would New York's Empire State Building, should anyone here ever see it. Out of their hymns and dances come Beethoven and Bach. Go back a few centuries and they are in their full glory—but I am in Africa, watching the conquerors arrive.

The rage of the disesteemed is personally fruitless, but it is also absolutely inevitable; this rage, so generally discounted, so little understood even among the people whose daily bread it is, is one of the things that makes history. Rage can only with difficulty, and never entirely, be brought under the domination of the intelligence and is therefore not susceptible to any arguments whatever. This is a fact which ordinary representatives of the *Herrenvolk*, having never felt this rage and being unable to imagine it, quite fail to understand. Also, rage cannot be hidden, it can only be dissembled. This dissembling deludes the thoughtless, and strengthens rage and adds, to rage, contempt. There are, no doubt, as many ways of coping with the resulting complex of tensions as there are black men in the world, but no black man can hope ever to be entirely liberated from this internal warfare—rage, dissembling, and contempt having inevitably accompanied his first realization of the power of white men. What is crucial here is that, since white men represent in the black man's world so heavy a weight, white men have for black men a reality which is far from being reciprocal; and hence all black men have toward all white men an attitude which is designed, really, either to rob the white man of the jewel of his naïveté, or else to make it cost him dear.

The black man insists, by whatever means he finds at his disposal, that the white man cease to regard him as an exotic rarity and recognize him as a human being. This is a very charged and difficult moment, for there is a great deal of will power involved in the white man's naïveté. Most people are not naturally reflective any more than they are naturally malicious, and the white man prefers to keep the black man at a certain human remove because it is easier for him thus to preserve his simplicity and avoid being called to account for crimes committed by his forefathers, or his neighbors. He is inescapably aware, nevertheless, that he is in a better position in the world than black men are, nor can he quite put to death the suspicion that he is hated by black men therefore. He does not wish to be hated, neither does he wish to change places, and at this point in his uneasiness he can scarcely avoid having recourse to those legends which white men have created about black men, the most usual effect of which is that the white man finds himself enmeshed, so to speak, in his own language which describes hell, as well as the attributes which lead one to hell, as being as black as night.

Every legend, moreover, contains its residuum of truth, and the root function of language is to control the universe by describing it. It is of quite considerable significance that black men remain, in the imagination, and in overwhelming numbers in fact, beyond the disciplines of salvation; and this despite the fact that the West has been "buying" African natives for centuries. There is, I should hazard, an instantaneous necessity to be divorced from this so visibly unsaved stranger, in whose heart, moreover, one cannot guess what dreams of vengeance are being nourished; and, at the same time, there are few things on earth more attractive than the idea of the unspeakable liberty which is allowed the unredeemed. When, beneath the black mask, a human being begins to make himself felt one cannot escape a certain awful wonder as to what kind of human being it is. What one's imagination makes of other people is dictated, of course, by the laws of one's own personality and it is one of the ironies of black-white relations that, by means of what the white man imagines the black man to be, the black man is enabled to know who the white man is.

I have said, for example, that I am as much a stranger in this village today as I was the first summer I arrived, but this is not quite true. The villagers wonder less about the texture of my hair than they did then, and wonder rather more about me. And the fact that their wonder now exists on another level is reflected in their attitudes and in their eyes. There are the children who make those delightful, hilarious, sometimes astonishingly grave overtures of friendship in the unpredictable fashion of children; other children, having been taught that the devil is a black man, scream in genuine anguish as I approach. Some of the older women never pass without a friendly greeting, never pass, indeed, if it seems that they will be able to engage me in conversation; other women look down or look away or rather contemptuously smirk. Some of the men drink with me and suggest that I learn how to ski—partly, I gather, because they cannot imagine what I would look like on skis—and want to know if I am married, and ask questions about my *métier*. But some of the men have accused *le sale nègre*—behind my back—of stealing wood and there is already in the eyes of some of them that peculiar, intent, paranoiac malevolence which one sometimes surprises in the eyes of American white men when, out walking with their Sunday girl, they see a Negro male approach.

There is a dreadful abyss between the streets of this village and the streets of the city in which I was born, between the children who shout *Neger!* today and those who shouted *Nigger!* yesterday —the abyss is experience, the American experience. The syllable hurled behind me today expresses, above all, wonder: I am a stranger here. But I am not a stranger in America and the same syllable riding on the American air expresses the war my presence has occasioned in the American soul.

For this village brings home to me this fact: that there was a day, and not really a very distant day, when Americans were scarcely Americans at all but discontented Europeans, facing a great unconquered continent and strolling, say, into a marketplace and seeing black men for the first time. The shock this spectacle afforded is suggested, surely, by the promptness with which they decided that these black men were not really men but cattle. It is true that the necessity on the part of the settlers of the New World of reconciling their moral assumptions with the fact—and the necessity—of slavery enhanced immensely the charm of this idea, and it is also true that this idea expresses, with a truly American bluntness, the attitude which to varying extents all masters have had toward all slaves.

But between all former slaves and slave-owners and the drama which begins for Americans over three hundred years ago at Jamestown, there are at least two differences to be observed. The American Negro slave could not suppose, for one thing, as slaves in past epochs had supposed and often done, that he would ever be able to wrest the power from his master's hands. This was a supposition which the modern era, which was to bring about such vast changes in the aims and dimensions of power, put to death; it only begins, in unprecedented fashion, and with dreadful implications, to be resurrected today. But even had this supposition persisted with undiminished force, the American Negro slave could not have used it to lend his condition dignity, for the reason that this supposition rests on another: that the slave in exile yet remains related to his past, has some means—if only in memory—of revering and sustaining the forms of his former life, is able, in short, to maintain his identity.

This was not the case with the American Negro slave. He is unique among the black men of the world in that his past was taken from him, almost literally, at one blow. One wonders what on earth the first slave found to say to the first dark child he bore. I am told that there are Haitians able to trace their ancestry back to African kings, but any American Negro wishing to go back so far will find his journey through time abruptly arrested by the signature on the bill of sale which served as the entrance paper for his ancestor. At the time—to say nothing of the circumstances—of the enslavement of the captive black man who was to become the American Negro, there was not the remotest possibility that he would ever take power from his master's hands. There was no reason to suppose that his situation would ever change, nor was there, shortly, anything to indicate that his situation had ever been different. It was his necessity, in the words of E. Franklin Frazier, to find a "motive for living under American culture or die." The identity of the American Negro comes out of this extreme situation, and the evolution of this identity was a source of the most intolerable anxiety in the minds and the lives of his masters.

For the history of the American Negro is unique also in this: that the question of his humanity, and of his rights therefore as a human being, became a burning one for several generations of Americans, so burning a question that it ultimately became one of those used to divide the nation. It is out of this argument that the venom of the epithet *Nigger!* is derived. It is an argument which Europe has never had, and hence Europe quite sincerely fails to understand how or why the argument arose in the first place, why its effects are so frequently disastrous and always so unpredictable, why it refuses until today to be entirely settled. Europe's black possessions remained—and do remain—in Europe's colonies, at which remove they represented no threat whatever to European identity. If they posed any problem at all for the European conscience, it was a problem which remained comfortingly abstract: in effect, the black man, *as a man*, did not exist for Europe. But in America, even as a slave, he was an inescapable part of the general social fabric and no American could escape having an attitude toward him. Americans attempt until today to make an abstraction of the Negro, but the very nature of these abstractions reveals the tremendous effects the presence of the Negro has had on the American character.

When one considers the history of the Negro in America it is of the greatest importance to recognize that the moral beliefs of a person, or a people, are never really as tenuous as life—which is not moral—very often causes them to appear; these create for them a frame of reference and a necessary hope, the hope being that when life has done its worst they will be enabled to rise above themselves and to triumph over life. Life would scarcely be bearable if this hope did not exist. Again, even when the worst has been said, to betray a belief is not by any means to have put oneself beyond its power; the betrayal of a belief is not the same thing as ceasing to believe. If this were not so there would be no moral standards in the world at all. Yet one must also recognize that morality is based on ideas and that all ideas are dangerous—dangerous because ideas can only lead to action and where the action leads no man can say. And dangerous in this respect: that confronted with the impossibility of remaining faithful to one's beliefs, and the equal impossibility of becoming free of them, one can be driven to the most inhuman excesses. The ideas on which American beliefs are based are not, though Americans often seem to think so, ideas which originated in America. They came out of Europe. And the establishment of democracy on the American continent was scarcely as radical a break with the past as was the necessity, which Americans faced, of broadening this concept to include black men.

This was, literally, a hard necessity. It was impossible, for one thing, for Americans to abandon their beliefs, not only because these beliefs alone seemed able to justify the sacrifices they had endured and the blood that they had spilled, but also because these beliefs afforded them their only bulwark against a moral chaos as absolute as the physical chaos of the continent it was their destiny to conquer. But in the situation in which Americans found themselves, these beliefs threatened an idea which, whether or not one likes to think so, is the very warp and woof of the heritage of the West, the idea of white supremacy.

Americans have made themselves notorious by the shrillness and the brutality with which they have insisted on this idea, but they did not invent it; and it has escaped the world's notice that those very excesses of which Americans have been guilty imply a certain, unprecedented uneasiness over the idea's life and power, if not, indeed, the idea's validity. The idea of white supremacy rests simply on the fact that white men are the creators of civilization (the present civilization, which is the only one that matters; all previous civilizations are simply "contributions" to our own) and are therefore civilization's guardians and defenders. Thus it was impossible for Americans to accept the black man as one of themselves, for to do so was to jeopardize their status as white men. But not so to accept him was to deny his human reality, his human weight and complexity, and the strain of denying the overwhelmingly undeniable forced Americans into rationalizations so fantastic that they approached the pathological.

At the root of the American Negro problem is the necessity of the American white man to find a way of living with the Negro in order to be able to live with himself. And the history of this problem can be reduced to the means used by Americans—lynch law and law, segregation and legal acceptance, terrorization and concession—either to come to terms with this necessity, or to find a way around it, or (most usually) to find a way of doing both these things at once. The resulting spectacle, at once foolish and dreadful, led someone to make the quite accurate observation that "the Negro-in-America is a form of insanity which overtakes white men."

In this long battle, a battle by no means finished, the unforeseeable effects of which will be felt by many future generations, the white man's motive was the protection of his identity; the black man was motivated by the need to establish an identity. And despite the terrorization which the Negro in America endured and endures sporadically until today, despite the cruel and totally inescapable ambivalence of his status in his country, the battle for his identity has long ago been won. He is not a visitor to the West, but a citizen there, an American; as American as the Americans who despise him, the Americans who fear him, the Americans who love him—the Americans who became less than themselves, or rose to be greater than themselves by virtue of the fact that the challenge he represented was inescapable. He is perhaps the only black man in the world whose relationship to white men is more terrible, more subtle, and more meaningful than the relationship of bitter possessed to uncertain possessor. His survival depended, and his development depends, on his ability to turn his peculiar status in the Western world to his own advantage and, it may be, to the very great advantage of that world. It remains for him to fashion out of his experience that which will give him sustenance, and a voice.

The cathedral at Chartres, I have said, says something to the people of this village which it cannot say to me; but it is important to understand that this cathedral says something to me which it cannot say to them. Perhaps they are struck by the power of the spires, the glory of the windows; but they have known God, after all, longer than I have known him, and in a different way, and I am terrified by the slippery bottomless well to be found in the crypt, down which heretics were hurled to death, and by the obscene, inescapable gargoyles jutting out of the stone and seeming to say that God and the devil can never be divorced. I doubt that the villagers think of the devil when they face a cathedral because they have never been identified with the devil. But I must accept the status which myth, if nothing else, gives me in the West before I can hope to change the myth.

Yet, if the American Negro has arrived at his identity by virtue of the absoluteness of his estrangement from his past, American white men still nourish the illusion that there is some means of recovering the European innocence, of returning to a state in which black men do not exist. This is one of the greatest errors Americans can make. The identity they fought so hard to protect has, by virtue of that battle, undergone a change: Americans are as unlike any other white people in the world as it is possible to be. I do not think, for example, that it is too much to suggest that the American vision of the world—which allows so little reality, generally speaking, for any of the darker forces in human life, which tends until today to paint moral issues in glaring black and white—owes a great deal to the battle waged by Americans to maintain between themselves and black men a human separation which could not be bridged. It is only now beginning to be borne in on us—very faintly, it must be admitted, very slowly, and very much against our will—that this vision of the world is dangerously inaccurate, and perfectly useless. For it protects our moral high-mindedness at the terrible expense of weakening our grasp of reality. People who shut their eyes to reality simply invite their own destruction, and anyone who insists on remaining in a state of innocence long after that innocence is dead turns himself into a monster.

The time has come to realize that the interracial drama acted out on the American continent has not only created a new black man, it has created a new white man, too. No road whatever will lead Americans back to the simplicity of this European village where white men still have the luxury of looking on me as a stranger. I am not, really, a stranger any longer for any American alive. One of the things that distinguishes Americans from other people is that no other people has ever been so deeply involved in the lives of black men, and vice versa. This fact faced, with all its implications, it can be seen that the history of the American Negro problem is not merely shameful, it is also something of an achievement. For even when the worst has been said, it must also be added that the perpetual challenge posed by this problem was always, somehow, perpetually met. It is precisely this black-white experience which may prove of indispensable value to us in the world we face today. This world is white no longer, and it will never be white again.

JACK KEROUAC

(1922–1969)

Jack Kerouac was a leading spokesman for the "beat movement" of the late 1950s. Described by some as "unwashed eccentricity," "orgiastic anarchy," or "adolescent violence," the movement, according to the Literary History of the United States, was defended by others as "rhapsodic dissent which harks back to Emerson and Whitman" or as a force speaking "for the beleaguered Self, for the holiness and spontaneity of the natural man." Kerouac himself saw a religious element in the beat view of life, once describing the term "beat" as meaning "beatific." On another occasion he wrote that "it is a new literary movement aimed at freer expression of highly personal impressions, and is, in that sense, modern individualistic romance for all it's worth."

Born Jean-Louis Kerouac at Lowell, Massachusetts, he went to high school in New York City and studied briefly at Columbia College and the New School for Social Research. He served in the Navy and Merchant Marine and traveled extensively about the United States and Mexico before writing the novel On the Road (1957), regarded by many as the "beat manifesto." This was followed by The Dharma Bums (1958), The Subterraneans (1958), Big Sur (1962), and Vision of Gerard (1963).

The brief excerpt from On the Road which follows has been seized upon by many commentators as characteristic of the beat vision of the Negro. Responding skeptically to this passage, Commentary editor Norman Podhoretz wrote, "It will be news to the Negroes to learn that they are so happy and ecstatic; I doubt if a more idyllic picture of Negro life has been painted since certain Southern ideologues tried to convince the world that things were just as fine as fine could be for the slaves on the old plantation." Another unfriendly critic, Sterling A. Brown, is reminded of the glorification of exotic black primitives during the Jazz Age, and he refers to beat views of the Negro as merely "A Greenwich Village refurbishing of old stereotypes." Nevertheless, Norman Mailer examined beat views of the Negro with sympathy in his essay "The White Negro," and Mailer's opinion is reflected in Eldridge Cleaver's Soul on Ice, wherein the following Kerouac passage is again excerpted.

From On the Road

. . . At lilac evening I walked with every muscle aching among the lights of 27th and Welton in the Denver colored section, wishing I were a Negro, feeling that the best the white world had offered was not enough ecstasy for me, not enough life, joy, kicks, darkness, music, not enough night. I stopped at a little shack where a man sold hot red chili in paper containers; I bought some and ate it, strolling in the dark mysterious streets. I wished I were a Denver Mexican, or even a poor overworked Jap, anything but what I was so drearily, a "white man" disillusioned. All my life I'd had white ambitions; that was why I'd abandoned a good woman like Terry in the San Joaquin Valley. I passed the dark porches of Mexican and Negro homes; soft voices were there, occasionally the dusky knee of some mysterious sensual gal; and dark faces of the men behind rose arbors. Little children sat like sages in ancient rocking chairs. A gang of colored women came by, and one of the young ones detached herself from motherlike elders and came to me fast—"Hello Joe!"—and suddenly saw it wasn't Joe, and ran back, blushing. I wished I were Joe. I was only myself, Sal Paradise, sad, strolling in this violet dark, this unbearably sweet night, wishing I could exchange worlds with the happy, true-hearted, ecstatic Negroes of America. The raggedy neighborhoods reminded me of Dean and Marylou, who knew these streets so well from childhood. How I wished I could find them.

Down at 23rd and Welton a softball game was going on under floodlights which also illuminated the gas tank. A great eager crowd roared at every play. The strange young heroes of all kinds, white, colored, Mexican, pure Indian, were on the field, performing with heartbreaking seriousness. Just sandlot kids in uniform. Never in my life as an athlete had I ever permitted myself to perform like this in front of families and girl friends and kids of the neighborhood, at night, under lights; always it had been college, big-time, sober-faced; no boyish, human joy like this. Now it was too late. Near me sat an old Negro who apparently watched the games every night. Next to him was an old white bum; then a Mexican family, then some girls, some boys—all humanity, the lot. Oh, the sadness of the lights that night! The young pitcher looked just like Dean. A pretty blonde in the seats looked just like Marylou. It was the Denver Night; all I did was die.

> Down in Denver, down in Denver
> All I did was die

Across the street Negro families sat on their front steps, talking and looking up at the starry night through the trees and just relaxing in the softness and sometimes watching the game. Many cars passed in the street meanwhile, and stopped at the corner when the light turned red. There was excitement and the air was filled with the vibration of really joyous life that knows nothing of disappointment and "white sorrows" and all that. The old Negro man had a can of beer in his coat pocket, which he proceeded to open; and the old white man enviously eyed the can and groped in his pocket to see if *he* could buy a can too. How I died! I walked away from there. . . .

LE ROI JONES

(1934–   )

A violent critic of American life and perhaps the most insistent
spokesman among contemporary Negro writers for a separate black
culture and aesthetic, LeRoi Jones has been condemned as a dema-
gogue and a nihilist. He answers his attackers, "My ideas revolve
around the rotting and destruction of America, so I can't really
expect anyone who is part of that to accept my ideas."

Jones was born in Newark, New Jersey, was graduated from
Howard University, and later did graduate work at Columbia University and the New School for Social Research. While
serving in the Air Force from 1954 to 1957 he traveled throughout
the world, and upon returning to civilian life he lectured in creative writing and theater arts at the New School and Columbia.
In the meantime he was writing for a number of avant-garde journals, including Yugen, which he founded himself, and soon his
work was appearing in such established magazines as Poetry, Saturday Review, Harper's, and The Nation.

Considering himself primarily a poet, Jones has produced three
collections of poetry: Preface to a Twenty Volume Suicide Note
(1961), The Dead Lecturer (1964), and Black Art (1966). He has
also written several plays, including Dutchman, which won the
Obie Award as the best off-Broadway play of 1964, The Slave
(1964), Baptism (1967), The Toilet (1967), Slave Ship (1967),

Arm Yrself or Harm Yrself (1967), and Home on the Range (1968). He is also the author of a semiautobiographical novel, The System of Dante's Hell (1965); a collection of short stories, Tales (1967); a book of social commentary, Home: Social Essays (1966); and two studies of Negro music in America, Blues People (1963) and Black Music (1967). He has been active in what has come to be called the "black revolutionary theatre," having helped to establish both the Black Arts Repertory Theatre in Harlem and Spirit House in Newark. His awards have included a John Hay Whitney Fellowship (1961–62) and a Guggenheim grant (1964–65). Like Walker Vessels, the poet turned revolutionary leader in The Slave, Jones had two children by a white wife from whom he was later divorced.

Jones was arrested for illegal possession of firearms during the 1967 Newark riots and sentenced to two and a half years in prison by a judge who quoted from Jones's work to illustrate the poet's violent intentions. This decision was widely denounced as an abridgement of freedom of speech, and early in 1969 the conviction was reversed for lack of evidence. Lately Jones has shown a growing interest in political action. He has been named, along with Roy Wilkins, Whitney Young, Senator Edward Brooke, and Rev. Ralph Abernathy, to membership on the National Advisory Council on Black Economic Development. He was defeated recently when he ran for election to a Newark community council charged with responsibility for the city's slum-rehabilitation program.

Jones's early poems, generally regarded as his best, reveal an existential outlook on life and are often concerned with suicide and the tenuous nature of reality. His later works have increasingly become vehicles for his separatist and revolutionary views, and it has become a common observation, at least among white critics, that he has traded art for propaganda. Thus a Newsweek review declares that Jones "writes and harangues himself out of the company of civilized men," while, according to critic Donald P. Costello, "Jones's art and philosophy are suicidal as well as murderous. His philosophy is ultimately a betrayal of all of humanity, and particularly of the black man." Edward Margolies, in Native Sons, concludes that "much of Jones's recent writing has lost its depth and sensitivity while as propaganda it fails to arouse the violence Jones urges because, ironically, it is too erudite and subjective."

Despite these views, Jones has become a cultural hero to an increasing number of young black nationalists.

The first four poems which follow were published in Preface to a Twenty Volume Suicide Note. *"A Poem for Black Hearts" appeared in the September 1965* Negro Digest.

Preface to a Twenty Volume Suicide Note

Lately, I've become accustomed to the way
The ground opens up and envelops me
Each time I go out to walk the dog.
Or the broad edged silly music the wind
Makes when I run for a bus—

Things have come to that.

And now, each night I count the stars,
And each night I get the same number.
And when they will not come to be counted
I count the holes they leave.

Nobody sings anymore.

And then last night, I tiptoed up
To my daughter's room and heard her
Talking to someone, and when I opened
The door, there was no one there . . .
Only she on her knees,
Peeking into her own clasped hands.

Ostriches & Grandmothers!

All meet here with us, finally: the
uptown, way-west, den of inconstant

moralities.
Faces up: all
my faces turned up
to the sun.

1.

Summer's mist nods against the trees
till distance grows in my head
like an antique armada
dangled motionless from the horizon.

Unbelievable changes. Restorations.
Each day like my niña's fan
tweaking the flat air
back and forth till the room
is a blur of flowers.

Intimacy takes on human form . . .
& sheds it like a hide.
      Lips, eyes,
tiny lace coughs
reflected on night's stealth.

2.

Tonight, one star.
eye of the dragon.
     The Void
signaling.
Reminding someone
it's still there.

3.

It's these empty seconds
I fill with myself. Each
a recognition. A complete
utterance.

Here, it is color; motion;
the feeling of dazzling beauty
Flight.

As
the trapeeze rider
leans
with arms spread

wondering at the bar's
delay

Way Out West

(For Gary Snyder)

As simple an act
as opening the eyes. Merely
coming into things by degrees.

Morning: some tear is broken
on the wooden stairs
of my lady's eyes. Profusions
of green. The leaves. Their
constant prehensions. Like old
junkies on Sheridan Square, eyes
cold and round. There is a song
Nat Cole sings . . . This city
& the intricate disorder
of the seasons.

Unable to mention
something as abstract as time.

Even so, (bowing low in thick
smoke from cheap incense; all
kinds questions filling the mouth,

till you suffocate & fall dead
to opulent carpet.) Even so,

shadows will creep over your flesh
& hide your disorder, your lies.

There are unattractive wild ferns
outside the window
where the cats hide. They yowl
from there at nights. In heat
& bleeding on my tulips.

Steel bells, like the evil
unwashed Sphinx, towing in the twilight.
Childless old murderers, for centuries
with musty eyes.

I am distressed. Thinking
of the seasons, how they pass,
how I pass, my very youth, the
ripe sweet of my life; drained off . . .

Like giant rhesus monkeys;
picking their skulls,
with ingenious cruelty
sucking out the brains.

No use for beauty
collapsed, with moldy breath
done in. Insidious weight
of cankered dreams. Tiresias'
weathered cock.

Walking into the sea, shells
caught in the hair. Coarse
waves tearing the tongue.

Closing the eyes. As
simple an act. You float

Notes for a Speech

African blues
does not know me. Their steps, in sands
of their own
land. A country
in black & white, newspapers
blown down pavements
of the world. Does
not feel
what I am.
        Strength
in the dream, an oblique
suckling of nerve, the wind
throws up sand, eyes
are something locked in
hate, of hate, of hate, to
walk abroad, they conduct
their deaths apart
from my own. Those
heads, I call
my "people."
        (And who are they. People. To concern
myself, ugly man. Who
you, to concern
the white flat stomachs
of maidens, inside houses
dying. Black. Peeled moon
light on my fingers
move under
her clothes. Where
is her husband. Black
words throw up sand
to eyes, fingers of
their private dead. Whose
soul, eyes, in sand. My color
is not theirs. Lighter, white man

talk. They shy away. My own
dead souls, my, so called
people. Africa
is a foreign place. You are
as any other sad man here
american.

A Poem for Black Hearts

For Malcolm's eyes, when they broke
the face of some dumb white man. For
Malcolm's hands raised to bless us
all black and strong in his image
of ourselves, for Malcolm's words
fire darts, the victor's tireless
thrusts, words hung above the world
change as it may, he said it, and
for this he was killed, for saying,
and feeling, and being/change, all
collected hot in his heart, For Malcolm's
heart, raising us above our filthy cities,
for his stride, and his beat, and his address
to the grey monsters of the world, For Malcolm's
pleas for your dignity, black men, for your life,
black men, for the filling of your minds
with righteousness, For all of him dead and
gone and vanished from us, and all of him which
clings to our speech black god of our time.
For all of him, and all of yourself, look up,
black man, quit stuttering and shuffling, look up,
black man, quit whining and stooping, for all of him,
For Great Malcolm a prince of the earth,
        let nothing in us rest
until we avenge ourselves for his death, stupid animals
that killed him, let us never breathe a pure breath if
we fail, and white men call us faggots till the end of
the earth.

CHESTER HIMES

(1909-)

<hr>

Chester Himes was born in Jefferson City, Missouri, and studied briefly at Ohio State University. For over a decade he has lived in France, where his detective novels, such as Cotton Comes to Harlem (1965), have been popular in French editions.

The first of Himes's serious novels, If He Hollers Let Him Go (1945), was a naturalistic social-protest novel in the tradition of Richard Wright which detailed the humiliations heaped on its Negro protagonist and examined his gradual emasculation by a racist society. Lonely Crusade (1947) dealt with the struggle of a Negro organizer to combat discrimination in labor unions and analyzed the racial subtleties underlying his relationships with his black wife and white mistress. Cast the First Stone (1953) was a novel of prison life with predominantly white characters, reflecting the movement toward racial assimilation popular among many Negro writers in the 1950s.

Himes's The Third Generation (1954), another "environmentalist" novel, employed autobiographical elements in a bitter attack on the Negro bourgeoisie while exploring the social disintegration of modern American city life. In The Primitive (1955) Himes dealt with an unsuccessful Harlem novelist whose humanity is acknowledged by society only after he murders his white mistress. Pinktoes (1965), a Rabelaisian farce which is probably Himes's best-known work in America, mocked the pretensions of white and

Negro liberals by tracing the activities of Mamie Mason, a Harlem hostess who attempts to advance race relations and her own social ambitions by promoting interracial seductions.

Edward Margolies writes that "Himes feels the trunk and roots of American society are so corrupted as to make normal growth and development impossible. His concern is not primarily with social protest, as has so often been alleged, for protest implies some hope of appropriate reform, and Himes, one suspects, regards the American scene as beyond redemption." Sterling A. Brown, who also notes Himes's bitter criticisms of America, characterizes his works in these terms: "As rebellious as Richard Wright but even more nihilistic and despairing, Himes has most fully presented the misanthropic, frustrated, furious young Negro, insulted and injured, uprooted and lost."

"Excursion in Paradox" was used by Himes as an Introduction to Pinktoes.

From Pinktoes

*Pinktoes is a term of indulgent affection
applied to white women by Negro men,
and sometimes conversely by Negro women
to white men, but never adversely by either.*

Excursion in Paradox

Nothing ever goes right. Nothing ever turns out as one has planned. How many times have you heard that said? How many times have *you* said it? And yet, it is never an expression of cynicism, defeatism or nihilism. It is always a confession of faith.

Despite the fact that nothing ever goes right, life goes right on. And, even though nothing ever turns out as one has planned it, the human race increases, develops, progresses. Mankind becomes wiser, healthier and happier; and all the various mechanisms it persists in developing for its own destruction do not one whit deter this steady movement toward the millennium, whatever and wherever that might be. So everything goes right for Some One, and everything turns out as Some One has planned. We ourselves, the billions of people who inhabit this earth, the unadorned fact of our existence, that during each and every day, every hour of the day, somewhere on earth there are people of all colors and races, all creeds and breeds, engaged in propagating, furnish the incontrovertible and absolute proof of our faith in the fact that everything turns out as Some One has planned it. Isn't it wonderful!

Take, for instance, the night Billie Hall fell in the Copa. Billie wanted to make a sensational entrance, capture everyone's full attention, become a cynosure of all eyes—*The Cynosure*. She wanted to inspire passionate inclinations, instigate magnificent propositions, be envied and coveted, as what girl doesn't?

The Copa, in case you do not know, is a big plush night club in Manhattan where the pinkest of Pinktoes dripping with furs and diamonds congregate in the late hours of the evening to seek and be sought, accompanied by male escorts whose chief function is to pay the bill—and at the Copa, this is not a minor consideration.

Billie, in case you don't remember her, was the star of an all-colored musical that was then having a brief success on Broadway. Naturally, Billie was a colored girl; it is only in the Opera further downtown that you will find white persons playing colored roles. Or does that make sense? "Colored roles" sounds like some way of doing it exclusive to the colored race.

Billie had jet black curls molded and polished by a Harlem coiffeur, and big dark eyes with a red underglow. Her skin was of the soft creamy texture of caramel pudding, and she had the beautiful, lovely, easy-to-take curves usually attributed to the Merritt Parkway. But no architect on earth, by whatever name, had designed her curves, regardless of who had made them. Because she felt the need to prove this about her curves to compensate for the color of her indescribably lovely skin, of which, naturally, she was somewhat ashamed, she wore only a fragile slip beneath her skin-tight rose silk evening gown.

Billie's escort for this occasion was a millionaire, the greenest, a white man-about-town who, during his night-life career, had spent enough money in the Copa to be assured of deference, despite the color of his girl; and from the moment his limousine drew up before the Copa entrance the Copa flunkies began hotfooting about to reindoctrinate him with his own sense of importance.

Their timing was perfect. The Copa was overflowing with Pink-toes just waiting to be impressed. The Copa chorus had just left the floor and the lights had come on briefly so the diners could identify their filets and not find themselves chewing on their souvenirs. But after one brief glance in Billie's direction, everyone studiously ignored her. After all, everyone who goes to the Copa is a celebrity. In fact, once you have gained admission to the Copa, you have automatically become a celebrity. Only a celebrities' celebrity, such as having a king of the last great empire forsake his throne for your love, or yourself forsake the fabulous notoriety of your role as motion picture queen to become a legend in smoked glasses, shabby clothes and secrecy, could have overwhelmed that antagonistic audience.

Billie felt her nerves tighten. Sweat broke out between her legs. She steeled herself against trembling. But her body lost its grace-ful flow of motion and her high heels wobbled. She was trailing her mink coat on the floor, according to the rigid ritual in such places as the Copa. In the center of the dance floor, as they were crossing it to their table reserved at ringside, her feet got caught in the soft folds of fabulous fur, and she fell forward toward the floor. Being an athletic girl, naturally she wasn't going to fall on her face, so she put forth her hands to catch herself. This posture of bending forward on her hands put too great a strain on the fabric of her dress, so that both her dress and her fragile slip ripped straight up the back, exposing to view the creamy hills of buttocks more captivating than ever seen in the Copa, or anywhere else in public for that matter. Needless to say, in such a posture it looked most inviting.

She had the instant attention of everyone present. Stovepipe pants became suddenly painful and young women were thrown into furious battle with their libidos. Old guys and nearsighted dames fumbled hastily in their pockets and purses for their glasses, mouths dribbling from the overflow of great gushes of saliva. There were several cases of hiccups and strangulation as gobs of half-chewed food went down the wrong pipes, and one old gentleman bit his tongue so severely he lost the services of his young chorus girl indefinitely.

It went as far wrong as it could possibly go. Nothing could have been further removed from the way Billie had planned it. Nevertheless, she accomplished what she had set out to do. She produced the most sensational entrance in the history of the Copa, an entrance that has become a legend.

On the other hand, consider the case of Henry Hill. All he wanted to do was make a little joke. He was one of five porters cleaning a new Horn & Hardart lunchette in Manhattan for the opening next day. They had all been laughing at old Fats, who had come to work all juiced up and kept trying to argue with the man. The man kept telling Fats to do this and Fats kept asking the man in a belligerent tone of voice, You mean do this? And the man would get mad and say, That's what I said, do this, don't you want to work? And Fats would say more belligerently than ever, Yessuh, I wants to work, of course I wants to work, that's why I'm here; if I didn't want to work I wouldn't have come to work. Then the man would say, Then what's the matter with you, if you want to work why don't you go to work and do some work. Fats would say, That's what I'm trying to do, is get to work. The man would ask, What's stopping you then? Fats would reply, I'm just trying to find out what you mean when you keep saying go to work, ain't I come to work?

Old Fats is a pistol, the other porters said.

Finally the man saw he wasn't going to get any work out of old Fats so he told Fats to take a ladder down into the basement, hoping Fats would have sense enough to stay down there out of sight. But Fats looked at the ladder and then looked at the man and said, You mean this ladder, boss? What other ladder is there, the man said disgustedly. Fats looked back at the ladder and said, Boss, it wasn't me who brought this ladder up here.

That knocked out the other porters. Even the man had to laugh.

All the rest of the night they kept laughing at old Fats and four o'clock the next morning, when they had about got the joint cleaned, the man told them to get some buckets of soapy water

and go outside and wash the marble posts alongside the old building. It was cold as hell outside and the porters looked at the man as
though he had gone crazy. It was then Henry Hill thought he
would make a little joke, being as they had to wash the posts anyway, so he said to the man, Boss, it weren't us who dirtied them
posts, it was them dogs that live around here.

Didn't nobody laugh. Like the spiritual says, "*Way down yonder
by myself, an' Ah couldn' hear nobody pray . . .*" Old Henry
couldn't hear nobody laugh. In fact, the other porters, all of them
being colored, got mad at him for insinuating before the white
man that they would stoop to dirtying posts in the broad open
street in the middle of Manhattan. And the white man got mad at
Henry for insinuating that he had ever even thought of any of the
colored fellows dirtying the posts. So one word led to another and
the man told Henry he had been working with colored fellows ever
since he had come into the organization, and in all that time he
had never once seen a colored fellow dirty anywhere but in the
lavatory and never once in all that time had he ever had any
trouble with the colored fellows who worked under him, and it
was people like Henry always agitating that caused the Negro
Problem anyway. Henry told the man it didn't have anything to do
with the Negro Problem, it was just that any time anything ever
came up about some colored fellows dirtying some street posts it
was people like the man who was always trying to make out as if
nobody but some colored fellows would dirty a post, whereas over
on Third Avenue and down on the Bowery he had seen white guys
dirtying all over the street; and if he wanted to get down to the
nitty-gritty it was only white guys he had ever seen dirtying in the
street or against a post at all, because the average colored man had
more respect for himself and those about him, and nine times out
of ten he would either go into a dark alley or duck into a doorway
out of sight so nobody could see him when he had to dirty. The
man was getting madder and madder, and said that was the entire
trouble with the Negro Problem; colored people like Henry was
always trying to draw a difference between white fellows and colored fellows, when people was just people, colored people was just
people like white people was just people. Henry was getting madder
and madder too and he said to the man, You don't act like colored

people is just people, like white people is just people, and I'd be willing to bet if we was white people instead of colored people you wouldn't ask us to go out there in the cold and wash them dirty posts.

The man got so mad at this he said, Give me a bucket and I'll go out and wash the posts myself, intending to prove by this that a white man would do anything he would ask a colored man to do.

But naturally the colored fellows wouldn't think of letting the white man go out into the cold and wash the posts while they stood inside and watched, so they went out grumbling and shivering and scrubbed down the posts and rinsed them with hot water until they shone white. Then Henry looked up and down the street and, seeing no one in sight, took out his black sprinkler and proceeded to dirty the marble white post he had just cleaned. The other porters did likewise, their black sprinklers silhouetted against the marble white posts and emitting streams of steaming water as though baptizing gigantic white legs in some inherited ritual of fertility. They were laughing to beat all hell when they returned inside.

The man wondered what they found so funny about washing the posts out in the cold, but being as they were black, and the posts were white, he was too sensible to ask. Instead he let them knock off and go home a half hour earlier, and after that Henry became his right-hand man.

Or for that matter, one may study the incident of two cats meeting one dark night in Harlem. It was on a side street in the Valley, and not a sound could be heard but the rustling of rats in the garbage cans; not a light could be seen but the dim red glow through the cracks in window shades.

The white cat looked east and west and north and south, then started catfooting obliquely toward the northern curb. The black cat waited until the white cat got in the middle of the street, then started walking toward the white cat, staggering as though drunk, and deliberately bumped into the white cat.

Why don'tcha watch where you're going? the black cat snarled.

The white cat saw right off that the black cat was looking for trouble, being as this was not the first time he had been in Harlem, so he hastened to apologize, I begs your pardon, sir, and tried to get past the black cat.

But the black cat wouldn't let him pass. Whatcha tryna do? he snarled. You tryna take all the street? I got as much right to this street as you is. This ain't Arkansas.

I'm sorry, the white cat kept apologizing. I didn't see you.

The black cat bristled. Whatcha mean you didn't see me? You tryna say I'm so black you can't see me in the dark?

Why don't you let me go about my business, buddy; I ain't looking for trouble, the white cat miaowed pacifically.

Don't call me your buddy; I ain't your buddy, you white son of a puss, the black cat spat.

The white cat began getting mad too. Don't call me a son of a puss, you black son of a bitch, he snarled.

You calling me a son of a bitch! the black cat yowled, whipping out his claws. This is where I'm gonna cut your throat, saying I'm mixed with dog!

Naturally, the white cat whipped out his own claws, and for a moment they stood there, yowling at each other.

Some of the colored residents along the way were awakened by all the caterwauling and opened their windows to throw some whiskey bottles at the cats. But when they saw it was a black cat squared off with a white cat they jumped into their clothes and rushed down into the street to see the black cat beat the hell out of the white cat.

But seeing the white cat with his claws unsheathed also, and in all four paws to boot, the black cat was not so anxious to fight anymore, so he asked the white cat chummily, Say, man, ain't you from Cincinnati, being as when home folks from places like Cincinnati ran across one another in New York they acted like bosom friends, regardless of color, and went off somewhere to get drunk.

The white cat was not anxious to fight either, so he replied with lots of enthusiasm, Yeah, man, I'm from Cincy, how could you tell? Although frankly this white cat was born and raised in Jersey City, and merely slipped across the river into Harlem every now and then to find some black pussy and change his luck.

But the black cat was so relieved to get out of fighting he replied with equal enthusiasm, Man, I could tell you was from Cincy the way you squared off there like Ezzard Charles; you know old Ez, don't you?

Do I know Ez! the white cat exclaimed. He wants to know do I know Ez. Me and Ez is running buddies.

By this time the colored spectators were impatient for some action. Come on and fight, they demanded. What's this supposed to be, a hugging match? You two cats ain't funny that way, are you?

But these two cats weren't paying any attention to these colored people urging them to fight. The white cat had his jive going about Cincinnati, where he had never been, and seeing how good it was taking asked the black cat jubilantly, You know old Smokey Joe? figuring that was going to be the clincher.

But he didn't figure on how sensitive black cats were about being black. Smokey Joe? Who he? the black cat snarled indignantly. How come I got to know somebody named Smokey Joe? You must figure all us black cats knows is somebody called Smokey.

So all of a sudden they were yowling at each other again, slashing the air with their claws and carrying on like two cats who really might want to fight if they could find anything to fight about.

The audience of black people figured they were seeing some action, and began jumping up and down and saying how that black cat was going to put together a Sugar Ray Robinson combination, and fold that white cat like all good cookbooks say "fold whipped egg whites into batter." But being as nothing happened, someone said finally, Them cats ain't fighting, them cats is just loving, them is fairy cats, or else they is bulldiking. These colored people got so mad at being cheated out of seeing the black cat whip hell out of the white cat they jumped on both of these cats and whaled them good.

Those cats took off north on Lenox Avenue and didn't stop running until they'd reached 135th Street.

Brother, the white cat said to the black cat as they were sitting on a stoop, catching their breath and licking their wounds, I don't mean to insinuate anything, but what made them black people get so mad at you, as black as you is too?

The black cat looked at the white cat sorrowfully and said,

Brother, that's what the trouble is: them is people and us is cats. So let's leave them people to their peopling and us cats go catting. I know where there is a cathouse near here with nothing but good pussies.

Pussy is all a tomcat needs, the white cat said, falling in beside the black cat as they catfooted for the cathouse.

Although Mama Meow, the madame, or landprop as they say in that part of the world, conducts a cathouse in a land of black cats, she is not at all opposed to serving white cats, which is more than can be said of the attitude of many white cats toward serving black cats. In fact, Mama Meow prefers serving white cats to black cats. If she were not a black pussy herself, cats might say she is prejudiced. But such is not the case. It is merely that she has found white cats easier to serve; they pay more for the pussy, demand less from the pussy, and are not always trying to take the pussy home.

So naturally Mama Meow greeted this white cat effusively, and even tolerated this black cat because he had brought such a fine white cat to buy some pussy. In fact, being as business was slow at that time she exhibited her whole stable of pussies.

These tomcats had never seen such an extraordinary collection of fine pussies. In fact there was such a variety of pussies offered, these tomcats could not make up their mind which they wanted. Obviously this aroused great suspicions in Mama Meow and she asked to see some green before these tomcats have come on a freeby. When it came out that this white cat was flat, and this black cat not even that, she threw them out into the alley.

Brother, the black cat said as they picked their way over the cold wet bricks, you know one thing, it's getting so nowadays the only friend a black cat's got is a pocketful of catnip.

Brother, the white cat said, it's just the same with us, only we got more pussies to feed.

All of which goes to demonstrate that nothing ever goes right for cats either.

Still cats keep right on catting, just the same as all these old bats one sees around keep right on batting, and as everyone knows who reads the daily newspapers, rats keep right on ratting.

FLANNERY O'CONNOR

(1925-1964)

———◆◆◆———

Flannery O'Connor was born in Savannah, Georgia, and grew up in the small Georgia town of Milledgeville. She received an A.B. at Women's College of Georgia and then studied creative writing at the State University of Iowa, where she was awarded a Master of Fine Arts in 1947. Her first published story appeared in Kenyon Review, and she became a regular contributor to Partisan Review, Sewanee Review, Mademoiselle, and Harper's Bazaar. Most of her stories were written against a background of personal suffering and heroism, since by 1951 she had developed disseminated lupus, a fatal disease which caused her retirement to Milledgeville and made her a partial cripple during the last nine years of her life. She produced two collections of short stories, A Good Man Is Hard to Find (1955) and Everything That Rises Must Converge (1965); her two novels were Wise Blood (1952) and The Violent Bear It Away (1960). A "writer's writer," she was admired by Caroline Gordon, John Crowe Ransom, T. S. Eliot, and many others.

Her works, usually set in rural Tennessee or Georgia, often display what Melvin J. Friedman termed a "Dickensian devotion to oddities of character." Her penchant for sensational incident and for grotesque or physically and spiritually deformed characters has caused some critics to place her writing in a "Southern Gothic" tradition, but Robert Fitzgerald has noted the influence of Nathanael West's Miss Lonelyhearts on her notions of the grotesque.

A devout Catholic, Miss O'Connor acknowledged that "I see from the standpoint of Christian orthodoxy. This means that for me the meaning of life is centered in our Redemption by Christ and that what I see in the world I see in relation to that." Richard Poirier has argued that her intense Christian commitment caused limitations in her artistry: "Caring almost nothing for secular destinies, which are altogether more various than religious ones, she propels her characters toward the cataclysms where alone they can have a tortured glimpse of the need and chance of redemption." But Walter Sullivan writes that "her vision was as clear and direct and as annoyingly precious as that of an Old Testament prophet or one of the more irascible Christian saints."

Miss O'Connor's favorite work among her stories is said to have been "The Artificial Nigger" (1956), in which a plaster figure of a Negro, with a face twisted by age and the elements into a "wild look of misery," helps an elderly white man and his grandson achieve insight into the workings of divine mercy: "They stood gazing at the artificial Negro as if they were faced with some great mystery, some monument to another's victory that brought them together in their common defeat. They could both feel it dissolving their differences like an action of mercy."

"Everything That Rises Must Converge," perhaps her most considered statement on race relations, was the title piece of a volume of short stories published posthumously in 1965. The phrase is derived from the Jesuit scientist and mystic Teilhard de Chardin, whose works Miss O'Connor began reading in 1961. (See, for example, the chapter on "The Convergence of the Person and the Omega Point" in Teilhard's The Phenomenon of Man.)

Everything That Rises Must Converge

Her doctor had told Julian's mother that she must lose twenty pounds on account of her blood pressure, so on Wednesday nights Julian had to take her downtown on the bus for a reducing class

From Everything That Rises Must Converge by Flannery O'Connor. Copyright © 1961, 1965 by the Estate of Mary Flannery O'Connor. Reprinted by permission of Farrar, Straus & Giroux, Inc.

at the Y. The reducing class was designed for working girls over fifty, who weighed from 165 to 200 pounds. His mother was one of the slimmer ones, but she said ladies did not tell their age or weight. She would not ride the buses by herself at night since they had been integrated, and because the reducing class was one of her few pleasures, necessary for her health, and *free*, she said Julian could at least put himself out to take her, considering all she did for him. Julian did not like to consider all she did for him, but every Wednesday night he braced himself and took her.

She was almost ready to go, standing before the hall mirror, putting on her hat, while he, his hands behind him, appeared pinned to the door frame, waiting like Saint Sebastian for the arrows to begin piercing him. The hat was new and had cost her seven dollars and a half. She kept saying, "Maybe I shouldn't have paid that for it. No, I shouldn't have. I'll take it off and return it tomorrow. I shouldn't have bought it."

Julian raised his eyes to heaven. "Yes, you should have bought it," he said. "Put it on and let's go." It was a hideous hat. A purple velvet flap came down on one side of it and stood up on the other; the rest of it was green and looked like a cushion with the stuffing out. He decided it was less comical than jaunty and pathetic. Everything that gave her pleasure was small and depressed him.

She lifted the hat one more time and set it down slowly on top of her head. Two wings of gray hair protruded on either side of her florid face, but her eyes, sky-blue, were as innocent and untouched by experience as they must have been when she was ten. Were it not that she was a widow who had struggled fiercely to feed and clothe and put him through school and who was supporting him still, "until he got on his feet," she might have been a little girl that he had to take to town.

"It's all right, it's all right," he said. "Let's go." He opened the door himself and started down the walk to get her going. The sky was a dying violet and the houses stood out darkly against it, bulbous liver-colored monstrosities of a uniform ugliness though no two were alike. Since this had been a fashionable neighborhood forty years ago, his mother persisted in thinking they did well to have an apartment in it. Each house had a narrow collar of dirt around it in which sat, usually, a grubby child. Julian walked with his hands in his pockets, his head down and thrust forward and his eyes glazed with the determination to make himself completely numb during the time he would be sacrificed to her pleasure.

The door closed and he turned to find the dumpy figure, surmounted by the atrocious hat, coming toward him. "Well," she said, "you only live once and paying a little more for it, I at least won't meet myself coming and going."

"Some day I'll start making money," Julian said gloomily—he knew he never would—"and you can have one of those jokes whenever you take the fit." But first they would move. He visualized a place where the nearest neighbors would be three miles away on either side.

"I think you're doing fine," she said, drawing on her gloves. "You've only been out of school a year. Rome wasn't built in a day."

She was one of the few members of the Y reducing class who arrived in hat and gloves and who had a son who had been to college. "It takes time," she said, "and the world is in such a mess. This hat looked better on me than any of the others, though when she brought it out I said, 'Take that thing back. I wouldn't have it on my head,' and she said, 'Now wait till you see it on,' and when she put it on me, I said, 'We-ull,' and she said, 'If you ask me, that hat does something for you and you do something for the hat, and besides,' she said, 'with that hat, you won't meet yourself coming and going.'"

Julian thought he could have stood his lot better if she had been selfish, if she had been an old hag who drank and screamed at him. He walked along, saturated in depression, as if in the midst of his martyrdom he had lost his faith. Catching sight of his long, hopeless, irritated face, she stopped suddenly with a grief-stricken look, and pulled back on his arm. "Wait on me," she said. "I'm going back to the house and take this thing off and tomorrow I'm going to return it. I was out of my head. I can pay the gas bill with that seven-fifty."

He caught her arm in a vicious grip. "You are not going to take it back," he said. "I like it."

"Well," she said, "I don't think I ought . . ."

"Shut up and enjoy it," he muttered, more depressed than ever.

"With the world in the mess it's in," she said, "it's a wonder we can enjoy anything. I tell you, the bottom rail is on the top."

Julian sighed.

"Of course," she said, "if you know who you are, you can go anywhere." She said this every time he took her to the reducing class. "Most of them in it are not our kind of people," she said, "but I can be gracious to anybody. I know who I am."

"They don't give a damn for your graciousness," Julian said savagely. "Knowing who you are is good for one generation only. You haven't the foggiest idea where you stand now or who you are."

She stopped and allowed her eyes to flash at him. "I most certainly do know who I am," she said, "and if you don't know who you are, I'm ashamed of you."

"Oh hell," Julian said.

"Your great-grandfather was a former governor of this state," she said. "Your grandfather was a prosperous landowner. Your grandmother was a Godhigh."

"Will you look around you," he said tensely, "and see where you are now?" and he swept his arm jerkily out to indicate the neighborhood, which the growing darkness at least made less dingy.

"You remain what you are," she said. "Your great-grandfather had a plantation and two hundred slaves."

"There are no more slaves," he said irritably.

"They were better off when they were," she said. He groaned to see that she was off on that topic. She rolled onto it every few days like a train on an open track. He knew every stop, every junction, every swamp along the way, and knew the exact point at which her conclusion would roll majestically into the station: "It's ridiculous. It's simply not realistic. They should rise, yes, but on their own side of the fence."

"Let's skip it," Julian said.

"The ones I feel sorry for," she said, "are the ones that are half white. They're tragic."

"Will you skip it?"

"Suppose we were half white. We would certainly have mixed feelings."

"I have mixed feelings now," he groaned.

"Well let's talk about something pleasant," she said. "I remember going to Grandpa's when I was a little girl. Then the house had double stairways that went up to what was really the second floor—all the cooking was done on the first. I used to like to stay down in the kitchen on account of the way the walls smelled. I would sit with my nose pressed against the plaster and take deep breaths. Actually the place belonged to the Godhighs but your grandfather Chestny paid the mortgage and saved it for them. They were in reduced circumstances," she said, "but reduced or not, they never forgot who they were."

"Doubtless that decayed mansion reminded them," Julian muttered. He never spoke of it without contempt or thought of it without longing. He had seen it once when he was a child before it had been sold. The double stairways had rotted and been torn down. Negroes were living in it. But it remained in his mind as his mother had known it. It appeared in his dreams regularly. He would stand on the wide porch, listening to the rustle of oak leaves, then wander through the high-ceilinged hall into the parlor that opened onto it and gaze at the worn rugs and faded draperies. It occurred to him that it was he, not she, who could have appreciated it. He preferred its threadbare elegance to anything he could name and it was because of it that all the neighborhoods they had lived in had been a torment to him—whereas she had hardly known the difference. She called her insensitivity "being adjustable."

"And I remember the old darky who was my nurse, Caroline. There was no better person in the world. I've always had a great respect for my colored friends," she said. "I'd do anything in the world for them and they'd . . ."

"Will you for God's sake get off that subject?" Julian said. When he got on a bus by himself, he made it a point to sit down beside a Negro, in reparation as it were for his mother's sins.

"You're mighty touchy tonight," she said. "Do you feel all right?"

"Yes I feel all right," he said. "Now lay off."

She pursed her lips. "Well, you certainly are in a vile humor," she observed. "I just won't speak to you at all."

They had reached the bus stop. There was no bus in sight and

Julian, his hands still jammed in his pockets and his head thrust forward, scowled down the empty street. The frustration of having to wait on the bus as well as ride on it began to creep up his neck like a hot hand. The presence of his mother was borne in upon him as she gave a pained sigh. He looked at her bleakly. She was holding herself very erect under the preposterous hat, wearing it like a banner of her imaginary dignity. There was in him an evil urge to break her spirit. He suddenly unloosened his tie and pulled it off and put it in his pocket.

She stiffened. "Why must you look like *that* when you take me to town?" she said. "Why must you deliberately embarrass me?"

"If you'll never learn where you are," he said, "you can at least learn where I am."

"You look like a—thug," she said.

"Then I must be one," he murmured.

"I'll just go home," she said. "I will not bother you. If you can't do a little thing like that for me . . ."

Rolling his eyes upward, he put his tie back on. "Restored to my class," he muttered. He thrust his face toward her and hissed, "True culture is in the mind, the *mind*," he said, and tapped his head, "the mind."

"It's in the heart," she said, "and in how you do things and how you do things is because of who you *are*."

"Nobody in the damn bus cares who you are."

"I care who I am," she said icily.

The lighted bus appeared on top of the next hill and as it approached, they moved out into the street to meet it. He put his hand under her elbow and hoisted her up on the creaking step. She entered with a little smile, as if she were going into a drawing room where everyone had been waiting for her. While he put in the tokens, she sat down on one of the broad front seats for three which faced the aisle. A thin woman with protruding teeth and long yellow hair was sitting on the end of it. His mother moved up beside her and left room for Julian beside herself. He sat down and looked at the floor across the aisle where a pair of thin feet in red and white canvas sandals were planted.

His mother immediately began a general conversation meant to attract anyone who felt like talking. "Can it get any hotter?" she said and removed from her purse a folding fan, black with a Japanese scene on it, which she began to flutter before her.

"I reckon it might could," the woman with the protruding teeth said, "but I know for a fact my apartment couldn't get no hotter."

"It must get the afternoon sun," his mother said. She sat forward and looked up and down the bus. It was half filled. Everybody was white. "I see we have the bus to ourselves," she said. Julian cringed.

"For a change," said the woman across the aisle, the owner of the red and white canvas sandals. "I come on one the other day and they were thick as fleas—up front and all through."

"The world is in a mess everywhere," his mother said. "I don't know how we've let it get in this fix."

"What gets my goat is all those boys from good families stealing automobile tires," the woman with the protruding teeth said. "I told my boy, I said you may not be rich but you been raised right and if I ever catch you in any such mess, they can send you on to the reformatory. Be exactly where you belong."

"Training tells," his mother said. "Is your boy in high school?"

"Ninth grade," the woman said.

"My son just finished college last year. He wants to write but he's selling typewriters until he gets started," his mother said.

The woman leaned forward and peered at Julian. He threw her such a malevolent look that she subsided against the seat. On the floor across the aisle there was an abandoned newspaper. He got up and got it and opened it out in front of him. His mother discreetly continued the conversation in a lower tone but the woman across the aisle said in a loud voice, "Well that's nice. Selling typewriters is close to writing. He can go right from one to the other."

"I tell him," his mother said, "that Rome wasn't built in a day."

Behind the newspaper Julian was withdrawing into the inner compartment of his mind where he spent most of his time. This was a kind of mental bubble in which he established himself when he could not bear to be a part of what was going on around him. From it he could see out and judge but in it he was safe from any kind of penetration from without. It was the only place where he felt free of the general idiocy of his fellows. His mother had never entered it but from it he could see her with absolute clarity.

The old lady was clever enough and he thought that if she had started from any of the right premises, more might have been expected of her. She lived according to the laws of her own fantasy world, outside of which he had never seen her set foot. The law of it was to sacrifice herself for him after she had first created the necessity to do so by making a mess of things. If he had permitted her sacrifices, it was only because her lack of foresight had made them necessary. All of her life had been a struggle to act like a Chestny without the Chestny goods, and to give him everything she thought a Chestny ought to have; but since, said she, it was fun to struggle, why complain? And when you had won, as she had won, what fun to look back on the hard times! He could not forgive her that she had enjoyed the struggle and that she thought *she* had won.

What she meant when she said she had won was that she had brought him up successfully and had sent him to college and that he had turned out so well—good looking (her teeth had gone unfilled so that his could be straightened), intelligent (he realized he was too intelligent to be a success), and with a future ahead of him (there was of course no future ahead of him). She excused his gloominess on the grounds that he was still growing up and his radical ideas on his lack of practical experience. She said he didn't yet know a thing about "life," that he hadn't even entered the real world—when already he was as disenchanted with it as a man of fifty.

The further irony of all this was that in spite of her, he had turned out so well. In spite of going to only a third-rate college, he had, on his own initiative, come out with a first-rate education; in spite of growing up dominated by a small mind, he had ended up with a large one; in spite of all her foolish views, he was free of prejudice and unafraid to face facts. Most miraculous of all, instead of being blinded by love for her as she was for him, he had cut himself emotionally free of her and could see her with complete objectivity. He was not dominated by his mother.

The bus stopped with a sudden jerk and shook him from his meditation. A woman from the back lurched forward with little steps and barely escaped falling in his newspaper as she righted herself. She got off and a large Negro got on. Julian kept his paper lowered to watch. It gave him a certain satisfaction to see injustice in daily operation. It confirmed his view that with a few exceptions there was no one worth knowing within a radius of three hundred miles. The Negro was well dressed and carried a briefcase. He looked around and then sat down on the other end of the seat where the woman with the red and white canvas sandals was sitting. He immediately unfolded a newspaper and obscured himself behind it. Julian's mother's elbow at once prodded insistently into his ribs. "Now you see why I won't ride on these buses by myself," she whispered.

The woman with the red and white canvas sandals had risen at the same time the Negro sat down and had gone further back in the bus and taken the seat of the woman who had got off. His mother leaned forward and cast her an approving look.

Julian rose, crossed the aisle, and sat down in the place of the woman with the canvas sandals. From this position, he looked serenely across at his mother. Her face had turned an angry red. He stared at her, making his eyes the eyes of a stranger. He felt his tension suddenly lift as if he had openly declared war on her.

He would have liked to get in conversation with the Negro and to talk with him about art or politics or any subject that would be above the comprehension of those around them, but the man remained entrenched behind his paper. He was either ignoring the change of seating or had never noticed it. There was no way for Julian to convey his sympathy.

His mother kept her eyes fixed reproachfully on his face. The woman with the protruding teeth was looking at him avidly as if he were a type of monster new to her.

"Do you have a light?" he asked the Negro.

Without looking away from his paper, the man reached in his pocket and handed him a packet of matches.

"Thanks," Julian said. For a moment he held the matches foolishly. A NO SMOKING sign looked down upon him from over the door. This alone would not have deterred him; he had no cigarettes. He had quit smoking some months before because he could not afford it. "Sorry," he muttered and handed back the matches. The Negro lowered the paper and gave him an annoyed look. He took the matches and raised the paper again.

His mother continued to gaze at him but she did not take

advantage of his momentary discomfort. Her eyes retained their battered look. Her face seemed to be unnaturally red, as if her blood pressure had risen. Julian allowed no glimmer of sympathy to show on his face. Having got the advantage, he wanted desperately to keep it and carry it through. He would have liked to teach her a lesson that would last her a while, but there seemed no way to continue the point. The Negro refused to come out from behind his paper.

Julian folded his arms and looked stolidly before him, facing her but as if he did not see her, as if he had ceased to recognize her existence. He visualized a scene in which, the bus having reached their stop, he would remain in his seat and when she said, "Aren't you going to get off?" he would look at her as at a stranger who had rashly addressed him. The corner they got off on was usually deserted, but it was well lighted and it would not hurt her to walk by herself the four blocks to the Y. He decided to wait until the time came and then decide whether or not he would let her get off by herself. He would have to be at the Y at ten to bring her back, but he could leave her wondering if he was going to show up. There was no reason for her to think she could always depend on him.

He retired again into the high-ceiling room sparsely settled with large pieces of antique furniture. His soul expanded momentarily but then he became aware of his mother across from him and the vision shriveled. He studied her coldly. Her feet in little pumps dangled like a child's and did not quite reach the floor. She was training on him an exaggerated look of reproach. He felt completely detached from her. At that moment he could with pleasure have slapped her as he would have slapped a particularly obnoxious child in his charge.

He began to imagine various unlikely ways by which he could teach her a lesson. He might make friends with some distinguished Negro professor or lawyer and bring him home to spend the evening. He would be entirely justified but her blood pressure would rise to 300. He could not push her to the extent of making her have a stroke, and moreover, he had never been successful at making any Negro friends. He had tried to strike up an acquaintance on the bus with some of the better types, with ones that looked like professors or ministers or lawyers. One morning he had sat down next to a distinguished-looking dark brown man who had answered his questions with a sonorous solemnity but who had turned out to be an undertaker. Another day he had sat down beside a cigar-smoking Negro with a diamond ring on his finger, but after a few stilted pleasantries, the Negro had rung the buzzer and risen, slipping two lottery tickets into Julian's hand as he climbed over him to leave.

He imagined his mother lying desperately ill and his being able to secure only a Negro doctor for her. He toyed with that idea for a few minutes and then dropped it for a momentary vision of himself participating as a sympathizer in a sit-in demonstration. This was possible but he did not linger with it. Instead, he approached the ultimate horror. He brought home a beautiful suspiciously Negroid woman. Prepare yourself, he said. There is nothing you can do about it. This is the woman I've chosen. She's intelligent, dignified, even good, and she's suffered and she hasn't thought it *fun*. Now persecute us, go ahead and persecute us. Drive her out of here, but remember, you're driving me too. His eyes were narrowed and through the indignation he had generated, he saw his mother across the aisle, purple-faced, shrunken to the dwarflike proportions of her moral nature, sitting like a mummy beneath the ridiculous banner of her hat.

He was tilted out of his fantasy again as the bus stopped. The door opened with a sucking hiss and out of the dark a large, gaily dressed, sullen-looking colored woman got on with a little boy. The child, who might have been four, had on a short plaid suit and a Tyrolean hat with a blue feather in it. Julian hoped that he would sit down beside him and that the woman would push in beside his mother. He could think of no better arrangement.

As she waited for her tokens, the woman was surveying the seating possibilities—he hoped with the idea of sitting where she was least wanted. There was something familiar-looking about her but Julian could not place what it was. She was a giant of a woman. Her face was set not only to meet opposition but to seek it out. The downward tilt of her large lower lip was like a warning sign: DON'T TAMPER WITH ME. Her bulging figure was encased in a green crepe dress and her feet overflowed in red shoes. She had on a hideous hat. A purple velvet flap came down on one side of it and stood up on the other; the rest of it was green and looked like a cushion with the stuffing out. She carried a mammoth red pocketbook that bulged throughout as if it were stuffed with rocks.

To Julian's disappointment, the little boy climbed up on the empty seat beside his mother. His mother lumped all children, black and white, into the common category, "cute," and she thought little Negroes were on the whole cuter than little white children. She smiled at the little boy as he climbed on the seat.

Meanwhile the woman was bearing down upon the empty seat beside Julian. To his annoyance, she squeezed herself into it. He saw his mother's face change as the woman settled herself next to him and he realized with satisfaction that this was more objectionable to her than it was to him. Her face seemed almost gray and there was a look of dull recognition in her eyes, as if suddenly she had sickened at some awful confrontation. Julian saw that it was because she and the woman had, in a sense, swapped sons. Though his mother would not realize the symbolic significance of this, she would feel it. His amusement showed plainly on his face.

The woman next to him muttered something unintelligible to herself. He was conscious of a kind of bristling next to him, a muted growling like that of an angry cat. He could not see anything but the red pocketbook upright on the bulging green thighs. He visualized the woman as she had stood waiting for her tokens —the ponderous figure, rising from the red shoes upward over the solid hips, the mammoth bosom, the haughty face, to the green and purple hat.

His eyes widened.

The vision of the two hats, identical, broke upon him with the radiance of a brilliant sunrise. His face was suddenly lit with joy. He could not believe that Fate had thrust upon his mother such a lesson. He gave a loud chuckle so that she would look at him and see that he saw. She turned her eyes on him slowly. The blue in them seemed to have turned a bruised purple. For a moment he had an uncomfortable sense of her innocence, but it lasted only a second before principle rescued him. Justice entitled him to laugh.

His grin hardened until it said to her as plainly as if he were saying aloud: Your punishment exactly fits your pettiness. This should teach you a permanent lesson.

Her eyes shifted to the woman. She seemed unable to bear looking at him and to find the woman preferable. He became conscious again of the bristling presence at his side. The woman was rumbling like a volcano about to become active. His mother's mouth began to twitch slightly at one corner. With a sinking heart, he saw incipient signs of recovery on her face and realized that this was going to strike her suddenly as funny and was going to be no lesson at all. She kept her eyes on the woman and an amused smile came over her face as if the woman were a monkey that had stolen her hat. The little Negro was looking up at her with large fascinated eyes. He had been trying to attract her attention for some time.

"Carver!" the woman said suddenly. "Come heah!"

When he saw that the spotlight was on him at last, Carver drew his feet up and turned himself toward Julian's mother and giggled.

"Carver!" the woman said. "You heah me? Come heah!"

Carver slid down from the seat but remained squatting with his back against the base of it, his head turned slyly around toward Julian's mother, who was smiling at him. The woman reached a hand across the aisle and snatched him to her. He righted himself and hung backwards on her knees, grinning at Julian's mother. "Isn't he cute?" Julian's mother said to the woman with the protruding teeth.

"I reckon he is," the woman said without conviction.

The Negress yanked him upright but he eased out of her grip and shot across the aisle and scrambled, giggling wildly, onto the seat beside his love.

"I think he likes me," Julian's mother said, and smiled at the woman. It was the smile she used when she was being particularly gracious to an inferior. Julian saw everything lost. The lesson had rolled off her like rain on a roof.

The woman stood up and yanked the little boy off the seat as if she were snatching him from contagion. Julian could feel the rage in her at having no weapon like his mother's smile. She gave the child a sharp slap across his leg. He howled once and then thrust his head into her stomach and kicked his feet against her shins. "Be-have," she said vehemently.

The bus stopped and the Negro who had been reading the newspaper got off. The woman moved over and set the little boy down with a thump between herself and Julian. She held him firmly by the knee. In a moment he put his hands in front of his face and peeped at Julian's mother through his fingers.

"I see yoooooooo!" she said and put her hand in front of her face and peeped at him.

The woman slapped his hand down. "Quit yo' foolishness," she said, "before I knock the living Jesus out of you!"

Julian was thankful that the next stop was theirs. He reached up and pulled the cord. The woman reached up and pulled it at the same time. Oh my God, he thought. He had the terrible intuition that when they got off the bus together, his mother would open her purse and give the little boy a nickel. The gesture would be as natural to her as breathing. The bus stopped and the woman got up and lunged to the front, dragging the child, who wished to stay on, after her. Julian and his mother got up and followed. As they neared the door, Julian tried to relieve her of her pocketbook.

"No," she murmured, "I want to give the little boy a nickel."

"No!" Julian hissed. "No!"

She smiled down at the child and opened her bag. The bus door opened and the woman picked him up by the arm and descended with him, hanging at her hip. Once in the street she set him down and shook him.

Julian's mother had to close her purse while she got down the bus step but as soon as her feet were on the ground, she opened it again and began to rummage inside. "I can't find but a penny," she whispered, "but it looks like a new one."

"Don't do it!" Julian said fiercely between his teeth. There was a streetlight on the corner and she hurried to get under it so that she could better see into her pocketbook. The woman was heading off rapidly down the street with the child still hanging backward on her hand.

"Oh little boy!" Julian's mother called and took a few quick steps and caught up with them just beyond the lamppost. "Here's a bright new penny for you," and she held out the coin, which shone bronze in the dim light.

The huge woman turned and for a moment stood, her shoulders lifted and her face frozen with frustrated rage, and stared at Julian's mother. Then all at once she seemed to explode like a piece of machinery that had been given one ounce of pressure too much. Julian saw the black fist swing out with the red pocketbook. He shut his eyes and cringed as he heard the woman shout, "He don't take nobody's pennies!" When he opened his eyes, the woman was disappearing down the street with the little boy staring wide-eyed over her shoulder. Julian's mother was sitting on the sidewalk.

"I told you not to do that," Julian said angrily. "I told you not to do that!"

He stood over her for a minute, gritting his teeth. Her legs were stretched out in front of her and her hat was on her lap. He squatted down and looked her in the face. It was totally expressionless. "You got exactly what you deserved," he said. "Now get up."

He picked up her pocketbook and put what had fallen out back in it. He picked the hat up off her lap. The penny caught his eye on the sidewalk and he picked that up and let it drop before her eyes into the purse. Then he stood up and leaned over and held his hands out to pull her up. She remained immobile. He sighed. Rising above them on either side were black apartment buildings, marked with irregular rectangles of light. At the end of the block a man came out of a door and walked off in the opposite direction. "All right," he said, "suppose somebody happens by and wants to know why you're sitting on the sidewalk?"

She took the hand and, breathing hard, pulled heavily up on it and then stood for a moment, swaying slightly as if the spots of light in the darkness were circling around her. Her eyes, shadowed and confused, finally settled on his face. He did not try to conceal his irritation. "I hope this teaches you a lesson," he said. She leaned forward and her eyes raked his face. She seemed trying to determine his identity. Then, as if she found nothing familiar about him, she started off with a headlong movement in the wrong direction.

"Aren't you going on to the Y?" he asked.

"Home," she muttered.

"Well, are we walking?"

For answer she kept going. Julian followed along, his hands behind him. He saw no reason to let the lesson she had had go without backing it up with an explanation of its meaning. She might as well be made to understand what had happened to her. "Don't think that was just an uppity Negro woman," he said. "That was the whole colored race which will no longer take your condescending pennies. That was your black double. She can wear the same hat as you, and to be sure," he added gratuitously (because he thought it was funny), "it looked better on her than it did on you. What all this means," he said, "is that the old world is gone. The old manners are obsolete and your graciousness is not worth a damn." He thought bitterly of the house that had been lost for him. "You aren't who you think you are," he said.

She continued to plow ahead, paying no attention to him. Her hair had come undone on one side. She dropped her pocketbook and took no notice. He stooped and picked it up and handed it to her but she did not take it.

"You needn't act as if the world had come to an end," he said, "because it hasn't. From now on you've got to live in a new world and face a few realities for a change. Buck up," he said, "it won't kill you."

She was breathing fast.

"Let's wait on the bus," he said.

"Home," she said thickly.

"I hate to see you behave like this," he said. "Just like a child. I should be able to expect more of you." He decided to stop where he was and make her stop and wait for a bus. "I'm not going any farther," he said, stopping. "We're going on the bus."

She continued to go on as if she had not heard him. He took a few steps and caught her arm and stopped her. He looked into her face and caught his breath. He was looking into a face he had never seen before. "Tell Grandpa to come get me," she said.

He stared, stricken.

"Tell Caroline to come get me," she said.

Stunned, he let her go and she lurched forward again, walking as if one leg were shorter than the other. A tide of darkness seemed to be sweeping her from him. "Mother!" he cried. "Darling, sweetheart, wait!" Crumpling, she fell to the pavement. He dashed forward and fell at her side, crying, "Mamma, Mamma!" He turned her over. Her face was fiercely distorted. One eye, large and staring, moved slightly to the left as if it had become unmoored. The other remained fixed on him, raked his face again, found nothing and closed.

"Wait here, wait here!" he cried and jumped up and began to run for help toward a cluster of lights he saw in the distance ahead of him. "Help, help!" he shouted, but his voice was thin, scarcely a thread of sound. The lights drifted farther away the faster he ran and his feet moved numbly as if they carried him nowhere. The tide of darkness seemed to sweep him back to her, postponing from moment to moment his entry into the world of guilt and sorrow.

ROBERT HAYDEN

(1 9 1 3 -   )

Robert Hayden was born in Detroit and received a bachelor's degree at Wayne State University and a master's at the University of Michigan. He joined the faculty of Fisk University, where he is now Professor of English, in 1964, after having taught at the University of Michigan. Arriving in time for the postwar influx of veterans, he helped the Fisk Herald, the student publication on which future novelist William Denby served as an editor, to produce what Robert A. Bone has termed "something of an intellectual renaissance at Fisk."

Hayden researched Negro history for the depression-era Federal Writers' Project and, in addition to his poetry, has written criticism, radio scripts, and a play. He is poetry editor of World Order, the Baha'i World Faith Magazine, and has edited an anthology, Kaleidoscope: Poems by American Negro Poets (1967). His books of poetry are Heart-Shape in the Dust (1940), The Lion and the Archer (written in collaboration with Myron O'Higgins, 1948), A Ballad of Remembrance (1962), and Selected Poems (1966). His honors include Hopwood Awards from the University of Michigan, a Rosenwald Literary Fellowship, and a Ford Foundation grant for travel and writing in Mexico. In 1965 A Ballad of Remembrance received the Grand Prize for Poetry at the First World Festival of Negro Arts, held in Dakar, Senegal.

Though some of his best works are rooted in a profound sense of

Negro history, Hayden refuses to limit his poetry to racial themes or to define himself as a "Negro poet." In the January 1968 issue of Negro Digest he rejected the notion of a "black aesthetic" and took odds with LeRoi Jones's black nationalism. The same issue of Negro Digest polled thirty-eight Negro writers on whom they considered the most important living black poet, with the result that LeRoi Jones ranked first, Hayden and Gwendolyn Brooks tied for second, and Margaret Walker was rated fourth.

"Tour 5" and "Runagate Runagate" appear in Hayden's Selected Poems (1966).

Tour 5

The road winds down through autumn hills
in blazonry of farewell scarlet
and recessional gold,
past cedar groves, through static villages
whose names are all that's left
of Choctaw, Chickasaw.

We stop a moment in a town
watched over by Confederate sentinels,
buy gas and ask directions of a rawboned man
whose eyes revile us as the enemy.

Shrill gorgon silence breathes behind
his taut civility
and in the ever-tautening air,
dark for us despite its Indian summer glow.
We drive on, following the route
of highwaymen and phantoms,

Of slaves and armies.
Children, wordless and remote,
wave at us from kindling porches.

From *Selected Poems*. Copyright © 1966 by Robert Hayden. Reprinted by permission of October House, Inc.

And now the land is flat for miles,
the landscape lush, metallic, flayed,
its brightness harsh as bloodstained swords.

Runagate Runagate

I.

Runs falls rises stumbles on from darkness into darkness
and the darkness thicketed with shapes of terror
and the hunters pursuing and the hounds pursuing
and the night cold and the night long and the river
to cross and the jack-muh-lanterns beckoning beckoning
and blackness ahead and when shall I reach that somewhere
morning and keep on going and never turn back and keep on going

      Runagate
            Runagate
                 Runagate

Many thousands rise and go
many thousands crossing over

                  O mythic North
                 O star-shaped yonder Bible city

Some go weeping and some rejoicing
some in coffins and some in carriages
some in silks and some in shackles

         Rise and go or fare you well

No more auction block for me
no more driver's lash for me

      If you see my Pompey, 30 yrs of age,
      new breeches, plain stockings, negro shoes;
      if you see my Anna, likely young mulatto

branded E on the right cheek, R on the left,
catch them if you can and notify subscriber.
Catch them if you can, but it won't be easy.
They'll dart underground when you try to catch them,
plunge into quicksand, whirlpools, mazes,
turn into scorpions when you try to catch them.

And before I'll be a slave
I'll be buried in my grave

North star and bonanza gold
I'm bound for the freedom, freedom-bound
and oh Susyanna don't you cry for me

Runagate

Runagate

II.

Rises from their anguish and their power,

Harriet Tubman,

woman of earth, whipscarred,
a summoning, a shining

Mean to be free

And this was the way of it, brethren brethren,
way we journeyed from Can't to Can.
Moon so bright and no place to hide,
the cry up and the patterollers riding,
hound dogs belling in bladed air.
And fear starts a-murbling, Never make it,
we'll never make it. *Hush that now,*
and she's turned upon us, levelled pistol
glinting in the moonlight:
Dead folks can't jaybird-talk, she says;
you keep on going now or die, she says.

Wanted   Harriet Tubman   alias The General
alias Moses   Stealer of Slaves

In league with Garrison   Alcott   Emerson
Garrett   Douglass   Thoreau   John Brown

Armed and known to be Dangerous

Wanted   Reward   Dead or Alive

     Tell me, Ezekiel, oh tell me do you see
     mailed Jehovah coming to deliver me?

Hoot-owl calling in the ghosted air,
five times calling to the hants in the air.
Shadow of a face in the scary leaves,
shadow of a voice in the talking leaves:

     Come ride-a my train

     Oh that train, ghost-story train
     through swamp and savanna movering movering,
     over trestles of dew, through caves of the wish,
     Midnight Special on a sabre track movering movering,
     first stop Mercy and the last Hallelujah.

     Come ride-a my train

       Mean mean mean to be free.

ELDRIDGE CLEAVER

(1935-   )

Black Panther Minister of Information, Peace and Freedom
Party candidate for President of the United States, challenger of
the California Board of Regents and the Oakland Police Department, Eldridge Cleaver is regarded by many as a symbol of black
militant activism. Yet he has exerted far more influence on educated opinion in America with one book, Soul on Ice (1968), than
through any of his Black Panther activities. Indeed, Maxwell
Geismar writes in his Introduction to the book that "Cleaver is
simply one of the best cultural critics now writing, and I include in
this statement both the formal sociologists and those contemporary
fictionists who have mainly abandoned this province of literature
for the cultivation of the cult of sensibility."

Born in Little Rock, Arkansas, in 1935, Cleaver has spent nearly
a dozen years in California prisons. He was first convicted at the
age of eighteen for possession of marijuana, and by 1958 he was
again in jail, this time serving a fourteen-year sentence for assault to
kill and rape. In California's Folsom Prison, where he wrote Soul
on Ice, he became an ardent Black Muslim but, gradually won
over to the views of Malcolm X, he left the Muslims when Malcolm X resigned from the organization. Paroled in December
1966, the self-educated Cleaver joined Ramparts magazine, where
he became a Senior Editor. Soul on Ice, published in 1968, combined love letters with a series of essays on American racism, the

Vietnam war, literature, prison life, American cultural heroes, the Third World, and Cleaver's own spiritual development. A constant concern in the book is the complex relationship between black men and white women, which Cleaver sees as central to an understanding of America's racial dilemma. So candid was Cleaver's handling of this theme, however, that New York Times reviewer Thomas Lask expressed the fear that "He has provided a couple of handy chapters for those who argue blandly that the aim of Negroes is not to live decently but only to be able to mix intimately with whites."

Following his release from prison, Cleaver joined the Black Panthers, described by the New York Times as a group of "gun-carrying Negroes who represent extreme militancy," and early in 1968 he was involved in a gun battle between Panthers and Oakland police. A Panther member was killed in the episode, and Cleaver and two policemen were wounded. His parole revoked as a result of the incident, Cleaver was returned to the California Prison Medical Center. A complex court battle followed in which Cleaver was released and then, after several months of freedom, ordered to return to prison. In 1968 he ran as the Peace and Freedom Party's presidential candidate and was invited to deliver a series of lectures in an experimental course on race relations at the Berkeley campus of the University of California. The invitation led to an elaborate debate, complete with sit-ins and other demonstrations, involving University students and faculty, Governor Reagan, State Education Superintendent Rafferty, and the State Board of Regents. While the debate was still in progress, Cleaver was ordered returned to prison in November 1968, and when he failed to surrender himself a fugitive warrant was issued. He is now residing in Algeria, but has announced plans to return to the United States.

Although he hesitates to call himself a revolutionary, Cleaver has said, "I don't believe it's possible for black people to have a good life under a capitalistic system." In a speech at Stanford University he described America as "the successor to Nazi Germany, the number one obstacle to human progress—not Russia, not China, but Babylon, right here in North America." Yet Grier Raggio, Jr., argues that "Cleaver basically hopes that social reform will be *enough. He is not a separatist, and he believes that the reforms can be made if enough people are aware of the problems and of the pain they cause. His writings, over and above the rhetoric and bravado, prompt the conclusion that Cleaver is an optimist; he assumes people can be influenced by argument, that their conduct is not wholly determined by racial, cultural or economic status."*

Eldridge Cleaver (1969), edited by Robert Scheer, is a collection of speeches and articles that Cleaver wrote during the time between his release from prison in 1967 and his becoming a fugitive from California parole authorities in 1968. The following selections are from Soul on Ice.

From *Soul on Ice*

On Watts

Folsom Prison
August 16, 1965

As we left the Mess Hall Sunday morning and milled around in the prison yard, after four days of abortive uprising in Watts, a group of low riders* from Watts assembled on the basketball court. They were wearing jubilant, triumphant smiles, animated by a vicarious spirit by which they, too, were in the thick of the uprising taking place hundreds of miles away to the south in the Watts ghetto.

"Man," said one, "what they doing out there? Break it down for me, Baby."

From *Soul on Ice* by Eldridge Cleaver. Copyright © 1968 by Eldridge Cleaver. Used by permission of McGraw-Hill Book Company.
* *Low rider.* A Los Angeles nickname for ghetto youth. Originally the term was coined to describe the youths who had lowered the bodies of their cars so that they rode low, close to the ground; also implied was the style of driving that these youngsters perfected. Sitting behind the steering wheel and slumped low down in the seat, all that could be seen of them was from their eyes up, which used to be the cool way of driving. When these youthful hipsters alighted from their vehicles, the term *low rider* stuck with them, evolving to the point where all black ghetto youth—but *never* the soft offspring of the black bourgeoisie—are referred to as low riders. [Cleaver's note.]

They slapped each other's outstretched palms in a cool salute and burst out laughing with joy.

"Home boy, them Brothers is taking care of Business!" shrieked another ecstatically.

Then one low rider, stepping into the center of the circle formed by the others, rared back on his legs and swaggered, hunching his belt up with his forearms as he'd seen James Cagney and George Raft do in too many gangster movies. I joined the circle. Sensing a creative moment in the offing, we all got very quiet, very still, and others passing by joined the circle and did likewise.

"Baby," he said, "they walking in fours and kicking in doors; dropping Reds* and busting heads; drinking wine and committing crime, shooting and looting; high-siding† and low-riding, setting fires and slashing tires; turning over cars and burning down bars; making Parker mad and making me glad; putting an end to that 'go slow' crap and putting sweet Watts on the map—my black ass is in Folsom this morning but my black heart is in Watts!" Tears of joy were rolling from his eyes.

It was a cleansing, revolutionary laugh we all shared, something we have not often had occasion for.

Watts was a place of shame. We used to use Watts as an epithet in much the same way as city boys used "country" as a term of derision. To deride one as a "lame," who did not know what was happening (a rustic bumpkin), the "in-crowd" of the time from L.A. would bring a cat down by saying that he had just left Watts, that he ought to go back to Watts until he had learned what was happening, or that he had just stolen enough money to move out of Watts and was already trying to play a cool part. But now, blacks are seen in Folsom saying, "I'm from Watts, Baby!"— whether true or no, but I think their meaning is clear. Confession: I, too, have participated in this game, saying, I'm from Watts. In fact, I did live there for a time, and I'm *proud* of it, the tired lamentations of Whitney Young, Roy Wilkins, and The Preacher notwithstanding.

* *Reds.* A barbiturate, called Red Devils; so called because of the color of the capsule and because they are reputed to possess a vicious kick. [Cleaver's note.]

† *High-siding.* Cutting up. Having fun at the expense of another. [Cleaver's note.]

Soul Food

Folsom Prison,
November 3, 1965

You hear a lot of jazz about Soul Food. Take chitterlings: the ghetto blacks eat them from necessity while the black bourgeoisie has turned it into a mocking slogan. Eating chitterlings is like going slumming to them. Now that they have the price of a steak, here they come prattling about Soul Food. The people in the ghetto want steaks. *Beef Steaks.* I wish I had the power to see to it that the bourgeoisie really *did* have to make it on Soul Food.

The emphasis on Soul Food is counter-revolutionary black bourgeois ideology. The main reason Elijah Muhammad outlawed pork for Negroes had nothing to do with dietary laws. The point is that when you get all those blacks cooped up in the ghetto with beef steaks on their minds—with the weight of religious fervor behind the desire to chuck—then something's got to give. The system has made allowances for the ghettoites to obtain a little pig, *but there are no provisions for the elite to give up any beef.* The walls come tumbling down.

On Becoming

. . . In the process of enduring my confinement, I decided to get myself a pin-up girl to paste on the wall of my cell. I would fall in love with her and lavish my affections upon her. She, a symbolic representative of the forbidden tribe of women, would sustain me until I was free. Out of the center of *Esquire*, I married a voluptuous bride. Our marriage went along swell for a time: no quarrels, no complaints. And then, one evening when I came in from school, I was shocked and enraged to find that the guard had entered my cell, ripped my sugar from the wall, torn her into little pieces, and left the pieces floating in the commode: it was like seeing a dead body floating in a lake. Giving her a proper burial, I flushed the commode. As the saying goes, I sent her to Long Beach. But I was genuinely beside myself with anger: almost every cell, excepting those of the homosexuals, had a pin-up girl on the wall and the guards didn't bother them. Why, I asked the guard the next day, had he singled me out for special treatment?

"Don't you know we have a rule against pasting up pictures on the walls?" he asked me.

"Later for the rules," I said. "You know as well as I do that that rule is not enforced."

"Tell you what," he said, smiling at me (the smile put me on my guard), "I'll compromise with you: get yourself a colored girl for a pin-up—no white women—and I'll let it stay up. Is that a deal?"

I was more embarrassed than shocked. He was laughing in my face. I called him two or three dirty names and walked away. I can still recall his big moon-face, grinning at me over yellow teeth. The disturbing part about the whole incident was that a terrible feeling of guilt came over me as I realized that I had chosen the picture of the white girl over the available pictures of black girls. I tried to rationalize it away, but I was fascinated by the truth involved. Why hadn't I thought about it in this light before? So I took hold of the question and began to inquire into my feelings. Was it true, did I really prefer white girls over black? The conclusion was clear and inescapable: I did. I decided to check out my friends on this point and it was easy to determine, from listening to their general conversation, that the white woman occupied a peculiarly prominent place in all of our frames of reference. With what I have learned since then, this all seems terribly elementary now. But at the time, it was a tremendously intriguing adventure of discovery.

One afternoon, when a large group of Negroes was on the prison yard shooting the breeze, I grabbed the floor and posed the question: which did they prefer, white women or black? Some said Japanese women were their favorite, others said Chinese, some said European women, others said Mexican women—they all stated a preference, and they generally freely admitted their dislike for black women.

"I don't want nothing black but a Cadillac," said one.

"If money was black I wouldn't want none of it," put in another.

A short little stud, who was a very good lightweight boxer with a little man's complex that made him love to box heavyweights, jumped to his feet. He had a yellowish complexion and we called him Butterfly.

"All you niggers are sick!" Butterfly spat out. "I don't like no stinking white woman. My grandma is a white woman and I don't even like her!"

But it just so happened that Butterfly's crime partner was in the crowd, and after Butterfly had his say, his crime partner said, "Aw, sit on down and quit that lying, lil o' chump. What about that gray girl in San Jose who had your nose wide open? Did you like her, or were you just running after her with your tongue hanging out of your head because you hated her?"

Partly because he was embarrassed and partly because his crime partner was a heavyweight, Butterfly flew into him. And before we could separate them and disperse, so the guard would not know who had been fighting, Butterfly bloodied his crime partner's nose. Butterfly got away but, because of the blood, his crime partner got caught. I ate dinner with Butterfly that evening and questioned him sharply about his attitude toward white women. And after an initial evasiveness he admitted that the white woman bugged him too. "It's a sickness," he said. "All our lives we've had the white woman dangled before our eyes like a carrot on a stick before a donkey: look but don't touch." (In 1958, after I had gone out on parole and was returned to San Quentin as a parole violator with a new charge, Butterfly was still there. He had become a Black Muslim and was chiefly responsible for teaching me the Black Muslim philosophy. Upon his release from San Quentin, Butterfly joined the Los Angeles Mosque, advanced rapidly through the ranks, and is now a full-fledged minister of one of Elijah Muhammad's mosques in another city. He successfully completed his parole, got married—to a very black girl—and is doing fine.)

From our discussion, which began that evening and has never yet ended, we went on to notice how thoroughly, as a matter of course, a black growing up in America is indoctrinated with the white race's standard of beauty. Not that the whites made a conscious, calculated effort to do this, we thought, but since they constituted the majority the whites brainwashed the blacks by the very processes the whites employed to indoctrinate themselves with their own group standards. It intensified my frustrations to know that I was indoctrinated to see the white woman as more beautiful and desirable than my own black woman. It drove me into books seeking light on the subject. In Richard Wright's *Native Son*, I found Bigger Thomas and a keen insight into the problem.

My interest in this area persisted undiminished and then, in 1955, an event took place in Mississippi which turned me inside out: Emmett Till, a young Negro down from Chicago on a visit, was murdered, allegedly for flirting with a white woman. He had been shot, his head crushed from repeated blows with a blunt instrument, and his badly decomposed body was recovered from the river with a heavy weight on it. I was, of course, angry over the whole bit, but one day I saw in a magazine a picture of the white woman with whom Emmett Till was said to have flirted. While looking at the picture, I felt that little tension in the center of my chest I experience when a woman appeals to me. I was disgusted and angry with myself. Here was a woman who had caused the death of a black, possibly because, when he looked at her, he also felt the same tensions of lust and desire in his chest—and probably for the same general reasons that I felt them. It was all unacceptable to me. I looked at the picture again and again, and in spite of everything and against my will and the hate I felt for the woman and all that she represented, she appealed to me. I flew into a rage at myself, at America, at white women, at the history that had placed those tensions of lust and desire in my chest.

Two days later, I had a "nervous breakdown." For several days I ranted and raved against the white race, against white women in particular, against white America in general. When I came to myself, I was locked in a padded cell with not even the vaguest memory of how I got there. All I could recall was an eternity of pacing back and forth in the cell, preaching to the unhearing walls.

I had several sessions with a psychiatrist. His conclusion was that I hated my mother. How he arrived at this conclusion I'll never know, because he knew nothing about my mother; and when he'd ask me questions I would answer him with absurd lies. What revolted me about him was that he had heard me denouncing the whites, yet each time he interviewed me he deliberately guided the conversation back to my family life, to my childhood. That in itself was all right, but he deliberately blocked all my attempts to bring out the racial question, and he made it clear that he was not interested in my attitude toward whites. This was a Pandora's box he did not care to open. After I ceased my diatribes against the whites, I was let out of the hospital, back into the general inmate population just as if nothing had happened. I continued to brood over these events and over the dynamics of race relations in America.

During this period I was concentrating my reading in the field of economics. Having previously dabbled in the theories and writings of Rousseau, Thomas Paine, and Voltaire, I had added a little polish to my iconoclastic stance, without, however, bothering too much to understand their affirmative positions. In economics, because everybody seemed to find it necessary to attack and condemn Karl Marx in their writings, I sought out his books, and although he kept me with a headache, I took him for my authority. I was not prepared to understand him, but I was able to see in him a thoroughgoing critique and condemnation of capitalism. It was like taking medicine for me to find that, indeed, American capitalism deserved all the hatred and contempt that I felt for it in my heart. This had a positive, stabilizing effect upon me—to an extent because I was not about to become stable—and it diverted me from my previous preoccupation: morbid broodings on the black man and the white woman. Pursuing my readings into the history of socialism, I read, with very little understanding, some of the passionate, exhortatory writings of Lenin; and I fell in love with Bakunin and Nechayev's *Catechism of the Revolutionist*— the principles of which, along with some of Machiavelli's advice, I sought to incorporate into my own behavior. I took the *Catechism* for my bible and, standing on a one-man platform that had nothing to do with the reconstruction of society, I began consciously incorporating these principles into my daily life, to employ tactics of ruthlessness in my dealings with everyone with whom I came into contact. And I began to look at white America through these new eyes.

Somehow I arrived at the conclusion that, as a matter of principle, it was of paramount importance for me to have an antagonistic, ruthless attitude toward white women. The term *outlaw* appealed to me and at the time my parole date was drawing near, I considered myself to be mentally free—I was an "outlaw." I had stepped outside of the white man's law, which I repudiated with scorn and self-satisfaction. I became a law unto myself—my own legislature, my own supreme court, my own executive. At the moment I walked out of the prison gate, my feelings toward white women in general could be summed up in the following lines:

TO A WHITE GIRL

I love you
Because you're white,
Not because you're charming
Or bright.
Your whiteness
Is a silky thread
Snaking through my thoughts
In redhot patterns
Of lust and desire.

I hate you
Because you're white.
Your white meat
Is nightmare food.
White is
The skin of Evil.
You're my Moby Dick,
White Witch,
Symbol of the rope and hanging tree,
Of the burning cross.

Loving you thus
And hating you so,
My heart is torn in two.
Crucified.

I became a rapist. To refine my technique and *modus operandi*, I started out by practicing on black girls in the ghetto—in the black ghetto where dark and vicious deeds appear not as aberrations or deviations from the norm, but as part of the sufficiency of the Evil of a day—and when I considered myself smooth enough, I crossed the tracks and sought out white prey. I did this consciously, deliberately, willfully, methodically—though looking back I see that I was in a frantic, wild, and completely abandoned frame of mind.

Rape was an insurrectionary act. It delighted me that I was defying and trampling upon the white man's law, upon his system of values, and that I was defiling his women—and this point, I believe, was the most satisfying to me because I was very resentful over the historical fact of how the white man has used the black woman. I felt I was getting revenge. From the site of the act of rape, consternation spreads outwardly in concentric circles. I wanted to send waves of consternation throughout the white race. Recently, I came upon a quotation from one of LeRoi Jones' poems, taken from his book *The Dead Lecturer:*

> A cult of death need of the simple striking arm under the street lamp. The cutters from under their rented earth. Come up, black dada nihilismus. Rape the white girls. Rape their fathers. Cut the mothers' throats.

I have lived those lines and I know that if I had not been apprehended I would have slit some white throats. There are, of course, many young blacks out there right now who are slitting white throats and raping the white girls. They are not doing this because they read LeRoi Jones' poetry, as some of his critics seem to believe. Rather, LeRoi is expressing the funky facts of life.

After I returned to prison, I took a long look at myself and, for the first time in my life, admitted that I was wrong, that I had gone astray—astray not so much from the white man's law as from being human, civilized—for I could not approve the act of rape. Even though I had some insight into my own motivations, I did not feel justified. I lost my self-respect. My pride as a man dissolved and my whole fragile moral structure seemed to collapse, completely shattered.

That is why I started to write. To save myself.

I realized that no one could save me but myself. The prison authorities were both uninterested and unable to help me. I had to seek out the truth and unravel the snarled web of my motivations. I had to find out who I am and what I want to be, what type of man I should be, and what I could do to become the best of which I was capable. I understood that what had happened to me had also happened to countless other blacks and it would happen to many, many more.

I learned that I had been taking the easy way out, running away from problems. I also learned that it is easier to do evil than it is to do good. And I have been terribly impressed by the youth of America, black and white. I am proud of them because they have reaffirmed my faith in humanity. I have come to feel what must be love for the young people of America and I want to be part of the good and greatness that they want for all people. From my prison cell, I have watched America slowly coming awake. It is not fully awake yet, but there is soul in the air and everywhere I see beauty. I have watched the sit-ins, the freedom raids, the Mississippi Blood Summers, demonstrations all over the country, the FSM movement, the teach-ins, and the mounting protest over Lyndon Strangelove's foreign policy—all of this, the thousands of little details, show me it is time to straighten up and fly right. That is why I decided to concentrate on my writings and efforts in this area. We are a very sick country—I, perhaps, am sicker than most. But I accept that. I told you in the beginning that I am extremist by nature—so it is only right that I should be extremely sick.

I was very familiar with the Eldridge who came to prison, but that Eldridge no longer exists. And the one I am now is in some ways a stranger to me. You may find this difficult to understand but it is very easy for one in prison to lose his sense of self. And if he has been undergoing all kinds of extreme, involved, and unregulated changes, then he ends up not knowing who he is. Take the point of being attractive to women. You can easily see how a man can lose his arrogance or certainty on that point while in prison! When he's in the free world, he gets constant feedback on how he looks from the number of female heads he turns when he walks down the street. In prison he gets only hate-stares and sour frowns. Years and years of bitter looks. Individuality is not nourished in prison, neither by the officials nor by the convicts. It is a deep hole out of which to climb.

What must be done, I believe, is that all these problems—particularly the sickness between the white woman and the black man—must be brought out into the open, dealt with and resolved. I know that the black man's sick attitude toward the white woman is a revolutionary sickness: it keeps him perpetually out of harmony with the system that is oppressing him. Many whites flatter themselves with the idea that the Negro male's lust and desire for the white dream girl is purely an esthetic attraction, but nothing could be farther from the truth. His motivation is often of such a bloody, hateful, bitter, and malignant nature that whites would really be hard pressed to find it flattering. I have discussed these points with prisoners who were convicted of rape, and their motivations are very plain. But they are very reluctant to discuss these things with white men who, by and large, make up the prison staffs. I believe that in the experience of these men lies the knowledge and wisdom that must be utilized to help other youngsters who are heading in the same direction. I think all of us, the entire nation, will be better off if we bring it all out front. A lot of people's feelings will be hurt, but that is the price that must be paid.

It may be that I can harm myself by speaking frankly and directly, but I do not care about that at all. Of course I want to get out of prison, badly, but I shall get out some day. I am more concerned with what I am going to be after I get out. I know that by following the course which I have charted I will find my salvation. If I had followed the path laid down for me by the officials, I'd undoubtedly have long since been out of prison—but I'd be less of a man. I'd be weaker and less certain of where I want to go, what I want to do, and how to go about it.

The price of hating other human beings is loving oneself less.

BIBLIOGRAPHY

GENERAL

The American Negro Writer and His Roots: Selected Papers from the First Conference of Negro Writers. New York: American Society of African Culture, 1960.

Baldwin, James. *Notes of a Native Son.* Boston: Beacon Press, 1955.

Bone, Robert A. *The Negro Novel in America.* New Haven: Yale University Press, 1965.

Brown, Sterling. "A Century of Negro Portraiture in American Literature," *Massachusetts Review*, VII (1966), 73–96.

———. *The Negro in American Fiction.* Washington, D.C.: The Associates in Negro Folk Education, 1937.

Chapman, Abraham. *The Negro in American Literature and a Bibliography of Literature by and about Negro Americans.* Oshkosh: Wisconsin Council of Teachers of English, 1966.

Ellison, Ralph. *Shadow and Act.* New York: Random House, 1964.

Gloster, Hugh M. *Negro Voices in American Fiction.* Chapel Hill: University of North Carolina Press, 1948.

Gross, Seymour L., and Hardy, John, eds. *Images of the Negro in American Literature.* Chicago: University of Chicago Press, 1966.

Hill, Herbert, ed. *Anger, and Beyond: The Negro Writer in the United States.* New York: Harper and Row, 1966.

Hughes, Carl Milton. *The Negro Novelist.* New York: Citadel Press, 1953.

Littlejohn, David. *Black on White: A Critical Survey of Writing by American Negroes.* New York: Grossman, 1966.

Locke, Alain. "The Negro in American Literature," in *New World Writing No. 1.* New York: Mentor Books, 1952.

Loggins, Vernon. *The Negro Author: His Development in America to 1900.* New York: Columbia University Press, 1931. Reprinted: Port Washington, New York: Kennikat Press, 1964.

Margolies, Edward. *Native Sons.* Philadelphia and New York: J. B. Lippincott, 1968.

Redding, Saunders. "American Negro Literature," *American Scholar,* XVIII (1949), 137–148.

————. *To Make a Poet Black.* Chapel Hill: University of North Carolina Press, 1939.

ON INDIVIDUAL AUTHORS

ANDERSON, SHERWOOD

Babb, Howard S. "A Reading of Sherwood Anderson's 'The Man Who Became a Woman,'" *PMLA,* LXXX (1965), 432–435.

Burbank, Rex. *Sherwood Anderson.* New York: Twayne Publishers, 1964.

Hoffman, F. J. "Three American Versions of Psychoanalysis" in *Freudianism and the Literary Mind.* Baton Rouge: Louisiana State University Press, 1957.

Howe, Irving. *Sherwood Anderson.* New York: William Sloane, 1951.

White, Ray B., ed. *The Achievement of Sherwood Anderson: Essays in Criticism.* Chapel Hill: University of North Carolina Press, 1966.

BALDWIN, JAMES

Bone, Robert A. "The Novels of James Baldwin," *Tri-Quarterly* (Winter 1965), 3–20.

Charney, Maurice. "Baldwin's Quarrel with Richard Wright," *American Quarterly,* XV (1963), 65–75.

Eckman, Fern Marja. *The Furious Passage of James Baldwin.* New York: M. Evans, 1966.

Gross, Theodore L. "The World of James Baldwin," *Critique,* VII (Winter 1964–1965), 139–149.

Hagopian, John V. "James Baldwin: The Black and the Red-White-and-Blue," *CLA Journal,* VII (1963), 133–140.

Klein, Marcus. "James Baldwin: A Question of Identity" in *After Alienation: American Novels in Mid-Century.* New York: World, 1962.

Murray, Albert. "Something Different, Something More" in *Anger, and Beyond,* ed. Herbert Hill. New York: Harper and Row, 1966.

Podhoretz, Norman. "In Defense of James Baldwin" in *Doings and Undoings.* New York: Farrar, Straus, 1964.

BONTEMPS, ARNA

Bone, Robert A. "Aspects of the Racial Past" in *The Negro Novel in America*. New Haven: Yale University Press, 1965.
Contemporary Authors, I (1962).

BOUCICAULT, DION

Faulkner, Seldon. "The *Octoroon* War," *Educational Theatre Journal*, XV (1963), 33–38.
Kaplan, Sidney. "*The Octoroon*: Early History of the Drama of Miscegenation," *Journal of Negro Education*, XX (1951), 547–557.
Quinn, Arthur H. "The Influence of Dion Boucicault" in *A History of the American Drama from the Beginning to the Civil War*, 2nd edition. New York: F. S. Crofts, 1943.

BROOKS, GWENDOLYN

Crockett, J. "An Essay on Gwendolyn Brooks," *Negro History Bulletin*, XIX (1955), 37–39.
Davis, Arthur P. "Gwendolyn Brooks: A Poet of the Unheroic," *CLA Journal*, VII (1963), 114–125.
Kunitz, Stanley. "Bronze by Gold," *Poetry*, LXXVI (1950), 52–56.

CABLE, GEORGE WASHINGTON

Arvin, Newton, ed. "Introduction" to *The Grandissimes*. New York: Hill and Wang, 1957.
Butcher, Philip. *George W. Cable*. New York: Twayne Publishers, 1962.
Pugh, Griffith T. "George Washington Cable," *Mississippi Quarterly*, XX (1967), 69–76.
Turner, Arlin. *George W. Cable: A Biography*. Durham, North Carolina: Duke University Press, 1956.
Whipple, James B. "Southern Rebel," *Phylon*, XX (1959), 345–357.

CHESNUTT, CHARLES W.

Ames, Russell. "Social Realism in Charles Chesnutt," *Phylon*, XIV (1953), 199–206.
Chesnutt, Helen M. *Charles Waddell Chesnutt: Pioneer of the Color Line*. Chapel Hill: University of North Carolina Press, 1952.
Gloster, Hugh M. "Charles W. Chesnutt: Pioneer in the Fiction of Negro Life," *Phylon*, II (1941), 57–66.
Hugley, G. "Charles Waddell Chesnutt," *Negro History Bulletin*, XIX (1955), 54–55.

Sillen, Samuel. "Charles W. Chesnutt: A Pioneer Negro Novelist," *Masses and Mainstream*, VI (1953), 8–14.

CLEAVER, ELDRIDGE

Geismar, Maxwell. "Introduction" to *Soul on Ice*. New York: McGraw-Hill, 1968.
Raggio, Grier, Jr. "Complex 'Black Voice' Called Eldridge Cleaver," *Wall Street Journal* (March 13, 1969), 14.

CRANE, STEPHEN

Nye, Russel B. "Stephen Crane as Social Critic," *Modern Quarterly*, XI (1940), 48–54.
Solomon, Eric. *Stephen Crane: From Parody to Realism*. Cambridge, Massachusetts: Harvard University Press, 1966.
Stallman, R.W. *Stephen Crane: A Biography*. New York: George Braziller, 1968.

CULLEN, COUNTEE

Bronz, Stephen H. "Countee Cullen" in *Roots of Negro Racial Consciousness: The 1920's: Three Harlem Renaissance Authors*. New York: Libra Publishers, 1964.
Davis, Arthur P. "The Alien-and-Exile Theme in Countee Cullen's Racial Poems," *Phylon*, XIV (1953), 390–400.
Ferguson, Blanche. *Countee Cullen and the Negro Renaissance*. New York: Dodd, Mead, 1966.
Smith, Robert. "The Poetry of Countee Cullen," *Phylon*, XI (1950), 216–221.
Webster, Harvey. "A Difficult Career," *Poetry*, LXX (1947), 222–225.

DREISER, THEODORE

Elias, Robert H. *Theodore Dreiser: Apostle of Nature*. Philadelphia: University of Pennsylvania Press, 1949.
Kazin, Alfred, and Shapiro, Charles, eds. *The Stature of Theodore Dreiser*. Bloomington: Indiana University Press, 1955.
Matthiessen, F.O. *Theodore Dreiser*. New York: William Sloane, 1951.
Swanberg, W. A. *Dreiser*. New York: Scribner's, 1965.

DUBOIS, W.E.B.

Bond, Horace Mann, *et al*. "The Legacy of W. E. B. DuBois," *Freedomways*, V (1965), 16–40.

Broderick, Francis L. *W. E. B. DuBois, Negro Leader in a Time of Crisis*. Stanford: Stanford University Press, 1959.

Duberman, Martin. "DuBois as Prophet," *New Republic*, CLVIII (1968), 36–39.

Howe, Irving. "Remarkable Man, Ambiguous Legacy," *Harper's Magazine*, CCXXXVI (1968), 143–149.

Rudwick, Elliott M. *W. E. B. DuBois: A Study in Minority Group Leadership*. Philadelphia: University of Pennsylvania Press, 1961.

DUNBAR, PAUL LAURENCE

Brawley, Benjamin. *Paul Laurence Dunbar: Poet of His People*. Chapel Hill: University of North Carolina Press, 1936.

Burch, Charles E. "The Plantation Negro in Dunbar's Poetry," *Southern Workman*, L (1921), 469–473.

Butcher, Philip. "Mutual Appreciation: Dunbar and Cable," *CLA Journal*, I (1958), 101–102.

Cunningham, Virginia. *Paul Laurence Dunbar and His Song*. New York: Dodd, Mead, 1947.

Daniel, T. W. "Paul Laurence Dunbar and the Democratic Ideal," *Negro History Bulletin*, VI (1943), 206–208.

Turner, Darwin. "Paul Laurence Dunbar: The Rejected Symbol," *Journal of Negro History*, LII (1967), 1–13.

ELLISON, RALPH

Baumbach, Jonathan. "Nightmare of a Native Son: Ellison's *Invisible Man*," *Criticism*, VI (1963), 48–65. Reprinted in *The Landscape of Nightmare*. New York: New York University Press, 1965.

Bone, Robert. "Ralph Ellison and the Uses of Imagination," *TriQuarterly*, Number Six (1966), 39–54. Reprinted in *Anger, and Beyond*, ed. Herbert Hill. New York: Harper and Row, 1966.

Glicksberg, Charles I. "The Symbolism of Vision," *Southwest Review*, XXXIX (1954), 259–265.

Klein, Marcus. "Ralph Ellison" in *After Alienation: American Novels in Mid-Century*. New York: World, 1962.

Rovit, Earl. "Ralph Ellison and the American Comic Tradition," *Wisconsin Studies in Contemporary Literature*, I (1960), 34–42.

Warren, Robert Penn. "The Unity of Experience," *Commentary*, XXXIX (1965), 91–96.

FAULKNER, WILLIAM

Edmonds, Irene C. "Faulkner and the Black Shadow" in *Southern Renascence*, eds. Louis D. Rubin and Robert D. Jacobs. Baltimore: Johns Hopkins University Press, 1953.

Howe, Irving. "Faulkner and the Negroes" in *William Faulkner: A Critical Study*. New York: Random House, 1962.

Nilon, Charles. *Faulkner and the Negro*. New York: Citadel Press, 1965.

Seiden, Melvin. "Faulkner's Ambiguous Negro," *Massachusetts Review*, IV (1963), 675–690.

Warren, Robert Penn. "Faulkner: The South and the Negro," *Southern Review*, I (1965), 501–527.

Wilson, Edmund. "William Faulkner's Reply to the Civil-Rights Program" in *A Literary Chronicle: 1920–1950*. New York: Doubleday, 1956.

HARRIS, JOEL CHANDLER

Gross, Theodore L. "The Negro in the Literature of the Reconstruction," *Phylon*, XXII (1961), 5–14.

Nelson, John H. "Uncle Remus Arrives" in *The Negro Character in American Literature*. Lawrence, Kansas: University of Kansas Department of Journalism Press, 1926.

Parsons, Elsie C. "Joel Chandler Harris and Negro Folklore," *Dial*, LXVI (1919), 491–494.

HAYDEN, ROBERT

Pool, Rosey E. "Robert Hayden: Poet Laureate," *Negro Digest*, XV (June 1966), 39–43.

HIMES, CHESTER

Margolies, Edward. "Race and Sex: The Novels of Chester Himes" in *Native Sons*. Philadelphia and New York: J. B. Lippincott, 1968.

HUGHES, LANGSTON

Davis, Arthur P. "The Harlem of Langston Hughes' Poetry," *Phylon*, XIII (1952), 276–283.

———. "Jess B. Semple: Negro American," *Phylon*, XV (1954), 21–28.

Dickinson, Donald C. *A Bio-Bibliography of Langston Hughes: 1902–1967*. Hamden, Connecticut: Archon Books, 1967.

Emanuel, James A. *Langston Hughes*. New York: Twayne Publishers, 1967.

Presley, James. "The American Dream of Langston Hughes," *Southwest Review*, XLVIII (1963), 380–386.

JAMES, G.P.R.

Dictionary of National Biography, X (1949–1950).
Ellis, S. M. *The Solitary Horseman: G. P. R. James.* London: Cayme Press, 1927.

JOHNSON, JAMES WELDON

Auslander, Joseph. "Sermon Sagas," *Opportunity*, V (1927), 274–275.
Bronz, Stephen H. "James Weldon Johnson" in *Roots of Negro Racial Consciousness: The 1920's: Three Harlem Renaissance Authors.* New York: Libra Publishers, 1964.
Collier, Eugenia W. "James Weldon Johnson: Mirror of Change," *Phylon*, XXI (1960), 351–359.
Potts, Eunice B. "J. W. Johnson, His Legacy to Us," *Opportunity*, XVIII (1940), 132–135.

JONES, LEROI

Costello, Donald. "LeRoi Jones: Black Man as Victim," *Commonweal*, LXXXVIII (1968), 436–440.
Dennison, George. "The Demagogy of LeRoi Jones," *Commentary*, XXXIX (1965), 67–70.
Major, Clarence. "The Poetry of LeRoi Jones," *Negro Digest*, XIV (March 1965), 54–56.
Margolies, Edward. "Prospects: LeRoi Jones?" in *Native Sons*. Philadelphia and New York: J. B. Lippincott, 1968.

KENNEDY, JOHN PENDLETON

McDowell, Tremaine. "The Negro in the Southern Novel Prior to 1850," *Journal of English and Germanic Philology*, XXV (1926), 455–473.
Ridgley, Joseph V. *John Pendleton Kennedy.* New York: Twayne Publishers, 1966.
Uhler, John E. "Kennedy's Novels and His Posthumous Works," *American Literature*, III (1932), 471–479.

KEROUAC, JACK

Askew, Melvin W. "Quests, Cars, and Kerouac," *University of Kansas City Review*, XXVIII (1962), 231–240.
Duffey, Bernard. "The Three Worlds of Jack Kerouac" in *Recent American Fiction: Some Critical Views*, ed. Joseph J. Waldmeir. Boston: Houghton Mifflin, 1963.

Tallman, Warren. "Kerouac's Sound," *Evergreen Review*, IV (1960), 153–169.

LINDSAY, VACHEL

Harris, Mark. *City of Discontent*. Indianapolis: Bobbs-Merrill, 1952.
Ruggles, Eleanor. *The West-Going Heart; A Life of Vachel Lindsay*. New York: Norton, 1959.

MC KAY, CLAUDE

Bronz, Stephen H. "Claude McKay" in *Roots of Negro Racial Consciousness: The 1920's: Three Harlem Renaissance Authors*. New York: Libra Publishers, 1964.
Butcher, Philip. "Claude McKay—'If We Must Die,' " *Opportunity*, XXVI (1948), 127.
Cooper, Wayne. "Claude McKay and the New Negro of the 1920's," *Phylon*, XXV (1964), 297–306.
Smith, Robert A. "Claude McKay: An Essay in Criticism," *Phylon*, IX (1948), 270–273.

MELVILLE, HERMAN

Carlisle, E. F. "Captain Amasa Delano: Melville's American Fool," *Criticism*, VII (1965), 349–362.
Gross, Seymour L., ed. *A "Benito Cereno" Handbook*. Belmont, California: Wadsworth, 1965.
Pilkington, William T. " 'Benito Cereno' and the American National Character," *Discourse*, VIII (1965), 49–63.
Rohrberger, Mary. "Point of View in 'Benito Cereno': Machinations and Deceptions," *College English*, XXVII (1966), 541–546.
Runden, John P., ed. *Melville's "Benito Cereno."* Boston: Heath, 1965.
Schiffman, Joseph. "Critical Problems in Melville's *Benito Cereno*," *Modern Language Quarterly*, XI (1950), 317–324.

NEGRO SONGS

Courlander, Harold. *Negro Folk Music, U.S.A.* New York: Columbia University Press, 1963.
Fisher, Miles Mark, ed. *Negro Slave Songs in the United States*. Ithaca, New York: Cornell University Press for the American Historical Association. Citadel Paperback, 1963.
Johnson, James Weldon, and Johnson, Rosamond J., eds. *The Books of American Negro Spirituals*. New York: Viking, 1940.

Jones, LeRoi. *Blues People: Negro Music in White America*. New York: Morrow, 1963.

Odum, Howard W., and Johnson, Guy B. *The Negro and His Songs: A Study of Typical Negro Songs in the South*. Chapel Hill: University of North Carolina Press, 1925.

——. *Negro Workaday Songs*. Chapel Hill: University of North Carolina Press, 1926.

O'CONNOR, FLANNERY

Burke, John J., Jr., S.J. "Convergence of Flannery O'Connor and Chardin," *Renascence*, XIX (1966), 41–47, 52.

Contemporary Authors, I–IV (1967).

Drake, Robert. *Flannery O'Connor*. Grand Rapids, Michigan: Eerdmans, 1966.

Fitzgerald, Robert. "Introduction" to *Everything That Rises Must Converge*. New York: Farrar, Straus, and Giroux, 1965.

Friedman, Melvin J., and Lawson, Lewis A., eds. *The Added Dimension: The Art and Mind of Flannery O'Connor*. New York: Fordham University Press, 1966.

Sullivan, Walter. "Flannery O'Connor, Sin, and Grace: *Everything That Rises Must Converge*," *The Hollins Critic*, II (1965), 1–8, 10.

POE, EDGAR ALLAN

Fiedler, Leslie A. "The Blackness of Darkness: E. A. Poe and the Development of the Gothic" in *Love and Death in the American Novel*. New York: Criterion Books, 1960.

Kaplan, Sidney, ed. "Introduction" to *The Narrative of Arthur Gordon Pym*. New York: Hill and Wang, 1960.

Levin, Harry. "Journey to the End of Night," in *The Power of Blackness*. New York: Knopf, 1958.

Moffitt, Cecil L. "Poe's Tsalal and the Virginia Springs," *Nineteenth-Century Fiction*, XIX (1965), 398–402.

Ridgley, Joseph V., and Haverstick, Iola S. "Chartless Voyage: The Many Narratives of Arthur Gordon Pym," *Texas Studies in Literature and Language*, VIII (1966), 63–80.

RUSSELL, IRWIN

Kendall, J. S. "Irwin Russell in New Orleans," *Louisiana Historical Quarterly*, XIV (1931), 321–345.

Shuman, R. Baird. "Irwin Russell's Christmas," *Mississippi Quarterly*, XV (1962), 81–84.

SIMMS, WILLIAM GILMORE

Burch, Charles E. "Negro Characters in the Novels of William Gilmore Simms," *Southern Workman*, LII (1923), 192–195.

McDowell, Tremaine. "The Negro in the Southern Novel Prior to 1850," *Journal of English and Germanic Philology*, XXV (1926), 455–473.

Ridgley, Joseph. "*Woodcraft*: Simms' First Answer to *Uncle Tom's Cabin*," *American Literature*, XXXI (1960), 421–433.

STOWE, HARRIET BEECHER

Baldwin, James. "Everybody's Protest Novel" in *Notes of a Native Son*. Boston: Beacon Press, 1955.

Duvall, Severn. "*Uncle Tom's Cabin*: The Sinister Side of the Patriarchy," *New England Quarterly*, XXXVI (1963), 3–22.

Nichols, Charles. "The Origins of *Uncle Tom's Cabin*," *Phylon*, XIX (1958), 328–334.

Nye, Russel B., ed. "Introduction" to *Uncle Tom's Cabin*. New York: Washington Square Press, 1963.

Wagenknecht, Edward. *Harriet Beecher Stowe, the Known and the Unknown*. New York: Oxford University Press, 1965.

Ward, John William. "*Uncle Tom's Cabin*, as a Matter of Historical Fact," *Columbia University Forum*, IX (1966), 42–47.

THURBER, JAMES

Morsberger, R. E. *James Thurber*. New York: Twayne Publishers, 1964.

Holmes, Charles S. "James Thurber and the Art of Fantasy," *Yale Review*, LV (1965), 17–33.

TOLSON, MELVIN B.

Randall, Dudley. "Melvin B. Tolson: Portrait of a Poet as Raconteur," *Negro Digest*, XV (January 1966), 54–57.

Shapiro, Karl. "Introduction" to *Harlem Gallery*. New York: Twayne Publishers, 1965.

Tate, Allen. "Preface to *Libretto for the Republic of Liberia*," *Poetry*, LXXVI (1950), 216–218.

TOOMER, JEAN

Bone, Robert A. "The Harlem School" in *The Negro Novel in America*. New Haven: Yale University Press, 1965.

Bontemps, Arna. "The Negro Renaissance: Jean Toomer and the

Harlem Writers of the 1920's" in *Anger, and Beyond*, ed. Herbert
Hill. New York: Harper and Row, 1966.
Munson, Gorham. "The Significance of Jean Toomer," *Opportunity*,
III (1925), 262–263.

TRILLING, LIONEL

Contemporary Authors, XI–XII (1965).
Hagopian, John V. "The Technique and Meaning of Lionel Trilling's
'The Other Margaret,' " *Etudes anglaises*, XVI (1963), 225–229.
Tanner, Tony. "Lionel Trilling's Uncertainties," *Encounter*, XXVII
(1966), 72–77.

TWAIN, MARK (SAMUEL CLEMENS)

Altenbernd, Lynn. "Huck Finn, Emancipator," *Criticism*, I (1959),
298–307.
Budd, Louis J. *Mark Twain: Social Philosopher*. Bloomington: Indiana
University Press, 1962.
Ellison, Ralph. "Twentieth-Century Fiction and the Black Mask of
Humanity" in *Shadow and Act*. New York: Random House, 1964.
Hoffman, Daniel G. "Jim's Magic: Black or White?" *American
Literature*, XXXII (1960), 1–10.
Marx, Leo. "Mr. Eliot, Mr. Trilling, and *Huckleberry Finn*," *American
Scholar*, XXII (1953), 423–440.

WALKER, MARGARET

Current Biography (1943).

WELTY, EUDORA

Hardy, John Edward. "Eudora Welty's Negroes" in *Images of the
Negro in American Literature*, eds. Seymour L. Gross and John Ed-
ward Hardy. Chicago: University of Chicago Press, 1966.
Isaacs, Neil D. "Life for Phoenix," *Sewanee Review*, LXXI (1963),
75–81.
Porter, Katherine Anne. "Introduction" to *Selected Stories of Eudora
Welty*. New York: Random House, Modern Library, 1954.
Trefman, Sara. "Welty's 'A Worn Path,' " *Explicator*, XXIV (1966),
Item 56.

WHITMAN, WALT

Allen, Gay W. *The Solitary Singer: A Critical Biography of Walt
Whitman*. New York: Macmillan, 1955.

Andrews, Thomas F. "Walt Whitman and Slavery: A Reconsideration of One Aspect of His Concepts of the American Common Man," *College Language Association Journal*, IX (1966), 225–233.

Glicksberg, Charles I. "Walt Whitman and the Negro," *Phylon*, IX 1948), 326–331.

Turner, Lorenzo Dow. "Walt Whitman and the Negro," *Chicago Jewish Forum*, XV (1956), 5–11.

WILLIAMS, WILLIAM CARLOS

Gregory, Horace. "Introduction" to *In the American Grain*. Norfolk, Connecticut: New Directions, 1925.

Holder, Alan. "In the American Grain: William Carlos Williams on the American Past," *American Quarterly*, XIX (1967), 499–515.

Koch, Vivienne. *William Carlos Williams*. Norfolk, Connecticut: New Directions, 1950.

Miller, J.H., ed. *William Carlos Williams: A Collection of Critical Essays*. Englewood Cliffs, New Jersey: Prentice-Hall, 1966.

Noland, Richard W. "A Failure of Contact: William Carlos Williams on America," *Emory University Quarterly*, XX (1964), 248–260.

WRIGHT, RICHARD

Baldwin, James. "Many Thousands Gone" in *Notes of a Native Son*. Boston: Beacon Press, 1955.

———. "Alas, Poor Richard" in *Nobody Knows My Name*. New York: Dial, 1961.

Ellison, Ralph. "Richard Wright's Blues" in *Shadow and Act*. New York: Random House, 1964.

Knox, George. "The Negro Novelist's Sensibility and the Outsider Theme," *Western Humanities Review*, XI (1957), 137–148.

Scott, Nathan A., Jr. "Search for Beliefs: The Fiction of Richard Wright," *University of Kansas City Review*, XXIII (1956), 19–24.

Webb, Constance. *Richard Wright, A Biography*. New York: Putnam's, 1968.